COMMITTEES AND COMMISSIONS IN INDIA

COMMITTEES AND COMMISSIONS IN INDIA

1947-1973

Volume IX : 1968-1969

VIRENDRA KUMAR

CONCEPT PUBLISHING COMPANY
NEW DELHI

First Published 1979

Virendra Kumar (*b.* 1933-)

Published by
Naurang Rai
Concept Publishing Company
H-13, Bali Nagar
NEW DELHI-110015 (India)

Printed by
Print Way India
at Print Master, Nabi Karim
NEW DELHI—110055 (India)

To

My Maternal-Aunt

Late Smt. Rajwati Devi Kulsreshtha

INTRODUCTION

This Ninth Volume attempts to understand and analyse the activities of the various "Committees and Commissions" during the period 1968-1969, which have received as far as the previous volumes are concerned, scant attention from even bibliographies and documentation experts. It is known that the government all over, the world largely rely on the Committees and Commissions for their decisions on particular subjects, Governments make an extensive use of the Instrument of the Public Inquiries which ultimately help in lessening managerial tensions as well as quietening the allegations of misrule. According to John Stuart Mill, "A man seldom judges right, even in his own concern, still less in those of the public, when he makes habitual use of knowledge but his own or that of some single adviser". Thus the "Committee System" greatly helps the proper functioning of a democratic set-up.

A Commission is a "Governmental Agency created to perform a particular function such as special investigations or on governmental regulations of business". It is appointed mainly when it is thought that a matter involves some financial questions. There are other reasons for which a Commission is appointed, e.g., in matters pertaining to the welfare of the State and its citizens and for improving the efficiency in an administration. The status of a Committee is also the same as that of a Commission, but it does not possess as wide powers as are enjoyed by a Commission and has to limit itself in relation to specific work assigned to it under its terms of reference. While arriving at decisions in the form of recommendations, a Committee or Commission ensures that such decisions are representative of interests of various types of people and also a safeguard against abuse of power.

The Committees and Commissions always advise a Government, offering valuable suggestions and recommendations for smooth operation and efficiency in administration for the welfare of the people.

A Committee or a commission comprises a Chairman, the Members and the Member-Secretary (sometimes there is also a Vice-Chairman and an Assistant Secretary). In some cases there are even One-Man Commission and enquiries conducted by such Commissions are entrusted to an Official-on-Special Duty or a Judge of the High Court.

The Chairman of a Commission is a person well versed in legal affairs and is often a retired Judge of a High Court or Supreme Court of India. Occasionally, a Member of Parliament is also appointed to the post of Chairman of a Commission. Regarding Committees, the Chairman is usually a specialist in the subject of the Committee. He can be a Leader or a Convener also if he heads a Panel, Study Group, Working Group or a Delegation etc.

The Members of a Commission, Committee, Panel, Study Group, Working Group, etc., are specialists in their respective fields and provide valuable guidance to the Commission in making recommendations.

The Member-Secretary or Secretary is nominated from among the experienced officials who have the requisite competent knowledge of the subject on which the Commission or the Committee is appointed.

The Study of the "Committees and Commissions" is divided into two main parts :

(i) **Pre-Independence** : From 1772 to August 1947 ; and

(ii) **Post-Independence** : From August 1947 to 1973.

The first Volume covers the period from August 1947 to 1954. The Second Volume covers the period from 1955 to 1957. The Third Volume covers the period from 1958 to 1959. The Fourth Volume covers the period from 1960 to 1961. The Fifth Volume covers the period from 1962 to 1963. The Sixth Volume covers the period from 1964 to 1965. The Seventh Volume covers the period from 1966. The Eighth Volume covers the period from 1967. The present Volume which is Ninth in the Series covers the period from 1968 to 1969.

The work provides information on subjects like **Bibliographical Data** of the Committees and Commissions, the **Chairman,** the **Leader,** the **Convener,** etc. **Appointments ; Terms of Reference ; Contents** and **Recommendations.**

Arrangements : The arrangements in the "Committees and Commissions" are **Chronological** and items have been arranged according to their dates of appointment and not according to their dates of publication.

I am sure that this reference work will continue into a number of volumes, for it is unique in nature. I have spared no efforts to make it a comprehensive reference work and it will be of great use to the research scholars, sociologists, historians, economists, students of political science, as well as to all those connected with the study of administration and legal affairs. I have tried my level best to rectify all errors and omissions that I noticed in the previous volumes. It will be my effort to go on improving these volumes. The introductory part in Volume I deals with the why, what and how of the "Committees and Commissions".

In the end I must express my gratitude to the Press that reviewed and appreciated the work. I am also indebted to my wife and children who have sacrificed their personal comforts by providing me every facility to make this Volume ready for publication within a reasonable short time.

NEW DELHI — VIRENDRA KUMAR

Vijay Dashmi
September 30, 1979

CONTENTS

1968

1969

1968

THE ADVISORY COMMITTEE ON THE PRESS COUNCIL 1968—REPORT

Delhi, Manager of Publications, 1969. 162p.

Chairman : Shri K.K. Shah.

Members : Smt. Nandini Satpathy; Shri Ganga Sharan Sinha; Shri Narla Venkateswara Rao; Shri Bhupesh Gupta; Shri Krishan Kant; Shri Mohan Manikchand Dharia; Shri T.N. Singh; Shri C.K. Bhattacharya; Shri P.C. Verma; Shri R.M. Hajarnavis; Shri Rajendranath Barua; Shri S. Supakar; Shri M.N. Naghnoor; Shri Manubhai M. Patel; Shri A.B. Vajpayee; Shri S.M. Joshi; Shri S.K. Sambandhan; Shri · Nath Pai; Shri Viren Shah.

APPOINTMENT

The Advisory Committee on the Press Council (1968) was constituted under the Government of India, Ministry of Information and Broadcasting vide Resolution No. 11/31/67—Pol PC dated January 17, 1968.

TERMS OF REFERENCE

The Committee shall study the existing Act under which the Press Council of India has been set up and suggest such amendments as may be considered necessary to enlist for the Council full and effective co-operation from all sections of the Press and Public and to enable it to play its due role in preserving the freedom of the Press and improve standards of journalism in the country which are in conformity with the basic objectives of the Council.

CONTENTS

Introduction; Need for a Press Council; The Present Council; Chairman of the Council; Composition of the Council; Regional Councils; Powers and Functions; Finances for the Council; Definitions; Press Council Members may Become Members of State Legislatures; Service Conditions of Employees; Summary of Conclusions and Recommendations ; Appendices I to VII.

RECOMMENDATIONS

The Committee is of the opinion that Government should bring forward an amending Bill for recognizing the Press Council on proper lines.

The Committee is in favour of retaining the Press Council as a statutory body and making it more effective.

The Committee recommends that the new Council should come into existence at the expiry of the term of the present Council and suggests that all necessary steps should be addressed to this effect. The Committee, also feels that it would be desirable if the terms of office of the present Chairman and other members of the Council could be made co-terminus which practice should obtain for future Council also.

The responsibilities attached to the Chairman are high and onerous and a part-time Chairman will not be able to spare either the necessary time or devote the constant attention required of him for the effective implementation of the various provisions of the Act. The Committee is, therefore, in favour of having a whole-time Chairman, his salary being fixed by the Central Government as already provided in the Act.

The selection of the Chairman need not necessarily be restricted to judges or any other categories of persons but should be kept open.

The Principal of election of the Chairman in such a small Council consisting of twenty-five members, divided into various groups, namely working journalists, editors, proprietors and others, is likely to lead to undesirable trends. The Committee, therefore, favours the system of nomination of Chairman in preference to election and suggests that the Chairman of the Council should be appointed by a Committee consisting of the Chief Justice of India, the Chairman of the Rajya Sabha and the Speaker of the Lok Sabha.

The Committee considers that the method of election on the basis of an electoral college, for electing the members of the Press Council will not be suitable. The selection of the members, representing the profession should continue to be made on the basis of nomination from panels. However, the Chairman of the Press Council should not be associated with selection of the members nor should Government or the President of India or his nominee be involved in the process. The Committee recommends that the selection of the members representing the profession should be made by a nominating Committee consisting of the Chief Justice of India, the Chairman of the Rajya Sabha and the Speaker of the Lok Sabha, from among the panels submitted by the organizations concerned. Those organizations should be requested to submi panels of names which should contain at least twice the number of members to be selected from that category.

The Committee does not consider it necessary to disturb the present size of the Council for the present. The distribution of seats in the Press Council should be as follows :

(1) Working Journalist :	
(i) editors who are working Journalists	6
(ii) working Journalists other than editors	7
(2) Persons who own or carry on the business of management of newspapers	6
(3) Other Members	6
	25

The Act at present provides that out of the thirteen Working Journalists, there should be "not less than" six editors. The Committee feels that the proportion of these two categories should be specifically determined and recommends that the editors who are Working Journalists should have six seats in the Council and no more or no less. The drafting of Clause (a) of Sub-section (3) of Section 4 should further be changed so that the qualifying words "who do not own or carry on the business of management of newspapers" apply not only to the editors but to the Working Journalists as well. It should also be provided that under each of the Sub-categories of Working Journalists in Para 34 of this Report, there should be atleast three persons belonging to the Indian languages newspapers.

As regards the six members representing the newspaper owners and managers, the distribution should be as follows :

(i) two members from among the big newspapers (by inviting panels).

(ii) two members from among the medium newspapers (by inviting panels).

(iii) two members from among the small newspapers.

For the purpose of categories will mean :

1. **Big** : Circulation—above 50,000.

2. **Medium** : Circulation—between 15,000 and 50,000.

3. **Small** : Circulation—less than 15,000.

The Council should notify the organizations from whom the panels are to be invited. Taking into account the present position, the Committee feels that the names of Indian and Eastern Newspaper Society and the Indian Languages Newspapers Association should be considered by the Press Council for inviting the panel for categories 1 and 2 respectively. As regards the small newspapers, it is noted that at present there is no All-India organization representing the small newspapers as such but that efforts are being made in this direction. Till such time as the Press Council recognises such an organisation for inviting panels, the selection of these two members Committee which may consult such associations or persons as it thinks fit. It should also be provided in the Act that out of the six members in the category of newspaper owners and managers at least three of them should be those belonging to the Indian languages newspapers.

As regards the organizations from which the panels are to be invited, the Press Council, as already provided in the Act, should periodically review the representative character of the organizations and notify the names of representative organizations from whom the panels can be invited.

The words "shall have due regard" appearing in Sub-sections (4) and (5) of Section 4 of the Act should be changed to provide that the considerations set out in those sub-sections will be binding on the nominating Committee and not merely be directory or recommendatory.

The idea of including in the Council persons from ourside the profession has been motivated by a desire to represent the opinion of the common reader on the Press Council. The Committee accepts it is as a wholesome principle and recommends the continuance of this practice.

The Committee is not in favour of the present system of nomination of three members from the special fields of experience by a Committee and suggests that the nomination of the three members may be entrusted to the following organizations :

1. University Grants Commission	One member from the field of education, science and allied matters;
2. Bar Council of India	One member from the field of law; and
3. Sahitya Akademi	One member from the field of literature and culture.

The Committee recommends the continuance of three seats for the Members of Parliament with the present system of nomination by the Chairman of the Rajya Sabha and the Speaker of the Lok Sabha.

There is no provision in the Act for dealing with non-cooperation by a particular organization in sending their members to serve on the Council. There is also no provision in the Act to consider any objections raised by any organization or body regarding the correctness or otherwise of the selection of members to the Council. As the nomination of the members of the Council is recommended to be made by a high level Committee, it will not be appropriate to provide in the Act for the establishment of an Appellate Authority over the decisions of that Committee. However, it would be desirable to made a specific provision in the Act to enable a review of its decisions by the nominating Committee either on receipt of a representation or otherwise. If any particular organization fails to submit panels when invited to do so, or otherwise does not cooperate in the constitution of the Council, the nominating Committee should be authorised to fill up their placed by nominating persons either from the panels submitted by other organizations of the same category or by selecting individuals belonging to these categories. The working of the Council should not be help us on this account.

The Committee feels that the question whether there should be separate regional councils or advisory bodies to the All-India Council might be considered after the Council has worked for sometime.

The Committee accepts the need for the association of experts and persons with adequate knowledge of the concerned languages or problems in enquiring into complaints concerning newspapers in Indian languages or in dealing with problems and difficulties of regional newspapers and recommends that the Council may be empowered to nominate to its Committees, set up under Section 8 of the Act, to deal with particular issues or situations, persons as ad hoc members who may not even be members of the Council for particular purpose.

There is no need to revise the functions mentioned in Clauses (a) to (e) of Section 12 (2) of the Act. Clause (f) may be amended suitably, as suggested by the Council, to enable it to review the cases of foreign assistance to Indian newspapers on a reference from the Central Government or of its own. Establishment of common services for the supply and dissemination of news to newspapers is not a proper function of the Press Council and so Clause (g) may be deleted. The Committee also recommends the retention of the functions mentioned in Clauses (h) to (i), except that Clause (i) may be amended suitably so as to exclude disputes under the Industrial Disputes Act from the purview of the Council.

The Committee does not accept the suggestion that in cases where censure is called for, it should be administered only to the editor and not to anybody else.

The Committee does not support the suggestion of the Press Council that it should be given powers to compel a newspaper complained against or, in the case of a working journalist, the newspaper in which he is employed, to publish the decision of the Council or of such portions of it as the Council deems fit.

The Press Council is primarily a professional body aimed at self regulation of the Press and its character should not be basically changed into a sort of inquisitorial body. It would neither be desirable nor appropriate to empower the Press Council to make statutory or judicial enquiries for performing its functions except to the extent the Act provides. The Committee is not in favour of the suggestion of the Press Council for amending Section 13 of the Act in order to enable it to make enquiries in the course of performance of all its functions under Section 12.

The Committee does not support the suggestion that, in case of recurring censures, the Council may be empowered to make recommendations to the Government suggesting the course of further action to be taken e.g. stoppage of the allotment of Government advertisements, allocation of newsprint, press facilities etc. Government can decide on their own what action is to be taken against a newspaper censured by the Council more than once. No specific provision need be made in the Act which might affect the functioning of the Press Council as a self-regulatory and independent body.

If there is any matter of urgent public importance and interest which is enquired into or reviewed by the Council a report on the same need not wait for inclusion in the annual report of the Council. The Committee recommends that the Council may be given the discretion to include reports on matters enquired into or reviewed by it within the scope of its functions, either in its annual report or to submit the same in the form of an interim report. The Government should lay the annual and other reports on the Table of both Houses of Parliament. A suitable provision to that effect should be incorporated in the Act.

In the context of the Press Council's suggestion that, for the purpose of performing its functions, it should be entitled to call for necessary information not only from the publishers of newspapers but also from the editor or any other person in the management or control of any newspaper or of any news service, the Committee is of the opinion that the purpose of the Council will be better served if sub-sections (1) and (2) of Section 14 are combined to read :

"For the purpose of performing its functions and while holding an enquiry under the Act, the Council shall have the same powers as are vested in a civil court while trying a suit under the Civil Procedure Code..."

"The Committee recommends acceptance of the suggestion of the Press Council that to remove any possible doubt about the limits of jurisdiction to the Council to summer witnesses, the Act may be amended to provide that the powers of the Council under Section 14 will extend to the entire territory to which the Act extends".

The Committee also accepts the suggestion of the Press Council for additional powers in regard to (i) requisitioning any public record or copy thereof from any public office and (ii) any other matter which may be prescribed.

Compulsion to disclose sources of news and information would be against generally accepted journalistic privilege and the Committee favours the inclusion of a proviso under Section 14 to provide that nobody shall be compelled to disclose the source of news of information published in a newspaper or a journals.

The Committee agrees to the Press Council's suggestion that Section 23 of the Act may be amended so as to empower the Council to frame regulations, inter alia, in respect of "any other matter for which under the Act regulations may be made".

After discussing the alternative methods of financing the Press Council, other than through grants-in-aid the Committee has come to the conclusion that for future flexibility the present arrangements whereby the budget of the Council is prepared depending upon its requirements annually and passed by the Parliament after due scrutiny, should continue.

For the reasons explained exhaustively in Chapter IX, there is no need to alter the existing definitions of the words "newspaper", "editor" and "working journalists". As regards the suggestions to exclude certain categories of press workers like the proof readers from the definition of the term "working journalist", the Committee feels that it would be advisable to depend upon the good sense firstly of the organisations concerned who are to submit the panels and secondly on the nominating machinery who will finalize the list of names.

The Committee accepts, in principle, the suggestion that a person, merely because of his membership of the Press Council, should not be disqualified from becoming a member of the State Legislature and recommends that the members of the State Legislature be given the same protection from disqualification as in the case of Members of Parliament.

The Committee recommends that the office of the Press Council should be treated as a Government department for purposes of accommodation and its employees should be treated for this and other service conditions on par with regular Government servants. Lack of adequate accommodation for the Council and its employees has created handicaps in the proper functioning of the Press Council and therefore the Committee recommends that the Government should give priority in allotting adequate accommodation to the Press Council and its employees.

WORKING PARTY ON EDUCATIONAL PLANNING, ADMINISTRATION AND EVALUATION, 1968—REPORT

Report on Educational Planning, Administration and Evaluation in Fourth Five Year Plan, 1969-74.

New Delhi, Education Division, Planning Commission, 1968. 91p.

Chairman : Shri J.P. Naik.
Members : Dr. M.B. Buch; Prof. D.A. Dabholkar; Dr. B. Dutta; Prof. R.K. Kapur; Prof. M.V. Mathur; Dr. S.N. Mehrotra; Shri B. Mehta; Shri D.P. Nayar; Shri V.V. Satav; Shri J.C. Saxena; Prof. N. Srinivasan; Shri N.D. Sundravadivelu.
Member-Secretary : Dr. S.N. Saraf.

APPOINTMENT

Planning Commission appointed the Working Party on Educational Planning, Administration and Evaluation under their letter No. 1/32/67-Edn. dated January 24, 1968.

TERMS OF REFERENCE

The Planning Commission broadly indicated that the Working Party should review the present position of educational planning, administration and evaluation, suggest long term of objectives of development in these sectors and make specific proposals for inclusion in the Fourth Five Year Plan and left at to the Working Party itself to define its detailed terms of reference.

The Working Party discussed this matter on its first meeting and adopted the following as its terms of reference :

1. To suggest ways and means of gearing educational administration to developmental needs;
2. To suggest needed improvement in the educational planning process;
3. To suggest reforms in educational administration with special reference to making the implementation of educational plans more effective; and
4. To discuss, in some details, the following major areas :

(a) administration at the national level;
(b) administration at the State level;
(c) special problems in educational ;
 (i) organisation ;
 (ii) procedures ; and
 (iii) personnel ;
(d) supervision and guidance ;
(e) evaluation ;
(f) broad-based and decentralised planning ;
(g) managerial aspects of Educational Administration ; and
(h) flexibility, dynamism and adaptability, among administrators and supervisors.

CONTENTS

Introduction; The Present Position—a View; Proposals for Reforms; The Planning Process; Proposals for Reform; Educational Administration; Evaluation; University Administration; Priority for Programmes of Educational Administration; Planning and Evaluation; Main Recommendations; Annexure I to III.

RECOMMENDATIONS

We give below our main recommendations for convenience and reference :

1. The plans drawn up, at present, merely, indicate financial allocations to selected educational programmes. Instead comprehensive educational plans should be formulated.

2. There is need to adopt a broad-based and decentralized system of educational planning and, to that end to prepare well-coordinated plans at the institutional, District, State and National levels.

3. The base for this new process of educational planning will be provided by Institutional Plans.

4. The District should be taken as the basic unit of educational planning, development and administration. District Plans should be introduced on a pilot basis in a few districts in every State with effect from next year. By the end of the Fourth Plan, planning at the District level should become universal.

5. The State Plans are very important and the centre of gravity of the entire planning process in education will have to be at the State level.

6. It is the responsibility of the Central Government to take a long-term and coordinated view of educational development and to ensure that regional imbalances between States are minimised. Special programmes will have to be developed in the National Plan from this point of view.

Planning should also be a two-way process from above as well as from below.

7. There is need to involve teachers intimately and effectively in the preparation and implementation of educational plans.

8. Necessary training should be provided to persons concerned with formulation and implementation of plans.

9. The project preparation technique for formulating educational development programmes should be adopted.

10. Expenditure orientation of our educational development programmes should be reduced and efforts should be made to develop and adopt techniques of planning suited for developing countries.

11. For effective educational planning, it would be necessary to decide priorities at different levels—National State, District and Institution.

12. There is an urgent need for securing better coordination between different agencies concerned with educational planning and for better coordination between the Centre and the States in the work of plan formulation and plan implementation.

13. The most urgent task in the field of improving the implementation of educational plans is to change the present "Maintenance Administration" to "Development Administration."

14. The new concept of "Developmental Administration" involves considerable reorganization of educational services of the Centre and in the States.

15. The organization of adequate programme of in service education for educational administrators should receive the highest priority in our Plans. On first appointment to the administrative or supervisory-side, every officer should be required to undergo an induction course. The duration and content of such courses will depend upon the level at which the appointment is made and the type of duties he is expected to perform. In addition, several different programmes of in-service education need to be developed to keep the departmental officers abreast of the latest developments in the field and the policies and programmes of Government. These may include annual seminars on education and administrative matters, conduct of journals, sabbatical leave, visits to other State, etc.

16. We attach the greatest importance to the Education Commission's recommendation regarding the establishment of a Notional Staff College for Educational Administrators and recommend that it should be set up immediately and developed to its full stature by the end of the Fourth Plan. The possibilities of developing it as an Indian wing of the Asian Institute of Educational Planning and Administration should be explored.

17. It is necessary to provide incentives for actual professional growth shown by officers of the Department.

18. While attempts to develop in service training programmes should be undertaken in earnest, it is equally essential to supplement them by a crash programme of inservice education in which all officers in educational administration at all levels will be reoriented to the complex and difficult tasks of educational reconstruction. The Centre and the State should fully cooperate in organising this programme which should be developed at the District, State and National levels for different categories of officers.

19. Appropriate institutional and personnal arrangements to look after programmes of qualitative improvement are necessary if educational administration is to be reformed. These will include the NCERT at the National level, the State Institutes of Education at the State level, appropriate organisations at the district level, and the school complexes.

20. Steps will have to be taken to provide better supervision and guidance to schools. This will include, amongst others an increase in the strength of inspecting officers where necessary and the appointment of subject inspectors. Efforts are also needed to improve the quality of inspection.

21. The departmental procedure and practices, which at present are very often unsatisfactory and unsuitable to the requirements of developments administration, should be reformed. Comparative studies of administrative practices will greatly help in this. Attention has also to be paid to such programmes as the adoption of the officer-oriented system, establishment of an O & M Organization in each State Education Department, and particularly to securing an adequate delegation of authority.

22. The functioning of the educational departments should be made flexible and dynamic.

23. It is suggested that in the years ahead, much

greater emphasis should be placed on evaluation and an educational research which should be vigorously promoted.

24. The Indian wing of the Asian Institute of Educational Planning and Administration should take up research studies in the administrative problems of universities in collaboration with University Grants Commission and arrange appropriate training programmes for the University staff of higher cadres. A Special Working Party should be set up immediately to work out the details of a programme of action.

25. The programmes for reform in educational planning, administration and evaluation need to be developed on a basis of high priority during the Fourth Five Year Plan. Adequate Funds should be provided for strengthening and improving educational administration. A satisfactory form in this respect would be that expenditure on educational planning, administration and evaluation, including research and inservice education of teachers, headmasters and educational administrators should be of the order of about five per cent of the total educational expenditure.

26. A provision of Rs. 22 crores is recommended for various schemes relating to improvement of educational planning, administration and evaluation. It will help to watch over the development of programmes relating to educational planning, administration and evaluation, if this expenditure is show as a separate sector in the Plans.

REVIEW COMMITTEE ON THE WORKING OF THE NATIONAL COUNCIL OF EDUCATIONAL RESEARCH AND TRAINING, 1968—REPORT

Future Development of National Council of Educational Research and Training.

New Delhi, National Council of Research and Training, 1969. 235p.

Chairman : Dr. B.D. Nag Chaudhuri.
Members : Shri P.N. Kirpal; Shri G.K. Chandiramani; Shri A.E.T. Barrow; Shri J.P. Naik; Dr. M.S. Gore; Dr. V.G. Bhide; Prof. N.V. Subba Rao; Shri L.S. Chandrakant.
Member-Secretary : Dr. S.K. Mitra.

APPOINTMENT

The Government of India appointed a Review Committee under Clause 6 of the Memorandum of Association of the National Council of Educational Research and Training vide its letter No. F.2-8/67 NCERT dated January 29, 1968.

TERMS OF REFERENCE

The Terms of Reference of the Review Committee were :

(a) To review the progress of the activities of the NCERT with particular reference to educational research and development programmes ; pre-service and in-service training of teachers, teacher-educators and educational administrators and extension services for elementary and secondary schools ;

(b) To evaluate the impact of NCERT programmes on educational problems in general and in particular, how far major programmes like curriculam development, text-books, examinations reform, science education, etc., are improving the quality and standards of school education in States ;

(c) To review the progress of Regional Colleges of Education and evaluate how far the concurrent courses conducted by them are contributing towards improving teacher-education in science, technology, commerce and other fields ;

(d) To lay down broad guidelines for the future development of NCERT in relation to our educational needs, together with recommendations for reorganising the organisational administrative and academic set up of the Units/Institution under control ;

(e) To prepare a broad estimate of the financial provision needed for the development of NCERT in the next five and ten years ; and

(f) To report on any other aspect of the present and future functioning of NCERT that is important to Indian education.

CONTENTS

Introduction ; Improvement of School Education and the Role of the NCERT ; Research and Development ; Programmes of Training and Extension ; Regional Colleges of Education ; The Institute of Education and Publications ; Organisation, Administration and Finance ; Main Findings and Recommendations ; Appendices.

RECOMMENDATIONS

Scope of the activities of the NCERT : Although the Memorandum of the NCERT visualises a wide range of activities covering all aspects of education at all stages, its programmes have largely been confined right from the outset, to the improvement of school education. In our opinion, this has been a health discipline imposed upon itself by the NCERT and the same policy should be continued over the next ten years. We would also like to suggest that primary education, which has been comparatively neglected in the past, should now receive greater emphasis.

Reorganisation Of The Nie

At present the NCERT has set up five different institutions of implement its programmes, namely, the National Institute of Education or NIE at New Delhi and the four Regional Colleges of Education at Ajmer, Bhubaneswar, Bhopal and Mysore. In our opinion, it would contribute to economy and greater efficiency if the Regional College of Education were deemed as single organisation responsible for carrying out the campuses of the NIE and if the NIE were to be made the objectives of the NCERT.

Department organisation of the NIE, New Delhi : At present, the NIE has eleven departments, namely; (a) Department of Foundations of Education, (b) Department of Psychological Foundations, (c) Department of Teacher Education, (d) Department of Educational Administration (e) Department of Field Services, (f) Department of Curriculum and Evaluation, (g) Department of Science Education, (h) Department of Audio-Visual Education, (i) Department of Adult Education, (j) Educational Survey Unit and (k) Central Science Workshop. In addition, there is a Publication Unit, whatever the differences in their names, these are all treated as Departments in practice and the persons in charge are designated as Heads of Departments. In our opinion, the number of Department, is too large and there is a great variation to their size-quality of work effort and emphasis on school education. Moreover, the difference between an academic department and what is, in effect, a service department has also been generally ignored. We, therefore, recommend that the existing set-up should be reorganised. With a view to improving efficiency, by reducing the number of departments and by clearly enunciating the difference between academic and service departments. From this point of view, we make the following recommendations :

(a) All the Departments of the NIE should be grouped under (1) those that are concerned with academic work and (2) those that are concerned mainly with service and technical assistance.

The programmes for the improvement of school education will, by and large, be initiated and implemented by the academic departments. The technical and service departments, generally, will provide the essential services for the developments of these programmes. The academic departments, however, should encourage initiative by the service and technical departments to suggest improvement of equipment and apparatus as well as ideas they may have on the modification or reinforcement in regard to programmes of school education. It should be the responsibility of the Director to ensure that these two arms of the NIE collaborate smoothly and prestige or hierarchy is not allowed to retard joint efforts.

(b) There should be only four academic departments, viz. (1) The Department of Primary Education which is to be newly established ; (2) The Department of Science Workshop ; (3) The Department of Social Sciences and Humanities and (4) The Department of Educational Psychology.

(c) The Department of Primary Education will deal with all problems of primary education such as curriculum, textbooks, methods of teaching and evaluation, single-teacher schools, multiple class teaching, inspection and supervision, wastage and stagnation, training of primary teachers, preparation of teacher-educators, physical education and art education for the primary stage.

(d) The Department of Social Education will deal comprehensively with programmes of science education at the secondary stage including curriculum, methods of teaching and evaluation, teacher preparation, supervision and inspection. The Central Science Workshop with a view to increasing efficient functioning and its services should be made available, where necessary, to other Departments. The Prototype Design Section of the workshop should be strengthened and its sections on Electronics and Optics should be developed more fully. The section dealing with design and preparation of prototypes and experimentation should be treated as distinct from the section which should devote itselt entirely to the pro duction of apparatus in large numbers for an accepted p ototype.

(e) The Department of Social Sciences and Humanities will deal with curriculum, methods of teaching and evaluation, teacher preparation, supervision and inspection with regard to the social sciences, languages, physical education, and art education at the secondary stage.

(f) Problems relating to work-experience and values will be dealt with by all these three Departments as part of their programmes of curriculum construction, development of improved methods of teaching and evaluation, preparation of teachers and production of text books and other teaching and learning materials.

(g) The Department of Educational Psychology will focus its attention on all aspects of the teaching and learning processes and on the psychology of the child and the adolescent. It can be developed out of the existing Department of Psychological Foundations by taking out the data-processing and psychometric units.

The technical and service departments will be (a) Department of Audio-Visual Education (b) Department of Survey and Data Processing, and (c) Department of Measurement and Evaluation.

(a) The Department of Audio-Visual Education which lacks expertise at the senior level should have a few senior staff to effectively use the large number of technicians at lower levels. It should provide technical and consultative services to the academic departments of the NIE as well as to state-level institutions. The Central Film library may continue to be a responsibility of the Department. A Copy of its catalogue and duplicate copies of its educational films should be kept at each of the Regional Colleges of Education for use in the regions concerned. The Department should concentrate in the immediate future on the production of filmstrips and other in-expensive teaching aids and devices.

(b) The Department of Survey and Data-processing will include the existing Educational Survey Unit and the Data Processing Unit carved out from the existing Department of Psychological Foundations. The Survey Unit will have to be strengthened to carry out periodical surveys on different aspects of educational development as recommended by the Education Commission. These will form bench-mark data in different sectors and will assist planning and policy formulation. The Data-processing Unit will also have to be strengthened to cope with the research and other activities of the NIE which we expect to increase considerably.

(c) An examination of the existing Department of Curriculum and Evaluation and that of the Department of Psychological Foundations shows that both have staff having similar qualifications in psychometrics and measurement. The examination reforms work has taken very much the characteristics of objective testing in which the group in the Department of Psychological Foundations concerned with developments of tests and psychometrics is also concerned. We, therefore, recommend that a Department of Measurement and Evaluation be established. It should incorporate the staff of the Department of Psychological Foundations and the Evaluation Section of the Department of Curriculum and Evaluation who have the necessary qualifications in psychometrics and measurement to work on the development of tools and instrument like questionnaires, aptitude and achievement tests, attitude scales, etc. The Department should take the responsibility of maintaining a comprehensive library of tests and provide consultative services in this respect.

The present library of the NCERT is an amalgam of the various departmental libraries. It is not housed properly nor is its work efficiently organised. It is of utmost importance that the library should be developed appropriately to serve the NIE.

A Documentation Centre and Information Services should be organised and an attempt should be made to collect all the necessary educational documents from all the States and Union Territories in purpose as well as for the promotional work.

The Department of Teacher Education has been weak from the start and its achievements have been mediore. Since the Regional Colleges of Education have to develop as primary centres for research and development in teacher education, the efforts of the NCERT in the years should be directed to this end. The Department of Teacher Education may therefore, be abolished.

The Department of Field Services tends to interfere with the establishment of direct relationship between academicians in the different fields at the national and state levels. Moreover, it would be better to organise such extension services from the Regional Colleges of Education than from New Delhi. The programme of financial assistance to Extension Centres, which is now being operated upon in this department, should be transferred to the Ministry of Education which should negotiate its transfer to the State Governments. The technical assistance to these Centres should be more conveniently provided from the Regional Colleges of Education. A Field Officer may be posted in each state for liaison and promotion. A Department of Field Services at the centre is therefore, not required.

The training of educational administrators as such is beyond the immediate programme we visualize for the NCERT and should preferable be undertaken by an organisation like the Asian Institute of Educational Planning Administration. In so far as supervision and inspection is concerned, we have suggested that these problems should be dealt with by the Department of Primary Education, Science Education, and Social Sciences and Humanities in their respective fields. School management however, should be a subject of study at the Regional Colleges of Education along with programmes of teacher education. The Department of Educational Administration in the NIE should therefore be abolished.

It is not possible, within the human and material resources available to the NCERT at present, to build up a really efficient department in the field of Philosophical and Sociological Foundations. For the next few years, efforts should be made to develop research in these fields in appropriate university departments. Although we recognise the importance of interdisciplinary research, for which this Department was established, we do not rule out the possibility of starting such a department at some future date. We are constrained to recommend its abolition, because it is essential that the NCERT should concentrate, at this stage of its development, on programmes directly related to the improvement of school education.

There is little or no relationship between the programmes of the Department of Adult Education and those of school education under other NIE Departments. We, therefore, recommend that this Department may be transferred to the Ministry of Education Unit which also forms a part of this Department may be transferred to the Department of Social Welfare in the Government of India or to the Commissioner of Scheduled Castes and Scheduled Tribes.

Programmes Of The NIE

We have indicated broadly the programmes to be developed in each of the four academic departments of the NIE. In addition, we make the following suggestions in respect of progrommes of the NIE in the fields of research, training and development.

Research: The Council has developed several programmes of research in the Departments of the NIE. The total quantum of work turned out is fairly large. But there is a great variation in standards from department to department and sometimes even within the same department. Another weakness is that a number of research projects draw their samples only from Delhi. To overcome these weaknesses and also to promote research on a large scale and in appropriate directives we recommend that :

(a) There should be rigorous screening of departmental research projects both within the departments and by the Academic Committee to ensure proper standards :

(b) The NIE should undertake studies which will serve felt national needs ;

(c) The NIE should adopt a policy of developing cooperative research projects with the university departments and other institutions of higher learning ; and

(d) In view of the limited resources available, there should be an allocation of priorities for research-programmes. The NIE Departments, the Regional College of Education, the State Institutes of Education and University Departments should be involved in the determination of such priorities.

As a premotional activity, the NCERT operates the GARP scheme of grants-in-aid for research projects under which schemes of individual research scholars are assisted. This scheme will contribute to reinforcing further the cooperative research with universities recommended earlier. In pursuing the scheme the scholars and research workers in the various institutions should be encouraged to consult the NCERT and get such assistance as is necessary. New research proposals for grants-in-aid should come up before the sanctioning authority twice a year at an interval of about six months. The time between the submission of the scheme and its disposal should on no account be more than six months.

The research projects of a department should be scrutinised and approved by a committee consisting of the Head of the Department and senior staff members. The projects of the NIE as a whole, as well as requests from outside under the GARP scheme should be scrutinised only at one level viz., by the Academic Committee. In each report in a research project, the contribution of every participant should be duly acknowledged.

The NIE should encourage individual research scholars to work at the doctoral and post-doctoral levels. This is expected to stimulate the members of the staff of the NIE in their own research and help them to develop insight into problems and create an in intellectual climate in the institute.

Curriculum, textbooks and examination reform: In the Department of Science Education, considerable work has been done on curriculum development and preparation of teachers' guides, instructional material, study kits, etc. There is, however, room for improvement in the direction of reducing costs on equipment and in the pedagogical approach to the content.

The programme of Summer Science Institutes has created an encouraging climate for improvement of science education in the country. It is necessary to follow this up effectively.

In the field of social sciences and languages, a

considerable volume of textbook and other instructional material has been produced by the Department of Curriculum and Evaluation as well as by the Panels/ Editorial Boards appointed by the Central Committee on Education Literature. This work should be continued.

There has not been an adequate appreciation of the textbooks produced by the NCERT in the States. More intensive efforts are needed for this purpose. What is even more important, the approach to the curriculum and textbook problems needs to be modified so as to reflect realistically the local needs in individual states and to provide for expert and consultancy services to State Governments. There has also to be a greater emphasis on production of textbook materials rather than on textbooks as such because these will be of greater use in helping the states to produced better textbooks of their own.

In making the above recommendations, we also feel that the Council should make periodic reviews of the textbooks that are in use in the various states. Through such periodic reviews the Council should attempt to establish norms of textbook production and generally strive to improve their standards. In making these reviews, the Council should carefully consider the textbooks from the point of view of national integration in addition to academic considerations. There should be an Advisory Committee for the textbooks programme consisting of the representatives of the State Governments and the Organizations in the State producing textbooks. Besides, periodic meetings should be held with authors and publishers of textbooks with a view to influencing their thinking.

Examination reform : The work done by the Council in the field of examination reform over the last several years has been largely confined to the training of paper-setters and examiners for the public examinations at the secondary stage in setting objective tests. Except Rajasthan, not much progress has been made in other States. The entire strategy of examination reform, therefore, needs closer review, especially because examination, among other things, has a social purpose and is wider than just objective testing. A cost-benefit analysis of the reform recommended should also be carried out.

Training programmes : We feel that training programmes should not be over-emphasized at the NIE. They can be more appropriately developed at the Regional College of Education. The training programmes to be developed at New Delhi should therefore be few, have a national character and should be restricted to those areas where the NIE has a special expertise and which cannot be satisfactorily developed at regional level.

The NIE has recently instituted an Associateship Course of one year's duration for improving the functional competence of workers in education. The course has not been popular firstly because it was not possible for the State Governments to depute persons for such a long period of twelve months and secondly because it was not recognised for purposes of promotion or additional qualifications. We therefore, recommend the discontinuance of the course. Instead, the NIE should organise a few courses, at an advanced level, for inservice education of workers in the field on the basis of an actual appraisal of needs made from time to time. In all such courses, care should be taken to relate the duration of the course, its contents and the qualifications of the trainees to the requirements of the practical situation.

As state-level organisation for improvement of school education are established and developed, they will take the work of training programmes more and more upon themselves. The responsibility of the NIE and the Regional Colleges of Education in this regard will then be correspondingly reduced.

Another important general principle which we would like to emphasise is that, in developing training programmes, whether at New Delhi or in the Regional Colleges of Education, a mere duplication of university courses or the organisation of courses which can be more appropriately and economically provided in the universities should be avoided.

The present programme of seminars and workshops is very large. Some of them do not appear to be linked closely with the developmental programmes of the NIE. The preparations made are often inadequate and the standard maintained often leaves much to be desired. We recommend that the number of seminars and workshops should be considerably reduced so that it becomes possible to link them effectively with the on-going programmes, to make adequate preparations, and to maintain high standards.

Leadership and staff : If the programmes of the NIE are to be developed on the lines indicated above, it will be necessary to provide leadership of the highest quality. The Director of the NCERT (who will also be the Director of NIE) should, therefore, be a whole-time officer of the Council with a high degree of competence in educational research as well as in administration. His status and emoluments should be similar to the Vice-Chancellor of a Central University or the Director of IIT and the mode of selection should also be similar. There should also be a joint Director.

We recommend that the Director of the NCERT should be relieved of other administrative work as far as possible, by the appointment of a whole-time Registrar, whose remuneration should be comparable to that of a

Head of the Department. To provide adequate academic leadership, the Director and the Heads of Academic Departments should act in close concert. The Director should be assisted by one Dean who will be one of the Heads of Academic Departments selected in rotation. The Dean will also be able to help in ensuring prompt and efficient assistance by the Technical Departments to Academic Departments.

We have recommended closer relation with Universities and state-level organisations. To Carry this out there should be effectively inter-change of staff. If necessary, supernumerary posts should be created for this purpose.

In view of what has been stated earlier, a proper ration between senior and junior posts will have to be maintained so that adequate guidance can be provided and supervision exercised. This will also provide avenues of promotion for those who show high qualities.

The number of class III and IV posts is large in comparison with the academic and technical staff, both in the NIE and in the Regional Colleges. However, to avoid problems of retrenchment, there should be a gradual reduction through rationalisation, transfer and other procedures.

The academic atmosphere in the NIE has not been developed properly because of status consciousness and heirarchical relationships. We recommend that the senior staff of the Council should make it their particular responsibility to create an atmosphere where communication between different levels and between different departments is easy and not affected by hierarchical consideration.

Regional Colleges Of Education

The setting up of the Regional Colleges of Education were motivated by two main considerations : (a) to prepare teachers for the scheme of multipurpose schools and (b) to improve the quality of teachers by adopting the pattern of integrated courses of general and professional education which prevails in the USA. We are not in favour of this programme for the following reasons, among others :

(a) This experiment of integrated courses is, and will always be, too costly to be repeated. It can however, make a marginal contribution to the improvement of teacher-education in India. The large scale allocation of scarce resources to this programme is, therefore, not desirable. If, for reasons of quality, such courses have to be organised, the experiment should be tried in universities with strong under-graduate departments in the subjects concerned and in education. In separate institutions like Regional Colleges, their costs mount up and efficiency tends to decrease.

For years to come, the average teacher of secondary schools in India will be a graduate of a University who receives professional training in a post-graduate course in the secondary Training Colleges. The efforts of the NCERT should therefore, be directed to research and improvement of this training course and towards the professional improvement of teacher-educators at this stage.

The multi-purpose schools are now a thing of the past. It is true that there will be new types of vocational courses corresponding to class VIII or classes XI—XII. But most of these courses will be provided, not in schools of general education, but presumably in separate institutions which would work in close collaboration with agriculture, craft or industry concerned. The provision of teachers for such courses should be the responsibility of the Ministry of Department concerned. For example, teachers required for agricultural schools or agricultural polytechnics will have to be trained by the Department of Agriculture and the Agricultural Colleges or Universities. The teachers required for courses in medicine and public health will have to be trained by the Ministry or Department of Health....and so on. The NCERT should not be saddled with the responsibility for the development of such varied courses which require an expertise which is not available in the NCERT Set-up.

We therefore, recommend that fresh admissions to the four year courses should be stopped with effect from the academic year 1969-70. The facilities thus released should be utilized for one-year courses and for expanding the programmes of the Regional Colleges for the training of teacher-educators and extension services and other developmental programmes.

The responsibility for continuing the course for the next three years will remain with the Regional Colleges because of the students already enrolled. There will be increasingly surplus staff and equipment during the next three or four-years courses taper off. The Ministry of Education should be apprised of the surpluses and the rate at which they will occur so that they can find suitable alternative use of the staff and equipment.

We offer the following suggestions regarding the different types of training courses which are now conducted in the Regional Colleges of Education.

(a) The fresh admissions to the technological courses have already been discontinued during the current year. However, the responsibilities of continuing the course for the next three years will remain with the Regional Colleges because of the students already enrolled. There will be a gradual surplus in staff and equipment.

(b) The facilities and staff released by the non-admission of students to the four-year courses in science should be utilised for expansion of programmes of science education in the region. Some staff may also be usefully transferred to the Department of Science Education, NIE, New Delhi.

(c) The staff and facilities released by the discontinuance of the four-year course in English may be utilised, to the extent possible, partly for increasing the enrolment in the one-year courses and partly for programmes of in-service education in the region.

(d) The one year courses in Science, English and Commerce may be continued, if necessary. The emphasis here should be on research and experimentation and not on reproducing what is being done in the Universities of Training Colleges not should the emphasis be on quality.

(e) The one year course in agriculture may be run, at one or two places, so long as there is a demand. It would, however, be preferable to transfer it to the Agricultural Universities or Colleges at any time that they are prepared to take over the responsibility.

(f) The NCERT has not carried out any experimentation so far in respect of preparation of teacher-educators for training institutions for primary and pre-primary teachers. This work should be developed at all the Regional Colleges of Education.

When the changes recommended by us are carried out, some staff will be released and it will be possible to use some of it in expansion programmes which we have indicated. If any retrenchment becomes necessary, persons who are on deputation should be returned to their original posts, unless there are strong reasons to the contrary. As far as possible, care should be taken to see that members of the staff do not get out of employment.

The Regional Colleges should in future be regarded as the campuses of the NIE with a free movement of staff and programmes between the Regional Colleges and the NIE. The activities to be emphasised at these campuses will be teacher education, both pre-service and in-service and research and extension programmes. Action research programmes in vocationalization of education could also be undertaken in these campuses.

Publication

The Publication Unit has brought out several text books, supplementary reading materials, year-books, pamphlets, journals, and reprints of some foreign books. Its work is naturally expanding. We recommend that this unit should be organised as a self-contained activities of the NCERT conducted largely on commercial lines.

To improve the efficiency of this Unit, we make the following recommendations :

1. There is no proper Advisory Committee which supervises the entire function of the Council in the matter of publications and gives guidance to the Publication Unit in all aspects of its publication policy. We recommend that such a Committee should be set up at any early date; and when that is done, the several Committees with limited jurisdiction which now exist should be abolished.

2. Some of the Departments of the NIE still handle some of their publications. This should be avoided and all publications should be centralised.

3. The present pricing policy needs revision. While the prices of the books should be kept at their lowest level, unnecessary subsidies should also be avoided.

Closer Relations With The State Governments

The main liaison between the NCERT and the States is the Council of which the State Education Ministers are members. But this is hardly enough and one of the reasons why the Council has not been able to make an adequate impact on the States is that it has not yet been possible to build up close working relations with the State Education Departments. We, therefore, recommend that immediate steps should be taken to build a closer relationship between the NCERT and the States by adopting the following measures :

(a) To bring the Education Secretaries in close contact with the working of the NCERT, they should be made members of the Council. Similarly, the Minister of Education should allocate definite time for discussion of the NCERT programmes in the periodical conference of Education Secretaries which it convenes.

(b) The Directors of Education/Public Instruction in the States are the key professional persons who provide leadership to the State Education Departments. A close association between the NCERT and the Directors of Education/Public Instruction will greatly facilitate the operation of the programmes of the NCERT. We, therefore, recommend that six DPIs/DEs, selected in rotation, should be members of the Governing Body. In addition, there should be an Advisory Committee consisting of all DPIs/DEs and the Director of the NCERT as the Chairman. The Committee will advise the NCERT on programmes of work and their implementation and will recommend research and development programmes to be undertaken, to meet the needs of individual States and of the Country in general.

(c) There should also be a Regional Advisory Committee for each Regional College of Education or NIE Campus. The Director of the NCERT will be the Chairman of all these Committees and their membership will include all Education Secretaries and Directors of Education/Public Instruction in the region; all Directors of State Institutes of Education in the region; Principles of two Training Colleges in the region and a few well-known educationists representing the different States in the region; Principal, Regional College of Education, to be Member-Secretary. These Committees will advise the NCERT on the development of programmes for the College of Education or Campus concerned with a view to matching them with the individual needs of the States in the region. It will also consider ways and means for adopting mutatis mutandis, the programmes developed by the NCERT in the different States of the region.

Closer Relations With Universities

It is essential that the NIE should work in close collaboration with University Departments. This will need effort, on the part of the Central and State Governments, to persuade the Universities to take increasing interest in the improvement of school education and the provision of necessary grants-in-aid by the University Grants Commission. We assume that these programmes will be developed on a priority basis. The NIE on its own part should develop collaborative programmes of research or improvement of school education with such Universities as show interest....in the problems. It should also provide facilities for exchange of staff between the Departments and the Universities.

The NIE should develop close liaison with outstanding school and university teachers and teacher's organisations.

Amendments To The Constitution

The NIE as such has no authority to award degrees nor is it affiliated to any university. The Regional Colleges are, however, affiliated to the universities within whose jurisdiction they are situated. When they are merged in the NIE, it will not be possible, nor desirable to affiliate the NIE to any university. It is, therefore, necessary to vest the NIE with the authority to grant its own degrees, especially in view of the experimental character of the work which it will undertake. This can be done either by declaring it as a deemed to be a university under Section 3 of the University Grants Commission Act, 1956, or by declaring it as an institution of national importance. We would recommend the adoption of the latter course, partly because of its intinsic value, but mainly because it will increase the status of the NIE and facilitate the dissemination of its ideas and practices in the country as a whole.

The composition of the Council and the other authorities of the NCERT gives an over representation to Delhi and does not represent the truly national character of the organisation. It also needs streamlining and building up of closer relations with the State Governments. From these points of view, the following amendments should be made to the Memorandum of Association and Rules and Regulations of the Council :

(a) **Council** : The Secretary to the Government of India, Ministry of Education, and the Director of the NCERT, should be members, Ex-officio. Instead of representation to universities being restricted to Delhi, four Vice-chancellers of Universities, one from each zone, should be nominated as members. Representation should be given to the Union Territory of Delhi and to such other Union Territories as have legislatures. The number of nominated educationists should be increased to sixteen and they should include persons of high academic standing in the field of agriculture, health, industry, art, letters, sciences, social sciences and technology. All Education Secretaries should be members of the Council ex-officio.

(b) **Governing body** : The Governing Body should be reconstituted as follows :

1. The Chairman of the Governing Body should be an eminent educationists, mentioned by the President of the Council;

2. The Director of the Council should be the Vice-Chairman of the Governing Body, Ex-officio;

3. Six eminent educationists with known interest in school education to be nominated by the President of the Council;

4. Six Directors of Education/Public instruction to be nominated by the President of the Council by rotation from among all the States and Union Territories which have representation on the Council ; and

5. Chairman of the U.G.C. and a representative each of the Ministries of Education and Finance.

The term of office of members, other than ex-officio members, should be for a period of three years. But an out-going member should be eligible for nomination for one more term and not more :

(c) **Academic committee** : At present there is a Board of Educational Studies with two Standing Committees and the Procedures of their operation lead to considerable delays. We therefore, recommend that these should be replaced by an Academic Committee consisting :

1. The Director of the NCERT—Chairman;

2. Five University Professors or Heads of Departments representing education and other related disciplines nominated by the Chairman of the Governing Body;

3. Five Directors of the State Institutes of Education to be nominated by the Chairman of the Governing Body in rotation from all the States and Union Territories ;

4. Joint Director and all Heads of Academic Departments of NIE;

5. Four Principals of Regional Colleges of Education; and

6. One Professor/Reader from each of the Academic Departments of the NIE to be nominated by Directors, NCERT.

The term of membership of the Academic Committee will be for two years.

It will be the responsibility of the Academic Committee to consider all plans, programmes, research proposal, applications for research grants or publication of the thesis, etc., to examine the academic aspect of the work of the NIE and to ensure coordinated approach to its programmes.

(d) **Bye-laws** : We were concerned to note that although the Council was set up in September 1961, it has not yet been able to frame even the essential bye-laws. Members of the staff have not yet been confirmed and even Provident Fund Rules are not in operation. We recommend that very early steps should be taken to regularise these and similar other matters by framing all essential bye-laws.

The details of the amendments needed to the Memorandum of Association, Rules and Regulations of the Council are given in Appendix X.

There has been a step rise in the expenditure of the Council. We feel that the Council has now reached a stage where it is more important to consolidate rather than to expand. The total financial provision of approximately Rs. 20 crores (including non-plan and plan) for the next five years should be sufficient to meet the requirements of work as envisaged by the Committee.

NATIONAL COMMISSION ON LABOUR, STUDY GROUP FOR THE CONSTRUCTION INDUSTRY, 1968—REPORT

Delhi, Manager of Publications, 1968. 35p.

Chairman : Shri Bagaram Tulpule.

Members : Shri N.S. Mankiker (Retired, Replaced by Shri S.R. Bhise) ; Shri B.V. Apte ; Shri M.A. Rehman ; Shri B.K. Kapadia ; Shri M.T. Shukla ; Shri N.N. Manna ; Shri K.A. Khan ; Shri K.P. Fadia.

APPOINTMENT

The Study Group for the Construction Industry was constituted under the National Commission on Labour vide their Memorandum No. 3 (40)/68-NCL dated February 6, 1968.

TERMS OF REFERENCE

To analyse available Information and Project its thinking on labour problems in the Construction Industry for the years to come taking into account the possible developments in the industry.

CONTENTS

Introductory; The Construction Industry; Employment; Working of Living Conditions; Safety; Workers' Organisations; Wages; Social Security; Summary of Conclusions and Recommendations; Annexure I and II.

RECOMMENDATIONS

The Government is the largest principal employer (sponsoring authority) in the construction industry. By devoting some care to the planning and coordination among different Governments and local authorities, it would be possible to phase the launching of major construction projects in such a way that a reasonably steady volume of work and level of employment are maintained.

The un-regulated entry of contractors into the industry regardless of qualifications or resources has been a major cause of chaotic labour conditions and much sub-standard and slipshod work. Hence, some system of classification and registration of contractors on the basis of their qualifications and resources should be introduced as suggested in Annexure I.

To ensure that contractor's labour gets proper amenities, it is necessary that the cost of such amenities is accepted as a permissible cost item in the tender and care is taken to ensure that the expenditure allowed under that head is in fact incurred and the amenities provided. Alternatively, a small cess on building materials may be imposed for financing these amenities.

Skilled workers in building trades are relatively

scarce, but arrangements for systematic training in such trades are very limited. It is necessary that adequate arrangements are made for such training in the Industrial Training Institutes and by the industry itself.

To provide greater security of employment to construction workers, the possibilities of introducing decasualisation schemes like those in the docks or in the Cotton Textile Industries in Bombay and Ahmedabad should be examined. Pilot decasualisation schemes should be tried out in one or two suitable not very large urban centres on an experimental basis and, if found workable, should be introduced in all other urban centres also.

Workers employed on major projects away from urban areas should be given employment cards for specified duration and should be entitled to get work for the duration.

Workers employed by Government or by local authorities on maintenance work on buildings, roads, airports, dams, irrigation canals, etc. should be deemed to be permanent and get all benefits of permanency, since their work is not of a casual nature.

As part of the amenities to be provided for construction workers, schools and shopping facilities need special attention.

A certain quota of tenements constructed by the State Housing Boards or authorities under the subsidised Industrial Housing or other schemes should be earmarked for allotment to construction workers.

Greater attention to safety in the industry on the lines proposed in the ILO conventions and the schemes prepared by the Chief Adviser of Factories needs to be given.

Only stronger Unions will be able to ensure real improvement in the workers' conditions as in the Western Countries.

Minimum wages fixed under the Act should be revised more frequently than the five-year interval prescribed under the Act.

Extension of the benefits of Health Insurance and Provident Fund to Construction workers will be feasible once some degree of decasualisation of their employment is achieved.

Systematic studies to evolve satisfactory norms of performance need to be undertaken, as, at present there is little reliable data available.

STEERING COMMITTEE OF PLANNING GROUP ON EDUCATION, 1968—REPORT

(Educational Development in the Fourth Plan 1969-74)
New Delhi, Education Division, Planning Commission, 1968. 194+11p. (Memiographed)

Chairman : Shri G.K. Chandiramani.
Members : Dr. O.P. Gautam; Prof. P.K. Doraiswami; Dr. P.J. Philip; Dr. A.R. Verma; Shri J.P. Naik.
Secretary : Shri D.P. Nayar.

APPOINTMENT

The Planning Commission set up an overall Planning Group on Education under the Chairmanship of Dr. B.D. Nag Chaudhuri, member (science), in March 1968, for undertaking preparatory work of formulating the Fourth Five Year Plan. The Group was asked to formulate proposals in regard to the size, content and strategies in the various sectors of educational planning. The first meeting of the Planning Group decided to set up a Steering Committee under the Chairmanship of the Union Education Secretary.

TERMS OF REFERENCE

(i) To examine the material already available ; the Draft Outline of the Fourth Plan, the Report of the Education Commission, the Reports of the various Committees that had discussed the Education Commission Report, etc. ;

(ii) To identify areas in which further work was necessary and specify problems which required further investigation ;

(iii) To prepare guidelines for preparing educational development programmes to be communicated to the State Governments after obtaining the approval of the

Planning Commission ; and

(iv) To prepare a tentative draft plan in education for the consideration of the Planning Group on Education.

CONTENTS

Introduction ; Present Position—A Review ; Priorities and Strategies for Fourth Plan ; Outlays and Targets ; Programmes and Policies (i) Pre-School Education ; (ii) Elementary Education ; (iii) Secondary Education ; (iv) University Education ; (v) Social Education ; (vi) Teacher Education ; (vii) National Service and Youth Programmes ; (viii) National Council of Educational Research and Training ; (ix) Development of Languages ; (x) Book Production ; (xi) Cultural Programmes ; (xii) Vocationalisation of Education ; (xiii) Development of Science Education ; (xiv) Technical Education) ; Planning, Implementation and Evaluation Machinery ; Annexures I to XIII ; Recommendations of the Planning Group on the Report of the Steering Committee ; List of the Members of the Planning Group on Education.

RECOMMENDATIONS

The Planning Group while discussing the report of the Steering Committee, desired that the various alternatives or choices before the country in the field of educational development might be posed squarely with their implementations to enable a fruitful debate to take place on the subject.

Basic Considerations

A certain number of considerations will have to underlie all possible alternatives. These are :

1. The inevitable expenditure must be met. This consists of maintaining the present momentum (leaving out the abnormal interrugnum of 1966-69) of educational development and providing for the commitments already entered into. The present momentum may again he reviewed from two angles : qualitative improvement and quantitative expansion. So far as quantitative expansion is concerned, it was agreed that providing for expansion on the basis of the past trend of increase in enrolment, which was a measure of the social demand for education, might be regarded as a priority in the sense that it might be difficult to resist it even if it might be desirable to do so on other considerations. Qualitatively, roughly speaking, it would be necessary to provide at least the expenditure which was incurred on these programmes in the Third Plan after applying the correction factor of increase in prices. The maintenance of the tempo of existing schemes does not rule out—as a matter of fact requires—the possibility of dropping some schemes that may have become redundent or comparatively unimportant.

2. As the demand for resources will always be greater than their availability, it is essential to provide for all the economies that are possible to effect through the use of improved technologies, a more intensive utilisation of facilities and creation of those facilities that are required more urgently in the economy or one more significant from the point of view of greater national cohension, as a first charge on the finances available.

3. For the same reason, it is essential to tap new resources in the community for educational development by the stimulus of suitable organisational changes such as linking the school more effectively with community needs, devising a machinery where the fruits of taxation are assumed for the Communities/Organisations which bear its burden, decentralisation of administration so that greater initiative is placed in the hands of the Community concerned and rights and responsibilities are more clearly linked, etc.

Inevitable Expenditure

4. The inevitable expenditure, duly rationalised in the light of the above considerations, is indicated below :

Table 1

Inevitable Expenditure

	(Rs. Crores)
Elementary Education	430
Secondary Education	195
University Education	195
Teacher Education	25
Social Education	12
Cultural Programmes	15
Physical Education	10
Languages and Books Production	28
Administration	10
NCERT	5
Other Programmes	5
Technical Education	105
Total	1080

5. The additional enrolment in the major sectors that will be obtained by the above expenditure will be as : (see table 2 on next page)

6. **The new departures in approach and strategy :** Apart from the three basic considerations mentioned para 2—that have been assumed for the above tasks and expenditure are :

Table 2

Additional Enrolment in Major Sectors

	Unit	Third Plan (additional achievement)	Fourth Plan (targets-additional)
Classes I-V	lakhs	165	150
Classes VI-VIII	lakhs	38	60
Classes IX-XI	lakhs	25	33
University Education	lakhs	5	9
Technical Education admission capacity	'000		
Diploma level		25	(—) 10*
Degree level		11	(—) 8*

(i) An average teacher-pupil ratio of 1 : 45** as against the present 1 : 40, for primary classes—mostly through the adoption of the shift system in Classes I & II. The average pupil-teacher ratio today in some States is as high as 55 and the adoption of the shift system should enable such States to bring the class size down to a manageable size within the limits of existing resources. The amount of Rs. 130 crores saved thereby is proposed to be ploughed back to improve the quality of primary education which is most urgently needed, especially to reduce the present heavy wastage and stagnation in primary classes. Many of the steps needed for the purpose do not require finance but purely organisational changes like limiting the admission in class I to the first one or two months of the year, discontinuation of examinations in early classes, adjusting the vacation to the need for labour at the time of the harvest and the sowing seasons, etc. Other measures which would have financial implications are :

(a) Paying an allowance to teachers who would work in the second shift or teach in part-time classes;

(b) Linking the school with the community and paying remuneration to teachers who would do adult education work;

(c) Providing free books to students;

(d) Providing tools for kitchen gardening;

(e) Providing guide books for teachers and interesting reading material and text-books for students; and

(f) Providing the minimum necessary teaching aids and other equipment required in primary classes.

(ii) Development of part-time education at the middle and college stages;

(iii) Correspondence courses for secondary and higher education and for teacher training;

(iv) Streamlining and modernising the administration

(v) Emphasis on functional literacy though on a limited scale;

(vi) Emphasis on languages and book production;

(vii) Emphasis on consolidation in technical education; and

(viii) All scholarships at the university stage to be generally loan scholarships.

7. If no additional resources are available and the above programme alone is implemented then the implications would be :

(a) The further postponement of the Constitutional Directive in the field of elementary education. The Education Commission had recommended that effective primary education of 5 years should be provided to everyone by 1975-76 and of 7 or 8 years by 1985-86. The target dates of the Steering Committee were 1980-81 and 1990-91 respectively. With the resources indicated for elementary education under the 'inevitable' expenditure the dates by which these goals could be achieved would get postponed to 1983-84 and 1993-94 respectively.

(b) Secondary education will continue to produce students who will only rush to the universities in the absence of effective alternatives.

(c) University education will continue to be at its present low quality and turn out people largely unemployable.

(d) The vast adult population will not be effectively brought into the developmental process.

Manoeuverability And Alternatives

8. If additional funds are provided the area of manoeuverability will be the amount provided minus Rs. 1080 crores and a number of choices will present themselves. Some of these will run through all sectors while others will pertain only to particular sectors. These are :

1. In regard to overall decisions it might be possible to take a view that we must link education effectively with productivity. So we could concentrate all the resources on these programmes which would increase productivity. These are :

—At the school stage (up to the matriculation), pro-

* As regards Technical Education, the Ministry of Education has advised the States to reduce their admissions in 1968-69 to this level in the light of the present unemployment among engineers (even if an optimistic rate of growth of the economy is assumed the present studies show that the supply from existing institutions will outstrip the demand) and with a desire to limit admissions to the extent of facilities available. More careful studies in the light of targets of industrial production, the rates of growth etc., that might be assumed for the Fifth Plan targets for technical education will be laid down and the figures revised, if necessary.

** This means an average attendance of 40 pupil per teacher.

viding work experience in agriculture and industry and creating through appropriate teaching methods those attitudes which are required for self-employment—initiative, resourcefulness, spirit of enquiry, leadership, etc.

—Provision of vocational education of an intensive character, especially oriented to self-employment, on a large scale, keeping in view the actual demand in the organised sector and the possibility of creating self-employment, at the end of the elementary and secondary stages.

—Provision of technical education on a large scale largely oriented to self-employment.

—Emphasis on research and design.

—Organisation of extension education including functional literacy on a large scale so that the practising farmer is brought under the impact of education. Part-time education and training ought to be provided for upgrading the labour force within industry. This is a most promising but hitherto neglected area.

The expenditure on each programme may be determined in the light of the resources available. Another limiting factor would be the feasibility of gearing up the educational system for various progrommes in the light of the limitations of personnel and the possibility of changing the present structure. Educational changes are very difficult to effect and, unless prepared carefully through a stage of, pilot projects, result in considerable wastage.

2. Elementary education may be expanded to the utmost possible extent. The limits here again are those of feasibility apart from financial resources. It is felt that it may be difficult to push forward this programme beyond what is visualised under the inevitable programme, except to bring in an additional 30 lakhs of children at the primary stage and another 10 lakhs (through part-time courses) at the middle stage. The funds required for this purpose are Rs. 50 crores. Considerable research and experimentation must be undertaken to evolve an effective programme to eliminate wastage and stagnation which is as high as about 60 per cent at the present time.

A view could be taken that as the entire nation shares the benefits accruing from elementary education and also as this stage could be enable us to shift and identity talent, it should get the highest priority and whatever resources are required for turning it into an effective programme ought to be provided. Such a course will not only be socially just but also ensure effective participation of the people as a whole in national programmes of social and economic development and lay a sound foundation for the growth of our basic institutions like the cooperatives and the Panchayats etc. In view of the fact that most of our people will not go beyond this stage of formal education and, therefore, whatever new in the matter of practices and attitudes we have to introduce, we should do so at this stage, the importance of concentrating our resources on this stage of education becomes obvious. Further, as we go to higher stages the benefit to the individual and to organised groups becomes more pronounced and hence it should be easier to shift the burden of education to the beneficiaries, which is not the case at the elementary stage. Again in developing countries the most important and difficult problem is to give the large mass of the people elementary skills through which they can process raw materials in the environment into usable goods. This task can best be accomplished through a suitably oriented elementary education. To put to productive use those trained at the higher stages requires capital which in developing countries is scarce.

3. A view can be taken to concentrate all additional available resources on the improvement of the quality of university education either over the entire field or in certain selected areas of excellence. It resources are spread over the entire field it may be difficult to produce appreciable impact. Concentration of resources on 'centres of excellence' could create focii of dynamism in our entire social, political and economical life.

4. A view can be taken that the teacher is the most important factor in education, and therefore, all additional resources ought to be concentrated on teacher education. The quantitative aspect is well taken care of by the funds provided under 'inevitable expenditure'. The quality of teacher training, however, could be emphasised and all its requirements met within the constraint of resources available and the feasibility of the programme.

5. The significance of functional literacy in a country, 50 per cent of whose national income comes from agriculture, is obvious. The limitations are the vast size of the problem, the limitations of personnel required for handling the programme effectively and the absence of effective techniques required to solve the problem with utmost economy. The problem of motivation is again serious. If functional literacy is to be provided to all within the age-group of 14-15 within the next 10 years the amounts required would be Rs. 450 crores.*

---

*The number of illiterates in the age-group 15-44 in 1978-79, i.e., ten years hence, will be 150 million. The cost involved in making an illiterate adult literate is estimated to be Rs. 30. On this basis the cost of eradication of illiteracy among 150 million illiterates would be Rs. 450 crores during the next 10 years. This means that the average cost per year would be roughly Rs. 45 crores.

6. In the filed of technical education are could follow other countries by increasing the output of engineers and technicians, as they bring in maximum returns if properly utilised. The demands of the organised sector, however, are seriously limited according to all indications. If we could orient our technical education towards self-employment, these personnel could became the means of building the country in addition to creating avenues of employment. The only limitation to advance in this direction is the capacity of the system to be oriented towards self-employment within the time period under reference. Considerable experiments will need to be conducted before any effective orientation of technical education on a large scale can be a reality.

Desirable 'Mix': Examination Of Steering Committee's Report

7. No single alternative could perhaps be accepted to the exclusion of others and the task before the Planning Group is to suggest the proper 'mix'. The Steering Committee has suggested one such 'mix'. Comments on this 'mix' are as follows:

(i) **The Requirements of elementary and secondary education:** Will need to be revised upwards as subsequent information about the existing pupil-teacher ratio has shown that the assumption that some of the additional enrolment will go into existing schools was not warranted. The requirements of elementary and secondary education will now be Rs. 391 crores and Rs. 229 crores respectively against Rs. 330 crores and Rs. 201 crores respectively. Secondly, the figures of elementary education are on the basis of the ratio of 1 : 45 through the introduction of the shift system. On the basis of the existing ratio of 1: 40, the expenditure will be Rs. 156 crores more for an enrolment of 180 lakhs assumed by the Steering Committee. The Planning Group supports the idea of the shift system in Classes I and II on the ground that the children of this tender age cannot remain engaged in academic work for more than 3 hours. They are, however, strongly of the view that this should not be used as a means of further lowering the already extremely in adequate per capita expenditure on primary education. The money saved thereby should be redeployed to strengthen primary education as indicated in para 5 (i) of this report.

2. **In teacher education**: The Planning Group tentatively suggests the reduction of outlays from Rs. 120 crores proposed by the Steering Committee to Rs. 84 crores in view of the fact that in June 1968 there were 1.5 lakh teachers who had registered themselves with the employment exchanges. The situation should be carefully reviewed by a small Committee. This Committee should go into the situation in each State.

3. While the Planning Group attaches the highest importance to the salaries and service conditions of teachers, then have not made any recommendations in this regard, because it has been decided to keep the improvement of salaries of teachers outside the Plan. Their estimate of this additional liability to government during the Forth Plan is roughly of the order of Rs. 200 crores.

4. In university education, while it is difficult to provide adequate quality in all our colleges and universities, it is necessary to create certain 'centres of excellence' where are provide all the facilities up to the optimum level so that top men can be produced who can occupy key positions in the various walks of national life. The Planning Group of the view that at least 15 per cent of the undergraduates* and post-graduate enrolment in science, which will mean 1.10 lakh students, may be provided laboratory and library facilities at the rate of Rs. 25,000 per student for post-graduates and Rs. 5,000 per student for under-graduates. This will mean an additional cost of Rs. 50 crores. A most immediate need and challenge in the field of higher education is the improvement of the quality of post-graduate work and research. To meet this challenge certain physical inputs are necessary. But what is even more imperative is the sense of urgency and commitment in the academic community and their initiative and resourcefulness.

5. In regard to the reduction already effected in admissions in engineering institutions the Planning Group is strongly of the view that any deliberate reduction of seats on the basis of the present unemployment among engineers would not be advisable. For any thing as institutional development is an integral whole and cannot be adjusted to reduced admissions later on, reducing admissions subsequently leads to underutilisation of facilities provided and higher per capita costs. Again, so far as the need of engineers in a developing country is concerned, it is unlimited. Only the country cannot employ them at the levels of wages to which they have got accustomed. If salaries could be lowered than many more engineers could be employed than are employed today. But this question of the salaries of engineers is connected with the total wage and salary structure in the country. These salaries are today much higher than the country can really afford to pay. The Planning Group realises the limitation of government operating a mixed economy to control salaries and wages over the entire range of the economy. Therefore, the best perhaps that government can do is to provide seats according to current demand and allow the market conditions of demand and supply

*Excluding the PUC and the Intermediate students.

to determine the salaries of engineers. Artificial limitation of admission by a government decision may not be desirable except in the case of institutions which do not have space, equipment or teachers. The government in the case of engineers, as in the case of others, however, takes no responsibility for providing employment at any fixed level of income to those who take up these courses of their own free will and over whose future deployment government has no control. The government could assist by orienting technical training towards self-employment so that the engineers through their increased competence to handle natural resources are able to find profitable openings for themselves and help open up the country in addition. An abundance of engineering graduates could also lead them to go into other than traditional channels and lead to the development of intermediate technologies. It could also lead them to go into sales, marketing, management, etc., which should have considerable impact on increasing returns from investments made in production, as has been so forcefully pointed out by Prof. Blackett.

6. In regard to the National Service Corps, the Planning Group recommends the appointment of a small Committee to suggest the activities that should be taken up under it and the phasing of the programme.

Adjusted for the changes indicated above, the allocations in the Steering Committee's Report will need to be revised as follows (Table 3):

The Planning Group realises that the allocations they have recommended for education are higher than those indicated in the Draft outline but in view of the National Policy Statement where the nation has resolved to spend 6 per cent of its national income on education, presumably in the next 15-20 years, this order of expenditure in the Fourth Plan becomes in escapable. This will raise the educational expenditure to 4 per cent of the national income in 1973-74.

Table 3

Distribution of an outlay of Rs. 1300 crores

(Rs. crores)

	Steering Committee's allocations	Revised allocations proposed
Elementary Education	330	486
Secondary Education	201	229
University Education	255	305
Teacher Education	120	84
Social Education	40	40
Cultural Programmes	20	20
Physical Education	30	30
Languages and Book Production	50	50
Administration	22	22
NCERT	10	10
Vocationalisation	4	4
Other Programmes	5	5
Technical Education	213	213
	1300	1498
		or Rs. 1500 crores approximately.

FINANCE COMMISSION, 1968—REPORT

Delhi, Manager of Publications, 1970. 282p.

Chairman : Shri Mahavir Tyagi.
Members : Shri P.C. Bhattacharyya ; Shri M. Seshachalapathy ; De. D.T. Lakadawala.
Member-Secretary : Shri V.L. Gidwani.

APPOINTMENT

This Finance Commission is the fifth Commission to be appointed Under Article 280 of the constitution and was constituted by an Order of the President dated the February, 29 1968, that "In pursuance of the provisions of Article 280 of the Constitution of India and of the Finance Commission (Miscellaneous Provisions) Act, 1951 (33 of 1951), the President is pleased to constitute with effect from March, 15 1968, a Finance Commission."

Shri Mahavir Tyagi shall render part-time service as Chairman of the Commission untill such date as the Central Government may specify in this behalf and thereafter, he shall render whole-time service as Chairman of the Commission. Of the other members Shri P.C. Bhattacharyya shall render part-time service as member of the Commission until such date as the Central Government may specify in this behalf and, thereafter, he shall render whole-time service as member of the Commission. The other three members will render whole time service.

TERMS OF REFERENCE

The Terms of Reference of the Commission are as follows:

The Commission shall make recommendations as to the following matters.

(a) The distribution between the Union and the States of the net proceeds of taxes which are to be or may be, divided between them under Chapter I of part XII of the Constitution and the allocation between the States of respective shares of such proceeds.

(b) The principles which should govern the grants-in-aid of the revenues of the States out of the consolidated Fund of India and the sums to be paid to the States which are in need of assistance by way of grants-in-aid of their revenues under Article 275 for purposes other than those specified in the provisions of Clause (1) of the article and other than the requirements of the Five Year Plan, having regard, among other considerations, to :

(i) the revenue sources of those States for the five years ending with the financial year 1973-74 on the basis of the levels of taxation likely to be reached at the end of the financial year 1968-69;

(ii) the requirements on revenue account of those States to meet the expenditure on administration, interest charges in respect of their debt, maintenance and keep up of Plan schemes completed by the end of 1968-69, transfer of funds to local bodies and aided institutions and other committed expenditure;

(iii) the scope for better fiscal management as also for economy consistent with efficiency which may be effected by the States in their administrative, maintenance, developmental and other expenditure;

(c) The changes, if any, to be made in the principles governing the distribution amongst the States of the grant to be made available to the States in lieu of the repealed tax on railway passenger fares;

(d) The changes, if any, to be made in the principles governing the distribution amongst the States under Article 269 of the net proceeds in any financial year of estate duty in respect of property other than agricultural land ;

(e) The desirability or otherwise of maintaining the existing arrangements under the Additional Duties of Excise (Goods of Special Importance) Act, 1957, inregard to the levy of additional duties of excise on sugar, textiles and tobacco in lieu of the States sales taxes thereon, with or without any modifications and the scope for extending such arrangements to other items or commodities.

(f) Irrespective of the recommendation made under item (e) above, the changes, if any, to be made in the principles governing the distribution of the net proceeds in any financial year of the additional excise duties leviable under the 1957 Act aforesaid on each of the following Commodities, namely :

(i) cotton fabrics; (ii) silk fabrics; (iii) woollen fabrics (iv) rayon or artificial silk fabrics; (v) sugar; and (vi) tobacco including manufactured tobacco, in replacement of the State's sales taxes formerly levied by the State Governments ;

Provided that the share accruing to each State shall not be less than the revenue realised from the levy of the Sales tax for the financial year 1956-57 in that State ;

(g) The principles which should govern the distribution of the net proceeds of such additional items or commodities as may be recommended under item (e) above for levy of a additional excise duties in lieu of the States sales taxes thereon ;

(h) The scope for raising revenue from the taxes and duties mentioned in Article 269 of the Constitution but not levied at present ;

(i) the scope for raising additional revenue by the various State Government from the source of revenue available to them ; and

(j) The problem of unauthorised overdrafts of certain States with the Reserve Bank and the procedure to be observed for avoiding such overdrafts.

CONTENTS

Introduction ; The Problems-Our Approach ; Income Tax ; Union Excise Duties ; Additional Duties of Excise ; Grants-in-Aid Under Article 275 of the Constitution ; Taxes and Duties Under Article 269 of the Constitution ; Scope for Additional Revenue ; Summary of Recommendations ; Minute by Shri G. Swaminathan ; Appendix from I to VI ; Annexures ; Interim Report of the Commission.

RECOMMENDATIONS

Our recommendations to the President in regard to devolution of taxes and grants-in-aid of the revenues of the States are set out below :

Income Tax

(a) In respect of distribution of the unadjusted balance of advance tax collections up to the year 1966-67 :

(i) out of the amount of such advance tax collections, as determined by the Comptroller and Auditor-General of India, a sum equal to 2-1/2 (two and a half) per cent thereof be deemed to be the portion which represents the proceeds attributable to Union territories, as constituted immediately prior to the Punjab Reorganisation Act, 1966 ;

(ii) the percentage of the amount of advance tax as determined by the Comptroller and Auditor-General of India except of the portion attributable to Union territories, to be assigned to the States should be 75 (seventy five) per cent.

(iii) the distribution among the States inter se of the share assigned to the States should be made on the basis of the percentages recommended by the Fourth Finance Commission, with appropriate adjustments in regard to the share of reorganised Punjab and Haryana States and Union Territories in accordance with the Punjab Reorganisation Act, 1966 ;

(iv) the share of each State should be paid to the State Government in three equal annual instalments during the years from 1971-72 to 1973-74.

(b) In respect of distribution between the Union and the States of the net proceeds of income-tax in the years 1967-68 and 1968-69, there should be no change in the distribution as prescribed in the Constitution (Distribution of Revenues) Order, 1965, in the event of the said net proceeds being certified by the Comptroller and Auditor-General of India on the revised basis;

(c) In respect of the distribution of net proceeds of income-tax in the financial years from 1969-70 to 1973-74;

(i) out of the net proceeds of taxes on income in each financial year, a sum equal to 2.6 per cent thereof be deemed to be the portion which represents the proceeds attributable to Union territories;

(ii) the percentage of the net proceeds of taxes on income, except the portion which represents proceeds attributable to Union territories, to be assigned to the States should be 75 (seventy-five) per cent; and

(iii) the distribution among the States inter se of the share assigned to the States in respect of each financial year should be made on the basis of the following percentages :

State	Percentage
Andhra Pradesh	8.01
Assam	2.67
Bihar	9.99
Gujarat	5.13
Haryana	1.73
Jammu & Kashmir	0.79
Kerala	3.83
Madhya Pradesh	7.09
Maharashtra	11.34
Mysore	5.40
Nagaland	0.08
Orissa	3.75
Punjab	2.55
Rajasthan	4.34
Tamil Nadu	8.18
Uttar Pradesh	16.01
West Bengal	9.11
Total	100.00

Union Excise Duties

(a) During each of the years 1969-70 to 1971-72 a sum equivalent to 20 (twenty) per cent of the net proceeds of Union duties of excise on all articles levied and collected in that year, excluding special excises, regulatory duties and cesses levied under special Acts and earmarked for special purposes, should be paid out of the Consolidated Fund of India to the States;

States	Percentages
Andhra Pradesh	7.15
Assam	2.51
Bihar	13.81
Gujarat	4.17
Haryana	1.49
Jammu & Kashmir	1.12
Kerala	4.28
Madhya Pradesh	8.48
Maharashtra	7.93
Mysore	4.65
Nagaland	0.08
Orissa	4.72
Punjab	2.17
Rajasthan	5.28
Tamil Nadu	6.50
Uttar Pradesh	18.82
West Bengal	6.84
Total	100.00

(b) During the years 1972-73 and 1973-74, a sum equivalent to 20 (twenty) per cent of the net proceeds of Union duties of excise on all articles levied and collected in the respective year, including special excises, but excluding regulatory duties and cesses levied under special Acts and earmarked for special purposes, should be paid out of the Consolidated Fund of India to the States; and

(c) The distribution among the States of the sum payable to the States in respect of each financial year should be made on the basis of the percentages : (See on page no. 23)

Additional Duties Of Excise

1. (a) It would not be desirable to maintain the existing arrangements in regard to the levy of additional duties of excise on textiles, sugar and tobacco, unless the Government of India, after discussing the matter further with the State Governments, can arrive at a general agreement for the continuance of the present scheme with suitable modifications;

(b) While the arrangements are continued, the rates of duties may be made ad valorem as far as possible, and may be revised periodically so as to secure reasonable incidence having regard to the prevailing prices and the general level of sales taxes on similar items levied by the States;

2. There is no scope at present for extending such arrangements to other items or commodities;

3. The net proceeds of the additional excise duties during each, financial year in which the existing arrangements continue, should be distributed on the following basis :

(a) A sum equal to 2.05 per cent of such net proceeds be retained by the Union as attributable to Union Territories;

(b) A sum equal to 0.83 per cent of such net proceeds be paid to the State of Jammu and Kashmir as its share;

(c) A sum equal to 0.09 per cent of such net proceeds be paid to the States of Nagaland as its share;

(d) Out of the remaining balance of 97.03 per cent of such net proceeds the sums specified below, representing the revenue realised in the financial year 1956-57 by each respective State from the levy of sales taxes on the commodities subject to additional excise duties, be first paid as guaranteed amounts to the following States :

State	Guaranteed amount (Rs. lakhs)
Andhra Pradesh	235.24
Assam	95.08
Bihar	130.16
Gujarat	323.45
Haryana	65.49
Kerala	95.08
Madhya Pradesh	155.17
Maharashtra	637.77
Mysore	100.10
Orissa	85.10
Punjab	96.07
Rajasthan	90.10
Tamil Nadu	285.34
Uttar Pradesh	575.81
West Bengal	280.41

(e) The balance be distributed among the States other than Jammu and Kashmir and Nagaland in accordance with their respective percentage shares of such balance as under :

State	Percentage distribution of excess amount
Andhra Pradesh	8.13
Assam	2.47
Bihar	8.40
Gujarat	6.33
Haryana	1.70
Kerala	4.84
Madhya Pradesh	6.34
Maharashtra	13.89
Mysore	6.00
Orissa	3.13
Punjab	2.98
Rajasthan	4.42
Tamil Nadu	9.63
Uttar Pradesh	12.99
West Bengal	8.75
Total	100.00

(f) In case the existing arrangements are discontinued during the course of a financial year, the sums specified in Clause (d) above, be reduced pro rata to the period for which the arrangements have continued.

Grants-In-Aid

The following States be paid the sums specified against each of them as grants-in-aid of their revenues in the respective years indicated in the table (See on next page) under the substantive part of Clause (1) of the Article 275 of the Constitution :

These sums are inclusive of the amounts specified in paragraphs as recommended by the májority of the members.

With reference to Clause (c) of paragraph 76 of our interim Report, we recommend that the payments made to the States on the basis of recommendation in Clauses (a) to (d) of that paragraph be adjusted against the respective amounts payable to them in accordance with the recommendations made in this Report.

The position regarding the estimated amounts of

transfer of funds to the States by way of their share of taxes and duties and grants under Article 275 (1) in the five years 1969-70 to 1973-74 in accordance with the recommendations made in our interim Report and in this Report, as compared with such transfers envisaged by the Fourth Finance Commission for the period 1966-67 to 1970-71, is shown in Appendix VI of this Report.

Rs. Crores

States	Total of the sums to be paid in the five years	Grants-in-aid to be paid in				
		1969-70	1970-71	1971-72	1972-73	1973-74
Andhra Pradesh	65.01	15.54	14.27	13.00	11.73	10.47
Assam	101.97	20.80	20.60	20.39	20.19	19.99
Jammu & Kashmir	73.68	16.81	15.77	14.74	13.70	12.66
Kerala	49.65	9.93	9.93	9.93	9.93	9.93
Mysore	17.99	6.48	5.04	3.60	2.16	0.71
Nagaland	77.95	17.40	16.49	15.59	14 69	13.78
Orissa	104.67	24.51	22.72	20.94	19.14	17.36
Rajasthan	51.49	12.36	11.33	10.30	9.27	8.23
Tamil Nadu	22.82	6.61	5.59	4.56	3.54	2.52
West Bengal	72.62	22.29	18.41	14.52	10.64	6.76
Total	637.85	152.73	140.15	127.57	114.99	102.41

ENQUIRY COMMITTEE ON FILM CENSORSHIP, 1968—REPORT

Delhi, Manager of Publications, 1969. 202p.

Chairman : Shri G.D. Khosla.

Members : Shri Lok Nath Misra; Shri M.P. Bhargava; Shri S.K. Vaishampayen; Shri P. Venkatasubhaiah; Shri Nath Pai (not attended); Shri R.D. Bhandare; Smt. Sharda Mukherji (replaced by Shri Balraj Sahni (resigned)); Shri Karni Singh (resigned); Shri K.A. Abbas; Shri R.K. Narayan; Shri Tapan Sinha; Shrimati Nargis (replaced by Smt. Tara Sapre); Shri A.V. Meiyappan; Shri Romesh Thapar; Shri Umashankar Jethalal Joshi; Shri M.V. Desai.

Secretary : Shri H.C. Khanna.

APPOINTMENT

In pursuance of the decision to enquire into the working of the existing procedures for certification of cinematograph films for public exhibition in India and allied matters, the Government of India in the Ministry of Information and Broadcasting constituted this Committee vide their Resolution No. 14/35/64-FC dated March 28, 1968.

TERMS OF REFERENCE

1. To study the effect of films exhibited in public on the people in the context of changing needs of society.

2. To enquire into the State of films in India in regard to their artistic content and healthy mass appeal in relation to the existing regulatory procedures.

3. To study the working of existing laws, machinery and procedures for the certification of Indian and Foreign cinematograph films for public exhibition in the country.

4. To recommend, on the basis of the above studies, measures for improvement in the existing censorship laws, machinery and procedures with a view to:

(a) enabling the Indian film to develop into an effective creative medium keeping in tune with the contemporary trends in social conduct and practices and responsive to the emotional and intellectual needs of the people.

(b) promoting between the film industry and the regulatory organisation a close understanding, which would be conducive to the production/exhibition of films of artistic excellence, high entertainment value and accepted moral standards.

(c) preventing the production/exhibition of films which offend against public taste.

CONTENTS

Introductory; History and Present Position; Film Censorship in Other Countries; The Legal Aspects of Film Censorship; Audience Rèaction; Evidence, Memoranda and Questionnaire; Forms of Censorship; Principles of Censorship; Improving Film Content; Summary of Conclusions; Notes from Members; Acknowledgements; Appendices I to IV; Bibliography.

RECOMMENDATIONS

History And Present Position

Before 1918, the censorship was haphazard and voluntary. The Cinematograph Act was passed in 1918. This was concerned both with the licensing of cinema houses and the certifying of films declared suitable for public exhibition.

In 1920, Boards of Film Censors were set up at Bombay, Calcutta and Madras. The Boards drew up General Principles for the guidance of Inspectors of Films based on the rules of censorship drawn up by the British Board of Film Censors. The lists of objectionable subjects was borrowed from the 43 rules formulated by T.P. O'Connor, the second President of the British Board of Film Censors. The whole aim of censorship in those days was to prevent the Indians from seeing a derogatory image of western life. The idea of a Central Board of Film Censors for the whole of India was also mooted at that time, but was dropped on the ground of postal delays in transmitting film prints. Censorship by the industry itself or a whole-time Board with whole-time paid Chairman was also suggested. Neither of the suggestions was accepted at that time.

In 1927, Rangachariar Committee was appointed to investigate into the whole question of film censorship. The Committee made various suggestions, including the setting up of a Central Board of Consorship. But it was not found possible to implement the recommendations of this Committee for some years.

At the end of 1948, the Governments of Bombay and Madras published a Production Code comprising a set of suggestions for the guidance of producers. The producers did not reject it altogether, but the Code was not adopted.

In 1949, two Acts were passed amending the Cinematograph Act of 1918. One Act introduced two categories, 'U' and 'A', and the other made provision for the appointment of a single Central Board of Film Censors. In the meantime, the Report of the Patil Enquiry Committee on Films was also received.

In 1952, the Cinematograph Act, repealing all previous enactments on the subject was passed. Under the Act, Cinematograph (Censorship) Rules were framed in 1958. The present Central Board of Film Censors consisting of a Chairman as a whole-time officer and nine non-official members who work in an honorary capacity, has been set up under these Rules. Advisory Panels have also been constituted at Bombay, Calcutta and Madras.

The General Principles and the application of General Principles which provide the guidelines to the Censors contain large and detailed instructions regarding what types of films or sequences in films must be considered objectionable. The procedure for certifying a film is that it is viewed in the first instance by an Examining Committee consisting of the Regional officer and three or four members of the Advisory Panel chosen by the Regional Officer. The Advisory Panels are appointed by the Government. Of the total number, two-thirds are to be appointed in consultation with the Board of Film Censors and one-third by the Government which virtually means the Minister in his discretion. There is a right of appeal against the views expressed by the Examining Committee and the Government has the ultimate power to decide the matter of certification in agreement with or against the views expressed by the Examining Committee or the Revising Committee.

Film Censorship In Other Countries

In most countries, there is a State Censorship. In the United States of America, the United Kingdom and Japan, however, the censors are non-officials appointed by the film industry. In Belgium and Uraguay, there is no censorship of films at all.

Censorship all over the world is tending to become increasingly liberal, particularly in relation to erotic themes. At the same time, there is emphasis now on the protection of children and young adolescents from the harmful effects of films depicting excessively erotic scenes, violence, cruelty and crime. For their protection, in certain countries rules have been framed classifying films into different categories. In some countries, children below a certain age are not allowed to go to the public cinemas at all and in others they are allowed only if they are accompanied by their parents or guardians. To see certain films, they are not allowed even if they are accompanied by parents.

There is a growing tendency not to have detailed

rules of censorship but to lay down briefly-worded general principles to promote greater flexibility in the matter of censorship, and to give wider discretion to censors in assessing films.

The Legal Aspects Of Film Censorship

Any law in regard to censorship must come within the ambit of Clause (2) of Article 19 of the Constitution of India and any directions or rules made under the Act must satisfy the test of reasonableness, which will ultimately be decided by a Court of Law. Some of the items under "Application of General Principles" which guide present day censorship· are beyond the terms of this clause and can well be questioned in a Court of Law. To extend the scope of censorship to considerations of public taste and ban a film which does not fall within the ambit of this clause would not be legal. The most sensible and the most rational way of dealing with the question is to declare that no film must transgress the reasonable restriction clause of the constitution and that the film must be judged as a whole.

To give protection to young and immature minds from the harmful effect of the films produced with a view to exploiting the gullible and innocent youth in order to make money, there is ample provision in the Constitution. The easiest and the most obvious measure is the classification of films into different categories, viz., suitable for children below a specified age, etc. Another measure which can be undertaken is the setting apart of special cinema-houses for children under the age of 13 and for young persons under the age of 18. But this is not feasible in India as conditions in India do not permit segregation of children and adults.

Thus, the recommendations are :

1. Any law dealing with film censorship should merely state that films must not be repugnant to the constitutional provision stated in Clause (2) of Article 19. There is no need to have a long catalogue of general principles or their application.

2. Classification of films may be three-fold :

(i) 'U' Fit for Universal Exhibition, including children, of all ages.

(ii) 'G' Fit for Universal Exhibition, but fit for children only if they are accompanied by adults.

(iii) 'A' Fit for adult audiences only.

Audience Reaction

No large scale study of audience reaction has been made in this country. In 1957, a pilot survey of audience reaction was conducted by the Central Board of Censors, assisted by the Tata Institute of Social Sciences. The area covered was Greater Bombay. At the request of the present Committee, another sample study was made by the Indian Institute of Mass Communication. Neither of these studies, however, was extensive or deep enough to convey a correct assessment of audience reaction in this country. Since it is a human problem of universal application with only minor regional differences, the surveys and studies made in America and England should prove of considerable interest and instruction.

The studies show that films have the greatest effect on young minds. The maturer mind can discount the unreality of the film, but the young mind cannot. Scenes of crime, violence and cruelty are prone to change the thinking and conduct of young children and adolescents. For example, when a young child sees love without marriage on the screen performed by popular film stars, a measure of sympathy and approval for illicit emotions is aronsed in him and he does not develop an aversion to adulterons or lascivious conduct. Crime films inspire delinquency. Many adolescents have been found to have been affected by films of this sort. Investigators believe that a great deal of liberty in sex matters claimed by the young minds to-day is due to the effect of films.

In the same way, films affect the minds of the unsophisticated, uneducated and simple adults also. Even if the seemings of such films does not make delinquents of innocent young men, it does have a very violent and depraving effect upon their minds. The continual viewing of such films makes them in sensitive to cruelty and violence, and they become prove to inflict violence on others. Above all, the young minds need protection from all types of highly emotional sequences, whether they be excessively erotic love scenes, scenes showing excessive or unusual cruelty or stories in which details of crimes are depicted in a way, which glamourises crime and the criminal.

Evidence, Memoranda And Questionnaires

There is almost universal criticism both of the film content and of the present mode of censorship. In this respect, the replies to the questionnaires are remarkably consistent with the conclusions derived from a detailed examination of the oral evidence tendered before the Committee and the numerous memoranda received by it.

Film Content

Quality of films: The poor quality of films has been attributed to the profit motive of the producer and to the star system. The film stars are blamed for demanding 'black' money, the producers for debasing the content of film and pandering to the lowest in human nature and the distributors for refusing to handle a film which has an aesthetic or artistic content, but no star cast. Films have been also criticised for the poor quality of the script and story used by the producers, for misrepresenting our ancient culture and for laying undue emphasis on sex and violence. They have been termed by some as mere cheap copies of foreign movies. Another criticism is that the Indian films are too long and far removed from reality. On the subjects of sex and obscenity in films the general opinion appears to be that though our attitudes have changed a great deal towards more liberality, there is a marked increase in excessive stress on sex themes in films.

Effect on Children : The replies showed that children are deeply affected by films dealing with crime, spying, violence and war, and a change in their behaviour is noticeable after they have seen such films. It was suggested by a witness that children upto the age of 13 or 14 should be allowed to see only films which are entirely devoid of the themes of crime, sex and violence. A critic felt that the responsibility for children in regard to films should be placed squarely upon the shoulders of the parents.

Film Censorship

Central board of film censors : The Board is criticised for not being a board of censors at all because in a large number of cases the final decision is aimed at without any member of the Censorship Board having seen the film. The Board has been categorised as a parking place for the Government officials who are due to move from one post to another but for whom suitable jobs cannot immediately be found. The members of the Advisory Panels have been criticised for being mostly ill-educated and not for taking sufficient interest in censorship. They work in an honorary capacity, and for each viewing they are paid a derisory amount of Rs. 10 to cover their expenses. This amount is insufficient even to cover conveyance charges. The members of the Examining and Revising Committees and the Board, according to some, treat the matter very casually and are sensitive to criticism from outside. Another weakness is that the Censorship Board is not an independent body and its decisions are subject to the over-riding power of the Government. The Board has also been criticised for inconsistency in their various decisions. Madras censors have been described as more liberal than the Bombay censors.

Chairman and other members of the board : For the post of Chairman, the appointment of a person with considerable judicial experience, such as retired judge of a High Court or Supreme Court, has been favoured though some producers suggested that someone drawn from the film industry would be more suitable. It is desirable to have as members persons with discrimination, possessing knowledge of Indian art, culture, traditions and, above all, persons with a liberal and modern outlook.

Representation of film industry : The absence of any representative of the film industry on the Advisory Panels has been stated as a reason for the neglect of the interest of the industry. It has also been suggested by some persons that the producer or his representative should be allowed to be present at the preview of the film.

Voluntary censorship : The majority thought that State Censorship was necessary in view of the present state of the country's development, and self-regulation was not possible, but the Board should be a completely independent body.

Censorship principles : The principles and their application have been criticised as being too explicit. If they are followed rigidly, not a single film, Indian or Western, is likely to be certified for public exhibition. It has been suggested that censorship in India should be broadbased and the censors should only have a few basic rules as guidelines.

Pre-censorship : Pre-censorship is not favoured by the respondents as the final shape of the film can be totally different in mood and manner from the original script.

Double standards : Opinions are divided as to the standards that should be applied in judging Indian and Foreign films. Producers feel that there is no justification for double standards while some witnesses contended that there is ample justification for evaluating foreign films on the basis of different standards.

Exported Films : Disapproval has been expressed of films being exported to other countries without having been viewed by the censors, as this results in many films with dubions artistic or cultural subject matter being sent to other countries and thus projecting a misleading and erroneous image of India.

Imported films : The consensus of opinion is that the import of films should be on a restrictive and selective basis.

Corruption among public servants and political graft : It was suggested generally that the producers should be free to deal with these themes.

'Predominantly educational' certificate : It has been felt that exclusively educational films should not be derived a PE Certificate simply because the 'credits' contain the name of the commercial concern which sponsored or financed the making of the film.

Certification fee : It has been suggested that this fee should be allowed to be remitted in cash, postal orders or bank drafts as the present system is irksome and time consuming.

Forms Of Censorship

Forms : Censorship may take the shape of a voluntary code of conduct drawn up and implemented by the film industry itself or it may be enforced by means of a State-imposed regulation, which may be entrusted to a Government department or to an independent statutory body.

Voluntary self-regulation : Voluntary self-regulation has obvious advantages. It eliminates protest against official curtailment of the right of freedom of speech and expression. Films which keep within the law and yet transgress the bounds of good taste can also be controlled. But the film industry in India, as testified by a large number of witnesses, is at present in a chaotic state. There are jealousies and rivalries between the various producers, studios, directors, etc. The industry is profit-oriented. To make money, some producers, produce films with scenes bordering on obscenity. In dealing with sex or love, no regard is paid to artistic or aesthetic values. Then, there is the 'star system'. Popular film stars are paid undisclosed and unaccounted for money. In the circumstances, voluntary censorship by the industry is wholly impracticable and impossible of achievement.

State control : State control has the disadvantage that any regulation dealing with censorship must keep within the reasonable restriction clause of the constitution. The present Board is not an independent body and suffers from lack of responsibility. This results in many delays and illogical decisions. Further, the decisions are likely to be set aside by the Government.

An independent board: An independent self-supporting Central Board of twenty fully paid members drawn from various regions and familiar with regional languages is, therefore, recommended. It will not suffer from any of the defects of the other two systems enumerated above and will make for consistency and uniformity in censorship policy.

Chairman and members of the board : The Chairman and Members should possess suitable educational qualifications and cultural background. The present system of entrusting the preview of a film to a panel of honorary examiners should be done away with. The Chairman should have the status of a High Court Judge and his salary may be in the neighbourhood of Rs. 4,000 p.m. The salary of the remaining members of the Board should be approximately Rs. 3,000 p.m.

Expenses of the board : The Board should be financially self-supporting. Its expenses should be met by increasing the previewing fees of films. A schedule for this purpose has been suggested at page 103 of this Report. The consequential burden on the industry will be negligible and the fees will represent a very small percentage of the total cost of the film. The industry will also benefit in the shape of prestige, respect and status, and earn for its members monetary dividends. The production of inordinately long films will be discouraged and a saving in foreign exchange expanded on the import of raw films effected.

Headquarters of the central board : It has been recommended that headquarters of the Board should be located either at Bangalore, Hyderabad or at Nagpur. These places are near enough to the main film industry centres and far enough to be impervious to constant influences of the industry.

Preview of films : Each film should be seen by not less than three Censors. In exceptional cases, they may associate with their advisers to give their views on local customs, linguistic antiguities or questions of good taste, etc. The list of such persons should be drawn up by the Central Board itself. They may be paid on honorarium of Rs. 100 for previewing a film. If there is difference of opinion between the censors viewing a film, the matter must be referred to the entire Board of Censors, the quorum for such previewing being seven.

Protection of children : To save the young and impressionable children and potential delinquents from the baneful effect of certain films, the Censors should be strict and forth right in the matter of classification. If the producer insists on a "U" certificate, the entire dance and song sequence which is vulgar should be deleted and not merely a few feet from it.

Outstanding merit certificate : To give a fillip to the production of better films, it is recommended that films which have outstanding artistic, aesthetic, cultural or educational merit should be awarded the "Outstanding Merit Certificate."

Modern viewing theatre : It is also recommended that a modern viewing theatre with adequate technical facilities and other literature dealing with film censorship question and other relevant matters must form part of the film censorship complex. This will lead to a better appreciation of the impact which films make on the society.

Principles Of Censorship

Need for censorship and constitutional validity : A film makes its impact by simultaneously arousing the visual and aural senses. The written word is understood by only a small fraction of the people, the spoken word reaches even fewer persons, but the film contains a complete and immediate appeal for everyone. And, if post publication penal action against objectionable films is to be taken, the remedy may be too long delayed, for before the producer can be punished and the film withdrawn, it already have done a great deal of irreparable damage. Therefore, in the case of films, censorship or pre-publication contr•l can be deemed to be a reasonable restriction on the right of freedom of expression.

Nature and extent of restriction : No rules framed by the Censor Board which go beyond the provisions of the Constitution can be legal. Censorship, therefore, must be within the terms of the Constitution, i.e., it must comply with the requirements of Clause 2 of Article 19. Freedom of expression is a fundamental right of the Indian citizen and the film artist has the right to express his ideas and communicate them as long as in doing so he does not transgress any law of the land.

Guidelines instead of the code : It is important not to have a Code drawn up by the Government under its rule-making authority, for such a Code assume the rigidity of a legal enactment, and does not permit the exercise of discretion. Therefore, the Censors should themselves drawn up the necessary guidelines. This will result in flexibility and the Censors will have•ample discretion in the matter of certification of films.

Imposition of reasonable restriction : The various matters with regard to which the Constitution permits the imposition of reasonable restrictions are these :

(a) **Sovereignty and integrity of India :** It is permissible to enact a law making it an offence to produce a film in which the sovereignty and integrity of India is attacked and to frame a regulation banning the exhibition of such a film. So, a film which advocates or argues a case for the ceding of any part of India or alleges that any part of the territory of India falling within the definition set out in Article (1) of the Constitution, is foreign territory or is not part of India may not be certified for public exhibition.

(b) **The Security of the state :** A matter which jeopardises or endangers the security of the State may be banned. The Board of Censors should, however, bear in mind the rulings of the Supreme Court and of the various High Courts. When an individual character in a film is shown representing a class or group and the film, by this device, aims at the inculcation of hatred against the entire group, it should be banned. But if no such inference of generalisation can be drawn, and it is clear from the film that it is only a particular individual who is being held up to ridicule, the shot should not be considered objectionable.

(c) **Friendly relations with foreign states :** Whenever any question of a film being declared objectionable or offensive to a foreign country arises, the film should be viewed by the Chairman of the Board of Censors and as many of the Censors as possible. The protest, if any, should be made through the Ministry of External Affairs and the matter should be discussed by an official of that Ministry with the Chairman of the Board of Censors. The ultimate decision must rest with the Board of Film Censors. The Government have, however, powers under the constitution to deal with an extraordinary case concerning the sovereignty and integrity of India or affecting friendly relations with foreign States.

(d) **Public order :** Incitement to act illegally and violently may be direct or indirect. Some films produced in foreign countries depicting detailed scenes of violence may be construed as indirect incitement. Methods of crime brutalise the mind by making it insensitive to pain and cruelty. Films should not be used for propagating anti-democratic and anti-social doctrines, nor for disseminating any kind of propaganda, political, social, regional, communal or religions which would make the film some thing that threatens public order. Reasonable freedom should be given to socially significant films. Depicting the character of a corrupt official may not be objected to as long as it does not transgress the law of libel and does not incite public order.

(e) **Decency and morality :** The principles laid down by the Supreme Court in regard to indecency and immorality reproduced at pages 118 and 119 of this Report must be carefully studied and applied by the Board of Censors. Films which do not fall within the mischief of these principles but may be considered in bad taste and unsuitable for young people can be easily rendered innocuous by the device of classification at the same time, a film must be taken as a whole, evaluated as a single integrated work of art or entertainment. If in telling the story, it is logical, relevant or necessary to depict a passionate kiss or a nude human figure, there should be no question of excluding the shot, provided the theme is handled with delicacy and feeling, aiming at aesthetic expression and avoiding all suggestion of unnecessary prurience or lasciviousness. This will give greater scope to the serious minded and sensitive creater of aesthetic films• The Censors should reject an entire film, which in its totality, is considered unwhole some because of many vulgar and obscene shots in it.

(f) **Contempt of court :** A scene casting aspersions on the integrity, impartiality and ability of the judges will be liable to be banned or deleted on this ground. Criticism of a judicial decision by attributing base motives to the judge will also bring the fil within the mischief of this clause.

(g) **Defamation :** Films containing matter defamatory of a national hero such as Mahatma Gandhi or Jawaharlal Nehru should be banned or the defamatory reference deleted. At the same time, it is unwise to develop a kind of hypersensitivity to even a humorous remark aimed at raising a length in reference to well-known public figures.

(h) **Incitement to an offence** : Incitement itself is punishable, whether it does or does not lead to the commission of the offence. A film containing a sequence which openly incites the audience to commit an offence should most certainly not be certified for public exhibition. Grue-some depiction of violence may be held to amount to incitement to commit an offence. The close association of erotic pleasure with the brutal infliction of pain in a film may indirectly incite an ordinary reasonable young man or workman to seek the sort of erotic experience displayed in the film. Cruelty and the infliction of pain move the viewers to perform similar acts. Therefore, any film in which violence is shown as a source of pleasure, erotic or otherwise, should be considered objectionable on the ground that it amounts to an incitement to commit an offence.

Scrutiny And Censorship Of Films Exported Out Of India

To discourage, and if possible, eliminate a distorted image of our social, political and cultural life being presented to other countries through exported films, only films approved by the Censors and granted a certificate for exhibition abroad should be exported :

(i) Newsreels and documentaries produced by accredited film producers, newsreel cameramen, or television teams may be sent out of the country without a certificate from the Board of Censors as at present.

(ii) Feature films produced by Indian producers should be censored and certified before their are allowed to be exported and exhibited abroad.

(iii) Films produced by foreign producers should be subject to the scrutiny of the final shooting script as at present.

Double Standard Of Censorship With Regard To Films Of Indian And Foreign Manufacture

The overall effect, the intention of the producer, the nature of the story, the country of origin and the effect on the type of audience viewing the film are all matters which must be simultaneously considered before deciding whether a particular shot or sequence in a foreign film should be passed or deleted. Having regard to the boldness with which many foreign producers treat human problems, it will be advisable to categories films containing too frank and intense a discussion of human relationship as films deserving the 'A' certificate instead of banning them completely.

Import Of Foreign Films

The following course has been recommended :

(i) Import of educational films through established importers may continue as at present.

(ii) Import of films by smuggling should be stopped altogether by the Censor Board's refusal to grant such films a certificate.

(iii) Like luxury goods, import of feature films should also be allowed to be made on a 'selective' basis. Let only those foreign films be allowed to be displayed which have outstanding cultural, social, scientific, aesthetic or educational value. Films having cheap and erotic entertainment should be banned.

(iv) Present trade agreements with foreign countries in regard to films may be allowed to run their life. But afterwards, all import of feature films must be processed under the advice of the Board of Censors.

Protection of children : Children and impressionable young boys and girls form a special class. Children between 10 and 15 are most vulnerable to evil influences. They must be protected from all evil and depraving impacts. The censorship applicable to films which the children may be prevented from seeing will be more extensive and wider in scope than the code for adults because a restriction which may well be deemed unreasonable when applied to adults may be adjudged reasonable in reference to young and immature minds. This can best be achieved by strictly classifying films as fit for universal exhibition (U), for general exhibition (G) and for exhibition to adult audiences only (A).

Improving Film Content

To improve the artistic and aesthetic quality of Indian films, the following measures are suggested :

1. Greater freedom should be permitted in the theme content of films. Producers should be allowed to deal with social and political questions and also the subject of sex. As far as films meant for adult audiences are concerned, greater freedom will not do any harm. The baneful effects, if any, of such films upon children and adolescents can be prevented by the classification suggested in Chapter VIII. Persons under the age of 18 will not be allowed to see 'A' category films. Children under the age of 16 will be permitted to see 'G' category films only if they are accompanied by adults. 'U' category films will be open to all audiences.

2. A stimulus for the production of better films can be provided by awarding an Oustanding Ment Certificate to films which have a high aesthetic, artistic and cultural value. In case of such films, the producer will be entitled to apply for exemption of Entertainment Tax. The refund can be authorised by the Film

Council.

3. The import of foreign films should be upon considerations of artistic, aesthetic, cultural or educational merit. It should be not commerce-and-politics-oriented.

4. The advice of the Board of Censors should be sought in choosing films for the President's Award and also for choosing entries for international film festivals.

5. The excessive length of Indian films should be discouraged by a higher slab of censorship fees for films exceeding three thousand metres in length. This will encourage production of good films and also effect a saving in foreign exhange used for the purchase of raw films from abroad.

6. The members of the Board of Censors should make themselves available to the film industry for consultation and advice in all matters concerning film production.

7. The state should undertake the construction of large number of small cinema houses which should not be controlled by commercial distributors. Small budget films of good quality can be shown in these cinema houses.

8. The Film Finance Corporation should be more discriminating, and use greater imagination in advancing loans to creative film makers. The competent producer who wishes to make an aesthetically good film should be encouraged.

9. Funds should be made available for research and experimentation in film production. Once the Corporation is satisfied that a producer has the imagination, competence and artistic talent required for the making of a good film, he should be encouraged without an eye on profit.

10. Predominantly educational films should not be refused a certificate simply on the ground that the film has been made by a commercial concern and the name of the concern appears in the credits portion of the film. As long as there is no open advertisement of the concern, the film should not be rejected on that ground.

11. The film society movement needs encouragement. This will help to develop taste and interest in the better type of films both Indian and Foreign. A link should be established between the Censor Board and the Socities. Exemption from censorship should given by the Board and not by the Ministry of Information and Broadcasting.

12. The Government may, in the event of Board of Censors finding themselves handicapped by the provisions of the constitution to control films debasing public taste, give consideration to the question of imposing social controls on the film industry, if there is no appreciable improvement in the content of films or in the purely profit-oriented attitude of the industry.

INQUIRY INTO THE ACCIDENT TO 12 DOWN DELHI-HOWRAH EXPRESS TRAIN AT LUCKEESARAI STATION EASTERN RAILWAY ON 14TH FEBRUARY, 1968—REPORT

Delhi, Manager of Publications, 1970. 11p.

One-Man Commission : Shri G.S. Pandor.

APPOINTMENT

The Commission was constituted under the Ministry of Tourism and Civil Aviation (Commission of Railway Safety) in accordance with Rule 10 of Railway Board's Notification No. 59-TTV/42/1 of April 11, 1966.

TERMS OF REFERENCE

To inquire into the accident in which prospective rail travellers were run over by No. 12 Down Delhi-Howrah Express Train at Luckeesarai Station on the Howrah-Mughalsarai Main Line section of the Eastern Railway at about 22.14 hours on 14th February.

CONTENTS

Corrigendum; Summary; Inquiry and Inspection; The Accident; Casualties; Relief Measures (Restoration of Train Services); Composition of Train and Damage (Composition of the Train; Damage); Local Conditions (Description of the Site; Maximum per missible Speed); Summary of Evidence; Discussion (Time of Accident; Speed; Visibility; Whistling by the Driver; Rules for Crossing Railway Lines; Responsibility); Conclusions; Recommendations and Incidental Observations and Recommendations Made by the Commission of Railway Safety in Connection with the Accident to 12 Down Delhi-Howrah Express Train at Luckeesarai Station, Eastern Railway at 22.14 hours on February 14, 1968.

CONCLUSIONS

Conclusions And Remaks

From the evidence available before me, I have arrived at the conclusion that the accident, which occurred at 22.14 hours at Luckeesarai on February 14, 1968 was the result of prospective rail travellers attempting to cross the Railway line in the face of the approaching Train No. 12 Down, Delhi-Howrah Express. The persons who died and who were injured are themselves to blame for the accident. They risked their lives by not using the foot over-bridge connecting the two platforms at the station. No responsibility lies on any railway employee.

Relief Measures

Within 20 minutes of the accident, a local Doctor rendered First-Aid to the injured. Kiul Railway Medical Van with 'A' class equipment, accompanied by the Railway Doctor reached the site within 3,4 hours 8 cases of grievous injuries were admitted in Jamalpur Railway Hospital within about 7 hours. I am satisfied that the relief measures were as effective as could be expected, in spite of the fact that the local public prevented the Assistant Medical Officer, Kiul, from attending to the injured persons.

COMMISSION OF INQUIRY ON GANGES WATER POLLUTION 1968—REPORT

Delhi, Manager of Publications, 1969. 156p.+2plates

Chairman : Shri Manohar Pershad.

Members : Shri N.V. Modak; Shri K.R. Bhide; Dr. M.G. Krishna.

Secretary : Shri N. Krishnamurthy.

APPOINTMENT

On March 3 1968, there was a blaze in the river Ganges near Monghyr in Bihar State. On the basis of the investigation made by the concerned authorities, the Government of India in the Ministry of Petroleum and Chemicals and Mines and Metals, Department of Petroleum decided to order a full investigation into what actually happened and to allocate the responsibility where necessary and to devise steps to guard against such events in future. The commission of Inquiry on Ganges Water Pollution was Constituted under the Commissions of Inquiry Act, 1952 Vide Resolution No. 22 (13) 68-OR dated April 20, 1968.

TERMS OF REFERENCE

(i) To determine the correct facts of the contamination with oil of the river Ganges near the downstream of the Barauni Oil Refinery during the last weak of February and the first week of March 1968 (or earlier);

(ii) To determine to what extent the Barauni Oil Refinery has been responsible for the happenings ;

(iii) To recommend the steps that must be taken to prevent the recurrence of such happenings in the refineries in the future;

(iv) To advice on whether there has been any negligence or carelessness on the part of the refinery management and staff in the discharge of their prescribed duties.

(v) Arising out of (iv) to recommend further action, if any, that must be taken;

(vi) To report on the loss or damage to the public caused by the pollution of the water and to recommend what, if any, restitution the Indian Oil Corporation should make in that connection to those adversely affected; and

(vii) Generally, to report on any other matter that is relevant in the opinion of the Commission.

CONTENTS

List of Abbreviations; Acknowledgement of Assistance; Introduction; Powers and Functions of a Commission Under the Act; Events That Led up to the Present Inquiry; Preliminary Proceedings and Directions; General Reference to the Memoranda of Barauni Refinery, Monghyr Municipality and the Bihar Government; Points that Emerge from the Memoranda of Barauni Refinery, Monghyr Municipality and the Bihar Government; Discussion of Points with Reference to the Evidence and the Finding Thereon; Cause of Contamination—Consideration of the Points of Difference Between the Versions of Barauni Refinery, Monghyr Municipality and the Bihar Government; Cause of Contamination—Discussion About Freezing and Melting; Cause of Contamination—Discussion About Discharge of ATF which has Gone Off—Specification; Cause of Contamination-Description of Plant for Treatment and Disposal of Effluent and Notes of Inspection of the Refinery; Cause of Contamination—Clarification Sought by Member of the Commission from the Then General Manager of the Refinery; Cause of Contamination—Technical Considerations; To Determine to what Extent the Barauni Refinery has been Responsible for the Happenings; To Recommend Steps that Must be Taken to Prevent the Recurrence of Such Happenings in Refineries in Future; To Advice Whether There has been any Negligence or Carelessness on the Part of the Refinery Management and Staff in the Discharge of Their Prescribed Duties; Arising Out of IV, to Recommend the Further Action; If any, that Must be Taken; To Report on the Loss or Damage to the Public Caused by the Pollution of the River and to Recommend What, if any, Restitution of the Indian Oil Corporation should Make in that Connection to Those Adversely Affected; Generally, to Report on any Other Matter that is Relevant, in the Opinion of the Commission; Annexure; Appendices from I to XV.

RECOMMENDATIONS

Regarding Item I Of The Terms Of Reference

1. There was a discharge of huge quantity of oil by the refinery from February 22, 1968 to February 28, 1968 and substantial quantities from October, 1967, onwards which were responsible for the pollution at Monghyr.

2. The capacity of different working units in Sector 6 to skim and store slops was not adequate to cope with the slop oil which was entering Sector 6 with the effluent.

3. There were constant and heavy leakages over a period of at least 3 to 4 months prior to the incident in the various pump glands, condensers, heat exchangers and other upstream units from which large quantity of oil might have entered the effluent streams.

4. Negligence on the part of the refinery management in not paying heed to the warnings given about the unsatisfactory conditions of Sector 6 and not trying to rectify the defects.

5. Non-inspection of the effluant pipe-line to see whether the effluent was mixing with the live current of the river which was the main consideration of the disposal scheme.

6. Absence of adequate facilities for inspection of the effluent upto the discharge point and improper roads and lighting conditions in Sector 6 which prevented the operators from exercising vigilance during night shifts and inclement weather.

7. No provision made for patrolling of the effluent pipe-line.

8. Lack of coordination between the officers and staff belonging to OM & SR and the Water Utilities Divisions operating in Sectors 6 and 7.

9. Measures not taken to provide the required pumping plant with adequate stand-bye for quick pumpage of storm water flowing into area of Sector 6 in order to ensure efficient operation of the units installed in it without their fooding in times of heavy rains.

Regarding Item II Of The Terms Of Reference

The Refinery has been wholly responsible for the contamination of river Ganga at Monghyr during the first week of March, 1968.

Regarding Item III Of The Terms Of Reference

1. The Commission has recommended what steps have to be taken by the Barauni Refinery and the Refineries in India, in general, to prevent recurrence of such happenings in future.

2. It has also recommended what steps have to be taken by the Government of India and the State Governments to ensure prevention of such happenings in future.

Regarding Item IV Of The Terms Of Reference

1. If BRD 39 was defective from its very inception it was the statutory duty of the refinery to get it rectified.

2. The refinery did not control the flow of larger quantities of oil beyond the permissible limit of 50 p.p.m. into the effluent pumping station and therefrom to the river through the 48″ rising main.

3. In the Guard Basin the effluent surface should not have had any noticeable stream units were operated and maintained properly even according to the thin

and almost unnoticable. The very fact that the thick layer of oil was constantly maintained for several months and years shows defective operation of the plants and gross negligence.

4. Untreated fecal sewage was allowed to pass and get mixed with the oil containing effluents which is well known as objectionable.

5. Adequate facilities for inspection of the pipeline were not provided which led to an obvious slackness in inspection.

6. Absence of proper co-ordination among the members of the staff of Sectórs 6 and 7 has aggravated the situation.

7. The three top officers of the management of the refinery, namely, Shri Balwant Singh, the ex-general Manager, Shri G.S. Harnal, the Deputy General Manager (Technical) and Shri C.D. Ayyar, Chief Electrical Engineer have failed to ensure the efficient treatment of the effluent and to discharge it in the proper manner into the river.

8. Poor maintenance of some of the epuipments in the production units has resulted in the generation of large quantities of slops during December 1967 to early March 1968 which has over-loaded the units of Sector 6.

Begarding Item V Of The Terms Of Reference

Arising Out Of IV, To Recommend The Further Action, If Any, That Must Be Taken

1. The Government of India should get a detailed inquiry made into the matters indicated under discussion on Clause 4 of the reference and also into the conduct of the officers of the refinery named therein and take suitable action.

2. The Government of India should direct the Indian Oil Corporation to make a thorough and careful study of the maintenance practices prevailing in the Barauni Refinery, if necessary, by using modern management techniques, for the efficient and better working of the refinery as the present maintenance of the various units is unsatisfactory.

3. The Government of India should also direct the Indian Oil Corporation to take suitable steps for maintaining better relations between the staff working in the various units and try to improve the co-ordination of functions allotted to its staff members.

4. The staff of the Inspectorate of Factories of the Government of Bihar do not seem to realise the importance of regular checks of the effluent pipeline running across fields upto the river Ganga and also of the effluent actually being discharged into the live current. The Commission, therefore, suggests that the Government of India should draw the attention of the Government of Bihar to this fact for future improvement.

5. The Government of India should ask the Government of Bihar to provide due facilities to the Barauni Refinery to protect the effluent pipeline and its fittings from being tampered with by the villagers as the attention of the commission was brought to this fact by the management of the refinery at the time of the inspection.

Regarding Item VI Of The Terms Of Reference

1. The Barauni Refinery is responsible for the loss and damage caused to the Monghyr Municipality and the individuals—MM 27, MM 28, MM 29, MM 30, MM 36 and MM 37.

2. It is also responsible for the loss and damage caused to the public in general of the Monghyr town for making arrangements to get supply of water which was suspended from the 3rd March to the 8th March, 1968.

3. Government of India should find ways and means of compensating the Municipality, the citizen of Monghyr town and the individuals who have suffered actual injury as indicated earlier.

Regarding Item VII Of The Terms of Reference

Generally To Report On Any Other Matter That Is Relevent In The Opinion Of The Commission

With regard to this clause of reference the contention of the learned lawyer for the Refinery is that this clause was ultra vires the powers of the Government in that the Government had failed to specify the definite matter of public importance and had left it to the Commission to report generally on any other matter which in its opinion was relevant. In other words it is urged that this term of referenc is vague in the sense that the Government which alone could form an opinion as to a definite matter of public importance has left this matter to be decided by the Commission without itself forming such an opinion. In this connection our attention is drawn to the terms of reference before Madholkar Commission of Inquiry. The contention of the learned lawyer for the Monghyr Municipality and the Bihar Government is that this clause is not ultra vires the powers of the Government.

We agree with the contention of the lawyer for the refinery that under the Commissions of Inquiry Act a Commission can be set up for making an inquiry into a definite matter of public importance, i.e., that the matter to be inquired into must be definite and it must also be of public importance. But in order to understand the clause of the reference are read together it appears to us that what the Government means by the use of the words "any other relevant matters" is that it wants the Commission to report on some other aspects which are not particularised by the preceding terms of reference and which are relevant in its opinion.

We need not go into details and discuss this point and express our view because we do not feel the need to recommend anything under this clause as what we had to suggest, we have done under clause 3 of the reference. In this view we are taking we need not discuss the terms of the Madholkar Commission of Inquiry or the other cases cited.

NATIONAL COMMISSION ON LABOUR, STUDY GROUP FOR TRIBAL LABOUR (AGRICULTURAL AND INDUSTRIAL), 1968—REPORT

Delhi, Manager of Publications, 1969. 120p.

Chairman : Dr. L.P. Vidyarthi.
Co-Chairman : Rev. Father M.V.D. Bogaert.
Members : Dr. B.N. Sahay; Prof. S.K. Chand; Shri Aroon Bose; (Shri Bhaiya Ram Munda (replaced Rev. Father J. Boel).
Member-Secretary : Mr. T.R. Sharma.
Associate Member-Secretary : Mr. T.S. Rao.

APPOINTMENT

The National Commission on Labour appointed the Study Group for Tribal Labour (Agricultural and Industrial) in and around Ranchi vide its letter No. 3 (64) 68—NCL dated Apirl 24, 1968.

TERMS OF REFERENCE

To undertake a study of tribal labour—both industrial and agricultural-to high light the problems and attitudes of this ethnic group as distinguished from, and parell to, those of non-tribal agricultural and industrial labour in terms of the objectives of the National Commission on Labour.

To ascertain facts and formulate recommendations for the amelioration of the conditions of the tribal labour on the basis of existing materials and information available to the Study Group.

CONTENTS

Introduction; Approach to Tribal Labour Problems; Tribal Labour Problem; The Background; Tribal Agricultural Labour; Tribal Forest Labour; Tribal Casual Non-Agricultural Labour; Tribal Industrial Labour; Conclusions and Recommendations; Appendices from I to XI.

RECOMMENDATIONS

General

Since Independence a number of large-scale industries have been set up in the tribal areas of Bihar, Orissa and Madhya Pradesh. Wherever it takes place, the process of industrialisation has vital impact on the economy and society of the people of the region. The impact is far more serious for folk societies like that of scheduled tribes. When the phase of change is rapid and overwhelming, it causes cultural crisis, economic disorganisation and social disintegration. This fact has been brought out by the several field studies made on this subject. They have pin-pointed the diverse and complex processes that are now operating on tribal life in these areas. There is a danger that if we do not make an honest attempt to understand the working of these processes and their effects on tribal culture from the unsettling effects, the tribal society may not be able to withstand these forces and may eventually disintegrate and disappear. This will be a great loss as we believe that development at the cost of human values is not worth it.

We believe that tribal people, if they are given time, will undergo a process of cultural evolution and would themselves work out a synthesis of traditional culture and modern culture.

We suggest that :

(a) Whenever a large industrial project is located in a tribal area, a study should be made of the possible consequences on the tribal life and culture;

(b) As far as possible, the resultant social change should be a planned process which should take into account the capacity of the tribal community to absorb change without losing the fundamental values of their own culture;

(c) Till this process works itself out, the tribal community should receive the necessary protection. Then alone the values of the traditional tribal culture will be satisfactorily integrated with modern culture.

The responsibility for helping this process of integration is that of the government and management of the industrial enterprises. Our view is that tribal labour force is not only willing but also competent to integrate itself into the industrial urban complex, provided it receives help and encouragement from the government and the management of industrial enterprises.

We are satisfied that the management has the scope to make adequate allowance for tribal values without detriment to productivity.

Tribal labour policy in the past has been either non-existent or inconsistent. We suggest that labour policies including that of recruitment, training, promotion, wages, etc., should be reviewed and reassessed from the point of view of the actual effects that they produce on tribal labour situation and a consistent and integrated labour policy should be evolved. It would be desirable for the government and the industrial concerns to consult the experts on these points.

We feel that it should be the duty of the government to ensure that none of its policies in respect to tribal labour gets circumvented or modified unwittingly or wilfully in the process of implementation to the detriment of the interests of the tribal labour.

The government should evolve a suitable employment policy for the tribals in industrial jobs and see that this policy is implemented not only public sector undertakings but also by private sector undertakings.

The most important reason which stands in the way of tribal people getting employment is lack of technical training. It is necessary that the government should provide suitable opportunities and encouragement for training.

Agricultural Labour

Almost all the problems of the tribal agricultural labour, whether it is inadequate employment or unjust service conditions or low wages, can be ultimately traced to the basic weaknesses of the tribal economy. Tribal indebtedness and agrarian insecurity add to the complexity of the problem. We, therefore, feel that an intensive programme for strengthening and diversification of tribal economy will go a long way to alleviate, if not solve, the problems of agricultural labour. As such it should be given the highest priority.

There should be adequate publicity of minimum wage rates fixed by government. A special study of the problem of agricultural indebtedness should be made to find out its causes, consequences and suggest solutions.

The policy of tribal development through the Tribal Development blocks has failed to improve the tribal economy to the desired extent for various reasons. The T.D. blocks are far too large and the tribal population is relatively too small for proper attention to the tribal economy. In our view, the correct approach will be to prepare plans for smaller areas, preferably a group of tribal villages. Plans for these tribal pockets should aim at the development and diversification of tribal agricultural improvement, of tribal cottage industries and extension of communication and irrigation facilities. In preparation of these plans, tribals should be more closely associated. There is considerable scope for providing more employment to tribal labour through rural works programmes in tribal areas. We recommend that an agency should be created with adequate funds for planning, implementing, co-ordinated and supervising tribal development plans.

We recommend that minimum wages should be fixed in tribal areas on a more realistic basis. In fixing up the wages, the various practices in tribal areas, in regard to payment of wages in cash or kind, should be taken into account.

Strict enforcement of minimum wages for tribal agricultural labour is necessary. If necessary, Labour Department personnel should be strengthened and necessary delegation of powers to field staff may be made.

Tribal Forest Labour

Forest satisfies deep-rooted tribal sentiments and helps them to meet some of their basic needs.

Changes in the forest policy have affected the tribals in general and the tribal labour in particular. Their rights in respect of the use of forest have been restricted and it has produced adverse effects on the tribal economy. On the other hand, intensive forest development has created employment for tribal labour for afforestation and exploitation of forest resources. In Ranchi alone, the employment is estimated to be about 35,000 workers.

There are several categories of forest labourers: (a) self-employed labour, (b) labour employed by the Forest Department, (c) labour employed by the contractors and (d) labour employed by co-operatives. The number and importance of self-employed forest labour is declining on account of the greater and greater restrictions being imposing by the forest department in respect of use of forest.

We came to know that supervisory staff of the Forest Department take advantage of the illiteracy of the tribal forest labour and pay less than the approved wages and take overtime work without payment.

Labour employed by contractors is exploited to a far greater extent. We recommend that :

(a) steps should be immediately taken for effective enforcement of Minimum Wages Act both in relation to labour employed by Forest Department and those employed by the contractors.

(b) Forest Labour Inspectors should be appointed to go round and investigate cases of under-payment of wages and overtime by the Forest Department and the contractors. The present procedure of enquiry by an officer of the Forest Department, which itself is one of the employers, is not conductive to the protection of the interests of the tribal labour.

(c) As far as possible, wage rates may also be prescribed according to the kind of operations undertaken.

(d) All those contractors against whom several complaints regarding non-payment or under-payment of wages and other types of complaints might have been lodged, should be blacklisted for purposes of grant of further contracts.

(e) More and more opportunities for employment should be provided to tribals in the service of the Forest Department as Mates, Fire watchers, Forests Guards and even Rangers if they qualify. This will provide incentives. Tribals residing in and around the forests should be given preference in employment.

(f) The Forest Department should draw up a plan of work for each year in such a way that as far as possible it does not interfere with the schedule of agricultural in operations and gives maximum employment to tribals in agricultural off-seasons.

(g) A real and long-term solution to end exploitation of forest labour and improvement of their condition would be to organise the forest tribal labour into co-operatives. Both the types of co-operatives—(a) Forest Co-operatives and (b) Forest Labour Co-operatives should be given all the necessary assistance and guidance. Voluntary organisations may be associated in organising such co-operatives. In dealing with these co-operatives there should be effective co-ordination between the Welfare, Co-operative and Forest Departments.

Casual Labour

Casual labour is an important category of tribal labour from the point of view of the number employed. Such work is popular among the tribals on account of its affinity to agricultural occupations and the income that it brings, which sees them through the lean agricultural months and helps them to improve their standards of living.

There are two categories of casual workers—(a) daily commuters and (b) shanty dwellers. In both the cases the tribal workers continue to maintain their strong ties on the land in the villages. Their main aim in taking up casual employment is to make some money to meet exigency and again go back to their lands. There is, thus, a lack of commitment to industrial life. They have not responded well to the opportunities to become skilled workers even when they were exposed to the work of skilled nature for long period.

On account of this lack of commitment to industrial-life, casual labour is not susceptible to organisation, and undue advantage regarding wages and overtime payment is taken by the employer. It has been found that casual workers are prepared to accept less wages when they get employment opportunities around their villages. Considerable diversity in wage-rates was found from one project site to another.

Overtime regulations are not strictly followed in respect of casual labour in construction sites. Overtime work is taken from casual workers, but they are not paid overtime wages or are given much below the scheduled rates.

Casual labour is deprived of a paid holiday on the seventh day of the week, which according to law he is entitled, if he has continuously worked for previous six days.

Casual workers are not given full payment of wages. Arrears are deliberately kept by the employers to prevent them from leaving their employment.

There is a fair percentage of women workers among the casual labour.

Indebtedness though prevalent among casual workers is not as rampant as it is thought to be. 78 per cent of the workers interviewed were not indebted.

Among casual workers there is hardly any unionisation. The trade unions have not shown any keenness or effectiveness in organising casual workers.

The tribal casual labour is still uncommitted to industrial life and deeply attached to agricultural economy. It is neither necessary nor desirable to tempt or force them out of this situation, so long as it is not possible to provide enough employment for casual workers.

However, the casual labourers do require to be protected against exploitation by unscrupulous employers and the government must take adequate steps to protect them.

Very few pieces of legislation are applicable to them and even when they are applicable, enforcement and implementation of the laws leave much to be desired.

There is an urgent need to tone up the existing legislative measures and introduce new measures to protect the interests of casual labour. Enforcement of labour laws applicable to casual labour, viz., Payment of Wages Act, Minimum Wages Act, is decidedly weak. As it has been established from the data collected, violation of the laws in regard to overtime payment, rest-day pay, withholding of wages are not, to put it mildly, uncommon. Various reasons put forward to account for these lapses include understaffing in the Labour Department, multiplicity of duties and insufficient delegation of authority to Enforcement Officers, etc.

Sometimes, effective enforcement of an Act is obstructed by administrative deficiencies. We are of the view that a Deputy Commissioner should not be appointed as Commissioner under the Workmen's Compensation Act.

Modern methods of building construction, dam and road works involve certain element of risk to the workers. It is necessary that some provision should be made regarding safety provisions more or less on the pattern of one existing in England.

Some schemes for insurance of workers against accident may be devised. The Study Group is aware of the difficulties in evolving a satisfactory scheme. If scheme like this is implemented, then only it would be possible to do away with the cumbersome processes of granting compensation. In any case, we strongly feel that measures should be strengthened and compensation procedures simplified without delay.

Whenever workers' camps are constructed or to put it more accurately, allowed to grow, health and sanitary regulations must be strictly enforced. Contracts may be drawn up in a form similar to that of the Railways general condition of contract which specifies measures in regard to health, sanitation and housing at labour camps.

Industrial Labour

Employment of tribal labour as factory workers has gone up as a result of setting up of a number of factories in and around Ranchi district. The position regarding their employment would have been still better if some steps were taken in advance for the purposes of making the tribal candidates employable. Mere reservation of posts have not helped the tribal labour in the past nor would it help in the future, if steps are not taken to make tribal labour fit for the jobs for which they apply.

We, therefore, recommend that whenever basic industries are established in predominently tribal areas, every step should be taken to ensure that local tribal workers, especially the displaced persons, get reasonable opportunities for recruitment to unskilled and semi-skilled jobs. It is necessary to arrange for the training of tribal workers for more skilled jobs even before employment opportunities are available.

The percentage of enrolment of scheduled tribe children at the primary, middle and secondary stages shows a progressive decline. This suggests heavy percentage of dropouts. The percentage of enrolment at higher educational levels and in engineering schools and colleges is also pityfully low. With such a low level of enrolment in the technical training institutions, it would be idle to expect that the position of employment of scheduled tribes would improve to any satisfactory degree in future.

We, therefore, recommend that steps should be taken for intensification of efforts for tribal education and training at all stages.

It has been noted that the tribal students are a little slow on comprehension of abstract sciences and as such find difficulty in matters of technical training. But when provided with adequate facilities for technical training and given time for acquisition of skill, the tribals do as good as other non-tribal workers. There is nothing which hinders them to respond to the demands of industrial-way of life. On the other hand, it should not be taken for granted that the non-tribals only are capable of such response. Studies on Patratu and Bokaro show that the high caste Hindus are lagging behind the tribal in their response to industrialisation. Even the tribal women have taken up the challenge, whereas the high caste Hindu women do not come out for industrial employment on account of restrictions imposed by traditions.

It has been found that the procedures of recruitment are not faithfully gone through in some cases. Sometimes the tribal candidates fail to impress at the selection interviews on account of their rural background and inborn shyness. It is, therefore, necessary to impress upon the selecting authorities that while interviewing tribal candidates they should take these characteristics of tribal people into account. We recommend that managerial staff of the private and public sector undertakings in and around Ranchi should receive a brief orientation in social anthropology and tribal culture. We feel that with this orientation they would have a proper appreciation of the tribal's psychology and there would be more understanding in matters of recruitment of tribal candidates.

We recommend that an officer, preferably of the Labour Department, should be given the specific duty of going round the industrial undertakings and keeping a vigilant eye on their recruitment practices with a view to check any deliberate attempt to keep out the tribal candidates. Wherever large-scale recruitments are advertised, the office may be associated with the processing of applications from tribal candidates and may also sit in as an observer on the Selection Boards.

We Recommend That

(a) Employment exchanges in tribal areas should ensure that there is a longer time span between the arrival of the call-cards at the job-seeker's address and the date of interview.

(b) A study should be made regarding the possibility of simplification of registration and placement procedures in the employment exchanges, particularly in the case of tribal candidates who are illiterate or possess very low educational qualifications.

(c) The method of record-keeping should be overhauled so as to make possible the statistical studies on labour-market behaviour of tribals and other communities over a longer period of time.

(d) A liaison may be established between the employment exchanges and the voluntary organisations interested in tribal welfare to secure the help of the latter in spreading employment information and assisting job-seekers in filling in application forms etc.

There is a fair percentage of commuters among the tribal industrial workers. Any attempt to force the tribal labour to cut off their connection with the land will not be a desirable proposition. We recommend that those who intend to commute, should be encouraged to do so. We would even suggest, that communications between the factory site and the neighbouring villages be improved for the facility of the commuters.

The habit of drinking is quite common among the tribal workers. The pre-existing drinking habits which has the sanction of the tribal culture gets accelerated with a change from the traditional rice-beer to distilled liquor. This leads to undesirable consequences like indebtedness and absenteeism. We recommend that no licence for opening liquor shops within three miles of an industrial establishment should be issued.

Indebtedness is common among the tribal workers, particularly the colliery workers. We recommend that facilities for credit co-operatives should be extended to as many factories as possible. In any case the factory should evolve some schemes for easy advancement of loans for fulfilling social and religious obligations.

Tribal workers do join trade unions but remain very such in the background. Where the unions have been organised on a truly universal basis and have paid attention to the problems of tribal workers, the latter have responded more positively. Where the unions are organised on caste or ethnic lines, the tribals have stayed away and have been making attempts to organise separate unions.

COMMITTEE OF ENQUIRY, COUNCIL OF SCIENTIFIC AND INDUSTRIAL RESEARCH, 1968—REPORT

New Delhi, Manager of Publications, 1970. 156+xlvip.

Chairman : Shri Justice A.K. Sarkar.

Members : Shri Akbar Ali Khan; Shri S.S. Bhandari; Dr. K. Ramiah; Shri P. Venkatasubbiah (replaced by P. Antony Reddy); Shri N. Dandekar (replaced by Shri K.P. Singh Deo); Shri Indrajit Gupta; Dr. C.R. Rao; Prof. M.G.K. Menon; Dr. M.S. Swaminathan; Dr. P.K. Kelkar.

Member : **Secretary** : Shri N. Sehgal replaced by Shri S.K. Sarkar.

APPOINTMENT

The Minister for Education announced in the Rajya Sabha on March 23, 1968 the decision to appoint a Committee consisting of Members of Parliament and Scientific experts to go into the overall functioning of the Council of Scientific and Industrial Research (CSIR) and suggest ways and means of improvement, wherever necessary. The formal constitution of the Committee and their terms of reference were notified by the CSIR Vide their Notification No. 9/5/68-PU dated June 1st, 1968. The text of this Notification is set out below :

"In terms of Article 57 of the Rules and Regulations of the Council of Scientific and Industrial Research, the Prime Minister, as President of the Council of Scientific and Industrial Research, has appointed a Committee consisting of the following members to enquire into the overall functioning of the Council and suggest ways and means of improving it.

TERMS OF REFERENCE

Following are the terms of reference of the Committee :

(i) To review the personnel policies followed at various levels with reference to the Rules and Regulations in force and, in particular, to look into the allegations of the irregularities brought to the notice of Parliament from time to time and to suggest any remedial measures necessary;

(ii) To enquire into the adequacy or otherwise of the existing policies in respect of payment of royalty, having regard to the following object prescribed in the memorandum of Association of the Council of Scientific and Industrial Research;

(iii) The utilization of the results of the researches conducted under the auspices of the Council towards development of industries in the country and the payment of a share of royalties arising out of the development of the results of researches to those who are considered to having contributed to the pursuit of such researches;

(iv) To review the overall functioning of the Council of Scientific and Industrial Research and to suggest ways and means of improvement.

CONTENTS

Introduction; Background; Procedure of the Committee; Rules and Regulations and Bye-laws Relating to Personnel Policies; Appointment of Persons without Scientific/Technical Qualifications to Posts Carrying Scientific/Technical Designations; Appointment to the Posts of Director-General and Secretary; Promotion of Hyderabad Officers; Appointment and Retirement of Some Directors; Conditions of Services; General Observations and Recommendations; Summary of Recommendations; Note of Dissent; Appendices from I to XI.

RECOMMENDATIONS

An officer, independent of the CSIR, may be selected by the Government of India to make thorough investigations into such of the complaints made to the Committee as disclose a prima facie case as a result of preliminary examination.

The CSIR should reclassify all the existing posts into scientific, technical and administrative according to the criteria mentioned in para 5.15 of this Report. For this purpose the Governing Body of the CSIR should appoint a broad based Committee.

The suggested reclassification of posts need not alter the grade, salary and status which have accrued to individuals from the existing classifications. However, with regard to their eligibility for future advancement the CSIR should be guided by the new classification provided it is not objectionable under the law.

The CSIR should take steps to prescribed certain minimum academic qualifications and ensure its implementation. Such qualifications could be subject to a praviso for relaxation inexceptional cases. The reasons for any deviation from the prescribed qualifications must be clearly recorded by the selection Committee and made available to the authority competent to make the appointments.

The decision concerning the transfer of an Institute/ Laboratory from one place to another should not be taken by the CSIR without a reference to the concerned Executive Council.

The CSIR should conduct an enquiry regarding the wrong qualifications given by H.P.S. Murthy, Assistant Director, National Metallurgical Laboratory, Jamshedpur.

The CSIR should obtain the approval of the Government of India at an early date to the changes made by them from time to time in the rules relating to the age of retirement and grant of extensions.

Posts should not be transferred from one laboratory to another or the headquarters or vice-persa. If any post becomes superfluous it should be abolished. Any new post which is needed for a specific purpose should be created by adopting the prescribed procedure.

It is not desirable to keep the sanctioned posts of Deputy Secretaries unfilled for a long period ; the posts should be filled or, if not required, should be abolished.

The proposals for creating new posts should be more rigorously scruitinised by the Executive Council so as to avoid excessive expenditure on salaries and allowances.

All the posts up to the level of Director should be advertised through the selections need not be confined only to those who apply in response to advertisements.

The CSIR should prescribed a set of model qualifications for different categories of posts and any deviation from these must be fully recorded. For each post precise job specifications must be laid down at the time of its creation and the qualifications advertised for the post should conform to such job specifications. In cases where special job specifications are considered necessary these should be specifically mentioned in the advertisement. The job specifications must be furnished to the screening authorities as well as the selection Committees.

The CSIR should examine whether Bye-law 60 needs

to be revised as strict adherence to it may give rise to practical difficulties.

The CSIR should designate the scrutinising and reviewing authorities responsible for selection of names of candidates to be put up before the selection Committees. The reasons for not placing the name of a candidate before the selection Committee should be precisely recorded.

If the view that a body competent to make selection for a comparatively junior post is acceptable, it would be desirable to make express provision in the Bye-laws for this purpose after examining the necessity of associating the members of the concerned Executive Councils in the selection of officers for the lower posts.

Supernumery posts may be created for appointing any additional persons recommended by the selection Committees. In view of their special talents. These posts should be regularised by following the prescribed procedure of advertisement etc.

Provisions of the Bye-laws relating to the composition of the selection Committees should be strictly adhered to.

Bye-laws 59 may be amended to provide that the Vice-President may nominate a suitable eminent person, not in the employment of the CSIR, as Chairman of the selection Committees for the posts of Directors/ in Joint Director/Deputy Director place of the Vice-President as provided in the existing Bye-law.

The CSIR should give adequate notice of the meetings of the selection Committees, both to candidates and to the members.

The selection Committees should record explicitly the reasons for recommending higher pay to the selected candidates or for proposing additional names for appointment etc.

All plant collectors doing the same type of work should get the same scale of pay. The Staff Car Drivers, when required to perform the duties of Heavy Truck Drivers, should be duly compensated. The scales of pay of Ferro Printers in the CSIR should be brought on par with those of their counterparts in the Government of India.

The CSIR may consider favourably, if the financial burden is not heavy, (a) payment of overtime allowance to Chowkidars, Farashes and Sweepers at the same rates as admissible to other Class IV employees and (b) grant of uniforms and shoes to Malis.

The reason for extending the period of probation should always be communicated in writing, if no decision extending the probation is communicated in writing to the persons concerned within three months of the expiry of the stipulated period of probation, they should be deemed to have completed the probation satisfactorily. The work of probationers should be periodically reviewed during the probationary period and shortcomings, if noticed by communicated in writing to them.

THE OIL PRICES COMMITTEE, 1968—REPORT

Delhi, Manager of Publications, 1970. 167p.

Chairman : Shri Shantilal H. Shah

Members : Shri B.N. Adarkar; Dr. B. Natarajan; Shri N. Krishnan;

Secretary : Shri N.R. Law.

APPOINTMENTS

The Government of India, by the Ministry of Petroleum and Chemicals (Department of Petroleum) set up a Committee to determine the ceiling selling prices excompanies storage points of various petroleum products in India, to be applied from the date of termination of the existing arrangement. The Oil Prices Committee was Constituted vide Resolution No. 101(22)/68-PPD dated June 14, 1968.

TERMS OF REFERENCE

Examination and report upon the—

(i) The determination of the ex-refinery prices of refined petroleum products, including bituments, produced by the refineries, whether on the basis of import parity as hitherto or by the adoption of the cost of production as the basis, or in any other appropriate manner, with due regard to the Government assurances having a bearing on the subject;

(ii) With reference to (i), the feasibility of introducing uniform prices all-India or on a regional basis;

(iii) The determination of landed prices in respect

of similar products which may be imported;

(iv) The feasibility of making all refineries (including the inland refineries) as the pricing points and the measures to be adopted to ensure that interests of the inland refineries are not adversely affected in consequence of the adoption of such a principle, regard, in this connection, being had to the basis of pricing indigenous crude;

(v) The determination of marketing and distribution charges and profit on the marketing operations and their allocation to the products mentioned in (i) and (iii) above, due account being taken also of the experience of the IOC in this behalf;

(vi) The determination of the ceiling selling prices in respect of lubricating oils, greases and specialities and in particular, (a) the pricing of lube base stocks produced/to be produced in India either from indegenous or imported crude, and (b) the pricing of mineral turpentine oil;

(vii) The determination of the rates of dealer's Commission in respect of motor spirit and high speed disel oil; with due regard to the representation of the Federation of All India Petroleum Traders; and

(viii) The determination of the rates of Commission in respect of kerosene to agents, dealers and retailers taking into account the losses/expenses incurred by them on account of leakage, handling charges etc., with due regard to the views of the State Governments and other interests.

CONTENTS

Introduction; Implementation of the Report of the Working Group on Oil Prices (WGOP); Structure and Working of the Oil Companies; Demands for Petroleum Products; Cost of Imported Crude Oil; Price of Indigenous Crude Oil; Control Over Prices; Determination of Ex-refinery Prices; All Refineries and Main Ports as Pricing Points; Uniform Prices All-India or on a Regional Basis; Pricing Formula; Landed Prices of Imported Products; Lubricants Greases and Specialities; Liquified Petroleum Gas (LPG); Naptha; Special Products; Pack/Bulk Differential for 18.5 Litre Tins; Future Estimate of Marketing and Distribution Charges; Return on Capital Employed in Marketing; Dealer's Commission on Motor Spirit and High Speed Diesel Oil; Dealers/Agents Commission; On Kerosene; Current Ceiling Prices as on the 28th June, 1969; Recommended Ceilling Prices; Comparison of the Current and Recommended Ceiling Prices; Period of Price Fixation and Provision for Adjustments; Additional (Non-Recoverable) Duties to be Borne by the Refineries; Some Ancillary Issues; Suggestions on Some Major Policy Aspects; Summary of Conclusions and Recommendations; Acknowledgements; Statements from 1 to 16; Appendices from I to III.

SUPPLEMENT

Introduction; Lube Base Stocks; Lubricants and Greases; Agents/Dealers Commission on Light Diesel Oil; Summary of Conclusions and Recommendations; Statements; Appendices from I to VI.

RECOMMENDATIONS

Our Conclusions and Recommendations are Summarised below :

1. An analysis of the working results of the oil companies, on the basis of their published accounts for 1967 (1967-68 for IOC and CRL), shows that except in the case Esso the gross profit on the integrated operation of refining and marketing and of refining only in respect of CRL has not been less than 11.50 per cent on capital employed.

2. For the years 1970 to 1972 an average annual sale of 23.29 million kilolitres of bulk refined products bitumens, lubricants, greases, specialists, naphtha and LPG is estimated for Burmah Shell, Esso, Caltex and IOC, the share of each being 20.39, 12.31, 6.67 and 60.63 per cent respectively.

3. The arrangements for supply of crude oil to ESRC, BSR and CORIL are designed to ensure that imports are made from their affiliates/associates abroad and the prices actually paid to the original suppliers of crude in the Middle East are not known.

4. The modified agreement in respect of CRL Provides for certain unusual incentives and concessions to Phillips.

5. The crude oil sales agreement for twenty two years in respect of MRL contains no provision for adjusting prices according to the discounts on crude available from time to time.

6. The agreement in question does not provide for sufficient assurance that the price chargeable for crude supplied to MRL will be reduced when transactions take place in the world maker at lower rates.

7. The agreement for the supply of crude oil to Haldia refinery leaves room for considerable uncertainty about a reduction in the contract price in the event of a fall in world prices.

8. BSR, ESRC and CORIL receive foreign exchange allocation for transportation of crude oil at INTASCALE with AFRA variation but it is not known whether marine freight is actually paid to the carriers on the same basis.

9. The entire requirements of crude oil of the country should be imported through a single agency by inviting competitive bids for supply over a specified period. The existing agreements/contracts may be re-negotiated to remove any impediments in the way

of crude oil being imported at world competitive prices.

10. The world supply and demand position of crude oil has undergone a radical change in recent past indicating the probability of a market downward trend in prices of Middle East crudes over the next few years.

11. Within three months and after formally communicating to the committee that it had failed to secure any reduction in the price of crude oil. Burmah-Shell informed Government that its suppliers had offered a reduction of 4 cents per barrel. Similar reductions were offered be Caltex and ESSO.

12. The following rates of discounts on the F.O.B. posted prices of crude oils are recommended :

		US dollar/bbi
1.	Iranian light (Aghajari)/ Arabian light	0.51
2.	Arabian medium	0.34
3.	Arabian heavy	0.37
4.	Iranian heavy	0.43
5.	Kuwait	0.38
6.	Darious	0.38

Government should build up their own system of intelligence regarding discounts available in the world market from time to time.

13. The post prices of products also are subject to discounts although the private oil companies deny the prevalence of discounts in this case.

14. Import parity is no longer an adequate basis for price fixation, however, Governments commitment to permit the oil companies to maintain the prices of their products at import parity makes it impossible to adopt any other basis.

15. After prices are determined for a period on the basis of import parity. Such prices should be kept unchanged for that period, except for major known variations in the cost of production actually incurred.

16. Taking into account the rate of discount recommended by us on light Iranian crude, principally in use in India, we have applied a uniform discount of 4 per cent to posted prices of products. If the discount on light Iranian Aghajari crude increases, the discount on posted prices of products should be increased by 4 per cent for every 10 cents extra discount on crude.

17. It would be anomalous to stick to a port based pricing system when a growing proportion of the country's requirements is being met from inland sources. The consumers in the region where the refineries are located have a right to benefit by the growth of local production. We, therefore, recommend that all inland refineries should be treated as pricing points in addition to the eight main ports and the supply areas should be revised.

18. When movements are regulated on an All-India plan, all under recoveries may be deemed to have resulted from movements considered necessary in the national interest and should, therefore, be borne by the general body of consumers and not by the oil companies. the latter should be reimbursed for the entire net under-recoveries incurred by them, including the under-recoveries a costal movement.

19. A surcharge be levied on the total consumption of major fuel products on a budgeted basis and the oil companies be compensated for their net under-recoveries out of the proceeds of this surcharge. The estimate of such a surcharge is Rs. 7.05 per kl.

20. The introduction of uniform all-India prices is not considered feasible. A regional pool is also not recommended.

21. The concept of free delivery zone currently applicable at main ports and concentrated up country markets for motor spirit and HSD should be extended to other products particularly finance oil.

22. The existing system of pool prices for motor spirit and kerosene in the Assam supply area should be continued. The rates of surcharge are presently revised only on the basis of AOC'S operation. In future the data for IOC should be also taken into account.

23. The under/over recoveries arising in the Assam supply area as a result of inland refineries being made pricing points should be taken into account along with the all India under-recoveries and not lumped with the pool account for motor spirit and kerosene applicable to supplies in that area.

24. In the pricing formula the national element of marine freight has been included at GP vessel rates for all products except furnace oil and bitumens for which it has been included at MR vessel rates.

25. The incidence of marine freight has been calculated on the basis of INTASCALE and should be modified according to WORLD SCALE from the date it comes into effect.

26. The rate of agents' commission for light diesel oil has been adopted at the existing rate, viz., R. 6.60 per kl.

27. In respect of bitumens, the bulk parity prices have been adopted for all the eight ports and cost of packing has been included as the basis of indigenous experience.

28. The selling prices of imported products may be at per with the ceiling prices recommended for domestic products.

29. With the increase in production of lubricants, the oil companies should be expected progressively to introduce specification grades in place of branded products.

30. For lubricants and greases, which are predominantly imported and are only blended and packed in the country, the existing system of Block control on

marketing/ distribution charges and profit should continue.

31. On the basis of the data for Burmah-Shell, Esso, Caltex and IOC, the ceiling rates recommended for marketing/distribution charges and profit are Rs. 84.12 and Rs. 23.60 per kl., respectively.

32. To remove the difficulties experience in the past in the operation of Block Control, the oil companies should review their prices at frequent intervals and make prompt adjustment to obviate large accumulations of over/under-recoveries.

33. The prices of those lubricants and greases which are predominantly produced in India together with the prices of lube base stock will be examined in the next part of the enquiry. For the present such lubricants and greases may also continue to be subject to the system of Block Control applicable to imported products.

34. Some aspects of the system of Block Control viz., regulation of blending and packing charges for individual products, groups of products, or on a block basis, will also be examined during the next part of the enquiry.

35. The selling prices of mineral turpentine and jute batching oils ex-companies storage points should continue at the existing levels and these products should be exempted from Block Control on marketing/distribution charges and profit.

36. SBP spirits/hexane/solvent oils, roofing materials and household specialities should be exempted from Block Control on marketing/distribution charges and profit because of their relatively small volume of sales.

37. A ceiling price need not be fixed for LPG supplied in bulk to industrial consumers.

38. The current selling prices of LPG of the private oil companies to domestic consumers should be reduced all over India by Rs. 207 per tonne or Rs. 3.00 per cylinder of 14.5 kg. As IOC is already charging 86 paise cylinder less, its price to domestic consumers should be reduced by Rs. 2.14 per cylinder of 14.5 kg.

39. The ceiling prices for naphtha have been determined on the basis of the import parity for light fuel.

40. A ceiling price has not been fixed for naphtha used as industrial fuel.

41. All the main eight ports and the inland refineries should be the pricing points for naphtha as for other bulk refined products.

42. No ceiling prices are proposed for carbon black feed stock, not heavy stock, Iomex, JP-5/JP-5, low sulphur heavy stock, malarial larvicidal oil, petroleum coke, pesticides, refinery gas and tea drier oil. The price of RFO to the Gujarat State Electricity Board and other consumers in Gujarat should be Rs. 45 per tonne.

43. Petroleum Coke should be used for industrial purposes to the maximum extent possible and its use as domestic fuel should be entailed and the possibility of exporting larger quantities should be explored.

44. The packed/bulk differential for 18.5 litre tins has been estimated a Rs. 3.60 per tin escalation being allowed on the basis of standard consumption of 1.15 kg. of tin plate per tin, for any variation in the average all-India price of tinplates compared with the price of Rs. 2.663 per kg.

45. IOC, Burmah-Shell, Esso and Caltex are expected to meet during the period 1970 to 1972 about 95 per cent of the total demand in the country. The future estimate of marketing/distribution charges has been based on the data relating to these companies.

46. The average charges during 1967-68 per kl. of sales came to about Rs. 20 in the case of IOC, while the same ranged in 1967 between Rs. 34 to Rs. 37 in the case of the foreign oil companies.

47. There is considerable room for economy in marketing charges in the case of the foreign oil companies, but they should be allowed reasonable time to affect such economy in order to soften its impect on employment and the establish channels of distribution.

48. The quantum of marketing/distribution charges allowed per unit of each productive given in paragraph 18.7.

49. A return of twelve per cent on capital employed is considered fair and reasonable for the marketing activity.

50. In respect of bulk refined products bitumens lubes and greases but excluding LPG, naphtha and specialities, the net value of the block has been estimated at Rs. 32.16 per kl., working capital at 10 per cent of the annual cost of sales at Rs. 53.19 per kl. and the total capital employed at Rs. 85.35 per kl. The return on capital employed in marketing is 2.09 per cent of the cost of sales.

51. The quantum of profit allowed per unit of each product is given in paragraph 19.4.

52. The dealers' commission for motor spirit may remain at the existing rate of Rs. 41.80 per kl. The rate of commission for high speed diesel oil, however may be revised to Rs. 37.60 per kl. Since this is inclusive of the service charge at present levied in some parts of the country, the dealers should not recover any service charge in future.

53. Licence fees charged to any dealer should remain unchanged at the average rate charged to that dealer during the last completed financial year of the company, but, if the commission earned by a dealer increases by substantially more than fifty per cent the licence fee may be raised by not more than five per cent of such increase provided such increase is essential to earn a reasonable return on the investment of the oil

company. The licence fee if levied on a new outlet in the first year of its operation should not exceed ten per cent of the commission earned by a dealer in that year.

54. Government should look into the dealership agreements to modify any harsh clauses creating a sense of in security for the dealers.

55. No increased is proposed in the existing rate of commission to kerosene agents/dealers of Rs. 7.70 per kl. but the local authorities should use their discretion to allow reimbursement of any extraordinary expenditure which the dealers may have to incur under local conditions.

56. The recommended ceiling prices exclusive of non-recoverable duties and dealers' retail commission wherever applicable are shown in paragraph 23.1. In the past the Government has followed the practice of keeping the current prices in changed and imposing non-recoverable duties at uniform rates on sales at all ports on the basis of the average difference between the current and the recommended prices. This system has some drawbacks, hence, certain modifications have been recommended in paragraph 23.4.

57. The pattern of sales for the future is based on the data furnished by Burmah-Shell, Esso, Caltex and IOC through the different ports during 1970 to 1972.

58. The reduction in the aggregate annual gross receipts of the four major oil companies from various products excluding naphtha resulting from the difference between the recommended ceiling prices and the current ceiling prices is estimated at Rs. 192.783 million.

59. The price structure recommended by us should remain valid for three years from the date of its implementation, subject to adjustments on account of the specified factors.

60. The price of packed bitumen is subject to adjustment for changes in the cost of drums on the basis of delivered price drum sheets to BSR over Rs. 1,486 per tonne of 24 gauge drum sheets for a consumption of 63.2 kg. per tonne of bitumen straight grades and Rs. 1,428 per tonne of 21 gauge drum sheets for a consumption of 90.3 kg. per tonne of bitumen cut backs.

61. The import parity for products should be adjusted for variations in marine freight and wharfage only to the extent of their effect on the cost of crude. But such variations may be allowed to be recovered in the case of imports of deficit products to the extent of actuals refineries moving products by coast to Indian ports should also be entitled to recover the actual increases in costs due to variations in wharfage.

62. The surcharges on ceiling prices applied from 1st May, 1968, to compensate the oil companies for the national increase in marine freight on products following the Middle East crisis should be united to the actual increase in the cost of crude oil to the refineries.

63. The additional (non-recoverable) duties levied on the refineries may, for the time being, be continued at the existing rates and the over/under-recoveries calculated in the light of the ceiling prices now recommended may be recalculated annually on the basis of the anticipated production pattern of the individual refineries for the years 1970 to 1972 and adjustments made in the existing rates of additional (non-recoverable) duties on the basis of such annual assessment.

64. Government may take suitable action to consider the feasibility of reducing expenditure in foreign exchange on account of marine freight a costal movement of products, which was of the order of Rs. 41 million in 1967 and Rs. 43 million in 1968.

65. The present situation is unsatisfactory from the point of securing the best prices for our exports of surplus products. The State Trading Corporation should equip itself to handle exports, so that better prices may be secured with proper planning and improved over arrangements for intelligence.

66. Action should be taken by Government to prevent the burning of defines by the refineries except where they are satisfied that separation of this material from the refinery gas is not feasible.

67. Government should review the basis on which the oil companies are being allowed to make remittances to their principle on account of overseas expenses and other services, with a view to reducing them and over a period of time eliminating them altogether.

68. The suggestions made by the oil companies for improvement of the existing system regarding levy and collection of duties and rail and road transportation of products are dealt with in paragraphs 27.8.1, 27.8.2 and 27.8.3.

69. There should be a proper investigation into the cost of indigenous crude by an independent agency.

70. A substantial quantity of Rostam crude has now become available to Government from the Iranian off-shore areas, but it is understood that Government is unable to sell this crude to the private refineries in India because of the right conceded to them to import crude from their own sources. It is anomalous that Government should have to seek foreign markets for the disposal of this crude when large quantities of crude of more or less similar quantity, are being imported at higher prices.

71. The concept of import parity ignores the cost of production of indigenous refineries and thus diverts attention from the relative levels of efficiency at the various refineries,

72. The commission's suggestions on some major policy aspects are given in chapter 28. In particular, it is recommended that a National Petroleum Commission be established as a statutory basis to renegotiate the agreement with the foreign oil companies and to serve as the policy-making and ordinating authority in respect of all aspects of this industry, from exploration and supply of crude to the marketing of products.

73. Greater attention should be devoted to increasing domestic production of kerosene.

74. The actual operation of Block Control on lubricants aid greases is not fair to the consumer as the oil companies are not asked to reduce prices suitably to prevent continuing over-recoveries in future.

SUPPLEMENT

Summary Of Conclusions And Recommendations

5.1. The Lube India Ltd., is permanently tied to Esso in regard to the Supply of its feed stock. This may become a handicap to it in certain circumstances.

5.2. The ceiling selling prices have been evolved for the specified products only and the prices of the products for which no ceiling prices have been recommended may continue to be fixed by the sellers as at present.

5.3. In respect of 1969 imports of Lube base stocks, there are wide variations in j.o.b. prices paid by the companies, which should be studied further in view of their foreign exchange implication.

5.4. The recommended ceiling prices for lube base stocks are given in the statement.

5.5. The recommended ceiling prices may remain in force for a period of three years subject to adjustments for variations in customs duty and the additional (non-recoverable) duty.

5.6. The present system of Block Control may be continued for the present in respect of lubricants and greases aid steps taken to obtain essential cost data from major products for the principal grades produced by them.

57. No charge is recommended in the existing rate of commission of Rs. 6.60 per kl. on light diesel oil supplied ex-godowns. The same rate should continue to apply to light diesel oil supplied from barrel and retail outlets. In these cases, the local authorities may allow recovery of any extra expenditure incurred by agents/dealers under local conditions.

5.8. Any committee appointed in future to consider major questions relating to the pricing of petroleum products should be given powers normally vested in a commission of inquiry to enable it to examine the books of accounts of the oil companies and independently to collect other evidence necessary for a proper investigation of their costs of production, imports and distribution.

COMMISSION OF INQUIRY INTO THE DEATHS OF STUDENT NURSES (IRWIN & WILLINGDON HOSPITALS, NEW DELHI), 1968—REPORT

New Delhi, Ministry of Health, Family Planning and Urban Development, 1968.

Members : Shri P.D. Sharma,
Secretary : Shri Inderjit Sharma.

APPOINTMENT

The Commission of Inquiry into the Death of Student Nurses (Irwin and Willingdon Hospitals, New Delhi) was constituted under the Ministry of Health, Family Planning and Urban Development, vide their Notification No. F. 6-124/68-H dated June 15, 1968.

TERMS OF REFERENCE

To make an inquiry into the deaths of :

(i) Prem Lata Sandil (died on 9.4.1968)
(ii) Shakuntala Daisy Mathias (died on 10.4.1968)
(iii) Sumitra Chaudhry (died on 14.4.1968)
(iv) Saroj Bala Chadha (died on 20.12.1967) student nurses of Irwin Hospital, New Delhi, and
(v) Jaswant Kaur (died on 9.3.1968), student nurse

of Willingdon Hospital, New Delhi.

CONTENTS

Report; Evidence Concerning Deceased Student Nurses of Irwin Hospital; Evidence Concerning Deceased Student Nurse of Willingdon Hospital; Maulana Azad Medical College and Associate Irwin and G.B. Pant Hospitals; Superintendent Nursing Services; Nursing Superintendent (Irwin Hospital); Nursing Superintendent Matron (G.B. Pant Hospital); Assistant Nursing Superintendent; Departmental Sisters; Sister Tutors; Nursing Sisters/Staff Nurses/ Student Nurses; School of Nursing, Irwin Hospital; Probationary Period; Examinations; List Examination of the Punjab Nurses Registration Council; 2nd Year Examination Held in the School; The 3rd Year (Qualifying Examination) held by the P.N.R.C. The Willingdon Hospital; School of Nursing, Willingdon Hospital and Nursing Home; Examinations; Miss Saroj Bala Chadha; Conclusions; Miss Prem Lata Sandil; Conclusions ; Miss Shakuntala Daisy Mathias; Conclusions; Miss Sumitra Chaudhry; Conclusions; Miss Jaswant Kaur; Conclusions.

RECOMMENDATIONS

(i) **Miss Saroj Bala Chadha** : Miss Saroj Bala Chadha committeed suicide by taking fatal dose of seconal, a type of barbiturate on the night between 13-14 December 1967 as a result of which she died at 2.45 a.m. on 20.12.1967. She did so in a depressed state of mind because of her failure in the Third Year Examination.

(ii) The administration concerned with the running of the Nursing School, Irwin Hospital have not followed the principles laid down by the Indian Council of Nursing in the syllabi and Regulations for the Courses in General Nursing and Midwifery. They should have appointed the required number of Tutors and Home Sister etc., as laid down therein. In addition, the appointment of a counsellor was very necessary who would be in a position to guide and assist the young student nurses in solving their difficulties connected with hostel or domestic life. Such a counsellor was very necessary who would be in a position to guide and assist the young student nurses in solving their difficulties connected with hostel or domestic life. Such a counsellor has already been appointed for the benefit of the Maulana Azad Medical College student. The ward duties of student nurses should be so phased they are left with enough time and energy to pursue their studies which are onerous in nature. I am of the confirmed view that if the guide lines laid down by the Indian Nursing Council had been faithfully followed, students like Miss Chadha who according to her two friends and class mates, Miss Soni and Miss Updesh and Master Baid (C.W. 15) was quite, well balanced, intelligent and serious about studies would have done better in her IIIrd Year Examination and thereby perhaps her life saved.

(iii) There is no evidence on the record to show that Miss Saroj Bala Chadha had any other serious complications in her life such as lack of funds for persuing her studies or entanglement in love affairs etc.

(i) **Miss Prem Lata Sandil** : Miss Prem Lata Sandil committed suicide by taking fatal dose of barbiturate and morphine because of the cruel and oppressive treatment given to her by her superiors particularly Mrs. A. Kuriakose, Department Sister who utterly lacked tact and understanding which was very essential for dealing with student nurses at this part of their career.

(ii) There was no avenue available to Miss Prem Lata Sandil to ventilate her grievances and to get justice against the tyrannical treatment meted out to her by her superiors in the ward. I feel that the Superintendent Nursing Services was treating such important cases in routine inasmuch as she directed the Departmental Sister to produce Miss Sandil before her not immediately but on April 5, 1961 a day which never came for Miss Sandil. Miss Sandil thinking that she would get more scolding from the Superintendent Nursing Service ended her life prior to appearing before her.

(1) **Miss Shakuntala Daisy Mathias** : Miss Shakuntala Daisy Mathias committed suicide by taking a fatal dose of Qninal barbiturate on the night between 2nd and 3rd April 1968 out of sheer helplessness. The administration of the Irwin Hospital of which the Nursing School formed an integral part was at a low ebb before and during the time when Miss Mathias committed suicide. It had colapsed both on organisational and functional wings. Indeed the administrative set up of the Maulana Azad Medical complex requires eareful scrutiny so that each person who participates in the administration knows his duties and is also invested with sufficieni powers to discharge them.

(2) The Nursing School should have the prescribed staff i.e. Sister Tutors, Home Sisters, Counsellor and if feasible a Nursing Advisery Committee as has been recommended by (i) Health Survey and Planning Committee presided by Dr. A. Lakshmanaswami Mudaliar, by (ii) the Nursing Committee to Review Conditions of Service, Emoluments, etc., of Nursing Profession presided by Shri A.B. Shetty and above all by (iii) the Indian Nursing Council in their book entitled "Syllabi and Regulations for the Courses in General Nursing and Midwifery". This school should have a Head of the rank of Matron so that she can inspire confidence amongst the nursing students and

can also take up their cause in the event of any difficulty. It should not run on the present lines where the student nurses are considered as part and parcel of the permanent nursing personnel with the result that they have neither the time nor energy left in them after ward work to pursue their studies leave aside their building of general character as useful members of the profession.

(3) The conduct of Mrs. A. Mathew in badly scolding Miss Shakuntala Daisy Mathias on a point the correctness of which she did not independently ascertain is not justifiable. Similarly, the conduct of other persons such as Dr. K.K. Srivastava, Dr. D.P. Bhatnagar, Miss A.D. Masih and Master P.A. Massey in the Orthopaedic Ward where Miss Mathias was working requires condemnation because they in a large way were responsible for creating circumstances which brought about the tragedy.

(4) The Resuscitation Ward should be located in a good commodious room and should have a bio-chemical laboratory and a poison laboratory attached to it for speedy and efficacious treatment of poison cases who require intensive and immediate care.

(i) **Miss Sumitra Chaudhry** : Miss Sumitra Chaudhry committed suicide on the night of April 10, 1968 by taking a fatal dose of barbitone. The treatment of Mrs. A. Mathew, Sister Tutor S. Gomez and Miss Lila Jadhav, Assistant Matron and her other aides towards Miss Sumitra Chaudhry was consistantly callous, cruel, unsympathetic which led her to believe that there was not other escape for her but to end her life.

(ii) The students in the Nursing School are being treated more as convicts in a jail than students in the Nursing School where they have to be handled with sympathy and understanding. The old saying of Spartan mothers that "spare the rod and spoil the child" no longer holds good particularly in the case of students in their late teens receiving training in technical schools and colleges. The very atmosphere in this school stood vitiated on account of mal-administration because there were not adequate number of sister tutors and Home Sisters. There was no Counsellor to give advice to the students when they were faced with difficulties which they thought were insurmountable in nature. In my opinion the administration of the School of Nursing, Irwin Hospital requires complete reorientation to bring in proper atmosphere for the training of young girls in Nursing.

(1) **Miss Jaswant Kaur** : Miss Jaswant Kaur committed suicide by taking a fatal dose of barbiturate late in the evening of 8th March, 1968. She did so in order to escape the displeasure of her father which she would have incurred on the two sister Tutors telling him that she was going out too often with Dr. R.K. Sharda and was neglecting her studies.

(2) Dr. R.K. Sharda in seducing Miss Jaswant Kaur who was not even eighteen years old acted in a manner which does not become a member of the noble profession to which he belonged.

(3) The Medical Superintendent failed to discharge his duty is not taking any disciplinary action against Dr. R.K. Sharda, Dr. Arvind Majupuria and Dr. Rajinder Singh Veerbhan was as already indicated by me above conducted themselves in an ignorable manner while working in the hospital towards the two student nurses.

(4) Dr. R.K. Seth in advising Miss R.D. Saini to show more tolerance to be successful in her career when she complained that Dr. Arvind Majupuria had molested her displayed utter lack of administrative acumen which a man in his position is expected to possess. He failed to discharge his duties in an appropriate manner.

(5) Dr. R.K. Sharda is still working as Casualty Medical Officer in the hospital. Disciplinary action can now be initiated and proper punishment awarded to him so that it could serve as an eye-opener to others who in their weaker moments are likely to conduct themselves in the manner he did.

(6) Doctors Arvind Majupuria and Rajinder Singh Veerbhan have left the hospital. Their cases deserve to be reported to the respective Medical Council for any action which it may deem fit in the matter.

COMMITTEE-BEGGING BY CHILDREN HOW MANY OF THEM ARE KIDNAPPED, 1968—REPORT

New Delhi, Central Bureau of Correctional Services, Department of Social Welfare, 1971. 91+vip.

Chairman : Dr. (Smt.) Jyotsna H. Shah.
Members : Shri S. Venugopal Rao; Shri J.J. Panakal; Smt. Sita Basu; Shri S. Ghosh; Shri H.C. Saksena.
Secretary : Shri J.S. Tyagi.

APPOINTMENT

The Government of India, Department of Social Welfare set up a Committee to go into all aspects of the problem of kidnapping of children and deforming them for the purpose of begging under their resolution No. F. 8/6/68-SW.5, dated the August 14, 1968. The resolution reads as follows :

"Attention of the Government of India has been drawn to the inhuman practice of kidnapping of children with a view to deforming them and using them as beggars. The question of providing for such children suitable services designed to promote their physical, mental and social well-being has, therefore, been under consideration.

Since this is a complex issue, it has been decided to appoint an Expert Committee to go into all aspects of this social problem and to suggest measures for a satisfactory solution.

TERMS OF REFERENCE

(i) To suggest measures for providing adequate shelter, education and other appropriate services to children who are kidnapped or deformed for being used as beggars.

(ii) To suggest suitable amendments to the existing legislation with a view to providing deterrent punishment for kidnappers.

(iii) To suggest appropriate preventive services.

(iv) To draw up a detailed scheme for the implementation of the various suggestions.

CONTENTS

Preface; Historical Background; Social Welfare Plans and Child Begging; Scope of Work; Meetings of the Committee; Limitations; General Trends in Child Begging and Kidnapping; Data on Children Kidnapped for Purposes of Begging; Role of the Police; Statutory Provisions Relating to Child Beggary and Kidnapping; Preventive Services; Services for Care and Protection of children; Summary of Recommendations; Appendices I to VIII.

RECOMMENDATIONS

Investigation, Statistics And Surveys

All cases of missing children should be fully recorded and investigated by the police to varify if any of those children are kidnapped for purposes of begging.

All children found begging should be interrogated and the bona fides of the 'so called' parents and keepers verified to ensure that they have not kidnapped the children for begging.

All handicapped children found begging should be fully investigated to see if any of them are deformed for purposes of begging.

Regional or state-wise surveys of the problem of kidnapping of children for purposes of begging with actual investigation of cases will furnish more useful data to help eradicate the problem.

No comprehensive research has been conducted on the problem of begging in general and child-begging in particular for over ten years. The Committee recommends that specific surveys on the problem of child begging should be sponsored in all the states by the Central Bureau of Correctional Services under the Department of Social Welfare, Government of India, with a view to discover the latest trends in the causation of child begging and to find out to what extent child-begging is due to neglect or connivance on the part of parents and guardians and what proportion of children are forced to beg under duress by other persons exploiting them for ulterior motives.

The administrative departments of the States and Union Territories concerned with Juvenile Courts and Child Welfare Boards, working under, the various Children Acts, should maintain the statistics in such a manner as to throw more light on the problem of child, begging and other forms of exploitation of children.

In the crime records of police departments, statistics of cases of kidnapping of minor under Section 363 Indian Penal Code should be registered separately from the whole group of Section i.e., 363 to 369 and 371 to

373 of Indian Penal Code. Covering the offences of kidnapping and abduction in general.

Role Of Police

The police play a major role in tackling the problem of kidnapping of children for purposes of begging. The responsibility of police extended to the sphere of location of victims of begging or other exploitation and the adoption of direct preventive measures which include surveillance over known criminals, watching the activities of dubious institutions and development of criminal intelligence.

Administrative arrangements and the investigation processes relating to missing children should be so designed that the real problem of kidnapping is not lost sight of and wherever the investigation suggests that the purpose of kidnapping is for begging, section 363-A should be invoked in all cases.

The Committee strongly recommends the creation and strengthening of the Missing Persons Bureau at the city, district and state levels and provisions of adequate facilities for thorough and persistent investigation of all cases of missing children as recommended by the Conference of Deputy Inspectors General of Police, CID.

There is need for an effective organisation of Missing Persons Squad in every city with a population of five lakhs and over. The functions of such Missing Persons Bureau will be to watch the progress of enquiry conducted by local police stations, provide necessary guidance, take over investigations in suitable cases, maintenance of central records and statistic and systematic patrolling.

Smaller towns in rural areas should also have smaller units of Missing Persons Bureau in District Headquarters under the Superintendent of Police.

The strength of the city, district and rural Missing Persons Bureau should be regulated according to workload.

The State Governments which have not set up the Missing Persons Bureau so far should take immediate action to initiate such units.

The Committee strongly recommends the maintenance of exhaustive records at police stations as regards reported missing persons so that important information may not be lost.

The Committee recommends close collaboration between the police and social institutions to rouse public consciousness through sustained propaganda and organising concerted drives to round up beggar children and their keepers to verify if these children were kidnapped.

Statutory Modifications

The Committee recommends that under Section 363-A (i) Indian Penal Code, a minimum sentence of 3 years should be provided so as to make the law more effective and deterrent.

The Committee recommends that the definition of begging under Indian Penal Code Section 363-A (4) (a) should be amended to make it more comprehensive in conformity with the anti-beggary legislation of some States.

The Committee strongly recommends that under Central Children Act, 1960 meant for Union Territories and various State Children Acts uniformity should be brought about in the punishment prescribed for causing, allowing or employing children to beg.

The Committee recommends that the offence of causing or allowing or employing children to beg should be declared as cognizable in Children Acts of all States which do not have such a provision.

There should be a uniformity in the punishment prescribed under the various anti-beggary measures of States for the offence of causing, allowing or employing children to beg.

The Committee recommends that the Legislative Department of the Union Ministry of Law and of various State Governments should examine the relevant provisions of Central and State Children Acts as well as the State anti-beggary legislations with a view to introduce basic uniformity in the definitions, procedures and punishment prescribed for the offence of using children for begging. Further, all these provisions may be examined in the context of Section 363-A of Indian Penal Code.

The Committee recommends that wherever enough evidence is available reasons should be prescribed under Section 363-A of Indian Penal Code as well as under relevant sections of Children Acts and Anti-beggary Acts for the offence of kidnapping and causing, allowing or employing children to beg.

Preventive Services

The Committee recommends better care of all destitute children through institutional services such as cottage homes and through adoption and foster-care, wherever possible.

Services under the Children Acts and under the Anti-beggary Acts should be well organised in all the States.

Welfare services for the physically and mentally handicapped children should be extensively developed.

The Committee strongly recommends that all States and Union Territories must enforce the Women's and Children's Institutions (Licensing), Act, 1956 or the Orphanages and other Charitable Homes (Supervision and Control) Act, 1960.

A special department or office at the State-level

should be made responsible for the services for neglected and handicapped children.

Help to migrant children and families should be systematically organised in all big cities.

Social security and social assistance programme should be progressively undertaken to assist needy families to help them to better provide for their children.

Special services should be organised for the children of weaker sections of society.

Non-official agencies such as Societies for Prevention of Cruelty to children and for Protection of children should be organised in all the States to combat the evil of child begging and other forms of exploitation and to help the law enforcement authorities.

Parental education for safety of children and public consciousness are necessary to prevant child kidnapping and begging.

Pilot projects of community chests should be organised to collect charities for eradicating child beggary and exploitation.

Services For Care And Protection Of Children

Children Acts should be enforced universally all over the country to take care of all needy children.

Adequate number of Juvenile Courts, Remand Homes and Children Homes should be set up under the Children Acts in all the States and Union Territories to take care of neglected and victimised children.

Sufficient number of Probation Officers should be appointed for all areas to attend to Juvenile Court inquiry and supervision work.

A diversified system of institutions for long term care of neglected, destitute, homeless, handicapped and begging children should be organised to take care of all such children in every state.

The Committee recommends proper after-care and follow-up services for all children who are brought up in institutions to help them rehabilitate in society.

ACCIDENT CAUSED BY FIRE IN COACH OF TRAIN NO. 2 FTD PASSENGER BETWEEN MARIPAT AND DADRI STATIONS, NORTHERN RAILWAY, ON 7TH AUGUST, 1968—REPORT

Delhi, Manager of Publications, 1970. 14p.

One-Man Commission : Shri C. R. Sule.

APPOINTMENT

The Commission was constituted under the Ministry of Tourism and Civil Aviation (Commission of Railway Safety) in accordance with Rule 10 of the Railway Board's Notification No. 59-TTV/42/1 dated April 11th, 1966.

TERMS OF REFERENCE

To inquire into the accident caused by Fire in Coach CR 4490 GTY of 2 FTD Down Passenger train between Maripat and Dadri Stations on Tundla-Ghaziabad Section of Northern Railway at about 15.00 hours on August 7, 1968.

CONTENTS

Corrigendum ; Summary ; The Inquiry ; The Accident ; Casualties ; The Train and the Affected Coach ; Damage Relief Arrangements; Local Conditions ; Inspection and Test; Summary of Evidence; Discussion (Time of the Accident; Speed of the Train; Sequence of Events; Precautions, Against Such Fires); Conclusion; Recommendations Made by the Commission of Railway Safety in Connection with the Inquiry into Five which Occurred in No. 2 FTD Down Passenger Train Between Maripat and Dadri Stations, Northern Railway, on August 7, 1968.

CONCLUSIONS

Cause

Having carefully considered all the evidence available and having carefully inspected the affected Coach, I have come to the conclusion that the fire in Coach No. CR 4490 GTY of FTD Down Passenger train was caused by ignition of petrol carried in that compartment. The can containing the petrol, accidentally got overturned, the petrol flowed out and got ignited by a live bidi or match stick thrown by some unknown passenger.

Responsibility

For the occurrence of fire and the passengers killed or injured, no responsibility is attributable to the Railway.

Relief Arrangements

The Relief Train and Medical Van reached the site about 2 hours after the accident. I feel, there has been some delay in the Relief Train reaching the site of accident.

Once the Relief Train reached the site of accident, however, the relief given to the passengers was satisfactory and the care they are now receiving is exemplary.

RAILWAY ACCIDENT INVESTIGATION ON THE REAR END COLLISION BETWEEN EC 281 DOWN GOODS TRAIN AND C 166 DOWN BURDWAN LOCAL (EMU) TRAIN AT GANGPUR STATION, EASTERN RAILWAY ON 18TH AUGUST, 1968—REPORT

Delhi, Manager of Publications, 1971.

One Man Commission : Shri G. S. Pandor.

APPOINTMENT

The above Commission was constituted under the Ministry of Tourism and Civil Aviation vide Rule 10 of Railway Board's Notification No. 59-TTV/42/1 of April 4, 1966.

TERMS OF REFERENCE

To inquire into the collision between EC. 281 Down Goods Train and C. 166 Down Burdwan Local (EMU) on the Down H.B.C. Line at Kml. 101/4-6 between the Down Distant and the Down Home Signals of Gangpur Station on the Quadruple Section of Howrah-Burdwan Main Line Electrified Section of the Eastern Railway at about 07.05 hours on August 18, 1968.

CONTENTS

Relief Measures; The Trains; Local Conditions; Summary of Evidence; Tests and Observations; Discussion; Conclusions and Remarks.

RECOMMENDATIONS

The Case Of The Accident

The collision occurred on August 18, 1961, was the result of EMU train No. C. 166 Down Burdwan Local being driven at excessive speed and without great caution and requisite care on Burdwan-Ganzpur Block Section which it had entered during total failure of all communications, when EC. 281 Down Goods which had preceded it was still occupying it while waiting at the Down Home Signal of Ganzpur station.

Full responsibility for the accident, lies on the Motorman of C. 166 Down, I.P. Singh, who failed to exercise due precaution as required by General Rules 89 (b), 122, 163 (a) (i) and printed instructions at the back of OPT/126 A which was issued to him.

The Guard of the EMU train, who was fully aware that the train was being drived at speed much inexcess of what was shown in the Caution Order, failed to act in time, as required by General Rules No. 121 and 126, to stop it to avert accident.

Service Records Of Motorman Of C. 116 Down

Shri I.P. Singh, who was 40 years of age, was originally recruited as Probationary Fireman Grade 'A' on May 21, 1951. He was promoted as Driver 'C' grade on November 21, 1962, which post he held up to the time of the accident. On completion of training for working EMU trains at Howrah Car Shed on June 19, 1968, he was put incharge to work such trains on short links from June 22, 1968 to July 23, 1968. He was entrusted with long distance EMU trains upto Burdwan on and from July 24, 1968. No punishment in connection with his train working duties was inflicted.

Service Records Of Guard Of C. 166 Down

Shri S. C. Moulik, aged 36 years, was initially appointed as Guard Grade II on January 21, 1945 but due to his unauthorised absence his service was considered terminated and was shown reappointed with effect from March 15, 1946. His record is clean in regard to his train working duties.

Relief Measures

Emergency calls were made without delay and they were met with prompt response. I am satisfied that the Medical aid at site was prompt and efficient. Relief Measures were satisfactory as could be expected in the circumstances.

THE COMMITTEE OF EXPERTS ON UNEMPLOYMENT ESTIMATES, 1968 —REPORT

New Delhi, Planning Commission, 1970. 203+xip.

Chairman : Prof. M. L. Dantwala.
Members : Prof. K. N. Raj; Prof. D. B. Lahiri.

APPOINTMENT

The Planning Commission set up a Committee of Experts on Unemployment Estimates under its Resolution No. L & E (E) 12-7/68, dated August 19, 1968 to "go into the estimates of unemployment worked out for the previous plans and the data and methodology used in arriving at them and advise the Planning Commission on the various issues connected therewith, in particular, the alternative methods of analysis, computation and presentation that may be adopted for the Fourth Five-Year Plan (1969-74) in the ten year perspective of 1969-79."

TERMS OF REFERENCE

To consider the following issues :

(1) **Concepts** : In the rural areas, the concept of unemployment, as the term is usually understood, is not applicable and the method of working out 'equivalent full time unemployment' from such data as may be available about the number of man-hours worked in a year is, as Prof. Mahalanobis himself admitted, arbitrary and not of the slightest value in making policy or administrative decisions. What is to be done ?

(2) **Methods of direct estimation of unemployment** : These methods are essentially based (a) for the urban areas on the Employment Exchange Data and (b) for the rural areas on the National Sample Survey (NSS) data of the 16th Round done in 1960-61. The limitations of Employment Exchange data as indicators of unemployment arise from (i) some persons already employed registering themselves, (ii) some persons not employed not registering themselves, (iii) some persons registering themselves at more than one Employment Exchange, and (iv) some persons from rural areas registering themselves at the exchanges. The limitations for the rural areas are even more serious because the latest available NSS data relate only to 1960-61 and the estimates of rural unemployment for subsequent years are based on the assumption that the proportions of unemployed in the rural population would be the same (i.e., 1.6 per cent) as in 1960-61. There is no means to verify the validity of this assumption.

"Because of the reasons set out above, the estimation of base year unemployment for a five year plan, or 'backlog' as it is called, is subject to serious limitation. Shall we continue to use the Employment Exchange and NSS data and if so, what corrective factors, if any, shall we apply ?

(3) **Methods of indirect estimation of unemployment** : This method consists in taking a previous direct estimation of unemployment in 1950-51 (subject to the limitation mentioned in (2) above) and adding to it the difference between the entrants to labour force in a five year period and the employment generated as estimated on the basis on investment made in public and private sectors by the use of sectoral investment employment 'norms' or 'coefficients'. The number of entrants to labour force is computed on the basis of population data for age-groups and the participation rate for males

and females as indicated by the latest population census returns. The estimation of employment generated takes the investment-employment norms for sectors or activities for which investment data are available and then makes an overall addition of about 50 per cent for the indirect employment. The result all along, has been an increase in the figure of 'back log'.

"Was the base figure of backlog in 1950-51 of 3.5 million, reliable or acceptable ? Is the present method of estimating employment generated in a five-year period correct ?

(4) If both the direct and indirect methods of estimation of unemployment are deficient and subject to limitations do we now state clearly that 'backlog' estimates of the past were exceedingly rough and need not be relied upon as a kind of overall guide to policy and action ? What other method of analysis and presentation shall we adopt ?"

CONTENTS

Introduction; Planning Commission's Estimates of Unemployment and Employement Generation ; An Outline; Evaluation of the Planning Commission's Methodology and Assumptions; A Framework of Analysis; The Major Sources of Data on Employment and Unemployment; Suggestions for Improvement; Summary and Conclusions; Appendices I to VII.

RECOMMENDATIONS

Planning Commission's Estimates Of Unemployment And Employment Generation : An Outline

The review below is confined to the Planning Commission's estimates and the methodology adopted in successive Plans for calculating :

(a) The backlog of unemployment or the number of persons unemployed at the beginning of the Plan;

(b) The additions to the labour force during the Plan period;

(c) The employment potential or the number of jobs likely to be generated through the implementation of the Plan as formulated; and

(d) The employment generated or achievements in terms of employment on the basis of the actual Plan performance.

Evaluation Of The Planning Commission's Methodology And Assumptions

Backlog of unemployment at the start of a Plan period.

(a) Backlog of unemployment at the start of the preceding Plan period plus.

(b) Net additions to the labour force during the period minus.

(c) Additional employment generated during the period.

The estimate of rural unemployment based essentially on the results of the First Agricultural Labour Enquiry was subject to several serious limitations.

The estimates of the backlog of unemployment in rural and urban India at the start of the second Plan must be regarded as very rough.

We also suggest that information on labour force, employment and unemployment should be disaggregated so that those who may need wage or salaried work could be distinguished from those whose preference would be for more work in family enterprises.

One might mention here the need to take into account not only the net additions to the labour force but also the gross number of entries into and withdrawals from the labour force. Men usually enter into the labour force before the age of 30 and withdrawals take place at older ages. The job requirements of the entrants into the labour force are different from the vacancies resulting from withdrawals. With a proper use of a age-specific participation rates, it should be possible to make separate estimates of entries and withdrawals.

The non-availability of detailed age-specific participation rates from the 1961 Census has been a handicap in making such adjustments. The NSS data do provide more detailed age specific participation rates but the age-groups have not always been comparable. The NSS tables on urban labour force participation rates distinguish between the States but, for rural areas, the State tables are not yet available. The NSS sample is probably not large enough to give sufficiently precise estimates of age-specific participation rates for all the States, that were necessary while making the labour force projections for the Fourth Plan.

The estimates of employment supposed to have been actually generated during a Plan period are based in part on the some norms as are used to estimate the "employment potential" at the beginning of the Plan period. Any difference between the two is, therefore largely attributable to divergence between the "planned" and the "actual" investment and output.

In view of the difficulties experienced in estimating the volume of investment in the non-corporate segment of the private sector, more particularly in agriculture and small-scale industries, the estimates of employment generation are necessarily subject to unknown margin of error. In particular, the estimates of additional employment generated in agriculture have been largely conjectural. In rural areas, persons from cultivating families who enter the labour force are customarily absorbed in the agricultural sector without regarded to the quantum of work they may get and do not normally "seek" alternative employment. Those who seek non-agricultural jobs might at times fall back on agriculture particularly if they, or their families, own or could lease in some land. Female workers in rural areas also work mainly on family farms or similar household enterprises; even the job-seekers among the night frequently drop out from the labour force and confine themselves to household work when the available opportunities are inadequate.

The evidence from the 1951 and the 1961 Censuses as well as the various Rounds of the NSS suggests that the number of persons working in the agricultural sector did increase substantially over the periods 1951-61 and 1955-66, though the quantum of work and/or income of the additional workers is not known. On the other hand, as noted earlier, the Planning Commission's estimates relating to agriculture appear to have been made in terms of the additional employment reckoned on a "full-time" basis.

The difference between the Planning Commission's estimates of employment generated in agriculture and the increase in the number of persons engaged in farming as recorded by the Censuses and the NSS is very large. Since large sections of the labour force in agriculture were exposed to under-employment throughout the period covered by these estimates, and no data are available for assessing the direction or extent of change of under-employment in this sector over the period, here is no way of comparing the realised growth of employment with the growth as anticipated in the Plans.

It is however worth noting that, according to the data collected by the NSS in rural India the percentage of the gainfully employed population that was "severely under-employed" (i.e. working 28 hours or less during the reference week and available for additional work) has shown some decline between the 14th and the 17th Rounds (1958-59) to (1961-62).

For the non-agricultural sector also, reliable data on employment generation are available only for enterprises in the private sector which employ more than specified minimum number of workers (generally referred to as the organised segment of the private sector) and for enterprises in the public sector. Under the Employment Market Information Programme (EMI) of the Directorate General of Employment and Training (DGET), data are normally collected for establishments employing 25 workers or more. For the Third Plan period one can thus obtain an estimate of actual increase in employment—about 3.12 million—in the civilian public sector and in the non-agricultural sector together (excluding small-scale establishments and plantations). The inclusions of increased employment in the defence sector would not raise this figure above 4 million. Since private sector establishments employing 25 persons or more and engaged it trade, commerce, transport etc., are covered by the EMI data, this figure of 4 million must be taken to include part of the increase in what was described as 'indirect' non-agricultural employment in the Planning Commission's estimates. However, for the other three-fifths of the estimated increase in employment of 10.5 million in the non-agricultural sector during the Third Plan, the statistical basis for cross-checking is totally inadequte.

The Planning Commission has made several attempts to refine the employment norms by consulting the various concerned agencies. Yet the outcome has been far from satisfactory. For estimating the employment potential of a plan, fairly reliable data are necessary on additional employment per unit of investment and/or per unit increase in output in different sectors. The relevant ratios not only differ from industry to industry but are seldom the same at the margin as on the average for the same industry changes in technology and organization introduce further problems. The projection of past experience into the future for estimating increases in employment is therefore, rather hazardous.

It is also important to recognise, that, given the organisational characteristics of house-hold and small-scale enterprises based largely on family labour, and the prevalent differences both in the attachment of family labour to such enterprises and in the intensity of their employment it is impossible to judge how a given increase in employment potential is likely to get distributed among the persons in the labour force even if such an increase could be somehow precisely estimated. In practice, when a norm has been used relating planned investment and increase in output to growth of employment, it has not always been made clear whether the additional employment estimated is full-time or at the level actually then prevalent in the industry. As mentioned earlier, if the norm used explicitly refers to full-time work (as has sometimes been the case) but the prevailing pattern of employment in a sector is seasonal and not full-time or perennial, a given amount of investment or increase in output would result in a large number of persons securing employment therefrom (though on a less than full-time basis) than would be estimated by the use of the norm.

This is best illustrated by the estimates of employment potential in the construction sector. During each of the plans, a significant proportion of the estimated growth of employment has been attributed to this sector. The additional employment potential was, however, estimated in terms of man-years, more specifically, in terms of full-time employment for 300 days. In reality, construction tends to be a seasonal activity and a substantial proportion of the persons working on construction projects tends to be employed on daily or weekly wages. The construction employment generated by the investment in the plans is therefore likely to have been spread over a larger number of persons than estimated.

We have given a good deal of thought to the question of refinement of the estimates of employment generation in different sectors but are unable to suggest any methods that would significantly improve such estimates, in the short or medium run, for the economy as a whole. The most that can be attempted by way of estimation is the likely growth of employment in a few segments of the economy such as in manufacturing industries (that too only within enterprises employing a specified minimum number of workers) and in certain types of services. For the rest, reliance has to be placed primarily on recording at frequent intervals changes taking place in the composition of the labour force (more particularly the numbers seeking wage employment), its industrial distribution, the wage rates for different types of labour, the intensity of employment, and the numbers seeking employment. This can perhaps be done through quinquennial sample surveys. The data thrown up by such surveys would help to throw light on the trends in the labour market and make possible more dependable projections of the trends in employment and unemployment in the future.

The available data on the number of persons on the Live Register of the Employm ent Exchanges do not, however, permit reliable estimates of the volume of urban unemployment because (i) some of those registered reside in rural areas and are not part of the urban unemployed; (ii) some of them are in fact employed or are students; (iii) not all the unemployed even in urban areas register themselves with the Employment Exchanges; and (iv) some of the urban unemployed probably register at more than one exchange. It is, therefore, necessary first to try and adjust the Live Register figures for these limitations.

The percentage of unemployed in urban areas indicated by the data from the Employment Exchanges, substantially exceeds the percentage estimated by NSS surveys. It has been suggested that this divergence is probably due to the fact that the NSS definitions would have the effect of classifying respondents as employed when for all practical purposes they may in fact be unemployed. Thus it has been pointed out that a person reporting some work, "however nominal it may be", during the reference period of one week is classified as "employed" by the NSS. The converse of this, however, is that many of those classified as unemployed during the reference period of "one week" might be employed during the rest of the year. Further, the NSS has tabulated the data on employed persons according to the number of hours worked by them and their availability for additional work. It would appear from these data that, even if persons reporting work for 28 hours or less during the reference week and available for additional work were included with the unemployed, the urban unemployed according to the NSS would not exceed 4 per cent of the urban labour force. On the other hand, the number of persons on the Live Register of the Employment Exchanges on December 31 1968, after adjustment for the various factors mentioned above (on the basis of the recent DGET survey and the NSS data on the proportion of the unemployed who register themselves with Employment Exchanges) amounts to about 7.5 per cent of the urban labour force.

We would like to note that one of the major shortcomings of the estimates of unemployment presented in the plan documents has been their high degree of aggregation, except for a separate reference to the problem of educated unemployed, i.e., those educated up to matriculation or higher level. The various estimates would be more meaningful for analysis and public policy, and at the same time more reliable, if distinctions are made in the demand and supply of labour in terms of their location (State or Zone), rural-urban residence, household and wage employment, and the characteristics of sex, age and education. Though lack of the necessary data has been the main reason for the presentation of aggregated figures for the net additions to the labour force and for the likely growth in employment opportunities, the Planning Commission can useful advise other agencies to collect and process disaggregated data of the kind required. Our recommendations on the subject of labour force data will be presented in the subsequent discussion.

A Framework Of Analysis

We believe that by introducing more clarity in the concepts of labour force and unemployment and by modifying them in consonance with the nature and the structure of the Indian economy, it would be possible to derive estimates which would reflect more accurately the different facets of the problem. It is also necessary to adopt survey techniques that would be more appropriate for measurement of these phenomena.

We emphasize the point that even the improved estimates of participation rates, industrial distribution of the labour force etc., pertaining to previous years would not be wholly adequate for the purpose of projections. The development process is likely to, in fact is meant to, alter the various elements which enter into such projections. The dynamics of changes in the demand and supply of labour should therefore, be constantly watched.

It is important to recognise that the labour supply available to the Indian economy for productive activity—whatever the criteria by which it is identified and estimated is of an extremely heterogeneous character. As table 3 would indicate, a significant proportion of the labour supply is self-employed or unpaid family labour within household enterprises, and only a part seeks wage or salaried employment. The relative importance of these components differs considerably between rural and urban areas. The unpaid family workers consist mainly of women and children whose participation in economic activity is generally limited and who might not ordinarily be suppliers of labour outside their own individual household. Unlike these family workers, the participation of the self-employed or own account workers is usually as complete as the pattern of economic activity in the given industry or occupation and the availability of land and/or capital stock permits. However, both among the self-employed and the unpaid family workers, even when the employment they obtain in their own enterprises is less than adequate, there would be many whose mobility is likely to be limited; and they may not, therefore, seek and/or be available for employment elsewhere.

Table 3

Percentage distribution of the gainfully employed in Rural and Urban India, according to Status, Specified Rounds of the NSS

Status	Rural India 17th Round (1961-62)			Urban India 15th Round (1959-60)		
	Males	Females	Persons	Males	Females	Persons
Employees	31.50	29.90	31.06	53.10	43.34	51.40
Employers	9.00	3.06	7.36	2.03	0.43	1.76
Own Account Worker	43.66	19.14	36.79	36.68	30.19	35.55
Unpaid Family Workers	15.84	47.90	24.79	8.19	26.04	11.29
All	100.00	100.00	100.00	100.00	100.00	100.00
Sample Persons	146,619	139,724	286,343	18,872	16,935	35,807

The suggestions for collecting data by seasons will remove one of the limitations of the present estimates of unemployment derived from NSS Surveys, since the employment situation revealed by the data for the reference week will not be regarded as reflections the position for the entire year but for the season covered by the sub-round. One important defect noted earlier will however still remain. According to the current definitions in use, persons working for only a nominal period of time during the reference week are classified as employed. In rural areas only those who, owing to lack of work, do not work even on a single day during the reference week and are currently available for work are classified as unemployed. In urban areas such persons must also be seeking "full time" work. The above criteria for distinguishing between 'employed' and 'unemployed' would have a tendency to underestimate the degree of unemployment actually prevailing, whether for the averaging process the period covered is a whole year or only a particular season.

It is necessary to abandon the practice of presenting the estimates simply in terms of 'employed' and 'unemployed' persons and instead try and obtain some measure of the level or rate of unemployment in the economy by reference to the daily recorded data on employment and unemployment. Essentially, this will amount to collection of data about the labour time disposition of each individual during a reference week, such as was attempted by the NSS in rural employment and unemployment surveys from the 11th to the 17th rounds. During these rounds, the data on labour time disposition were collected only for persons who were classified as gainfully employed during the reference period. Under the new approach suggested by us, such information would be collected for every individual in the sample.

It appears to us that while the collection of data on hours of work is useful, it would be better if data are collected about the number of days on which a person is employed or unemployed during the reference week, without recording the number of hours of work on each day, and the present estimates of unemployed are replaced by a measurement of the rate of unemployment during a season.

It should be emphasized that the estimate of unemployment derived from the above procedure will not correspond to the Planning Commission's estimates of the unemployed.

Those who are unemployed for a long period, say for a year or more, can reasonably be considered as needing full-time jobs and can be called chronically unemployed.

We need to have a better idea about the degree of commitment or non-commitment of those who withdraw from the labour market after seasonal work. Do they withdraw because of the compulsions of their "non-gainful" activity (such as household work) or do they do so because of the presumed or real non-availability of particular types of work? Without a few probing questions, no precise idea about their motivation for 'not-working' after certain peak season would be available and their classification as 'outside the labour force' or 'unemployed' would remain a debatable issue.

In view of such fluctuations in the characteristics of the labour force, it would be useful if the employment/unemployment data obtained for the season or sub-round are also analysed in terms of the usual status of the respondents. The usual status characteristics, that might be taken into account, would include (a) labour force status (in the labour force/outside the labour force, i.e., house-workers, students and others); (b) employment status (employed/unemployed); (c) industry (agriculture/household manufacturing/non-household manufacturing/others); and (d) status or class of worker (employer, employee, self-employed and unpaid family worker).

In urban labour force surveys, an attempt should be made to ascertain how many of those classified as 'employed' had actively sought (a) alternative or (b) supplementary part-time or full-time jobs and the reasons for the same (for example, inadequate income or dissatisfaction with the utilisation of skills and/or educational training). Periodical canvassing of such probing questions would permit better comparability between the NSS data and those reported by the employment exchanges. In addition, they would indicate the extent to which the employed persons view themselves as under-employed.

For unemployed persons who had worked at some previous time, it would be useful to find out their industry, occupation, and status in the last job held by them. Such information will make it possible to understand the factors responsible for their unemployment and devise programmes of creating employment opportunities suitable for their experience and skills gained during periods of employment.

A view was apparently held in the Planning Commission around 1958-59 that "with the stage in development we might reach in 1976, it would be safe to assume that the labour force participation rate will increase to 45 per cent from the level of 40 per cent indicated by the 1951 Census and 42.5 per cent assumed for the Third Plan. While it is true that the 1961 Census indicated a higher aggregate participation rate of 43 per cent, there is reason to believe that this was partly due to the very liberal definition adopted for the enumeration of workers in seasonal industries. Apart from this, there is no evidence to suggest that the participation rate tends to increase with development. The NSS data on crude male participation rates for the urban India from the 9th Round (1955) to the 21st Round (1966-67) indicate, if anything, a slightly declining trend. For females in urban India, the trend is not clear. For rural India, the crude rate fluctuated from Round to Round and does not indicate any significant trend after the 9th Round. The rate for rural males, however, shows some decline from the high levels of the 14th and the 15th Rounds 57 and 59 per cent to about 52-54 per cent during the 17th to 21st Rounds.

It may be mentioned that, as a general rule, in the developed countries, the overall participation rates do appear to be higher than those in the developing countries. But this is mainly due to the difference in the age-structure of the population in the developed and developing countries. It will be evident from Table 4 below that the age-specific participation rates in the ages 15 to 60 are not very different for the two categories of countries; in fact, the rate for the age-group 0-24 is lower in the developed countries. As far as India is concerned, for the next few years at least, the percentage of the young (i.e., those below 25 years of

Table 4

Estimates of Sex-age-specific Participation Rates in Countries of North-West Europe and Less Developed Countries, 1965.

Age	Males		Females	
	Less Developed countries	North-West Europe	Less Developed countries	North-West Europe
0-14	6.5	1.1	4.0	0.9
15-24	78.1	76.2	36.9	60.2
25-54	96.3	96.8	40.1	41.3
55-64	86.8	83.3	29.2	28.9
65+	57.5	23.4	14.5	7.4
All ages	53.2	61.1	22.9	28.6

age) in the total population is likely to increase rather than decrease. Therefore, a decline in the participation rate of persons aged less than 25, associated with the process of development, would tend to depress the overall participation rate.

Two factors appear to be particularly relevant to the impact of development on participation rates, namely, urbanisation and decline in the share of agriculture in labour force and increasing school enrolments. An increase in school enrolments delays entry into the labour force and lowers the participation rate. The effect is observed significantly in the age-group 10 to 14 and to a lesser extent in the age-groups 15 to 19 and 20 to 24. As for urbanisation, it may be noted that urban participation rates are lower than those for rural areas, particularly for females (See Table 5 below). This is probably due both to higher school enrolment rates and fewer opportunities for self-employment or work within household enterprises in urban areas. Thus, if development leads to greater urbanisation, it would result in lower participation rates.

Table 5

Labour Force Participation Rates in Rural and Urban India according to 1961 Census (per cent)

	Rural	Urban
Males	58.51	54.15
Females	31.45	11.25

Another consideration to be kept in mind in analysing the likely trends in employment and unemployment is that since the various components of the labour force are likely to be affected differently by different patterns of development, it would be difficult to quantify or analyse probable changes from the supply side of labour independently of the likely changes on the demand side. Changes on the supply side will be affected particularly by factors such as the extent of increase in productive employment opportunities within the household enterprises, increase in school enrolments, and literacy and wage/income differentials associated with particular patterns of development.

If the growth of productive employment opportunities on family farms or within other household enterprises is not adequate to absorb the increase in this category of the labour force, two kinds of response could be expected. One is withdrawal of some from the labour force, a response often noticed from among females in the rural labour force. Another possible response is an increase in the supply of labour seeking employment on contractual basis as "employees". Whether the net balance of these responses is positive or negative will depend on a variety of factors such as the minimum income requirements of the "self-employed", opportunities for wage employment in the vicinity, the degree of literacy, the skills acquired etc.

On the basis of our present knowledge, it is difficult to predict with any accuracy either the direction of change in the labour participation rate on account of such factors or the kind of transformation that might take place in the pattern of labour supply. All one can say is that it would be a serious mistake to proceed on the assumption that the entire labour force is of a homogeneous character and make estimates of increases in the labour force simply on the basis of population projections and aggregate sex-age-specific participation rates reflected in data relating to the past.

There is some evidence that the participation rate in some parts of the country (such as Kerala) has tended to fall over the decades a phenomenon attributable in part to the decline in the share of agriculture in the total labour force (since the participation of women and children in productive activity tends to be relatively high in this sector) and in part to increased school enrolment and literacy which delay the age of entry into the labour force. Evidence of such fall is also available from data relating to the urban sector of the economy in recent years; the explanation in this case may be largely growth of literacy. But there is as yet no evidence of a noticeable decline in the participation rate in the rural sector of the economy taken as a whole.

We recommend separate estimation for the different segments of the labour force, taking into account such important characteristics as region (State), sex, age, rural-urban residence, status or class of worker and educational attainment. Attempts could then be made to identify the demand likely to be generated in the various regions (States) for different categories of labour as a result of various developments envisaged under the Five Year Plans. Such effort should concentrate initially on sectors where the personnel or labour requirements can be clearly recognised.

We would like to emphasize is the need for disaggregation and for checking on the estimates for each plan period with the help of data collected or derived independently of those employed in making the original projections.

The Major Sources Of Data On Employment And Unemployment : Suggestions For Improvement.

The tabulation of the data on workers by broad age groups and industrial categories undertaken in the 1961 Census was not adequate for obtaining labour force projections that would permit drawing a distinction between the entries into and withdrawals from the labour force or the pace of change in the sectoral distribution of workers with age. As a result of some cooperative research by the University of Bombay and the Census authorities, such data have been tabulated by five year age groups, and for females by marital status as well, for the State of Maharashtra. Similar tabulations are currently being prepared for some other States as well. Our understanding of the pattern of participation by economic activity is likely to be considerably enriched when these data became available. If similar tables can be compiled from the data collected by the 1971 Census, it will be possible to study not only the effect of the differences in the concepts used in the two censuses on the size and composition of the working force but also the inter-sectoral mobility of workers during the inter-censal period, 1961-71. We, therefore, recommend that the 1971 Census should endeavour to compile a basic table on the economic activity distribution of the population by five year age groups, at least for the age range 10-34 and 55 and over.

In the 1961 Census different age groups have often been used to tabulate the same data for rural and urban India. This has particularly been the case for the classification of the unemployed. A similar difference exists in the age-classification of the unemployed seeking work for the first time and the other unemployed. Also, the class of worker distribution was obtained only for workers engaged in activities other than cultivation. The use of computers for the 1971 Tabulation Programme should make it possible for the Census authorities to adopt uniform age groups for compiling tables on the same items for different groups of the population and to prepare the class of worker distribution for the entire working force, by sex and five year age groups.

Finally, we wish to emphasize the need for a more detailed cross-classification of workers by sex, five year age groups, educational level, and industry.

Some efforts at collecting data on unemployment have been made in the last three censuses. The data collected on the subject by the 1941 Census were not tabulated. In the 1951 Census, data were collected only in the three States of Uttar Pradesh, Bihar and Bombay, Saurashtra and Kutch, under the option provided to the Superintendents of Census Operations of various States to introduce an additional question in the Census Schedule. The number of unemployed reported in each of these States was very small.

In the 1961 Census, while identifying the status of those who were classified as non-workers, some information was obtained on persons 'seeking employment' for the first time, and 'persons employed before, but now out of employment and seeking work', although the instructions given to the enumerators did not elaborate the concept of 'seeking work'. The total of these two categories was taken as representing the unemployed. The number of unemployed enumerated by the 1961 Census was only 1.4 million, of whom 0.8 million were in urban areas. The very small number of 'unemployed in rural areas (0.6 million)' was perhaps a natural consequence of the definition and the reference period used to classify the workers. Any one engaged in a seasonal activity such as agriculture, animal husbandry and household industries, who had worked for "at least one hour a day throughout the greater part of the working season", was considered a worker. These activities predominate in rural areas where most of the unemployment is essentially seasonal in character. In other words, anyone seeking work would ordinarily be able to find it for at least short periods during the peak season in agriculture. It is not surprising, therefore, that the number of rural unemployed enumerated by the 1961 Census was very low.

The 1961 Census estimate of the unemployed males in urban areas was a little higher than that indicated by the data from the 16th and 17th Rounds of the NSS covering the period July, 1960—July 1962 and relating to the urban sector. This will be evident from Table 6 below :

Table 6

Unemployed As Per Cent Of The Labour Force Aged 15 Years And Over In Urban India, According To The 1961 Census And The 16th And The 17th Rounds Of The NSS

	Males	Females
1961 Census	3.25	1.48
NSS 16th Round	2.40	2.64
NSS 17th Round	3.02	3.31

It may be noted that, like the 1961 Census, the 1971 Census will initially classify and individual as a worker or a non-worker. Non-workers are proposed to be classified as (1) those engaged in household duties, (2) students, (3) retired persons or rentiers, (4) dependents, (5) beggars etc., (6) persons in institutions, and (7) other non-workers. The job seekers (unemployed) are proposed to be included under the last category. Unlike in a labour force survey, those who report their main activity to be other than work (non-workers) will not be asked by the Census enumerators whether they were "seeking or not seeking but available for work". Without such a question, a specific identification of persons as unemployed is not feasible. (With a reference period of one year, few persons in rural India would in any case be in the category of wholly unemployed). It would thus appear that the Census organisation has practically given up the idea of collecting data which could be considered as indicating unemployment. Presumably, this procedure has been adopted because the Census enumerators undertake their work on an essentially honorary basis and do not generally have the training to ask detailed probing questions to ascertain whether a person is unemployed. This is a valid reason, and therefore we do feel that the Census organization should not be burdened with the task of collecting data on unemployment.

We recommend that the NSS should resume its rural labour force surveys, taking into account the various suggestions made in this Report.

While we recognize the inter-State differences in regard to the importance of various problems, problems of employment and unemployment are of sufficiently high importance to require close cooperation between the States and the Centre for the processing of these data.

We recommend that an attempt be made to identify separately the proportion of such unemployed in urban areas as well.

It is advisable to collect the information, on the persons seeking or not seeking but available for work, for all persons irrespective of age.

It is advisable to obtain initially [for two or three Rounds and subsequently at a certain interval, monthly estimates of labour force characteristics. The sole additional requirement for this purpose is appropriate tabulation and the concerned authorities should explore the possibility of accommodating this requirement in their tabulation plans.

The extent to which persons, who are usually (i.e., according to 'usual status') outside the labour force—such as students and house workers—undertake some casual work. However, this objective may not be fulfilled if the interviewers, avoid asking the necessary questions to ascertain the labour force status of all sample respondents on each day of the reporting week. Due care should be taken to minimise this possibility.

In some of the NSS Rounds, an attempt can usefully be made to ascertain the extent of such movement and its effect on the estimates of unemployment, with due attention to the difference in the characteristics of towns in different size classes.

It would be useful if the conventional classification of the population of each sex by age, activity and status or class of worker could include an additional variable about the number of hours of work during the reference week. It would indicate the difference, if any, in the hours worked by workers of different status categories, such as employers, self-employed and unpaid family workers.

The planning of the various surveys and tabulations of the NSS is done by a committee consisting of officials of the State and Central Governments and the Technical Wing of the NSS. We feel that the inclusion of non-official experts from universities and research institutions interested in the use and interpretation of empirical data on the subject will contribute substantially to improvements in the concepts, procedures and tabulation plans adopted.

While we recognize the physical constraints in processing the data for a national sample in a country as large as India, we recommend immediate efforts to shorten the time interval. The disadvantages of delay in the publication of reports can also be mitigated to some extent if the draft reports are made available to universities and research institutions for comments and study as soon as the draft reports are prepared.

The EMI should aim at covering all establishments using power and employing 10 or more workers as well as establishments not using power but employing 20 or more workers (i.e. the "factory" establishments). At the same time, figures for establishments employing 25 workers or more should be provided separately. The advantage of such a procedure would be that, from time to time, the EMI data could be fruitfully compared with the data thrown up by the Annual Survey of industries (ASI) for sectors common to both the EMI and the ASI. This is particularly necessary on account of the serious problems involved in keeping the list of establishments up-to-date and because the ASI, unlike the EMI, relies on trained investigators who interview all the respondents. This would provide a valuable cross-check on the EMI data and ensure that it is an efficient and sensitive barometer of changes in the urban employment situation.

The EMI should also separate urban establishments from the rural in their tabulations, so that we would have separate figures relating specifically to the urban sector.

Since the EMI data are an important "barometer", attempts should be made to collect the data by the interview method (as in the case of ASI) instead of the present postal method. This would improve the response and the quality of the data collected. This might involve important administrative and financial considerations; given the great potentialities of the EMI data in our statistical system, it seems worthwhile, perhaps, as an initial measure, the interview method might be restricted to establishments employing 25 or more workers.

The need to conduct frequent surveys to estimate appropriate correction factors to adjust the Employment Exchange data is obvious. The distribution of registrants on the Live Register by age, sex, educational levels, rural-urban residence, and employment status (employed or unemployed) is likely to vary over time, and correction factors be available for such categories of registrants at the State level. This would probably require a large sample from the Live Register. We recommend that such surveys should estimate also the extent of multiple registrations, and attempt to provide reliable and up-to-date correction factors so that the rural registrants as well as the urban employed and the student registrants could be separately estimated and excluded from the urban unemployed.

It is important that efforts be made to ensure that the personnel employed for such surveys are independent of those in the Employment Exchanges, so that respondents may not be unwilling to admit that they are employed persons or students.

Some research workers from universities and other academic institutions should be associated with the planning and analysis of these surveys.

The educational level classification used in the NSS and in the Live Registers of the Employment Exchange should be uniform in order to facilitate the application of the relevant correction factor to convert urban unemployed registrants into urban unemployed persons. In particular the tabulation of job-seekers by sex, age-group, and educational level should distinguish illiterates from literates "below middle school standard".

The renewal period for registration should be uniform all over the country. At present, it varies between States and even within a State as between those with different educational attainments. Uniformity is essential if the data are to be comparable and useful for interpretative purposes of the kind we have in mind.

We note that the decennial censuses provide information on the size and composition of the Indian labour force once every ten years, while the NSS rounds attempt to furnish the material to build up a time series based on annual data. A suggestion has been made that an intensive quinquennial survey devoted specifically to the measurement of the size and composition of the labour force and unemployment would be a valuable supplement to the pool of available data. However, the quinquennial surveys are subject to a possible disadvantage that results might be affected by various contingencies, such as a drought if the latter coincide with the year of survey. An alternative seems to be the pooling of the NSS data collected during successive Rounds and preparation of a kind of moving average series. The reference point of such a series would like at some time in the past; for example, an average picture built up from five annual Rounds would have its reference point approximately at the mid-point of the quinquennial period. However, with a reasonably large sample size (that would be necessary also to meet the various requirements outlined by us earlier), the pooling together of the data for a five-year period would permit separate estimates of different labour force characteristics for states and other regions, that are presently wanting. The NSS field staff has had the training and experience in collecting data on various aspects of the labour force for a long time; and it would probably be a more effective agency than any special cadre of investigators appointed for the quinquennial survey. Of course, if the NSS data for successive Rounds are to be pooled together, frequent changes in the concepts, such as have been made in the past, will have to be kept at a minimum or else an attempt will need to be made to obtain appropriate adjustment factors through a simultaneous use of the alternative approaches. If these factors are recognized adequately, a continuous serious built-up from the NSS data is likely to be more useful than ad hoc quinquennial surveys.

Summary And Conclusions

As a result of the various suggestions made by us, two types of improvements will be brought about in the estimates of unemployment. First, even without a change in the concepts of employment and unemployment currently in use, we shall obtain separate estimates of the level of unemployment during different seasons of a year among various homogeneous groups of the labour force and/or population identified through the 'usual status' approach.

Secondly, we have suggested a change in the present procedure of classifying a person as employed or unemployed. Our alternative envisages the identification of the employment and labour force status of the population studied in various surveys on the basis of the activity of the respondents on each day during the reference week. The estimate obtained under this approach will indicate the average rate of unemployment during the season, or in other words, the extent of under-utilization of the available labour supply in the rural economy. It will not indicate the number of unemployed persons or the requirement of additional full-time jobs. The latter figure can be estimated through some supplementary questions about the duration of unemployment, etc., to be asked to those who report unemployment throughout the week. If our suggestions are accepted, the resulting estimates of the level of unemployment in different sectors of the economy will not only become more realistic but will be more useful for the formulation of appropriate public policy.

We have also proposed some additional probing questions to be asked to persons in various categories of the labour force. These questions are intended to enhance our understanding of the factors underlying the changes taking place in the labour market. From the response to these questions, we shall be able to gain an insight into (a) the reasons for the apparent withdrawal from the labour market by many unpaid family workers after seasonal work and (b) the extent to which the employed persons in urban areas actively seek alternative or supplementary jobs, and the underlying reasons.

The problem of unemployment is most serious for workers who seek wage employment. As such, it would be appropriate to take special care to collect information in greater depth and at short intervals regarding their position. In the course of development, both their proportion (in the labour force) and their characteristics are likely to change. In any case, the impact of economic pressures is felt mainly and directly by this class. We, therefore, suggest that special studies should be made continuously of the conditions of the employee class, suitably defined, in various parts of the country and in different sectors of the economy, taking into account the frequency of cropping, the supply of irrigation facilities and the pattern of land use, the nature of the industry, etc. Simultaneously, information should also be collected on wage rates for different categories of labour in selected centres; such data could be useful indirect indicators of the employment situation

CENTRAL MUSEUMS REVIEW COMMITTEE, REPORT—1968

New Delhi, Ministry of Education and Social Welfare, 1972. 242p.

Chairman : Dr. M. S. Randhawa.
Members : Prof. S. Nurul Hasan; Prof. H.D. Sankalia, Dr. Moti Chandra; Dr. S. T. Satyamurti.
Member-Secretary : Shri B. B. Lal.

APPOINTMENT

During the discussion, held on the 30th August, 1968, in the Rajya Sabha, on the theft in the National Museum, New Delhi, the Minister of Education agreed to the setting up of a Committee to review the working of the Central Museums, viz. National Museum, New Delhi, Salarjung Museum, Hyderabad and Indian Museum, Calcutta. The last two Museums are autonomous institutions, and hence a request was made to their Chairman to agree to the review by the proposed Committee, which they accepted. Government of India vide its Resolution No. F.3-53/68-CAI-5, set up a Committee to Review the working of the Central Museums, namely the National Museum, New Delhi, the Salarjung Museum, Hyderabad and the Indian Museum, Calcutta, and the existing arrangements for the security of arts objects in the Museums as well as in protected Archaeological monuments and sites.

TERMS OF REFERENCE

The following are the terms of reference of the Committee :—

(i) to review the working of the three Central Museums and to make recommendations for their improved functioning and in particular to suggest measures for improving the security arrangements in the Museums, and

(ii) to review the existing security arrangements of the protected archaeological monuments and sites to recommend measures for strengthening them.

Although in the terms of reference there was no specific mention about the security arrangements at the Archaeological Museums, maintained by the Archaeological Survey of India, the Committee at its first meeting held on the 4th and 5th December 1968 felt that, as these Museums are usually associated with the protected monuments or sites, the security arrangements thereat should also be regarded as being within the terms of reference, and decided that two site Museums and a few monuments in the charge of the Archaeological Survey of India may also be visited.

CONTENTS

Introduction; National Museums, New Delhi—External Security Arrangements; Internal Security Arrangements; Review of Various Sections; Paintings, Prehistory and Protohistory, Stone Sculptures; Bronzes, Preservation; Photographic; Modelling, Education Service; Library; Manuscripts; Arms; Coins, Central/Asian Antiquities, Publications, Anthropology, Display, Archaeology; Admission fees, Administration;

Recommendations of the Estimates Committee (1968-69); Indian Museum, Calcutta — External Security Arrangements; Internal Security Arrangements, General Organisational set-up; Salarjung Museum, Hyderabad—External Security Arrangements, Internal Security Arrangements, General Arrangements in Respect of Museum Objects; Admission fees; Review of Various Galleries, Manuscripts and Library, Publications, Education—Service. Administration; Archaeological Monuments, Sites and Museums—Sites and Monuments, Archaeological Museum, Konark, Archaeological Museum, Nagarjunakonda; General Recommendations; Appendices from A to K.

RECOMMENDATIONS

The Committee noted with disquiet that in the National Museum, the posts of the Director, and Assistant Director have been lying vacant since long. It expressed surprise that a Deputy Secretary was looking after this work on a part-time basis. It was learnt that the Director General, Archaeological Survey of India, had been given the charge of the National Gallery of Modern Art, but the Ministry had not considered it worthwhile to give him the charge of the National Museum which is nearer the discipline of Archaeology. The Committee recommends, therefore, that, pending the appointment of a permanent Director, an ad hoc appointment of a temporary Director with suitable qualifications be made immediately, if necessary on a part-time basis. The Committee is of the view that the Ministry should set up, under an Act of Parliament, an autonomous Governing Body. Pending such a legislation, an Advisory Committee of experts should immediately be set up. This Committee should be allowed to function as an autonomous body.

The Committee feels that the Government should normally have the working of the Central Museums reviewed after every five years. Furthermore, the Committee is of the view that a Conference of the Directors of the Central Museums, presided over by the Minister, should be held annually.

For defining the scope of the Museum, the Committee feels that a joint meeting of all the three Governing Bodies and other specialists, presided over by the Minister, should be convened. Meanwhile, the Committee suggests that the National Museum should be a Museum for study of the Indian Culture and Civilization and its development. It should develop all sections including sculpture, paintings, textiles, porcelain, China-ware, jewellery, anthropology, etc. The sections should be carefully defined and demarcated, so that the Museum develops as the foremost institution in Asia for research purposes. The Museum should also prepare dioramas showing ways of living in different cultural periods so that glimpses of the cultural life of all parts of India are available in the National Museum.

The National Museum should also start developing sections dealing with cultures of other countries, particularly those of Asia.

Regarding future recruitment, the Committee is of the view that the Governing Bodies of the respective Museums should lay down qualifications for each post. In case of existing incumbents, however, the Committee recommends that they should be required to specialize in one branch or the other.

As regards the scope of the Indian Museum, Calcutta, the Committee feels that it should pay special attention to Natural History as also to the cultural history of Eastern India. At the same time, it should present Indian heritage (in broad outlines) in all its aspects for the benefit of the people living in that part of the country. Coordination should also be built up between the different sections, namely Geology, Anthropology, Zoology and Archaeology.

For the Salarjung Museum, the Committee suggested that it should specialize in handicrafts, medieval art and culture of peninsular India and paintings of Western Europe, especially of the Renaissance period. At the same time, it should present Indian heritage (in broad outline) in all its aspects for the people living in South India. The Committee feels that special attention should be given to the preservation of the existing collection. Facilities should also be developed for photostat and microfilming of manuscripts.

The Committee feels that the Ministry should consider the desirability of placing the three Central Museums at par with each other insofar as the strength of technical, administrative and other staff is concerned.

Regarding the staff strength, the Committee is of the view that the requirement should be determined not by the Staff Inspection Unit but by an expert body appointed by the Government. This Expert Body should also prescribe qualifications for the posts of the Director, etc. The Staff Inspection Unit may continue to assess the requirement of the administrative and ministerial staff.

For the constitution of the Governing Bodies/Boards of Trustees, the Committee proposes the following core composition : Two officers of the Government of India, one from the administrative Ministry and the other from the Finance Ministry; three experts on the subject in which the Museum is specialising, at least one of them being from the Universities; three Museologists, including technical experts in preservation; and the Director of the Museum as Member-Secretary. Besides the above, the Governing Body of the National Museum will have the Director General, Archaeological

Survey of India, and a representative of the University Grants Commission as ex-officio Members. Similarly, for the Governing Body of the Indian Museum, Calcutta, the Director General, Archaeological Survey of India, the Director General, Geological Survey of India, the Director, Anthropological Survey of India, the Director, Zoological Survey of India, the Director of the Botanical Survey of India and a representative of the State Government would be ex-officio Members. And, for the Governing Body of the Salarjung Museum, the Director General, Archaeological Survey of India, a representative of the State Government and two specialists, one with a sound knowledge of medieval Indian History and Persian and Arabic and the other in Western art and European History should be made members, the first two being ex-officio.

The Committee views with alarm the smuggling of art objects out of the country and feels that export of all antiquities should be done through the State. It also feels that a permanent body should be set up for advising on the sale of surplus antiquities, including sculptures, coins, paintings, etc. in the overseas market. The function of this body should also be to advise on exchange. Ragarding the composition of this Body, the Committee suggests the following pattern: one nominee of the Director General, Archaeological Survey of India; one nominee each of the other surveys, five museologists, including Directors of the Central Museums or their representatives; some distinguished public persons which would include historians of the different periods of Indian History; and one representative each of the State Trading Corporation and the University Grants Commission. This Body can function through sub-committees. While considering the exchange or sale of the objects, this Body should see that no rare or unique object is allowed to be exported. A duplicate may be exported in exchange for an equally important object from abroad. Triplicates and quadruplicates, etc. should be judiciously exchanged for important objects, or sold. The foreign exchange earned in this manner should be utilized for purposes of purchase of art objects from abroad. This Body should also serve the requirements of the State Governments and University Museums, and function as a coordinating house for the exchange of objects.

The Committee discussed the problem of drain of art objects from the country through the art dealers. The Committee is of the view that most of the sale is clandestinely done and as such the question of payment of sales tax or taxes of any kind does not arise. The dealers sell art objects to foreigners because they get ready cash. As against this, the art purchasing done by the Museums is dilatory and the prices offered in many cases are not attractive enough. As such, the Committee feels that the problem can be partially met if substantial grants are given to the Museums for the purchase of old paintings, bronzes, illustrated manuscripts and sculptures.

On the point of appointments, the Committee feels that when a person serving in one Central Museum is appointed to another, he should have the benefit of carrying with him leave, previous service, seniority, fringe and other benefits etc. This facility should also be given to those who are appointed to the Central Museums from the Government of India and State Governments, and vice versa.

The Committee is of the view that there is a great necessity for building up a separate Science Museum so that the advancement in science and technology is made known to a large public.

The Committee felt that it was necessary that the employees of the Museums, working in the various disciplines of archaeology and anthropology, are kept in touch with field-work. For this purpose, the Committee recommends that the staff should be encouraged to carry on research and write articles. The employees who publish their findings should be awarded advance increments to serve as an incentive, and entry to this effect should be made in their confidential reports. The Museums should be recognized as centres for research on art, archaeology and anthropology by the Universities. The Committee further recommends that the employees of the Museums while attending seminars and delivering lectures in Universities or research institutes should be counted as on duty.

It further recommends that the Museums should organize archaeological and anthropological exhibitions independently or in collaboration with the Archaeological Survey of India or a University.

Regarding the preparation of casts, the Committee felt that the restriction on the production of casts from sculpture was not necessary. It was of the view that there was no danger of an original object being substituted by a plaster cast, which could be so easily detected. The Committee noted that this restriction had affected the sale of casts. As such, it recommends that the Museum should be allowed to prepare casts in original size from all sculptures, especially because the educational institutions urgently needed them for teaching the history of Indian culture. At the college and university levels, neither photographs nor miniature replicas serve the purpose.

The Committee considered the following extract from the Fourth Report of the Estimate Committee (Fourth Lok Sabha) concerning the National Gallery of Modern Art, New Delhi:

"The Committee understand that at present there are no restrictions on the sale of art objects less than

100 years old to foreigners or on their export. Under such circumstances, works of art of eminent Indian artists can easily find their way to foreign galleries which can afford to pay handsome prices for the same. The Committee suggest that the law may be suitably amended so that foreign buyers may not export Indian art pieces in original without the permission of the Government."

The Committee feels that there is no need of amending the law, It will cause great hardship to Indian artists some of whom are able to sell their works outside, and thus they earn foreign exchange for their country apart from making their living. It has to be borne in mind that there is a very little purchasing of such paintings in the country and if this avenue, which is now available, is shut out, it will give a setback to Indian art.

While examining the existing pay scale of the Curators of the Archaeological Museums, the Committee felt that it was not commensurate with the duties and responsibilities attached to the post. The Committee recommends, therefore, that the Curators should have a pay-scale conforming to at least Class II gazetted cadre of the Central Services.

TRIPARTITE EXPERT COMMITTEE FOR CALCUTTA DOCKS REPORT—1968

Delhi, Manager of Publications, 1970. p.103

Chairman : Shri N.N. Chatterjee.

Members : Shri P.K. Ganguly; Shri A. Ahad Khan; Shri N. Dutt-Mazumdar; Shri M.R. Das; Shri A.S. Mehta; Shri D.S. Bose; Shri K.N. Banerjee; Shri R. Roy.

APPOINTMENT

At a meeting presided over by the Hon'ble Labour Minister at Calcutta on the July 4, 1968 it was decided that since the remaining items of the terms of reference of the One-Man Committee were largely of a technical nature involving intimate study of the Port and Dock Industry in Calcutta, it would be better if the matter were looked into by a tripartite body of experts. It was generally felt that such a body of experts with tripartite characteristics would be in the better position to assess the various problems of the Dock Industry at Calcutta and to suggest remedial steps. It was also decided at that meeting to enlarge the scope of the enquiry by adding to it certain other urgent problems of the port in general and Dock Labour Board in particular. The Hon'ble Labour Minister mentioned at this meeting that he would be very glad to set up such a Tripartite Committee and he hoped that both the Unions and the Employers would give him agreed names for the suggested Committee.

The Government of India in the Ministry of Labour, Employment and Rehabilitation thereafter appointed a Committee for Calcutta Docks Vide their letter No. 53/18/67-Fac. II dated October 11, 1968.

TERMS OF REFERENCE

(1) To study generally the output of Dock Workers in Calcutta Port compared with that of Dock workers in other ports and to investigate the reasons for the low output;

(2) To investigate why the existing incentive schemes have not given the expected results in terms of output an to suggest remedial measures;

(3) To examine whether further incentive schemes should be introduced and, if so, to suggest the principles on which these should be based;

(4) (i) To examine in the light of experience how far the categories covered by the registered and the unregistered schemes are appropriate and whether they require any modification;

(ii) To examine further whether any categories not covered by either of the two schemes should be brought within the scope of these schemes; and

(iii) To examine and recommend how flexibility in employment to ensure reasonable equality of opportunity for work amongst different categories can be achieved.

(5) To examine generally the working of the Dock Labour Board Schemes at Calcutta and to report how far the objectives of the schemes have been realised

and to suggest measures to remedy any shortcomings;

(6) To examine in particular the working of the unregistered scheme and to suggest what the future policy should be in the light of Vasist Committee's recommendations and experience;

(7) To examine why the employment of workers on a monthly basis has dwindled and to suggest how such employment on an increasingly larger scale may be ensured;

(8) To examine the causes of the high cost of chipping and painting work and the decline of such work in the Port of Calcutta and to suggest how this once flourishing and necessary industry can be restored and developed further;

(9) To examine the future manpower requirement on the basis of normal output and manning, scales prevailing at other ports and to indicate the extent of surplus, if any, taking into account the following factors:

(i) future traffic trends;

(ii) future trend in the methods of handling;

(iii) transfer of bulk cargo traffic to the new Haldia Dock which will be fully mechanised;

(10) If the examination mentioned in the preceding clause reveals a surplus, to suggest what practicable measures, including any voluntary retirement schemes, can be devised to deal with the problem of surplus.

CONTENTS

Introductory; General Background and Main Findings; The First Term of Reference; The Second Term of Reference; The Third Term of Reference; The Fourth Term of Reference; The Fifth Term of Reference; The Sixth Term of Reference; The Seventh Term of Reference; The Eighth Term of Reference; The Ninth Term of Reference; The Tenth and Last Term of Reference; Summary of Recommendations; Conclusion; Annexures from I to XXX.

RECOMMENDATIONS

Introductory

A summary of recommendation made by the Committee in this report is given hereunder. For findings on specific issues mentioned in the terms of reference, the relevant chapters should be referred to.

In case the Government accepts its recommendations the Committee would strongly urge that the recommendations should be regarded as one integrated whole, designed to cure the ills of the dock industry in general, and Dock Labour Schemes in particular, at Calcutta. The Committee would also like to state emphatically that no piecemeal solution of the complex problem is possible and such an attempt will only result in aggravating rather than relieving the situation.

In the Committee's view the basic requirement for the solution of the entire problem is the reduction of the workforce to a rational level by the implementation of an effective voluntary retirement scheme.

Since the Committee itself is tripartite and all the concerned interests are represented on it and in view of the urgency of the need to relieve the situation in the Calcutta Port, the Committee suggests that further detailed consultations with these interests in regard to the recommendations of the Committee, may not be necessary.

The First Term Of Reference

To study generally the output of Dock workers in Calcutta Port compared with that of dock workers in other ports and to investigate the reasons for the low output:

(1) For better control and supervision of work all the Deck Foremen and Hatch Foremen should be directly employed by the stevedores on a monthly basis. No pool for such supervisory categories should be maintained by the Board.

(2) The stevedores in co-operation with the Port Authorities should arrange to make the gangwise output known to the members of the gangs at the end of the shift or soon thereafter.

(3) Definite standards as to permanent supervisory staff, stevedoring gear and monthly gangs should be laid down by the Port Commissioners and any stevedore unable to fulfil these requirements himself should not be licensed. The amount of actual work performed by each stevedore during the last two years should be checked and the licenses of those who fail to achieve the minimum stipulated figures should not be renewed.

The Second And The Third Terms Of Reference

To investigate why the existing incentive schemes have not given the expected results in terms of output and to suggest remedial measures;

To examine whether further incentive schemes should be introduced and, if so, to suggest the principles on which these should be based :

The Central Wage Board for Port and Dock Workers has set up a Sub-Committee to evolve an incentive scheme for dock workers at Calcutta. Three members of this Committee are also members of this Sub-Committee. The scheme prepared by this Sub-Committee has been largely on the lines suggested by this Committee. The guidelines suggested for preparation of the incentive schemes for dock workers are as follows :—

(a) The piece-rate scheme for dock workers must

support and be complementary to the existing scheme for shore workers.

(b) The new scheme should take into account the operation of the existing unofficial incentive scheme in the Calcutta Docks.

(c) There must be a fall-back wage, and

(d) Gangwise output figures should be made available to the workers shortly after the shift.

We recommend that Government should implement this scheme expeditiously on its publication.

The Fourth Term Of Reference

(i) To examine in the light of experience how far the categories covered by the registered and the unregistered schemes are appropriate and whether they require any modification;

(ii) To examine further whether any categories not covered by either of the two schemes should be brought within the scope of these schemes; and

(iii) To examine and recommend how flexibility in employment to ensure reasonable equality of opportunity for work amongst different categories can be achieved :

The existing difinition of 'Dock Worker' is too wide. The term 'Dock Worker' should apply only to persons mainly or wholly engaged in loading and unloading operations on board ships. The question, as to whether any other category of workers not covered by either of the two current schemes should be included in the scheme, should be viewed in the light of the above definition of Dock Workers.

In making the following recommendations for new categories the Committee has applied the above basic standards :—

(a) For Baggers, Stitchers and Salt Workers—it is recommended that they should be brought under a suitable registration scheme after an incentive scheme with a fall-back wage has been introduced and as soon as the number of workers has been reduced suitable by the implementation of the voluntary retirement scheme proposed under the tenth term of reference. The majority of workers should thereafter be on the monthly register with the stevedores.

(b) For cleaning gang workers, markmen, carpenters (i.e., coopers), etc. it is recommended that since their work is of a general nature, these workers should be merged within one category of general purposes worker and put in a separate scheme of registration under the present Dock Labour Board and the existing Administrative Body of the Stevedoring Association. The scheme should have provisions that would permit the employers to draw upon the pool for work ashore or even outside the port;

(c) For watchmen and the gear handling workers we recommend that they be directly employed on a monthly basis by the present Watchmen Contractors, Shipping Companies/Steamer Agents and the Stevedores respectively, under a statutory scheme.

(d) Ore handling workers are essentially shore workers engaged in a trade that will be shifting to Haldia early in 1971. In view of this we cannot recommend that these workers be brought under any schemes of the Dock Labour Board. It is understood, however, that their earnings are of a highly fluctuating nature and we feel that steps should be taken to stabilise them.

(e) Bargemen are engaged more in the transport of cargo rather than in its handling and they therefore do not fit in with our definition of dock worker. They are also workers who have to be attached to or employed at particular barges and are not therefore underemployed. We recommend that the Government should make an early investigation into their conditions of services, emoluments etc. which are stated to be highly unsatisfactory.

(f) For the dock supervisory and clerical staff we make no separate recommendation because it is learnt that negotiations have reached an advanced stage between the Stevedores' Association and the Dock Sramik Association for evolving a scheme for these workers under the Act. It is also understood that the Ministry of Labour is seized of the matter. We urge however that the Stevedores' Association should settle details regarding their conditions of service and other matters by direct-negotiation with the unions as early as possible.

We have proposed that where possible, workers of comparable categories should be clubbed together to serve the demands of 2 or 3 types of commodities so that employment levels of a larger section of workers can be made uniform.

It is strongly felt that in the event of further registration or listing of any categories of workers in future efforts should be made to restrict the number of categories by having such flexibility of employment of workers, as far as possible. Any particular tendency of having several sub-categories within one category should be scrupulously avoided.

(g) For the workers handling scrap, pig iron, mill scale etc., it is recommended that the existing arrangements between the workers and the contractor should be improved under a bipartite agreement ensuring better opportunities for higher benefits and emoluments and improved conditions of service.

The Fifth Term Of Reference

To examine generally the working of the Dock Labour Board Schemes at Calcutta and to report how far the objectives of the schemes have been realised and to suggest measures to remedy any shortcomings :

(1) We suggest the following amendments to the 1956 scheme :

(a) The relevant clauses of the scheme should be amended in such a way that the system of payment by results is embodied in the scheme itself. A suitable provision under the application clause should be inserted binding both the employers and the workers to fulfil their respective obligations.

(b) The term 'stevedore' should be replaced by the word 'employer' wherever it appears in the scheme. Suitable words should be suffixed to this term to identify any particular type of employer, ie. Employer (Salt Stevedoring), Employer (General Stevedoring) etc.

(c) The age of superannuation for new entrants should be set out in the scheme and it should be fixed at 55 years. For these entrants, the maximum age of recruitment should not exceed 25 years.

(d) The present practice of allowing workers to continue work beyond 60 years on being certified fit by the medical officer should stop forthwith.

(e) In the matter of enforcement of discipline, the Board's Inspectors should be empowered under the scheme to take summary action like suspension on the spot against workers violating standing orders or rules. It is necessary to increase the present deployment of 2 or 3 Inspectors per shift to 4 per shift. The Inspectors' offices should be located in close proximity to the offices of the Asstt. Traffic Superintendents of the Labour Supervisors of the Calcutta Port Commissioners.

(f) The Administrative Body of Employers should be vested with sufficient executive authority to administer and implement effectively the scheme and all the decisions of the Board. The Chairman, Administrative Body, will be the appellate authority for any punishment which is meted out by the Labour Officer. For offences of a major nature, where the power of awarding higher punishment than what is vested in the Labour Officer is required, the Chairman, Administrative Body, should be the punishing authority and the Deputy Chairman of the Board, the appellate authority. It will be necessary then for the Employers' Association who forms the Administrative Body to appoint a whole time Chief Executive who should have sufficient delegated powers from the employers as has been done at Bombay. He should have powers to suspend summarily a worker who is found to be violating the obligations under the scheme.

The staffing pattern of supervisory-cum-executive staff suggested above is for the interim period pending the transfer of 75 per cent of the workers to the monthly employment of the stevedores.

(g) The Board should only be a policy-making body and should not interfere in the day to day administration of the scheme.

(h) The Administrative Body should also be vested with sufficient financial powers to carry out day to day administration including the administration of the Welfare Schemes. It should be the only authority for the control and maintenance of day to day administration.

(2) The present set-up of the offices of the Administrative Body and the Dock Labour Board should be streamlined through a proper organisation and Methods study of the establishments. For this purpose the services of a qualified body of efficiency experts may be obtained. A part of the Dock Labour Board's surplus staff can perhaps be absorbed by the stevedores since they have to take on a lot of workers on their monthly roll. A good many may be induced to take advantage of an attractive voluntary retirement scheme to be framed for them.

(3) The Traffic Manager, Calcutta Port Commissioners, should be nominated by the Government as one of its nominees on the Board.

(4) Labour booking should be made on individual basis instead of the present practice of booking on gang basis. To enable this to be achieved, it will be necessary to break up the present gangs and maintain a list of workers category-wise. It will also be necessary to abolish the present practice of one stage promotion within a gang whenever a vacancy arises in it.

(5) Recommendations on the industrial relations, communication system and grievance procedure :

(a) The sections of the Administrative Body's office which deal with personnel matters should be in-charge of officers who have had some training in personnel management which is now a well-developed science;

(b) An adequate Grievance Procedure should be formally laid down and communicated to the individual worker;

(c) The management should establish direct and easy lines of communication with the workers and disseminate all necessary information among them by issuing booklets in different languages and by other means;

(d) A bipartite joint consultative body should be set up supported by joint committees at lower levels. The joint consultative body should deal with all serious matters of dispute and other important issues and the joint committees should discuss problems of discipline, welfare, day-to-day working of the schemes and so on;

(e) A distinction should be made between an individual grievance and a collective grievance and there should be a separate procedure for each;

(f) An easy and friendly access to a number of

designated persons should be ensured so that workers' complaints are entertained promptly, their grievances removed, doubts clarified and they receive other kinds of help to present their case; and

(g) Dock work should be treated as an industry and therefore the Administrative Body should evolve a system of effective communication between labour and management.

The Sixth Term Of Reference

To examine in particular the working of the unregistered scheme and to suggest what the future policy should be in the light of Vasist Committee's recommendations and experience :

(1) The Listing Schemes having failed to achieve their objectives should not be preserved with. These schemes should be replaced by suitable Registere l Scheme.

(2) This should be done only after the number of the listed workers has been reduced to the workable level by implementing the voluntary retirement scheme.

(3) If the Listing Scheme has perforce to be retained at all, a very careful assessment of the number of men required in each category should be made before listing is done in future. There should however be a provision that under no circumstances should there be a gap of more than 2 years between the listing and the final registration of a worker. In case all the listed workers cannot be registered after this period, the number that can be safely registered should be taken on the Registered Pool or Monthly List. The Committee commends such a step only as a bad second best as this would create a fresh problem viz. the men still left in the Listing Scheme.

The Seventh Term Of Reference

To examine why the employment of workers on a monthly basis has dwindled and to suggest how such employment on an increasingly larger scale may be ensured :

(1) Restrictions imposed on employment of monthly workers under clause 29 of the scheme should be withdrawn.

(2) The emoluments of monthly workers should invariably be higher than those of the pool workers.

(3) Depending upon the annual employment of workers by individual employers, the employers should be required to maintain a certain number of workers, supervisory staff etc. on their monthly registers as a prerequisite for holding a stevedoring licence.

The employers whose own labour force and indents on the pool are below a specified norm for a period of 2 years should have their names removed from the Employers' Register. The employers would, of course, be free to form groups for the purpose of maintenance of specified work force on the monthly register.

Eventually with effective implementation of the voluntary retirement scheme 75 per cent of the workers should find their place on the monthly registers of the stevedores who are the operational employers.

(4) The monthly workers should also work in all shifts like pool workers.

(5) Deck Foremen and Hatch Foremen should be employed directly by the stevedores.

(6) In case all the workers of a particular category are taken into the monthly gangs of stevedores, individual employers or groups of employers should be allowed to borrow services of monthly workers from other employers who are in a position to spare them temporarily.

The Eighth Term Of Reference

To examine the causes of the high cost of chipping and painting work and the decline of such work in the Port of Calcutta and to suggest how this once flourishing and necessary industry can be restored and developed further :

The following suggestions are made which, in the opinion of the Committee, would help to restore normalcy in the chipping and painting trade in the Calcutta Docks :

(i) Serangs/Sardars should all be put on monthly register on emoluments that would be attractive for them and allocated to different employers. The Dock Labour Board should not maintain a pool for them.

(ii) The feasibility of further reduction in the number of categories should be fully explored and action taken to merge categories wherever possible.

(iii) Depending on average work availability individual employers should maintain a stipulated number of workers on the monthly register.

(iv) There is an excessive number of employers in this trade. The Committee feels that there should not be more than 20 employers in the field. The employers may be allowed to form groups or consortia for the purpose of booking within the groups.

(v) A new incentive scheme should be prepared and a fall-back wage should be provided at the one-unit level performance. Details of this scheme should be worked out separately.

(vi) A minimum administrative charge of Rs. 4,000 per annum should be imposed in place of the existing amount of Rs. ˆ0 per month.

(vii) The Board should be empowered in the scheme to remove the name of the employer who has had no work for two consecutive years.

(viii) The workers should be brought under a suitable registration scheme with a separate administrative body. This should be done immediately after the voluntary retirement scheme has reduced their numbers to a workable level. The age of retirement in this scheme should be fixed at 55 years.

(ix) Government should make suitable statutory provisions for the supply of safety belts and other necessary personal protective equipment to chipping and painting and other workers.

The Ninth Term Of Reference

To examine the future manpower requirement on the basis of normal output and manning scales prevailing at other ports and to indicate the extent of surplus, if any, taking into account the following factors :

(i) future traffic trends,

(ii) future trend in the methods of handling cargo,

(iii) transfer of bulk cargo traffic to the new Haldia Dock which will be fully mechanised :

Categorywise requirement of labour has been worked by the Dock Labour Board office on the basis of the average or normal output obtained at the ports of Bombay and Madras and taking into account the... manning scale of one gang per book as prevalent in these ports. The other premises on which these calculations have been made have also even set out in the report. Another set of calculations for assessment of required manpower have been made taking 1.5 units of performance (as per the incentive scheme being considered by the Wage Board) as the normal output per gang-shift. The Committee considers this to be a more practical approach to the problem. If flexibility in the placement of labour, as suggested in an earlier chapter, could be achieved then the requirement of manpower would be even less.

The Tenth Term Of Reference

If the examination mentioned in the preceding clause reveals a surplus, to suggest what practicable measures, including any voluntary retirement schemes, can be devised to deal with the problem of surplus.

The extent of surplus as indicated in item 9 of the term of reference is considerable. To deal with it, no measure of retrenchment is recommended. It is, however, suggested that workers should be induced to leave the industry through a sufficiently attractive scheme of voluntary retirement. Such schemes for both Registered and Listed workers and Temporarily Listed workers have been worked out by the Committee and set out in the main body of the report. The main features of the scheme are summarised as follows :

(a) For Registered Workers :

A worker retiring at the age of 40 will be compensated at the rate of one and a half month's pay for each remaining year of service. For every year above this age, the compensation shall be less by one months' pay. The scheme will not be applicable to workers who have completed the age of 60 Beyond 60 years there would be an ex gratia payment equal to 6 months' pay.

(b) For Listed Workers :

The scheme is in two parts—

(1) They will get the same compensation for loss of career as for the registered workers suggested above.

(2) In addition, they should have one months' pay for each year of completed service.

(c) For temporarily Listed Workers :

The Committee recommends an ad hoc payment of Rs. 2,000 to all these workers irrespective of their age of length of service.

The schemes shall remain operative for only 6 months from the date these are introduced.

The voluntary retirement schemes should be financed by the Board obtaining an interest free loan from Government. The loan will be recovered from the employers (and naturally from the a various users of the port) through the normal channel of the levy imposed on wages by the Dock Labour Board.

As soon as the Government accepts the recommendation of the Committee the Dock Board should give the widest possible publicity about the details and implications of the scheme and give guidance to the workers on the proper carriage and investment of the considerable sums of money to be received by them.

A whole time officer should be placed at the disposal of the Dock Labour Board to be in charge of the implementation of the voluntary retirement scheme. He should be supported by other officers and a Cell adequately staffed.

General

As the widest possible consultations have taken place in formulating these recommendations and as the situation development in the Calcutta Port is critical, the Committee feels that it may not be necessary for Government to hold detailed consultations with the concerned interests (which include labour, shipping interests, stevedores, etc.)

Conclusion

1. The Committee appreciates the fact that the major recommendations made by it have wide financial and administrative implications and a good many of them are not unanimous. In examining these recommendations the Government would normally invite the

comments of the Dock Labour Board, Port Commissioners, Associations of Employers and Workers and other interests. Since the Committee itself is tripartite and all the concerned interests are represented on it, the Committee ventures to suggest that wide consultations at this stage, when speedy implementation is called for, might only make matters difficult all round. Several members of the Committee are also members of the Dock Labour Board. The ex-Chairman of the Port Commissioners and the present Chairman have discussed all the issues with the members of the Committee in detail. All the relevant interests have been consulted, their written representations examined and their representatives interviewed.

2. The composition of the Dock Labour Board is such that it cannot possibly come to unanimous views on the very important issues raised in this report. Instances of representatives of particular interests appearing in different and contradictory roles in different forums are so common here that any hopes of an agreed view emerging in a reasonable period of time would be remote indeed. The Committee therefore feels that it may not be necessary to hold detailed consultations with the concerned interests (including labour, shipping interests, stevedores, etc). Keeping in view the urgency of the situation developing in the Calcutta Port.

3. The Committee would reiterate that in case the Government accept its recommendations, these should be regarded as parts of one integrated whole; and that in its view a piecemeal solution of this huge and complex problem should not be attempted as it would only make matters worse. The Committee wishes to emphasize the fact that the basic approach to the whole problem has to be the implementation of an attractive voluntary retirement scheme which will leave the Calcutta docks with a normal work force.

1969

RAILWAY LABOUR TRIBUNAL, REPORT—1969

New Delhi, Railway Board, 1972. 235p.

Chairman : Justice N.M. Miabhoy (one-man Commission).
Secretary : Shri Anand Prakash.

APPOINTMENT

The Railway Labour Tribunal was appointed by the Government of India, Ministry of Railways vide Resolution No. ERBI69CO1/8 dated January 28th 1969, referring the demands of National Federation of Indian Railwaymen, in regard to which agreement between Railway Board and National Federation of Indian Railwaymen could not be arrived at under the Permanent Negotiating Machinery which is outlined in Railway Board letter No. E51 FE1-22 dated December, 29th, 1951 addressed to General Managers of All India Railways.

TERMS OF REFERENCE

(i) Night duty Allowance should be calculated at 1½ times the normal rate of pay to all employees performing duty at night, irrespective of their Classification under the Hours of Employment Regulations.

(ii) In respect of workshop staff :

(a) All vacancies, which occurred since the introduction of the incentive scheme should be filled up;

(b) Proper proportion of skilled, semi-skilled and unskilled staff should be maintained and other measures taken to ensure adequate scope for promotion to the semi-skilled and unskilled staff;

(c) The posts of supervisory staff in the mechanical workshops should be redistributed amongst the various grades in conformity with their responsibilities and an adequate channel of promotion should be provided for them;

(iii) Casual labour on the Railways should be paid wages at the rate of 1/30th of the minimum of the time-scale plus appropriate Dearness Allowance applicable to the corresponding categories of staff in regular employment in the Railways.

(iv) The disparity between the hours of work and annual gazetted holidays at present prescribed for clerks of Railway Stations, sheds and depots on the one hand and those prescribed for clerks in administrative offices on the other should be removed by granting the former the privileges available to the latter. If this is not possible the former should be monetarily compensated for the extra hours and days of work done by them.

(v) The present Hours of Employment Regulations, which govern hours of work, periodic rest and overtime in respect of Railways staff, other than those employed in workshops, falling under the definition of 'Factories' in the Factories Act, should be completely reviewed.

(vi) All gangmen in Civil Engineering Department of the Railways should be granted an Arduous Duty Allowance of Rs. 3/9 per month.

(vii) The scale of pay of gangmates in the Civil Engineering Department of the Railways should be raised to skilled grade. Along with this, the scale of pay of keymen and head trolleymen of the Civil Engineering Department should be suitably enhanced.

(viii) The scale of pay of all running staff should be enhanced.

CONTENTS

Introduction; Terms of Reference No. 1—Night Duty Allowance; Terms of Reference No. 2—Workshop Staff; Terms of Reference No. 3—Payment of Wages to Casual Labour; Terms of Reference No. 4—Hours of Work and Gazetted Holidays for Clerical Staff; Terms of Reference No. 5—Hours of Employment Regulations; Terms of Reference No. 6 and 7—Scales of Pay etc., of Gangmen, Keymen, Gangmates and Head Trolleymen of Civil Engineering Department; Terms of Reference No. 8—Scales of Pay of Running Staff; Appendices from A to F.

RECOMMENDATIONS

Night Duty Allowance

The demand of the Federation that night duty allowance should be granted to all railway employees irrespective of their classification or irrespective of the pay limit which is at present imposed, is granted.

The demand for calculation of night duty allowance at the rate of one and a half times the normal pay is rejected.

The demand that the "normal rate of pay" should include not only dearness allowance but also compensatory allowance (other than house rent) is also granted.

The demand of the Federation that dearness allowance as revised or reviewed from time to time should be included for calculation of the ordinary rate of pay is granted too.

Workshop Staff

Workshop administrations should prepare incentive cadres in the light of the principles enunciated by the Deputy Director and in the light of the provisions contained in paragraph 202 of the Mechanical Code. The incentive cadres must be fixed with due regard to the minimum requirements of each workshops and provision must be made for temporary additional posts which may be filled up at the discretion of the Works Manager. Attempts must be made, as far as possible, to fill up vacancies in the permanent incentive cadre, unless, in the opinion of the Works Manager, the filling up of such vacancies is not immediately justified, but in such a contingency, the Works Manager must be directed to give up the excessive posts if the same are not required to be filled up within a certain period of time, say about six months, if any change is to be made in the permanent cadre strength, it must be made on the principles enunciated by the Deputy Director as regards the non-filling up of vacancies. In making such variations, emphasis should be more on local conditions prevailing in a workshop rather than its effect upon productivity targets. In filling up vacancies in future, railway administration should not make a fettish of the manpower ratio. They must bear in mind that the ratio is an all-India generalization, not necessarily intended to be applied to each and every workshop irrespective of local conditions. In working the ratio, the administration must have regard to the local conditions prevailing and the promotional prospects of workmen. On the whole it is not proper to arrest or retard a promotion due to a worker solely on the ground that all-India manpower ratio will be affected. Having regard to the fact that the manpower ratio has been considerably reduced on an all-India basis, the administrations can, with justification, permit suitable variations in regard to individual workshops.

In determining the cadre strength of various categories of staff in a particular railway workshop, if the railway administration comes to the conclusion that the average team of three workers in a shop requires more than or less than one semi-skilled or unskilled worker, it should not be fettered in fixing a proper ratio in respect of these categories by reason of the fact that it will not conform to the all-India ratio of 3 : 1 : 1.

The principles which justify off loading or private purchase of items should be reiterated by the Board and the workshop administrations should be impressed that off loading or private purchase should not take place in violation of those principles.

The workshop administrations must be impressed about the desirability of holding trade tests at regular intervals so that vacancies may not remain unfilled on the ground that qualified workmen are not available for promotion.

Directions should be reiterated to the workshop administrations that BTMs should be regarded as trainee workers, that they should be promoted if found fit as skilled workers after their period of training is over, that they should not form part of incentive cadres or leave reserve cadres and that they should not be used as skilled workers without paying them as such.

If an unskilled or semi-skilled worker/BTM has stagnated in the scale for more than twelve years even though he has otherwise qualified himself for promotion, then, he should be granted one increment at interval of every three years thereafter.

The order in regard to the pooling of the unskilled workers should be amended so as to remove the proviso that the ratio of 3 : 1 : 1 should be maintained.

Recruitment of Trade Apprentices does not require to be banned permanently.

In those cases where Mistries supervise the work of highly skilled grade-I workman or workmen, they should be in the higher grade of Rs. 175—240 instead of Rs. 150—240.

Posts of Mistries holding independent charge of a section should be upgraded to those of chargemen C.

The demand of the Federation that the quota at present allotted to skilled workers for promotion as chargemen C and for recruitment as Apprentices-Mechanic should be increased is rejected.

In some workshops, percentage distribution of grades of Chargemen, as agreed to by the Board and the Federation, is not being maintained. Immediate steps should be taken to implement the percentage distribution in those workshops so as to conform to the agreed percentage.

The demand of the Federation that the staff of the PCO should be excluded in determining the percentage distribution of chargemen on the agreed basis in all workshops is rejected.

The demand of the Federation for an increase in percentage distribution of the various grades of chargemen is rejected.

The demand of the Federation that the percentage distribution of the two grades of Foremen A and B should be in the ratio of 40 : 60 is rejected.

The demand of the Federation in regard to grant of a special pay of Rs. 150 per month to Foremen A is granted.

As regards the demand of the Federation to grant a special pay of Rs. 100 per month to Foremen B, it is decided that, instead of such special pay, Foremen B should be given the higher grade of Rs. 450—575.

Percentage distribution of the grades of chargemen A, B and C in the Electrical and S & T Workshops should be in conformity with that agreed to by the Board and the Federation in the case of Mechanical Workshops.

Decisions given in this Report in regard to the upgradation of the posts of Mistries exercising supervision over highly skilled grade-I workmen to Rs. 170—250 scale and of Mistries in independent charge of sections to those of chargemen C grade should also be applied to 'lectrical Workshops and Signal and Telecommunication Workshops.

Decisions given in regard to grant of special pay of Rs. 150 per month to Foremen A and Upgradation of Foremen B to Rs. 450—575 scale in Mechanical Workshops should also be made applicable to Foremen working in Electrical and Signal Telecommunication Workshops.

Workmen and Sub-Supervisors in Power Houses are not entitled to the benefits of decisions made herein.

The demand of the Federation that the avenues of promotion for posts of Assistant Mechanical Engineer should be further widened is rejected.

Payment Of Wages To Casual Labour

The Board should issue immediate directives in regard to the grievance referred to in relation of concepts of Casual Labour so that the rules regarding the definition of 'Casual Labour' are not contravened and also so that they may be implemented in their true spirit. The Board should also devise a proper machinery to see that breaches of the above rules that are committed are set right immediately and it must also see that employment cards are issued to casual labourers so that evidence regarding the continuity of service is not destroyed.

The broad contention of the Federation that casual labour should be treated in the matter of payment of wages, on a par with regular labour is not, subject to the decisions mentioned hereinafter, accepted.

(i) Definite instructions should be issued to the effect that whatever figures of local rates are obtained from the localities concerned must be taken as the figures at which casual labourer is to be paid in respect of the locality from which the figures have come and that the practice obtaining in one of the divisions of extracting an artificial rate by tabulating the various rates should not be followed.

(ii) Although it is open to each railway administration to fix the date from which the ascertained rates should become effective, the time-lag between the date in respect of which the local rate is collected and it is made effective should never be more than three months. If, for some reasons, the time-lag is longer than 3 months, then, casual labour should be paid, for the period previous to such 3 months, at the new local rate if the same happens to be higher than the previous local rate.

(iii) If, for some reasons, the local rates are not or cannot be ascertained for a period of more than one and a half years, then casual labourer should be paid at the rate of 1/30th of the minimum of the time scale plus dearness allowance payable to the corresponding railway worker.

(iv) The period of maximum service for earning temporary status should be fixed at four months instead of six.

(v) If casual labourer is engaged on works which automatically expire on 31st March, the continuity of his service shall not be regarded as broken if sanction for that work is given subsequently and the same casual labourer is employed to finish the work, provided further that no casual labourer shall be prevented from working on such job so as to deprive him of earning the status of a temporary railway worker.

The present provision made in the Manual for payment of wages to scheduled labour should be scrapped and, instead, a new provision should be introduced which would bring scheduled labour on a par with non-scheduled labour in the matter of payment of wages, i.e., it must be provided that scheduled labour also will be paid either at the local rate, subject to the further provision that if either of these rates happens to be less than the minimum, then, scheduled labour will be paid the mimimum wage fixed by the appropriate authority.

The provision contained in the Manual in regard to project casual labour should be amended as to provide that such casual labour will also be paid the scale rate if the same happens to be higher than the local rate, if the project casual labour is employed for a continuous period of six months in the same type of work. It may be clarified that, as a result of this decision, a project casual labourer will not acquire the status of temporary servant, nor will he have the benefit of any future increments.

If casual labour is remunerated on the basis of the minimum wage fixed by Central Government, then, if there is any further rise in the index of the cost of living after such minimum wage was so fixed, that further rise must be neutralised by granting casual labour neutralization on the same conditions and scale as recommended by the Dearness Allowance Commission.

The overall effect of the above decisions is as follows :

All casual labour of whatever category will be paid at the local rate or, if such local rate is not available, at the scale rate, subject to the provision that if either of these two rates happens to be less than the minimum prescribed by the M. W. Act either for scheduled employees or employees comparable to such scheduled employees, it will be paid at the minimum wage fixed by the M.W. Act, with a further proviso that if there is any rise in the index of the cost of living after such minimum rate was fixed by Government, then, such further rise will be neutralised on the same conditions and scale as recommended by the Dearness Allowance Commission. However, in the case of casual labour employed under emergent circumstances or in the case of specialised casual labour, power will vest in the relevant authority to pay wages at a higher rate provided the conditions which are at present prescribed for such payment are fulfilled. Non-Project casual labour will acquire the status of temporary service if it is employed continuously for a period of four months in the same type of work. However, project labour under similar circumstances if employed for a period of six months will be paid only the scale rate if it happens to be higher than the local rate, but such labour will not earn future increments in the scale or be entitled to any fringe benefits. If the scale rate happens to be less than the minimum wage prescribed by the appropriate authority, such project labour will be paid minimum wage rate with the benefit of neutralization as mentioned hereinbefore in case there is any further rise in the index of the cost of living after the minimum wage was fixed by the authority concerned.

Hours Of Work And Gazetted Holidays For Clerical Staff

The demands of the Federation for removal of disparities and for grant of compensatory relief are rejected.

Having regard to the order of the Board that the field staff may, if necessary, be required to work the same hours as the other staff in the concerned establishments when duties of clerks are such that their presence throughout is necessary for efficient working of the entire staff, it becomes the duty of the officers controlling the field offices to examine the question as to whether the presence of the clerical staff of their offices is or is not necessary for efficient working of their other staff. Therefore, the Federation can have a grievance only if the above order of the Board has not been properly and correctly implemented by any of the officers. If there are any cases which violate the above order, it is upto the Federation to bring the breaches to the notice of the concerned authorities and, I am sure that such individual cases will be examined and suitably redressed by the concerned authorities consistent with the main principle that ordinarily, both the field and the non-field staffs, should have the same hours of work.

The disparities at present in existence in regard to

hours of work and holiday entitlements, if they are inevitable, must be shared equitably by the staff as a whole and the burden thereof should not fall upon a section of the staff only and means may be devised by which the concerned clerks are rotated between the field and the non-field offices in such a way that none of them has to put in inordinately long periods of service in the field offices or none of them has an entire period or unnecessarily long period of service in the non-field offices. In this connection the practice deposed to by witness Madhav as prevailing in the Integral Coach Factory Offices commends itself. I am not quite sure as to whether that practice can be followed effectively in regard to all the non-field offices, but, in my opinion, a scheme can be devised in such a way that the field staff and the non-field staff are interchanged at the initial stages of their service and/or at the initial stages of their promotion to a higher grade.

In regard to those establishments where clerical staff is required to put in more hours of work per week than 48, and if this is being done in any establishment on the ground of tradition only, then, in my opinion the tradition may well be disregarded. It can be preserved if it is necessary on the basis of the principle that the working hours of the field staff must synchronise with those of the non-field staff.

In the matter of holidays, specially in those offices where there is sufficient number of clerks who can be rotated on different holidays, some relief can be granted prima facie the number of holidays granted in the field offices appears to be inadequate. In this connection, the recommendation of the National Labour Commission is noteworthy. The Commission recommends, besides three National holidays, five festival holidays for all Government servants including the industrial staff. If and when this recommendation comes to be accepted, there is no doubt that the field staff will also get the benefit thereof. But even if this recommendation does not come to be accepted, in my opinion, if no violence is done to the main principle that efficiency of the other staff should not suffer, the question may be examined in regard to individual offices as to whether those five festival holidays can or cannot be given wholly or by rotation.

The Federation is at liberty to put forward a scheme before the Board or the other concerned authorities for arranging the rostered hours of the field staff in such a way that whilst bringing all the members of that staff on par with the non-field staff, efficiency of the other staff does not suffer. I feel confident that if and when such a scheme is submitted by the Federation, the same will be examined carefully and the Board or the concerned authorities will make a sincere attempt to put the same into practice without violating the principle and the rider accepted by me.

Hours Of Employment Regulations

Hours of employment shall be those during which an employee is at the disposal of his employer at the employer's instance i.e. duty of an employee commences when he places himself at the disposal of his employer at the latter's instance, and such duty continues until he is full at liberty to leave the place of duty.

Existing classification of workers into Continuous, Intensive and Essentially Intermittent should be maintained. No decision is recorded regarding Excluded Classification, except in cases of Gatemen, Saloon Attendants, Care-takers of Rest Houses etc., and Bungalow Peons residing at or close to the place of work, as no demand has been made in regard to such classification.

Demand of the Federation that new classification or a series of new classifications of employments should be introduced in between Continuous and Intensive classification, is rejected.

Except as otherwise provided herein :—

(1) Daily and Weekly hours of employment of Continuous and Essentially intermittent workers should be fixed at 8 and 48 respectively.

(2) Daily and Weekly hours of Essentially Intermittent workers may be increased by such number of hours as may be necessary, but not exceeding those mentioned in sub-para (8) herein below.

(3) Weekly hours of employment of Intensive workers will continue to be maintained at 42.

(4) (a) Preparatory and/or complementary work, which expression also includes taking over and handing over charges, can be demanded from workers in regard to work which must necessarily be carried on outside the limits laid down for the general working of an establishment, branch or shift.

(b) The concerned administrations will determine, in the light of the propositions hereinafter mentioned, the time required for preparatory and/or complementary work in regard to each classification of worker or workers and, if such time requires to be included in rosters, it shall be so done.

(i) For Continuous, Intensive and Essentially Intermittent workers who are called upon to do preparatory and/or complementary work for a period of less than 15 minutes per day and may not be mentioned in the rosters of such workers.

(ii) Preparatory and/or complementary work between 15 and less than 45 minutes per day in the case of continuous worker will be treated as half-an-hour's work, will be reflected in rosters and considered as period of duty.

(iii) Continuous workers who are required to do

preparatory and/or complementary work for a period between 45 minutes and one hour per day will be considered to have rendered duty for one hour. The same will be reflected in their rosters and will be considered to be period of duty. However, continuous workers cannot be required to do preparatory and/or complementary work so as to violate the statutory limits.

(iv) As regards intensive workers, preparatory and/or complementary work for a period between 15 and 30 minutes will be considered to be duty for 30 minutes and rosters will be prepared accordingly. However, no Intensive worker shall be required to do so such work as to violate the statutory limits.

(v) In the case of Essentially intermittent workers, preparatory and/or complementary work for a period between 15 and 30 minutes will be considered to be duty for 30 minutes and rosters will be prepared accordingly. However, the maximum additional hours for such type of work should be fixed at 3 hours per week in the case of Class 'C' Gatemen, Saloon Attendants and Care-takers of Rest Houses and Reservoirs, etc., and EI workers at roadside stations who are given residential quarters within a radius of 5 kilometres from their places of duty. As regards the rest of EI workers, the maximum additional hours should be fixed at 4½ hours per week.

(vi) Existing practice in regard to running staff of treating the whole period from signing-on to signing-off as period of duty will continue.

In addition to the hours of works as fixed above, all railway workers governed by HER can be called upon to render duty beyond statutory limits applicable to them in the circumstances mentioned in and by an order of temporary exemption made under section 71-C of the Railways Act by a competent authority.

(a) Principle of averaging is warranted in railway working in regard to :

(i) running staff, (ii) operating staff, (iii) shift workers and (iv) those workers whose work is bound up with the work of workers comprised in the above three categories. The concerned administrations will examine cases falling within category (iv) in the light of the principles enunciated in Article 5 of Washington Convention, and determine within 2 years from the date of this Report whether averaging should or should not be permitted in their cases.

(b) Averaging period for intensive and continuous workers should be fixed at two weeks and for EI workers at one week.

(c) Continuous and intensive workers will earn overtime if they put in more than 96 and 84 hours respectively in two weeks plus, in those cases where they are required to do preparatory and/or complementary work, such additional number of hours as they are required to work on that account during that period.

(d) EI workers will earn overtime if they are required to put in more hours in a week than determined for them plus, in the case of those EI workers who are required to do preparatory and/or complementary work, such further number of additional hours during the week in which they may be required to do preparatory and/or complementary work.

(e) In the case of those railway workers whose cases are decided by administrations as not falling within the purview of Article 5 of Washington Convention, overtime will be that which the concerned worker renders everyday beyond daily limit.

(f) Daily rate of overtime should be calculated on the basis of the total number of rostered hours during averaging period fixed for the concerned employee.

(g) Rate of overtime shall be one and a half times the ordinary rate for overtime work beyond rostered hours but within statutory limits, but, it shall be twice the ordinary rate for overtime worked beyond statutory limits.

Subject to the following two exceptions, all time spent for travelling spare on duty should be considered as period of duty. The exceptions are (1) when a worker is provided with facility of crew rest van, and (2) when a worker does not travel on any day beyond a radius of 8 kilometres from his place of duty. It is clarified that if he so does on any day, then, the whole time spent for travelling spare on duty including distance within radius of 8 kilometres will also be considered as period of duty.

(a) Demand of the Federation that Essentially Intermittent Classification should be abolished is rejected.

(b) Class C Gatemen, Saloon Attendants and Caretakers of Rest Houses and Reservoirs etc. and Bungalow Peons, who reside at or within a short distance from the residence of their officers, should be removed from Excluded classification and should be classified as Essentially Intermittent workers.

(c) Subject to ceilings mentioned hereinafter, an Essentially Intermittent worker can be called upon to render duty for additional hours which may be fixed. The ceilings are as follows :

(i) Class C Gatemen, Saloon Attendants, Caretakers of Rest Houses and Reservoirs etc. may be required to do duty for additional four hours per day and 24 hours per week. However, their averaging period will be two weeks so that the total number of hours which the above class of workers can be called upon to work may be 144 per two weeks on an average.

(ii) Essentially Intermittent workers at roadside stations who are provided with residential quarters within a radius of 5 kilometres from their places of duty may be called upon to do duty for four hours per day and 24 hours per week. Their averaging period will be one week, so that the above class of workers can be called upon to do work for 72 hours a week on an average.

(iii) The rest of the Essentially Intermittent workers can be called upon to do duty for an additional number of 2 hours per day and 12 hours per week. Their averaging period will be one week, so that such workers can be called upon to work for 60 hours on an average in a week.

(d) Decisions Nos. (B) to (C)(iii) should be implemented within two years from the date of this report.

The concerned administrations should take immediate steps for job-analysing the work and finalising the classification of Wireless Operators (including Operators who do partially controlling work but excluding monitoring Operators and excluding Operators who do exclusively controlling work) who are at present classified as continuous, that is, those operators who are engaged in the work of transmitting, receiving and watching messages, within one year from the date of this Report and that, if administrations fail to do so, then, at the expiration of the period of one year, such operators whose cases have not been so finalised should be presumed to be Intensive workers and their hours of work fixed accordingly. In the latter contingency, it will be open to the administrations thereafter to begin or complete the analysis of such jobs at any time in future and, if any such analysis justifies the finding that the work of any particular operator is continuous, job of such a worker may be re-classified as continuous.

The concerned railway administrations should undertake and finish the job analyses in regard to employments of all Continuous Section Controllers and the prescribed authority should pass orders in accordance with law on the basis of such job analyses within two years from the date of this report. If, within the latter period, a decision on the classification of any Continuous Section Controller is not reached by the concerned prescribed authority, then, with effect from the expiration of the above period of two years, the Concerned Section Controller will be deemed to be an Intensive worker and classified accordingly. In the latter case, it will be open to the prescribed authority to reach a final decision on the subject at a later stage on merits in accordance with HER and if and when such decision is reached, effect may be given to the same.

Demand of the Federation for Automatic Intensive Classification of (1) Yard Masters, (2) Assistant Yard Masters, (3) Yard Supervisors, and (4) Shunting team is rejected.

Demand of the Federation for automatic Intensive classification of Telegraph Signallers on heavy circuits is rejected.

Demand of the Federation that Station Staff at a crossing station where commercial work is nil or negligible should be classified as Intensive straight-off is rejected.

Demand of the Federation that Station Staff at stations where 16 trains run each way on a single line in a cycle of 24 hours should be classified as Intensive straight-off is rejected.

Demand of Federation that a Cabinman at a crossing station and at stations where 16 trains run each way on a single line in a cycle of 24 hours should be automatically classified as Intensive is rejected.

Demand of Federation for automatic Intensive classification of Platform porters at crossing station and at stations where 16 trains run each way on a single line in a cycle of 24 hours is rejected.

Demand of the Federation for automatic Intensive Classification of Station Staff at junctions is rejected.

Demand of the Federation for automatic Intensive Classification of Operational Staff General ASM, at junctions where there are marshalling and/or goodsyard is rejected.

Demand of the Federation for automatic Intensive Classification of yard staff at junctions and at stations where more than 16 trains pass each way on a single line in a cycle of 24 hours is rejected.

Running duty at a stretch of running staff should not ordinarily exceed 10 hours, but such duty may extend to a maximum of 12 hours provided concerned authority gives at least 2 hours' notice before the expiration of 10 hours to the concerned staff that it will be required to perform running duty for 2 hours more; provided further that total maximum hours of duty from signing-on to signing-off does not exceed 14 hours; provided further that total maximum hours should progressively be reduced by half-an-hour every 2 years from the date of this report till the period of 12 hours is reached, i.e., at the end of 8 years from the date of this Report, total maximum hours of duty at a stretch from signing-on to signing-off shall not exceed 12 hours.

When an administration wants any railway worker to come earlier and/or remain later by a total period of 15 minutes or more, the railway worker is not bound to do so unless and until the period or periods for which he is required to come earlier and/or remain later are mentioned specifically in his roster.

As regards Wireless Operators, the present practice of reporting for duty before rostered hours by such period as may be less than 15 minutes will continue to be followed. However, if the concerned administration requires any Wireless Operator to report for duty for a period or periods earlier than his rostered hours by a period of 15 minutes or more, it may prepare his rosters accordingly.

The controversy regarding time to be taken by Deputy Chief Controllers for taking over and/or handing over should be dealt with and solved in the same manner in which the controversy in regard to Section Controllers is decided.

As regards Section Controllers, whilst the present practice as regards the time for taking over and/or handing over on different boards may be continued, the concerned administration should make up its mind on the subject within 6 months from the date of this Report and issue specific instructions as regards the time for taking over and/or handing over and get specific rosters prepared for all Section Controllers or for such of them as may be required to perform preparatory and/or complementary duties for 15 minutes or more and, in that contingency, fix the extent of time for such early arrival and/or late departure. If any Section Controller is required to come earlier and/or depart later by 15 minutes or more, overlapping rosters shall be prepared for him.

As regards SMs and ASMs including Platform and Cabin ASMs, the concerned railway administrations shall determine each particular case within 6 months from the date of this Report whether the required period of time for taking and/or handing over is less than 15 minutes or otherwise and if it is 15 minutes or more, definite rosters will be prepared for all such SMs and ASMs. Unless such definite rosters are prepared SMs and ASMs will be deemed to be required to come earlier and/or depart later by a total period of less than 15 minutes only before and/or after rostered hours.

As regards Booking and Parcel Clerks, if the concerned administration requires such staff to come and/or depart earlier and/or later than rostered hours, specific rosters will be prepared for them, except when they are required to come and/or depart for such purpose by less than 15 minutes.

As regards yard staff i.e. Yard Master and Assistant Yard Master and Shunting Jamadar, there is reliable evidence that they require 15 or more minutes for taking over and/or handing over charges.

A Cabinman does not require 15 minutes or more for handing over and/or taking over charge.

Existing provisions relating to periodic rest do not require any change except that Class IV Excluded workers should be put on a par with EIs in the matter of periodic rest.

Demand of the Federation that the ratio of rest givers and railway workers should be 1 : 6 is rejected.

Scales Of Pay Etc. Of Gangmen, Keymen, Gangmates And Head Trolleymen Of Civil Engineering Department

The claim of gangmen for payment of an arduous duty allowance of Rs. 3 per month is rejected.

A gangmate should be given the scale of Rs. 105-3-135 instead of the existing scale of Rs. 80-1-85-2-95 EB-3-110.

A Keyman should be given the scale of Rs. 75-1-85-EB-2-95-EB-3-110 instead of existing scale of Rs. 75-1-85-EB-2-95.

The claim of head trolleyman for granting the scale of Rs. 75-1-85-EB-2-95 is rejected.

Scales of Pay of Running Staff

All inter-divisional and long distance passenger trains should be upgraded to Grade A, provided the total run is not less than 250 kilometres.

Subject to above, the claim made by the Federation for revising pay-scales of various categories of running staff is rejected.

BANKING COMMISSION, REPORT—1969

Delhi, Manager of Publications, 1972. 760p.

Chairman : Shri R.G. Saraiya
Members : Shri N. Ramanand Rao; Shri Bhabatosh Datta
Member-Secretary : Shri V.G. Pendharkar

APPOINTMENT

In pursuance of the policy statement on social control over Commercial Banks made in the Parliament on the December 14th, 1967, it has been decided to set up a Banking Commission. The Banking Commission was appointed by the Department of Economic Affairs, Ministry of Finance, Government of India vide Resolution No. F. 4 (70)-BC/68 dated the February 3rd, 1969.

TERMS OF REFERENCE

(i) To enquire into the existing structure of the Commercial Banking system having particular regard to size, dispersion and area of operation and to make recommendations for improving the structure;

(ii) To make recommendations for extending the geographical and functional coverage of the commercial banking system;

(iii) To make recommendations for improving and modernising the operating methods and procedures and the management policies of Commercial banks;

(iv) To examine the cost and capital structure and to review the adequacy of available surplus and reserves, having regard to the developmental needs of the banking system and to make recommendations in the light of the findings;

(v) To review the existing arrangements relating to recruitment, training and other relevant matter connected with manpower planning of bank personnel and to make recommendations for building up requisite professional cadre of bank personnel at all levels of management;

(vi) To review the working of co-operative banks and to make recommendations with a view to ensuing a co-ordinated development of Commercial and Co-operative banks, having regard, in particular, to (ii) above;

(vii) To review the role of various classes of non-banking financial intermediaries, to enquire into their structure and methods of operation and recommend measures for their orderly growth;

(viii) To review the working of the various classes of indigenous banking agencies such as multanis and shroffs, evaluate their utility in the money market complex and to make recommendations in the light of the findings;

(ix) To review the existing legislative enactments relating to commercial and co-operative banking;

(x) To make recommendations on any other related subject-matter as the Commission may consider germane to the subject of enquiry or on any related matter which may be specifically referred to the Commission by the Government.

CONTENTS

Introduction; Banking in India—A Review; Existing Structure of the Banking System; A Review of Services Provided by Commercial Banks in India; Improving the Geographical Coverage of Commercial Banks; Functional Coverage I: Deposit Mobilisation by Banks; Functional Coverage II: Advances with Particular Reference to Financing of Priority Sectors; Small Artisans and Small Scale Industries; Co-ordination Between Commercial and Co-operative Banks I: Geographical Coverage at the Primary Level; Coordination Between Commercial and Cooperative Banks II: Loan Policies and Procedures; Co-ordination Between Commercial and Co-operative Banks III: Resources and Certain Organizational Aspects of Cooperative Banks; Bank Operating Methods and Procedures; Costs and Capital Structure of Banks; Information System for Banks; Management Development in Banks; Restructuring of the Banking System; The Need for Specialised Financial Institutions; Non-Banking Financial Intermediaries; Indigenous Bankers; Banking Regulation; National Banks; Other Laws Affecting Banking; Banking Research and Education; Concluding Observations; Summary of Recommendations; Appendix from I to XI; Index.

RECOMMENDATIONS

Banks should not be allocated 'Lead' districts which are away from their respective principal areas of operation.

Techno-economic surveys of the districts should be preferably conducted by the planning authorities because only they can establish the targets taking into account the availability of the financial as well as physical resources.

District authorities i.e., the District Collector (or his equivalent) and his staff should be in charge of district planning of which credit planning will be an integral part. Banks acting in consortium can help in the preparation of credit plan for the particular district.

Increasing deposits with the banks will held to bring to the organised market savings that are idle or are wasted, or are used in creating assets which are low in the scale of the plan priorities. As new bank deposits constitute a rather low proportion of current savings and of current income, even a small positive change in the two ratios should have a large effect on the total amount of deposits. Large and quick changes that will be required to achieve this objective will have to be induced by positive action by the banks for the mobilisation of deposits.

Various investigations showed that an addition of the existence of the institutional structure, proximity of the institution to the depositor and the availability of varying schemes tailored to suit the liquidity and other considerations which weigh with the depositors, the return on deposits appeared to be of some significance. Hence, the effects of administered interest rates on bank deposits in a highly competitive market for deposits need to be studied carefully and a well thoughtout comprehensive approach to the question of the structure of interest rates on deposits worked out. Such a study can examine the proposal to have a dual structure of interest rates from the point of view of mobilising deposits in the rural areas.

It is necessary for banks to take into account the motivation for savings to attain a larger measure of success in deposit mobilisation from small persons.

While the efforts which the banks have been making to mobilise deposits have to continue, it is important for them to see that the standard of services for the existing depositors is also maintained at a high level. The availability of ancillary banking services also is an important factor influencing the depositor's choice particularly in the smaller towns.

While during the promotional period after introducing a new deposit scheme, the cost factor could be ignored to some extent, once the scheme proves successful in attracting deposits on a sizeable scale, it would be useful for banks to make a proper cost-benefit analysis of these schemes from time to time.

As the saving-income ratio is smaller in the rural sector than in the urban sector, a concerted effort has been and is necessary to raise the rate of savings in general and the rate of savings in the form of bank deposits in particular, especially in this sector. Deposit mobilisation in rural areas will continue to be the responsibility mainly of cooperative banks. However, several steps as recommended in Chapter 8 and 10 will have to be taken to overcome their present difficulties in order to enable them to offer a wider range of services to their customers and introduce new deposit schemes.

The important policy objective of promotion and development of small units has to be realised by measures that effect not only the credit aspect but also other aspects.

Eligibility for participation in the credit guarantee scheme for small loans should be extended so as to include non-scheduled banks as well as co-operative credit institutions extending credit to industrial co-operative credit societies and small borrowers.

Commercial banks need not insist on maintenance of proper books of account for gauging the credit-worthiness of small artisans. Often, informal enquiries about the financial position and personal integrity and character of artisans in the localities where they live would prove useful in assessing the creditworthiness of artisans.

Commercial banks should evolve schemes that combine in them both savings and borrowing operations of artisans and other small borrowers in order to promote and develop banking habit among them.

Interest rates charged to small artisans should be reasonable and the banks should attempt to reduce the costs by resorting to simpler procedures as also to a properly designed policy of differential interest rates.

Small artisans and other self-employed persons may be encouraged to form themselves into co-operatives or associations wherever feasible, which could look into the financial operations of artisans and help the credit agencies with information about them when processing loan applications, as also issue certificates, if needed, to vouch for the operations of the artisans concerned.

There should be non-financing multi-purpose agencies functioning as purely advisory bodies, providing advice and guidance to small industrial units regarding the availability of raw materials, other resources, marketing prospects and institutional sources of finance and technical matters. Advice to the unit on the management of its resources or collecting information about the prospective borrowers should not be expected of these agencies.

The State Governments should take the main initiative in setting up the multi-service agencies which should serve both the commercial and co-operative banks. Commercial banks could, however, render help in this regard and should be encouraged to provide consultancy and other technical services wherever they can.

The location and area of operations of the proposed agencies would depend on the amount of business that each agency will have. They would require the services of technically qualified persons but should not be overburdened with a large permanent staff.

Banks should give advance to viable small industrial units with an eye on the end-use of their loans and simplify loan procedures.

The Institute of Chartered Accountants of India can effect some simplifications in accounting practices and procedures to suit the small borrowers. The proposed multi-service agencies also may provide facilities of accounting at reasonable charges.

Banks may consider whether they can grant soft term loans in collaboration with other term-lending institutions to bridge the gap in equity capital which the small unit face.

Where technically qualified and competent persons are able to bring forth technically feasible projects but equity capital for them is not adequate, banks as also term-lending institutions should consider providing a certain amount of soft loans.

Some of the credit problems which small units face can be solved if there is close co-ordination among the lending agencies.

A borrowing unit should maintain its loan account for working capital purposes with only one bank or lending agency. Any loss incurred by the constituents owing to dislocation of work for any reason in their banks should be reimbursed by the concerned bank. Besides, the constituent if he so desires, should be able to shift his account to another bank without any difficulty in case he is not satisfied with the operation of his account.

Extension of credit to the priority sectors should not be at the expense of meeting the legitimate credit needs of other sectors. In allocating credit, the linkages between the different sectors of the economy should be borne in mind as economic activities are interconnected and denial or insufficient sanction of credit to one sector will have repercussions on other related sectors.

The structure of banking institutions in the rural sector should be improved by strengthening the primary credit societies in such a way that they can provide adequate credit, and develop the banking habit in this sector by providing a wide range of banking services and certain closely allied non-banking services. For this purpose, they have to become rural banks. The primary credit societies can do this if (i) they are well managed efficiently run units, (ii) they get technical assistance to enable them to provide the credit and the banking and the non-banking services, and (iii) certain legal steps are taken to enable them to function as rural banks. Where the central co-operative bank of the district is strong, the primary unit would get most of the assistance from the central bank, where the central bank is weak, the apex bank could give such assistance. Such rural banks in the co-operative sector, called 'rural co-operative banks', will obviate the need for opening branches by central or State co-operative banks merely for providing banking facilities to the rural areas and the latter can concentrate on meeting the needs of other co-operativised productive and distributive activities. A number of societies which satisfy the criteria of potential viability can be converted into rural banks provided they can get technical assistance from the central or State co-operative banks. Since, however, in many States both the district and State co-operative banks need to strengthen themselves, commercial banks may have to provide such assistance.

Besides formation of rural co-operative banks, banking facilities can be provided to rural areas by commercial banks through (i) opening of branches or (ii) adoption of villages or (iii) financing of primary credit societies. The first two can result in the extinction of co-operative credit institutions from the concerned areas. The third method can strengthen the co-operative societies provided satisfactory solutions can be obtained to the various difficulties (referred to in paragraph 8.41) experienced by commercial banks; in due course many of the primary societies can become rural banks. The emphasis on rural banks does not imply that other methods of providing banking facilities are ruled out. In the present Indian context the need is to try out various alternatives with a view to finding out which particular method is suited to an area of a given type. What is essential is that the banking and credit arrangements in any area are capable of making a significant impact on the development of agriculture and the local industry in that area.

In areas where the co-operative credit structure is generally weak, a rural bank may be established either by making a good primary agricultural credit society to work as a subsidiary of a commercial bank or by the commercial bank setting up its own subsidiary. Such a rural bank may be called a rural subsidiary bank. It should retain the useful features of co-operative credit institutions such as local participation, flexibility as regards increasing share capital, arrangements for selling shares to local people, etc. The parent bank will provide it with full technical and financial support.

Where a commercial bank sets up a 'rural subsidiary bank', it should offer to the residents in the area of operation of such rural bank about 49 per cent of the share capital of the rural bank. In cases where such local participation in shares is not forthcoming, the promoting bank should increase its participation in shares is not forthcoming, the promoting bank should increase its participation in the share capital to make up the shortfall in the minimum capital required, if necessary, by subscribing wholly to the share capital. Later, it may offer to the residents of the area, its holdings of shares in the rural bank, always retaining the controlling holding of shares and management control.

Those primary societies which are converted into rural co-operative banks should create a new class of members called 'associate' members who can avail themselves of the facilities of the bank but will not be entitled to any rights of voting or to patronage dividend. However, in order to retain the essential co-operative character, the loan business with 'associate' members may be restricted to a reasonable limit, say 25 per cent to the total loan business.

In order to encourage local participation in the rural banks, these banks should give, in their dealings, some preferences to the members over 'associate' members in the case of 'rural co-operative banks', and shareholders over non-shareholders in the case of 'rural subsidiary banks'. Thus the interest rate charged to a member/shareholder for his borrowings would be somewhat lower than that charged to an 'associate' member/non-shareholder.

The various functions which a rural bank may be expected to assume in due course are :

(i) mobilise local savings;

(ii) provide short-term and medium-term credit for agriculture and other purposes on its own and long-term credit as agent of the land development bank;

(iii) implement programmes of supervised credit tailored to the needs of individual farmers;

(iv) provide various ancillary banking services to local people;

(v) set up and maintain godowns;

(vi) undertake supply of inputs and agricultural and related equipments, and in appropriate cases, equipment leasing;

(vii) provide assistance in the marketing of agricultural and other products through marketing organisations; and

(viii) generally help in the overall development of the villages in its area.

A rural bank may be described as a primary banking institution set up to serve a compact group of villages covering a population from 5,000 to 20,000, generally, working as a co-operative bank or as a subsidiary of a commercial bank. However, in sparsely populated areas, it may be necessary to organise a rural bank for as big an area as a development block to start with.

A rural bank should cater to the full credit needs of all medium and small cultivators. Those cultivators and other rural producers who may be in need of a different type of technical help and of a much larger volume of loans than what a rural bank would be in a position to provide, should have access to a branch of a commercial bank. Some of the uneconomic primary agricultural credit societies which have been operating in the area covered by the rural bank may continue to do so till they are wound up. The Reserve Bank should ensure through appropriate directives that the commercial or co-operative banks should not continue to finance such uneconomic and weak credit societies while at the same time financing rural banks in the same area. The members of such societies should be eligible for finance from the rural banks. In such circumstances, the provision empowering the Registrar of Co-operative Societies to order winding up of societies which are uneconomic and poorly managed, may be invoked, in the public interest, wherever there is such a provision. Where it does not exist, it may be provided for.

Since rural banks under the scheme will be either subsidiaries of commercial banks or will be supported by strong co-operative banks and in either case they are likely to be under the effective control and supervision of the parent bank apart from that of the Reserve Bank, it is not necessary to fix any maximum borrowing power for these banks.

The financial strength of the rural bank should be increased more by way of ploughing back the profits into the reserves than by increasing the proportion of share capital to be held by a member to the maximum amount he can borrow. This can be done by placing a ceiling on the rate of dividend.

The co-operative principle of distribution of patronage dividend to the borrowers should be applied to rural banks. The business surpluses after providing for statutory reserves and other funds may be distributed to borrowers and depositors in the shape of patronage dividend when the rural banks are in a position to do so.

It should be ensured that lack of resources for the purpose of making share capital contribution to the rural banks does not stand in the way of either co-operative or commercial banks for sponsoring rural banks wherever it is considered necessary. The resources for the purpose may be made available from the National Agricultural Credit (Long-term Operations) Fund set up by the Reserve Bank of India.

The rural bank should be allowed to offer a somewhat higher rate of interest on deposits than that offered by the parent commercial or co-operative bank. The extent to which the rate can be higher on different deposits may be fixed by the Reserve Bank from time to time. The Deposit Insurance Scheme may also be extended to the rural banks.

The Food Corporation of India and its authorised agents who make purchases of foodgrains and other commodities from the agriculturists may make payments to the producers through the rural banks on an experimental basis wherever these are set up. Similarly, where the system of compulsory procurement exists, the State Government may utilise the rural banks for payment to farmers.

A good part of the resources of the rural banks would come from higher level banks, whether co-operative or commercial. Rural co-operative banks may supplement their resources by borrowing from a commercial bank as and when necessary. However, rural banks should also get some concessional credit facilities. The policy regarding concessional credit facilities from the Reserve Bank should be a uniform one irrespective of the channel through which they are made available. The rural borrower should pay the same interest whether he borrows from a primary co-operative or from a rural bank.

It is not desirable for the rural banks to seek direct refinance from the Reserve Bank. The higher level institution, viz., the central co-operative bank or the sponsoring commercial bank will be the link with the Reserve Bank. It is, however, necessary to ensure that the borrowings of the commercial bank for financing its rural subsidiary do not result in penalising the commercial bank in obtaining refinance for its own purpose. The Reserve Bank may make appropriate changes in its policy in this regard.

The norms for maintenance of liquid assets by rural banks should be lower than those for other banks. Further for both types of rural banks, the balances maintained by them with the higher level banks should be regarded as liquid assets.

The rural banks should be given by parent banks, remittance facilities free of cost and training facilities for personnel including technical personnel and personnel on a loan basis at subsidised costs in the initial years.

The rural banks should be eligible for participating in the guarantee schemes designed for ensuring adequacy of credit facilities to small and neglected sectors.

The success of a rural bank depends on the type of men put in charge of it. The staff of the rural banks should have the requisite background and training consistent with its functions. It is important that either the manager or the official next in line should have proper training in farm management and agricultural credit.

The first priority in establishing rural banks should be given to the well-tun primary agricultural credit societies. Each central cooperative bank which has the necessary organisational strength should select a few such primary societies every year for conversion into rural banks. Where such societies exist in the area of operation of a weak central co-operative bank, the concerned State co-operative bank can take such action if it can provide the necessary technical support. Otherwise, the primary credit society may be allowed to become a subsidiary of a commercial bank. Where the whole co-operative structure is weak, the commercial banks should set up rural subsidiary banks on their own on an experimental basis for a period of five years and establish rural subsidiaries in some of their lead districts. The experience gained during this period will decide the future of the scheme.

There are two types of districts where this type of organisation can be tried out initially. The districts which are known as package districts, the cash crop districts and parts of those where high-yielding varieties programmes have been introduced in a big way come under the first category. The other, comprises the areas which have been identified as having considerable potential for development of agriculture, agro-industries and related rural activities but much development has not taken place on account of lack of banking and credit facilities.

Since the Reserve Bank will have to license/notify the rural banks, it should also have the responsibility for ensuring that the Scheme of rural banks is implemented properly. It will have to co-ordinate the rural bank programmes of the commercial and co-operative banks and formulate guidelines for their working.

A separate legislation should be enacted by the Parliament in order to enable rural banks being set up quickly and in a fairly simple way without straining too much the organisation and resources of either co-operative or commercial banks.

Pending the enactment of the new legislation, appropriate amendments may be made to Co-operative Laws in different States to enable the setting up of rural co-operative banks expeditiously along the lines suggested.

A sound and progressive system of credit, whether followed by cooperative or commercial banks, should have certain well understood goals. It should (a) provide integrated and comprehensive credit facilities to all the producers, (b) be based on the purpose of the loan and in particular the improvement of productivity it can achieve through modernisation and diversification of farming, and (c) be responsive to individual needs, in matters like the quantum, timing of sanction, spacing of disbursements and the degree of technical help and supervision needed.

It is important under a progressive loaning system to increase the capability of the farmer to increase his overall income, resulting from his improved productivity and efficiency of management. The system of credit should increasingly emphasise building up of these qualities in the borrower which make tangible security a matter of secondary importance. At the same time, such a system of credit should also enable farmers to acquire assets which help improve their productivity and risk-bearing ability.

The implementation of the programmes of the Small Farmers Development Agency should continue on an experimental basis. However, as small farmers are not concentrated in any one district but are dispersed all over the country, their problems will have to be viewed in the wider perspective of equipping the institutional structure designed to cater to rural needs in order to satisfy their needs also to the maximum extent.

The problems of small and marginal farmers call for an integrated approach to their requirements combined with supervised credit. Unless the institution which is in direct touch with the rural producers is adequately equipped to provide integrated services combined with credit, a complete answer to their problems is not likely to emerge.

The Commission endorses the recommendations of the "Expert Group on State Enactments having a bearing on Commercial Banks Credit to Agriculture" which deal with removing the restrictive features of the State enactments particularly those relating to rights of alienation of land or interest therein in favour of commercial banks and with providing certain facilities which are now available to borrowers from co-operative to borrowers from commercial banks also (See also Recommendations Nos. 122 and 397).

The authority for laying down guidelines for policies for all banks in the field of agricultural finance should be the same, as in the past, i.e., the Reserve Bank of India.

In the case of co-operative banks there is need for greater flexibility in their loan policies than exists at present. This is particularly important on account of the flexibility that is available to commercial banks. Towards this end, the policy making body at the State co-operative banks level should be sufficiently broad-based to include representatives of agricultural departments in charge of extension work, a farm management specialist and a representative of the 'lead bank' in the area.

The Reserve Bank may take steps to encourage the State co-operative banks to take decisions regarding details of loan policies subject to broad guidelines laid down by it as in the case of commercial banks.

As regards the loans granted to individual borrowers it is necessary to consider the purpose of the loan from the point of view of the improvement it can bring about in the productive, efficiency of the borrowers and their income. In particular, diversification of farming is essential for improving the income and risk-bearing ability of the farmers. It is, therefore, necessary that the institutions at the primary level should be functionally equipped to provide credit facilities for all productive purposes to the farmers whether undertaken jointly with agriculture or independently, and whether they help production directly or indirectly. The primary units will also have to finance small scale and agro-industries like flour mills, oil crushing units, etc., for financing which there may be no separate institutions in the area.

The proposed rural banks as well as the recognised viable primary credit societies should be equipped to provide production loans for all purposes which help either directly or indirectly in improving the production capacity and income of the farmers. In the matter of eligibility of purpose for loans, a farmer borrowing from a co-operative should not be at a disadvantage as compared with a borrower from a commercial bank or its subsidiary rural bank.

The loaning system should provide for accepting as security those assets, real as well as financial, which farmers may acquire to improve their production and rapaying capacity. The commercial banks, the rural banks and recognised primary credit societies should be equipped to reorient their loaning system in this manner.

It would be useful to find out whether 'credit rating' of borrowers on the basis of certain personal data developed in a number of countries is applicable under Indian conditions [See also Recommendation No. 165 (ix)].

Farm guidance and supervised credit programmes are important factors in ensuring efficient use of credit. For farm guidance, the best course would be to make use of the agricultural extension machinery at the government level. Arrangements for credit supervision is the responsibility of banks and there should be suitably co-ordinated supervised credit programme.

Since the primary credit societies are too small to be in a position to appoint specialists for credit supervision, the central/apex co-operative banks should appoint a suitable number of specialists and make their services available to the societies for undertaking supervised credit programmes as in the case of rural banks. Where necessary, co-operative banks may be sanctioned suitable subsidies by the Government in the initial years.

The proposed rural banks and recognised viable primary credit societies should receive adequate guarantee support for undertaking financing of small and marginal farmers and other producers of similar categories in an integrated way. In view of the special factors affecting agricultural production, it may be necessary to augment the resources of the Credit Guarantee Corporation by an adequate subsidy from the Government. It may also be necessary for the Corporation to suitably decentralise its work. As the Reserve Bank of India has already opened branches of the Agricultural Credit Department in most of the States, these branches should be able to do the work of the Corporation in regard to loans to small farmers.

The scope of guarantee cover extended by the Credit Guarantee Corporation should be so widened as to extend its coverage to all institutions which give production credit to small farmers and other borrowers. The proposed rural banks and recognised primary credit societies and co-operative banks where they finance producers directly, should be made eligible for suitable guarantee cover, under the schemes of the Credit Guarantee Corporation.

In the case of wilful defaulters, the societies and the rural banks, where these are set up, should take prompt legal action. Wherever it has not already been done, the co-operative banks should be enabled to proceed directly against the borrowers where the societies have failed to take action. In the case of commercial banks, the legal impediments that stand in their way of taking action against defaulters should be removed by the State Governments expeditiously.

When the borrowers satisfy the primary institution, regarding the purpose of the loan, their repaying capacity and security, it should be possible for the primary lending institution to defer repayment of loan by a suitable period in all cases of default for reasons beyond the control of the borrowers. In such cases upto a reasonable level of their resources, the institutions at the primary level should be allowed to grant extensions.

Both Central Banks and the higher financing institutions including the Reserve Bank should treat such extended loans as current loans to the extent they are satisfied about the soundness of the purpose of the loans and the repaying capacity of the borrowers. The apex bank and the Reserve Bank may from time to time cause investigations to be made of such extensions granted by the primary institutions in order to make sure that the powers to sanction extension are not used injudiciously. This practice of granting extension should be confined to the proposed rural banks and recognised viable primary credit societies.

It is necessary to introduce a flexible system of making recoveries in those areas where : (a) both the crops are not equally good or certain, (b) there are periodical crop failures. The long-term solution to this problem lies in encouraging the farmers to undertake improvements on the farm and undertake supplementary non-farm activities so as to ensure steadily growing income and to develop a system of loaning and recovery that will be appropriate to such areas. In areas where one of the crops is more important than the other, a major part of the loan extended for the whole year may be recovered from out of the crop that is more important and the remainder from out of harvest of the other crop or other incomes of the farmers. Similarly, in areas subject to periodical droughts once every three or four years, the recovery system should be so adapted that the repayment of that part of the loan which remains unpaid during the lean years is spread over the two or three years during which good crops can be expected. Wherever co-operative and commercial banks have the resources, and have introduced the supervised credit system, recovery may be spread over periods of two to three years.

The existing conditions for converting short-term loans into medium-term loans on account of widespread crop failure should be relaxed. The eligibility of co-operative Banks for conversion facilities from the National Agricultural Credit (Stabilisation) Fund of the Reserve Bank should not be linked to the State Governments declaring annawari short-fall of less than 6 annas in 16 annas (i.e., 37-1/2 per cent) in the affected area. The decision whether or not the crop failure in the area justifies conversion facilities should be left to the Committee headed by the seniormost officer in charge of agricultural production in the State.

Considering that a rural bank is designed essentially to cater to the needs particularly of medium and small farmers as well as those sections which have been hitherto denied credit facilities, all these types of farmers should be adequately served by the rural banks or the viable primary societies, unless they are directly served by commercial banks. If needs of individual farmers for credit exceed a specified level, they should be financed by the nearest branch of a commercial bank and not by a rural bank or a primary agricultural credit society. In their case, there is a definite need for their using a good part of their own resources for current operations and investment in farming which can be better ensured by a commercial bank. These farmers should not be eligible for subsidized credit. They should be charged the usual rates of interest on loans. Further, they need not be brought under the supervised credit programme which is necessary in the case of small farmers.

As far as possible, a borrower should get his entire credit from one single institutional agency. Rural banks and recognised primary credit societies should be enabled to make long-term loans also as agents of the land development bank. It would be useful to avoid 'splitting of security' among the lenders and enable the lending institution to have complete control over the assets offered by the borrower and help improve his production and income. Where farmers have outstanding dues to any other institutional agency, the institutions providing complete credit facilities may arrange to repay those dues and get the pledged security released in its favour, to have a better control over the assets of the borrower.

Where members of primary co-operatives are unable to obtain loans to the full extent of their needs, the society should enable them to raise the balance from a commercial bank. This can be done by entering into a participation arrangement with the commercial bank or a rural bank, or by permitting the borrower in writing to approach the commercial bank.

Unless there are special circumstances like the commercial bank or co-operative bank adopting a group of villages for providing complete credit facilities and related services, demarcation of areas between commercial banks and co-operative banks does not appear as a practicable method of ensuring co-ordination between the two.

In areas where either commercial banks or co-operative banks launch their schemes of village adoption and seek to provide complete credit facilities for all the rural producers, other institutional agencies should not be allowed to operate.

In areas where there is scope for development loans, but co-operatives have not been able to make development loans but are in a position to make adequate short-term loans, it would be preferable for commercial banks to confine their lending for development purposes by entering into suitable arrangements with the co-operatives. Close co-ordination between the concerned co-operative and commercial banks is necessary to ensure that the total finance provided is adequate and is properly utilised.

It is necessary to have regular machinery at the district level in all the States which will take a co-ordinated view of the credit problems of the various productive activities in a district. Co-ordination committees at the district level, with representatives of the lending agencies as members and the seniormost officer of the State Government in charge of development of the district as the Chairman should, therefore, be formed.

One important aspect of co-ordination is the exchange of information between the co-operative and commercial banks by obtaining standardised type of information. Exchange of information would be useful in regard to crop prospects, availability and prices of the different agricultural inputs, etc. It will be one of the main functions of the district level co-ordination committee to look into all such practical aspects of field level co-ordination and evolve suitable procedures to keep all the agencies lending to rural producers in a district properly informed.

The co-operative banks should appoint well qualified and trained staff. The Deposit Insurance Scheme should be extended to the co-operative banks. It is necessary that the Reserve Bank of India should link the rate of interest charged on its loans to co-operative banks to the deposit mobilisation efforts put in by them. The Reserve Bank should formulate a scheme at any early date for this purpose.

At present there is considerable variation in the regulation of co-operative banks, their inspection and the assistance they get from State to State. This had led to difficulties in the efficient management and functioning of the co-operative banks. As these banks are the main channel for providing institutional credit to agriculture, the differences mentioned above create a number of difficulties in effective implementation of the monetary and credit policy of the country. Moreover, the financial assistance provided by the States to these banks is mostly from the resources of the Reserve Bank or the Central Government. Therefore, from the point of view of ensuring a unified monetary and credit policy, uniformity of laws and regulations relating to credit supplying agencies and ensuring a high quality of management of these agencies through programmes of training and exchange of information, co-operative credit should be transferred to the Union or the Concurrent List. (See also Recommendations No. 309).

Wherever weak central banks exist, the co-operative structure should be reorganised. This can be done in the following manner :—

(i) In those States where all the district central banks are weak, it will be better to reorganise the structure so as to have only branches of the apex bank;

(ii) In those States where there is a small number of strong central banks and a large number of weak banks, the apex should open branches in places where the weak central banks exist at present;

(iii) In a State where the majority of the district central co-operative banks are strong, it is not advisable to disturb the existing structure. In such cases, the weak banks which form the minority, may be converted into branches of apex bank till such time as they are transformed into strong viable banks;

(iv) However, in States where both the apex and district central co-operative banks are strong, the present structure may be allowed to continue.

It is possible that the reorganised State co-operative banks in some States are likely to acquire deficits on account of taking over the assets and liabilities of the central co-operative banks already under 'rehabilitation' programmes are likely to be brought under such programmes. In all such cases, the net owned funds position of the reorganised banks should be ascertained and where necessary suitable share capital contributions be made from the National Credit (Long-term Operation) Fund of the Reserve Bank of India, taking care to see that the capital base is not thereby made excessive.

The policy regarding owned funds of co-operative banks is baded partly on the principle of maximum borrowing power being a definite multiple of the owned funds and partly on the principle of increasing such funds for the purposes of absorbing overdues. For the co-operative credit agencies, the share capital base has become rather large in relation to the volume of business resulting in a low rate of return to the individual shareholder. For the individual members, a good part of the share capital is collected from loans as compulsory deductions. From the point of view of the shareholder it is more advantageous if the co-operatives concentrate on deposit mobilisation rather than on raising more share capital. The requirements of owned funds should be related to such factors as (i) the fixed capital requirements of the credit agency, (ii) bad and doubtful debts, and (iii) quality of other loans, and not linked up with the considerations of maximum borrowing power. The Reserve Bank should review the policy in this light and revise the requirements for share capital contribution. (See also Recommendation No. 151).

The proposed reorganisation of weak central banks as branches of apex banks and granting of a 'scheduled' status to strong co-operative banks may create some difficulties for these banks in raising resources from the Reserve Bank because of the requirement of two good signatures to be furnished on the promissory notes submitted for obtaining accommodation from the Reserve Bank. In this connection the Reserve Bank of India Act 1934, may be suitably amended to enable it to provide financial accommodation against a single good signature.

As a result of the proposed reorganisation in some States, the offices of the central banks as branches of apex banks, will acquire the status of the branches of a 'scheduled' bank, so long as the present distinction between the 'scheduled' banks and other banks remains. This could mean, however, that those central co-operative banks which continue their independent existence because of their good performance will remain non-scheduled. If the banks wish to be included in the Second Schedule to the Reserve Bank of India Act, 1934, it should be possible for them to be so included. In order that central co-operative banks are also enabled to be scheduled, the Central Government should notify them as eligible institutions under section 42 (6) (a) (iii) of the Reserve Bank of India Act, 1934.

In order to enable the central and the State co-operative banks to finance small scale industries in their States, individual membership in such banks should be allowed upto a limit to be specified by the Reserve Bank of India.

In those States where co-operative banks are generally strong and re-organisation is not considered necessary, steps should be taken to simplify the existing documentation and procedural formalities that are required to be observed between apex and central banks.

With the introduction of credit planning, it may be expected that broad sectoral allocations of the total available credit will be made from time to time by the credit planning authorities. However, because of the inadequacies of both the commercial and co-operative banks at the primary or the field level, there is likely to be a problem for some time to come of credit to agriculture and other productive activities in the rural areas not being made available fully. In particular, it is likely that while the deposits raised by the co-operative banks will be fully utilised for this purpose the allocation out of commercial banks deposits remains unutilised. The Agricultural Credit Board of the Reserve Bank of India should keep this matter under constant review and devise ways and means of utilising the allocation from commercial banks deposits more fully. There is no case for establishing a National Co-operative Bank.

What is of utmost importance is that lending at the level of ultimate borrowers should be sound. To what extent the Reserve Bank may finance a co-operative bank should be determined not so much by the audit classification and prescribed multiples of owned funds, but by the extent to which it has been in a position to make sound use of resources. Where the co-operative banks are financially sound, managed efficiently and when sound loaning policies are followed, they should be able to get credit facilities for meeting their actual needs. This may mean relaxation of or altogether dispensing with the existing multiples.

In the case of banks which are weak and are not so sound, what the Reserve Bank provides by way of credit limits should be part of a total 'package' consisting of credit plus management guidance, plus a concrete annual programme for improving the loaning system. This would enable weaker co-operative banks to draw larger loans from the Reserve Bank.

There is a strong case for combining the Agricultural Refinance Corporation and the Agricultural Finance Corporation. The new institution will be in a better position to help promote development financing to a much greater extent by both co-operative and commercial banks. This would also ensure effectiveness of co-ordination between term-financing, technical assistance and finance for current operations within the Reserve Bank complex. The new institution formed by merging the two corporations can serve the purposes the proposed Agricultural Development Bank of India is expected to serve.

Urban co-operative banks do useful work in mobilising deposits and financing the sector of small borrowers such as small scale industries, professionals, retailers and so on. Another useful activity is the financing of house construction and repairs, for members of the banks. Also this type of banking provides a useful avenue for those who have the necessary ability to set up a bank.

The establishment of urban co-operative banks should be encouraged by the authorities, by such means as (i) according to the status of a 'scheduled' bank to the well managed urban co-operative banks if they so desire; (ii) counting towards liquid assets the deposits which these banks place with the national banks; and (iii) asking the national banks to give such of the urban co-operative banks which remain non-scheduled, free remittance facilities and borrowing facilities on reasonable terms.

In order to ensure that the productive and distributive activities are adequately financed by urban banks, (i) there should be a system of ceilings on the borrowings by individual members on the basis of the purpose for which the loan is obtained instead of linking it only to the amount of shares held; (ii) lending for long-term purposes, such as house construction, should be allowed subject to a ceiling that may be specified by the Reserve Bank of India regarding the proportion of such lending to the total loans given by the bank; and (iii) there should be a ceiling on the proportion of total loans for consumption purposes; this ceiling need not apply in the case of employees' co-operative credit societies.

*In order to create a good image in the minds of customers for retaining existing business and attracting fresh business, it is necessary that their waiting time at the counters should be minimised, proper guidance should be given to them by providing enquiry counters and behaviour of the staff with them should be courteous and helpful.

For expediting the transactions at the counters, the teller system should be adopted in all banks at all important branches for encashment of cheques and receipt of a cash for credit to accounts. Where the teller system is not in operation and where it is not proposed to be introduced immediately, the first line supervisors should be permitted to pass cheques for payment in cash up to a specified amount.

The waiting time of customers paying in cash at the counter can be reduced by authorising the cashier to issue the counterfoil without its being countersigned by another official. In order to maintain an independent record of cash receipts, the Scroll Book should, however, be maintained by a member of the Accounts Department who should sit near the cash counter.

Cheques and bills tendered for collection and credit to accounts should be allowed to be received by the bills clerk who should be authorised to sign the counterfoils singly.

Banks should discontinue the practice of obtaining balance confirmations for credit balances in deposit accounts except where the branch agent considers it necessary to obtain them in the light of his personal knowledge about the depositors and operations in their accounts. The internal auditor should be required during the course of audit to request a few depositors, selected at random, to confirm their balances and send the confirmations direct to him.

A planned programme for use of regional languages for account opening forms, pay-in-slips, cheque books, pass books, statements of account, etc., should be adopted and implemented by banks, so that within a period of three years or so dealing with customers are carried out entirely in the languages they fully understand. Government departments, local bodies, educational institutions, public utility concerns, public sector undertakings, etc. should encourage the use of cheques in their financial transactions with the public, where necessary, by suitably amending their rules and regulations.

Banks should take expeditious steps to encourage the members of the staff and officers to learn local languages and to dispense with the practice of obtaining letters of indemnity for vernacular signatures of the depositors and of transcribing and attesting such signatures. Banks should also make arrangements for taking and keeping on record photographs of illiterate depositors for facilitating their identification.

Commercial banks which close their accounts at the end of June each year should discontinue the practice of half-yearly closing of accounts.

Banks should issue cheque books with crossing printed thereon to the customers who require them. A similar system should be followed in respect of bank drafts.

Increased use of ultra-violet ray equipment should be made by banks at their urban branches and they should also supply protectograph machines to all offices which are authorised to issue drafts.

Mechanisation should be introduced by banks, especially at larger branches, by adopting a phased programme. The Government should take positive steps to help the banks in getting over the difficulties such as non-availability of machines and opposition, if any, of the staff. Indigenous manufacturers should be encouraged to produce machines to suit the requirements of Indian banking.

The feasibility of opening clearing houses at places with population of more than 50,000 which are served by more than 3 or 4 banks should be examined by the concerned authorities. The State Bank of India should take a lead in this matter. At centres where the State Bank of India is not established but other banks or their customers feel a need for establishment of a clear-

---

*A number of recommendations relating to improvement in customer services, simplification of credit procedures, measures for making internal control systems more effective and those for improving organisation and management of banks, besides a few miscellaneous suggestions have been made in paragraph 11.8 to 11.127 of which the major ones are summarised in recommendations 97 to 142.

ing house, the initiative should be taken by the banks themselves, preferably by the lead banks.

The feiasbility of opening additional clearing houses in large cities to serve sub-urban or other composite areas should be expeditiously considered by the Reserve Bank of India. The question of admitting non-scheduled banks as full-fledged members of clearing houses as also liberalising the clearing houses rules should be examined by the Reserve Bank of India and the State Bank of India.

Expeditious steps should be taken for extension of the 'Courier Service' for transmitting instruments, documents, advices, etc., in order to cover all important trade centres in the country connected by air; the Government should render such help, as may be necessary, in resolving the legal and technical difficulties which might arise.

In order to avoid inconvenience to customers and as a measure of self-discipline, banks should issue instructions to their branches that the cheques and drafts sent by them to outstation branches for collection should be considered as realised and proceeds credited to the customers' accounts if they are not returned unpaid or information regarding their dishonour is not received from the collecting branches within specified periods.

To bring about an improvement in procedures, a suitable manifold system should be introduced by banks, which have not so far adopted it, for outward and inward bills for collection.

First line supervisors should be authorised to sign drafts singly up to a specified amount. Further, the introduction of manifold draft requisition form, with a carbon attached is likely to reduce the waiting time of customers.

A bank Giro should be established by banks, with mutual collaboration, as an independent institutions, to clear inter-bank credit transactions relating to transfer of funds from one bank account to another and also remittance of funds by a non-account holder to an account holder and vice versa. It may also undertake issue of travellers cheques and drafts.

A comprehensive scheme should be drawn up by the Reserve Bank of India for on-the-job training of co-operative banks' personnel at various levels in commercial banks. In turn, the members of the staff in commercial banks dealing with agricultural finance may also receive training in co-operative banks and training institutes in order to acquaint themselves with the procedures adopted by these banks.

In regard to advances to small borrowers, only essential information of a simple nature relating to the borrower and his credit requirements should be required to be followed in the application form. The information so obtained may be supplemented by a bank official by questioning the applicant and perusing his books of account and other relevant papers.

It is necessary to create a separate organisation which could be named as Credit Intelligence Bureau as a statutory corporation for compiling and furnishing credit information to various financial institutions in the country.

While assessing the credit requirements of a borrower, the branch agent should take into consideration the borrower's requirements for different types of facilities. The head office/regional office should also give discretion, to some extent, to the branch agent to interchange various limits in favour of a borrower according to requirements from time to time.

If a constituent has been borrowing from other sources for his business purposes, the bank should endeavour to persuade him to repay such borrowings and deal exclusively with it for all his credit requirements. The borrower should, however, have freedom to shift their entire dealings from one bank to another. Where the requirement of a borrowers are large, he may be allowed to borrow from more than one bank, i.e., by a consortium of banks entering into participation arrangements or by mutual arrangements between banks. Borrowings from more than one institution may also be allowed in other reasonable circumstances.

In order to ascertain the end use of funds, the branch officials during their periodical visits to the places of business of the borrowers, should try to test and check whether large drawings made from the accounts were for genuine business purposes, whether the inflow of cash in the business was regularly deposited in the account and whether the production and marketing activities of the concerns have been running smoothly.

In regard to direct advances to agriculturists, the Regional Offices of commercial banks should issue instructions to branches in their respective areas indicating the scale of finance applicable to different types of crops. As far as possible, banks should disburse credit by making direct payments to the suppliers of inputs taking care to see that finance in respect of a particular input is commensurate with the requirements of the farmers.

Expeditious steps should be taken to ensure that commercial banks are not made to suffer from any direct or indirect legal disabilities which co-operative banks are not subjected to and also to ensure that all the privileges and concessions enjoyed by those banks are extended to commercial banks.

The extent of the area served by a rural branch of a commercial bank should depend upon the nature of available communication and conveyance facilities.

Normally, such area should not be larger than about 15 to 20 kilometres from the branch. Larger areas may have however, to be served in suitable cases, particularly in respect of under-banked regions until banking are adequately spread out.

The terms and conditions usually prescribed by banks in the case of advances to medium sized and large scale industries should be relaxed suitably while considering the limits in favour of deserving small scale industries. Further, the various limits granted to them should, in suitable cases, be consolidated in a smaller number of limits as multiplicity of limits, causes hardships when there are seasonal variations in business. In regard to working capital advances to small scale industries, technical reports from consultancy firms or institutions need not be insisted upon as a matter of course.

The number of centres where banks provide intensive export finance facilities should be increased. In order to provide facilities to the costomers and guidance to the branch agents, banks should post at least one officer with adequate knowledge of foreign exchange procedures at the regional offices which do not have full-fledged Foreign Exchange Department.

The Industrial Development Bank of India should be in a position to obtain information regarding export opportunities as also exchange control and customs regulations in different countries, to keep it up-to-date and make it available to commercial banks and others on request. The Indian Institute of Foreign Trade should be strengthened for rendering better assistance to small exporters in exploring foreign markets.

In regard to financing of small borrowers banks may insist upon guarantees of third parties only when there are reasonable doubts about the repaying capacity of the borrower. The banks should introduce night safe facility at suitable centres to enable customers to deposit their daily cash collections in the bank after banking hours.

Mechanisation to the extent possible, including the use of electronic computers, should be adopted by banks for reconciling the inter-branch transaction. The outstanding entries should be promptly followed up and reasons for their remaining outstanding should be ascertained.

During the course of audit of a branch, the internal auditor should make a test check of the entries in the inter-branch account on a random sampling basis and a complete scrutiny of the long outstanding entries.

For the purpose of exercising an effective control over the working of the branches, proper attention has to be paid by banks to the organisation of the Audit and Inspection Department, selection of inspection staff, preparation of reports and follow-up action on them. The major suggestions in this regard are as under :

(i) The inspection staff of banks should normally consist of Internal Auditors, Branch Inspectors, and Godown Inspectors. Internal Auditors should have a thorough knowledge of the procedures and at least five years' experience of handling different types of work in responsible capacities. Branch Inspectors should be senior and experienced enough to be in a position to comment critically on and assess the quality of business conducted by the branch officials.

(ii) The Audit and Inspection Department should be directly responsible to the Chief Executive Officer of the bank. For the sake of convenience and in the interest of economy, members of the inspection staff may be posted at different regional offices but they should be under the direct administrative charge of the head office.

(iii) The internal audit and inspection should ordinarily be conducted once every year on a surprise basis. The verification of stocks pledged or hypothecated to the bank (which should also be on a surprise basis), should be carried out once in each quarter. While drawing up the inspection programme, it should be ensured that an official does not visit the same branch consecutively.

(iv) In the case of large branches, the audit and inspection may be taken up simultaneously and one or more Internal Auditors may be deputed to assist the Branch Inspector. The size of the inspection team should be sufficiently large so as to complete the audit and inspection expeditiously. It would also be desirable for banks to carry out concurrent audit of their large offices in metropolitan cities.

(v) Apart from the examination of various assets and liabilities of a branch outstanding at the time of audit, a test check of some of the transactions effective since the date of last audit on random sampling basis and a percentage check (say 5 to 10 per cent) of the account opening forms, specimen signature cards, notings in respect of cheque books issued, recording of stop payment instructions, compliance with standing instructions, etc., should be made by the Internal Auditor.

(vi) In order to ensure that audit and inspection are thorough and exhaustive, a check list on the lines of the 'Hand Book for Bank Inspectors' prepared by the Bankers Training College should be supplied to the inspection staff.

(vii) The Branch Inspector should arrive at an overall assessment of the working of the branch on the basis of the findings of audit and inspection as also financial and management ratios of its working and classify it according to its standard of efficiency. A research institution like the National Institute of Bank Management may compile a suitable scheme for rating of the branches on scientific basis for adoption by banks.

(viii) The inspection staff should make efforts not only to detect frauds, if any, committed by employees and/or others but also to find out laxity or loopholes in the procedures.

(ix) Any serious irregularity reported to the head office by the Internal Auditor or the Branch Inspector should be immediately brought to the notice of the Chief Executive Officer of the bank, who may, if considered necessary, refer it also to the Board of Directors/Executive Committee. The irregularities should be followed up vigorously till they are rectified. At the end of each quarter, the Audit and Inspection Department should prepare a memorandum on the basis of the inspection and audit reports received during the quarter for submission to the Board of Directors, bringing out, inter alia, major irregularities observed and action taken or proposed to be taken to rectify them.

There is a need for bringing about uniformity in various forms, documents, nomenclature, terms, accounting procedures and norms used for deciding various matters by the National Banks as also for creation of a common agency, in due course, to carry out internal audit and inspection of the branches of these banks. A committee may be appointed under the auspices of the Reserve Bank of India : (i) to consider the question of creation of a common internal audit and inspection agency and (ii) to formulate standard forms and procedures, keeping in view the advantages of mechanisation on a planned basis for rendering better customer service. The standardised procedures and forms should be reviewed from time to time and necessary changes made in them to ensure maximum efficiency and customer convenience.

Branches should not be required to submit statements of all outstanding advances (other than Uniform Balance Book returns) at frequent intervals and it will be adequate if such statements are called for once every year at the time of the annual closing. Branches should not also normally be required to submit periodical returns giving details of advances sanctioned by the branch officials within their discretionary powers. The control of head office over advances through periodical returns should relate mainly to irregular advances, the position of other advances being examined during the course of annual inspection of branches. Separate statements of irregular advances may be prepared for different categories of advances and sent on different dates of the month so as to stagger the work at the branch and facilitate scrutiny at the head office. As regards the advances involved in litigation, a return may be sent at quarterly intervals.

The control returns should be scrutinised at the head office by the supervisory staff and, where necessary, prompt follow-up action should be taken through the regional offices. All advances indicating serious irregularities should be immediately brought to the notice of the top management. Internal Auditors, during their visits to branches, should make test check of the statements sent to the head office and regional office.

Banks should organise and/or strengthen Organisation and Methods, Economic and Statistics, and Public Relations Departments. They should also have separate departments for Management Development and Budgetary Control (See recommendations 173 and 214). The heads of the Organisation and Methods Department of different banks should meet periodically, say one every half-year, for exchanging information regarding the studies made by them; the Reserve Bank of India may take the initiative in this matter. Further, the banks which have not so far introduced a scheme for obtaining suggestions from their employees for improving methods and procedures should do so at an early date.

Banks having a sizeable network of branches should create or reorganise regional offices keeping in view the need to decentralise authority. Regional Offices should be granted adequate powers not only for sanction of the bulk of the advance proposals emanating from branches but also in regard to administrative matters. They should be placed under the charge of experienced and capable senior officers who should not be overburdened with routine work. Such offices should maintain specialised cells on functional basis with adequate trained staff for assessment of advances proposals from different sectors and for supervision and review of advances granted to them. They should also maintain a close contract with the branches and review their working periodically.

Delegation of discretionary powers to branch agents to sanction advances to small borrowers should be liberalised keeping in view the needs of different areas in which the branches function. While vesting discretionary powers, the head office should prescribe an overall ceiling on the total amount of credit that could be advanced at each of the branches to various categories of borrowers based on their annual plans in order to ensure equitable distribution of credit in relation to the bank's total available resources and in the context of liquidity requirements. Delegation of authority should be reviewed at least once in two or three years and discretionary powers should be varied, if necessary, according to requirements.

The provisions of Section 292 of the Companies Act, 1956, may be suitably amended so that in the case of banking companies, the Board of Directors is enabled to authorise the Chief Executive Officer or a Committee of Directors to exercise the powers of the Board in regard to specifying the total amount up to which loans may be made by the delegates, the purposes for which the loans may be made and the maximum amount of loan which may be made for each such purpose in individual cases.

The question of standardising the form of import letter of credit and the form of payment order relating to foreign mail and telegraphic transfer as also revision of monthly statement of import letters of credit may be considered by the appropriate authorities.

A committee may be appointed by the Reserve Bank of India to thoroughly examine the various procedures prescribed under the Exchange Control Regulations. There should be adequate representation ont his committee of different interests, e.g., authorised dealers, exporters, importers, travellers etc.

In order to ensure expeditious and proper disposal of complaints, complaint-cum-suggestion boxes should be provided at all branches of banks for use of the public. Regional manager or development officers attached to regional offices, on their visit to the branches should spare some time to hear the grievances and suggestions of the local constituents.

Banks should take steps to improve the layout in their offices in order to enhance the efficiency of the staff as also for improving the customer service after conducting studies of office routine.

To begin with and on an experimental basis, administrative offices of banks may remain fully closed on Saturdays and, to compensate for the loss of man-hours, the working hours on other week days should be suitably enhanced. The question of introducing similar change in the bank offices dealing with the public may be considered later.

Branches of banks at rural and mandi centres should be kept open in the evening, if necessary, by suitably reducing the working hours in the day time. In the residential areas at urban centres, wherever feasible, working hours should be in the mornings and evenings to suit the convenience of the clientele.

There is a scope for modifying the pricing system of the banks, particularly those in the public sector, in such a way that in fixing charges levied on the different customers, the use they make of the banking system is taken into account.

The profit objective of the national banks should be such as to ensure : (i) the return at a specified rate to the Government of India on its investment after meeting the requirements for purposes of expansion and modernisation as well as for strengthening the various units, and (ii) adequate cover for risk assets. In order to cover the risk assets adequately, the national banks should be required to classify their loans and advances (including bills purchased and discounted) into different categories, say, (i) regular advances, (ii) substandard advances; (iii) doubtful advances, and (iv) bad debts. The Reserve Bank should lay down the guidelines for being followed by banks in making such classification and should also specify the percentages at which provision should be made for different categories of advances. The external auditors should be required to examine, during the course of their audit, the classification and also the provision made, and certify that it is adequate. The Reserve Bank may, if necessary, vary the rates of provision for all banks or for any particular bank from time to time. Adequate provision should also be made for depreciation in assets other than advances. The banks in the private sector should also be persuaded to follow similar policy in regard to making provisions and appropriation of profits.

With the nationalisation of major banks the public are entitled to know the true and fair position of banks through their published accounts. Further, the protection afforded to the depositors by the Deposit Insurance Corporation and to banks by Credit Guarantee Organisation/Corporation in respect of advances to small scale industries and small borrowers, render the maintenance of secret reserves superfluous. Also as larger provision for risk assets is expected to be made by banks in terms of the Recommendation No. 144, banks in India need not keep a part of their reserves secret.

From the point of view of maximum deposit mobilisation, the deposit interest rate structure has to conform to the expectations of the public about the appropriate rates for deposits of different terms. Research to determine which rates need revision and in what direction should be initiated by the appropriate authority.

The effects on servicing costs because of shifts in the distribution of deposits between current, savings and fixed, consequent on changes in interest rates for deposits, is also an area in which research is needed to ascertain the direction and the magnitude of such efforts. This research should also be initiated by the appropriate authority.

The main elements of the pricing system for deposit accounts should be the following (i) minimum balances should be prescribed for each type of account; (ii) the extent of free facilities should be dependent on the size of the account, (iii) a charge per transaction should be made if the balance in the account is below the minimum, or the total number of transactions in a period exceeds the maximum allowed for the account, and (iv) consideration should be given to the need to encourage the banking habit particularly amongst the small account holders. In the case of advances, emphasis should be on cost reduction through procedural improvements, especially in the case of priority sectors. The schedule of charges should be fixed on the basis of comprehensive data on costs. A more correct way in this regard would be to fix the maximum levels of charges according to the size groups of the banks and the average costs of banks in the group, rather than on the basis of the averages for all banks. It is also important to keep a watch on how the revision of charges actually works out in practice; if it results in overfulfilling the profit objectives, suitable adjustments should be made to lower the schedule in the interests of spreading the banking habit.

Banks should examine carefully their existing procedures and methods of handling foreign exchange transactions and also for developing methods of cost and profitability analysis in this field. The implications of changes such as the exchange rate adjustments of currencies and use of wider margins for spot rates, on the banks and their customers, need to be studied. Further work in this matter should be done by bankers who have the necessary expertise.

The relevance of the prescription of minimum rates by Foreign Exchange Dealers Association (FEDA) for the different types of commission charges in the present context needs to be examined. In this field, the maximum should be related to the average of the cost of the banks.

The profitability of co-operative apex and central banks can be improved : (a) by bringing down excess cash reserves for which the authorities should 'notify' for the purposes of the Banking Regulation Act, 1949, all National Banks with whom balances are maintained to facilitate remittances and other operations, and the co-operative banks giving attention to better management of resources, and (b) by efficient management of liquid assets, by diversifying activities and improving the absorbing capacity of primary societies. Also, the validity of policies being pursued now to increase the capital base of co-operative banks through members' contribution as well as Government participation has to be re-examined to ensure a reasonable return on capital.

In evolving a method for profitability analysis of bank branches, it should be ensured that the method truly and fairly measures the profit performance of a branch against the background of the policies of the bank. The banks, particularly those in the public sector, should adopt a practice in regard to transfer prices which is suitably designed to the needs of the times. A method based on the Central Pool concept and weightage on the basis of various priorities should be adopted. This will assist banks in making their branches conform to their overall policies and objectives. The calculation of rates to be charged for transfer price mechanism should be done at quarterly intervals. Whenever a major change affects either the level of the interest rates or their pattern, the transfer price should be revised. Institutions engaged in banking research should do further work on this and similar matters.

Research should be carried out bankwise in order to find out the scope for increasing banks' profitability by increasing the business of their branches.

One of the major organizational weaknesses of the banks in India is the absence of a well designed Management Information System (MIS). The MIS in banks should be organised in such a way as to provide in compact, comprehensive and condensed form all the requisite information necessary for the purposes of policy formulation, performance evaluation, control, economic analysis, etc., Information for the Manager must be regular, prompt and in a form which serves as an effective aid to decision-making and in signalling approaching events and developments. Regular needs of the various parts of an organisation should be taken into consideration.

The MIS for the banking sector has to serve the following purposes :

(i) to ensure from time to time that the requirements prescribed by the law relating to banking are satisfied;

(ii) to ensure satisfactory implementation of the monetary and credit policy;

(iii) to ensure a high level of operational efficiency; and

(iv) to provide information to the general public regarding the working of the banking sector.

The information system should provide for tabulations at State and district levels apart from the All-India level in respect of the following :

(a) Banking Services—
- (i) Deposits,
- (ii) Advances including Bills,
- (iii) Foreign Exchange,
- (iv) Remittances, and
- (v) Other services.

(b) Geographical Spread; and

(c) Operational Efficiency—
- (i) Profitability of different services;
- (ii) Profitability of Branches,
- (iii) Management of Liquid Assets, and
- (iv) Personnel.

At all levels, the information should provide a basis for control, evaluation of performance and development of business.

Instead of the present practice of prescribing the former of returns under the statute, the Reserve Bank should be given powers to prescribe it.

If it is not found feasible for any reason to adopt the suggestion that the Reserve Bank should be given powers to prescribe the formats of statutory return (see previous recommendation), these returns should be amended as recommended by the Inter-departmental Committee on Banking Statistics set up by Reserve Bank.

Different authorities ask for information which varies only slightly in content. There is, therefore, great need at the Reserve Bank of India and in the Government as also in each individual bank, for well-defined points which prescribe what returns may be called for, receive these returns and from where all information is disseminated to various user departments.

It is necessary that each bank has a statistical cell which is responsible for: (i) planning and developing statistical series; (ii) securing timely and accurate statistics in periodical returns, (iii) training branch level staff concerned with this work; (iv) rationalising the data needs and returns; and (v) processing and analysing the trends and patterns in the data. This cell should be attached to the Planning or Development Department and not to any operational department. No new form or return should be prescribed without reference to this cell.

It is necessary that, wherever possible, and particularly in situations where 100 per cent accuracy need not be aimed at, collection of figures by the Reserve Bank of India or the Government is organised on a sample basis. This will have the effect of reducing costs and providing known margins of errors.

Bank should increasingly take to codification of accounts and use high speed machinery for processing the data. The system of ledger keeping should be such that information can be readily called out for different sectors of the economy such as Government-sector companies, private-sector companies, individuals, priority sectors, etc.

The information flow for deposits should be based upon:

(i) A monthly return by all branches of the bank giving total deposits and the number of accounts under various heads and total advances on the lines of Form M-1 with certain conditions.

(ii) An annual return on the lines of Uniform Balance Book (UBB), giving figures for individual accounts. This information could be collected for all branches for all deposit accounts showing a balance of say, Rs. 5,000 or over. For the rest it could be collected only from a sample of branches. A complete picture of deposit distribution among regions, among different classes of ownership, and by size of deposits and patterns of interest rates of deposits can be built up. For the study of the velocity of bank money, summations of debits can be incorporated in the return. Such a return should be obtained once a year The Department of Statistics of the Reserve Bank of India may be requested to evolve a suitable sampling design.

(iii) For quick information as regards changes in deposits by categories, it would suffice to keep the figures of certain large branches under constant observation.

The Uniform Balance Book form needs to be redesignated in a manner which would enable banks to use it as a fan-fold of the balance book. To avoid repeating the fixed information every month, each account could be given a reference number at the time of opening the account. The fixed information in respect of each account should be submitted to the Reserve Bank of India as soon as it is opened and in monthly returns the reference number and the amount outstanding should be supplied. The fixed information can be updated on an early basis.

For advances, the data flow structure should be:

(i) The UBB should be the main form for detailed information and for analytical purposes. In view of the markedly skew distribution of advances by size, it may not be necessary to prepare tabulations on the basis of all entries. A cut-off point can be prescribed while processing the data.

(ii) The frequency of the modified UBB return should be monthly. The processing of data may be done so as to have tabulations based on (a) all entries twice a year (e.g., March and September), (b) on loans and advances of Rs. 10,000 and above for two other quarters of the year (June and December), and (c) monthly for all advances of Rs. 1 lakh and above. In addition, the figures of total advances should be obtained, classified according to district, State and for all-India population groups, etc. Quick feed-back should be arranged for.

(iii) For the purpose of watching the movement of advances against the security of commodities under the selective credit controls, it would suffice if 800 to 900 largest branches relevant to sensitive commodities, i.e., commodities subject to selective credit control, are selected for quick information purposes and tabulations of advances by security are prepared for these selected branches. A purposive sample of branches can be selected to give information for about 80 per cent or more of total advances against each given important security.

(iv) The data collected for priority sectors should not be in different sets of forms for the purposes of different authorities. A common set of forms as part of the UBB should be evolved for each priority sector. These forms should all be received in one department in the Reserve Bank of India from which information can be made available to different agencies.

(v) Banks should also base their information collection of these forms as far as possible and refrain from prescribing additional forms. Though there may be arrangements for feed-back of data on the basis of tabulations of the UBB, banks may need to compile data on advances to priority sectors according to district, region and State.

(vi) With a view to enabling banks to submit purposewise returns without difficulty as well as to underscore the basic change in lending policy, the banks' ledgers should be maintained according to purposes rather than according to the type of account. This change has to be done gradually and would need loose-leaf ledgers.

(vii) For the banking system as a whole, the Reserve Bank of India and for its own purposes each individual bank should constantly keep under review the movement of hypothecated and pledged commodities (in physical terms), particularly the speculative commodities or those brought under selective credit control, on the basis of stock statements submitted by borrowers. Study of variations in these movements will be useful for control as well as analytical purposes.

(viii) The information from the UBB can be used for the purpose of Credit Intelligence Bureau (see Recommendation No. 117) which could conveniently work in co-operation with the organisation which processes the data from the UBB.

(ix) Systems of credit scoring for borrowers from priority sectors should be developed on the basis of the association between personal data relating to the borrowers and the recovery of the loans. The Credit Intelligence Bureau should organise such research.

The information tabulated by the Reserve Bank of India for the purpose of compiling the balance of payments data would be of considerable use to individual banks in judging their performance vis-a-vis the total volume of work handled by all the banks. There should be a system of feed-back of information from Reserve Bank to individual banks, by supplying to each bank consolidated statements showing the various types of exports, imports and other business handled by it as a proportion of the total.

Information on the numbers and amounts of remittances of main types issued and paid by the various branches will be valuable for giving geographical pattern of money flows. The banks can suitably classify the information at the point at which the inter-branch reconciliation is handled and supply it to the authorities.

As regards geographical expansion of branches, each branch should be properly briefed on the type of information it has to supply to the various authorities and its frequency. Standard booklets giving the various proformae and instructions on filling them up should be prepared and supplied to the branches.

The MIS should clearly bring out the inter-relationships between the levels of volume of business, costs and related income so that the managerial decision-making leads to improved profitability. For this purpose, the accounting system of banks in India should be reoriented by the blending of the cost and financial accounting into an integrated system which combines and co-relates the collection, analysis, interpretation and reporting on each of the three aspects, viz., the output, cost and income.

(i) A regular record needs to be maintained at the branch level of all physical outputs, e.g., vouchers, number of drafts handled, etc., according to the type of services besides the data on deposits and advances.

(ii) It is also necessary to organise a sample survey on a regular basis to obtain accurate estimates of unit costs and income for the different types of outputs for representative types of branches. Such estimates of unit costs and income used in conjunction with the record of the physical outputs and the monetary data and of the earnings and expenses relating to the branches will enable evaluation of efficiency and profitability of branches.

(iii) The sample survey should be conducted by a central agency which may be either the Reserve Bank of India or an agency set up by it in collaboration with the scheduled banks—both commercial and co-operative.

(iv) This Agency should prepare the sampling frame for commercial banks and co-operative banks, conduct pilot studies to effect necessary improvements in the sampling frame, collect suitable data and analyse it. The methodology followed by the Study Group on Banking Costs in the survey conducted by it would be useful as a starting point though it can be improved upon in the light of further experience.

(v) The Agency should advise each bank of the costs and income for representative types of branches and also the average costs and income for each of the large and medium sized banks taking into account the details of their branch network. It should also calculate all-India averages for the various costs and income so as to help the authorities in framing their policies in regard to interest rates on deposits and advances and the various charges levied by the banks.

On the basis of quarterly returns received from branches showing the particulars of their outputs, the head office can work out what the total costs for the branch should have been by using the unit cost figures for the different activities supplied by the Agency, for the representative branch type. The ratio of the actual cost at the branch to the estimated costs would be the cost index for the branch. This will provide the management with a fairly good idea of the efficiency at branch level and would enable it to take appropriate corrective action.

Banks can improve profitability through the use of proper techniques in respect of the cash held by themselves at the various branches. As regards holdings of cash, the techniques of inventory control can be applied with suitable modifications. The MIS for this purpose can consist of collecting regular information on holdings of cash by the important branches accounting for say 75 per cent of the cash balances. This together with the data on types and amounts of deposits, advances and remittances would enable appropriate action.

Operational efficiency can be achieved through a proper planning of the year's activities sufficiently in advance and by fixing targets for performance and income, and limits for expenditure. On the basis of business survey reports received from the branches and the prevailing monetary policy, the head office of each bank should formulate its overall performance targets for the year and invite each branch to fix its own share of the overall targets through budgets prepared separately for different types of activities. Budgets may be prepared for the calendar year with a system of monthly reporting. The banks' Boards of Directors should review each month the consolidated budget reports in order to compare the actual working result with targets. The exercise of budgetary control should be made as simple and understandable as possible, and willing co-operation at all management levels should be ensured.

For measuring productivity of the employees, it will be necessary to fix man-hours required (officer and clerical) for various types of jobs. This should be done by the bank itself for internal use, i.e., inter-branch comparison and by the central agency in respect of representative branches for facilitating comparison of inter-bank efficiency. Once this is done, it should be the responsibility of the Personnel Department to evolve methods by which a reduction in unit cost can be brought about.

Compilation of stock statements can be organised at the Reserve Bank of India level, in respect of trade particularly, and time series maintained for different States, in order to provide additional information which is lacking at present and which would be very useful for policy purposes.

Banks can give information on income and expenditure, value added, capital invested, sources and uses, etc., in respect of small scale industries. Banks should be in a position to canvass a simple, short schedule for the annual accounts and balance sheet data for their clients in this sector. The data could be centrally processed by the Reserve Bank of India.

The information needed periodically for judging the impact of a new scheme can be called through a special progress report, the format and the periodically of which would depend upon the type of the scheme and its importance. The information content in such a return should, however, be restricted to the purpose for which it is called. Once this scheme has been accepted and has settled down, the return should be discontinued.

A central institution like the Reserve Bank of India should have a Survey Organisation for conducting large scale surveys from time to time with competent field staff spread over the country. A Standing Committee of Direction could be vested with the function of planning and the content of surveys. It could plan a series of surveys so that each type of survey is repeated every few years. Thus, for instance, surveys on rural debt and investment, urban incomes and savings, small scale industries, etc., could be taken up in rotation.

To develop the feed-back system to serve not only different levels of management in banks but also of the Reserve Bank of India and the Government of India it is necessary to ensure prompt submission of accurately filled up returns by branches and banks and organise computerisation of data processing. A common feed-back system should be based on a common set of tabulations. Any changes in the set should be made only after careful consideration of the various requirements that may have been intimated.

Properly organised data processing centres with adequate mechanical equipment should be created after carefully considering the recommendations proposed to be made in this regard by the NIMB study Group on Information systems. A Committee of Direction or a Steering Committee may be set up to consider the feasibility of the various system, a separate corporation, or a Reserve Bank system.

The recommendations on Management Development for commercial banks can also be applied after suitable modifications to urban co-operative banks. Facilities for training the employees of urban cooperative banks, rural banks, chitties, nidhis and other similar financial institutions should be provided by commercial banks in their training colleges and centres on reasonable payment.

In the field of training co-operative bank personnel and research on problems relating to co-operation, the Vaikunth Mehta National Institute of Co-operative Management should play a role similar to that of the National Institute of Bank Management in relation to commercial banks. The Vaikunth Mehta National Institute should make use of the training methods and techniques developed by the National Institute of Bank Management, the Bankers Training College and similar other institutions while designing the training programmes for the staff of co-operative banks. While formulating a comprehensive scheme for on-the-job training of co-operative bank employees in commercial banks (See Recommendation No. 115), it should be ensured that there is proper co-ordination between the theoretical and practical training.

Banks should maintain proper inventories of their existing personnel on branch, regional and circle level, formulate business plans and, make estimates of the requirements of personnel of different categories. The plans should be reviewed periodically in the light of business development and number of persons actually employed for banks.

The search for suitable talent should not be restricted to the first point of entry in a bank (the clerical level), but should also be extended to attract sufficient number of persons who possess executive potential. With the functional enlargement of banking and the adoption of customer-oriented approach, the need for specialists in banks has increased considerably. Apart from the subordinate staff, the requirements in banks should, therefore, be at three levels, viz., clerical, junior officers and specialists.

For recruitment at clerical and cashier level (excluding typists, telephone operators and other technical personnel) an applicant should at least be a graduate and of an age not exceeding 24 years. Suitable relaxation in the minimum qualifications and the maximum age limit may, however, be allowed in respect of candidates belonging to scheduled castes and tribes; but even in their case the standard should not be lowered below matriculation. Extraneous considerations such as sons of the soil, relations of existing employees, etc., should not be given any weight as they tend to fetter objective selection on the basis of merit. Selection tests should be so devised that graduates with rural background are not barred from getting selected.

The advertisements for recruitments should not only indicate the minimum qualifications for the job but should also describe the range of duties, the service conditions and the future prospects.

The selection process should consist of written tests and interviews. The time lag between the receipt of application and selection should be restricted to a reasonable period of say three months.

A set of written tests should be formulated in the light of the experience gained as a standard examination procedure for clerical candidates aspiring for employment in banks. Tests should judge not only the candidate's ability to perform clerical duties but also evaluate the potential to shoulder the responsibilities of an officer in due course. A carefully designed test of general knowledge covering a wide range of subjects including those relating to rural background should form part of the examination and sufficient option should be given to the candidates for answering questions of their choice, so as to eliminate bias against candidates coming from rural areas.

Interview should follow the written test and should be restricted to those candidates who have passed the written test. The interview should be considered as one of the subjects of examination having about 20 per cent of the aggregate marks. It should be obligatory for a candidate to obtain minimum pass marks for each test (including viva voce) to become eligible for selection. The ranking for placement in the waiting list should depend upon the aggregate marks obtained in written as well as oral examinations.

Opportunities for competing for recruitment at Junior Officers' level should be kept open to the existing staff. The proportion for internal promotions and recruitment from open market should be two to one for the present, subject to review after a few years.

The minimum qualification for the junior officers' post should be graduation with high second division marks (over 55 per cent) and the maximum age limit should be 27 years. The recruitment should be open to graduates in any subject but preference should be given to those holding degrees in commerce, economics and business administration by allotting to them specified additional marks in the selection test. For the candidates who are already in the employment of banks, the age limit should be relaxed by three years. Outside candidates belonging to scheduled castes and scheduled tribes should also be allowed relaxation in the age limit by the same number of years.

The selection procedure for junior officers, as in the case of clerical staff, should consist of a written test and interview with accent on testing initiative and enterprise, general intelligence and logical thinking. Standard tests for selecting officer staff should be evolved in the light of experience gained.

As the major portion of the banking industry is now in the public sector, there should be a common agency for recruitment of staff for these banks both at the clerical and junior officers' level. This agency could be named the 'National Banking Service Commission'. To vest it with proper authority, it may have to be created statutorily. The provisions for its membership, functions, jurisdiction, etc., may be on the lines of those for the Union Public Service Commission.

The National Banking Service Commission may conduct examinations at regional levels for clerical staff and an all-India competitive examination for junior officers' cadre. Waiting lists of selected candidates current for a specified period, say two years, may be prepared and allotment may be made to different banks according to their requirements. The allotment in the case of junior officers may be on all-India basis and that in the case of clerical staff on regional basis. Before the Commission can start functioning effectively, salaries and other emoluments of the staff of the National Banks at various levels will have to be standardised and this work should be taken up in right earnest by the Government of India. Expenses of the Commission should be shared by the National Banks.

The co-operative banks have also to adopt a systematic recruitment policy in order to improve the quality of their staff. They should avail of the services of the National Banking Service Commission on mutually agreed terms. Commercial banks in the private sector desiring to make use of the services of the Commission should be able to do so on mutually agreed terms.

Recruitment of specialists may be made as and when required through the National Banking Service Commission, which may prescribe appropriate eligibility standards, procedures and test for the purpose. To provide adequate career development opportunities to these categories of employees, there should be a common pool for each type of specialists for all the National Banks and the incumbents may be transferable from one bank to another.

For judging the ability of employees for promotion, banks should maintain proper service records and introduce scientific procedures for performance appraisal. Standard forms and methods should be devised for evaluating job performance of varicus categories of bank employees. The appraisal should bring out with clarity the strengths and weaknesses of the employee which should be discussed with him in a post-appraisal interview in order to give him an opportunity for self development. The appraisal reports together with job analysis should be used for proper placement of personnel in post suited to their skills, interests and abilities.

It is necessary for banks to formulate specific programmes for grooming suitable people to occupy executive posts. Maintenance of 'Management Chart' will be helpful in this regard.

All posts below the junior officer's level should be filled in by promotions on the basis of seniority-cum-merit as revealed by the appraisal reports without any written examination and/or interview. However, for filling in the posts of junior officers reserved for internal promotions, a qualifying examination should be conducted at various centres by the National Banking Service Commission for the National Banks. The co-operative banks should also arrive at an arrangement with the National Banking Service Commission for conducting a qualifying examination for their staff. Banks in the private sector may either hold their own examinations or make an arrangement with that Commission in this regard. The employees who have completed at least five years' service in the clerical cadre with satisfactory performance record irrespective of their age, should be allowed to appear for the qualifying examination. Those who pass the examination should be ranked on the basis of seniority for the purpose of promotion. The maximum number of chances to be allowed to an employee to appear for these tests should be three.

Once an employee has either been selected or promoted as a junior officer, he may be allowed to reach the middle management level, without further screening, on the basis of seniority-cum-ability. There should, however, be a selection grade for posts carrying senior executive responsibility. Post which involve control over branches in a region or taking policy decisions or which carry at the beginning of the scale total emoluments (including perquisites) of Rs. 2,000 and above, may be covered by the selection grade. For the National Banks the selection may be made by the National Banking Service Commission. The candidates selected should be transferable from one national bank to another.

A clerical employee after recruitment should be given induction training for a short period. He should then receive a week's training in a particular banking service on the basis of programmed learning material. The employee should, thereafter, work in a branch on that particular desk for six months. This process should be repeated in regard to other banking services so that the employee works on all the different desks in a branch in about 4 to 5 years.

The direct recruits to the junior officers' cadre should also be given induction training and on-the-job training with the help of programmed learning material, but the duration of their training period should be about one year. All junior officers (internal promotees as well as direct recruits) after about three years' working in that capacity should be given training in a general banking course designed to equip them to discharge the duties of accountant/Branch Manager. They should also be trained in short duration specialised courses e.g., finance to priority sectors, organisation and methods, management of human resources, etc. Their entire training on the above lines should be completed with 5 years from the date of their becoming junior officers.

Training should be an integral part of the general organisational process and there should be a proper link between training and overall personnel policies. Selection of employees for training should be made on the basis of well-planned policies of career development and executive succession. A person trained in a specialised aspect of banking should be given an opportunity to make use of the knowledge and skill gained by posting him in an appropriate position.

The banks which do not have adequate facilities for training their officers and other staff should make the necessary arrangements by extending the scope of the existing training centres and colleges and/or by opening new colleges and centres. They should also make sufficient arrangements for infrastructure. For proper co-ordination of the training programme; training centres should work as wings of the training colleges of the respective banks. Small banks may not, however, be in a position to afford their own training colleges or centres. Such banks in contiguous areas should join together and establish joint colleges. Where, however, a small bank still has a difficulty in imparting training to its staff, larger banks should afford the necessary facility in their staff training colleges and centres. The officers of small banks should also participate in courses conducted by the National Institute of Bank Management and the Bankers Training College. At a later stage, when the banks adopt uniform procedures and methods, it may be desirable to organise training colleges and centres on a regional basis with collaboration of the concerned banks rather than each bank having its own college.

The faculty of the training colleges and centres of commercial banks should be strengthened. The principals of colleges should be chosen from experienced but dynamic senior executives with a penchant for development work. About 50 per cent of the total strength of tutors should remain in the training colleges on a permanent basis and the others should be taken on a deputation basis. The salary scales and promotion potentialities in the colleges will have to be suitably revised to make this suggestion workable. Every endeavour will, however, have to be made to ensure that the tutors keep themselves in touch with current banking problems and developments. Care should also be taken to see that those who go back to the operational work in the bank are not effected adversely in their prospects for promotion, merely because of their deputation to the colleges. Experience in the college should be considered as a point in favour of the concerned employee.

In view of the magnitude of the problem of training bank staff, the National Institute of Bank Management should undertake the task of planning, co-ordinating and directing the training programme. It should work on the lines of a University and the colleges of all commercial banks as well as the Bankers Training College should be its constituent units. To ensure proper co-ordination and synthesis of various views on matters pertaining to the planning and execution of training, a body on the lines of Academic Council of a University comprising the representatives of the Reserve Bank of India, National Institute of Bank Management, Bankers Training College, other constituent colleges and experts in various fields connected with training may be constituted by the National Institute of Bank Management. A representative of the Institute should also be on the Managing Committee of each constituent college. Once the above arrangements come into effect and the provision of necessary physical facilities is made by the banks, the training programme should be so planned and implemented that, within a period of three years or so, the entire backlog of training the bank staff is cleared and adequate arrangements are made to meet the current training needs.

Apart from planning, co-ordination and directing the training programme, the National Institute of Bank Management should design training courses and teaching material. The training of senior officers should also be undertaken by the Institute. In such training, the emphasis should be on managerial aspects rather than on banking techniques. The Institute should also continue its research and consultancy work. It should further consider conducting, in due course, diploma, degree and post-graduate courses in banking for the bank employees.

The internal set-up of National Institute of Bank Management should be strengthened by having a good admixture of the academic personnel and bankers with experience in commercial and central banking. These bankers should be invited to serve on the faculty as full-time members for the periods of three to five years, so that their experience is fully drawn on in the operation of the Institute's programme.

In addition to providing training facilities to the Reserve Bank Officers, the functions of the Bankers Training College should continue to be to train bank officers in specialised courses. The College should also carry on the work of designing new courses, revising existing courses and that of imparting training to trainers in collaboration with the National Institute of Bank Management. By virtue of its special position, the Bankers Training College should function as the most important constituent college of National

Institute of Bank Management.

The C.A.I.I.B. examination should be redesigned by changing the syllabus suitably so as to make it more practical. Banks should run evening or morning teaching programmes at their training colleges and centres and at some of their branches for preparing their employees for these examinations, and, for this purppse, arrangements should be made for designing teaching courses and preparation of suitable teaching material. In these and other similar matters, there should be a close collaboration between the Indian Institute of Bankers and the National Institute of Bank Management.

For building up of an efficient professional cadre in the banking industry, it is necessary to introduce a deliberate policy of worker participation. At different levels of the organisation and for important segments of activities, informal committees should be constituted in which the officials should be encouraged to participate, to deal with matters relating to the developmental activities, performance targets and operating efficiency.

Banks should offer incentives in the form of grant of honoraria to employees who acquire knowledge of languages other than their mother tongue.

There is need for increasing the element of responsibility in a larger number of jobs and the National Institute of Bank Management should conduct research in this subject for issuing suitable guidelines to banks. It is also necessary for bank managements to eliminate as far as possible, irritants arising from status consciousness as they act as impediments in proper co-operation and understanding.

Banks should organise a separate department under a senior executive qualified to handle personnel matters for proper formulation of management development programme and its effective implementation with functions as described in paragraphs 14.61 and 14.62. Committees should also be formed at top management level to direct the programmes of management development.

Early steps should be taken for reorganising the national banks into two or three all-India banks and six other banks each specialising in developing banking services in a broad region, on the lines described in paragraph 15.36. There should be a time-bound programme for mergers or amalgamations of the Indian commercial banks in the private sector which have not shown good performance.

There should be no slowing down of the rate of opening new branches, but the new branches of the national banks should be in areas selected on the basis of the principles indicated in paragraph 15.36. Thus, the constituent bank of the proposed regional banks should be asked to open branches within the area of the States in which the regional bank is expected to operate. An All-India bank should concentrate on opening branches at district centres or large towns, whenever there is need for new branches in these centres.

Wherever there are too many branches of the national banks in a restricted area, the number should be reduced. The banks, whose branches are closed down, on account of such rationalisation, should utilise the release of manpower in opening branches in areas allotted to them, particularly in unbanked areas. This may require some inter-bank exchange of personnel.

In metropolitan cities, both the all-India and the regional banks should be allowed to open branches, so that every bank can have a reasonable share of the business in these centres.

At the end of 10 years from the commencement of the re-organised banks, there should be a comprehensive review of the manner in which these banks have worked, the size which they have attained and the further organisational changes that will be necessary in the light of the future development of these banks.

The organisational set-up of the restructured National banks should be on the following lines :

(a) Decentralisation of work at branch offices depending on the size to give the Branch Manager sufficient time to devote attention to planning, co-ordination, control, training, etc.

(b) Setting up of Zonal Offices for control and guidanee of 200 to 300 branches depending on factors like transportation and communication. This should be backed up by delegation of discretionary powers to the zonal and divisional managers.

(c) Formation of 'Areas' for purposes of collection and processing of statistical data.

(d) The Head Office should do planning and budgeting for the bank as a whole and attend to essential central office functions.

(e) The top executives should be free to assess matters relating to policy and should divest themselves of routine matters by delegating proper powers.

A standing committee of the Chairman of the reorganised national banks should be established for the purpose of securing co-ordination of the regular banking activities of these banks.

This Committee should function as an advisory body to the policy-making authority.

An important function of the Committee of national banks' Chairmen would be the supervision and control of the Lead Bank's system.

The foreign banks may be allowed to continue as at present as they have only a limited geographical and functional spread.

Unless there are some exceptional circumstances, it is not necessary for the present to establish new commercial banks either as independent units or subsidiaries of the existing banks except rural subsidiary banks mentioned in Chapter 8.

Merchant banking institutions are needed in India to offer the following types of services :

(a) Syndication, financing and promotion of Indian projects,

(b) Investment, management and advisory services to medium and small savers and to provident funds, pension funds and trusts of various types.

Initially, there could be four merchant banking institutions located at Bombay, Calcutta, Madras and New Delhi set up by the commercial banks and specialised financial institutions. These merchant banking institutions can later set up branches at other important centres.

Subject to proper safeguards, other agencies also may be allowed to set up merchant banking institutions.

Under the present circumstances, merchant banking institutions need not take up acceptance and discounting business because commercial banks are well in a position to do this business. When the bill market is sufficiently developed, merchant banks may also enter it; also specialised acceptance and discount houses may be formed as joint stock companies for this business as well as for functioning as a money market intermediary. These institutions should work under the conditions prescribed by the Reserve Bank.

The machinery for providing export credit is adequate and hence there is no justification for the creation of an Export-Import Bank. The present credit arrangements, however, need improvements in the following respects :

(a) Arrangements should be made to provide exchange cover on reasonable terms in respect of exports made on long-term deferred payment basis.

(b) Export credit facilities at inland centres in the country.

(c) Co-ordination between all export financing institutions should be ensured through Consultative Groups and Informal Groups of I.D.B.I.

(d) For pooling information on foreign markets, creditworthiness of foreign importers, etc., and arranging it systematically, IDBI should obtain information, keep it up-to-date and make it available to commercial banks and others.

In view of the satisfactory performance of the existing financial institutions in the field of financing of small scale industries and small business and of the costs involved in raising resources for a specialised institution for the purpose, there is no need either to set up a new specialised financing institution or for some commercial banks to specialise in making credit to these sectors.

Resources of the existing institutions should be increased, their technical personnel should be improved and conditions be created whereby small industrial units can obtain loans from the organised banking system.

Credit may be required by consumers for meeting medical, educational and other urgent expenses and the purchase of durable consumer goods. The health and educational insurance and other welfare schemes of the Government should provide for medical, educational and other contingent expenses. For credit for durable consumer goods and consumer consultancy services public limited companies may be formed in the public or private sector.

From the point of view of regulation, the institutions to be set up should be brought under the control of the Reserve Bank of India or any other agency which might be set up for the purpose. It will be useful to have a uniform legislation for the country as a whole with allowances for regional characteristics insofar as the terms and conditions of consumer finance are concerned.

Though there is scope for mobilising and institutionalising savings, especially in rural areas, an entirely new organisation of specialised savings banks need not be created.

A two-tier system of housing finance should be created with apex housing finance institution at the national level and local housing finance institutions at the district or regional level sponsored by the local community with active encouragement of central finance institution.

The primary function of local institutions should be to attract savings linked to provision of credit for construction or purchase of houses and that of the apex institution should be to encourage, supervise and provide temporary finance to local institutions.

Either the Housing and Urban Development Corporation may be vested with the functions of the central institution in which case it will have to shed its existing non-financial activities, or the central agency should be sponsored by the Reserve Bank of India, which may create a special housing fund to assist the proposed housing finance system.

Wherever feasible, Housing Boards and Nidhis may be vested with the functions of the proposed local or regional institutions.

Co-operative Housing Societies should be strengthened particularly with a view of mobilising resources from members and eliminating malpractices. An apex co operative finance should be set up in each state to refinance affiliated primary societies all over the State.

Commercial banks may give short and medium-term credit to the builders in order to enable them to undertake mass housing construction programmes. Prospective purchasers of houses may borrow from the specialised institutions to purchase houses from the builders, who in turn can repay their loans to commercial banks.

To the extent their administrative and personnel resources permit commercial banks may also give credit to individuals desiring to own or construct houses.

The central agency proposed in Recommendation No. 238 should extend refinance facility to apex co-operative societies as well as to commercial banks extending housing loans.

DIC and general insurance institutions should devise a scheme to guarantee housing loans.

Steps should be taken to create and develop a secondary mortgage market and impart liquidity to housing loan.

As the financial and personnel rosources in India are limited, specialised financial institutions should be created only if there is a clearly identified credit gap which, for some reason or the other, cannot be filled by the existing financing institutions.

NBFIs should be regulated with a view to :

(a) safeguarding the depositors interest;

(b) creating conditions for the growth of dynamic and forward looking NBFIs; and

(c) ensuring effective implementation of monetary policy.

To facilitate regulation, the NBFIs should be given inducements to form themselves into corporate bodies.

For purposes of regulation, NBFIs should, in general, be classified into two categories, viz., 'approved' and 'non-approved'. While a specified minimum degree of control may be exercised on all NBFIs, the 'approved' ones which will be only corporate bodies and which satisfy certain additional requirements of the regulating authority should be accorded a special and favourable treatment such as refinance from the banking system, coverage of their loans under the Credit Guarantee Scheme and extension of Deposit Insurance Corporation. Institutions in each category will be 'approved' on the basis of the judgement of the regulating authority regarding the quality and scope of their operations.

Reserve Bank or the regulating authority set up for the purpose will have to strengthen and build up its inspecting machinery so that these institutions can be inspected at least on a sample basis.

The existence of a large number of small non-corporate bodies is a weak link in the chain of hire-purchase finance institutions. In order to strengthen the financial position of these agencies, facilitate regulation, bring down the level of finance charges, the policy objective should be to institutionalise hire-purchase credit and encourage formation of strong units.

All hire-purchase finance units should compulsorily be licensed and the licensing authority should be given powers to revoke the license in case it is satisfied that the operations of a particular unit are unsatisfactory.

Hire purchase financiers should be required to indicate clearly the true rate of interest along with the flat rate of finance charges.

In order to induce smaller units to organise themselves into bigger ones, the permissible equity-debt ratio and liquidity ratio should be so prescribed that they are higher for small units and lower for bigger units.

Benefit of Credit Guarantee Scheme for small borrowers should be extended to other institutions like non-scheduled commercial banks, urban co-operative banks and hire-purchase finance companies in appropriate cases.

The scheme of classification of NBFIs into 'approved' and 'non-approved' should be applied to hire-purchase finance institutions.

Commercial banks may enter hire-purchase credit business by having special departments or by setting up subsidiaries.

It would be desirable for leading banks to form a few hire-purchase finance companies in participation and acting together particularly in the Eastern region where this form of credit is not institutionalised. This will require amendment of Section 19 of Banking Regulation Act so that banks will be enabled to promote subsidiary hire-purchase companies.

Small local commercial banks and urban co-operatives should take more interest in hire-purchase credit as their structure and intimate knowledge of local conditions make them specially suited for this form of credit.

In the immediate future there may not be scope for setting up new unit trusts and investment companies. They should be encouraged when suitable conditions exist in the capital market.

The following criteria may be laid down for identifying a genuine investment company :

(a) it should have an independent management and investment policy; (b) it should have a diversified investment portfolio both in terms of companies and groups of companies; (c) it should have adequate public participation in its share capital and it should ensure listing of its shares on the stock exchange; (d) a major portion of its funds should be invested in shares, stocks and bonds and other securities; (e) it should regularly distribute not less than a specified proportion of its net income to its members. The investment companies which satisfy the above criteria can play useful role in the economy. Hence, Government should consider the question of exempting such companies from intercorporate tax.

Although the number of genuine investment companies at present is small and hence no separate machinery is required to regulate them, it would be useful to pass legislation with the object of protecting the interests of members of these companies The proposed legislation should be modelled on the lines of the Investment Companies Act of U.S.A. and also incorporate provisions for bidding investment companies from doing certain types of business such as dealing in real estate.

No industrial or trading company should be permitted in any event to hold shares in an investment company.

To ensure independent management policy, Government should have powers to appoint a nominee on the board of directors of a genuine investment company in appropriate cases.

An examination of chit fund business from various aspects and the effect of the institutions on the economy such as the safety of funds of chit fund subscribers, shows the need for measures to regulate chit funds.

It is essential to have a uniform chit fund legislation applicable to the whole country. Depending upon the Constitutional position, whether chit funds come under the Union List, Concurrent List or the State List, either an All-India Chit Fund Act may be enacted or a model law may be prepared for adoption by all the States. It will be desirable to provide in the legislation that only public limited companies can run chit funds.

Pending such uniform legislation, as an interim measure, existing State laws regulating chit funds registered within the State should be made applicable to their branches in States having no legislation.

As a measure towards introducing discipline in the chit business, it will be useful for commercial banks to run chit funds subject to proper safeguards as formulated by the Reserve Bank of India.

The State Governments may, wherever they think appropriate, consider starting chit funds at strategic places as model foremen with the object of offering effective competition to private chit funds and thus acting as a disciplining factor.

The ultimate solution to the problem created by chit funds is for commercial banks to provide saving and lending schemes which can take the place of chit funds without the weaknesses and disadvantages associated with chit funds.

In the interest of the public and of those who participate in Prize Chit Schemes, which are really a form of lottery, the offence under section 294A of the Indian Penal Code should be made a cognisable one. Also the Registrar of Chit Funds should be authorised to take note of any 'Prize Chit' that may be run and may either himself initiate action against those responsible or request the police to do so.

'Finance Corporations' are para-banking institutions which accept deposits from the public and make loans and advances. It is necessary to regulate their activities on the same lines as is in the case of commercial banks.

For safeguarding the interests of the depositors and to utilise the advantage of local knowledge of the 'finance corporations' for country's benefit :

(a) no institution of the type may be allowed to work without a licence from the monetary authorities ; (b) a ratio may be prescribed between the owned funds of an institution and its deposit liabilities; (c) liquidity ratio may be prescribed for them which may, however, be lower than that in the case of commercial banks; (d) periodical inspections of the 'corporations' may be undertaken on a sample basis by the regulating authority; (e) a ceiling on interest rates on deposits may be prescribed which may, however, be higher than that prescribed for commercial banks; (f) since they are not bodies incorporated under the Indian Companies Act, they should not be allowed to use the word 'corporations' in their names; and (g) 'Finance Corporations', loan companies finance companies, etc., may be subjected to scheme of classification into 'approved' and 'non-approved'.

The solution to the problem created by the operations of 'finance corporations' and other similar institutions should ultimately be sought in commercial banks offering effective competition to them in their lending business.

As nidhis are performing useful functions through their operations in the localities where they operate, growth should be encouraged.

To safeguard the depositors' interest and to make these institutions more useful to the economy—(a) they may be licensed by the Reserve Bank or such other regulating authority as may be set up for the purpose; (b) a minimum level of liquidity ratio may be fixed which may, however, be lower than that of commercial banks; (c) a minimum amount for paid-up capital and reserves may be prescribed and every nidhi should allocate a certain specified proportion of its profits to reserves; and (d) periodical inspection may be conducted by the regulating authority.

While these regulations may be made applicable to all the nidhis, incentives may be offered to those among them which satisfy certain requirements. For this purpose, nidhis may be classified, like other NBFIs, into two categories, viz., 'approved' and 'non-approved'. Besides according to the advantages like the availability of refinance, guaranteeing of loans and insurance of deposits to approved nidhis, Government may also consider extending to the depositors of these nidhis the same tax concessions as are available to the depositors of the banks.

For meaningful analysis of the operations of NBFIs and their regulation, statistics relating to the different aspects of their working should be collected and processed in a systematic manner.

Pending the Constitutional amendment suggested in Recommendation No. 309, a model legislation should be drafted for adoption by all States to regulate the activities of those indigenous bankers who rely entirely on bank credit as external source of finance for the conduct of their business.

The best way to control the business of indigenous bankers would be through commercial banks. The Reserve Bank of India should exercise indirect influence over the business of indigenous bankers through the medium of commercial banks by laying down guidelines for their dealings with indigenous bankers. The Reserve Bank of India should review from time to time whether commercial bank financing in respect of multani hundi business is in accordance with the guidelines laid down by it.

Commercial banks should call for regular returns from indigenous bankers and require them to maintain adequate internal inspection procedures and be subject to regular outside audit.

The requirements which the indigenous bankers should fulfil in order to be entitled to discounting facilities commercial banks are: (a) such indigenous bankers should not engage themselves in trading activity; (b) an indigenous banker should have Rs. 1 lakh as the minimum owned resources. In turn, there should be a ceiling on the total discounting limits which should be fixed as a multiple, say, 5 times of the owned funds of each indigenous banker; (c) the indigenous banker has to agree to maintain books of account in the usual recognised manner and have them annually audited and certified by a recognised firm of auditors; (d) a summary statement of the volume and nature of business (in the form indicated in Annexure 18.1 to Chapter 18) should be furnished annually by each indigenous banker to the Reserve Bank. The Reserve Bank and the commercial banks should review annually the activity of indigenous bankers in order to ensure that the advances granted by them are for socially desirable purposes; (e) as far as possible, indigenous bankers should not be encouraged to borrow from more than one bank; (f) indigenous bankers should preferably be members of an association.

At present the volume of hundis discounted by the commercial banks is not so large as to warrant separate refinancing facilities; and the refinancing requirements of commercial banks can easily be met from the facilities that are customarily given to them. The matter could be reconsidered if the volume of this business assumes significant proportion.

Some understanding should be reached between the commercial banks and the indigenous bankers regarding the level of interest rates that such bankers should charge on advances to their customers. It should be made incumbent on commercial banks to see that no indigenous banker availing himself of bank credit facilities charges interest rates higher than those agreed upon.

The Reserve Bank should periodically indicate the interest spread considered adequate for this business. Further, where the banks are satisfied that the lending by the indigenous bankers is for priority sectors, they should charge a reasonable discount rate and also ensure that the indigenous bankers pass on the benefit to the borrowers.

There is a good case for commercial banks re-examining the policy of charging the high rates on advances to multanis, from various aspects such as liquidity, cost and end-use of such credit and reconsidering whether there is a case for reducing the discount rate even though such advances are classified as unsecured. Further, commercial banks should make every effort to verify on a random basis the rates charged by the indigenous bankers to the ultimate borrowers.

A code of conduct should be formulated for the operations of indigenous bankers. Such bankers as are found to be indulging in malpractices should not be allowed any further bank accommodation.

It should be made mandatory for the indigenous banker to disclose the terms of loan transactions to the customer fully. Incidental charges such as brokerage and charity which vary from region to region should be standardised. In addition to indicating the amount of the loan and the interest, the indigenous banker should be required to express the interest and other charges, if any, in terms of the effective rate per cent per annum. The legislation referred to in Recommendation No. 279 should impose penalties for charges in excess of the standardised ones or for failure to disclose the full terms to the customers and in cases of flagrant violation, the authorities should have the power to suspend the licences of indigenous bankers.

A systematic evaluation of the financial statements of indigenous bankers should be undertaken by commercial banks.

Also commercial banks should satisfy themselves at least on a random basis that the credit has been used for the purpose for which it was given.

Once the present approach of commercial banks to credit analysis of indigenous hundi business is replaced by systematic credit analysis, the flow of assistance from commercial banks to the indigenous bankers should be steady and uninterrupted.

Multani bills need not be accorded the status of liquid assets under Section 24 of the Banking Regulation Act.

It may be desirable to gradually raise the maximum value of multani hundi from Rs. 5,000 to Rs. 10,000 and in the case of creditworthy borrowers up to Rs. 25,000 to facilitate increasing amounts of indigenous banking funds being channelled to meet the working capital requirements of small scale industries.

It is necessary to codify the practices and usages applicable to hundis and bring such indigenous negotiable instruments within the framework of the codified law. Standard forms of Darshani (Sight) and Muddati (Usance) types of hundis should also be drawn up.

Payments by Darshani Hundi may be recognised as an eligible mode of payment under Section 40A (3) of the Income Tax Act.

With their banking acumen and traditional skills the more efficient of the indigenous bankers could transform themselves into discount and acceptance houses provided they adopt to the corporate form of organisation.

The definition of 'Banking' should cover acceptance of all forms of deposits, independent of their mode or withdrawal.

The purpose for which deposits are accepted by a person from the public should not be relevant for the definition of 'banking', though it is relevant while considering the scheme of banking regulation.

The expression "from the public" should be clarified as covering also the acceptance of deposits by a body from its member or shareholders.

The expression 'deposit' should be defined as including also borrowings by way of loans, but excluding :

(i) borrowings by companies or other corporate bodies by way of debentures; and

(ii) borrowings from Governments, banks, financial institutions established by statute, and any other financial institution that may be notified by the Central Government.

'Banking' should be defined as the acceptance of deposits of money from the public. Further, 'deposit' for the purpose of this definition should be statutorily clarified to include borrowings by way of loans, but it should exclude :

(a) borrowings by companies or other corporate bodies by way of debentures, and

(b) borrowings from Governments, banks, financial institutions established by statute, and any other financial institution that may be notified by the Central Government. The expression "from the public" should also be statutorily classified to include also acceptance of deposits by a body from its members or shareholders. Such a definition of 'banking' should not affect or cover :

(i) casual or stray transactions of borrowings as they are not to be regarded as "acceptance of deposits of money from the public",

(ii) payments by the persons who are, or who may be under an obligation to the person accepting the payment, such as security deposits, or advance payments intended for adjustment towards supply of goods or service by the person receiving such payments,

(iii) indebtedness arising on account of particular relationships, such as principal and agent, doctor and patient, etc.,

(iv) every indebtedness, but only a debt created as a loan or deposit.

Undertakings which do 'banking' can be broadly classified, on the basis of the forms of banking they do, into those :

(i) accepting chequeable deposit;

(ii) accepting non-chequeable deposits for the purpose of lending or investment; and

(iii) accepting non-chequeable deposits for financing their own business such as manufacture or trade.

For the purpose of regulation, concerns doing (i) above may be termed as 'banks' those doing (ii) above as 'financing institutions' and those engaged in (iii) above as 'deposit receiving institution' (See Chart 19.1). The scheme of the regulation that should apply to these categories of banking undertakings should take note of the differences in the legal status and the objectives of the concerns.

Private limited companies accepting 'non-chequeable deposits' from their shareholders, companies taking such deposits from their partners need not be brought within the scope of the banking regulation connected with the acceptance of such deposits.

The reference to 'cheque' in section 49A of the Banking Regulation Act, 1949, should be substituted by the expression "cheque or other negotiable instrument payable on demand". The expressions 'deposit' and 'from the public' should also be given, for the purpose of this section, the meaning given to them in the definition of 'banking'.

It is only those concerns that are authorised to

accept chequeable deposits which should be allowed to accept demand and near demand deposits from the public.

It is only institutions which are authorised to carry on all forms of banking, that is, the acceptance of all kinds of deposits including chequeable deposits, that should be required and permitted to use as part of their business names the expression 'bank', 'banker' or banking', and others, including other undertakings carrying on other kinds of 'banking', should be precluded from using such terms as part of their business names.

For the effective implementation of the regulation of the business of accepting chequeable deposits, the carrying on of such business should be allowed to be undertaken only by corporate bodies. Non-corporate entities, such as firms and individuals, which are already doing such business should be allowed a reasonable time within which they could either bring their undertakings under corporate ownership and get the licence to carry on such business, or eschew such business. A period of two years should be allowed for this purpose from the date such a requirement is made statutory. Indigenous bankers who are accepting deposits withdrawable by hundis should be required either to incorporate their undertakings and get the licence from the Reserve Bank, or to eschew the acceptance of 'chequeable deposits', within the prescribed time.

Banks could be classified, as follows, on the basis of their legal status :

(i) banking corporations set up under separate Acts of Parliament and which are wholly or substantially owned by the Central Government directly or indirectly (national banks);

(ii) co-operative societies accepting chequeable deposits and which are registered under the Co-operative Societies Acts of the States (co-operative banks);

(iii) co-operative banks, or subsidiaries of national banks or of 'other banks' established as 'rural banks';

(iv) 'Companies' authorised to accept chequeable deposits ('other banks').

Government may consider what type of regulation is necessary to govern Post Office Savings Banks.

As things stand, the best way of reconciling the claims of the Central and the States' jurisdictions in regard to co-operative societies doing banking is to make them subject to banking regulation in matters which will not encroach on the States' jurisdiction. The regulation of persons carrying on the business of banking and providing credit and others who merely provide credit without undertaking any form of banking is now the concern of different jurisdictions, the responsibility for the former rests with the Union, and the responsibilities for the latter rests with the States. For economic and also operational reasons, it is not desirable to have such divided jurisdiction or dual jurisdiction over those providing credit. Hence, the jurisdiction to regulate money-lenders and money lending and also co-operative credit agencies should be transferred either to the Union List or to the Concurrent List, by a constitutional amendment.

The scheme of rural banks envisages provisions to facilitate the conversion of good primary credit societies at the primary level into rural banks which may continue to be in the co-operative structure and may be called "rural co-operative banks". It also visualises the setting up of new banking undertakings, in rural areas, as subsidiaries of commercial banks called 'rural subsidiary banks'. To ensure unified policy regarding their development and a meaningful comparison of their performance and effectiveness, these banks should come (except for the differences inherent in the organisational pattern relating to their set-up) under one set of common regulations relating to authorised business and other matters as specified later. Moreover, in its application to rural banks, banking regulation should be appropriately modified. This requires enabling and supporting legislation both of the Centre and of the States; Central legislation would suffice on the implementation of our recommendation to confer on the Union the power to legislate on matters relating to the incorporation, regulation and winding up of co-operative credit societies. The legislative provisions relating to rural banks may have to comprise those necessary :

(a) to facilitate the selection of good primary credit societies as rural banks;

(b) to enable the setting up of fresh units as subsidiaries of commercial banks and other incidental matters;

(c) to provide for conversion of category (a) into (b) and vice versa;

(d) to ensure that rural (of both categories) function effectively; and

(e) other matters that require attention in relation to the above.

While the Union can provide for most of the matters specified above, there may have to be complementary State legislation in certain matters, especially (c) above. In certain matters, such as the concessions in relation to payment of stamp duty, registration charges, etc., to be made available to 'rural subsidiary banks', and in certain other respects, it may be necessary for the States to make appropriate provisions. The matters which the Union could provide for should become a part of banking legislation. The necessary changes to the Co-operative Laws may be effected by the States by passing appropriate legislation.

Rural banks should be set up in a manner that would provide for them the benefits that accrue to co-operatives, while avoiding their drawbacks. This implies that a separate statutory framework should be provided for the formation of 'rural subsidiary banks'.

A rural bank may be defined as a notified co-operative bank, or a licensed subsidiary bank of a commercial bank, functioning or set up in a rural area for the purpose of providing banking and credit facilities in that area. The definition of 'rural area' should be on the basis of well-accepted criteria, such as, the Census classification. Where the area in which a rural bank has been set up is subsequently considered as non-rural, this should not per se affect the powers, functions and provisions applicable to such rural banks. The actual area of operation may be specified by the Reserve Bank taking into account the local conditions. The determination of the areas where rural banks are to be set up, and whether any primary credit society, existing or proposed, should be notified as a 'rural bank' in any area or a commercial bank should start a subsidiary (and if so, the particular commercial bank which should be given this responsibility) may be left to the assessment of the Reserve Bank. The Reserve Bank may from time to time set out the principles it follows for such determination.

'The rural subsidiary banks should be registered by the Reserve Bank rather than by the Registrar of Companies. The functions which the Registrar of Companies at present performs as regards companies could be entrusted to the Reserve Bank as regards 'rural subsidiary banks'. For this purpose, the Reserve Bank may have to open a branch or branches in each State which could inter alia act as the registering authority for such rural banks.

Where a promoting commercial bank decides to sever its links with the 'rural subsidiary bank', then another commercial bank could take the place, and perform the functions, of the promoting bank. It should also be possible, in appropriate cases, for a 'rural subsidiary bank'. It should also be possible, in appropriate cases, for a 'rural subsidiary bank' to become a 'rural co-operative bank'. The Reserve Bank may also initiate action for the substitution of a promoting bank, or for conversion of a 'rural subsidiary bank' into a 'rural co-operative bank' suo motu when it considers that such action is necessary in the interest of banking development.

It is necessary that a simple procedure is evolved for expeditiously dealing with the applications for licences from 'rural subsidiary banks' and that as far as possible the licences are not refused except on substantial grounds.

It is necessary that the Reserve Bank should draw certain minimum and objective criteria that the primary credit societies should be required to fulfil. If, on a prima facie assessment, the Reserve Bank is of the view that these criteria are fulfilled, then the Bank should notify the primary credit societies fulfilling such criteria as 'rural co-operative banks'. If, at any time, the Reserve Bank is of the view that the affairs of any such 'rural co-operative bank' are not being conducted on healthy and sound lines, then it should be in order for the Reserve Bank to denotify it from the list of 'rural co-operative banks' and to ask any commercial bank to start a 'rural subsidiary bank' in the area earlier served by a 'rural co-operative bank'.

It is desirable to provide for primary co-operative credit societies, which wish to do so, to merge with the 'rural subsidiary banks'. The provisions that could be thought of may be somewhat on the lines of Section 44A of the Banking Regulation Act, 1949, and the Reserve Bank should be given the necessary powers to sanction the schemes of amalgamation.

Where a primary credit society which fulfils the eligibility standards of the Reserve Bank to be classified as 'rural co-operative bank' wishes to come under the umbrella of a commercial bank, subject to the fulfilment of conditions, such rural banks should be removed from the Register of Co-operative Societies maintained by the Registrar of Co-operative Societies and should be included in the Register of Rural Subsidiary Banks maintained by the Reserve Bank. It would be necessary to have complementary State legislation to effectuate this.

The minimum paid-up capital of a 'rural co-operative bank' or a 'rural subsidiary bank' should be Rs. 50,000 and consequentially the minimum authorised capital of Rs. 1 lakh. The existing restriction of transferability of shares in co-operative societies only to bona fide residents of their areas of operation should apply also to shares of 'rural co-operative banks' and of 'rural subsidiary banks'.

The commercial banks should deal with and hold the shares in the 'rural subsidiary banks' in the manner specified in Recommendation No. 29.

The principle of limitation on the exercise of voting rights by individual shareholders (excepting the commercial bank promoting a 'rural subsidiary bank') should apply to all rural banks.

The Reserve Bank of India Act, 1934, may be suitably amended to enable that Bank to advance from out of the National Agricultural Credit (Long Term Operations) Fund loans also to any commercial bank for enabling it to subscribe to the share capital of a 'rural subsidiary bank' which it is promoting. If any primary agricultural credit society, for whose share capital a State Government has subscribed, decides to merge or otherwise amalgamate with a 'rural subsidiary bank' set up in the area, the share capital held by the State Government could be transferred to the promoting bank. There should be necessary provisions for this.

A rural bank should be required to give only prior intimation to the Reserve Bank of the places where it would be carrying on business within the area of its operation; it should not be required to apply for and obtain from the Reserve Bank a licence for each such place. Where a rural bank desires alteration in the area specified for its operation the question of approving such alteration should be left to be determined by the Reserve Bank. The powers to be exercised on behalf of the Reserve Bank in this regard should be delegated to the authorities of the Bank at the branch level.

It should be statutorily provided that the Reserve Bank, in granting refinance to a rural bank, may do so through the promoting bank in the case of a 'rural subsidiary bank', and through the concerned district/State co-operative bank in the case of a 'rural co-operative bank'.

In States where the deposit insurance has been extended to cover deposits with co-operative banks, that insurance should also cover deposits with the 'rural co-operative banks'. The Deposit Insurance Corporation Act should be suitably amended to extend insurance to cover deposits with 'rural subsidiary banks'.

The legislation relating to 'rural subsidiary banks' should provide for an expeditious and inexpensive procedure for the winding up of a 'rural subsidiary bank' when circumstances so warrant.

The fiscal concession, which would be available to 'rural co-operative banks', should be enlarged to cover also income arising on account of banking and credit transactions of 'rural co-operative banks' with non-members. The concession should also be allowed to 'rural subsidiary banks' in regard to their liability to pay tax on their income. The tax concessions available to dividends on the units of the Unit Trust of India should also be available in respect of dividends on the shares held in rural banks.

The exemptions from payment of stamp duty and registration charges would be available to 'rural co-operative banks'; State Governments may consider the granting of similar exemptions in respect of transactions with 'rural subsidiary banks'. The provisions which facilitate the creation of charges on borrowers' assets and the giving of priority for the claims of the banks over such assets would now be available only to 'rural co-operative banks'; State Governments may consider the making of appropriate provisions which would provide such facilities also to 'rural subsidiary banks'. The Co-operative Societies Acts have special provisions which provide for a simple procedure for reconciling the claims of co-operatives and their members inter se; the Acts also provide for expeditious recovery of loans and advances granted by co-operative societies. These provisions would ensure to the benefit of 'rural co-operative banks'. The question of making similar provisions which would be applicable to 'rural subsidiary banks' should be examined.

With reference to 'rural subsidiary banks', the District Court may be specified as the court having jurisdiction to decide disputes concerning such rural banks unless provisions similar to those applicable to Cooperative Societies are made. In the revised scheme of banking regulation now recommended there is no need for the present distinction between scheduled and non-scheduled banks.

The position of banking companies which have applied for a licence on or before September 16, 1949, and, pending a decision on their application, are carrying on banking business so far, is anomalous. An expeditious decision on the applications of such banks, which have been pending for over two decades, would remove this anomaly.

In the conditions prevailing in our country, it is necessary that banks should be allowed to undertake the business of buying machinery and other equipment and leasing them. There should also be a statutory provision providing that banks could undertake any form of business which the Reserve Bank may notify with the prior approval of the Central Government. For this, the Reserve Bank may undertake reviews from time to time.

Section 19 of the Banking Regulation Act, 1949, may be amended to provide that banks may form subsidiaries for :

(a) carrying on business which banks are permitted to do under section 6 of the Banking Regulation Act, 1949; and

(b) any purpose considered by the Reserve Bank in consultation with the Central Government as conducive to the spread of banking or otherwise useful or necessary to be undertaken by banks in public interest.

There should also be a statutory clarification that in the aforesaid circumstances the national banks are allowed to form subsidiaries.

On the model of the proviso to section 42(1) of the Reserve Bank of India Act, 1934, a proviso should be added to the sections providing for the maintenance of other liquid assets, specifying a range within which the requirements as to other liquid assets may be varied. The Central Government in consultation with the Reserve Bank may decide on the particular range within which the Reserve Bank may be enabled to raise or revise the requirements as to maintenance of liquid assets.

The provisions relating to the balance sheet and profit and loss account of banks may be modified to ensure full disclosure by banks of all their assets and liabilities. Consequentially, section 34A of the Banking Regulation Act, 1949, may have to be repealed. Having regard to the purpose for which secret reserves are maintained, such reserves of banks, existing on the date on which the provisions providing for full disclosure become effective, should be required to be transferred to the banks' general reserves. In order to ensure that profits that would have gone to reserves are not utilised to meet other needs, there should also be a provision requiring banks to transfer to their general reserves (which are to be disclosed) a larger percentage (than the present 20 per cent) of their net profits. The exact percentage to be specified may be laid down by the Central Government in consultation with the Reserve Bank.

Acceptance of deposits (non-chequeable) by loan companies, investment companies and hire-purchase finance companies really comes within the sweep of the regulation as set out in the Banking Regulation Act, 1949, having regard to the definition of 'banking' given in that Act and the objectives of banking regulation. There is no reason to deal with such financing institutions accepting non-chequeable deposits from the public as non-banking companies.

Concerns accepting non-chequeable deposits for the purpose of lending or investment, that is, financing institutions, should really be regulated as part of scheme of banking legislation. However, there may have to be appropriate differences in the nature of the regulation to which concerns taking chequeable deposits and concerns accepting non-chequeable deposits for lending or investment, i.e., banks and financing institutions, are subjected. Nidhis, Bangalore type financing 'corporations', Hire-Purchase Companies and Investment Companies should be brought within the framework of the banking regulation. Housing finance institutions which accept non-chequeable deposits from the public for mobilising the necessary resources may also come under the scheme of banking regulation. The scheme of regulation that should apply to financing institutions may be as described in Chapter 17

The distinction between a person doing banking and a person doing money-lending really rests on the presence or absence, as part of such person's business, of the acceptance of deposits from the public. As the definition of 'banking', since 1936, has essentially centred around the deposit-taking function, to distinguish banking from money-lending we have per force to rely on the question whether or not the person accepts deposits from the public.

There is no legal impediment and the Union should legislate to regulate private banking.

While incorporation of private banking undertakings is highly desirable, this need not be enforced by compulsion. Alternatively, there could be appropriate differentiation between corporate bodies and firms and individuals carrying on private banking. In particular, in prescribing the conditions to qualify as eligible concerns for any concession or inducement, incorporation could be made one of the conditions. Subject to the above, all the provisions that apply to corporate financial institutions should also apply to firms and individuals doing private banking, with necessary modifications for the difference in their legal status. A private banker should be required to obtain a certificate of authorisation and to satisfy certain specified conditions. There should also be special provisions for facilitating either the conversion of private banking undertakings into corporate institutions, or their disolution.

The objectives of the regulation would be met in the case of deposit receiving institutions if the regulation deals with the terms (including the terms relating to the period of repayment, payment of interest, etc.) subject to which deposits could be accepted, and contains necessary provisions to ensure that the borrowing concerns have adequate repaying capacity. Having regard to public interest, the provisions may also enable authorities to restrict, regulate or prohibit the acceptance of deposits. The regulating authorities should also be given the necessary powers to enforce the observance of the regulations by the deposit receiving institutions by inspection and other measures. But the licensing of such institutions should not be necessary for the purpose of banking regulation.

The administration of banking regulation over financing institutions and deposit receiving institutions may be left to an independent agency which should be closely associated with the Reserve Bank. This agency would comprise separate licensing/regulating authorities at the State level with an apex body at the all-India level. The apex body would be concerned with questions of policy and matters of all-India importance while State level bodies could deal with administration of the regulatory/licensing provisions. As an alternative to such machinery the Reserve Bank itself may be vested with such responsibility which it could discharge, if necessary, departmentally and by opening its branches in all the States.

It is desirable that the regulation of the different banking undertakings is considered as parts of one comprehensive scheme. That would ensure that there is a proper perspective over the control that is exercised in regard to the different categories of banking institutions having regard to certain common objectives, such as, the protection of the interests of the depositors, the safeguarding of public interest and the effective implementation of the monetary policy and credit policy. For this, there should be a comprehensive banking code. We recommend a comprehensive banking code suited to the conditions of India and covering all types of deposit-taking institutions. The banking code can appropriately differentiate between the different categories of persons doing one or the other form of banking. The statutory provisions applicable to the national banks could become a part, or parts, of the banking code (see Recommendation No. 372). Chapter III-B of the Reserve Bank of India Act, 1934, may be repealed and the provisions to be made with reference to financing institutions and deposit receiving institutions may be placed as separate parts of the code. The provisions necessary for regulating firms and individuals doing private banking could be made a part of the code. The provisions of the Banking Regulation Act, 1949, in relation to their application to banks could be retained in the code, subject to necessary modifications. The schemes governing the rural banks and the housing finance institutions, could find appropriate places as parts of the banking code. The suggestion for a comprehensive banking code should not, however, delay the promotion of legislation necessary for banking regulation.

If necessary, legislation can deal separately with the different categories of banking institutions with the ultimate aim of fitting in all the pieces of legislation for the regulation of banking into one comprehensive banking code.

If the national banks are to have a common programme of functions and responsibilities in the development of the banking/credit system of the country, it is necessary that they are governed by a uniform scheme. In evolving such a uniform scheme, such features, as have more a historical rather than a present day value, may be discarded. However, such a uniform scheme may have to be evolved gradually and not brought about suddenly.

A statutory provision may be made for the capital of any national bank being revised by it in consultation with the Reserve Bank and with the approval of the Central Government.

When Government reviews the schemes governing the national banks, the question whether or not the outside shareholdings in the capital of the State Bank and the subsidiaries should continue may be taken up and decided. Until then, the placing of the annual accounts and of the report on the working of the State Bank and the Subsidiaries may continue to be made before their general bodies.

The provision, which requires the boards of the State Bank and the Subsidiaries to act 'on business principles, regard being had to public interest', should also apply to the 'new banks', as all the national banks should have the same objectives.

The provisions regarding the persons who should head the boards of directors of the national banks and those regarding the persons who should be entrusted with powers to act as their chief executives should be uniform in pattern for all the national banks.

In the national banks there should be a whole-time Chairman and a whole-time chief executive. In no case the two offices should be combined. Of the two whole-time directors, provided by the Scheme for the 'new banks', one should be made whole-time Chairman and the other whole-time chief executive. The Chairman and the chief executives of all the national banks should be made on uniform lines in the statutes governing the national banks for the appointment of chief executives and for the determination of the remuneration payable to them.

The question of extending representation on the Boards of the State Bank and the Subsidiaries to men engaged in specified occupations, namely, farmers, workers, artisans, as also the depositors and the employees of banks could also be considered, when a uniform scheme is evolved for all the national banks.

In the appointment of the representative(s) of the Central Government, the choice of that Government need not be restricted only to its officials.

The number of whole-time directors necessary for the State Bank and the 'new banks', as at present provided for, seems to be adequate; however, Government may review the situation from time to time in consultation with the Reserve Bank and provide for any changes that may be considered necessary. In the Subsidiaries, the General Manager should be made a member of the board and designated as Managing Director.

In our view, even in the State Bank there does not seem to be much necessity for a Vice-Chairman. But if a Vice-Chairman is at all to be appointed, he should be a professional banker.

The reference to election in the 'new banks' Act for the selection of the representatives of farmers, workers, artisans and depositors may be deleted. However, it should be statutorily provided that the representatives of employees should be chosen always through secret ballot.

The principle underlying section 10A of the Banking Regulation Act, 1949, has validity for all the banks and it is necessary to make provisions on similar lines with reference to the national banks as well.

(i) Provision should be made in the statute of the 'new banks' itself for the setting up of a managing committee and the entrustment of powers to it;

(ii) Following the pattern of the State Bank and the Subsidiaries, it should be provided that any director (including the whole-time director) of a national bank, though he is not named a member of the managing committee, may participate in the meetings of the managing committee as a member if he is able to attend its meetings; and

(iii) Provision should be made for the setting up of other committees, and for the power to associate outsiders with such committees, in the enactments of the national banks.

In the case of national banks having 300 or more branches deputy chief executives should be appointed, and to enable this, necessary provisions should be made in the enactments governing the national banks on the lines of the provisions found in the State Bank Act.

(i) Provision should be made to enable the constitutions, for the 'new banks', of regional boards with statutory powers and responsibilities as in the case of the State Bank. These regional boards may cover the branches under the control of one or more zones.

(ii) In the matter of the composition of the regional boards for the 'new banks', it is necessary to make provision, on the lines of Section 10A of the Banking Regulation Act, 1949, for including also at the local level persons with special knowledge or experience.

(iii) In the case of the 'new banks' provisions should also be made for constituting committees of local boards having regard to relevant factors, such as their size, area of operation, etc.

(iv) The State Bank Act empowers its Central Board to constitute local committees for any area to exercise such powers and perform such functions as the Central Board may confer on, or assign to, such committees. Such enabling provisions should also be made with reference to the 'new banks'.

(v) Appropriate statutory provisions should be made for the 'new banks' having regional chief executives on the pattern of the provisions applicable to the Secretary and Treasurer of the State Bank.

(vi) The existing restrictions, arising from sections 33 and 34 of the State Bank Act, in regard to certain types of transactions being undertaken by the State Bank should be removed and that bank should be statutorily empowered to engage in all forms of business which the 'new banks' and the Subsidiaries can undertake.

(vii) In relation to the transaction of Central Government business, all the national banks should be treated equally. Section 45 of the Reserve Bank of India Act, 1934, may be suitably amended to embody this principle.

(viii) The mechanism of the Currency Chests enables the State Bank (including the Subsidiaries) to operate with slender cash balances. The 'new banks' should also be given this privilege.

(ix) Statutory provision should be made so that any of the national banks may be entrusted with State Government business.

(x) Government should modify suitably its administrative instructions issued earlier to enable all the national banks being entrusted with the banking business of Local Bodies and statutory corporations.

(xi) The statutory and other applicable provisions in, or under, other Central and State enactments should be suitably modified so as to provide for the banking business of Trusts and other statutory bodies being given to any of the national banks.

The justification for the State Bank or any of the other national banks continuing to exercise intermediate central banking functions, such as those specified under the provisions of sections 18 and 24 of the Banking Regulation Act, 1949, and section 42 of the Reserve Bank of India Act, 1934, has to be examined by the monetary authorities. Pending a decision on this basic question, the references to the State Bank in sections 18 and 24 of the Banking Regulation Act, 1949, and section 42 of the Reserve Bank of India Act, 1934, may be substituted by a reference to the 'national banks'.

As the intention is that the 'new banks' should also be enabled to build up adequate reserves by transferring a portion of their net profits to their general reserves, it may be specifically provided that the transfer by them of the surplus to the Central Government would be only the balance of net profits remaining after such transfer.

The Integration and Development Fund for the State Bank Group may be discontinued.

The provisions that specify who should sign the annual accounts of the national banks and the time for their completion and submission should be modified providing for uniformity in all these matters.

It should be statutorily provided that notwithstanding the statutory form of declaration of secrecy provided for the officials of the national banks, the banks are not precluded from disclosing information relating to their affairs, as distinct from those of their customers.

The provisions applicable to the national banks in relation to the appointment of their auditors, the carrying out of special audit, the remuneration of auditors, the form of auditors' certificate, and the submission and verification of the auditor's report should be uniform for all the national banks.

It is necessary to have provisions similar to those found in the Companies Act, 1956, and the Rules framed thereunder for the audit of branches of the national banks. The formula for granting exemption from audit of the branches of the national banks should ensure that all the branches of a national bank are audited at least once in three years. The selection of branches in a particular year may be left to be determined by the Reserve Bank. The branch auditor should be approved by the statutory auditor for the national bank from out of a panel of auditors maintained by the Central Government. The statutory auditor's right to inspect any branch office and obtain necessary information should not also be affected.

There should be a statutory provision to the effect that Government's directions to the national banks should be in writing.

To give effect to the recommendations in Chapter 15, suitable amendments should be made in the enactments governing the national banks.

The Central Government may be vested with powers to make Rules, in consultation with the Reserve Bank, to give effect to the provisions of the 'new banks' Act.

(i) Section 35 of the State Bank Act and Section 38 of the Subsidiaries Act enable these banks to acquire other banking undertakings pursuant to a Scheme framed by the Central Government. Provisions on similar lines should be made for the new banks as well.

(ii) Provisions that should apply to the new corporations that may come into existence by reason of the break-up or amalgamation of any of the new banks should be laid down in the status itself.

(iii) Generally, the provisions found with reference to the Schemes that could be framed under the Banking Regulation Act, the State Bank Act and the Subsidiaries Act may be taken as the pattern for the provisions to be made for the framing of schemes under the 'new banks' Act. The State Bank and the Subsidiaries Acts, as also the Banking Regulation Act, 1949, contain enabling provisions specifying in detail the matters that can be provided for in the Schemes framed thereunder. Similar provisions should be made in respect of the Schemes framed under the 'new banks' Act.

(iv) There are specific provisions in the enactments governing the State Bank and the Subsidiaries, providing that in the event of the transfer of the services of the staff, pursuant to any Scheme, the employees will have no claim for compensation (like that payable under the Industrial Disputes Act, 1947). It is necessary to make such statutory provisions, with reference to the Schemes framed under the 'new banks' Act.

The setting up of a statutory body like the Regional Consultative Committees envisaged under the scheme for the 'new banks' may not be either necessary or desirable. Such consultations and co-ordination of activities may be provided for by administrative arrangements rather than by legislation. In this view, there will be no need for the Regional Consultative Committees envisaged in the Scheme for the 'new banks'.

The provisions relating to the capital structure, ownership pattern and the management of the State Bank, the Subsidiaries and the 'new banks' may be given as separate sections, and the provisions which could apply in common to all the national banks, e.g., provisions relating to the organisational set-up, forms of authorised business, could be made another section of the part of the Banking Code that would deal with all the national banks. The aim should be to have all the relevant provisions relating to banking legislation placed in the Banking Code.

The banks' obligation to observe secrecy as regards the affairs of their customers should continue subject, however, to recognised exceptions and qualifications.

There should be a statutory clarification to the effect that the obligation to observe secrecy as to the affairs of customers is not to affect in any manner the banks furnishing information of a general nature relating to the affairs of their customers without revealing the identity of the individual constituents.

The qualifications for the banker's duty to observe secrecy regarding their customers' affairs should be :

(1) where disclosure is under compulsion by law;

(2) where there is a duty to the public to disclose;

(3) where the interests of the bank require disclosure; and

(4) where the disclosure is made with the express or implied consent of the customer.

A statutory provision may be made in the Banker's Book Evidence Act to the effect that during police investigations it should be sufficient for a bank to produce before police authorities certified copies of the relevant extracts from its books, unless the production of copies thereof is considered as not adequate by an authority of a rank not lower than a Superintendent of Police.

A statutory provision may be made in the Banker's Books Evidence Act specifically clarifying that if the original documents a e destroyed by banks, in the regular course of business, and the documents have been micro-filmed before such destruction, the relative positives of the films are admissible as evidence provided they are properly produced and proved in court.

A separate statutory provision should be made for specifying the minimum period for which the banks should be required to preserve their several records. Such period should be fixed for each type of record, having regard to :

(i) the period for which it would be desirable for banks to maintain the records for their own needs;

(ii) the period upto which such records could be usefully required in connection with tax or other regulatory proceedings; and

(iii) the practical difficulties the banks may face in preserving their records beyond a reasonable length of time.

The period of preservation of various records may be prescribed from time to time by the Central Government in consultation with the Reserve Bank. The provision should also apply to all co-operative banks other than primary credit societies.

A statutory provision should be made fixing the period of preservation of paid instruments by banks. When, for valid reasons, customers require the return of the paid instruments before the specified period, they may be returned only after they are micro-filmed. The cost of micro-filming should be borne by the customer. This provision should be applied also to the return of paid instruments drawn by Government Departments and statutory Corporations.

Banks need not be required to identify parties coming to them for all types of transactions.

The State Governments may, in terms of State laws, in proper cases, call for information available with banks regarding their customers. While making such provisions, and administering the existing provisions in their laws, State Governments should act in consultation with the Reserve Bank.

Questions of law and propriety arise with reference to information available with the foreign branches of Indian banks, when such information is required to be disclosed pursuant to orders served on their controlling offices in India. There should be a statutory provision clarifying this. This question has also to be considered keeping in view other practical considerations, such as the repercussions of such disclosure on the business of the foreign branches of the Indian banks. In such cases, we should have regard to international practice and agreements between countries.

There should be a statutory provision clarifying that banks should disclose in public interest information relating to the affairs of their customers :

(a) when a bank is asked for information by a Government official concerning the commission of a crime and the bank has reasonable cause to believe that a crime has been committed and that the information in the bank's possession may lead to the apprehension of the culprit;

(b) When the bank considers that the customer is involved in activities prejudicial to the interests of the country;

(c) where the bank's books reveal that the customer is contravening the provisions of any law; and

(d) where sizeable funds are received from foreign countries by a constituent.

The statutory provision can also lay down that if and when a bank forms bona fide an impression that it owes a duty to the public to disclose, it is relieved of its obligation to maintain secrecy if it discloses the relevant information to the concerned authorities.

Different periods may be prescribed for the disclosure of the affairs of individual-customers and those of corporate entities; in relation to the former, information relating to a period anterior to 50 years and in relation to the latter, information relating to a period anterior to 20 years may be furnished by banks for research purposes.

Government may be empowered by law to declare, from time to time, the names of Commissions/Committees appointed by Government to whom banks are obliged to disclose information relating to the affairs of their customers in public interest.

There should be adequate statutory provisions which would enable banks and financial institutions to exchange freely credit information on the affairs of their customers.

There should be full, free and frank communication of credit information between the national banks. For this purpose, there should be a special provision in their statutes.

Since the major banks and financial institutions which are in need of credit information are in the public sector, specialised credit information agency or agencies may have to be set up by legislation. Government may take appropriate measures to set up these as statutory corporations. On the setting up of such agencies, there will no longer be the need for continuing the Credit Information Bureau in the Reserve Bank, and Chapter III-A of the Reserve Bank of India Act, 1934, could thereafter be repealed.

There should be provision requiring banks and other financial institutions to furnish credit information agencies with such information, and in such form, as the agencies may specify in consultation with the Reserve Bank.

It is necessary to provide for credit reporting agencies adopting reasonable procedures in a manner which is fair and equitable, and for an opportunity being given to the person reported on to ask for correction of any error in the report on him.

There should be a statutory provision for indemnifying the credit reporting agencies from any action for damages or other losses which may be suffered by any person consequent on the credit information being given on, or for the use of, such person, so long as such agencies exercise their powers and functions bona fide. Such protection should also be available to banks while they furnish credit information on their constituents.

Legislative measures should be taken to provide that financial statements furnished to banks by their borrowers (including prospective borrowers) shall be true and correct and that any wilful breach of this obligation is punishable.

Statutory provisions should be made :

(i) on the lines of the provisions found in the banking codes of the States of the United States of America, (a) for the repayment by banks of deposits held in accounts opened in the names of more than one individual, and (b) to facilitate bank's dealing with adverse or conflicting claims to deposits held in bank accounts;

(ii) for giving nomination facility in relation to deposits by individuals with banks, the effect of a nomination being provided for on the lines of the provisions contained in the Public Debt Act, 1944, and banks being permitted to make payment to the nominee(s) unless restrained by an order of a competent court;

(iii) for an individual borrower availing of credit facilities from a bank nominating a person(s) who could be allowed, in the event of the death of the borrower, to repay the debt and obtain redemption of the assets charged to the bank by the borrowers. Such redemption while giving a good discharge to the bank, should not affect the rights and claims of other parties to the assets of the deceased;

(iv) for the nominee obtaining release of the charged assets having a prior claim for getting himself reimbursed of the expenditure incurred by him to obtain the release of the charged assets. Such a nomination should not also affect any other rights the bank may have for realising any of its other dues recoverable from the estate of the deceased;

(v) in relation to immovable properties mortgaged to banks, for a nominee indicated by the mortgagor having the right, on the death of the mortgagor to redeem the mortgage by repaying the amount due to the bank in respect of such mortgage. Such a provision could also be made by way of an amendment to the Transfer of Property Act. It should also be provided that the rights of the nominee so redeeming the property are subrogated to the rights of the banks vis-a-vis other persons who may have claims on the property. Such a nomination should not, however, affect the rights inter se of individual parties claiming under the mortgage;

(vi) for enabling banks to return the articles kept in safe custody with them to the nominees of the depositors so as to relieve the banks from any obligation in relation to such asset, but not so as to affect the rights inter se of the nominee and other claiming under the deceased depositor;

(vii) for those renting safety lockers from banks indicating the persons to whom access may be allowed to the lockers on their death, or on the death of any one jointly renting the lockers; before any such access is allowed :

(a) the tax authority specified by the Central Government for the particular area should be notified of the date; and

(b) the locker would be opened in the presence of two responsible bank officials, or a responsible bank official and the representative of the tax authority specified by the Central Government, and an inventory taken of the contents of the locker(s) in their presence.

There should not be a wide disparity in the regulation applicable to the lending function of those doing 'banking' and those doing 'money-lending'. Hence. there should be a review of the laws governing 'money-lending' with a view to eliminating the wide disparity in the regulation that is now present.

The business of those who carry on the business of dealing in usance hundis but do not accept deposits and rediscount the hundis with banks should be regulated.

Pending the implementation of our recommendation to vest the Union with the responsibility to regulate 'money-lending', a model legislation should be drafted for the consideration of the States for the regulation of the Multani business, as stated in recommendation No. 279.

The following matters require further review :

(i) the laws relating to negotiable instruments and negotiable documents and those relating to loans and advances, laws relating to non-banking financial intermediaries and the provisions of the Company Law insofar as they have a bearing on the working of the banking system, in the light of the developments in other countries;

(ii) codification of the law relating to bank deposits and collections;

(iii) codification of usages and incidents applicable to different types of indigenous negotiable instruments (which should be continued) excluding those which need not be given legal recognition;

(iv) codification of the law relating to the negotiation of negotiable documents like debentures, bonds issued by companies, bearer bonds, bearer scrips, bearer debentures, etc. for the payment of money;

(v) consideration of the desirability of having separate legislation on the lines of Article 7 of the Uniform Commercial Code of the U.S.A.;

(vi) (a) the facilities available for investigation of title in general, and the ascertainment of encumbrances on land, notice of lis pendens, etc., in particular; (b) the system of registration of title deeds; (c) the question of issuing title deeds which would facilitate the ready ascertainment of the encumbrances on the land; (d) review of the provisions of the Transfer of Property Act and other relevant laws pertaining to the cost of creation and the enforcement of charges over immovable property; (e) the extending of the special provisions available to co-operative societies to commercial banks lending to agriculture (see also Recommendation Nos. 56 and 122); (f) depending on inclusion of earlier point, consideration of legal handicaps faced by co-operative banks in carrying on their business vis-a-vis commercial banks carrying on similar business, and legal measures to remove them; (g) streamlining of the procedures to be adopted while making advances against immovable properties and measures to ensure that such procedures are not cumbersome but are simple and leave scope for commercial flexibility;

(vii) the legal effect and the reconciliation of the claims of third parties who deal with movable assets with or without notice of the claims of the bank in respect of the goods, the applicability of the reputed ownership clause in the event of the insolvency of the borrower and related questions and the technicalities of the documents that are now taken for evidencing the creation of the various forms of security interest, e.g., pledge, hypothecation charge, floating charge, trust receipt, hire-purchase interest, with a view to safeguarding the interests of the lending institution and reconciling the interests of third parties vis-a-vis the lending institution;

(viii) the legal status of trust receipts;

(ix) consideration of the Hire-Purchase Bill, 1968;

(x) the law relating to charge on fixtures;

(xi) the law relating to guarantees and letters of credit;

(xii) evolving a legal framework that would help to ensure that credit given even on an unsecured basis is not allowed to fail, including questions, such as the giving of adequate level basis for advances against the security of negative lines or negative pledges;

(xiii) evolving a legal framework that would help to ensure that credit given even on an unsecured basis is not allowed to fail, including questions, such as the giving of adequate level basis for advances against the security of negative lines or negative pledges;

(xiv) the question of making suitable special provisions which would be available to all banks to facilitate the expeditious recovery of the loans, if necessary by enforcing the charge in favour of the banks on the lines of special provisions applicable to co-operative societies, Industrial Finance Corporation of India, State Financial Corporations, etc;

(xv) consideration of the setting up of an appropriate special machinery for deciding on the disputes between commercial banks and their customers on the analogy of arbitration provisions in the Co-operative Societies Acts, and the question of constituting commercial courts which would deal with the settlement of disputes relating to, and the recovery of, loans and advances granted by banks and financial institutions;

(xvi) (a) review of the provisions of the Company Law insofar as they have a bearing on the working of the banking system. In particular the provisions bringing in a sort of dual control over companies doing 'banking' by the Reserve Bank and the Registrars of Companies have to be reviewed; (b) consideration of the special requirements that are to be complied with, or to be observed, by reason of banks and banking undertakings dealing with companies, and the effect of such provisions on banking business.

In the interest of banking development and in public interest, there should be a constant review in India of the laws concerning and affecting banks which fall either within the ambit of the Union List or the State List or the Concurrent List of the 7th Schedule to the Constitution. The review should include the examination of the prevailing laws concerning and affecting banking, of the Union and of the States with a view to bringing them in line with the developments in other countries and having regard to the local conditions. Such a review would keep the States informed about (i) the developments in other countries in regard to such laws; and (ii) assist the different States for promoting legislation. Such review should provide a forum for mutual discussions and periodical reviews of the laws in force in the Union and the different States on the subjects with which bankers and banking are concerned.

Having regard to the conditions in India and the fact that banking system is expected to fulfil certain social and economic objectives, a special machinery should be set up by the Central Government for a constant review of the laws concerning and affecting banking. It should be presided over by a jurist, and its members should be drawn from the legal profession, from legal experts who have worked or are working with banks, and from experienced bankers and others possessing expert knowledge and experience considered necessary or useful for such review. The Reserve Bank may be asked to give such assistance as may be required by the reviewing body. It should review all the laws concerning and affecting banking and falling within the jurisdiction either of the Union or of the States, and suggest appropriate measures.

The objectives of banking research and development should include the following : (i) to study the manner in which the banking system as a whole functions in the context of the problems of development of the Indian economy; (ii) to study the inter-relationship between the working of the different parts of the banking system and the special features of the contributions made by these parts to economic development; (iii) to discover and devise methods to develop banking habit; (iv) to find ways of improving the quality of bank services; (v) to assist in creating new opportunities for mobilisation of savings and in extending the geographical and functional coverage of banks, (vi) to bring about reduction in costs—capital as well as operational costs; and (vii) to study the impact of loan policies of banks on its environment.

Further work needs to be done in all the fields in which research was sponsored by the Commission. (See Appendix IV).

The history of individual commercial banks may be written so as to throw light on the evolution of Indian commercial banks.

Recent information of a general nature regarding the operations of banks not involving disclosure of affairs of any individual customers should be made freely available by banks for research. Data useful for purposes of policy and for information of the public about the functioning of the banking system should be published regularly by the Reserve Bank.

To avoid waste and duplication of work, the findings of research should be published and widely distributed without delay. Findings of consultancy projects on particular banks should be made available to other banks.

There is need for a properly indexed and periodically updated bibliography of articles, books and reports on banking with special reference to India.

There should be a scheme for reprinting certain studies and reports (like the Report of the Indian Central Banking Enquiry Committee) which are in demand but have gone out of print.

To bring theory and practice together and improve banking research, reciprocal arrangements for training of staff between financial institutions and between universities and financial institutions can be worked out.

Large banks can sponsor Chairs in Banking in colleges and universities around the country. Alternatively, the Government and the Reserve Bank can set apart a certain amount from the profits of the national sector banks received by them for such a purpose.

Research workers for the Reserve Bank sponsored research fellowships may be allowed to do their work at universities and under teachers of their choice, subject, however, to the approval of the Reserve Bank.

The banks should also consider tie-ups with schools, specially in rural areas, where banking facilities are slowly spreading.

As part of educational aids, a basic reading list on banking topics should be prepared and suitable text books brought out.

The Field Level Organisation

We shall not discuss the steps that need to be taken to improve the structure of banking institutions as what might be called the field level. It is obvious that the starting point for these improvements is the strengthening of the primary credit societies in such a way that they are able to provide not only adequate credit but develop the banking habit in the rural sector by providing it with a wide range of banking services as well as certain closely allied non-banking services. In short, they have to become rural banks. Under certain conditions the primary credit societies can do this. These conditions are, first, the society itself must be a well managed efficiently run unit. Second, the society should have an assurance of the kind of technical assistance that is required to enable it to provide the credit and the banking services necessary. Where the central co-operative bank of the district in which the primary society is located is itself a strong unit, it should be possible for the primary to get most of the assistance from the central bank. Where the central bank of the district is weak, the apex bank could be the agency to give such assistance. In both these types of cases, establishment of rural banks in the co-operative sector or rural co-operative banks will obviate the need for opening of branches by central or the State co-operative banks merely for the purpose of providing banking facilities like deposit accounts, remittances, etc., to the rural areas. The central and State co-operative banks can concentrate their attention on meeting the needs of other productive and of distributive activities in the co-operative sector. Since however, in many States both the district and the State level co-operative banks need to strengthen themselves. It will be necessary to think in terms of commercial banks providing such assistance. Third, certain legal steps are necessary to enable the primaries to function as rural banks. These have been dealt with in Chapter 19.

It was mentioned earlier that out of the 1.63 lakhs of societies, around 51,000 satisfy one of the indices of potential viability, viz., appointment of a full-time paid Secretary. However, upto March 1971 only about 30,000 societies had received Government share capital contribution which is another index of potential viability. A number of such societies which satisfy both these indices can be converted into rural banks provided they are able to get the requisite technical assistance from the central or the State co-operative banks. In view, however, of the relatively small number of such higher level co-operative institutions which can do so, it is necessary to think of other solutions to the problem of extending the geographical coverage of banks. Three methods are being tried out at present for this purpose. Two of them, namely, opening of branches by commercial banks and financing of a group of primary agricultural credit societies by commercial banks have already been mentioned. The third method which has been tried out by the State Bank Group is the village Adoption Scheme. The object of this scheme is to make intensive efforts to reach all economically viable farmers, irrespective of the size of their holdings. Even small farmers who are potential producers for the market are covered and for determining their repaying capacity, their income from all productive activities is taken into account. The scheme also provides for the system of group 'guarantee'. By the end of June 1971. as many as 1,145 villages are reported to have been covered under the scheme. The number of farmers assisted directly stood at 2.56 lakhs, 76 per cent of whom had holdings of 4 hectares and less and those having holdings of 2 hectares and less formed 51 per cent.

Of these three methods, opening of branches by commercial banks or village adoption can develop the banking habit and provide the full range of banking services to the rural sector. At the same time, they can result in the extinction of the co-operative endeavour in the field of credit institutions. The method of financing primary societies by commercial banks can strengthen the co-operative institutions provided satisfactory solutions can be obtained to the various difficulties mentioned in paragraph 8.41. In due course many primary societies in this group can become rural banks.

It is doubtful whether all these three methods will suffice to give adequate geographical coverage of the rural sector in the foreseeable future. It is, therefore, necessary to consider whether in areas where the co-operative credit structure is generally weak an institution like a rural bank cannot be established either by making a good primary agricultural credit society to work as a subsidiary of a commercial bank or by the commercial bank setting up its own subsidiary. Such a rural bank which may be called a rural subsidiary bank to distinguish it from the rural co-operative bank mentioned earlier (paragraph 8.42) should be an organisation which retains the useful features of co-operative credit institutions such as local participation, flexibility as regards increasing share capital, arrangements for selling shares to local people, and so on. At the same time, the parent bank will provide it with full technical and financial support and exercise control over its management. Thus, of the total capital of a rural subsidiary bank, the sponsoring bank will hold 51 per cent and the remainder will be available for the people in the area of operation of the rural subsidiary bank. In such an arrangement, the rights of the individual share holder in respect of the balance of the capital should be of the same kind as those of a primary credit society. In those cases where no local participation is forthcoming, the sponsoring bank has to provide the whole of the capital for the rural bank. It should, however, be the endeavour of the sponsoring bank to sell a part of its holding to the people residing in the area of the rural subsidiary bank.

Since the object of setting up a rural bank whether as a co-operative or a subsidiary is to extend credit and other banking facilities to all members of the public in its area, it would be necessary for those primary societies which are converted into rural banks to make some departure from their practice of not lending to non-members by creating a new class of members called 'associate' members who can avail themselves of the facilities of the bank but will not be entitled to any rights of voting or to patronage dividend. However, in order that the rural co-operative bank retains its essential co-operative character, the loan business with 'associate' members may be restricted to a reasonable limit, say 25 per cent of its total loan business. There is nothing new in admitting non-members as 'associate' members of co-operatives. Indeed, the International Co-operative Alliance Report on Co-operative Principles finds it a desirable way of inducing the smaller proportion of rural residents in the area of a co-operative, who may have remained outside the co-operative fold for some reasons, to eventually become full-fledged members.

In order to encourage local participation in the rural banks these banks should give in their dealings, some preference to the members over 'associate' members in the case of 'rural co-operative banks', and shareholders over non-shareholders in the case of 'rural subsidiary banks'. Thus the interest rate charged to a member/shareholder for his borrowings would be somewhat lower than that charged to an associate member/non-shareholder.

Functions of Rural Banks

While the rural banks are basically banks and will perform all the banking functions, it will be desirable to enable them to perform certain non-banking functions, such as constructing and maintaining godowns on their own, supplying, as agents, agricultural inputs and acquiring of agricultural and other equipment for leasing it out, providing assistance in the marketing of agricultural and other products and generally helping in the overall development of the villages in their areas. Thus the various functions which a rural bank may be expected to assume in due course may be listed as below:

(1) Mobilise local savings by means of the various types of deposits;

(2) Provide short-term and medium-term credit for agriculture and other purposes to rural producers and provide long-term loans to agriculturists as agent of the land development bank.;

(3) Implement programmes of supervised credit tailored to the needs of individual farmers;

(4) Provide various ancillary banking services to local people, such as remittance of funds, acceptance of insurance premia, safe deposit lockers, etc. ;

(5) Set up and maintain godowns ;

(6) Undertake supply of inputs and agricultural and related equipments to farmers as agents and in appropriate cases equipment leasing ;

(7) Provide assistance in the marketing of agricultural and other products through marketing organisations;

(8) Generally help in the overall development of the villages in its area.

Outline Of The Scheme Of Rural Banks

Location and Area of Operation : A rural bank may be described as a primary banking institution set up to serve a compact group of villages generally, working as a co-operative bank or as a subsidiary of a commercial bank. Its object is to provide at one place the special type of credit and banking facilities and other related services needed by agriculturists and other rural producers. Generally, it should be possible to organise a rural bank for a compact group of villages covering a population ranging from say, 5,000 to 20,000. However, in sparsely populated areas, it may be necessary to organise a rural bank for as big an area as a development block to start with.

It is intended that a rural bank should cater to the full credit needs of all medium and small cultivators. There may be in its area some cultivators and other rural producers who may be in need of a different type of technical help and of a much larger volume of loans than a rural bank would be in a position to provide. Such producers should have access to a branch of a commercial bank. Further, it is possible that some of the uneconomic primary agricultural credit societies which have been operating in its area for some time may continue to do so till they are wound up. Considering that the setting up of rural banks by either commercial or co-operative banks will be in pursuance of a national policy designed to bridge the credit gaps adequately, the Reserve Bank should ensure through appropriate directives that the commercial co-operative banks should not continue to finance such uneconomic and weak credit societies while at the same time financing rural banks in the same area. The members of such societies should be eligible for finance from the rural banks.

We recommend that the provision empowering the Registrar of Co-operative Societies to order winding up of societies which are uneconomic and poorly managed, may be invoked in the public interest, wherever there is such a provision. Where it does not exist, it may be provided for.

Share Capital and Borrowing Power : Where a rural bank is set up as a subsidiary of a commercial bank (the rural subsidiary bank) its minimum authorised capital should be Rs. 1 lakh of which Rs. 50,000 should be paid-up. At least 51 per cent of the paid-up share capital should be held by the sponsoring bank, the other 49 per cent being offered to the local people for subscription. Where a primary society becomes a rural bank (the rural co-operative bank) it should also have Rs. 50,000 as its minimum share capital. The special law we have recommended provides for the share capital of a rural subsidiary bank being increased suitably as and when necessary in a simple manner.

In areas where local participation is not readily forthcoming, the sponsoring bank should be in a position to put up the entire minimum capital prescribed under the law. However, the bank should offer for public subscription an appropriate part of its share capital as and when there is possibility of attracting local participation in share capital.

Irrespective of the amount of share capital held by any member of the public, the voting power of the shareholders other than the sponsoring bank should be regulated by the principle of 'one-man-one-vote' as prescribed in the special law. The sponsoring bank will have the right to nominate the majority of directors on the board which should consist of between 5 and 9 members.

We do not consider that there is need for fixing any maximum borrowing power in the case of rural banks. Maximum borrowing power fixed as a multiple of owned funds of an institution is a device of rather limited utility. Where the institution is well managed, it becomes necessary to increase the maximum borrowing power and where it is badly managed the ceiling is not required because the institution is unable to borrow up to the limit. Moreover, since rural banks under the scheme will be either subsidiaries of commercial banks or will be supported by strong co-operative banks and in either case they are likely to be under the effective control and supervision of the parent bank apart from that of the Reserve Bank, we do not consider it necessary to fix any maximum borrowing power.

Nevertheless, it is important to emphasize the need for building up the financial strength of the rural bank and this should be done, in our view, more by way of ploughing back the profits into the reserves than by increasing the proportion of share capital to be held by a member to the maximum amount he can borrow. This can be done by placing a ceiling on the rate of dividend.

The co-operative principle of distribution of patronage dividend to the borrowers is a healthy principle and should be applied to rural banks proposed under the scheme. The surpluses arising from the business after providing for statutory reserves and other funds in the normal course may be distributed by the rural bank to borrowers as well as to depositors in the shape of patronage dividend in order to encourage the patronage of the local people, when the financial position of the rural bank is adequately built up.

Contribution to Share Capital : The amount of resources that the commercial and co-operative banks might need every year for the purpose of enabling them to subscribe to the share capital of rural banks depends on the number of rural banks proposed to be sponsored. This is discussed later. It is important to ensure that lack of resources for the purpose of making share capital contribution to the rural banks does not stand in the way of sponsoring rural banks wherever it is considered necessary. Accordingly, we recommend that resources for the purpose may be made available from the National Agricultural Credit (Long Term Operations) Fund set up by the Reserve Bank of India which is being used for the purpose of, among other things, making long-term loans to State Governments for enabling them to participate in the share capital of co-operative banks and primary credit societies. The resources of the Fund should also be available for the purpose of making contributions to the share capital of the rural co-operative banks. The Reserve Bank of India Act may be amended for enabling it to make loans from the Fund to commercial banks directly for facilitating their sponsoring of such banks.

OTHER RESOURCES

(a) **Deposits** : As the rural banks develop their business in the rural areas, they should be in a position to mobilise, through deposits from the local people, an increasing part of their requirements for loaning. We recommend that the rural bank should be allowed to offer a somewhat higher rate of interest on deposits than that offered by the parent commercial bank or co-operative bank, as the case may be. The extent to which the rate can be higher on different deposits may be fixed by the Reserve Bank from time to time. In terms of the special legislation recommended, the Deposit Insurance Scheme will also be extended to the rural banks.

We also expect that rural banks, as in the case of the sponsoring banks, would be increasingly involved in making payments to the agriculturists on behalf of the Food Corporation of India and its authorised agents who make purchases of foodgrains and other commodities from them. There are definite advantages in the long run if the Food Corporation of India makes payments to the producers through the rural banks. We recommend that the Food Corporation of India may do this, on an experimental basis, wherever rural banks are set up. Similarly, where the system of compulsory procurement exists the State Governments can utilise the rural banks for their payments to farmers.

(b) **Borrowings** : A good part of the resources of the rural banks, however, would come from the higher level banks whether co-operative or commercial. Those set up by co-operatives may, however, supplement their resources by borrowing from a commercial bank as and when necessary. It is important, however, that the rural banks get some concessional credit facilities in order to off-set to an extent the relatively high interest cost on the deposits they collect locally. These concessional credit facilities should be the same as are available to the co-operative credit system. That is to say, there should be a uniform policy regarding concessional credit facilities from the Reserve Bank, irrespective of the channel through which they are made available. The rural borrower should pay the same interest whether he borrows from a primary co-operative or from a rural bank.

For practical considerations, we do not consider it desirable for the rural banks to seek direct refinance from the Reserve Bank of India. The higher level institution, viz., the central co-operative bank or the sponsoring commercial bank will be the link with the Reserve Bank. It is, however, necessary to ensure that the borrowings of the commercial bank for financing its rural subsidiary do not result in penalising the commercial bank in obtaining refinance for its own purposes. The Reserve Bank will have to make appropriate changes in its policy in this regard.

Requirements Regarding Liquid Assets : In view of the fact that the rural banks will operate in areas where current deposits of a significant order are not likely to be collected, we recommend that the norms for maintenance of liquid assets by rural banks should be lower than those for other banks. Further for both types of rural banks, the balances maintained by them with the higher level banks should be regarded as liquid assets.

Other Facilities : These banks should be given by parent banks, remittance facilities free of cost and training facilities for personnel including technical personnel and personnel on a loan basis at subsidised costs in the initial years.

We also recommend that the rural banks should be eligible for participating in the guarantee schemes designed for ensuring adequacy of credit facilities to small and neglected sectors and that the dividends on shares held in rural banks by individuals should receive the same exemptions as are available to the dividends paid on units of the Unit Trust of India.

Personnel : We should like to emphasise here that the success of a rural bank depends on the type of men put in charge of it. The staff of the rural banks should have the requisite background and training consistent with its functions. It is important that either the manager or the official next in line should have proper training in farm management and agricultural credit.

Implementation

The first priority in establishing rural banks should be given to the well-run primary agricultural credit societies. Each central co-operative bank which has the necessary organisational strength should select a few such primary societies every year for conversion into rural banks. Where such societies exist in the area of operation of a weak central co-operative banks the concerned State co-operative bank can take such action if it can provide the necessary technical support. Where it is not practicable for the higher level co-operative banks to undertake such responsibility, the primary credit society may be allowed to become a subsidiary of a commercial bank. Where the whole co-operative structure is weak, the commercial banks should set up rural subsidiary banks on their own. The establishment of the rural subsidiary banks will necessarily be somewhat slower than those of the rural co-operative banks as it will take time to sort out the various practical problems of running such banks. We recommend, therefore, that commercial banks should take up this work on an experimental basis for a period of five years and establish rural subsidiaries in some of their lead districts. The experience gained during this period will decide the future of the scheme.

In particular, we consider that there are two types of districts where this type of organisation in our view can be tried out first. First, there are the agriculturally advanced districts with a rich deposit potential as well as scope for further agricultural development. What are known as 'package' districts, the cash crop districts and parts of those where high yielding varieties programmes have been introduced in a big way come under this category. Secondly, there are areas which have been identified as having considerable potential for development of agriculture, agro-industries and related rural activities but much development has not taken place on account of lack of banking and credit facilities.

Since the Reserve Bank will have to license the rural banks, it should also have the responsibility for ensuring that the Scheme of rural banks is implemented properly. It will have to co-ordinate the rural bank programmes of the commercial and co-operative banks and formulate suitable guidelines of their working*.

Need for Special Legislation

Under the existing laws, co-operative banks are registered under the Co-operative Law, and others under the Company Law. In either case a new 'bank' requires a licence before it can start its business. While rural banks can be established both in the co-operative sector and outside it, the present legislation needs to be changed to facilitate speedy establishments which will be subsidiaries of the commercial banks, the Company Law is very cumbersome and costly. There are also disadvantages in registering rural banks sponsored by them under the Co-operative Law. For one thing, such rural banks would have to confine their operations only to members of co-operatives. This means that in areas where the membership of co-operatives is low such rural banks will not be able to bridge the credit gaps and thus the whole purpose of setting them up would be defeated.

Secondly, the commercial banks will find it hard to implement the programmes, if they are required to deal with several State Governments at the same time, not only for the setting up of rural banks but also in the process of running them. Besides, the co-operative principle of democratic management would come in conflict with the controlling interest of the sponsoring bank in a co-operative rural bank.

---

*The detailed procedure is given in Chapter 19, paragraph 19-71

Thirdly, registration of rural bank sponsored by either the commercial or co-operative banks under the Co-operative Societies Act of States imposes heavy burdens on the co-operative department in several States both for registering the banks as well as for the administration of the provisions of Co-operative Laws in relation to such banks. Under the existing laws, the Registrar of Co-operatives has wide-ranging powers over co-operative banks particularly relating to compulsory amalgamation, financing of non-members, borrowings, loans, investments, etc. Since under the proposed scheme, the Reserve Bank has the responsibility to ensure that the scheme is implemented properly, it is necessary that all such powers should also be vested in the Reserve Bank.

In view of the above, the Commission recommends that separate legislation should be enacted by the Parliament in order to enable rural banks being set up quickly and in a fairly simple way without straining too much the organisation and resources of either co-operative or commercial banks. The lines along which such legislation should be framed are given in Chapter 19.

Pending the enactment of the new legislation, we recommend that appropriate amendments may be made to Co-operative Laws in different States to enable the setting up of rural co-operative banks expeditiously along the lines recommended by us.

General Observations Concerning Rural Banks

Under the scheme outlined in the preceding paragraphs, rural banks will in most cases represent the logical development of the well-run primary agricultural credit societies. Where the primaries though strong are not able to get assistance from the higher level co-operative institutions they may have to become subsidiaries of commercial banks in order to get the necessary technical and financial support. But they can still retain the advantages of being a co-operatively organised institutions. Even where both the primaries and the higher level co-operative institutions are weak and a rural bank is to be established as a subsidiary of a commercial bank the scheme envisages such a rural bank to incorporate the advantages of a co-operatively organised institution. This emphasis on co-operation is essential in our view because the co-operative credit institutions have played an important role in many areas of the country, have built an organisation at the grass root level and have acquired insight into the rural problems. Properly managed and operated, co-operative banking and credit structure can be a source of strength to the whole credit structure of the economy. Under certain conditions, the local participation, democratic management and responsiveness to local needs and urges that co-operative organisations characterise make them the ideal type of institutions to be sought after.

In recommending the establishment of rural banks, we are not unaware of the difficulties and problems that such banks, especially those to be sponsored by commercial banks, will face. The right type of local participation, which is an essential feature of the scheme, may not be forthcoming. The problem of management and staffing may prove to be difficult in many areas. The sponsoring banks may find the supervision and control of their subsidiaries more difficult and even more costly than control of branches. Some of these difficulties may, however, be expected to fade out after the initial stage. What is more important is that in the large and complex situation in the field of rural credit in India, there will remain a large gap even after the maximum possible branch expansion has been tried by the commercial banks. There cannot be any one solution to this extensive residual problem and all possible alternatives should be tried. Rural banks established by transforming good co-operatives into all-purpose credit institutions will be the logical culmination of the process of evolution of the co-operative system. Here the rate of conversion should proceed as rapidly as practicable. We have recommended for the subsidiaries of commercial banks, an initial experimental phase of five years, during which only a limited number of such banks should be established.

The experiment will indicate the strong points as well as the weak points of the new institutions. It is not unlikely that the experiment will have different degrees of success and create different types of problems in different areas. The emergence of the problems during the experimental period should not be taken as a reason for the abandonment of the scheme. The objective should be to discover how these problems can be solved, so that the scheme can be expanded to cover all the rural areas which remain without banking facilities.

The rural banks will succeed in discharging the wider responsibilities they are required to assume only if they get adequate technical and financial support so that they can be run on sound banking lines. The initial selection of the primary society or the area in which the rural bank is to operate, the training its staff gets, the managerial support it can get from the central co-operative or the commercial bank, the kind of discipline these banks are able to maintain, all such factors count. The early years of the operation of the scheme are crucial from this point because they will throw up the various practical problems these banks are likely to face. But we have no doubt that once such problems are successfully handled, the rural hands will go a long way in providing the kind of banking facilities. Indian agriculture needs over the coming years. At the same time the emphasis on rural banks does not imply that other methods of providing banking facilities are ruled out. In the present Indian context the need is to try out various alternatives with a view to finding out which particular method is suited to an area of a given type. What is essential is that the banking and credit arrangements in any area are capable of making a significant impact on the development of the agriculture and the local industry in that area

The Commission endorses the recommendations of the All-India Rural Credit Review Committee regarding the need for the co-operative banks appointing well qualified and trained staff and the extension of the Deposit Insurance Scheme to them. The Commission also considers that it is necessary that the Reserve Bank of India should link the rate of interest charged on its loans to co-operative banks to the deposit mobilisation efforts put in by them and recommends that the Reserve Bank should formulate a scheme at an early date for this purpose.

At present there is considerable variation in the regulation of co-operative banks, their inspection and the assistance they get from State to State. This had led to difficulties in the efficient management and functioning of the co-operative banks. As these banks are the main channel for providing institutional credit to agriculture, the differences mentioned above create a number of difficulties in effective implementation of the monetary and credit policy of the country. Moreover, the financial assistance provided by the States to these banks is mostly from the resources of the Reserve Bank or the Central Government.

The Commission feels, therefore, that from the point of view of ensuring a unified monetary and credit policy, uniformity of laws relating to credit supplying agencies and ensuring a high quality of management of these agencies through programmes of training and exchange of information, co-operative credit should be transferred to the Union or the Concurrent List. The Commission has made recommendations regarding this in Chapter 19.

Thus the policy regarding owned funds of co-operative banks is based partly on the principle of maximum borrowing power being a definite multiple of the owned funds and partly on the principle of increasing such funds for the purposes of absorbing overdues. For the co-operative credit agencies the share capital base has become rather large in relation to volume of business resulting in a low rate of return to the individual shareholder. On the other hand, for the individual members, this has resulted in a good part of the share capital being collected from loans as compulsory deductions. From the point of view of the shareholder it is more advantageous if the co-operative concentrates on deposit mobilisation rather than on raising more share capital. The Commission feels that the requirements of owned funds should be related to such factors as (i) the fixed capital requirements of the credit agency; (ii) bad and doubtful debts; and (iii) quality of other loans and recommends that the Reserve Bank should review the policy in this light and revise the requirements for share capital contribution.

The policy of establishing a central co-operative bank for each district does not take into account such facts as differences in the physical endowments of the districts, inadequacy of rainfall and the consequent possibility of recurrent crop failures, etc. The central banks established in districts with poor agricultural potential are considerably handicapped and, therefore, remain weak. Unless the economy of such districts is improved through programmes which generate productive activities other than agriculture, these banks are not likely to improve.

Apart from districts of this type, weaknesses have developed for one reason or another in central banks in a number of other districts also. Weak central banks are unlikely to be useful instruments of credit policy. The Commission, therefore, recommends that wherever such weak central banks exist, the co-operative structure should be reorganised. In the Commission's view, this can be done in the following manner :

(i) In those States where all the district central banks are weak, it will be better to reorganise the structure so as to have only branches of the apex bank;

(ii) In those States where there is a small number of strong central banks and a large number of weak banks, the apex bank should open branches in places where the weak central banks exist at present;

(iii) In a State where the majority of the district central co-operative banks are strong, it is not advisable to disturb the existing structure. In such cases, the weak banks which form the minority, may be converted into branches of apex bank till such time as they are transformed into strong viable banks;

(iv) However, in States where both the apex and district central co-operative banks are strong, the present structure may be allowed to continue.

The additional share capital requirements, if any, for such reorganisation may be made from the National Agricultural Credit (Long-term Operations) Fund of the Reserve Bank of India.

The strong central co-operative banks may be accorded the status of a 'scheduled' bank if they so desire.

The proposed reorganisation of weak central banks as branches of apex banks and granting of a 'scheduled' status to strong co-operative banks may create some difficulties for these banks in raising resources from the Reserve Bank because of the requirement of two good signatures to be furnished on the promissory notes submitted for obtaining accommodation from the Reserve Bank. The Commission recommends that the Reserve Bank of India Act, 1934, may be suitably amended to enable it to provide financial accommodation against a single good signature.

In order to enable the central and State co-operative banks to finance small scale industries in their States, the Commission recommends that individual membership in such banks should be allowed upto a limit to be specified by the Reserve Bank of India.

In providing finance through the central co-operative banks, the Reserve Bank should not proceed on the basis of the Reserve Bank finance being given up to a fixed multiple of the owned funds of the bank or on its precise audit classification. Financial soundness and efficient management should be the basic criteria to be employed for such a purpose.

The Commission has examined the suggestions for setting up either a National Co-operative Bank or an Agricultural Development Bank of India on the lines of the Industrial Development Bank of India. In the Commission's view, the major part of the difficulties in providing credit needed by agriculture are with the field level organisation and the Commission has made several recommendations to meet them. As regards the problem of resources, it is the primary responsibility of the Reserve Bank of India to regulate the availability of credit to the different sectors and it has the necessary powers and the expertise for this purpose. Establishment of a National Co-operative Bank is not likely to mobilise any more resources for this purpose. On the other hand, by creating one more tier, it is likely to add to the cost of the distribution of credit. Besides, it is important that all short-term credit, which has an important bearing on the money supply, should be under the control of a single authority and that authority can only be the Reserve Bank.

With the introduction of credit planning, it may be expected that broad sectoral allocations of the total available credit will be made from time to time by the credit planning authorities. However, because of the inadequacies of both the commercial and co-operative banks at the primary or the field level, there is likely to be a problem for some time to come of credit to agriculture and other productive activities in the rural areas not being made available fully. In particular, it is likely that while the deposits raised by the co-operative banks will be fully utilised for this purpose, the allocation out of commercial banks deposits remains unutilised. The Commission recommends that the Agricultural Credit Board of the Reserve Bank of India should keep this matter under constant review and devise ways and means of utilising the allocation from commercial banks deposits more fully. The Commission, therefore, considers that there is no case for establishing a National Co-operative Bank.

As regards the establishment of an Agricultural Development Bank of India, the Commission is of the view that the Agricultural Refinance Corporation and the Agricultural Finance Corporation may be combined so that the resources available in both the institutions are put to the best use. The Agricultural Refinance Corporation which is a subsidiary of the Reserve Bank of India has already developed considerable expertise in project oriented loaning. The Agricultural Finance Corporation which has been established by commercial banks, the majority of which are now in the national sector, has also developed its own expertise for identifying and formulating potential agricultural projects and organising consortia of commercial banks. The new institution formed by merging the two Corporations can serve the proposed Agricultural Development Bank of India is expected to serve.

Urban and Industrial Co-operative Banks

Urban Co-operative Banks : The main objectives of urban co-operative banks are to promote thrift by collection of deposits from members and others and to advance loans to members. They cater to the banking and credit needs of mainly the urban middle class consisting of traders, businessmen, artisans, factory workers and salaried persons with a fixed income in urban and semi-urban areas. These are important mainly in five States, i.e. Maharashtra, Gujarat, Tamil Nadu, Andhra Pradesh and Mysore.

The area of operation of an urban co-operative bank is normally restricted under its bye-laws to the municipal area or town where it is located. More than one urban co-operative bank may, however, function in the same area as there is no demarcation of areas within a city amongst various urban co-operative banks.

Membership : Generally, there is a preponderance of individual membership in urban co-operative banks and institutions such as joint stock companies and firms constitute a negligible proportion of the total membership.

The Study Group on Credit Co-operatives in the Non-Agricultural Sector (1963) had recommended that no restrictions should be placed on the size of the urban banks. It stressed that the banks should have a strong base for raising adequate resources so that they could effectively cater to the requirements of their members. Regarding the size of membership, it recommended that the banks should aim at a minimum membership of 1,500. In areas where urban co-operative banking is well developed, it exceeds this limit but in most cases there is scope for increasing membership.

Branches: Branch banking is not yet a common feature among the urban co-operative banks. There are reported to be around 220 branches. Most urban banks have to introduce systems of effective branch control and inspections. For opening of branches urban banks are required to take permission of the Registrar of Co-operative Societies as well as of the Reserve Bank of India. Urban banks urged, in their evidence, for proper co-ordination between them and commercial banks in the matter of branch expansion.

Owned Funds: The position of urban banks is presented in Table 10.5. The owned funds of banks range from about 10 to 30 per cent of their working capital. The maximum borrowing power of a bank is fixed generally at 8 to 12 times of the owned funds. There are instances of banks finding these limits inadequate. In some States (e.g., Maharashtra), they are at a disadvantage if they accept deposits in excess of this limit, because they are required to invest such funds in Government securities and keep them in safe custody with the apex bank.

Deposits: The urban banks accept all types of deposits, viz., current, savings, fixed and other deposits, such as recurring deposits, home savings deposits, etc. The performance of the urban co-operative banks in deposit mobilisation has generally been satisfactory and several institutions depend to a small extent on borrowings.

In some cases, urban banks are not eligible to accept deposits from local bodies and other similar institutions. Some urban banks have suggested to the Commission that those with a standing of more than 5 years should be allowed to accept deposits from such bodies.

The urban banks generally allow a slightly higher rate of interest on deposits than what the local commercial banks offer. They are required to deposit their surplus funds with the concerned apex co-operative bank. Some banks have pointed out that, as a result they stand to lose, because the rate of interest paid by the apex bank does not correspond to the rate paid by them on their deposits. The apex bank makes profit by investing the surplus resources outside the co-operative sector but urban banks have no such facility.

In terms of the Banking Regulation Act, 1949, urban banks have to maintain cash reserves and liquid assets. However, when balances are kept with the banks outside the area of operation, banks are required to obtain the permission of the Registrar of Co-operatives. The balances kept with the national banks do not count for liquid assets.

Table 10.5—Urban Co-operative Banks

(Rs. in crores)

	Position as on			
	30.6.1969		30.6.1970	
	Amount	% to working capital	Amount	% to working capital
1. Owned Funds	31.14	18.9	33.88	18.4
2. Deposits	125.92	76.4	140.63	76.4
3. Borrowings	7.68	4.7	9.58	5.2
4. Total working capital	164.74	100.0	184.09	100.0

Table 10.6—Industrial Co-operative Banks

(Rs. in crores)

	Position as on			
	30.6.1969		30.6.1970	
	Amount	% to working capital	Amount	% to working capital
STATE				
1. Owned Funds	1.70	33.8	1.90	38.1
2. Deposits	1.16	23.1	0.98	19.7
3. Borrowings	2.17	43.1	2.10	42.2
4. Total working capital	5.03	100.0	4.98	100.0
CENTRAL				
1. Owned Funds	2.03	22.9	2.17	20.9
2. Deposits	3.25	36.6	3.89	37.5
3. Borrowings	3.60	40.5	4.30	41.6
4. Total working capital	8.88	100.0	10.36	100.0

Source: Statistical Statements Relating to the Co-operative Movement in India.

Loans and Advances : Urban banks make loans and advances for various purposes including building or repairing of houses, petty trade and industry, purchase of immovable property, ceremonial and educational expenses, redemption of prior debts, purchase of agricultural machinery, livestock, etc. There is linking of shareholding with borrowing, the ratio in the case of unsecured loans being higher than in the case of secured l oans.

The bye-laws generally provide for limits upon which advances can be made. These vary from Rs. 3,000 to Rs. 75,000 for different banks. In some states (e.g., Maharashtra and Gujarat) there is preponderance of short-term loans while in certain others, medium-term loans (3 to 5 years) constitute a larger proportion. For making long-term loans, many urban banks do not possess the required expertise.

Urban banks have argued before the Commission that they should be enabled to expand their business. Towards this end, they should be allowed to finance co-operative marketing societies for fertiliser business, etc. Some undertake financing of small scale industries. But many are yet to develop expertise in this regard. The limitations placed on unsecured loans should be lifted. It was also suggested that credit guarantee facility for small industries should be made available through the State Bank of India. One bank pleaded for removal of present ceiling on advances and on holding of shares per person.

Some banks make loans against three guarantors. Where such loans formed a sizeable proportion of total loans, banks found it administratively difficult to manage. They suggested a guarantee scheme for small loans so that the practice of obtaining sureties could be dispensed with.

Security : Loans and advances are made against the security or mortgage of unencumbered immovable property, personal surety of other members, pledge of agricultural produce, mercantile or industrial goods, gold and silver ornaments. Government and other trustee securities, fixed deposits, insurance policies, etc.

Quite a few banks in Tamil Nadu, Andhra Pradesh, West Bengal and Mysore have a high proportion of secured advances, while unsecured advances figure prominently in the loans portfolio of some banks in Maharashtra, Gujarat and Madhya Pradesh. Some of these banks have stressed the need for relaxing the limit on loans and advances.

Needs of Urban Banks : In their replies a number of urban banks expressed themselves in favour of accepting deposits with a maturity exceeding 5 years in order to enable them to finance block capital needs of small scale industries.

The need for concessional remittance facilities under the Reserve Bank of India scheme was also stressed by some urban banks. Some of the banks have stressed that they should be allowed to have all the privileges of a 'Scheduled' bank when they reach a certain level of business.

Future Rule : The Working Group on Industrial Financing through Co-operative Bank set up by the Reserve Bank (1967) envisaged a prominent role for the urban co-operative banks in securing adequate finance for small scale industrial units which are run by individuals, firms and joint stock companies.

Following its recommendations, the Reserve Bank decided to sanction long-term loans to State Governments to enable them to contribute to the share capital of urban co-operative banks. The banks are also made eligible for refinance facilities under Section 17 (2) (bb) of the Reserve Bank of India Act, 1934, in respect of their finance to 22 broad groups of small industries. The State Governments/urban banks have yet to avail themselves of these facilities in a significant way.

State Industrial Co-operative Banks : At the end of June 1970, there were 3 apex industrial co-operative banks, one each in Mysore, Rajasthan and Tamil Nadu in the country. In the case of apex industrial co-operative banks in Tamil Nadu and Rajasthan, there is no separate organisation at the district level for financing industrial co-operative societies ; while in the case of Mysore there are district industrial co-operative banks. The financial position of the apex and central industrial co-operative banks is presented in Table 10.6.

Central Industrial Co-operative Banks : There were 24 central industrial co-operative banks in the country as at the end of June 1970. The majority of the central industrial co-operative banks, viz., 20 were established in Mysore State alone. Of the remaining 2 banks were located in Gujarat and one each in Maharashtra and Punjab. In the case of central industrial co-operative banks there was a preponderance of individual membership and individual financing.

The Working Group on Industrial Financing through co-operative banks appointed by the Reserve Bank in June 1967 made the following recommendations in regard to the State and Central industrial co-operative banks :

"...No strong justification exists...to request the Reserve Bank to depart from its policy of not recognising state-level industrial co-operative banks independently of the state co-operative banks either for the provision of financial accommodation from the Reserve Bank or for the purposes of the Credit Guarantee Scheme.

(i) Such of the existing industrial co-operative banks as have already developed into viable institutions should be encouraged to continue to function by extending to them the facilities to which the central co-operative banks are entitled. Specifically, this means that they should be (a) considered on merits for licensing under the Banking Regulation Act, 1949; (b) recognised as approved institutions for purposes of the Credit Guarantee Scheme; and (c) recognised also for the purpose of channelling financial accommodation from the Reserve Bank.

(ii) Such of the existing industrial co-operative banks as are not viable at present but can be developed into viable institutions over a period of time should be given an opportunity to develop in this direction. As soon as the Reserve Bank is satisfied that a particular central industrial co-operative bank shows promise of functioning as a viable unit, it should be given the same facilities as the institutions under the first category.

(iii) Industrial co-operative banks which do not satisfy the criteria of viability or potential viability should be merged with central co-operative banks in suitable cases, or if they have a large membership of individuals, reorganised into primary co-operative banks.

(iv) If the above courses are not practicable or warranted, the central industrial co-operative banks concerned should be taken into liquidation without any delay."

Urban co-operative banks do useful work in mobilising deposits and financing the sector of small borrowers such as small scale industries, professionals, retailers and so on. Another useful activity is the financing of house construction and repairs for members of the banks. Also, this type of banking provides a useful avenue for those who have the necessary ability to set up a bank.

The Commission recommends that establishment of urban co-operative banks should be encouraged by the authorities, by such means as (i) according the status of a 'scheduled' bank to the well managed urban co-operative banks if they so desire; (ii) counting towards liquid assets the deposits which these banks place with the national banks; and (iii) asking the national banks to give such of the urban co-operative banks which remain non-scheduled, free remittance facilities and borrowing facilities on reasonable terms.

The Commission further recommends that in order to ensure that the productive and distributive activities are adequately financed by such banks (i) there should be a system of ceilings on the borrowings by individual members on the basis of the purpose for which the loan is obtained instead of linking it only to the amount of shares held; (ii) lending for long-term purposes, such as house construction, should be allowed subject to a ceiling that may be specified by the Reserve Bank of India regarding the proportion of such lending to the total loans given by the bank; and (iii) similarly, there should be a ceiling on the proportion of total loans for consumption purposes; this ceiling need not apply in the case of employees' co-operative credit societies.

The Commission recommends that steps should be taken to enable the urban co-operative banks to make better use of the financial assistance available from the Reserve Bank of India.

The Commission supports the recommendations of Working Group on Industrial Financing through Co-operative Banks, some of which have been mentioned earlier.

RAILWAY ACCIDENT INVESTIGATION ON THE ACCIDENT THAT OCCURRED TO UNAUTHORISED TRAVELLERS ON THE ENGINE AND ROOFS AND COACHES OF NO. 114 UP MADURAI-MADRAS JANTA EXPRESS BETWEEN VALLAMPADUGAI AND CHIDAMBARAM STATIONS, SOUTHERN RAILWAY ON 4TH FEBRUARY, 1969—REPORT

Delhi Manager of Publications, 1971. 16p.

One-Man Commission : Mr. H. S. Hart

APPOINTMENT

The above Commission was constituted under the Ministry of Tourism and Civil Aviation vide Rule 10 of the Railway Board's Notification No. 59-TTV/42/1 dated April 11, 1966.

TERMS OF REFERENCE

To inquire into the accident that occurred to unauthorised travellers on the engine and roofs of coaches of No. 114 UP "Madurai-Madras Janta Express" between Vallampadugai and Chidambaram stations on the morning of the 4th February, 1969.

CONTENTS

Preamble ; Relief Measures ; Local Conditions ; Summary of Evidence ; Conclusions ; Annexures.

RECOMMENDATIONS

From the evidence available, I have no hesitation in concluding that the accident was brought about as a result of the roof travellers themselves insisting on travelling on the roof of the carriages and on the engine of the train and that they themselves are solely responsible.

In the circumstances prevailing, I have also to conclude that the Railway Administration and the Railway Staff are not to be blamed for this accident.

The relief arrangements were satisfactory. Several have drawn attention to the help rendered by the scouts on the train in picking up the injured and dead at the site of the accident. No doubt the Railway Administration will convey its appreciation to them, and also to the Civil Doctors at Cuddalore and Chidambaram who responded so promptly to the call for assistance.

COMMISSION OF INQUIRY INTO THE AFFAIRS OF THE BHARAT SEVAK SAMAJ, 1969—REPORT

New Delhi, Ministry of Agriculture, Department of Community Development 1973. Vols. XV

Chairman : Mr. Justice J. L. Kapur.

APPOINTMENT

In exercise of the powers conferred by Section 3 of the Commission of Inquiry Act, 1952 (Act No. 60 of 1952), the Central Government appointed this Commission vide their notification dated February 21, 1969 for the purpose of making an enquiry into definite matters of public importance.

TERMS OF REFERENCE

(i) The extent to which Central Government assistance in grants, loans and other advances to the Bharat Sevak Samaj, has been utilised by it for the purposes intended;

(ii) The extent to which the Central Government loans and advances given to the Bharat Sevak Samaj are duly secured, and measures required for timely recovery;

(iii) The statement of accounts of the Bharat Sevak Samaj in respect of the Central grants, loans and advances made to it, the extent to which these have been or can be prepared and furnished, and the measures in which they conform to the procedures prescribed for assistance to voluntary organisations.

CONTENTS

Introduction; A. History of the Bharat Sevak Samaj; B. Assistance Given by the Government to the Bharat Sevak Samaj; Terms of Reference of the Commission; Interpretation of Rule 149(3) of General Financial Rules; Jan Jagran Scheme; Labour and Social Service Camps; Lok Karya Kshetras (Rural); Lok Karya Kshetras (Urban): Training Centres (A. Lok Karya Kshetra Training Centre; B. Training Centres for the Training of Supervisory, Accounts and Organizer Staff); Family Planning Clinics; Family Planning Orientation Training Camps; Welfare Extension Projects (Urban); Night Shelters; Occupational Therapy Institute; Tools and Equipments; National Consumer Service; Allotment of Government Lands, Buildings etc. to Bharat Sevak Samaj; Construction Activities of the Bharat Sevak Samaj and the Concessions and Facilities given by the Government, Loans given by the Government for the Construction Activities: Central Construction Service Delhi Works Unit; Central Construction Service Gorakhpur Unit; Central Construction Service Bidar Unit: Central Construction Service Varanasi Unit; Central Construction Service Purnea Unit; Construction Service, Yamuna Barrage; Central Construction Service Agra Unit; Satbari and Hastsal Kilns; Working of the Central Construction Service Units; Andhra Pradesh; Bihar; Delhi Pradesh; Goa; Gujarat; Himachal Pradesh; Kerala; Madhya Pradesh, Maharashtra; Manipur; Mysore; Orissa; Punjab; Rajasthan; Tamil Nadu; Uttar Pradesh; Gorakhpur Unit; Varanasi Unit; Railway Construction Units; Working of the Pradesh Bharat Sevak Samaj Units; Advantages Claimed for Bharat Sevak Samaj Participation in Construction Contracts; Other Assistance or Concessions given to the Bharat Sevak Samaj; Accounts of the Bharat Sevak Samaj of Activities not Financed by Government; Availability of Accounts and the State of the Accounts; Conclusions; List of Witnesses; List of Exhibits; List of Annexures; Evidence.

RECOMMENDATIONS

The Bharat Sevak Samaj was started in 1952 and the initiative for creating the Samaj was taken by Mr. Gulzari Lal Nanda who was at that time Deputy Chairman of the Planning Commission. It was conceived by Mr. Nanda as a new national non-political agency which was to educate the people so that they might have a better understanding of the facts and their own needs and problems which confronted the people as a whole so that they might be ready to join in a large scale constructive effort.

The Bharat Sevak Samaj was registered on December 17, 1952 under the societies Registration Act of 1860 but the constitution of the Bharat Sevak Samaj was prepared by Mr. Gulzari Lal Nanda and approved by the National Advisory Committee on Public Co-operation in the Planning Commission on August 12, 1952. The objects of this society as mentioned in the constitution are as follows :

(i) To find and develop avenues of voluntary service for the citizens of India (a) to promote national sufficiency and build up the economic strength of the country. (b) to promote the social well-being of the community and to mitigate the privation and hardships of its less favoured sections.

(ii) To draw out the available unused time, energy and other resources of the people and direct them into various fields of social and economic activity.

(iii) To take all steps which are necessary for the fulfilment of the aforesaid objects.

There was no specific object showing the power of the Society to carry on commercial pursuits e.g. taking construction contracts, or producing other market table materials such as first aid kits nor did the objects clause contain power of borrowing money or charging and hypothecating the properties of the Bharat Sevak Samaj.

In the first year of its existence the Samaj raised resources for its functioning but from the second year onwards, i.e. from 1953-54 the Government started giving assistance to the Bharat Sevak Samaj in various forms under different schemes starting with the scheme of Jan Jagran. This assistance from the Government was in the form of cash grant, loans and advances. There were also various other types of assistance from the Government to the Bharat Sevak Samaj, such as the giving of Government accommodation either free of rent or at concessional rates both for the housing of the offices of the Bharat Sevak Samaj and for residential purposes for the officers and workers of the

Bharat Sevak Samaj. Then there were free railway passes (1st Class) for use by the workers of the Bharat Sevak Samaj and also various concessions for its constructional activities like exemption from payment of earnest money and security deposits, non-insistence of previous constructional experience before entrusted with construction works and above all exemption from payment of income tax on the incomes derived from the commercial activities like construction contracts or brick manufacturing which the Samaj took up.

The number of schemes for which the Bharat Sevak Samaj were given grants by the Government of India was 30 and the information given by the various Ministries of the Government of India shows that the total grants given from 1953-54 to 1966-67 by the Government of India to the Bharat Sevak Samaj amounted to about 3 crores, to be exact Rs. 2,93,55,275.44 (Table I-B). It cannot, however, be said that the information given by the various Ministries is complete because the Commission in the course of the enquiry found the Ministries in many cases did not keep a consolidated record showing grants given to the Bharat Sevak Samaj from time to time. Besides the grants by the Government of India given directly to the Bharat Sevak Samaj, grants were also given by the Government of India to Bharat Sevak Samaj through the State Governments for the Local Development Works from 1953 but the exact amount of the grants so given cannot be ascertained. From the information available for some of the years the grants for Local Development Works totalled Rs.71,37,855.00.

The procedure adopted by the various Ministries of the Government of India was to release grants to the Bharat Sevak Samaj for the different sehemes on the basis of estimates. The Bharat Sevak Samaj on receipt of the grants credited them in their General Branch account. The Samaj had a number of activities, some financed by Government grants, some run from out of their own funds and some activities were of a commercial nature like the Construction Service or the manufacture of bricks. The Samaj had also units at the Central, State, District and lower levels all of which were financed out of Government grants and in activities which were not so financed. The detailed procedure of accounting varied but the basic feature was that the grants were credit into the general accounts of the Bharat Sevak Samaj and later they were expended on the different schemes for which Government had given the assistance as and when required or they were taken out from the general funds in instalments and kept in separate accounts which were maintained for different schemes. As the grants were merged with the general balances at least for some periods and were not kept in separate accounts for individual schemes right from the beginning, the grants were used for all the activities of the Bharat Sevak Samaj until they were taken out of the General Funds for specific schemes or they were actually expended on those separate schemes.

Another difficulty which the Commission found in ascertaining the utilisation of the grants was that the Samaj rendered accounts for the different schemes either after the entire scheme was over or at the end of different financial years and the Ministries accepted the utilisation on the basis of final expenditure that was incurred on the different schemes. There was no attempt to ascertain how the Bharat Sevak Samaj used the grants in the intermediate period. Even though the grants were given to the Central Bharat Sevak Samaj in many cases, the actual expending was done by the units at the lower levels i.e. the Central Bharat Sevak Samaj received the grants, then distributed the same to the Pradesh units or to the Regional units and then in turn distributed the amounts to the District units and the village units and it was at the lower levels that the money was actually expended. In many cases, either the Pradesh units merged the grants along with their general funds and the lower level units did not keep the grants separately and in some cases they were even merged with the personal funds of the persons incharge. No distinction was made by those persons between personal and Samaj moneys and there were occasional cases where the moneys were used for personal purposes like marriages, business etc.

Even though the grants given by the Ministries from 1953-54 to 1966-67 amounted to about Rs. 3 crores, the Ministries by and large did not have any proper machinery to control and ensure the proper utilisation of the grants by the Bharat Sevak Samaj or to scrutinise and examine and channelise the working of the schemes. The Ministries released the grant, got accounts from the Bharat Sevak Samaj and in some cases some reports also showing the working of the scheme and the grants were considered as utilised if they were supported by accounts. The accounts were in some cases not audited by Chartered Accountants but in some cases were audited by some minor officials or in some cases were not audited at all. Even in the cases where the accounts were audited, no complete accounts were obtained showing the receipts and payments at various levels, the income and expenditure and the assets and liabilities for the different years to which the accounts related. In some cases, the accounts obtained merely showed the expenditure on the scheme and the Ministries did not even ascertain what the receipts were or if there were deficits, how the deficit was met.

In many cases, the reports sent to the Ministries

were not comprehensive. They were merely a review of the scheme and the details of the work done by the different units under the scheme were not given therein which alone could have enabled a proper assessment and evaluation of the work done by the different units.

In the case of the schemes for which the Bharat Sevak Samaj was given assistance, it was all the more necessary to obtain detailed reports on the working of the different units because the schemes were so nebulous in character that in the absence of proper reports for the units, no proper assessment could be made unless the performance by the different units was analysed and then consolidated.

Jan Jagran

The scheme of Jan Jagran was the first to receive assistance from the Government of India and its objective was Plan Publicity, i.e. the Samaj was to popularise the Five Year Plan with a view to obtaining maximum cooperation from the public for the success of the Five Year Plans. It may be observed that the Samaj virtually had no experience of any publicity whatsoever not to speak of Plan Publicity before they were entrusted with the task. They did not have any cadre of workers trained enough to carry on propaganda regarding the Plan or its publicity. It appears however that the working of the scheme was little different from propaganda for the Samaj itself and those employed in this scheme were more a cadre of paid Bharat Sevak Samaj workers at the Central, State, Regional and District levels, who went about organising the Bharat Sevak Samaj units in the various parts of the country, collected subscriptions for the Bharat Sevak Samaj, popularised the ideals of the Bharat Sevak Samaj and did propaganda work for and in favour of the Bharat Sevak Samaj and its leaders.

Under this scheme, grants were given for publishing a journal by the Central Organisation in Hindi and English and some bulletins at the state level in the regional languages but these did virtually only propaganda of the Bharat Sevak Samaj and its leaders. The Plan Publicity for which the grants were given was not in practice the dominant activity and whatever publicity was done was more or less a repetition of the publicity done by the Government publicity agencies.

Another item for which assistance was given under the Jan Jagran Scheme was publication of brochures and the Samaj virtually utilised the grants for bringing out either some pamphlets containing the speeches of the leaders of the Bharat Sevak Samaj or such material as did propaganda for the Bharat Sevak Samaj and its leaders or brought out such publications which were plagiaristic copies of the material brought out by the Government agencies who according to some officials of the Ministry were more competent to bring out such publicity material. The grants given for these brochures were also used by the Samaj for bringing out reprints of some novels and short stories from religious books and this appears to the Commission a misutilisation of the grants given for Plan Publicity and not subserving the ideals of a secular State.

The journals and brochures were restricted in circulation to the Bharat Sevak Samaj workers and their leaders or some Government officials and they hardly reached the public for whose benefit the scheme was claimed to have been formulated. The Samaj was unable to sell or distribute even free the material they brought out from out of the grants and large stocks were accumulated from time to time, which could not be sold even as waste paper.

The Commission is constrained to remark that the very scheme of Plan Publicity under the Jan Jagran was unplanned and wanting in exactitude and it would not be an exaggeration to call it nebulous. Further the reports that were obtained in regard to the execution of the scheme were inadequate and the scrutiny by the Ministry was casual and ineffective. So much so that on this record it is not possible to give a finding of the proper utilisation of the grants, which amounted to as much as Rs. 36,18,535.00 between the years 1953-54 and 1965-66.

The reports regarding the performance of the different Public Cooperation Centres set up by the Bharat Sevak Samaj are only for two half years. They give the work done by the workers of the Jan Jagran Scheme at the Central, State and District levels.

The record shows that a large number of workers were employed at the Central, State and District levels under the Jan Jagran scheme and they were more interested in popularising the Samaj and its leaders than popularising the Five Year Plans.

There is no proof before this Commission that these workers employed under this scheme were of a sufficiently high intellectual level as to be able to understand the implications of the Plan or to be able to explain them to the general public.

The publications which the Samaj undertook under the Jan Jagran scheme, as has already been said, did more propaganda for the Samaj than it did for the Plan. The nature of those publications were either records of what the Samaj was doing or its leaders were doing or they were largely reprints of what had appeared in other papers. And surprisingly no objection was taken to these infirmities by the Ministry.

The evidence supporting any Plan Publicity done by the Samaj is meagre and as has been said earlier, the calibre of the workers employed by the Samaj or at least a large majority of them was not such as was capable of doing intelligent propaganda of the Plan.

Labour And Social Service Camps

One of the most important schemes entrusted to the Bharat Sevak Samaj by the Central Government was the Labour and Social Service Camps. During the period 1954-55 to 1964-65 a total amount of grant given for this scheme was Rs. 1,13,74,312.24. Under the scheme, the Samaj was to hold camps for the students in rural areas, the objective being to inculcate a sense of discipline among the students and "to break the dislike of manual work among the educated youth".

As originally conceived, the camps were mainly for students with a very small percentage of non-students being allowed to join the camps but as time passed the camps were sanctioned for rural youth also which was the opposite of the original objective. The camps were originally to be held under the auspices of or by educational institutions through their Principals and Head Masters and the role of the Samaj was to assist in holding of the camps. But when this scheme started operating, the Samaj itself was asked to hold the camps and the grants were given to them instead of to educational institutions. Thus, the role of Bharat Sevak Samaj and the educational institutions was reversed and it was left to the discretion of the Samaj to seek cooperation of the heads of educational institutions as and when they required it.

The Samaj held as many as 9,701 camps during a period of 11 years. In the beginning of the operation of the scheme, other institutions also participated in its working but by 1962-63 the Samaj got a virtual monopoly of the scheme. Out of 1,236 camps held during 1962-63 other institutions including the National Cadre Corps, Bharat Scouts and Guides got 34 camps and the rest 1,202 were given to the Bharat Sevak Samaj.

The scheme operated like this. The Samaj got a yearly grant on the basis of probable number of camps to be held in the year. Although large amounts of money were paid to the Samaj both for holding camps on the basis of camper days and also supervision charges on the same basis, the Ministry itself had no proper machinery for the supervision of the camps held or for the assessment of the work done there. Thus, the Ministry had neither supervision nor the control except to the extent of being entitled to receive accounts of the camps sent by the Central Samaj and also calling for some reports.

Although 9,701 camps were held, the officials of the Ministry or its nominees inspected only 46. Some of the nominees were Professors in the various universities or they were State Government officers.

When these camps were held no information was given to the State Governments. They were not therefore asked to exercise any supervision or control over camps. Without a proper machinery it was not possible for the Ministry to keep a check on the Samaj so as to see the proper working of the scheme, not even to find out when and where the camps were actually held and also whether they were a useful scheme.

The Samaj was paid a considerable amount of money based on camper days both for the Central Samaj and for the Regional Units of the Samaj but there is no proof showing as to how the Central Samaj kept control and supervision over these camps atleast no reports properly drawn up seem to have been sent to the Central Samaj by the persons who were alleged to have been employed to keep supervisory control over the holding of the camps.

Thus, although the Samaj was paid for the purpose, it has not been proved that there was a proper or regular arrangement for the inspection and supervision of the camps and, therefore, the Samaj cannot be said to have discharged this most important function for which both the Central Samaj and its regional units were separately paid on the basis of camper days.

The reports of the inspections carried out by the Professors nominated by the Ministry or by its own officers were not flattering to the Samaj because quite a number of irregularities were pointed out by them. Unfortunately, these inspection reports do not seem to have received attention by the Ministry and no attempt was made by it to investigate the irregularities and defects pointed out nor was a proper machinery devised for a periodical check and inspection of camps either by officers of the Ministry, its special nominees or by officers of the State Governments. At a very late stage, the States were asked to conduct inspections. These inspections were instituted towards the fag end of the operation of the scheme and could not have been of much utility.

It appears that serious complaints about the irregularities in the camps came to the notice of the Bharat Sevak Samaj and some to the notice of the Planning Commission and even of the Prime Minister. The allegations were serious such as claims being made although no camps were held and inflation of camper days in the accounts.

That the Samaj itself was aware of the complaints about the camps is shown by its appointing Mr. B.V. Radhakrishnan a retired Under Secretary of the Government of India to look into the complaints against the camps. He gave a voluminous report, a copy of which seems to have been sent to the Ministry also and it was produced by the Ministry before the Commission but an important part of it, an annexure, containing particulars of the complaints were not produced before the

Commission. The Samaj did not produce the report or its annexure.

The inspection reports referred to above made by the officers of the Ministry or by Professors or by the State Government officers were evidently ignored by the Ministry and the grants were continued without any proper evaluation.

It appears that in spite of the fact that complaints were made to the Bharat Sevak Samaj and the Planning Minister who was its Chairman, the Samaj itself did not take any effective measures to have a proper supervisory control over the camps and there is nothing to show that the officials visited the camps regularly or periodically. It is not even clear as to whether any officers of the Samaj were asked to conduct the inspections and to make reports. If they did make any reports, they have not been produced before the Commission.

When the Commission went to Simla to record evidence there, in regard to Himachal Pradesh, it found on inspection of the record that there were complaints of irregularities in the accounts of the camps and that some action was taken thereupon by the District authorities. This was also disclosed by some evidence produced before the Commission. The complaints were serious in nature, which amounted to falsification of books and accounts and making claims about the camps which were not held at all. It also came to the notice of the Commission that the allegations were of forged vouchers, misappropriation of funds, falsification of accounts. It was also stated that some criminal cases had been started which were still going on.

It must be mentioned that Mr. G.L. Nanda in his evidence before this Commission has stated that it was at his instance that criminal action was taken because he had directed action to be taken when he got reports of extremely unsavoury character of the holding of the camps and of their accounts.

Another feature of the scheme was that in the beginning each camp was sanctioned by the Ministry and grants given therefor and the accounts of these camps were submitted to the Ministry separately. From the year 1958-59 this practice was discontinued and a lump sum grant was given to the Samaj and it was left to the discretion of the Samaj to hold the camps at such places as it thought fit, so the decision as to the number of camps, the location of the camps and the appointment of organisers of the camps were the sole responsibility of the Samaj and at their alsolute and uncontrolled discretion. These lump sum grants were given at the beginning of the year but they were released in instalments depending upon the rules that the Ministry had prescribed.

This has led to a state of affairs which the Commission has found extremely difficult to enquire into. The practice was this that the Central Samaj sent certain amount of money to each individual Regional Camp Committee and they rendered a Receipt and Payment Account which have been produced but not for all the years nor for all the Regional Camp Committees. Similarly, moneys sent by Regional Camp Committees to the individual camp organisers are difficult to investigate because individual camps have not produced Receipt and Payment accounts. What has been produced is their expenditure account without disclosing how much was received from the Central or Regional Organisation and what was raised by them or spent out of their own funds. This has happened even when the expenditure was more than what was shown in the accounts of the Regional Committees as having been sent to that particular camp.

The Commission has, therefore, not been able to find out where the moneys claimed to have been spent over and above what was received by the individual camp came from or whether they remained mere liabilities.

Another defect that the Commission has found in the camp accounts is that the accounts of the individual camps were not audited by any trained Accountant and the report on those accounts was in the nature of certificate that the expenditure had been verified from the vouchers in support thereof and it has been utilised for the purpose for which it was sanctioned. This is a vague kind of a certificate and it is unlike certificates of the Chartered Accountants. But it appears that this was the form which was prescribed but by whom is not clear. It seems to be a defective kind of a certificate, without certifying that it was in accordance with the books of accounts and other necessary proof of income and expenditure. Normally the Auditors certify accounts after an inspection of books and vouchers which must tally before Chartered Accountants give their certificates.

In any case, this account does not show where the money came from, how much was received and whether the whole of the expenditure was met out of that amount or from some other source.

The Programme Evaluation Organisation of the Planning Commission inspected different Lok Karya Kshetras located at different places. It had been claimed by some of these Kshetras that they had held camps which the Programme Evaluation Organisation found not to have been held.

As has been stated above, the various complaints made and irregularities committed were brought to the notice of the Ministry but in spite of adverse criticism against the Bharat Sevak Samaj, it had no effect on the

Ministry and it continued to give grants for the camps. It appears to have showed blissful ignorance and disregard of the complaints and criticisms brought to its notice.

Besides the accounts which were received by the Ministry of Education, it also received reports from the Samaj relating to the work done at these camps. Besides this there is no proof of the holding of the camps or the work done by them. The least that the Ministry of Education could have done was to nominate its own officers or if that was not possible, asked the State Governments to nominate their officers to inspect the working of the camps and certify the correctness of the claims of holding the camps and in regard to the work done therein.

Unfortunately the Central Bharat Sevak Samaj have produced only a portion of the records of the Regional Camp Committees and that also not for the whole period during which they were in existence. The records pertaining to the individual camps, i.e. books of account, registers showing the particulars of the campers or of the names of the organisers or of the work done or even audited Receipt and Payment accounts or income and expenditure accounts of these individual camps have not been produced before this Commission. The Commission has, therefore, had to restrict its enquiry only to such accounts and documents which the Ministry or the Samaj has chosen to submit before it.

In the absence of those particular documents it is difficult to verify the correctness of the expenditure that is claimed to have been incurred on the individual camps.

The accounts of the Regional Camp Committee contain the names of the organisers but no particulars are given of the camps organised by them or by whom. The duties of organisers are nowhere given nor is it shown which camps were inspected by them and with what results.

It has been said above and it is worth reiterating that the accounts submitted by the different camps were inadequate in as much as they do not show what moneys were received from the Regional Camp Committees. They only show the expenditure claimed to have been incurred by them. In cases where the grants received were not adequate to meet the expenditure, it is not shown how the difference between the expenditure and income was met. Unfortunately, the primary accounts were not properly checked and scrutinised by trained or qualified Accountants and as has been said above, the certificates given by the personae disignatae were wholly insufficient. In the opinion of the Commission, this was not a satisfactory mode of scrutinising the accounts.

The Ministry paid organisational expenses at the rate of 13 paise per camper day for the Central Organisation and 12 paise per camper day for the Regional Organisations. These moneys are not shown to have been utilised for appointing proper inspecting staff nor was any provision made for proper inspection by the organisers who had been appointed by the Regional Camp Committees. At least, no proper reports have been produced before this Commission.

It may also be mentioned that it was only the Bharat Sevak Samaj which was paid organisational expenses for the Central and Regional Organisations; the Central Organisation was paid Rs. 7,03,959.75 and the Regional Organisations Rs. 4,64,907.17. This was up to the year 1961-62. Besides this there is a claim by the Samaj pending for Rs. 1.98 lacs.

As far as the Commission has been able to see in practice the work of organisation, both by the Central as well as by the Regions, consisted of distribution of grants, keeping and having the accounts audited by the Central Organisation and submitting them to the Ministry. The Samaj was asked to definite question to submit a list of persons employed on these organisations. Their reply was that the Commission had got the ledgers and could look for them itself from the ledgers. But even that would not specify the function each one of the persons so employed was performing or did perform.

The tour particulars produced by the Samaj show that the persons employed under this scheme by the Central and Regional Organisations were more interested in the propaganda for and in the furtherance of the interests of the Samaj and raising its membership than in ensuring the success of the Labour and Social Service Camps or in inspecting them.

The documents show that up to the year 1964-65 the Regional Camp Committees had received a sum amounting to Rs. 3,22,376.08 from the Central Samaj which had not been expended or accounted for. And no efforts had been made to recover the same. Further, from out of the grants the Central Samaj had not paid to the Regional Camp Committees sums amounting to Rs. 4,34,294.61. These two sums must therefore be held to be unutilised.

Two Committees were appointed by the Ministry of Education—one under Dr. Hirday Nath Kunzru, M.P. and the other under Mr. Ashok Mehta, M.P. The former was appointed in 1959 to enquire into the schemes relating to physical education and youth welfare and had as its members very eminent people, who were Members of Parliament or Secretaries in the Central Government or educationists of note and the latter was appointed in 1962 to examine the scheme of Labour and Social Service Camps. It consisted of two important members of the Bharat Sevak Samaj, one representative of the Planning Commission, one of the Ministry of Education and another of the Ministry of Community Development. What offices they held is not clear from the report. The former gave its report in December 1963 and the latter in February 1963. It may be pointed out that Mr. Ashoka Mehta was a member of both the committees and is signatory to both the reports.

The recommendation of the Kunzru Committee was that outside agencies must be excluded from managing the Labour and Social Service Camps the holding of which should be entrusted to educational institutions. The Ashoka Mehta Committee found that the scheme had proved useful in meeting the gaps in the educational programme of our youth and needs to be promoted and expanded more effectively. But they also held that the camps should be organised either by the educational institutions themselves or by voluntary organisations with the requisite experience. They even said that voluntary organisations with their valuable built-in experience had done good work in the past and they should be encouraged to spread the movement far and wide.

It is difficult for this Commission to adjudicate on the findings of either of the two committees or to reconcile them. It will be both impolitic and unnecessary but this Commission would like to emphasise that no objective test has been suggested either by the Government or by the Samaj by which the success or otherwise of this movement could or can be tested and on the evidence before the Commission it is unable to say whether the movement has done any good to the student community because the evidence is wholly insufficient for the purpose and is scrappy if not existent.

Grants were received by the Bharat Sevak Samaj from State Governments also for the camps and contributions were also raised from local people but the evidence shows that there was no proper machinery to see proper accounting of all the receipts in the camps' accounts and the State Government grants have not been accounted for in full. For the local contributions the records of the individual camps have not been produced before this Commission.

The evidence produced is not sufficient for the Commission to be able to give a finding as to the age, qualification and quality of a majority of the boys and girls who were recruited for the camps nor the qualifications of the organisers who organised them. As has been said above, there is no material to show that the staff appointed by the Regional Committees was qualified to keep a proper control or to properly inspect the camps held in different parts of the country. But there is some evidence to show that boys, who were underage or were non-youths, were also recruited.

Lok Karya Kshetras (Rural)

For the Lok Karya Kshetras in the Rural Sector, substantial grants were given during the period from 1958-59 to 1966-67 which amounted to Rs. 45,00,170.00. The scheme was started in order to provide two or three paid workers in the selected areas who were to mobilise public cooperation for the successful implementation of the schemes and programmes of the Community Development Blocks and of the Government. These workers were to act as "catalytic agents" for the successful implementation of the Plan programmes but the State Governments or the Community Development Blocks were not even informed of the opening of these Lok Karya Kshetras or about their functioning and the Lok Karya Kshetra workers functioned in complete isolation. Instead of moblising public cooperation Samaj itself started a few Balwadis, craft centres in the Lok Karya Kshetra areas and the salaries of the teachers employed therein were debited to the Lok Karya Kshetras in total violation of the conditions of the grant and against the spirit of the entire scheme.

The Planning Commission exercised very little control over the functioning of the Lok Karya Kshetras. All that they did was to release the grants and they did not even know where the kshetras were opened, when they were opened and who were working in the kshetras. They got an audited account of the grant and a general combined report for the whole country giving a general review of the scheme. Even the report of the individual Kshetra, which alone could have enabled the Planning Commission to find out what was being done in each Kshetra, was never obtained and the general report sent by the Bharat Sevak Samaj was wholly inadequate to enable the Planning Commission to know the progress of the scheme or its utility.

The Planning Commission did not have any machinery for inspecting the Lok Karya Kshetras and during the entire period of 8 years during which the scheme functioned, not even a single Lok Karya Kshetra was visited by any official of the Planning Commission.

The Bharat Sevak Samaj also did not have any effective machinery for inspection and control of the Lok Karya Kshetras even though they claimed grants for organisational expenses totalling Rs. 4,01,634.03. The reports of the few inspections carried out, which have been produced before this Commission, show some of the irregularities in the functioning of the Lok Karya Kshetras, e g. workers being paid salaries even though the Kshetras were not functioning and misuse of equipment, furniture etc. purchased from out of the Lok Karya Kshetra funds.

The approved pattern provided for the payment of

organisational expenses for the Central Samaj at Rs. 150.00 per Kshetra, per annum and Rs. 150.00 per Kshetra per annum for State Organisation but the Planning Commission allowed Rs. 2,08,013.93 in excess of the approved pattern for organisational expenses from 1958-59 to 1965-66. For the year 1966-67 the Samaj appears to have claimed excess grants for the organisational expenses but the accounts for the year have not been settled and are under scrutiny of the Government of India.

Even though the grants have been finalised up to the year 1965-66, the Samaj has not remitted to the respective Kshetras the full grant due to them ; Rs. 71,488.04 has not been remitted to these Kshetras. Grants to this extent cannot therefore be said to have been utilised for the purpose for which they were given.

It is claimed by the Samaj vide its accounts submitted to the Ministry that the Kshetras had spent a sum of Rs. 4,14,964.75 in 1966-67 up to March 31, 1967. The Ministry had released only the first instalment of Rs. 2,37,500.00 for the year 1966-67 and no further instalments were released. There is no proof on the record as to where the moneys alleged to have been spent by the Kshetras came from or whether they are only liabilities. Unless the accounts are scrutinised by the Ministry and passed and it is also shown that Rs. 4,14,964.75 were actually spent and were not mere liabilities, and it is also shown where the money came from it is not possible to give a finding as to their utilisation.

The accounts rendered by the Bharat Sevak Samaj to the Planning Commission were not complete but were only partial accounts showing what was received by the Central Bharat Sevak Samaj and what was spent at the Central level and by the different Kshetras. It did not show the amount remitted by the Central Samaj to the different Kshetras and the amounts received by them. The accounts of the individual Kshetras have been produced for only three years, i.e, 1964-65, 1965-66 and 1966-67 and they show differences between what is shown in the accounts of the Central Bharat Sevak Samaj rendered to the Planning Commission.

The accounts of the individual Kshetras for the three years also show that the Kshetras have not accounted for amounts sent by the Central Samaj in full.

The Bharat Sevak Samaj have not produced the records of the individual Kshetras nor have they produced all the records of the Central Bharat Sevak Samaj relating to the inspection of the Kshetras.

The Planning Commission had no regular inspectorial machinery excepting two Evaluation Teams which went into the working of the Lok Karya Kshetras and the schemes. The two Evaluation Teams found many defects in the working of the scheme like non-coordination between the Lok Karya Kshetras and Community Development Blocks, inexperience and unsuitability of the workers employed, opening of Lok Karya Kshetras in the areas of influence of political leaders and Ministers etc. The second Evaluation Team wanted the role of the Lok Karya Kshetras to be specified more clearly.

The available records shows that many of the Kshetras were allotted to Ministers and important politicians or leaders of the Bharat Sevak Samaj and it was not unusual for the workers and funds of the Kshetras in some cases to be used to promote the political interests of the Convenor or of the Sahyogi who was working in the Kshetra. There were also some cases where the workers used the Lok Karya Kshetra offices for their political purposes like fighting elections.

The workers in the Lok Karya Kshetras were required to function as "catalytic agents" for development work and were to mobilise public co-operation and all these tasks would normally have required persons of high calibre. But the evidence shows that persons of rather ordinary and even low educational status with little, if any, aptitude for social work were appointed for reasons which may be called extraneous. In some cases, persons with political ambitions were appointed as Sahyogis and then used Lok Karya Kshetras as a mere stepping stone to further their political interests and spheres of influence. The Lok Karya Kshetras were in some places either reduced to an instrument for giving employment to a few associates or relatives of the Convenors or means for furthering the political ambitions of individuals. There is no evidence of any effective work done in most of the Lok Karya Kshetras.

In the reports on the Lok Karya Kshetras submitted to Government, a number of achievements were claimed but there was no machinery to check the facts reported and a few reports of inspection and reports of the Programme Evaluation Organisation Teams show that the reports were exaggerated and the achievements of other organisations and agencies were very often claimed as the achievements of the Lok Karya Kshetras. Neither the Government nor the Bharat Sevak Samaj had any machinery to verify these claims.

In the absence of an objective test the work of these Lok Karya Kshetras cannot now be properly checked and claims raised by the Samaj can neither be verified nor assessed.

The Commission has been handicapped in finding out the utilisation of the grants for the Rural Lok Karya Kshetras. Because of the non-production of the records of the individual Kshetras by the Bharat Sevak Samaj, it has not been possible to find out who and what the Sahyogis were and when the Kshetras were actually opened and where they were functioning. The Planning Commission's control was so slender that they have not been able to supply information about the number of Kshetras functioning from time to time or about the places where they were functioning. A verification of the claims made of the achievements of the Kshetras is also not possible because the details given are so meagre that even the identification of the works is not possible but the reports of the inspectors of the Bharat Sevak Samaj and of the Programme Evaluation Organisation show that the reports about the achievements were mostly exaggerated. There is precious little evidence of the mobilisation of public co-operation. At least no lasting results have been brought to the notice of the Commission.

Lok Karya Kshetras (Urban)

There was also a scheme of Lok Karya Kshetras (Urban) which was started at the instance of the Bharat Sevak Samaj. For this scheme grants given amounted to a toal of Rs. 21,41,481.00 during 1957-58 to 1966-67. The object of the scheme was to have two or three paid workers in the slum area who were to mobilise public cooperation for slum improvement work, to promote self-help among the slum dwellers and to educate them to avail themselves of the facilities made available by the Municipalities and Corporations in a better way.

The Bharat Sevak Samaj, however, instead of mobilising any public co-operation, used grants mainly for starting some balwadis and craft classes and for running a few activities from out of the Lok Karya Kshetra funds and the mobilisation part of the scheme was completely lost sight of. The result was that no voluntary effort from the local people has been proved to have been generated but instead the grants were used for salaries of teachers, and craft inspectors. As soon as the grants were discontinued for the scheme, a mojority of these institutions collapsed. The exceptions were largely in Bombay and Kerala. There is no proof showing the identity of persons running them.

There was no control of the Planning Commission on the working of these Kshetras. There was no verification of the claims of achievements of the Kshetras and all that the Planning Commission did was to give or release the grants, get the audited accounts and get a report of the working of the scheme for the year. These reports in most of the years were merely a review of the scheme as a whole and no details were given of what was being done in the different Kshetras or of the persons who were employed or what they had achieved.

Even though the Bharat Sevak Samaj were paid organisational expenses for this scheme also, there is no evidence of much control or supervision by the Samaj. Only very few reports of inspections have been produced and these reports are not very complimentary to the Samaj.

Welfare Extension Projects

Grants were given for the Welfare Extension Projects from 1958-59 to 1966-67. The amount paid for this scheme was Rs. 10,45,127.78. The scheme envisaged the Samaj employing some community organisers and social service organisers and also taking up specific activities like Balwadis, craft centres, adult education classes etc. This shows that there was little difference between the two schemes, the Lok Karya Kshetras (Urban) and this scheme.

The major activities taken up by these Welfare Extension Projects were two, i.e. running of Balwadis and Women's Craft Centres and the inspection by the State Social Welfare Board inspectors showed that the majority of them were not functioning properly but still the grants were continued to be given. There were irregularities in the accounts e.g. not keeping proper accounts of the fees collected or not having proper account-books. In many cases, high fees were charged from these who should have been benefited. It made the institutions in many cases inaccessible to the slum dwellers and the poor people for whose benefits these projects were started.

Family Planning Centres

From the year 1957-58 to 1966-67 grants were given for the 37 family planning centres and the total grants paid amounted to Rs. 8,72,652. The records do not show how the Bharat Sevak Samaj, which was not a body of medically trained persons and had no background of medical service or family planning promotion was chosen for this work. Very little control was exercised by the Ministry of Health and there are reports of inspection only in respect of six clinics over a period of nine years during which grants were given and these reports show the unsatisfactory functioning of the clinics.

The reports which the clinics submitted every half year also showed that in many clinics either no work or very little work was done towards the promotion of family planning. The reports also show that only very few people visited the clinics but still grants were continued from year to year. There were instances where the clinics were used for residential purposes by the doctors incharge and also of the clinics being attached to private dispensaries or clinic in violation of the conditions of the grant.

Family Planning Orientations Camps

From 1962 63 to 1965-66 grants amounting to Rs. 12,74,912.58 were given for the Family Planning Orientation Training Camps. None of the Camps held by the Bharat Sevak Samaj was inspected by any officer of the Department of Family Planning and there is very little evidence of any control by the Department. The Ministry did not take any interest in the scheme except of releasing grants, getting audited statements for the same and getting reports which in many cases were incomplete.

The Bharat Sevak Samaj were paid organisational expenses and the expenditure on account of the Family Planning Orientation Camps, which for four years amounted to Rs. 2,50,523.61; but there is no evidence of any inspection conducted by any Central or State Bharat Sevak Samaj officer of any of the Camps. No reports of the inspection have been produced before this Commission.

The Bharat Sevak Samaj did not render to the Ministry any accounts of the organisational expenses received for the Family Planning Camps but still the grants on account of this were admitted. The Samaj was called upon by this Commission to produce the accounts and pursuant to that order it did produce the audited Receipt and Payment accounts which show that upto 1964-65 the Samaj was given grants for organisational expenses in excess of the admissible grants and the excess amounted to Rs. 1,70,175.68.

In the organisational expenses the Samaj included expenses for the Coordinator-cum-Accounts Officer amounting to Rs. 93,639.40 even though no Coordinator-cum-Accounts Officers were separately employed by the Bharat Sevak Samaj.

The records of the individual camps have not been produced by the Bharat Sevak Samaj and, therefore, the Commission has not been able to verify the factum of the holding of the camps. The Ministry also did not appear to have conducted any verification. But the evidence shows that in some cases grants were claimed for camps which were actually not held.

The Commission has no material on which it can decide as to how successful the camps were in achieving the objectives for which they were held viz. to popularise family planning. The criteria laid down by the Minister before sanctioning the scheme was the number of persons seeking advice for family planning and taking contraceptives from the clinics in the area and the number of sterilisation operations. But no data relating to this information was obtained from the State Governments. There is no evidence to show that individual camps were inspected by State Government officials.

The machinery for supervision and inspection devised by the Government was so defective that in the years 1962-63 and 1963-64 the Government asked the Municipal Health Officer, Delhi, to countersign the accounts of the camps held all over the country and the accounts were accepted on the basis of the countersignature of the Municipal Health Officer, who never knew and could know nothing of the holding of the camps or about the correctness of the amounts spent. Counter signatures of the local officers which were meant to certify the holding of the camps and their expenditure thus became an utter farce.

Tools and Plants

In March 1957 a grant of Rs. 4,80,000 was given to the Bharat Sevak Samaj at the insistence of the Planning Commission Vice-Chairman for the purchase of tools and equipments stated to be required for the Labour and Social Service Camps and other Shramdan works of the Samaj entrusted with this work because the matter was considered very urgent and the Department of Community Development who were approached, wanted more time to purchase the tools. But the Samaj which was chosen specially to complete the purchase expeditiously did not even place any orders for nine months and even after 14 months they had spent only Rs. 61,000 out of the grants and they were asked to refund Rs. 2,65,000 after objections were raised by the Finance Minister himself.

Even though the tools and equipments were made out to be urgently required for the holding of camps and for Shramdan work very little use was made of those tools and equipments. The reports about the use made were received from very few agencies among whom they were distributed even small items like hurricane lanterns and pick axes were purchased at Delhi or Calcutta and they were sent to the remote corners of the country spending considerable sums on railway freight.

Night Shelters

The Central Social Welfare Board gave grants to the Bharat Sevak Samaj totalling Rs. 4,38,687.34 for starting night shelters for pavement dwellers who could not afford a shelter at night. The Samaj in many cases perverted the user of these shelters by running them as cheap lodging houses which were used by students, government servants and in some cases by fairly well-paid persons like the Principals of colleges. The object of the scheme was thus entirely defeated and the places chosen by the Bharat Sevak Samaj and the efficiency with which they worked could not attract many pavement dwellers. In a majority of the places the shelters were a total failure and they could hardly attract two or three inmates.

Voluntary Workers

It has been one of the claims of the Bharat Sevak Samaj that it had a band of voluntary workers, but the Government had to give grants out of which they were paid what was termed honorarium. Besides the Government had to give grants for "training centres". For this purpose the amount of grant for the years 1958-59 to 1966-67 was a sum of Rs. 6,44,737.00 for the running of two training centres. Thus, not only had the Government to pay for the workers whom the Bharat Sevak Samaj employed for different schemes, the Government had also to give grants for training those workers who in many cases were just raw freshers. The Samaj did not keep any proper record showing how the persons trained were used in the different schemes or whether they were used at all.

Training for Construction Service

Even for the training of workers to be employed in the Construction Service of the Bharat Sevak Samaj the Government gave grants amounting to Rs. 3,37,080.00. This is an indirect subsidy for a commercial activity undertaken by the Bharat Sevak Samaj. The Bharat Sevak Samaj has not produced the records relating to these training centres.

National Consumer Service

Grants were given from 1963-64 to 1966-67 totalling Rs. 72,194.54 for another scheme of the Samaj, the National Consumer Service started by the Bharat Sevak Samaj, which was envisaged as an agency for the collection of price intelligence which would be independent of Government agencies. Even though grants were given for four years, only for a few months price intelligence of some sort was collected by persons engaged by the Samaj whose educational status in many cases was not up to mark and the utility of this intelligence can be judged by the little use made of this price intelligence, so collected.

The Bharat Sevak Samaj were given grants for a number of other small schemes and the utilisation of those grants has been discussed in the earlier chapters.

A part of the grant given for the different schemes was used by the Bharat Sevak Samaj for purchasing furniture and other assets. The Government assistance for these schemes was used by the Bharat Sevak Samaj for purchasing furniture and other assets. The Government assistance for these schemes stopped in the year 1966-67. The total expenditure incurred on the acquisition of these assets under the different schemes was Rs. 16,38,436.89. Though the schemes were stopped in 1966-67, even upto this date the various Ministries have not issued any instructions as to how these assets should be utilized. The Central Bharat Sevak Samaj also has no precise information about the persons with whom these assets were lying or the manner in which they were being used. They have merely stated that they should be lying "in the places where the activities were functioning".

For every scheme for which Government assistance was given, the Bharat Sevak Samaj claimed and was given organisational expenses. In some it was for organisational expenses at the Centre and in the others it was both at the Centre and in the states or regions. From 1953-54 to 1966-67 organisational expenses claimed under the different schemes amount to Rs. 18,06,272.91.

Even though under the terms of the grants for the different schemes the grants were to be used for the purpose of those schemes only and the persons employed were for the purposes of those specific schemes, it has been noticed that the Samaj did not conform to this injunction; and the organisation of the Bharat Sevak Samaj was being run mostly out of the grants given for specific schemes. The State Units apart from the grants given to them from out of the central grants, also received grants from the State Governments which from 1954-55 to 1968-69 amounting to Rs. 86,03,099.76. Not only the services of the personnel appointed under individual schemes were being used by the Bharat Sevak Samaj for all its activities, the rent-free accommodation given by the Government and the facility of the office organisation available under the different schemes were also freely used by the Samaj for building up its organisation and propagating its own achievements.

During the period between 1953-54 to 1966-67 the amount spent by the Bharat Sevak Samaj on its organisation from out of its own funds was only Rs. 7,49,123.93. The Bharat Sevak Samaj had during this period a network of activities and units spread over the country in the various districts and even in the villages and this vast machinery was mainly maintained out of the grants and assistance given by the Government.

Grants given for 30 schemes

From 1953-54 to 1966-67 the various Ministries of the Government of India gave to the Bharat Sevak Samaj grants amounting to Rs. 2,93,55,275.44 for 30 schemes. Out of this amount the various Ministries have issued utilization certificates or finalised the accounts for Rs. 2,46,25,595.48. The Bharat Sevak Samaj has refunded Rs. 17,19,535.99 in cash. For the balance Rs. 30,10,143.97 accounts have either yet to be submitted or have yet to be finalised. The Bharat Sevak Samaj is reported to have submitted accounts for Rs. 23,90,185.66 but these accounts are stated to be under the scrutiny of the Ministries. The grant admissible under these accounts can only be determined when the Ministries finalise the accounts. It must be mentioned that the grants to the Bharat Sevak Samaj were released for the last time in 1966-67 and even after 7 years, accounts of these grants have not been finalised. The reason for this is stated to be either the non-furnishing by the Samaj of some essential particulars about the utilisation or non-fulfilment of some conditions attached to the grants. In either case, it is no credit either to the Bharat Sevak Samaj or to the Ministries that even after the lapse of such a long time the accounts have not been finalised and the matters settled.

The Commission has found that for grants amounting to Rs. 6,19,958 31 the Samaj has not rendered accounts and the Ministries have not been able to recover the same from the Samaj even after the lapse of more them six years from the date of stoppage of grants. The records do not show that the Ministries of the Government of India took any precaution to ensure the recovery of outstanding moneys from the Samaj.

In the accounts submitted by the Bharat Sevak Samaj for different schemes, liabilities were also included and the Ministries worked out the admissible grants on the basis of expenditure including those liabilities. The Samaj did not follow a uniform practice in the preparation of accounts. The accounts submitted by them were in some cases Receipt and Expenditure accounts and in other they were a mere statement of the expenditure. No uniform practice was adopted or insisted upon by the Ministries. Even the Balance-Sheets were not submitted along with the accounts which alone would have shown the position of liabilities at the end of different years. The result is that the Ministries issued utilisation certificates for amounts including liabilities and left it to the sweet will of the Samaj to meet or not to meet these liabilities. The result is that not only were the accounts submitted by the Samaj incomplete, the grants also were admitted including liabilities without the Ministries satisfying themselves about the discharge of the liabilities and thus without the full amount being proved to have been expended.

On March 31, 1967 the uncleared liabilities for 8 schemes given in the table attached hereto and which have been prepared from the accounts of the Samaj before the Commission, amounted to Rs. 14,78,570.99. But even this figure cannot be said to be a complete and correct representation of the correct state of affairs because the Samaj never drew up regular Balance-Sheets for the different years and therefore there is no means of verifying whether the balances were correctly carried forward from year to year.

It has already been mentioned that the Samaj utilised the services of the persons employed under and for individual schemes for other activities of the Bharat Sevak Samaj, which in many cases included the promoting, supervising and executing the construction activities and other commercial activities of the Bharat Sevak Samaj or help in the popularisation of the Samaj itself.

Local Development Works

Another scheme for which the Planning Commission gave assistance to the Bharat Sevak Samaj was the programme of Local Development Works. The assistance for the scheme given by the Government of India alone and its extent was upto 50 per cent of the cost. The procedure in the beginning was that the schemes were sent to the Planning Commission by the Central Bharat Sevak Samaj and were approved for sanction by the Planning Commission. The State Governments were asked to nominate Liaison Officers who were to satisfy themselves about the completion of the works and then to disburse the grants to the Bharat Sevak Samaj Units. The Bharat Sevak Samaj was required to raise the contributions either in kind or cash for an amount not less than 50 per cent of the cost of the works subject to certain limits. Generally the Collectors of the different districts were nominated as Liaison Officers. In the later years, certain schemes were not got approved by the Planning Commission but funds were placed at the disposal of the State Governments who disbursed the grants on the same basis as mentioned above. In either case, grants came from the Government of India.

The Planning Commission has not been able to supply to this Commission information about the grants paid under this scheme to the Bharat Sevak Samaj due to the records connected therewith having been destroyed. But in the annual reports of the Bharat Sevak Samaj for the years 1953-54, 1955 to 1957 and 1959 the number of schemes sanctioned, the total cost of the Local Development Works and the grants sanctioned by the Planning Commission are given. Unfortunately for the other years there is no mention in the reports about these grants for Local Development Works. However, the Commission has been able to collect some information about these grants given in the State of Gujarat from 1954-55 to 1964-65. The Commission has also been able to get the total amounts of grants received by the Rajasthan Pradesh Bharat Sevak Samaj from the years 1955-56 to 1958-59. The Planning

Commission has also made available the files connected with grants given for some local development works in the year 1962 and from the available records the Commission has been able to collect information for some years which show that 1,426 local development works were sanctioned the total cost of which was Rs. 1,64,63,006.00 and grants paid therefor amounted to Rs. 71,37,855. The Samaj was asked to produce the accounts of these Local Development Works but they have not produced any accounts. The Commission when it visited the different states also tried to get the accounts but no accounts were produced by the different units of the Bharat Sevak Samaj. The Commission also finds that the Collectors did not obtain any accounts but actually released the grants on the basis of measurements taken by revenue authorities but these measurements did not and cannot show the amount of grants received for the different works, the local contributions received from the beneficiaries of the local people and the total expenditure. Thus, the position comes to this that the Samaj had no accounts for the Local Development Works and the information about the total grants paid for the Local Development Works and the local contributions that were raised is not complete as the relevant files of the Planning Commission have not been produced before this Commission. Besides no accounts of these works have been produced.

Free accommodation for the Central Samaj

From its very inception the Bharat Sevak Samaj was allotted Government accommodation for its office and for the residences of some of its office bearers and workers in Delhi. In the beginning only a nominal rent of Re. 1 per month was charged for the premises but in the year 1954 the Planning Minister, Mr. G.L. Nanda, wanted the Bharat Sevak Samaj to be given rent-free accommodation describing the Samaj as a limb of the Planning Commission and consequently it was so treated for the purpose of allotment of accommodation with effect from April 1954. For no other purpose, however, was the Bharat Sevak Samaj treated as a limb of the Government. It may be remarked that the Government had no control over the activities of the Samaj except that it received accounts of the grants given by the Ministries but no other accounts.

The Samaj has claimed that it was a non-official and non-political organisation and it was given assistance to promote non-official effort for working the Five Year Plans and if it was such a limb then all these grants and assistance given to the Bharat Sevak Samaj must be taken to have been given by the Planning Commission to itself and not to a non-official and non-political body. Further the Samaj carried out its activities with the help of large grants given by the Government of India, which also helped it by concessions and loans and equipment.

The Bharat Sevak Samaj were allotted 13 different buildings by the Director of Estates in different parts of Delhi for its various activities. These included office accommodation in the heart of the city at no rent. A portion of this accommodation was even given on rent to some of the units of the Bharat Sevak Samaj, financed out of Government of India grants. Apart from office accommodation, the Samaj was also given residential accommodation for some of its workers at very nominal rent and some of these residences were requisitioned flats.

The Commission is of the opinion that the use of the power of requisitioning for providing accommodation to officers or servants of the Bharat Sevak Samaj was not a proper use of the powers of requisitioning. There was a further misuser by the Samaj inasmuch as it allowed these premises to be used by the Bharat Sevak Samaj for residential purposes by persons who were not even in the service of the Samaj. Some of the permanent servants of the Bharat Sevak Samaj designated as its workers got Government accommodation on the ground that they were workers of the Bharat Sevak Samaj and were doing voluntary services.

In the opinion of the Commission it was a graver misuse of the powers of eminent domain to allow requisitioned premises to be passed on by the Bharat Sevak Samaj to the Bharat Sadhu Samaj; and it was still graver misuse when the Bharat Sevak and the Sadhu Samajes compelled the Estate office not to derequisition the premises for such a long period of time.

The Commission also finds that two Community Halls built by the Government for the welfare of the Government Servants residing at Kidwai Nagar and Sarojini Nagar were allotted to the Bharat Sevak Samaj for its use and the Government servants for whose benefit these buildings were constructed, were denied the use of the same and the Bharat Sevak Samaj collected rent from other parties who made use of the same and also from other organisations which were housed in those buildings.

Inspite of serious complaints about charging of high rent the Samaj was allowed to continue the use of the buildings and the buildings still continue to be with them. The Samaj used these buildings for raising resources for its own organisation. The activities run by the Samaj in those buildings e.g. the Nursery Schools or craft classes were activities for which fees were charged. The Samaj appears to have allowed the possession of the building at Kidwai Nagar to pass in to the hands of another society which was in violation of the terms and conditions of the allotment.

It does appear to be an unfortunate result of this allotment to the Bharat Sevak Samaj that when Government had inadequate accommodation for its own offices and officers, it was providing accommodation to the Samaj either free or at concessional rates and for such a long period of time.

As a result of the criticism by the Public Accounts Committee, Government issued orders withdrawing the concessions about accommodation to the Bharat Sevak Samaj with effect from July 1, 1965 but the Samaj has not paid any rent for the accommodation in its possession and still continues to remain in occupation of those premises. The arrears of rent which had accumulated up to November 30, 1972 amounted to Rs. 3,57,496.33. There is no evidence as to what the Government proposes to do about this amount.

If the Government charged the usual rent from the Bharat Sevak Samaj, the rent recoverable for the period for which rent-free accommodation was given would have amounted to Rs. 11,40,055.89. This is an indirect assistance and subsidy to the Bharat Sevak Samaj from the Government of India calculated up to June 30, 1965.

The office accommodation given to the Samaj was used by the Bharat Sevak Samaj also for its commercial activities like the Construction Service and the brick kilns but no rent was recovered from the Bharat Sevak Samaj for that portion which was used for construction activities upto June 30, 1965.

Aims and Objects of the Bharat Sevak Samaj

The aims and objects of the Bharat Sevak Samaj under its Memorandum of Association are as follows :

(i) To find and develop avenues of voluntary service for the citizens of India—

(a) to promote national sufficiency and build up the economic strength of the country,

(b) to promote the social well-being of the community and to mitigate the privations and hardships of its less favoured sections.

(ii) To draw out the available unused time, energy and other resources of the people and direct them into various fields of social and economic activity.

(iii) To take all steps which are necessary for the fulfilment of the aforesaid objects.

Commercial Activities

Construction Service : Despite these aims and objects not authorising the taking up of commercial activities for profit, the Samaj from the year 1954 took up construction contracts for execution starting with the embankment works in Kosi River Valley Project in Bihar. The initiative for this activity was that of Mr. G. L. Nanda, who was at that time the Union, Minister in charge of Planning, Irrigation and Power.

The purpose of starting this activity was stated to be to mobilise public co-operation but the Samaj instead of merely mobilising public co-operation itself took up construction contracts. Later on their construction activities extended to Rajasthan, Andhra Pradesh and Delhi.

In 1958 a separate Construction Service was organised with a separate constitution. But this Construction Service was not registered as a separate society and it is doubtful if they would have been covered by the preamble of the Societies Registration Act of 1860.

In the year 1968 this activity was registered as a separate company under the Companies Act.

Neither the Government of India nor the various State Governments which gave contracts to the Bharat Sevak Samaj appear to have examined the legal competence of the Bharat Sevak Samaj to enter into construction contracts. In the Kosi Project, the Bharat Sevak Samaj was inducted at the instance of Mr. G. L. Nanda, the Union Minister for Planning, Irrigation and Power, at that time and later on other works were given on the basis of their performance in Kosi. The Samaj when it started its contracts possessed neither the machinery nor the expertise to take up construction contracts but still they were entrusted with these contracts and at no stage was the competence of the Samaj to take up construction works tested as is done in the case of other contractors.

The advantages claimed for the participation of the Samaj in construction programmes more particularly in the case of the Kosi Project included :—

(i) Giving of employment not only to landless labourers but also to the agriculturists ;

(ii) the execution of work at cheaper rates due to elimination of the middleman's profit ;

(iii) elimination of graft and other corrupt practices ;

(iv) creation of a feeling of national pride among the labour and a sense of participation.

(v) Achievement of better targets as compared to the contractors who were not fully equipped ;

(vi) considerable savings to the public exchequer ;

(vii) utilisation of the profits earned by the Bharat Sevak Samaj for social welfare activities and consequent reduction of the burden on the Government to provide social welfare measures ;

(viii) as the Bharat Sevak Samaj was a public agency, this method of work, accounts, etc. were open and available for close scrutiny by the officials ;

(ix) Promotion of honest dealings in the working of the construction industry ; and

(x) Provision of better and more amenities to the

labour.

On the basis of the claim of these advantages, the Ministry of Irrigation and Power and the Planning Commission took the initiative to have various concessions extended to the Bharat Sevak Samaj for its construction activities. These were—

(i) Preference was given to the Bharat Sevak Samaj in the matter of allotment of contracts. Works were to be allotted in some cases without calling for tenders and in other cases at negotiated rates and in some cases certain weightages were given to the Bharat Sevak Samaj. In the beginning, certain limits were imposed for alloting of works to the Bharat Sevak Samaj but these limits were observed more in the breach. In no case, however, was the previous construction experience or the organisational set-up of the Samaj subjected to a scrutiny before alloting the works to the Bharat Sevak Samaj.

(ii) Giving initial advances to the Bharat Sevak Samaj to be recovered according to certain set formula.

(iii) No earnest money or security deposit was to be taken.

(iv) Grants totalling Rs. 3,37,080.00 for setting up training centres for staff employed by the Bharat Sevak Samaj in the construction units were sanctioned.

(v) Loans totalling Rs. 45.80 lacs were sanctioned by the Government of India to the Central Construction Service and loans totalling Rs. 36.50 lacs were sanctioned by the Planning Commission to the various State units of the Bharat Sevak Samaj through the State Governments. Apart from these the Samaj was also given rent-free accommodation for its office, a part of which was used for construction activities. The officers of the Planning Commission more particularly the Director of Construction Service and the Director of Public Co-operation were not only doing day to day supervision of the Construction Service and were also members of the Managing Committee of the Central Construction Service but were also using the power and prestige of the Planning Commission to have decisions made in favour of the Bharat Sevak Samaj in various construction contracts. The Government also lent services of some of its senior engineers to the Bharat Sevak Samaj for its construction activities.

Apart from these concessions and advantages, there was exemption from income-tax which if translated into monetary terms would have amounted to a very considerable amount, as a matter of fact quite a few lacs. While alloting the different works to the Bharat Sevak Samaj, the monetary equivalent of these concessions was not taken into account. In view of this, the claim of savings to the exchequer became considerably weakened. These claims were even incorporated in the Five Year Plan documents.

The loans given by the Central Government direct to the Bharat Sevak Samaj amounted to Rs. 45.80 lacs (Table 18-A) ; the Samaj has repaid the principal and interest but the last instalment was paid only as late as on August 4, 1972. The exact figures for the initial advances sanctioned by the Ministry of Works, Housing and Supply are not available for all the works entrusted to the Bharat Sevak Samaj but the figures made available for 34 works show that for those works advances totalling Rs. 28,49,926.00 were paid and these have been recovered from the Bharat Sevak Samaj.

As regards the loans given through the State Governments amounting to Rs. 36,50,000.00 (Table 47-B); the Samaj has not repaid the balance of principal amounting to Rs. 23,84,968.74 and the interest on the principal is also due for various periods.

Complete information has not been made available about the advances given by the State Governments to the Bharat Sevak Samaj for the different works, which advances were the result of directions issued by the Planning Commission, but from the available information it appears that the Samaj is yet to pay back initial advances totalling Rs. 23,32,632.02 (Table 47-B).

The records of the State Governments do not show that there are sufficient assets to pay these amounts outstanding against the Bharat Sevak Samaj. The only assets available are the machinery and equipments purchased out of the loans and which were hypothecated but after so many years of use, these assets are not of much value except as scrap and virtually there are no securities available for these outstanding loans and advances.

Even though in the Consolidated Accounts of the Construction Service as on March 31,1966, the value of fixed assets has been shown as Rs. 13,30,935.17, the Commission during its visits to the different States found that most of these assets are only on paper and in many cases even the whereabouts of the assets were not known to the various office-bearers of the Bharat Sevak Samaj. In some cases when the State Governments took over the assets with a view to realise their debts, they found that they could be sold only as scrap.

Commencement of Construction Service

The construction activities of the Bharat Sevak Samaj started in 1954. In the beginning, activities were to be managed by the local units of the places where construction was going on. The Central Construction Service was started only in 1958 but the accounts of the Central Construction Service have been produced before this Commission only from 1961-62.

There were 8 units of the Central Construction

Service which took up 101 works of the tendered value of Rs. 11,14,11,089.00. The accounts of four of these units have been produced upto the year 1966-67 and for four other units upto 1967-68 and these accounts show the payments received were Rs. 9,70,05,517.09, and there was a net loss of Rs. 74,212.16. All these losses are in spite of various concessions given by the Government which have already been enumerated. (See Table 27-A).

Immediately after the Chinese aggression in 1962, the Samaj was assigned certain emergency works connected with the improvements of aerodromes and the Samaj made large profits in those emergency contracts. In the Kusmi Aerodrome work at Gorakhpur alone there was a profit of Rs. 37,21,825.82 in the contract of the value of Rs. 1,71,78,967.29. In another aerodrome work at Bidar, the Samaj made profits amounting to Rs. 7,31,771.26 in a contract of the value of Rs. 22,06,303.08. In the Bidar Aerodrome the workmanship of the Samaj was found to be of a poor quality because the quantities of bitumen used were insufficient and the method adopted by the Samaj for laying the runway was defective and consequently the aerodrome could not be used for training jet aircrafts for which it was designed and virtually the entire outlay became a waste. But still the Samaj were paid full contract amounts which shows that the authorities were not careful both in the matter of expenditure of public moneys and in the utility of works executed. This performance was neither a credit to the Bharat Sevak Samaj nor to the M.E.S. authorities.

All the profits made in the aerodrome works were wiped out in other construction contracts of Delhi whereon works of the value of Rs. 2,94,45,618.56 the Samaj lost as much as Rs. 62,32,197.41. It may be mentioned that disputes about these works are still pending. (see Table 27-A).

The information supplied by various Government Departments about the payments made to the Bharat Sevak Samaj shows that as much as Rs. 40,15,591.91 are not accounted for in the accounts produced by the Bharat Sevak Samaj before this Commission.

As a consequence, the Consolidated Accounts of the Construction Service prepared by the Bharat Sevak Samaj were defective and the first balance sheet prepared for the year ending July 31, 1963 included certain items carried forward from the previous year and the accounts for those years were not produced. There are no details of the expenditure of Rs. 1,16,581.10 shown in the expenses met out of the Central Development Fund in the Profit and Loss Accounts for the year ending July 31, 1963.

In the Balance-Sheet as on July 31, 1963 profits of previous years have been carried over were Rs. 3,11,620.74 but these are not verified from the accounts as the accounts for the previous years were not produced. The details given by the Samaj show that Rs. 48,104.08 have not been properly accounted for and certain transactions shown between the Construction Service and the Central Development Fund are not properly reconciled and certain assets have been shown both in the Construction Service and Central Development Fund affects away the correctness of the Balance-Sheet of the Construction Service.

Loss in Construction Service

Even though the net result of the working of the Construction Service shows a loss, the Samaj either donated or contributed amounts totalling Rs. 13,96,098.29 to the different Sections and Units of the Bharat Sevak Samaj or to its sister institutions. Barring two small donations of Rs. 5,101.00 to a college and a gurudwara in Bidar, there are no items of expenditure on any social welfare activities. These donations and contributions were made either for the payment of the salary bills of the office expenses or of some Sections of the Central Bharat Sevak Samaj or for advancing moneys to the Pradesh and District Units in which in turn advanced them to individuals from whom no accounts were received in many cases. No contributions are shown to have been made towards any of Government aided schemes except for some very small amounts. The payments to the Government aided activities were not shown in the accounts of those schemes nor are they shown as contributions ; they were only loans. Thus, the primary objective of starting the Construction Service to provide a source of income for the social welfare activities and thereby reducing the burden on the Government for providing funds for those activities was not achieved.

Upto March 19, 1968, amounts totalling Rs. 10,08,233.01 from out of the advances given by the different Units to the piece workers, suppliers and officials of the Bharat Sevak Samaj were written off in the accounts of the Construction Service. The records do not indicate what these advances were given for and the particulars of the amounts written off are also not available. Therefore, it appears that some individuals who either took up sub-contracts from the Bharat Sevak Samaj or who were the workers of the Bharat Sevak Samaj derived financial advantage which was not the object of the Construction Service and was contrary to the professed objectives.

Defects in Accounts

In the Consolidated Balance Sheet as on March 31, 1966, an amount of Rs. 7,28,122.32 is shown under the head "Central-inter-Unit Account" representing transactions between the different Units of the Central Construction Service. Had the accounts been properly prepared there should not have been any balance under this head. The existence of such a large balance indicates that the accounts of the Construction Service of the Central Bharat Sevak Samaj were not properly kept or prepared.

One of the basic objectives of inducting the Bharat Sevak Samaj into the construction activities was to eliminate middle-man's profit which the contractors would have made. The evidence shows however that in the Central Construction Service the Bharat Sevak Samaj did not execute a major part of the work themselves and engaged sub-contractors for the execution of works. The Samaj has not produced the contracts made with the sub-contractors except in very few cases, These sub-contractors were variously described as piece workers, group leaders, petty contractors etc. A scrutiny of the available records shows however that they were nothing but sub-contractors and the Samaj did not observe the terms of the contract with the Central Public Works Department and other departments in regard to subletting. Agreements with the sub-contractors were also not produced before the auditing Chartered Accountants and, therefore, they could not verify whether the payments made to the sub-contractors were in accordance with the contracts made with them. Even in cases where contracts were said to have been executed through departmental labour, the Samaj did not actually employ any dapartmental labour but got the work done through labour Mukaddams to whom they made lump sum payments.

The auditing Chartered Accountants said in their reports in many cases that the Contractor's labour and so called departmental labour were working side by side and the necessary records showing the work respectively done by the two were not kept and consequently they could not verify whether the expenditure for the departmental labour was commensurate with the work done.

Thus, the claim of the Bharat Sevak Samaj that the middleman's profit was eliminated and that labour benefited by the Samaj entering the field of construction are not made out and are disproved by the very method of working adopted by the Bharat Sevak Samaj and by their employing sub-contractors or labour contractors for the different works.

The major expenditure on the various contracts taken up by the Bharat Sevak Samaj was on building materials like cement, bricks, steel, etc. The Samaj has not produced the accounts showing receipts, issue and consumption of construction material for the works which they executed. The auditing Chartered Accountants have also reported the non-maintenance and non-production of the accounts of construction material during the years. The total expenditure on building material for the different Units of the Central Construction Service for the years for which accounts have been produced amounted to Rs. 6,33,69,123.56 and the fact that no accounts whatsoever of material of such a large value have not been produced considerably detracts from the proper working of the Construction Service and from the correctness of its accounts. The available records also do not show that there was any proper inspection done by the Samaj itself even though the expenditure on building materials went up to crores of rupees. If the Samaj had a machinery, the records relating to its functioning have not been produced. Whatever records were produced before this Commission, and they are very few they go to show that there were instances of shortages of materials noticed in almost all the works and that matter has been discussed in the relevant chapters by the Commission. The Samaj did not take any action to investigate these shortages or take appropriate measures at least, no action has been proved.

Loans to the Samaj

The loans given to the Bharat Sevak Samaj for the construction activities carried a nominal rate of interest and no securities were taken for these loans except that the machinery and equipments purchased out of the loans was hypothecated to the Government. Even this hypothecation was not done in all cases. Even though the Bharat Sevak Samaj had some landed property, those properties were not taken as security for the loans except in cases of the brick kilns where the land purchased or taken on lease was itself mortgaged to the Government.

The loans given had a specific condition of the loans being utilised for the specific purposes of purchase of machinery and equipments or financing the works taken up by the Bharat Sevak Samaj and accounts were also required to be rendered to the Government showing utilisation. The Samaj did not keep separate accounts of the loans and the loans were merged with their other moneys and they did not restrict the user of the loans only for the specific purposes for which they were given. The loans and advances were used for whatsoever activities, the Samaj had in hand. Further the Samaj did not adhere to the time schedule for the repayment of the loans and even after there were breaches in the repayments, further loans were given to them.

The Samaj had no funds of their own for investing in the construction works and practically the whole of the finances required for construction contracts came from out of the loans given by the Government of

India and the advances given by the Central and State Governments at the beginning of the work. The entire construction activity of the Bharat Sevak Samaj was financed out of Government funds but still the Government had no control over the manner in which loans were utilised or the method in which the construction service of the Samaj functioned. The Commission has been at a great disadvantage in ascertaining the utilisation of the individual loans and advances given by the Government because the Samaj never kept a separate account of those loans and advances but merged the loans and advances with their other funds and in the utilisation also no distinction was made between the purposes for which the loans and advances were given and the general activities of the Bharat Sevak Samaj.

The Samaj as mentioned above was irregular in the repayment of loans and advances and the Government had to take stringent measures like the appropriating of payments due to the Bharat Sevak Samaj for works done and the recovery of the loans, due from the Central Bharat Sevak Samaj together with interest was completed only in August 1972.

Construction activities in the States

The construction activities in the States started earlier than those under the Centre and from 1954 a large number of construction contracts were taken up by the different State Units of the Bharat Sevak Samaj. The information made available by the State Governments and the different Units of the Bharat Sevak Samaj show that 2,122 works of the value of about Rs. 8.50 crores, to be exact Rs. 848,21,423.29, were taken up by the different Units of the Bharat Sevak Samaj (see Table 47-B). In the absence of authentic information, the Commission is not in a position to say whether these were all the works that were taken up or whether there were also some others because the Bharat Sevak Samaj had a number of Units in the different parts of the country and even the Central Bharat Sevak Samaj did not have a precise idea of the works taken up by them. The information collected from the different State Governments cannot be said to be complete because a large number of Public Works Divisions had entrusted these contracts to the Bharat Sevak Samaj and the State authorities did not have their complete records.

The Central Bharat Sevak Samaj had laid down certain rules for the recognition of different units to enable them for taking up construction contracts and these rules were framed after the construction Service was formed as a separate agency in 1958. The basic reason for this recognition was to enforce uniform standards of efficiency and observance of rules regarding accounts and for accounting of receipts and utilisation of profits. The records relating to the recognition of the different Units have not been produced by the Bharat Sevak Samaj even though they were specifically asked to produce them. But from the available records, the Commission finds that 79 Pradesh and District Committees were recognised by the Central Samaj but out of these there is evidence of only 62 Units functioning. Apart from those recognised Units, there were 20 unrecognised Units functioning which shows that the system of recognition was not an effective method of control. Whether there were more unrecognised Units functioning or not cannot be verified because the relevant files of the Bharat Sevak Samaj has not been produced before the Commission. (see Table 47-A).

The accounts of as many as 31 Units have not been produced before this Commission. Therefore, it has not been possible to verify as to how the funds of those units and profits, if any, were utilised. Even the accounts of the Units which were produced were not complete or for the entire period of the functioning of the Units. In the case of 50 Units, the accounts are available only for a part of the period of their functioning. Out of the 2122 works taken up by the Bharat Sevak Samaj of the value of Rs. 8,48,21,423.29, accounts have been produced only for 1,601 works of the value of Rs. 4,30,07,220.60. (see Table 47-B). For the remaining there are no accounts. The records available show a net loss of Rs. 6,93,003.35 in respect of the works taken up by the different Units. As to whether the other Units had made any profit or not or what happened to their funds or accounts cannot be ascertained.

In the Consolidated Accounts of the Construction Service for the years 1964-65 and 19.5-66, the total value of works shown was only Rs. 1,77,15,578.47. These accounts were of the Central Construction Service of the Bharat Sevak Samaj which they collected when they wanted to consolidate the accounts. The profit shown in those accounts was Rs. 1,34,364.87 but the latest accounts produced before the Commission show that this profit has been converted into a loss of Rs. 6,93,003.35. (see Table 47-B).

The main source of finance for the works undertaken by the Pradesh and District Units of the Bharat Sevak Samaj was the loans given by the Planning Commission through the State Governments totalling Rs. 36.50 lacs. Besides this, the State Governments also gave initial advances at the beginning of the work as a result of instructions received from the Central Ministry of Irrigation and Power and the Planning Commission as a part of the concessions extended to the Bharat Sevak Samaj. No precise information is available about the advances given but the Commission finds that out of these loans and advances Rs. 23,84,968.74 plus interest was outstanding against the Samaj Units and out of the advances Rs. 23,32,632.02 was outstanding (Table 47-B). Besides the advances given by the State Governments for the works given by them, advances were also given by the Central Government departments in respect of the works given by the Central departments to the State Units. The advances given by those Central departments have been recovered by the States but the record shows that the financing of the works of the State Units was also done out of the Government loans and advances given by the Central or State Governments.

On the basis of the instructions issued by the planning Commission, no securities were taken for the Planning Commission loans distributed through the State Governments except that the machinery and equipments purchased out of those loans were hypothecated to the Government.

Even though the construction activities of the Bharat Sevak Samaj in the States were also financed out of Government funds virtually there was no control over the activities of the Construction Service. Accounts of the Construction Units or of the utilisation of the loans were not obtained except before sanctioning the loans.

The Government had also given various concessions like exemption from payment of earnest money and security deposit, allotment of works to the Bharat Sevak Samaj on the basis of negotiated basis without calling for tenders and alloting works upto certain monetary limits at scheduled rates, or at certain fixed rates. Still there was hardly any control exercised and the funds could be used by the Bharat Sevak Samaj in any manner the Samaj wanted. As a consequence of this lack of vigilance and control, the Samaj has not repaid as much as Rs. 47,17,600.76 together with interest thereon as far as the Commission has been able to see. (see Table 47-B).

The records produced by the State Governments show that the State Governments had paid for the works executed by the Bharat Sevak Samaj a sum of Rs. 6,70,76,930.61 out of which the Samaj has produced the accounts only for Rs. 4,28,70,043.66 and for the balance of Rs. 2, 40,69, 710.61 no accounts have been produced. (See Table 47-C). Whether the non-production is due to the non-existence of any accounts or due to the Samaj withholding the accounts, it is difficult to say. The major part of the unaccounted receipts pertains to the Kosi Unit of the Bharat Sevak Samaj which had done work of Rs. 2,26,09,753 81 but has produced accounts for only three years, i.e. 1963-64 and 1965 for the works of the value of Rs. 40,51,184.61. For the balance of Rs. 1,85,58,569.20, (see Table 47-C) no accounts have been produced. Even for the three years for which accounts have been produced, the accounts are only Receipt and Payment accounts and no Balance Sheets or Profit and Loss Accounts have been produced.

The contracts entrusted to the Samaj State Units were executed mainly through sub-contractors and the agreements with the sub-contractors have not been produced before the Commission except in a few cases. The records show that these agreements were also not produced before the auditing Chartered Accountants who could not verify whether the expenditure shown in the accounts was rightly chargeable to the accounts of the works.

A major part of the expenditure of the works in the States also was on account of materials used in the works in the State Units but no quantity accounts showing the material received issued and consumed were kept nor were the auditing Chartered Accountants given any consumption statements for the different works which would have enabled him to ascertain the reasonableness of expenditure on material. Thus, for a major portion of the expenditure on its construction activities, the Bharat Sevak Samaj had no accounts, at least, none were produced before the auditors or the Commission.

Another major item of expenditure in the Construction activities was on "departmental labour" but even for these no proper accounts were kept. What was called departmental labour was not actually employed directly by the Bharat Sevak Samaj but only through the labour contractors who were called Mukkaddams.

There is no proof that the various advantages which were claimed for the Bharat Sevak Samaj participation to arise, did arise in fact. A major part of the works taken up by the Bharat Sevak Samaj were got executed through sub-contractors who were euphemistically and variously described as "piece workers", "labour contractors", "Unit leaders", "group leaders" etc. The contracts entered into with them varied from complete assignment of the contracts as to sub-contractors as in the case of Bombay to splitting up the works into different convenient reaches and portions and giving them to small contractors. The details varied but the basic feature remained the same, i.e.. the actual execution was in the hands of agencies other than the Bharat Sevak Samaj itself. In the case of Bombay particularly the records show that the Samaj provided no finance ; they did not engage any supervisory staff except for preparing the bills to be submitted to the Government or for tendering for works. Even in cases where the Samaj had shown some work done through departmental labour, the departmental labour was mostly the labour employed through Mukkaddams as labour contractors and the direct employment and payment by the Bharat Sevak Samaj was the exception rather than the rule. This was the mode of execution of the works in Punjab also. Consequently, all claims that the contractors and the middle men were eliminated in the system of execution of Government contracts by public co-operation agencies like the Bharat Sevak Samaj are not made out. Similarly, the claim that the middle man's profit was eliminated is also not borne out by facts. In fact, the Samaj became an extra agency which took a part of the profit. What is really surprising is that even in cases where the works were got done through sub-contractors, the Samaj kept a big complement of staff and the justification for this is not clear and so also the reason for losses because in the case of sub-contractors being employed there should be no loss.

The Commission has also not been able to find any support for the claim of the Samaj that more agricultural labour got employed under them than under the works taken up by other contractors. Further the Samaj had the patronage of some Union and State Ministers and political leaders and also high officials of the Planning Commission who pleaded their cases and even interfered in the working of the Government Departments in the interest of the Samaj. Thus, undue influence was not eliminated but there is no proof of the bribing of the officials.

The officials of the Government Departments were subjected to such pressure that they could not take decisions according to their judgements and discretion and some of them who found fault with the working of the Bharat Sevak Samaj in the execution of contracts were complained against to the higher authorities including Central Ministers by the Bharat Sevak Samaj and they suffered both indignity and in their official career. This was particularly true of the Bombay Unit of the Samaj and of Bidar.

In the execution of the contracts taken up by the Samaj there were delays but no action was taken by the officials and when it was it had to be withdrawn on the ground of the Samaj being a voluntary organisation working without a profit motive.

In many cases the Samaj did not complete the work and abandoned the contracts and the departments had to incur extra expenditure on getting the works completed through other agencies. Delay was the usual feature of the working of the Samaj and the instances where the works were completed in time were more an exception than a rule. But this extra expenditure on completion was not recovered in accordance with the terms of the contracts.

The Samaj and the Planning Commission had made various claims about the savings to the exchequer due to Samaj entering the field of construction activities but these claims are not supported by any details and no verification of the claims is possible because of the concessions given to the Samaj which were not available to other agencies.

These concessions were inter alia the following :—

(i) Exemption from security deposits and earnest moneys ;

(ii) advances to the extent of 25 per cent of the value of the work ;

(iii) giving of contracts without tenders on negotiated basis ;

(iv) exemption from payment of income tax ;

(v) grant of loans on liberal terms ;

(vi) lending of Government officials to the Bharat Sevak Samaj ;

(vii) the help rendered by the Planning Commission and Ministers in getting the matters sorted out in favour of the Bharat Sevak Samaj , and

(viii) giving assistance for training centres for training workers engaged for construction activities.

Even in the case of Kosi the rates of the Samaj were actually higher in some of the years or equal to that of the other contractors and the volume of work done by the Samaj was only a little more than Rs. 2 crores in a project costing more than Rs. 65 23 crores. It must in fairness be added that the coming in of the Samaj did help in bringing down the rates which were in the beginning demanded by the contractors although there were other factors also operating like malaria prevention measures.

The claim of the Samaj about the savings to the exchequer has to be taken in conjunction with the likely losses to the exchequer on account of the unrepaid loans by State Units and advances given to the Bharat Sevak Samaj Units which, as mentioned earlier, comes to Rs. 47,17,600.76 plus interest (see Table 47-B).

Though the Samaj was a society registered under the Societies Registration Act, normally the funds of the society could not be used for private gains. The Samaj had engaged a number of piece-workers for its contracts and had given large amounts of money to them, to various office-bearers and staff and to others. Out of these advances, Rs. 12,75,519.02 were written off and how far these advances were bona fide business advances, it is not clear from the records because necessary details are not given in the ledgers. The authority for making these advances has also not been proved but one thing is clear that some private individuals were benefited out of the write off of these amounts.

In the Consolidated Accounts as on March 31, 1966, the amount of advances outstanding against the Bharat Sevak Samaj workers and piece-workers was

Rs. 70,32,211.50. How much out of this was subsequently recovered is not clear as the accounts of all the units have not been produced but the records produced show that a major part of these advances was not recovered even as late as 1968 and substantial part of these advances made had to be written off ultimately. It is surprising that the full details about the persons from whom these advances were due are not available on the records produced.

Further, in Units like the District Unit of Varanasi, large amounts of expenditure have been shown in the accounts without any supporting details of expenditure and the fact that the accounts of many Units are not audited makes it impossible to determine the correctness of the items of expenditure.

In these circumstances, the correctness of the claim of the Bharat Sevak Samaj that the profits of the Samaj did not go into private pockets remains unproved.

In some places and particularly in Bombay the managers looking after construction activities of the Samaj were themselves contractors of the Class I. That considerably eroded the image of the Samaj and detracted from its claim of being a body of selfless workers working for altruistic motives. This damage was further increased by the association of some ambitious people who wanted to use the Samaj as a means of making money for themselves.

The Bharat Sevak Samaj had also claimed that its methods of work and accounts were subject to the examination and scrutiny of the officials. There is no proof that the accounts of the construction service or of other activities of the Samaj were regularly submitted to the Government or its officials for scrutiny except that some accounts were submitted for the grants-in-aid schemes and in a few cases for the sanctioning of loans. Complete accounts were never produced before the officials and in the case of Kosi Project which was the first venture in the construction activities of the Samaj, the Samaj resisted all attempts by the Government to get the accounts. In fact, even the accounts of the community savings which were credited to the Government accounts initially from out of the deductions from the unit leaders and were subsequently withdrawn from the Government were not given to the Government in spite of the criticism in the Press and legislature right from 1962 and even after the Chief Minister suggested submission of those accounts to the Government. The Samaj has consistently refused to have the accounts produced before any official agency and even before this Commission then took the stand that the Commission is not entitled to look into the accounts.

There were constant quarrels and bickering between the Bharat Sevak Samaj and the Government Departments in regard to the execution of the contracts. The Samaj was in many cases unhelpful and its tendency to make allegations against Government servants who attempted to enforce the terms of the contracts can be found in almost all the construction contracts. In the opinion of the Commission it was an unhealthy trend.

The history of the different contracts shows that in many of the cases the Samaj was not equipped to take up the contracts whether due to lack of machinery or lack of personnel or expertise and experience and there were many instances of delays, some of even abnormal delays and many were the instances of bad workmanship and poor quality of work. The poor workmanship and bad quality of work were tolerated and even over-looked due to its being a voluntary non-profit making body but it cannot be ruled out that its important connections and patronage from high quarters was the reason of this rather lenient and overlooking attitude of the officials. In many cases, no compensation was recovered and where it was recovered it was almost negligible. One of the important reasons for inducting the Samaj into construction works was the hope that the savings made by the Bharat Sevak Samaj would be available for social welfare activities and the burden on the Government for such activities would be reduced. The record, however, shows that the Central Bharat Sevak Samaj spent precious little on social welfare activities, only a few hundreds. A major part of the savings of some aerodrome works was offset by the losses elsewhere and on the whole there was a loss. Some amounts of money were paid for the organisational section of the Samaj for maintaining a complement of staff but on welfare activities as such there was practically no expenditure.

There were some loans given to the section of the Samaj dealing with central grants and the Samaj has put forward claims against the Government in regard to all those schemes; and there is no evidence of burden on the Government for social welfare activities being reduced.

In Kosi, various claims were made about the savings being used in activities beneficial to the community but the Samaj has contumaciously kept away records from the Commission and in absence of the requisite records, the Commission is unable to verify those claims of moneys having been expended on community projects.

This Commission has to enquire into the extent to which accounts have been rendered by the Bharat Sevak Samaj for central assistance and the extent to which these accounts conformed to the procedures prescribed for the submission of accounts. From the record it appears that in the letters sanctioning assistance to the Bharat Sevak Samaj the form of accounts to be rendered by the Samaj were not clearly set out and the different Ministries followed different procedures in the matter of accounts and consequently the accounts submitted were also different and indifferent in character. The General Financial Rules laid down a definite procedure for obtaining the accounts and under Rule 149(3) of the General Financial Rules an overall consolidated account showing the financial position of the institution was required to be submitted by the organisation receiving the grant. The Consolidated Accounts of all the activities of the organisation and of its units and these accounts have to be :—

(i) Receipt and Payment accounts;

(ii) The Income and Expenditure account or the Profit and Loss Accounts; and

(iii) The Balance-Sheet at the end of the financial year.

The various Ministries giving assistance to the Bharat Sevak Samaj obtained only the accounts of the particular scheme for which assistance was sanctioned by that Ministry and even these accounts did not reflect the financial position of the grantee or the utilisation of total assistance. Only in the year 1965, after the Public Accounts Committee pointed out the need for obtaining the consolidated accounts of the Bharat Sevak Samaj was an attempt made to obtain consolidated accounts when perhaps it was too late. After that the Bharat Sevak Samaj rendered the following accounts to the Government of India :—

(i) Consolidated statements of accounts of central and State Units (excluding construction service) for the years 1962-63, 1963-64 and 1964-65 24-5-1966

(ii) Consolidated statements of Receipts of and Payments against Central Government grants for the years, 1953-54 to 1961-62 26-10-1966

(iii) Consolidated Statement of Receipts and Payments of Central and State Units (excluding construction activities) for the year 1965-66 31-5-1968

(iv) Recasted Consolidated Balance-Sheets of Bharat Sevak Samaj Construction Service for the period ended 31-3-1965 and 31-3-1966, supported by Profit and Loss Accounts, Contract Accounts and Manufacturing and Training Accounts of Brick Kilns, duly certified by a Chartered Accountant. 8-1-1969

These accounts are not the overall accounts of the Bharat Sevak Samaj as the Samaj has not prepared the consolidated accounts from the beginning. Actually the consolidated accounts for the general activities are only for four years, i.e. 1962-63 to 1965-66 and for the construction services these accounts have been rendered only for two years namely for 1964-65 and 1965-66. The defects, omissions and deficiencies of these accounts have been discussed at length in an earlier chapter. But the main deficiencies are :—

(i) As the consolidated accounts have not been prepared from the beginning, the balances shown in the accounts for the years for which the consolidated accounts have been prepared are not verifiable.

(ii) The accounts of a number of schemes have been left out of these accounts, particularly the accounts of the Local Development Works Programme for which grants given were more than Rs. 71 lacs and the outlay more than Rs. 165 lacs.

(iii) The accounts of the District Units of the Bharat Sevak Samaj were not included in the consolidated accounts.

(iv) The accounts of a number of construction units were not included in the consolidated accounts.

(v) In the case of Kosi Unit of the Bharat Sevak Samaj the construction works executed by the Samaj were of the value of Rs. 1.85 crores. It was claimed that out of these works of the value of Rs. 1.85 crores, there was a saving to the Samaj of Rs. 16 lacs during the period 1954 to 1962. But there are no accounts produced to show as to what happened to these Rs. 16 lacs nor has it been shown how the figure of Rs. 16 lacs was arrived at.

(vi) Under an agreement contained in the contract between the Unit leaders and the Administration and by the Samaj, a certain sum of money was to be deducted, the percentages of which varied from time to time, from out of the payments to be made to the Unit leaders. These moneys were to be used for the Community Savings Fund and the Organisational Fund. Out of this amount, a sum of Rs. 14,93,318.00 was withdrawn by the office bearers of the Samaj and it is claimed that they were expended. The Commission has been unable to verify this as no accounts have been produced. The position taken by the Samaj was that these moneys were its own and, therefore, it was not bound to give any accounts of these moneys. The Commission is unable to accept this contention because even on the plea taken by the Samaj they were moneys clothed with a trust and had to be expended on particular and specified objectives. They had to be spent according to the contract with the concurrence of the Kosi Administration, a condition which in the opinion of the Commission was illegally abrogated. At the most the Samaj were the trustees of these moneys and so was the Kosi Administration and they had to be expended for the benefit of cestuiqui trustent and should have been proved to have been so expended.

(vii) The records produced by the Bihar Government and other records before this Commission show that out of the advances given by the Kosi Project to the Unit Leaders, a sum of Rs. 19,01,526.26 was outstanding. What happened to these advances and how they were utilised has not been shown as no accounts have been produced. The Central Bharat Sevak Samaj made efforts to get the accounts of the Kosi Construction Unit to the Central Samaj but both were unaudited, one on September 27, 1965 and the other on October 11, 1965. The former showed the advances against the Unit Leaders to be Rs. 26,16,174.16 and the latter showed no outstandings at all. This makes these accounts unacceptable in the absence of books of accounts by means of which the Commission would have been able to verify these figures. Unfortunately these were withheld by the Samaj when the Commission visited Patna.

(viii) Mr. G.L. Nanda in a letter which he sent to the Commission has stated that he has personally checked that labour was paid its share of payments out of the moneys paid by the Kosi Administration. The Commission has no reason to disregard this assurance but this does not apply to those moneys which were deducted for the special purpose of Community Savings and Organisational Funds from out of the wages payable to labour for which no accounts have been produced.

(ix) The assets of the Bharat Sevak Samaj such as buildings and land etc. are not included in the Balance-Sheets which were prepared.

(x) The accounts of the General Section and other funds like the Central Development Fund and the Special Fund operated by the chairman are not included in the Consolidated Accounts.

(xi) There were large amounts under the Inter-Unit suspense account which have remained unexplained and unadjusted.

(xii) The consolidated Accounts have been prepared from the accounts of the different schemes and of the different Units but these accounts of the different units and of the different schemes were not prepared on a uniform pattern, i.e. Receipt & Payment Account, the Income & Expenditure or Profit & Loss Account and the Balance Sheets were not prepared for all the Units of the scheme. Very often the accounts prepared were hybrid accounts, i.e. they were not exclusively maintained on cash basis nor on mercantile basis with the result that sometimes liabilities were included and sometimes they were not. In the absence of a uniform pattern of accounts for the different Units, the Consolidated Accounts do not reflect the correct state of affairs.

(xiii) In the Consolidated Accounts, the accounts of a number of Units which were unaudited were included and the books of accounts of those Units also have not been produced. In the absence of any audit certificate and the books of accounts, it was not possible to verify the unaudited accounts which have been included in the Consolidated Accounts.

The Consolidated accounts prepared by the Samaj for the few years above set out are incomplete. Further the accounts for a number of years have not been included in those overall accounts. In many of the states and districts the Units had ceased to function and it is not known as to where or in whose custody the books of accounts are. The present office-bearers of the Samaj are unaware of the whereabouts of the portion of the records. Even if the books could be traced the accounts would have to be recast into a uniform pattern and this will be a stupendous task as the Samaj has not maintained their books of accounts on a uniform pattern. The Commission, therefore, finds that it will be almost impossible to reconstruct the overall consolidated accounts for the Bharat Sevak Samaj for all the years and unless the overall accounts are prepared from the beginning, the balances for the subsequent years cannot be correctly carried forward and without these balances the uptodate balances of the assets and liabilities cannot be worked out.

The Commission, thus, finds that out of the grants given by the Government of India accounts are yet to be rendered by the Bharat Sevak Samaj for amounts totalling Rs. 6,69,958·31 and the accounts rendered for Rs. 23,90,185.66 are yet to be finalised by the various Ministries in accordance with the principles herein suggested. How much of these accounts will be admitted will be known only when the scrutiny is completed by the Ministries. Further the amounts tatalling Rs. 3,57,496.33 are due from the Bharat Sevak Samaj on account of the arrears of rent of buildings allotted by the Estate office ; Rs. 6,14,287.15 is due from the Bharat Sevak Samaj on account of arrears of rent, lease money and damages on the lands and buildings allotted by the Land and Development officer.

The Commission finds that out of the loans sanctioned by the Planning Commission to the State Units of the Bharat Sevak Samaj, Rs. 23,84,968.74 is still due and for these are unsecured loans except that the machinery and equipments purchased were hypothecated to Government. Apart from this, out of the advances given by the various State Governments to the State Units of the Bharat Sevak Samaj, Rs. 44,78,677.60 plus interest was outstanding.

The Samaj is one entity under its constitution and the State Units cannot be said to be separate bodies and they cannot be even termed legal entities as they were not separately registered and are not legal personae except as units of Central Bharat Sevak Samaj. The Commission in the absence of any specific claim by the Government and in the absence of specific pleas of the Samaj does not propose to hazard an opinion on the liability of the Central Samaj which has now disowned any liability but that was in the course of arguments.

But in the absence of a special power of borrowing or carrying on of a commercial activity in the Memorandum of Association, it is difficult to hold in favour of legality of these loans or of the liability of the Samaj. But that plea also was not raised by the Samaj ; on the other hand, it has submitted that its constitution allowed it to do the work of a building contractor and also to borrow.

Apart from the cases of shortages of materials reported in the different Constitution Units, there were also instances where there were complaints of misappropriation against some of the Bharat Sevak Samaj officials. These complaints were in respect of the Varanasi Unit of the Central Construction Service where the ex-Accountant of the Unit has been charged with misappropriation totalling Rs. 40,458.27. The records of the Varanasi Unit have not been produced before this Commission by the Bharat Sevak Samaj on the ground that the First Information Report lodged by them against the Accountant is still being inquired into and the records are with the police. Similarly, in the Bidar Unit of the Central Construction Service also there were complaints of misappropriation against the Accountant. The Commission has already discussed at another place the complaints against the District Convenor of the Bharat Sevak Samaj about the misappropriation and falsification of accounts in respect of the camps. There are also allegations of misappropriation by the various office bearers and others in different states. These have been discussed in detail in the respective chapters. There were many serious financial irregularities in the Nahan unit of the Bharat Sevak Samaj where amounts totalling Rs. 85,838.02 shown in the cash book as deposited into the bank were not traceable in the bank accounts and Rs. 1,99,198.22 withdrawn from the bank were not accounted for. Other irregularities noticed in the unit were (1) the Chairman showing the contributions received from the public totalling Rs. 1,47,727.26 as loan given by himself, (2) non-issuing receipts for and non-accounting of public contributions and (3) maintenance of duplicate sets of books of accounts.

The Government allotted three plots of land for the construction of an office building and an occupational therapy institute to the Delhi Pradesh Bharat Sevak Samaj but these buildings were not constructed and the land passed into the hands of another society called the Society for the Aid of Crippled and Handicapped. The allotment of the land to the Bharat Sevak Samaj was later cancelled by the Government but during the period the land was in possession of the Bharat Sevak Samaj, some barracks which according to the terms and conditions of the allotment were to be dismantled were not so dismantled and the barracks were hired out to a college and rent collected from it.

Two plots of land were allotted on Magazine Road to the Bharat Sevak Samaj one for construction of an office building for the Patharthoda Society and another for a labour camp for workers of the said society.

Another piece of vacant Government land vacated at Kutab Road were allotted to the Bharat Sevak Samaj for running a school and a dispensary.

A building in Khyber Pass market was also allotted to the Bharat Sevak Samaj for its use.

The Samaj was also allotted an area of 151.01 acres for two seasons for removal of sand from the river bed. The Samaj also encroached on a plot of land in Nauroji Nagar for use of a school.

Some of these plots of land were not vacated by the Samaj even after the expiry of the lease. Arrears of rent and lease money and damages in all these plots of land amounted to Rs. 6,14,287.15 as on January 31, 1970.

It appears to the Commission that in most of the cases, the schemes, which were subsequently approved and passed by the Planning Commission or its Coordination Committee, emanated in the first instance from the Samaj and the Samaj had asked for large amounts of grants, for each scheme though the grants were not made on that ground scale. It is unfortunate that the schemes were more or less nebulous in their scope and objective and vague in concept and it has not been possible to find or devise any objective test by which the success or otherwise of those scheme could be measured.

The working of these schemes also suffered from an avoidable infirmity and that was that the Government had divised no machinery for the supervision of the work done under the various schemes for which large amounts were given as grants and there is no material on the record showing that the Government took any interest in the execution of those schemes after Bharat Sevak Samaj was entrusted with the task of carrying them out. It further appears to the Commission that the Ministry did not have any machinery at New Delhi which could carefully supervise the working or scrutinise the results of the carrying out of the schemes by the Samaj or be able to discover the various defects which crept in the execution of the schemes. The entire working of these schemes was left to the Bharat Sevak Samaj and it was paid a special grant for an overall supervision of these schemes but there is little evidence to show that the Samaj carried out its obligations of inspections and supervision or even proper guidance. In these circumstances it would be difficult to hold that supervision grants were well or even properly utilised. Therefore, the Commission would venture to recommend that whenever assistance is given to voluntary or non-official bodies by the Government an adequate official machinery should be devised for keeping supervision and control over the execution of those schemes and there should be an assessment of their success during the course of execution. It would not be advantageous for the Central Government to associate the states and their employees in the matter of supervision, whenever grants are given to organisations executing schemes which are more easily capable of inspection and control by officers of the states.

Even though grants and other assistance were given to the Bharat Sevak Samaj by the Government of India from the year 1953 no consolidated accounts showing the overall financial position of the Bharat Sevak Samaj were called for or obtained by the Government of India till the Public Accounts Committee in its 34th Report for the year 1964-65 commented adversely about it. Even after these adverse comments grants were released for the years 1965-66 and partly for 1966-1967 and time was allowed to the Bharat Sevak Samaj to furnish the consolidated accounts. The Samaj could not prepare a complete and current consolidated account for all the years it was functioning, and only for some years in-a complete accounts were prepared which did not show the true financial position of the Bharat Sevak Samaj as a whole. The Samaj could not obtain the accounts from a large number of units either due to the non-cooperation of those units or due to their becoming defunct. The Commission recommends that in order to avoid such contingencies the General Financial Rules should be suitably amended in order to make it compulsory on the part of the grants receiving bodies to submit consolidated accounts of the body as a whole showing its overall financial position both before sanctioning of assistance as well as after the assistance is utilised. These accounts should be obtained not only from such bodies to whom grants-in-aid is given but also from all such bodies to whom other assistance is given.

The Commission finds that the General Financial Rules as they stand now do not specify the form of accounts to be submitted by the grant receiving bodies. The Commission, therefore, recommends that General Financial Rules may be suitably revised and amended in order to provide for the submission of the following sets of accounts by all organisations and institutions receiving assistance from Government for each financial year :

(1) Audited Receipt and Payment Accounts of the body as a whole for the financial year.

(2) Audited Income and Expenditure Accounts or Profit and Loss Account for the body as a whole for the financial year.

(3) Audited Balance Sheet of the body as a whole for the year ending with March 31 of the year.

The Commission recommends that all institutions receiving assistance from the Government may be asked to adopt the same financial year as that of the Government. These accounts mentioned above should also be invariably accompanied by the Auditor's report on the accounts.

The Commission finds that under the Societies Registration Act, 1860 there is no provision making it compulsory for the societies registered under the Act to file their audited accounts with the Registrar of societies. The Commission recommends that suitable amendments in the Societies' Registration Act be made so as to provide for the filing of the audited annual accounts of Societies with the Registrar of Societies.

On the evidence before the Commission the experiment of giving construction contracts requiring technical knowledge of carrying them out was not a success in the case of non-official agencies even like the Bharat Sevak Samaj. In the case of the Bharat Sevak Samaj the work done was no uniformly good or the working free from squabbles with the Government engineers and has in a majority of cases led to litigation in the Courts or before private Tribunals which is neither a credit to the Departments nor to the Bharat Sevak Samaj.

The evidence shows that the Construction Service of the Samaj both at the Centre and in the States was not properly managed and resulted in an overall loss and also both damaged the Bharat Sevak Samaj materially and also tarnished its name and reputation.

STUDY GROUP ON WAYSIDE AMENITIES, 1969—REPORT

Delhi, Controller of Publications, 1974. 77p.+13 Photos+6 Charts,

Chairman : Shri S. N. Sinha.

Members : Shri S. R. Ratnakar; Shri A. P. Verma; Shri C. L. Mehta; Shri C. V. K. Murthy Rao; Shri T. Kumaran; Shri B. Ramu replaced by Shri T. N. Nagendra.

Convenor : Shri R.K. Sharma replaced by Shri K.C. Joshi again replaced by Shri B.S. Singh.

APPOINTMENT

Long distance road traffic has increased steadily in the last few years and will continue to develop further with the economic growth of the country. Such traffic makes it necessary that provision is made on our highways for certain basic amenities for the road-users including large number of tourists arriving in India by land route or taking to the road for local sight-seeing. The matter was considered at the seventh meeting of the Transport Development Council held at Mysore in June, 1968. It was decided that a small Study Group should be set up, consisting of representatives of the Government of India from the Ministries of Shipping and Transport and Petroleum and Chemicals, the Department of Tourism, and Oil, tyre and automobile manufacturing companies, to formulate a programme of providing wayside facilities on the National and State Highways. In pursuance of the Council's recommendation, the Government appointed a (part-time) Study Group on Wayside Amenities to examine the problem vide the Ministry of Shipping and Transport Resolution No. 3-T (49)/68, dated the 22nd February, 1969.

TERMS OF REFERENCE

(a) To suggest what roadside amenities should be provided on the National and State Highways; and

(b) To formulate an action programme for the provision of such amenities including also the estimated cost of providing them.

CONTENTS

Introductory; Procedure of Study; Need for Basic Wayside Amenities; Concepts of Wayside Amenities in Certain Foreign Countries; Evidence of Local Conditions; Suggested Roadside Amenities; Recommended Action Programme for Amenities and Agencies for Implementation; Summary of Conclusions and Recommendations; Annexures I to IX; Figures.

RECOMMENDATIONS

Need For Basic Wayside Facilities Increase In Traffic:

Road traffic is gaining fast upon rail traffic. The share of roads in total goods tonnage carried by rail and road together increased from 16 per cent in 1961 to 24 per cent in 1969. Over the same period, the share of roads in passenger traffic rose from 42 to 48 per cent. The share of roads in the total traffic carried by rail and road may increase to 35 per cent and 51 per cent respectively for goods traffic and passenger traffic by 1974.

There has been a steady increase of 10-12 per cent per year in the motor vehicle population of country.

Increasing road length, improvement in the quality of the highways and rising car and scooter ownership present the prospect of steady expansion of traffic on highways which is likely to reach 14 per cent per year in the near future and improve further in the years to come.

Road Tourism : A new concept of road tourism is in the advent, that of people travelling just for the pleasure of being on the road in a motor vehicle to visit beauty and picnic spots. If the highways are beautified with wayside picnic and rest areas, they are likely to become a source of popular outdoor recreation.

There is an increasing tendency for bus travel by school children and groups of young student over long distances in pursuit of historical and other interests or just for holidaying.

There is a steady increase in foreign tourists comparing favourably with the general increase in world tourism. A well-conceived programme of highway amenities is bound to attract more tourists to road travel, whether for pleasure, education or business.

In view of the progressive nationalisation of passenger road transport services, and the attendant improvement in their operation, more and more people within the country are travelling by road, particularly during pilgrim seasons. This necessitates a minimum programme of shelters, sanitation and food inspection.

Inter-State Traffic : The Inter-State traffic which is already heavy on many long-distance routes is likely to further increase by 50 to 60 per cent by the end of Fourth Plan period.

The bulk of traffic on highways, especially on approaches to big cities, comprises commercial vehicles which necessitates the provision of rest areas where the drivers could ease their limbs after a long drive and also give rest to their vehicles.

Benefits to Local Business: The provision of ancillaries and amenities should benefit business in the locality from where supplies to the catering establishments on roadsides will have to be drawn.

If the amenities are standardized and properly spaced, they would generate more employment. In fact, in due course a need may arise for a suitable programme to train staff for restaurants, snack-bars, rest-houses, motels etc.

The New Challenge: Considering average vehicle occupancy, 30,000 to 60,000 people are on the move every day on several sections of highways for which facilities by the roadside must be provided. Thousands of kilometres on highways are still berest of any facilities whatsoever.

Although fuel stations erected on the highways by oil companies have been catering to some of the basic needs of passengers, these stations must be equipped to provide more of these facilities. A large number of privately run snack bars etc. have sprung up on the highways but the service provided by them is generally unhygienic and below par.

The challenge for improved facilities must be taken up by the Government who should ensure these with the help of private operators and agencies connected with road building, automobiles and oil distribution.

Concept Of Wayside Amenities In Certain Foreign Countries

In many foreign countries, notably U.S.A., U.K, Germany, France, Netherlands and Japan, great importance has been attached and concerted attention paid to the provision of basic wayside amenities at certain minimum intervals along the highways. Stress is mainly on facilities like fuel stations, service areas, lay-byes, rest areas, scenic overlooks, motels, restaurants, emergency telephones, traffic patrols and tourist information. Beautification of the roadside is also considered an important requirement.

Evidence Of Local Conditions—General Deficiencies

Road travel in India does not always present a pleasant prospect. Mixed traffic, uncontrolled intersections, lack of byepasses and numerous checkposts on the way cause irksome delays. Dangerous litter and construction material strewn on the road are additional deterrents. Clean food and water are not available easily. There is absence of repair facilities for vehicles at a proper scale, as also of telecommunications and information regarding the route to be travelled upon. Because of insufficient police vigilance, night driving is unsafe in many sections.

Fuel Stations: Refuelling arrangements, checking of oil, water and air pressure and normal repair and serving are essential facilities for vehicles. But of the 10,255 fuel stations owned by six oil companies in the country on 1st January, 1971, only 1838 possessed service and repair facilities.

The oil companies have not been particular about maintaining a maximum or minimum distance between two fuel stations. The result is that whereas in some states fuel stations are located between 35 and 75 kms. apart, in others these are not available even at 150 kms. Convenience in supply and availability of land have led to the clustering of pumps at various points along the highways. In the circumstances, the idea of a fully equipped station with repair facilities, parking space, canteen etc. is not considered a good proposition by the oil companies unless it is located at a key point.

The supply of air is one of the basic requirements for a vehicle, next only to fuel and oil. But at a number of stations, the pressure gauge/air tower was either found to be out of order or non-existent.

Drinking water is usually available every where but mostly in unhygienic condition. Tube wells by the side of fuel stations are rare. In many cases, the nearest well or reservoir is only source of supply.

Next to drinking water, the need of a traveller is a toilet room. The new designs of fuel stations all provide for a toilet room with sanitary arrangements. But these have not been built everywhere. Even where a few have been built and are open for use, generally either the flushing system is out of order or the toilet is maintained very unhygienically. In order to keep a toilet clean, some dealers have kept them locked, not to be used by all and sundry.

Most of the fuel stations now keep of a few spare parts but the stocks do not cover the whole range of essential items such as tyres, tubes, radiator hoses etc.

The necessity of installing a telephone, a fuel station is now being recognised. Presently on some of the heavily trafficed highways telecommunication facilities are not available at the fuel stations for hundreds of kilometres.

The need for maintaining a minor repair establishment at a fuel station is being increasingly felt. About 10 per cent of the stations offer this facility at present. The facility of major repairs can however be had only at fuel stations located near the towns with a sizeable population of car owners.

Very few of the fuel stations have canteens or snack bars due to regulations which prohibit the cooking of food inside the premises. Snack bars are an easier proposition but many fuel stations do not have them either. It is so because a number of eating and drinking stalls have come up in the vicinity or else the traffic is not enough.

Parking space is a facility which has not been considered in the layout of many fuel stations.

A fuel station where a vehicle has to stop for refuelling, is a very suitable spot for disseminating information about the highway and facilities available en route. But advantage has not been taken of these stations to display such publicity material.

Service Stations : Service areas are infrequent on the National Highways and practically non-existent on the State Highways except in the vicinity of towns. Generally, service facilities are provided by oil companies within the premises of the fuel stations but only around 10 per cent of the stations possess these. On many busy routes, the facility of repairs or spare parts is not available for long distances.

State Road Transport Undertakings have service arrangements at their larger depots but these are meant mainly for the maintenance of their own fleet. Normally, a stranded motorist cannot avail himself of these facilities even at payment.

In places where the distance between service stations is considerable, the lot of the motorist whose car breaks down is really unenviable on account of absence of telecommunications and the non-existence of mobile patrols or break-down vans. However, some organisations and big transport operators maintain their own break-down vans and also help stranded motorists in trouble.

The Automobile Associations help their members if they are stranded in the city but unfortunately their activities do not extend beyond the city limits to open highways.

Rest Houses : Most of the highways in India are studded with Rest Houses, Inspection Houses, Dak Bungalows, Travellers' Bungalows, Tourist Lodges and Circuit Houses. But barring some exceptions these are meant mainly for the use of officials on duty and cannot be availed of by the private motorists.

Some Government Rest House located in places of tourist interest are open to tourists and Government officers alike but there is a difference in charges for the same accommodation.

In many of the Rest Houses, Tourist Lodges etc. run by the State Governments, the services offered are below par even for middle-class tourists.

There is great deal of difference in the facilities available at Government Rest Houses and Tourist Rest Houses even though the latter also are maintained by the Government. While up-keep of the Government Rest Houses is far superior, that of the Tourist Rest Houses is allowed to lapse.

There is no organised motels at present, However, many State Governments and private concerns has started construction of rest houses on the highways with an eye on the tourists. Also India Tourism Development Corporation is planning to build some standard motels.

There is a general inadequacy of roadside information advising the Motorist-tourist about possibilities of lodging in a nearby Inspection House/Rest House.

Roadside restaurants have developed haphazardly in most cases to cater for requirements of bus passengers and truck drivers. The bulk of these eating places are unclean, though food of different kinds is available.

Rest areas, safety areas, lay-byes : There is no rest areas as such on our highways. In many areas the passengers have to wait on the road without any shelter to catch their bus. Maharashtra State Road Transport Corporation has, however, attended to this problem and constructed 1000 pick-up sheds.

During some of the big fares, such as Dussehra festival at Mysore, motorists are forced to park their cars on any available open space. In the absence of appropriate facilities for parking and rest at such places, sanitary conditions are bound to deteriorate.

Great difficulty is experienced by foreign tourists, particularly women, requiring toilet facilities even on short journeys.

There are no arrangements on the roadsides for occasional parking, either for rest, cooling the engine of the vehicle or any personal convenience.

Traffic Posts : The Government of Maharashtra has set up Traffic Aid Posts on important highways. The service is available to all roadusers. Such a measure has not been adopted by the other States.

The provision of mobile traffic police patrols for the highways has not yet been made in any State.

Health Services : There are no regular First Aid Posts on the highways, and dispensaries also are very few. Some fuel stations, however, keep a first-aid kit with them.

In places where dispensaries hospital exist a little away from the highways, no effort has been made to indicate this fact by means of sign posts.

Scenic or Historical Spots : There has been no organised programme to provide special resting spots at places overlooking beautiful scenery.

Where a place of interest is some distance away from the roadside, sign posts often do not exist to indicate its location or the nature of interest. Quite often the roads leading to such places are rough.

Road Obstructions : The most annoying obstruction on the roads is that of parked heavy vehicles at the large number of check-posts studying the highways. At such checkposts the rise of a small colony of eating shops, booths and temporary huts adds to the congestion.

Obstructions are also common in the form of litter on the roads near townships and stones left behind by truckers who are in the habit of parking their vehicles for repairs in the middle of the road.

Information Signs : Road signs on some of the State Highways are in the regional language which is not understood by foreign tourists or travellers coming from other States. In some States numerals on kilometre stones have been inscribed in regional characters.

The sign posting of beauty spots and places of historical or other interest besides or near the road is quite inadequate or even non-existence.

Coordination in Planning amenities : There has been no effort in any State to develop roadside amenities in a coordinated fashion keeping in view the requirements of other Departments like that of Transport and Tourism.

Facilities at borders : There are three border posts on the Asian Highways with Pakistan, Nepal and Bangla Desh. In the West and Attari, there are stalls for eating and cold drinks at the post itself but facilities for fuel are located some distance away. On the eastern border, refuelling arrangements and stalls providing eatables and cold drinks exist at Bongaon but amenities like hotels and rest houses are available only at Calcutta 80 km from the check-post. At Raxaul, on the Nepal border, all facilities are available.

Suggested Roadside Amenities

Fuel Stations : The provision of well-equipped fuel stations which satisfy some of the basic needs of passengers also falls within the domain of oil companies who have to play a principal role in organising the much-needed wayside amenities.

At present, except in some sections of the road fuel is generally available within 100 kilometres. We recommend that on highways which are carrying a traffic of over 1000 vehicles per day, this distance should normally 50 kilometres, while for other highways 80 kilometres would suffice for the present.

The present arrangement of distribution of fuel by M/s. Indian Oil Corporation should make it possible to achieve judicious spacing of fuel stations and the provision of new ones only where these are really needed. The installation of new stations should be so regulated as to prevent any further clustering of fuel stations.

The Indian Roads Congress has evolved standards for siting fuel stations but these are not being observed strictly. We recommend that concerned authorities in the States should review the position of all the fuel stations in their area and in cooperation with the oil companies draw up plans to bring them up to the IRC standards to the extent these are deficient. For new installations, the concerned authorities should be firm in enforcing the standards.

On some erstwhile single lane highways, the fuel stations have become closer to the road due to subsequent widening of the carriageway. It is important that these stations should be redesigned. While doing so, it would be more appropriate to follow the recommendation of the Transport and Communications Committee of ECAFE that the distance of the fuel pump from the nearest edge of the carriageway (including cycle tracks and footpaths) should not be less than 12 metres.

Rather than green and red lights, the use of sparklers/neon signs is recommended at fuel stations at night to guide the motorists.

For optimising the spacing of fuel stations, existing clusters along the highways should be broken up and oil companies parsuaded to shift the surplus stations to other spots.

A double system of installations is recommended i.e. one station on one side and the other on the opposite side of the road. The intervening distance between adjacent petrol stations on the same side should not be less than about 1200 metres.

Openings in medians opposite the exits or entrances of fuel stations should not be allowed on any highway having a median dividing strip.

So far as the architectural treatment of fuel stations is concerned, the road authority may be able to lend its expertise on landscape architecture to the oil companies so as to avoid the monotonous repetition of type design.

Control over fuel stations should be exercised finally by the road authority.

With regard to the provision of other basic facilities, the fuel stations on the highways may be grouped under four categories viz. (a) fuel stations near the metropolitan cities, (b) fuel stations near large towns, (c) fuel stations at other points of the National Highways, and (d) fuel stations at other points on State Highways. In addition to petrol, diesel oil and lubricants, the fuel stations in all these categories must offer facilities of air pressure, drinking water, toilets, spare parts and information material.

Every fuel station on a National Highway or near metropolitan cities or large towns should have a telephone. Public call booths may be installed where installation of a telephone at the dealers' expense is not feasible.

All fuel stations near metropolitan cities and large towns, and at other points of the National Highways, must keep equipment and helpers for certain minor repairs. The arrangements could vary according to demand. If necessary, duties of the pump operator could be combined with that of a mechanic.

Fuel stations on the highways should keep some tinned food and drinks which might be displayed for the choice of the motorists. It should be possible for the stations in vicinity of metropolitan cities and big towns to offer a greater variety in this respect.

Fuel stations near the metropolitan cities and large towns should further offer major repair facilities.

There should be no charge for parking of vehicles, cleaning of wind screen, air pressure service or drinking water, even godown space for a limited period. There may be an adequate charge for telephone calls for washing the vehicles and use of toilet, towels and soap.

Service stations and service areas

Service stations have been more popular with the oil companies. Some automobile manufacturers have also arranged with their distributors to maintain service stations. Some of the larger fuel stations should be encouraged to instal service facilities on selected heavily trafficked sections of highways. It is recommended that on National Highways service stations should be available every 150 kilometres or so.

Service areas providing comprehensive facilities for vehicles and passengers do not exist on our highways. We would suggest that such service areas should be developed in the vicinity of motels (where these are to come up) so that each may generate customers for the other. These should specially be provided at places frequented by the tourists. The concerned State Governments should study the situation and take steps to set up service areas, with the help of central loans if necessary.

Rest houses, inspection houses, youth hostels, pilgrim shelters etc. : An inventory of all the inspection houses, Rest Houses etc. along the highways should be prepared and those having large compounds and durable buildings selected for extension and improvement. These could provide an excellent chain of overnight stay facilities for the weary motorists.

In places where it is not possible to extend and improve the Inspection Houses, small toilets along with change rooms and bath rooms should be constructed at the edge of the compound along the highway for use of motorists, who may be permitted to park their cars inside the compound and make use of these facilities on a nominal payment.

Where possible, the practice of Jammu and Kashmir and Himachal Pradesh should be emulated by other States by making a portion of all the Government Inspection Houses available to tourists on "first come, first served" basis.

Extensive compounds of Inspection Houses should be made available to the young students and children travelling in groups for the purpose of parking and camping on nominal charges.

A very welcome facility would be the provision of tents, mosquito curtains and sleeping bags in Inspection Houses for being hired to tourists. For such users, bath rooms and change rooms should also be provided which may be away from the main building.

All the Inspection Houses should be equipped with telephones which would be of help to motorists. There may be an appropriate charge for the use of the telephones.

The concept of motels is catching up, although some State Governments Union Administrations think that these are not as yet justified having regard to the present traffic. In view of the cost involved, it is recommended that instead of laying emphasis on a motel programme, drive-in rest houses should be constructed along the highways near places of tourist importance. A drive-in rest house need not have more than a few double-bed rooms nor need it provide full meals. Breakfast, drinks and snacks should suffice.

Arrangements of cheap lodging for the middle and lower middle income travellers should be made. For this purpose, the cooperation of private agencies should be enlisted.

To mitigate inconvenience to foreign tourists, fuel stations located in and around major cities should be made to accept Travellers Cheques in payment of the fuel bills.

More youth hostels, based on the simple dormitory system, should be constructed at places having scenic, historical or educational significance. Facilities at Shantiniketan and Porbunder which are associated with two of the greatest men of modern India, should be developed so that young people are encouraged to visit these in greater numbers.

Accommodation facilities should be provided for the periodic mass pilgrim traffic. After surveying traffic on different routes, the State Road Transport Undertakings should construct pilgrim shelters with basic amenities at appropriate locations. At least one per cent of its gross operational revenue should be set apart by each undertaking for the creation of passenger facilities.

Eating Establishments : Good restaurants should be set up on the highways with the cooperation of private agencies including automobile Associations at selected places made available for the purpose by the Road Authority.

Steps should be taken to contain the over-extension of facilities like tea-stalls, dhabas, etc. indiscriminately cropping up at check-posts and other points. In no case should these be allowed to locate within the road right-of-way. Also suitable restrictions should be imposed on their exit and entry etc. The cooperation of the food inspection units of states and local bodies should be enlisted to remove the unhygenic booths and improve and remodel others.

Rest areas, picnic places, scenic overlooks and historical markers : At places of scenic or historical interest, it is recommended that parking-cum-entertainment areas of about one acre may be set up. The land, after development, may be allotted to a private entrepreneur on public tender. Where possible, the construction should be undertaken by the Road Authority itself. It should be aimed to construct such areas at distances of about 100 km. on National and State Highways. Establishments of this type will also be able to provide cheap service for truckers and low income group travellers.

A start should be made with rest area development by covering at least places of scenic or other special interest. Such rest areas should have canteen facilities besides shelters with picnic tables, drinking water, toilet and change rooms. Publicity material about the highway should also be made available here.

Small lay-byes are a more immediate requirement of the heavily trafficked routes. Such lay-byes should be constructed at distances of 80 kilometres on the National Highways on land already acquired for construction.

Clustering of ancillary facilities like eating stalls should not be allowed to occur near the check-posts. Check-posts should be constructed in accordance with the type designs recommended by Indian Roads Congress which provide for side lay-byes to store heavy vehicles so that the main carriageway is kept free for car traffic.

Lay-byes for disabled vehicles should be built at frequent intervals according to designs included in the report. These need not have any provision for drinking water or a toilet. Often these could be combined with scenic overlooks or historical markers.

Public Works Departments should help the State Road Transport Undertakings by releasing land to them for construction of passenger shelters equipped with drinking water, snack-bars and toilets.

Traffic aid posts and highway patrols : Traffic aid posts should be established on National Highways which are having a comparatively greater volume of traffic.

In heavily trafficked sections, the State Governments concerned should also consider the establishment of mobile highway patrols covering about 80 kms. in either direction. The duty of such patrols, apart from prevention and control of accidents on the highway, should be the promotion of facilities meant for easy movement of traffic like rendering assistance to disabled motorists.

First-aid arrangements : To start with, first-aid arrangements should be made at the fuel stations and traffic posts. In due course, dispensaries should be set up in the service areas, in the vicinity of motels and at terminal stations.

State Road Transport Undertakings should make it incumbent for every passenger bus to carry a first-aid kit with it, as has been done by the Maharashtra State Road Transport Corporation.

Obstructions and encroachments : A serious problem is that of encroachments on the right-of-way of highways. Safety of traffic is also endangered by the indiscriminate stacking on road of litter, stones and construction material. In the removal of encroachments, litter, etc. highway patrols assisted by the PWD staff could plan an effective part. It is necessary that all the states should have adequate legal powers to speedily remove encroachments from the roads. In fact, there is case for a comprehensive highway legislation through which check could also be exercised on unauthorised growth like ungainly clusters along the highways.

Information : Printed information about the highway and facilities available en route should be supplied to each fuel station, rest house, etc. The Tourist Departments of the States should also bring out road maps of the region showing side by side the facilities available and places of interest.

Sectional maps of the road and roadside area should be prepared by the Automobile Association State Transport Departments showing standard facilities and sports of interest. These should be updated regularly.

Road signs and kilometre stones on State Highways should not be in regional language alone which will not be intelligible to all road users. The system of inscription as adopted on the National Highways should be followed for this purpose.

Beauty spots, historical monuments and places of interest beside the road or within a short distance from it, should be adequately sign posted. Signs should also be provided to indicate the presence of rest houses, inspection houses etc.

Highway beautification : The future programme of road development impose a duty on the highway authorities to beautify the roadside landscape right at the time of initial construction. This involves development of scenic spots, roadside parks, plantation of trees etc. For these activities land should be acquired together with the land required for construction of the road.

The landscaping of roadsides, development of lay-byes, roadside parks etc. should be so done as to be in architectural harmony with the surroundings.

The Road Authority should take steps to protect features of natural, historical, educational, recreational or ecological significance and provides access to them.

As in the U.S.A., here too the setting up of wayside amenities and their architecture should be the function of a special cell within the Road Authority at its headquarters. The development of amenities should be in coordination with the Tourist and Transport Departments.

The position regarding advertisements by the side of highway, which generally divert the attention of the drivers, should be looked into by the road authorities for necessary action. The space inside rest areas away from the main road would be a good place to advertise but the advertisements there should be so sited as not to obstruct the view of the road or scenery around.

Problems of hill States : After assessment of traffic requirements, emergency telephones should be provided in hilly areas as necessary. There is need for constructing frequent lay-byes as well.

Small repair and service stations should be set up at distances of about 80 kilometres along the hill roads, as well at the terminals.

Shelters as protection against rain should be constructed for passengers at all necessary points, but in any case at the terminal stations.

Documentation : A uniform system of maintaining the records should be followed by all the concerned Departments of State Governments and Union Administrations as regards information about roadside facilities and travel. The data must be updated periodically.

Facilities at the borders : The construction of a motel somewhere on the outskirts of Amritsar is recommended. Arrangements for the distribution of information about facilities available along routes nearly and distances of places etc. should be made at the border customs posts.

Spare parts for taxies : The Department of Tourism should press the Chief Controller of Imports & Exports to liberalise import of spare parts required by tourist taxi-operators.

Study of terminal facilities : Since the various services at a terminal depot have an important bearing on the neighbourhood and these are still in a disorganised state, the Ministry of Shipping & Transport should take steps to have a separate study made of their employment potential and other benefits. A well-developed terminal station in a rural background can result in a number of benefits.

COLLISION BETWEEN 2 AGA DOWN PASSENGER TRAIN AND E 460 DOWN GOODS TRAIN AT BHARWARI STATION NORTHERN RAILWAY ON 30TH MARCH 1968—REPORT,

Delhi, Manager of Publications, 1970. 24p.

One-Man Commission : Shri G. S. Pandor.

APPOINTMENT

The Commission was constituted under the Ministry of Tourism and Civil Aviation (Commission of Railway Safety) in accordance with Rule 10 of Railway Board's Notification No. 59-TTV/42/1 of 11th April 1966.

TERMS OF REFERENCE

To inquire into the collision between 2 AGA Down Passenger train and E 460 Down Goods train on the Down Main Line at Bharwari station on Fatehpur-Allahabad Electrified Broad Gauge Double Line section of Northern Railway at about 22.20 hours on 30th March 1968.

CONTENTS

Summary; Inspection of Site and Inquiry; The Accident; Casualties; Relief Measures (Intimation of the Accident; Medical Attention; Relief and Breakdown Trains; Restoration of Lines); Composition of Trains and Damage (Composition of the Trains;

Damage and Disposition); Local Conditions (Description of Site; Permanent Way; Signalling and Block Working); Summary of Evidence; Observation and Tests; Discussions (The Time of the Collision; Speed of the Train; Track; E 460 Down Goods Train; Route Set and Signalling Aspect before the Collision; Defective Signalling; Extraneous Feed and Tampering); Conclusions; Annexure I.

CONCLUSIONS

Cause of the accident: After full consideration of all the facts and the material and circumstantial evidence, I have reached the conclusion that the collision between 2 AGA Down Passenger train and E 460 Down Goods train an 30th March on the Down Main Line of Bharwari station was caused by K.A. Khan, Driver of E 460 Down Goods train, who in contravention of General Rule 78 (reproduced in Annexure 1) passed the Down Home Signal of Bharwari at 'ON' for which full responsibility lies on him. The driver of the offending train also contravened the provisions in General Rule 76 (reproduced in Annexure 1).

Service record of Driver held responsible: Driver K.A. Khan aged 30 years, who died in the accident, was appointed on 18th April 1957. He was promoted as Driver 'C' Grade on 8th November 1965 and in that capacity he was working upto the time of the accident. He had passed the previous medical examination on 8th April 1968 for A II category without glasses. His service record in respect of train working duties is clear.

Relief Measures: Emergency calls were made without delay and they were met with prompt response. I am satisfied that the Medical aid at site was prompt and efficient. Relief Measures were satisfactory as could be expected in the circumstances.

IRRIGATION COMMISSION, 1969—REPORT

New Delhi, Ministry of Irrigation and Power, 1972. 4 Vols.

Chairman : Shri Ajit Prasad Jain

Vice-Chairman : Dr. S. R. Sen (on his appointment as Executive Director of International Bank for Reconstruction & Development. Dr. S.R. Sen left on in June 1970 and replaced by Shri L. J. Johnson.

Members : Shri O. P. Gupta; Shri K. V. Ekambaram; Shri D. V. Reddy.

Part-time Member : Shri N. S. Pardasani (resigned on 29th January, 1970).

Member-Secretary : Shri K. S. S. Murthy.

Consultant : Shri Balwant Singh Nag.

APPOINTMENT

Since Independence the country has made substantial progress in irrigation development. The area under irrigation has been nearly doubled from what it was at the time of Independence. Even so, about four-fifths of the country's cultivated area still depends exclusively on rainfall. The drought conditions in the last four years in several parts of the country and the continued food shortages have brought into sharp focus the importance of providing greater irrigation facilities. In this context the maximum exploitation of both surface and ground water resources within the next four to five plan periods needs greater emphasis and attention. The Government of India have therefore, decided in consultation with the State Governments and Administrations of Union Territories, to set up an Irrigation Commission to go into the question of future irrigation development in the country in a comprehensive manner. So the Government of India appointed the Irrigation Commission vide its Resolution No. DW. 11-28 (52)/67 dated April 1,1969.

TERMS OF REFERENCE

(1) To review the development of irrigation in India since 1903, when the last Irrigation Commission submitted its recommendations, and report on the contribution made by irrigation to increasing the productivity of land, and in providing insurance against the vagaries of rainfall.

(2) To examine in detail the irrigation facilities available in chronically drought affected and food deficit areas, and suggest essential and minimum irrigation work to be undertaken promptly in such areas.

(3) To draw up a broad outline of development of

irrigation of all types, for achieving self-sufficiency in cereals, and for maximising the production of other crops, and to make a broad assessment of the funds required for the purpose.

(4) To examine the administrative and organisational set-up for the planning, execution and operation of irrigation work, particularly with a view to the speedy completion of projects, and reduction of their gestation period.

(5) To suggest criteria for the sanctioning of irrigation projects and

(6) To examine any other matter incidental or related to the development of irrigation in the country, and make suitable recommendations.

CONTENTS

Letter of Transmissal; India—Physical and Other Features; Land and Water Resources; Progress of Irrigation—A Review; Planned Development of Water Resources; Policies and Considerations in Irrigation; Ayacut Development; Drought Affected Areas; Improvements to Existing Irrigation Systems; A Perspective of Irrigation Development; Economics and Financing of Irrigation Works; Administration and Organisation; Waterlogging, Drainage and Floods; Sedimentation of reservoirs; Inter-State River Dispute; Irrigation Acts and Codes; Research, Education and Training; Irrigation Statistics; Summary; Appendices.

RECOMMENDATIONS

Physiography: The sub-continent of India covers an area of 328 million hectares and supports a population of 547 millions. It has a land frontier of 15,200 Km. and a coastline of 5,700 Km.

The perennial rivers of the Himalayan region and the rivers of peninsular India constitute the main river systems. The Himalayan rivers are fed by the melting snow and glaciers of the Great Himalayan ranges. They are often uncertain and capricious in their behaviour and sometimes subject to drastic changes of course. In the dry weather, the flow in these rivers is significantly enhanced by water from the melting snow and glaciers. The flow is considerably reduced in the winter, but never to the same extent as in the peninsular rivers. The peninsular rivers originate at much lower altitudes and flow through areas which are geologically more stable, so that they are more predictable in their behaviour. Their flow is characterised by heavy discharges during the monsoons, followed by low discharges during the dry months.

Climate: The great mountain mass formed by the Himalayas and its spurs on the north, and the ocean on the south are the two major influences of cold winds from Central Asia, and gives the sub-continent the element of the tropical type of climate. The second is the source of cool moisture-laden winds which reach India and give it the elements of the oceanic type of climate.

India has a very great diversity and variety of climate and weather conditions. The climate ranges from continental to oceanic, from extremes of heat to extremes of cold, from extreme aridity and negligible rainfall to excessive humidity and torrential rainfall.

The South-West monsoon is responsible for 80% or more of the total annual precipitation outside Assam, Bengal, Coastal Orissa and parts of the peninsula. In Gujarat, Saurashtra, Kutch and adjoining Rajasthan and Madhya Pradesh, it accounts for more than 90 per cent. The States of Orissa, Bihar, West Bengal, Assam and eastern Madhya Pradesh, the West Coast and the Ghats as also the sub-montane belt which extends from North Bihar to Jammu receive more than 100 cm. of rain during this season. Southern Punjab, North-West India from Veraval in Saurashtra through Delhi to Jammu receive 50 cm. of rain or less. The rainfall decreases repidly towards the West and on the Western Border of Rajasthan it is less than 10 cm. In the rain-shadow of the Western Ghats, the rainfall is only 40 to 50 cm. during this season. In some patches, it is 30 cm. or less.

Soils: The four major soil groups in India are (i) alluvial soils, (ii) black soils (regur), (iii) red soils, and (iv) laterite soils. Of less importance are forest soils, desert soil, saline and alkaline soils. The behaviour of soil under irrigation is of primary importance. The capacity of the soil to take in water and hold it and its effective rooting depths are important criteria for determining irrigability. The depth and frequency of irrigation is a function of soil properties. The greater the water-holding capacity, the greater will be the irrigation depth, and in consequence the lower the irrigation frequency. From the point of view of drainage, the main criterion is the hydraulic conductivity of the sub-soil or the sub-stratum.

Utilisable Water Resources: The total utilisable water resources of the country have not been systematically studied or analysed except for the Indus River System. Preliminary studies relating to the Godavari, the Krishna, the Narmada and the Tapti indicate the entire water resources of these rivers can be utilised. The waters of the Cauvery have already been almost fully utilized.

Of the 493 t.m.cu.m. (400 MAF) of water in the Ganga, it should be possible to utilise about 185 t.m. cu.m. (150 MAF) for irrigation. A higher utilization is precluded for reasons of topography and the shortage of storage sites so that most of the water will still continue to flow into the Bay of Bengal. There is very little possibility of utilising the waters of the Brahmaputra except through a few medium and minor lift irrigation scheme in Assam. Nearly 370 t.m cu.m. (300 MAF) of the Brahmaputra is likely to continue to flow annually into the Bay of Bengal.

The west-flowing rivers of India (excluding the Tapi and Narmada) are also important sources of water. They carry on an average, nearly 247 t.m.cu.m. (200 MAF) but due to the narrowness of the coastal plains through which they flow, the possibilities of using these waters for irrigation are very limited. Some water may, however, be diverted eastwards for irrigation.

The Mahanadi and other east-flowing rivers have a sizeable water potential but not all of it can be utilised. About 74 t.m.cu.m. (60 MAF) of these rivers would continue to flow into the Bay of Bengal.

The utilisable water resources of the country are roughly as indicated below :

1.	Narmada, Tapi, Godavari, Krishna, Cauvery and other Southern rivers	246,700 m.cu.m. (200 MAF)
2.	The Indus System	49,300 m.cu.m. (40 MAF)
3.	The Ganga System	185,000 m.cu.m. (150 MAF)
4.	The Brahmaputra System	12,300 m.cu.m. (10 MAF)
5.	The Mahanadi and other east-flowing rivers	123,400 m.cu.m. (100 MAF)
6.	West-flowing rivers, excluding the Tapi and Narmada	49,300 m.cu.m. (40 MAF)
	Total	666,000 m.cu.m. (540 MAF)

Progress of Irrigation : On the eve of partition, the net irrigated area in the Indian sub-continent was about 28.2 million hectares amounting to about one-fourth of the total cultivated area. 54 per cent of the area was irrigated by canals, 23 per cent by wells, 12 per cent by tanks and 11 per cent by other miscellaneous sources. The partition of India brought about sudden and drastic changes. It greatly depleted the irrigation potential of India as shown in the table below :

Country	Net shown Area	Net irrigated Area	Col. 3 as per cent of Col. 2
1	2	3	4
Undivided India	116.8	28.2	24.1
India	98.5	19.4	19.7
Pakistan	18.3	8.8	48.1

Since Independence, the gross irrigated area from major, medium and minor works has risen steadily to 28.0 million hectares in 1960-61 and to 33.13 million hectares in 1967-68. A sum of over 30 billion rupees has been spent up to the beginning of the Fourth Plan on irrigation schemes.

Planned Development Of Water Resources

A comprehensive strategy to ensure the success of agriculture should aim at meeting the water requirements of crops through the economic and judicious use of water.

A river basin and, in the case of a large rivers, a sub-basin is the natural unit for planning water resources. This planning should be based on an assessment of the surface and sub-surface water resources of the basin, and their utilization.

The Commission recommends the following policy for formulating river basin plans, on the basis of the feasibility status of individual projects :

(a) The basin plan should present a comprehensive outline of development possibilities of land and water resources to meet the anticipated regional and local needs.

(b) The plan should,

(i) indicate a broad framework of various engineering works to be taken up in the basin giving reasons for their choice from the alternatives considered and inter-relationship between those works;

(ii) establish priorities in respect of water use for various purposes;

(iii) indicate inter se priority of projects; and

(iv) indicate the need for earmarking water for any specific future purposes.

(c) The basin plan should be periodically reviewed and revised to take into account changes in storage capacity and the extent and pattern of water use.

Domestic requirements should have the highest priority in the allocation of water, followed by industry and then by irrigation. As between irrigation and power generation, the Commission recommends that priority be given to irrigation.

The Commission recommends that instead of the Irrigation Department determining the cropping pattern in consultation with the Agriculture Department, as is done at present, the latter Department should determine the pattern in consultation with the Irrigation Department.

While designing future canals, the result on soil-plant-water relationships, the contribution of rainfall in the growth period of crops and the interaction of other inputs like fertilizers, should be taken into account, and duties, deltas and water allowances fixed accordingly.

There is a large scope for the conjunctive use of

surface and sub-surface water, particularly in the Indo-Gangetic Plain, the coastal areas of Orissa and Andhra Pradesh, the Cauvery Delta and part of the Narmada basin. It can also be applied to a lesser extent elsewhere in the country where canal supplies can be supplemented by open wells or tube wells.

The Commission recommends that areas where conjunctive use is feasible, should be identified, particularly in the commands of existing canal systems.

There should be a number of fully investigated schemes kept ready for choice, so that financial resources may not get deployed on relatively uneconomic schemes. The quality of investigations should not be sacrificed to speed up project formulation. The investigation of irrigation projects and their ayacut development should be undertaken simultaneously. Also, studies of soil conservation measures, particularly for the more critical areas in the catchment should be taken in hand at the same time.

Policies And Considerations In Irrigation

For judicious use of limited irrigation supplies, it is important to determine critical periods during which deficiency of moisture in the soil can seriously reduce the yield of crops. Irrigation system should provide water not only in the required quantity but at the required time.

Rice requires much more water than other cereals, but its productivity per unit of water is much lower than that of the others. The Commission, therefore suggests that the need for adequate support from rainfall should be kept in view while planning for rice production. It further recommends that a second rice crop, particularly in the non-rainy season, should be grown in an area only if the irrigation supplies cannot be put to better use.

Broadly, the goals for irrigation policy may be classified under three heads viz.,

(i) maximum production per unit of area, as in the Brahmaputra Valley, Kerala and the Indo-Gangetic Plain;

(ii) maximum production per unit of water as in regions of medium and low rainfall, in which about 70 per cent of the cultivated area of India lies; and

(iii) maximum area served, as in drought affected areas.

In the southern States, the heavier black cotton soils are generally located in the valleys, and the lighter red soils higher up. Growing paddy in the higher light soils leads to a comparatively larger consumption of water and the problem of waterlogging, paddy should, therefore, be localised, as far as practicable, on the heavier soils at lower levels and the lighter red soils reserved for light irrigated crops.

Lining must be resorted to where water resources are inadequate and particularly where the percolated water cannot be retrieved or, when retrieved, is unfit for use The Commission recommends that in all future projects, the main canals and branches should, in general, be lined and lining of distributaries undertaken as and when resources become available. As an alternative to lining small water courses, pipelines may be worth considering.

There are many areas in the country where the use of sprinkler or drip irrigation would be more useful. There is, however, need for research, experimentation and demonstration to identify the areas, conditions and crops which are most suitable for this mode of irrigation.

Farmers should be encouraged to lift water for irrigating areas in canal commands which cannot be served by flow. Drain water should be utilised for irrigation in an authorised manner and the farmers be charged lift irrigation rates for it.

Some major rivers, particularly the Ganga and Brahmaputra offer considerable scope for Floating Pump Irrigation Schemes. The Commission recommends that these possibilities should be fully explored in Assam, Bihar, Uttar Pradesh and West Bengal and on some major rivers in other states.

At present, irrigation projects are designed on the basis of a 75 per cent dependability. Availability can be improved by providing a carry-over capacity in storage reservoirs at an additional cost. The economics of this device needs consideration. The more precious the water in an area, as in drought areas, the greater is the justification for providing a carry-over.

Ayacut Development

Systematic ayacut development in India has taken shape because of delay in the utilisation of water in some command areas. Its aim is to ensure rapid utilisation of the irrigation potential of new irrigation projects. This calls for a series of co-ordinated measures. The command areas of projects should be fixed in advance. Soil surveys should be undertaken, and only those crops which are suited to local soil and climate conditions should be encouraged. Scattered holdings should be consolidated. Farmer's fields should be properly levelled, shaped and kept ready with field channels, so that the water can be utilised without delay. The supply of inputs needs to be streamlined, and research and extension efforts geared to support a forward looking agriculture. Attention should also be paid to the need for additional roads, markets and storage and other infrastructure facilities.

The Commission recommends that a comprehensive plan of ayacut development should be prepared for every major and medium irrigation project, simultaneously with the preparation of a plan for the project.

The Commission is of the opinion that a special administrative agency for the co ordinated and expeditious development of command areas under medium and major projects is very necessary. No separate cadres should be created for the ayacut development programme and the relevant departments of the State Government, such as Irrigation, Agriculture, Co-operation, etc. should continue to discharge their respective functions within the ayacut could, however, set out specific task for various departments and institutions, co-ordinate their activities and ensure implementation of the agreed programme. Each irrigation project deserves a separate ayacut development agency.

The States are unanimous that the absence of field channels has been a major reason for serious lags in the utilization of irrigation potentials. In 1966, Mysore State took upon itself the responsibillty of excavating field channels. This brought about a spectacular improvment in the utilisation of the irrigation potential. Andhra Pradesh took action on similar lines in the Nagarjunasagar project and this also had a salutary effect.

We have made recommendations for land-levelling and land-shaping and also their financing from institutional sources.

We have also recommended that research should be conducted in command areas of projects to encourage the farmers to adopt improved irrigation practices and crop patterns with confidence. Demonstration plots, training programmes and the use of television for educating the farmers have been recommended.

During the formulation of the Fourth Five-Year Plan, the Government of India felt that the development of regulated markets, all-weather roads and storages had lagged behind, because the State Governments could not find the funds for it. It led to the acceptance of the area Development Programme as a centrally sponsored scheme, and was to be executed through the State Governments. Before any command area became eligible for inclusion in the programme, the State Governments concerned have to provide funds for all other services and works which form part of the plan. The Commission hopes that the tempo of these activities will gain momentum and have a larger coverage.

Drought Affected Areas

The India Meteorological Department has defined drought as a situation occurring in any area when the annual rainfall is less than 75 per cent of the normal. Areas where drought has occurred in 20 per cent of the years examined, are considered 'drought areas' and where it has occurred in more than 40 per cent of years, as 'chronic drought areas'. A persisting adverse water balance has also been found to be a characteristic of the drought areas.

On the basis of the annual and south-west monsoon rainfall data from 1901 to 1960 for about 500 stations, drought and chronic drought areas have identified as follows :

(a) Drought areas (20 per cent probability of rainfall departures of more than (—)25 per cent from the normal	(1) Gujarat, Rajasthan and adjoining parts of Punjab, Haryana, West Uttar Pradesh and West Madhya Pradesh. (2) Madhya Maharashtra, interior Mysore, Rayalaseema, Southern Telengana and parts of Tamil Nadu. (3) A small portion of north-western Bihar and adjoining East Uttar Pradesh. (4) A small portion of north-eastern Bihar and adjoining portion of West Bengal.
(b) Chronically drought affected areas (40 per cent probability of rainfall departure of more than (—)25%	Western parts of Rajasthan and Kutch.

As the chronically drought areas are part of the same meteorological phenomenon and the difference between the two is one of degree, for our purposes no distinction has been made between the two.

We have accepted the taluk as a unit for identifying and planning for drought areas. From the list of the taluks furnished by the State Governments, the Commission has excluded (i) those which lie outside the drought zone; (ii) those where 30 per cent or more of the cropped area is irrigated; and (iii) those which comprise only a small portion of the districts with an adequate rainfall or irrigation. After these adjustments, most of the drought areas which need special attention lie in the States of Mysore, Andhra Pradesh, Gujarat, Rajasthan, Maharashtra and Tamil Nadu. The hard-core areas of drought comprise about 16 per cent of the total geographical area of the country and account for over 11 per cent of its population.

At present, about 13 per cent of the cropped area of the drought affected region is irrigated. This is likely to rise to about 19 per cent when the schemes under execution are completed. In the drought areas of Madhya Pradesh, Mysore, Maharashtra and Gujarat, where the present level of irrigation is lower than 13 per cent, the position may be worse. The extent of the area irrigated in the drought districts is not likely to go above 25 per cent of the cropped area when all the works proposed by the States for these areas are completed.

The needs of the drought areas will not be adequately met by any minimum programme of irrigation. What is needed is a maximum programme because even if such a programme is implemented, drought areas will lag behind. In drought areas only 25 per cent of the cropped area will come under irrigation, as against the 50 per cent for the country as a whole.

The Commission recommends that high priority should be given to irrigation works in drought areas.

If rigorous tests of productivity are applied, it may not be possible to take up as many new schemes as is desirable for drought areas. The likely expenditure on famine relief also needs to be kept in mind because the introduction of irrigation would reduce, if not eliminate such expenditure.

Only a few States, like Gujarat and Maharashtra have given thought to the special needs of drought areas in determining criteria for financing irrigation projects. The Gujarat Government has relaxed the benefit cost ratio in respect of major and medium schemes in drought and other backward regions upto unity. The Maharashtra Government allows the same relaxation but only in respect of irrigation scheme costing less than Rs. 30 million. Both these Governments have fixed more liberal yardsticks in respect of minor works like storage tanks, percolation tanks, check dams, etc. The Gujarat Government has removed all cost restrictions on medium or minor irrigation schemes in scarcity areas, under certain conditions. The Commission supports a liberal policy for irrigation work in drought areas and recommends that the benefit cost ratio of major and medium works in those areas may be relaxed up to unity. The States should be provided with loans at the concessional rate of half the normal rate to facilitate the construction of irrigation works in the drought areas.

Improvements To Existing Irrigation Works

Many of the irrigation systems in the country date back to the 19th century or earlier, and need remodelling. Among such systems are the Eastern and Western Yamuna Canals, the Cauvery Delta System, Upper Ganga Canal and the Godavari Delta System. The usefulness of these systems is limited by structural handicaps, such as out-moded headworks, the absence of silt excluding devices and unsatisfactory cross drainage. Faulty irrigation practices and poor drainage add to these handicaps. As a result the systems cannot meet the exacting demands of water for the new high-yielding varieties of crops.

Irrigation from wells of all kinds forms 30 per cent of the total irrigation in the country. Many of these wells and tubewells lie wthin the command areas of canal system.

The Commission recommends that the inadequacies in run-of-the-river systems should be met by the increased use of groundwater, by the construction of storage reservoirs and by supplementing supplies by transferring water from an adjacent basin. Farmers should be encouraged by providing them financial assistance, technical guidance and electricity, to sink wells or tubewells so as to make up any inadequacies in supply from canals and to extend irrigation.

Other measures recommend to mitigate the effect of inadequacies are the lining of canals, the control of drainage, the provision of regulators and escapes, the substitution of weirs by barrages and the improvement of headworks.

The hydraulic performance of some systems has been reduced by the addition of temporary outlets, by changes in canal sections due to silt, erosion, cross-bunding and the cutting of banks. This calls for remodelling. Periodic examination of each system once in twenty or thirty years should be done to make systems up-to-date. The remodelling project undertaken in the Cauvery Delta illustrates the big gains accruing from planned remodelling. Remodelling schemes should include, inter alia, (i) measures for working the system with greater efficiency and minimum loss of water; (ii) measures to supplement supplies by pumping water from neighbouring rivers or from sub-soil reservoirs and by transferring water from adjacent basins; (iii) changes in cropping patterns; and (iv) measures to enlarge areas under irrigation and to increase its intensity.

Existing methods of conveying water from the outlet, and field-to-field irrigation of rice are causes of a heavy waste of water. The Commission recommends that effective steps should be taken gradually to replace field-to-field irrigation of rice by the system of field channels. There should also be separate drains serving individual fields.

The Future Perspective

A third of the country is prone to drought, which makes for low yields. Improved dry-farming practices can improve yields, but the results can at best be a fraction of those from irrigated areas. The growing disparity between irrigated and dry regions can be reduced only if vigorous steps are taken to improve irrigation facilities in the dry zones. The perspective of development is thus not confined to the limited aim of increasing agricultural production, but has been extended to include the broader objectives of removing social and regional disparities.

The provisional totals of the 1971 census reveal that the total population of India on 1 April, 1971 was 547 millions. The growth rate of 24.66 for the decade 1961—70 closely tallied with the projected growth rate of 24.6 for the quinquennium 1966—70.

The demographers have worked out firm population projections only upto the year 1985. The Commission proceeds on the assumption that the expected population growth rate of 14.5 per thousand per annum, attained during the quinquennium 1981—85, will be maintained in the subsequent 15 years. On this basis, India's population in the year 2000 A.D. would work out to around 900 millions, an increase of 65 per cent over the 1971 population.

The food and fibre requirements at the end of the century will, however, increase by about 100 per cent because of the likely rise in living standards. The country must, at the very least, produce twice its present output of food and fibre. This increase is possible if more areas are brought under irrigation.

Scope for extention of agriculture to new areas is almost exhausted, and future increases in yield must be secured from intensive and double cropping.

An analysis of yields and irrigated areas under principal crops—rice, wheat, pulses, oilseeds and cotton-made by us lead to the inescapable conclusion that the crop yields are high in States which have a high percentage of irrigated area under the crop, and low where the irrigated percentage is less.

We are of the opinion that significant results in increasing yields of these crops can be achieved if proper attention is given to irrigation, particularly in the States mentioned below :—

Rice	: Bihar	West Bengal	Uttar Pradesh	Orissa
Wheat	: Uttar Pradesh	Madhya Pradesh	Rajasthan	Bihar 4
Pulses	: Madhya Pradesh	Rajasthan	Maha-rashtra	Bihar
Oilseeds	: Uttar Pradesh	Gujarat	Andhra Pradesh	Madhya Pradesh
Cotton	: Maha-rashtra	Gujarat	Mysore	Madhya Pradesh

Many States have not furnished a reasonable accurate assessment of future possibilities of irrigation development by surface and ground waters. In some cases it appears that the figures were based on a rough assessment.

As the inter-State disputes over the waters of the Krishna, the Godavari and the Narmada are pending before inter-State water tribunals, the total irrigation potential of Andhra Pradesh, Mysore, Maharashtra, Madhya Pradesh, Orissa and Gujarat cannot be worked before the tribunals allocate water to the various States.

In some cases the projects proposed by two or more States in the same river valley are mutually exclusive. Which of these projects would be sanctioned ultimately and in what form, can be determined only after the completion of river basin plans and agreement among the States concerned. The total irrigation potential suggested by such States is liable to be reduced.

A great deal of work has been done in the past few years to assess the ground water potential, but a complete assessment for the whole country has not so far been carried out. At best, the estimates of ground water potential are based on certain assumption which may or may not turn out to be correct.

Of over 500 medium irrigation schemes taken up during the last 20 years, more than three-fifths have been completed. With better planning and co-ordination, it should be possible to complete the investigation of the remaining schemes in the next 5-7 years. If necessary funds are allocated, it should not be difficult for the States to complete all medium works in about 15 years. Minor works should be completed within a period of 10 years.

Of the total irrigated area of 40.5 million hectares, the perennial flows of the Himalayas account only for about four million hectares. Tubewells account for another 2.4 million hectares. The rest of the area depends for its water supply on storages and river diversion schemes, and shallow aquifers.

More than 90 per cent of the river flow occurs in the monsoon months of June to September. It is imperative that storages should be built to impound monsoon flows for utilising that water for irrigation in winter and summer. Big storages have big catchment areas, and variations in rainfall do not affect them to the same extent as they do small tanks. These reservoirs provide assured irrigation.

The Commission estimates the total irrigation potential of the country, both from surface and ground water resources, including 20 million hectares of the Godavari, the Krishna and the Narmada, as of the order of 81 million hectares. This would provide irrigation facilities to about 50 per cent of the total cropped area.

If this potential is developed by the turn of the century it would double the production of food and fibre in the country, including increases in yield effected by improved varieties of seeds, fertilizers, pesticides etc. This increase would not only ensure self-sufficiency in 2000 A.D. but also lay a sound foundation for higher production in subsequent years.

The cost of the major and medium irrigation

projects sanctioned during the last few years varies from Rs. 1500 to Rs. 3000 per hectare and average around Rs. 2000. The future projects will be more expensive than the present or those now under way, because of difficult locations and complex technology involved. It may, therefore, be reasonable to assume that the future schemes, on an average, will cost Rs. 3000 per hectare at current prices. On a rough basis, the cost of future development may work out to about Rs. 100 billion.

The Ganga-Cauvery link will operate as a grid to make up periodical shortages in the Son, Narmada, Godavari, Krishna and Cauvery systems. This gigantic project should be investigated.

We are of the opinion that proper attention should be given to maintain the ecological balance in the planning of major irrigation works.

Economics And Financing Of Irrigation Works

The Commission supports the adoption of the benefit-cost ratio criterion in sanctioning projects. It, however, recommends that the financial return of the projects should also be examined. The present practice of accepting projects only if the benefit-cost ratio is more than 1.5 is a prudent precaution. The Commission, however, recommends that this rule should be relaxed in favour of irrigation projects in the drought affected areas where a lower limit of unity may be accepted.

In working out the benefit-cost ratio, the investment on Ayacut development comprising land-levelling and construction of field channels and field drains should also be taken into account. The investment which may be necessary for soil conservation measures in the catchment area need not be considered.

The Commission wishes to emphasise that once a scheme is taken up for implementation, it must be constructed at an optimum pace determined by technical considerations and the necessary funds must be provided for it. Where an irrigation scheme is too large for proper financing from the State's own plan resources, the State should negotiate with the Union Government for special financial arrangements for the scheme.

Irrigation works in India were making a net annual contribution to the exchequer of over Rs. 10 million, at the time of Independence. There was an annual loss of Rs. 566 million in 1967-68. The Commission is of the view that irrigation works in a State should, give an annual income at least equal to the annual cost of operation. No part of the burden for providing irrigation should fall on the general tax-payer.

Essentially, the value of irrigation is the benefit it gives to the farmer. From the irrigator's point of view, therefore, the water rate should be related to the benefit which irrigation confers rather than to the cost of an irrigation project. There can be no precise formula for the fixation of water rates, which remains a matter for administrative decision. As a guideline, the Commission recommends the following principles :—

(i) Water rates should be levied on a 'crop basis', except in the case of irrigation from tubewells ;

(ii) The rate should be related to the gross income from the crop and not to the cost of the project. It should range between 5 per cent and 12 per cent of gross income, the upper limit being applicable to cash crops;

(iii) The rates should be within the paying capacity of irrigators and aim at ensuring full utilization of available supplies;

(iv) As between regions with a similar class of supply, there should be the minimum disparity, if any, in the rates charged;

(v) For fixing rates, irrigation should be divided into A, B and C categories on the basis of the quantity and timeliness of supplies of water. Lower rates may be fixed where, on account of good rainfall, the demand for irrigation water is less or where the supply is inadequate and uncertain;

(vi) The general level of rates in a State should be such that, taken as a whole, the irrigation schemes do not impose any burden on the general revenues.

Irrigators in drought affected areas derive larger benefits from irrigation than those in other areas. The Commission is of the opinion that farmers in these areas should be charged the normal irrigation rate.

In canal commands, a lower rate should be charged on the basis of the quantity of water supplied at the tubewell in some States, and in others on the basis of the electricity consumed. The Commission is of the view that the former is more equitable.

The Commission recommends that water rates should be reviewed and revised by all the States in the fourth year of every plan.

In order to remove difficulties experienced in enforcing the existing laws for betterment levy, the Commission recommends that these laws should be amended so that half of the capital cost of the irrigation projects is recovered from the beneficiaries.

Administration And Organisation

The massive programme for the development of water resources calls for a streamlining of the procedures and agencies dealing with both at the Centre and in the States. Our recommendations in this connection are :

A Directorate of Hydrology should be set up under a Director-General. The functions of the Directorate will be to collect hydrological data, standardise procedures and publish the data.

Prospecting and mapping of ground water has been the responsibility of the GSI. Recently a decision has been taken to transfer the division doing this work from the GSI to the CG&WB. The Commission recommends that the decision may be reviewed and the GSI allowed to continue to do this work.

The CG&WB which is at present under the Ministry of Agriculture, should be transferred to the Ministry of I & P.

Each river basin has its peculiar characteristics and would need a plan of its own, To formulate twenty major river basin plans will be too heavy a task for a single Commission. We have recommended that seven river basin Commissions should be set up for the whole country. To begin with, the work may be entrusted to four Commissions.

Each Commission would consist of four whole-time members nominated by the Union Government; two engineers, an agricultural economist and an agronomist. The Chairman of the Commission will be nominated by the Union Government. Each State Government concerned with the basin shall be represented by a Chief Engineer. The small States and the Union Territories may be grouped and given representation by rotation.

The basin plans prepared by the Commission will be sent to the States for opinion, and, thereafter, the plans with the views of the States and the comments of the Commission, if any, will be submitted to the National Water Resources Council. The plans will then be forwarded to the States and the Union Government.

The Commission recommends the setting up of a high level authority 'The National Water Resources Council' to take policy decisions relating to the conservation, utilization and inter-basin transfers of water; to lay down priorities for the use of water; to keep a continuous watch on the working of the River Basins Commissions and problems of inter-State rivers, and to ensure that the formulation and execution of irrigation projects is in accordance with the highest national interest.

The Prime Minister of India should be the Chairman of the Council and the Union Minister for Irrigation and Power, its Vice Chairman. The Ministries of Finance, Agriculture, Community Development, Planning, Health, Industry and Tourism should be represented on it through their Ministers.

Major States should be represented on the Council either by Chief Ministers or by the Irrigation Ministers. The smaller States and the Union Territories would have group representations by rotation.

Two eminent irrigation engineers and the Chairman, CW&PC should also be Members of the Council. The CW&PC will act as the Secretariat of the Water Resources Council.

The National Water Resources Council and the River Basins Commissions should be created by an Act of Parliament.

The Chairman of the CW&PC should be ex-officio Special Secretary in the Ministry of Irrigation & Power.

The work of exploitation of ground water in the State should be entrusted to two divisions; one under the Irrigation Department dealing with planning, operation and maintenance of heavy duty State tubewells, and the other under the State Agriculture Department dealing with drilling, boring of private wells and shallow tubewells.

The Governments of the Southern States and Maharashtra should consider proposal to make their Irrigation Departments responsible for the management of water from the source to the field as practised in the Northern States.

The present system of keeping the Secretariat separate from the Department is sound.

One of the Chief Engineers should be appointed as an Additional or Joint Secretary in the State Irrigation Department.

The Commission is of the opinion that in the appointment of the Secretary, Union Ministry of I&P and Secretaries to the State Irrigation Departments, technocrats should be treated at par with generalists.

Early steps may be taken to set up the Indian Service of Engineers.

Water Logging, Drainage And Floods

Large Tracts in the Indo-Gangetic plain suffer from water logging. The State of Punjab before its second re-organisation, had the largest affected area. Signs of water logging also appeared in Maharashtra in the commands of the Deccan Canals. Even in recent projects like the Chambal in Rajasthan and Madhya Pradesh water-logging has become a problem. As Irrigation is extended and developed, necessary precautions should be undertaken in advance to avoid water-logging.

The Presidency of Bombay, as it was then known, was the first to set up an irrigation research division in 1916. This division made valuable studies and Maharashtra has implemented a number of drainage schemes.

Other States have also constructed drainage works and other schemes like flood embankments, pumping out drainage water, and seepage drains. However, the Commission is of opinion that a more vigorous and planned action on the lines of what has been done in Punjab, is called for in many other States.

The Commission feels concerned about dangers of serious water logging in the command areas of the Gandak and Kosi Projects. The high water table heavy rain fall, perennial irrigation and the flat nature of the terrain are conditions that can create serious problems in these areas. The Commission recommends that the dangers of water-logging in the Gandak and Kosi projects should be vigorously dealt with from now on.

The Commission hopes that the States will continue to take steps to improve drainage in their irrigated areas. The drains should be excavated to adequate sections, and bad curves should be eased.

The Commission has drawn attention to the need for examining the water-ways at bridges, on roads and railway embankments, and cross drainage structures across the canals and water-ways across drains.

The Commission has not been specifically asked to examine the problem of floods. But irrigation cannot be introduced in areas prone to flooding unless they are freed from it. For instance, the extension of irrigation to Purnia and Saharsa districts would not have been feasible but for the flood control works built on the Kosi river.

Floods cause heavy damage to numerous irrigation works and irrigated areas. The sudden floods in the Ganga in 1970 led to heavy silting up of the Upper Ganga Canal which resulted in the closure of the canal for nearly nine weeks during critical parts of the kharif season.

Complete protection from floods can seldom be achieved, even if it were technically feasible. Works for cent per cent protection from floods may not be economically justifiable. Most flood control works aim at minimising the flood damage and protecting the maximum area. Steps should also be taken for flood forecasting to reduce the loss of life and property.

Sedimentation Of Reservoirs

Recently, studies of selected reservoirs to assess the sediment load carried by rivers, and the rate at which silt is deposited have been carried out by the Soil Conservation Directorate of the CW&PC, who have collected data for 22 reservoirs. In the Tungabhadra reservoir against the assumed siltation rate of 42,861 cu.m. per hundred sq. km. of catchment, the observed rate is 181,927. At this rate, its dead storage will be filled in 22 years, and the live storage in 74 years. In all reservoirs, the observed rate of siltation is very much higher than the rate initially assumed.

Soil conservation is the normal method of protecting the water-shed. It includes such measures as afforestation, pasture development, protection of river fringes, road-sides and the shore-lines of reservoirs, and the control of forest fires.

For an effective soil conservation programme, rivers and streams which carry a heavy silt load should be identified. The next step should be to locate the sources and assessment of sediment. This entails a systematic study of silt loads and discharges at selected observation stations. We have recommended that new observation stations on all important projects should be set up early.

A centrally sponsored scheme now covers 21 major projects for soil conservation. The Commission recommends that the States should make an early assessment of the erosion problem in the catchment areas of reservoirs not covered by the central scheme. Soil conservation should be taken up urgently in the more vulnerable areas.

The Commission recommends that the problem of soil conservation in all major projects should be completed in the next 20 years. In projects where the problem is acute, it should be completed within ten years.

A special problem, which deserves consideration, is the silting of canals, as has been observed in the Kosi irrigation system. Such silting affects the functioning of the irrigation system. The Commission, therefore, recommends that the silt problem of the Eastern Kosi Canal should receive urgent attention.

Inter-State Water Disputes

At present, the riparian States in a river valley are free to reach agreement among themselves for sharing the river flows in the valley. Should no agreement be reached, the issues in dispute can be referred by the Union Government to a tribunal on a request made by all or any of the States concerned. Although resort to a tribunal may occasionally be necessary in inter-State water disputes, adjudication is less satisfactory than negotiation.

Joint Commissions, such as the European Commission for the Danube, the International Water and Boundary Commission set up by Mexico and the United States and the Niger River Commission and others have provided useful forum to facilitate international agreement between riparian States. The functions of these Commissions include the investigation of the potentialities of a basin, the collection and collation of technical and other data and the formulation of schemes which provide the basis for eventual agreement. A body of this nature creates a climate of negotiation. It helps to define and limit the major issues in dispute. The Commission recommends that the machinery of River Basin Commissions should be used to marshall facts and to clarify issues involved in inter-State disputes.

In the past, the Union Government has played the role of mediator in settling inter-State water disputes. In some cases, it set up committees to assist the contending riparian States to reach agreement. The Union

Government provides substantial funds for plan projects of the States. Since an early settlement of inter-State disputes is important in nation's interest, the Union Government should step in when necessary. It can suggest alternative schemes and can expedite agreements by providing loans and grants or other forms of assistance to balance the scales.

We are of opinion that the Union Government should assume the same active and beneficial role in the settlement of inter-State water disputes as the World bank did in bringing about the Indo-Pakistan Treaty in Indus Water Dispute.

Irrigation Acts And Codes

There are different irrigation Acts and Codes which regulate irrigation in the States. The Acts vary because of the differences in irrigation practices in different parts of the country. These practices are influenced by such factors, as the incidence of rainfall, soil characteristics, topographic features and the agricultural practices.

In most States there exists a multiplicity of laws covering various aspects of irrigation management and administration. This accounts for multiple lines of authority. The diversification of control diffuses responsibility.

After the reorganisation of States in 1957 irrigation works in certain areas of the same continue to be administered by the laws of their parent States prior to reorganisation. The Commission recommends that the irrigation laws in each State should be consolidated into a single statute. Within the State the statute should apply uniformly to all regions.

The existing Irrigation Acts do not define the ownership of sub-surface or ground water. In view of the vital importance of ground water for agriculture, it is essential to extend control of Government over it to provide control and regulation. The Commission recommends that State Governments should assume legal power to regulate deep aquifers. However, ground water up to a certain depth, say 30m. in alluvial plains, being voluminous, may be exempted. The Union Government has prepared and circulated a model bill for this purpose.

The Commission recommends that the law relating to water courses and field channels should make provision for : (1) construction of water courses at Government's cost and their maintenance by the beneficiaries; (2) construction and maintenance of field channels by the beneficiaries; (3) on failure to construct to maintain a water course and/or field channel, the State's right to construct and maintain such works and recover the cost from the beneficiaries; (4) the State's power to construct field channels suo moto or on a request made by a majority of irrigators holding more than 50 per cent of land to be benefited; (5) to enact laws on the lines of the Northern India Canal and Drainage Act as applicable to Punjab for the purpose of acquiring land for water courses and field channels; and (6) for recovery of compensation for land acquired for field channels from the beneficiaries.

Experience of entrusting certain function of irrigation administration to the Panchayati Raj institutions and irrigators' cooperatives has not proved satisfactory. The Commission is of opinion that some sort of body composed of irrigators has to be created to share responsibility. The Commission recommends that State Governments should examine the nature of organisations or societies of irrigators to be set up.

Research Education And Training

Research in hydraulics and construction material can play an important role in effecting economies and improving quality in the massive programme of construction ahead of us.

The use of standardised precast members in various structures not only reduces the cost but also improves the quality and speed of construction. We are of opinion that research stations should work in closer collaboration with the design centres to promote standardisation.

Local materials should preferably be used to cut down the cost of transport. If suitable local materials are not available, research should be done to improve their quality.

Research activities would need the support of well-equipped libraries and documentation. The Commission recommends that the library maintained by the CBI&P/CW&PC should be provided with a proper building and modern equipment. A systematic extension of library facilities to different regions for research and designing is called for.

A significant portion of the literature on irrigation originates from non-English speaking countries such as the USSR and Japan. Translation facilities in English and Indian languages should be provided at CBI&P/CW&PC library.

Irrigation engineers should acquire a basic knowledge of agronomy. The education and training of irrigation engineers should include a basic course in agronomy.

Irrigation Statistics

Delay in the publication of land use statistics which include irrigation statistics, is frustrating. The Commission has been compelled to use statistics which are at least three years old.

The Commission recommends : (i) computerisation

of irrigation and agricultural statistics at the State headquarters; (ii) training of patwaries; (iii) strengthening of statistical set-up in districts; (iv) preparation of statistical extracts for each village, each district and each State with the aid of computers; and (v) routing back abstracts to appropriate levels of administration.

The Commission hopes that this process will ensure that the statistics are available within twelve months of the close of the relevant period.

COMMITTEE ON TELANGANA SURPLUSES, 1969—REPORT

Delhi, Manager of Publications, 1969. 116p.

Chairman : Justice Vashishtha Bhargava.
Members : Prof. Mukut Vehari Mathur; Shri Hari Bhushan Bhar.
Secretary : Shri T.N. Krishnasami.

APPOINTMENT

In a statement made in the Lok Sabha on April 11th, 1969 in regard to Telengana the Prime Minister had indicated certain specific measures which the Government of India proposed to take with a view to accelerating the place of development and expansion of employment opportunities in Telangana Region and creating conditions for balanced economic development of the State of Andhra Pradesh as a whole. It was indicated that a high-powered Committee would be appointed to determine the surplus relatable to Telangana which was expected to have been spent on the development of Telangana Region. Accordingly, the Government of India, Ministry of Home Affairs appointed the Committee on Telangana surpluses vide its Resolution dated April 22, 1969.

TERMS OF REFERENCE

The Committee shall take into account the agreements reached between the representatives of Andhra and Telangana Regions of the State of Andhra Pradesh regarding the utilisation of the surpluses from the Telangana Region for expenditure on development of that region, and in the light of those agreements :—

(a) examine the varying estimates made of such surpluses during the period 1st November, 1956 to 31st March, 1968 and of the unspent portion of such surpluses and also any representations made against these estimates ; and

(b) determine the sum which ought to have been spent on the development of the Telangana Region in accordance with the agreements but remained unspent on the 31st March, 1968.

Keeping in view the agreements aforesaid, the Committee shall also evolve and recommend precise principles on which the surpluses from the Telangana Region should be determined in future.

CONTENTS

Resolution ; The Procedure : Interpretation of the Terms of Reference ; Principles for Calculation of Surplus of Telangana and Development Expenditure ; Unspent Surplus ; Acknowledgment ; Annexures from A to G.

RECOMMENDATIONS

Interpretation Of The Terms Of Reference

In the Resolution laying down the terms of reference the Government of India mentioned that we were to take into account the agreements reached between the representatives of the Andhra and Telangana Regions of the State of Andhra Pradesh regarding the utilisation of the surpluses from the Telangana Region for expenditure on development of that region. There was considerable controversy as to the "agreements" which were thus referred to by the Government of India. Three documents were brought to our notice in that connection. The first was the agreement known as the "Gentlemen's Agreement" of 1956 (Annexure B). The second was a so-called "agreement" between the Chairman of the Regional Gommittee and the Government of Andhra Pradesh arrived at in the year 1959, laying down the principles for allocation of revenue receipts and expenditure between the two regions. The third was an "agreement" dated the 19th January, 1969, described as an all party accord arrived at between representatives of the various political parties in the whole of the State of Andhra Pradesh.

In the representations made before us, as well as during the course of personal interviews, all persons representing the views of either region were agreed that our determination under the terms of reference had to be based on the "Gentlemen's Agreement" of 1956. As regards the principles for determination of the surpluses laid down in the documents of 1959, it was represented on behalf of Telangana Region and particularly by the Chairman of the Regional Committee that this document embodied principles which had been enunciated by the Regional Committee and which had been accepted by the State Government, so that they should be treated as binding and unalterable for purposes of our culculations. The persons representing the views of Andhra Region attempted to challenge the principles contained in this document and urged that these principles had been laid down without taking into consideration the views of persons who could legitimately be considered as representing the interests of the Andhra Region. After a detailed discussion with all the representatives, we have come to the view that these principles embodied in the document of 1959 cannot be given the status of an agreement binding on persons representing the two regions of Andhra and Telangana, though the principles laid down appear to us to be, by and large, the correct principles which had to be applied available for development in Telangana in accordance with the "Gentlemen's Agreement" of 1956 and for purposes of discovering to what extent those surpluses had actually been spent on the development of Telangana. It appears to us that, in some details and in respect of some items, the principles applied may not be strictly fair and, consequently, where we intend to part from those principles, we shall indicate in our Report subsequently the reasons in brief why we have not strictly followed the norms laid down in this document. The third "agreement" of 19th January, 1969 was repudiated by the representatives of both the sides, so that we were not inclined to give that "agreement" the status of a binding agreement which necessarily had to be given effect to by us. However, in working out the principles which are to be applied in fairness to both the parties, we have kept this agreement in view and adopted it to the extent to which we consider that it would be fair to do so.

In this connection, we may also mention that during his interviews with us, the Chairman of the Regional Committee informed us that, from time to time, there were agreements on various principles between the Regional Committee and the Andhra Pradesh Government having bearing on the question of giving effect to the "Gentlemen's Agreement" of 1956 and all such agreements should also be treated as binding. For the reasons that we have come to the view above in respect of the document of 1959, we have come to the view that any such arrangements arrived at are to be given due weight and to be taken into consideration in working out the available surpluses, but they cannot be held to be of a binding nature, as they were not agreements arrived at between representatives of the two different regions.

There was also some controversy as to the actual contents of the "Gentlemen's Agreement" of 1956. It appeared from the records produced before us that a meeting was held on the 20th February, 1956, at Hyderabad Guest House, New Delhi, when the States of Andhra and Hyderabad existed as two separate units. The State of Andhra was represented at that meeting by Sarvashri B. Gopala Reddy, Sanjeeva Reddy, G. Latchanna and A. Satyanarayana Raju, while the State of Hyderabad was represented by Sarvashri B. Ramkrishna Rao, K.V. Ranga Reddy, Chenna Reddy and J.V. Narsinga Rao. A note was published in the Indian Express dated the 24th January, 1969, purporting to contain a "Gentlemen's Agreement" of Telangana safeguards containing details of the points which, in the opinion of the meeting, arose out of the unification of Telangana and Andhra, and the conclusions arrived at on those points after the discussions. We have verified from Government records that this note correctly reproduces the minutes of the meeting. On the basis of these minutes, the Ministry of Home Affairs, Government of India, prepared a note on safeguards proposed for the Telangana area which was placed on the table of the Lok Sabha on the 10th August, 1656. Both parties were agreed that the terms contained in this note placed on the table of the Lok Sabha on the 10th August, 1956, formed the subject matter of the "Gentlemen's Agreement" of 1956 which is to be the basis of the Report by our Committee ; but the representatives of Andhra urged that we should also take into account, in addition, some of the clauses which were not contained in this note but which were included in the minutes of the meeting. This contention was raised primarily because in the minutes there was a paragraph which prescribed a limitation for the period during which the revenue surpluses of Telangana were to be reserved for expenditure on the development of that area. That paragraph was as follows :—

"The expenditure of the Central and general administration of the State should be borne proportionately by the two regions and the balance of income from Telangana should be reserved for expenditure on the development of Telangana area. The arrangement will be reviewed after five years and can be continued for another five years if the Telangana members of the Assembly so desired".

The last sentence of the above term of the agreement contained in the minutes drawn up did not from part of the note placed before the Lok Sabha which was communicated by the Central Government to the State Government for being giving effect to. In these circumstances, we were not inclined to accept the argument put forward on behalf of the Andhra Region that the calculation of surpluses which were to be utilised for development of Telangana region should be limited to a period of only five years, because there was no review at the end of five years and there was no request by the members of the Legislature of Telangana region in that behalf. It was also urged in the alternative that, in any case, the computation should be limited to a period of ten years.

These arguments could not be accepted by us for two reasons. The basic reason is that when interpreting an agreement like the "Gentlemen's Agreement" of 1956, we cannot be very technical and base our decision on the mere language. The interpretation should be made on the basis of the purpose of such an agreement and the object to be achieved under it. It is obvious that this agreement was arrived at, because the residents of Telangana area were prepared to join the residents of Andhra to form a single State only subject to the condition that, being more backward, special considerations should be shown to them for their development and, since such development could hardly be achieved by limiting the period of agreement to five years only, acceptance of that limitation would defeat the purpose of the agreement itself. The second reason is that, by the very terms of our reference, we are excluded from accepting such an interpretation. In the Resolution of the Government of India, we have been asked to determine the surpluses for a period beginning from the 1st November, 1956, and ending with the 31st March, 1968. This is a period which exceeds ten years and on the face of it, therefore, the Government of India have already indicated that this period limitation contained in the note of minutes of the meeting was not treated as binding part of the "Gentlemen's Agreement" at all, and that appears to have been the reason why no such clause was included by the Government of India in the note placed on the table of the Lok Sabha. We are, consequently, inclined to accept that the "Gentlemen's Agreement" that is to be given effect to by us is the one contained in the note placed by the Government of India on the table of the Lok Sabha.

It is in the light of our decisions indicated above that we have to fulfil our terms of reference by examining the varying estimates made of Telangana surpluses during the period 1st November, 1956 to the 31st March, 1968 and of the unspent portion of such surpluses and also any representations made against those estimates. In order to do so, we consider that three steps have to be gone through. The first step is to determine the revenue income accruing to the Telangana region during this period and next to determine the revenue expenditure during the same period, dividing that period into financial years, except for the initial period limited to five months from the 1st November, 1956 to the 31st March, 1957. The difference between the revenue income and the revenue expenditure on development of Telangana region in accordance with the Agreement of 1956. The third step is to determine what part of that surplus was spent in each of those years. On behalf of the Andhra region, it was argued before us that, if the figures are scrutinised, it will be found that, in each of those years, the amount actually spent on development work in Telangana would exceed the amount of surplus calculated as mentioned above, so that there cannot possibly be any surplus remaining unspent. The argument is, on the face of it, fallacious. The agreement did not envisage that on development of Telangana the expenditure will be restricted to the surplus accruing in Telangana as a result of excess revenue income as against expenditure. That surplus was to be spent as a special concession to Telangana region over and above any other expenditure which should have been incurred there is view of the availability of funds for purposes of development in the State from all other sources, whether those sources were sources of income or tapped by resorting to borrowing. In our opinion, the proper approach would be to find out what total amount was actually spent on the development of the whole of the State and then to determine from that total amount. Thereafter, if it is found that the amount actually spent on Telangana out of the total exceeds that fair share of Telangana, it would be held that this excess amount was utilised out of the surplus of Telangana. In a converse case, if in any year the actual amount spent on Telangana is found to be less than its fair share of the total, the conclusion must be that the amount actually spent for development of Telangana did not include any surplus at all and Telangana was, in fact, deprived of part of its fair share. The extent to which Telangana is held to be thus deprived of its fair share of the actual total development expenditure should be added to the surplus of the year to determine the amount which should be reserved for development of Telangana in accordance with the "Gentlemen's Agreement".

Then, we have to examine the proportion according to which the Telangana region should be entitled in the development expenditure actually incurred in the State. During the discussions before us, only two alternative suggestions were put forward. The first was that the expenditure in the two regions should be in proportion to the areas of the two regions, and the second was that it should be in proportion to the population. The first suggestion was not seriously pressed by any party nor does it appear to be appropriate to us, because development expenditure cannot be based on the mere existence of a larger area in one region that the other, ignoring the nature of the lands and the needs for development. We are of the view that it would be much more equitable that expenditure for development in different areas should, as far as possible, be in proportion to the number of persons residing in each area who are to benefit from the development schemes and whose needs have to be taken into account. The All Parties' Conference on the 19th January, 1969 also appears to have arrived at the same view when it laid down that "the Telangana surpluses for each year will be computed by adding to the net revenue surplus of Telangana region of that year the difference between one-third of the total capital expenditure of the State in that year and the actual capital expenditure in the Telangana region in that year." The proportion of one-third of the total was envisaged on the basis of the approximate proportion between the population of the two areas. In addition, we have before us the circumstance that, in the principles for calculation of surplus agreed upon between the Regional Committee and the State Government, it was laid down that receipts and expenditure from common sources will be divided in the proportion of 2 : 1. The information given to us shows that, according to the census of 1951, the population of the region now forming Telangana was about one-half of that of the area now forming the Andhra region. This appears to have been the principal reason for applying this proportion of 2 : 1 between Andhra and Telangana. Our attention was drawn to the latest census figures of 1961 according to which there has a small variation in this percentage of population inasmuch as the population is in the proportion of about 65 : 35. The variation, in our opinion, is very small and, if we were to alter the proportion for the purpose of working out fair share of each region in the total development expenditure, it would also mean revising the principle of dividing receipts and expenditure in that proportion earlier, the Chairman of the Regional Committee was insistent that we should give effect to the principles laid down in that document without any alteration. In the circumstances, we hold that even in the case of working out proportionate share of Telangana in the total development expenditure of the State, the same proportion should be maintained, so that the proportionate share of Telangana in each year would be one-third of the total expenditure. The difference between this fair share and the actual expenditure in Telangana region in each year will have to be added to or subtracted from the surplus in order to determine the unspent surplus as indicated by us above.

Principles For Calculation Of Surplus Of Telangana And Development Expenditure

Before we proceed to deal with the actual method of calculation of revenue income and expenditure in Telangana area and the amounts spent on development in the two regions, it is necessary to consider the nature of the investments, receipts and expenditure of Boards and Corporations functioning in the whole of the State. In the present times, the Government, in addition to its function of administration, undertakes a number of commercial activities which result in development of the area where they are carried on. Three different systems are adopted in carrying on those activities. The first is that all the activities are carried on by the Government directly through its Departments or Boards which work under the orders of the Government Secretariat. The second method is to create statutory corporations by passing laws which define the functions and powers of such statutory corporations. The third is that the Government, in order to encourage industrial development, makes investments in corporations registered under the Companies Act and these corporations function as separate autonomous entities.

So far as the activities carried on by the Government directly through its Departments or Boards functioning under the Departments are concerned, it is clear that all expenditure, revenue or capital, has to be treated as expenditure or development investments by the Government and the receipts accruing through such activities are receipts of the Government. All such activities can be divided into two parts. Some activities would be confined exclusively to one region and some to the other. In those cases, the investments treated as development expenditure and the income and expenditure arising out of that activity will have to be treated as the income or expenditure of that separate region. Then there may be cases where the activity is a State-wide activity and it is not possible to identify each item carried out as pertaining to one region or the other. For such cases, the obvious method is to treat it as a common activity meant for the entire State and on the principle we have indicated above, all items relating to such activity will be divisible between the two regions of Andhra and Telangana in the proportion of 2 : 1.

The position in respect of statutory boards and corporations is, in our opinion, exactly similar. It has already been decided by the Supreme Court that statutory boards and corporations are included in the word "State" as used in part III of the Constitution dealing with fundamental rights even though those boards or corporations may be carrying on commercial activities. Even on general principles it is clear that such statutory boards and corporations are created merely for the sake of administrative convenience while the activity entrusted to the board or corporation is an activity which the State undertakes to carry on for the benefit of the people in the State. All investments in, as well as income and expenditure of such statutory boards and corporations must be allocated on the footing that they are similar to activities carried on directly by a Government Department. Special mention, in this connection, may be made of the State Financial Corporation which it appears, is functioning on the basis of investments made not merely by the State or the Central Government, but even by others such as Scheduled Banks, Cooperative Societies and individuals. All other statutory boards or corporations, we have found are working on the basis of investments made only by the State Governments or the Central Government. Investments by Central Government in such boards and corporations partake of the nature of money invested for the development of the State by the Central Government and in allocating development expenditure, these moneys have to be taken into account as utilised for development of the region in which that statutory corporation or board is functioning. In the case of State Financial Corporation also, we consider that this principle need not be departed from because the major investment in that corporation is from resources which can be identified either with the State Government or the Central Government or institutions like the Reserve Bank of India. The investments obtained from others such as Scheduled Banks, Cooperative Societies or private individuals have to be treated as funds raised by the Government for purposes of carrying on the activities of the State Financial Corporation in successfully working out development schemes in the State, and if such funds are raised by the Government by issue of shares for a corporation constituted by a statute, the utilisation of these funds should also be treated on the same basis as investments made by the Government itself. Consequently, statutory boards and corporations are to be treated on the same footing as a Department of the Government for purposes of calculation of surplus of income over expenditure as well as amounts for development in the various areas. The important corporations which claim mention are : the Electricity Board, the Road Transport Corporation, the State Housing Board, the State Warehousing Corporation and the State Financial Corporation.

We have then to consider the cases of corporations registered under the Companies Act in which Government funds have been invested either by the State Government or the Central Government. Such corporations discharge their functions according to, and derive their powers from, the Memoranda of Association and the Articles of Association which are agreed to by the share-holders, so that they are markedly different from statutory corporations which derive their powers from a statute passed by the Legislatures and have to work within the scope of that statute. The former cannot be equated with the State which has to carry out its functions in accordance with the Consitution or the statutes and are separate legal entities which have the right to frame their own rules in the Articles of Association to regulate their conduct. It is true that investments by purchases of share in such corporations are frequently made by the Central or State Government in order to ensure that the industry to be started by the corporation works successfully and results in development of the area where the factory is established. The actual activity of running the factory is, however, not carried on by or on behalf of the Government, so that the actual income and expenditure of such corporations cannot be treated as revenue and expenditure pertaining to any Government activity. The revenue income and expenditure belong to the corporation which is a separate legal entity distinct from either the Central Government or the State Government. The Government can only claim dividends on the amounts invested in shares or interest in case the investments are in the form of loans. Consequently, in making our calculations, it appears to us to be fair to hold that only the dividends and interest received are to be treated as income of the Government from those corporations while investments made in shares are to be treated as amounts invested for development of the industry in the region in which that particular corporation is carrying on its activity.

For calculation of revenue income and expenditure of Telangana in order to arrive at the surplus available for development of Telangana in accordance with the agreement of 1956, we are of the view that the principles laid down in the document of 1959 should be followed as they are equitable and have been enunciated in order to give effect to the agreement of 1956 as explained by us above subject, of course, to proper interpretation or minor variations which are indicated below :

(1) **Sales Tax** : According to the norms laid down in 1959, the amounts of sales tax deposited in the two separate regions of Telangana and Andhra are to be treated as receipts of those regions with the exception of the receipts at Headquarters for which the principle rightly laid down is that the entire amount deposited will be treated as receipts of Telangana

region, except for such amounts as can be shown to specifically relate to Andhra region. The controversy between the representatives of the two regions on this interpretation centered mainly on sales tax realised from dealers who had their Head Offices in Hyderabad but were carrying on business through their branches in the region. In such cases, the procedure in vogue was that a single return was filed for the sales by the Head Office as well as the Branch Office before the assessing authority at Hyderabad, but in those returns the turn-overs of the Head Office and the Branch Office were separately shown and the sales tax due separately could be worked out, even though, at the time of assessment, the entire turn-over was taxed as one unit. There were also a few reverse cases where the Head Office was situated in Andhra region and Branch Offices in Telangana region and, in such cases, the tax for the Head Office as well as the Branch Office was assessed and realised in Andhra region. It was also found that the Branch Offices in one region were conducting their sales in that region only and not in the other region. In these circumstances, it was clear that the sales tax due in respect of the transactions carried out by the Branch Office accrued to the State Government in the area in which the Branch Office accrued to the State Government in the area in amount was assessed and taxed at the place where the Head Office was located. The sales tax accruing in respect of the transactions of the Branch business was clearly a receipt relating to the region in which the Branch business was being carried on and, on the principles agreed in 1959, that sales tax should have been treated as a receipt of the area in which the Branch Office is located and not the area in which the Head Office was located. Thus, in respect of business concerns having Head Offices at Hyderabad, the amounts received at Hyderabad for business carried on by their branches in the Andhra region should be excluded from the income of Telangana regions, while the sales tax due from branches in Telangana region of dealers who had their Headquarters in the Andhra region should be included in the income of Telangana region.

In his last representation before us, the Chairman of the Regional Committee in interpreting the 1959 Agreement, urged that only if any particular remittance specifically pertaining to Andhra region is credited to Hyderabad city, its credit should be given to Andhra region. He has added that the wording of the exception cannot be extended to reopen cases where the receipts themselves accrue in Hyderabad city and are paid here. This argument proceeds on a misconception. Sales tax does not accrue where returns are filed or assessments are made. Sales tax accrues, under the Sales Tax Act, at the place where the sale itself takes place. As soon as a sale is completed, the amount of sale money becomes a part of the turn-over at the place where the sale has taken place and that amount becomes liable to sales tax immediately at the place of the sale. Consequently, in respect of sales conducted by a branch situated in the Andhra region and entering into sale transactions only within Andhra region, the tax accrues to the State Government in Andhra region and not at Hyderabad even though, for convenience, the returns in respect of such sales are filed and the assessment of tax on those sales takes place at Hyderabad, the State Headquarters. In varying the calculations of sales tax made by the Shri Kumar Lalit in this respect, we are, thus only giving effect to the principles agreed upon in 1959 by the Regional Committee and the Government.

In this connection, it was also urged before us that the figures supplied by the Sales Tax Department in respect of transactions of branches in one region having Head Office in a different region may not be correct. To set at rest this doubt, we had a test check made by our Secretary in a number of cases and we have only accepted figures after being satisfied that they have been properly worked out. The receipts from the sales tax have been allocated between the two regions on the basis of these figures and on the basis of the further principles indicated above.

(2) Grants under Article 275 of the Constitution : The grants under Article 275 of the Constitution were not specifically dealt with in the document of 1959 which only mentioned grants-in-aid from Central Government against which the method of allocation was "on schemes if they are there". Shri Kumar Lalit, when making the calculations for purposes of determining the Telangana surpluses, sought clarification from the State Government and the State Government, in their letter dated the 22nd February, 1969, laid down that these grants should be allocated between Andhra Telangana regions in the ratio of 2 : 1. This method of allocation was challenged before us by representatives of the Andhra region, primarily on the ground that grants under Article 275 are meant to cover revenue deficit of a State and since the Telangana region is surplus in revenue and the deficit in revenue occurs in the Andhra region only, the entire amount received as grant under this head should be treated as a receipt for Andhra. In our opinion, this argument cannot be accepted for two reasons. One is that the grants under Article 275 are not meant merely for covering the revenue deficit but also take into account the factor of backwardness and need for development of a State. The second reason is that even though the grants under Article 275 in the past were necessitated primarily by the revenue deficit accruing as a result of heavier expenditure than income in Andhra region, the position would have been different if Andhra region did not have such a deficit in which event larger amounts could have been spent in Telangana while the deficit so created would still have been covered by the grants under this Article. The benefit of a common grant for the entire State cannot justifiably be claimed by a region merely because there is over-expenditure in that region. For these reasons we hold that the principle laid down by the Government in the letter dated 22nd February, 1969, does not need any alteration.

(3) **Other Grants-in-Aid from Central Government:** The grants received from Central Government can be divided into two broad sub-heads, viz., Plan grants and non-Plan grants. In respect of the Plan grants, the document of 1959 envisages distribution between the two regions in proportion to the Plan outlay of those regions. The only further explanation required is to make it clear that the expression "Plan outlay" is not to be interpreted as the projected outlay, but as the actual Plan outlay whether in the form of capital investment, loans and advances or revenue expenditure. In the case of non-Plan grants which cannot be co-related to a particular scheme or expenditure on it and such grants, therefore, have to be treated as common grants for the whole State and must be allocated on the general principle in the proportion of 2 : 1 between Andhra and Telangana. The figures incorporated in our calculations have been worked out on these principles after obtaining from the State Government lists of grants meant for specified schemes and treating those amounts only as common grants for the whole State which are ascertainable but cannot be identified as intended for any particular scheme.

(4) **Interest on investments.** In the norms laid down in the document of 1959, provision was made for crediting to the Receipts accounts forming part of the investments of the funds of the State. Some of these investments are specified and the manner in which the interest on those investments is to be credited is clearly indicated. The provision in respect of these specified items appears to us to be quite fair and equitable. Then, there is a residuary clause which reads as follows :

"The other amounts realised at Headquarters will be allocated between the two regions in the ratio of 2 : 1".

This clause in its application, creates a little difficulty, because other amounts of inetrest which are not specified in that document itself relate to two types of investments. Some are investments which have been debited as capital outlay in the accounts of the Telangana region, while some are common to both the regions. It is but fair that interest realised in respect of investments debited entirely to Telangana region is credited to the revenue account of Telangana region, while the amounts of interest realised in respect of common investments is allocated in the ratio of 2 : 1.

(5) **Common Offices** : According to the norms in the document of 1959, expenditure incurred at Headquarters, on common services and establishment is to be allocated between Andhra and Telangana regions in the ratio of 2 : 1. This appears to be a very fair provision. At Headquarters, there is expenditure incurred on the Governor, the Ministers, the Legislature and the Secretariat. There are other institutions of similar nature, like the High Court and the Board of Revenue. Then there are located at Headquarters a number of heads of Departments like Inspector General of Police, Director of Public Instruction, Director of Medical Services etc. Since these function for the entire State though the expenditure on them is shown in the accounts at Hyderabad, the capital of the State, it is reasonable that the expenditure so incurred is shared in the proportion of 2 : 1 by Andhra and Telangana regions. In view of this provision, it was urged before us by the representatives of Andhra region that even on the income side the receipts by such common services and establishments should be allocated between Andhra and Telangana in the same proportion of 2 : 1. The norms of 1959 do not contain any such provision. On the receipt side, the provision is that all receipts of Headquarters are to be credited to the Telangana region except in cases where they specifically relate to Andhra region. In the case of such common services and establishments as mentioned above, it is not easy to say what proportion of receipts by such an institution can be said to specifically relate to Andhra region. Then there is another consideration which has to be kept in view. Apart from these services and establishments, there exist in Hyderabad a number of other social services and amenities from which benefit is derived even by the residents of Andhra. Since Hyderabad became the capital of the State, a large number of persons originally residing in Andhra have shifted to Hyderabad, particularly those who are concerned with the administration of the Government at the capital of the State. Such persons take full advantage of amenities provided in the city of Hyderabad in the form of medical aid, water supply, education, sanitation etc. According to the accounting system adopted, expenditure incurred on the amenities is going to be debited towards the revenue expenditure by Telangana and is not going to be divided in the proportion of 2 : 1. Any receipt from a few institutions like the High Court or the Board of Revenue in the form of Court fee would be more than offset by the expendi-

ture attributable to the benefit derived by residents of Andhra through services of the nature mentioned above by us. When division of expenditure and income has to take place between regions within the same State, there cannot be two watertight compartments and calculations have to be made on equitable basis. Keeping this principle in view, we think that the method of allocating receipts as well as expenditure from common services and establishments laid down in the document of 1959 is fair and equitable and needs no variation.

(6) **Employees' State Insurance Scheme**: Under the Employees' State Insurance Scheme, a number of institutions, particularly dispensaries, were started at various places in both the regions. The expenditure incurred on them has been debited in the accounts of the respective regions. That expenditure incurred by the State Government is partially reimbursed by the Employees' State Insurance Corporation. The amounts received from that Corporation were all credited of Hyderabad and were meant to cover a proportionate expenditure on the various dispensaries, etc., maintained in the entire State. In order to arrive at the correct figure of income allocable to each region, we have divided these receipts at Hyderabad in proportion to the expenditure incurred in the two regions under this scheme.

(7) **Receipts from Taxes on Road Transport Corporation Vehicles**: The representatives of the Andhra region put forward a complaint that taxes due on vehicles run by the Road Transport Corporation even exclusively in the Andhra region had been credited in the Government accounts at Hyderabad and that it was incorrect to treat the amounts so received as income of Telangana when, in fact, these receipts were in respect of taxes which accrued to the State in the Andhra region. The accounts were examined to see how far this grievance was justified. It was found that, except for two years, in all other years the taxes paid on the Road Transport Corporation vehicles were deposited in the same region in which the vehicles were running. So far as the other remaining two years are concerned, re-allocation has been made so as to ensure that taxes paid in respect of vehicles plying in one region are treated as receipts of that very region.

(8) **Electricity Board.** There was very considerable controversy on the question of allocation between the two regions of the capital expenditure as well as the revenue income and revenue expenditure of the Electricity Board which is a State-wide organisation. It was first urged by the representatives of the Telangana region that the activities of the Electricity Board should not be treated as a Government activity saparately in the region in which that activity is carried on, but the entire work being carried on by the Electricity Board should be held to be a single unit serving the entire State, so that all capital expenditure should be divided between the two regions in the proportion of 2 : 1. It was further urged that the revenue income and expenditure of the Electricity Board should not be taken into account at all. The main reason advanced in support of the latter is that the Telangana surpluses have to be determined on the basis of expenditure incurred on Government account and it would be wrong to introduce extraneous figures into this determination which have no bearing on the State Exchequer and are not reflected in the Government budgets and accounts. This view put forward on behalf of the Telangana region cannot be accepted in view of our decision indicated with reasons above that the Electricity Board being a statutory corporation carrying on a Government activity has to be equated with the Government itself, so that investments by the Board stand on the same footing as investments by Government, and income earned and expenditure incurred by the Board are to be equated with income earned and expenditure incurred by the Government.

So far as the capital expenditure by the Electricity Board is concerned the plea put forward on behalf of the Telangana region was based on the ground that the high tension electricity lines now maintained in the State by the Electricity Board formed one single grid so that all the electric schemes serving that one single grid must be treated as one single unit serving the entire State. We are not prepared to accept this argument either. Even though there is inter-connection through a grid between various sources of electric supply in the State, our information elicited from the Chairman and Officers of the Electricity Board is that various sources of supply can be separately identified as intended to serve separate areas with a few exceptions where one single source may serve more than one area. Since it is possible to find out which source of electricity is going to serve which particular region it appears to be fairer to treat the investment on that source as development expenditure in that region. Further, if we were to accept the view put forward on behalf of Telangana region and to hold that all the electricity schemes for the entire State are to be treated as one common unit, it would be very difficult to arrive at a suitable principle for allocating the share of expenditure on the various schemes between the two regions. There can be only two possible methods for allocation. One is the proportion of 2 : 1 based on population which is being adopted in respect of ordinary items of revenue and expenditure. In the case of electricity, we do not think that principle can be applied because the consumption of electricity and the benefits derived from electric supply cannot bear any relation to the population, particularly because large portions of the power supplied are used for industrial purposes. The other method of allocation in proportion to the number of units of power used in each region is inappropriate because the power consumption will vary from day to day and the proportion at present existing may have no relation with the proportion in future when various areas have been developed or new industries set up. Allocation of capital expenditure on the basis of the existing proportion of energy consumption will then appear very anomalous after that proportion alters very materially. In the circumstances we hold that it is proper to treat the activities of the Electricity Board as separate ones depending on whether a particular source of supply is serving one region or the other.

On a discussion with the Chairman and officers of the Electricity Board, we have come to the view that apart from the two Power Houses situated at Kothagudem and Srisailam, which are under construction, all other sources of supply are really intended to supply distinct areas falling either under the Andhra region or the Telangana region. Consequently, all investments made on those sources of supply as well as on high tension lines maintained for the purpose of transmitting the power to the sub-stations which step down the electricity for supply to consumers must be treated as representing capital development expenditure in the region in which that source of supply is situated. In the case of Kothagudem Power House, our information was that it is intended primarily to serve Telangana region but has now been so connected with the supply lines in Andhra region that a portion of the energy produced by the Kothagudem Power House is going to be utilised in the Andhra region. On an estimate based on information given to us, we have come to the conclusion that in these circumstances it would be fair to allocate two-third of the capital investment in Kothagudem as intended to serve Telangana, while one-third as intended to serve Andhra. In the case of Srisailam Power House, the proportion is just the reverse. That Power House, when completed, is likely to serve primarily the Andhra region and Telangana can only be held to benefit to the extent of one-third of the power generated at that station. We have had to take this decision with regard to Srisailam immediately, because capital expenditure on its construction is going on and has been going on during the years with which we are concerned and that expenditure must be allocated between the two regions in the manner just indicated.

So far as revenue expenditure is concerned, it consists of the day-to-day running cost and all such cost incurred on running and maintenance of the source of supply together with high tension lines connected with that source of supply must follow the same method of allocation as the capital expenditure in respect of that source of supply. Apart from the sources of supply, viz., Hydro-Electric Generators or coal-based Power Houses and the high tension lines needed to carry the electric power up to distributing sub-station. The question arises as to the capital and revenue expenditure incurred on construction and maintenance of the sub-stations and the actual supply lines for distributing electricity to the consumers. So far as these sub-stations and lines from sub-stations to consumers are concerned, they have been identified as separately relating to one region or the other and, consequently, all expenditure on them is to be treated as expenditure of the region in which the sub-stations and the lines are situated. The revenue income to the Electricity Board only accrues at this stage of supply to the consumers and, consequently, that income is also allocable to the region in which the supply is made and the supply charges become due to the Electricity Board.

(9) **State Road Transport Corporation :** A grievance was made before us that, in view of the fact that this Corporation did not maintain separate accounts of income earned and expenditure incurred in the two regions. Shri Kumar Lalit was not right in allocating its earnings and expenditure in the manner he did, nor should any such allocation be made by us. An examination of the records and accounts maintained by this Corporation has led us to the conclusion that a proper manner of allocation between the two regions is feasible and we have adopted that course. In the case of capital expenditure, we found that accounts were maintained in such a manner that it was possible to find out the separate expenditure incurred on construction of buildings, acquisition of land and purchase of vehicles and spare parts for vehicles running in the two regions. So far as revenue income earned by this Corporation is concerned, the income accruing from a route wholly situated within one region or the other could clearly be attributed to that region and treated as its income. In the case of inter-region routes, the income can, on principles of fairness, be divided between the two regions in proportion to length of the route situated in each region. As regards expenditure, it appears that the Corporation has divided the entire road scheme within the State into five divisions and accounts of expenditure are maintained at one place for each division. The road mileage within each division situated in each of the two separate regions has been worked out and the expenditure incurred by the division has been divided in proportion to the road mileage of the division in each region.

(10) **Milk Scheme :** It appears that for the purpose of supplying milk to the twin cities of Hyderabad and

Secunderabad, milk used to be purchased in the Andhra region, primarily at Vijayawada. The cost of that milk purchased was debited in the Andhra region. The milk thereafter was supplied to the consumers in the twin cities of Hyderabad and Secunderabad and the sale proceeds were credited at Hyderabad. Obviously, the receipts at Hyderabad representing the price of milk sold cannot represent revenue receipts of Telangana region unless the cost incurred in purchases is first deducted. This activity carried on by the Government is in the nature of a business activity. The cost of the materials purchased and the price realised on their sale must be first balanced against each other and then only can the net gain or loss be worked out. It was, therefore, incorrect to debit the cost to the Andhra region and credit the entire sale price to the Telangana region. We consider that the Milk Scheme is an activity meant for Telangana region which benefits from the transactions under the Scheme and hence the cost of the milk purchased in Andhra region is being debited by us as expenditure of the Telangana region so as to give effect to the correct position.

(11) **Andhra Pradesh Text-book press** : This Press is being run at Hyderabad by the State Government for printing of text-books for use in educational institutions in the entire State. The main object of starting the Press was to ensure that well-printed and well got-up text-books are made available to the students without risk of the books getting out of print and the studies of the students suffering therefrom. The further object was to ensure that the books are supplied at reasonable prices. This Press is clearly, in these circumstances, a service undertaken by the State Government for the students of the entire State and has, therefore, to be treated as a common institution. Consequently, the capital expenditure on the Press must be treated as a development expenditure for the whole State and so also the income and expenditure in running the Press from day to day are to be treated as common income and expenditure of both the regions. We may mention that we are taking the income and expenditure of this Press as common receipts and expenditure of the entire State because, besides being a service for the entire State, it also partakes of the nature of a commercial undertaking inasmuch as this Press is not run on a 'no profit no loss' basis. The investment in the Press as well as its income and expenditure, in these circumstances, has to be allocated in the proportion of 2 : 1 between by Andhra and the Telangana regions on the principle enunciated by us earlier.

(12) **State Trading Schemes** : One question that has arisen is whether State Trading Schemes of the nature of purchases and sale of fertilizers and foodgrains should be taken into account in working out the surplus or in determining the amount spent on development. In the case of fertilizers, the purchases by the State Government are primarily from public or private sector manufacturers outside the State of Andhra Pradesh or from stocks imported by the Government of India. The fertilizers are then sold in both the Telangana and Andhra regions for use by the cultivators. In the case of foodgrains, the purchases are both within as well as outside the State. The sales of foodgrains so purchased are to other States as well as within the State for purposes of price control through fair-price shops. In both cases, these transactions are carried out by the State Government on a 'no profit no loss' basis. Consequently, these transactions are not expected to result in either increase in revenue over expenditure or in bringing about a deficit. For purposes of calculation of surplus of revenue over expenditure, therefore, these transactions should have no bearing. Further, the accounts that are invested by the Government in purchasing the fertilizers or the foodgrains are reimbursed as soon as the goods purchased are sold, so that there is no such investment over a substantial period which could possibly be treated as development expenditure. In these circumstances, it is clear that these Trading Schemes do not have any effect on the calculations which we are required to make and we are, consequently, leaving them out of our calculations.

(13) **Nagarjunasagar Dam** : The Nagarjunasagar Dam is one of the biggest development schemes in the State. The total cost of construction of the Dam and the canals is going to exceed Rs. 150 crores. Naturally, therefore, there was considerable controversy about the allocation of this development expenditure between the two areas.

The reports received by us show that the work on this Dam is going to be taken up in several phases and during the period covered by our report only the first phase of construction had been going on. That phase has progressed to such an extent that benefit from it is already available to both the regions for irrigation through the canals and for regulating the water supply in the middle channel which serves the Krishna Delta area in the Andhra region. The information furnished by the Government and the Chief Engineer shows that the right canal is intended to serve Andhra region alone, while the left canal will serve partly the Andhra region and partly the Telangana region. In the first phase the present plan is that 177 T.M. Cft. will be utilised through the two canals in the Andhra region and benefit which the two regions will derive from the canals to be fed by this Dam. In addition, it appears that 30.45 T.M. Cft. are going to be available for perennial irrigation in the Krishna Delta. There was no dispute that in working out the proportion of investment on this Dam representing benefit to each area, the separate supplies through the canals must be taken into account, but it was urged before us by the representatives of the Andhra region as well as by the P.W.D. and Finance Secretary to the Andhra Pradesh Government who also appeared before us, that the quantity of 30 T.M. Cft. envisaged for utilisation in the Delta area should not be taken into account because, even without this Nagarjunasagar Dam, the Delta area would have received the irrigation facilities through the existing river channel.

In order to examine whether it would be fair to take into account water supplied in this original river channel from the Dam, we obtained additional information from the P.W.D. and the Finance Secretary to the Government. It appears from the information supplied by them that during the twelve years from 1953-54 to 1964-65, the average withdrawals at Vijayawada available for irrigation purposes in the Krishna Delta area were 53.07 T.M. Cft. Out of this, on an average 37.41 T.M. Cft. were available from the natural flow of the river at Krishna Delta while the deficiency was made up by letting down water from the Tungabhadra Reservoir. The water so withdrawn from the Tungabhadra Reservoir was, on an average, 15.66 T.M. Cft. or in round figure 16 T.M. Cft. These figures were supplied in respect of the water requirements between 1st January to 30th April each year which is the lean period when the level of water in the river goes down to its minimum and yet water is needed for irrigation of the Rabi crops. The further information supplied to us shows that from the time that this Nagarjunasagar Dam has become useful by having been erected up to a suitable height, the water withdrawals at Vijayawada have been larger. In the three years 1966-67, 1967-68 and 1968-69, the withdrawals were 63.3 T.M. Cft., 91.7 T.M. Cft., and 62.5 T.M. Cft., respectively, giving an average of 72.5 T.M. Cft. These withdrawals were possible even without letting down any water at all from the Tungabhadra Reservoir. It is true, as stated in the letter of the Finance Secretary, that subsequently when the full water supply in the two left and right bank canals is utilised for irrigation of lands meant to be served by those canals, the same quantity of water may not be available for withdrawals at Vijayawada because some of these withdrawals are based on unutilised water in the canals which flows back into the Central river channel. However, one thing is clear viz., that in any case the effect of this Nagarjunasagar Dam is that no further withdrawals of water are required from the Tungabhadra Reservoir so that the middle river channel serving the Delta area in Andhra region will benefit to the extent that water supply needed by it will be ensured without drawing upon the Tungabhadra Reservoir. The natural consequence is that the water which was being withdrawn from the Tungabhadra Reservoir would be available for use elsewhere and since this is water which was being received by the State of Andhra Pradesh that quantity of water would now be available to this very State for utilisation in the areas which can be conveniently irrigated from channels coming out of the Tungabhadra Reservoir. That area which can be so served lies entirely in the Andhra region. The construction of the Nagarjunasagar Dam thus results in an additional benefit to the Andhra region to the extent of 16 T.M. Cft. which are supplied at Vijayawada for the Krishna Delta area by this Dam and which thus enables the Andhra region to obtain an additional 16 T.M. Cft. of water for irrigation of other areas in that region which can be served from channels fed by the Tungabhadra Reservoir. The benefit from the Nagarjunasagar Dam, therefore, to Andhra region must be held to be to the extent of 177 T.M. Cft. plus 16 T.M. Cft., i.e. total 193 T.M. Cft., while the benefit to the Telangana region will be 87 T.M. Cft. It is in the proportion of 193.87 that the investment made by the State of Andhra Pradesh in the construction of the Nagarjunasagar Dam must be divided as representing the development expenditure in the two areas of Andhra and Telangana. So far as the expenditure on construction of canals is concerned, the right canal being meant for irrigation of areas in the Andhra region alone, the entire cost of that canal system must be treated as expenditure for the benefit of Andhra region while expenditure on the left canal which is to serve both the Andhra and Telangana regions is to be treated as development expenditure in the two regions in the proportion of 45 : 86 which is the proportion in which the water from this canal is planned to be utilised in the two regions.

(14) **State Housing Board** : The activities of this Board, as we have indicated earlier, are to be equated with State Government activities. Consequently, any expenditure incurred by this Board in a particular region must be treated as expenditure on that region with the exception of Hyderabad, the Headquarters of the State. The Board's activity of construction of residential accommodation has been primarily concentrated in Hyderabad where there was acute shortage due to the city being made the capital of the unified State. The constructions made in Hyderabad were intimately connected with the requirements arising on account of its becoming the capital of the State and this accommodation had to be made available to whoever required it there for purposes of serving the Government or for purposes connected or arising therefrom. This accommodation was, therefore, needed by residents of both the areas of Andhra and

Telangana who were required to live in Hyderabad. In these circumstances, it is clear that the benefits arising out of the activities of this Board would be availed of by the two regions as common amenities so that the expenditure incurred by the Board at Hyderabad had to be allocated in proportion of 2 : 1 between Andhra and Telangana.

(15) **Common Institutions at Hyderabad** : The Chairman of the Regional Committee, in his Supplementary Memorandum presented to us, gave a list of 52 institutions which, according to him, were meant for the entire State of Andhra Pradesh and consequently, it was urged that the expenditure incurred on these institutions should be divided between the two regions in the proportion of 2 : 1. We have carefully examined the list to see how far this argument can be accepted in respect of each of these institutions. It is correct that a large number of these institutions are of such a nature that they are intended to serve the entire State or to be utilised by the residents of the entire State. For example we may mention that Research Institutes will be of State-wide importance even though they may be located at Hyderabad. Similar is the position with regard to Specialised Training Institutions. Facilities of the nature of a Zoological Garden or a Stadium are also meant for the residents of the entire State and the location at Headquarters is only considered desirable because it is here that the largest number of persons from both the areas reside as well as come to visit. A list of the Institutions which we consider should be included in this class is attached at Annexure 'C'. Some of the institutions included in the list of the Chairman of the Regional Committee in our opinion, cannot be treated as State wide organisations because they are meant to benefit primarily the residents of Telangana, such as the schools for deaf and dumb and for the blind as similar institutions already exist in the Andhra region. In this list we have also included institutions which are not entirely maintained by the Government but to which the Government gives grants-in-aid. It was found that quite a large number of these institutions were treated as common by Shri Kumar Lalit who divided the expenditure on them in the proportion of 2 : 1 between Andhra and Telangana. We have now corrected these figures so as to take into account all the institutions mentioned in Annexure 'C'.

(16) **Expenditure on Development of State Capital** : Shri Kumar Lalit, in accordance with the advice of the State Government, debited to Andhra region the entire expenditure incurred on construction of Government building at Hyderabad up to the year 1961 whereafter the expenditure has been debited to the two regions in the proportion of 2 : 1. The representative of the Andhra region urged that the allocation of the entire expenditure up to 1961 to Andhra region was not fair. The reason why the Government approved of this manner of allocation is obvious. When Hyderabad became the capital of the unified State, a number of buildings in Hyderabad, which were contributed by the Telangana region, were made available for use by the Government and that contribution by Telangana must be taken into account when allocating expenditure on the city for providing accommodation to other offices of Government. Construction of new buildings in Hyderabad was necessitated by the merger of Andhra with Telangana. The Government envisaged that the expenditure incurred on construction of new buildings upto the year 1961 would represent a fair share of Andhra region, taking into account the buildings contributed by the Telangana region at the very inception of the joint State. We are unable to hold that this arrangement approved by the Government is at all unfair to any of the two regions. Subsequently, of course, all the expenditure on the capital and building constructions has been rightly allocated in the proportion of 2 : 1 between Andhra and Telangana.

(17) **Interest on loans and advances taken to meet the ways and means difficulties of the State Government** : During the period with which we are concerned, the State Government had to obtain loans and advances from the Reserve Bank of India or the Central Government to meet its overall deficit. In almost all the years, the Andhra region has had a revenue deficit, while the Telangana the interest on these loans and advances should be debited to the Andhra region and not allocated at all to Telangana region. It is for this reason that we are making a departure from the principle laid down in the document of 1959 in this behalf.

(18) **Milk powder factory, Vijayawada** : A factory for preparing milk powder was erected at Vijayawada. The officer who was in-charge of the construction had his Headquarters at Hyderabad, with the consequence that all the expenditure incurred on construction of the factory was debited in the accounts at Hyderabad even though the building was constructed at Vijayawada. It has, therefore, become necessary to transfer from the expense account of Telangana the cost of the factory constructed at Vijayawada into the account of expenditure for Andhra region.

(19) **Purchase of machinery by Agriculture Department** : Machinery of the value of Rs. 146.65 lakhs were purchased by the Director of Agriculture during the years 1965-66, 1966-67 and 1967-68 for development of Ayacut in connection with the new canals flowing out of the Nagarjunasagar Dam. The information elicited

by us from the Chief Engineer of the Nagarjunasagar Canals and the Director of Agriculture, through the State Government, shows that this machinery was needed for development of Ayacut of the left canal only. The further information is that the Ayacut of the left canal will be 5.2 lakh acres in Telangana region and 3.6 lakh acres in Andhra region. There is no specification possible whether the machinery is needed for the entire Ayacut in each region; but the communications received indicate that the machinery is meant for development of the land which is to be irrigated by the left canal. Consequently, it will be fair to allocate the expenditure on that machinery in the proportion of 36 : 52 between Andhra and Telangana.

(20) **Expenditure on Police :** The figures compiled by Shri Kumar Lalit showed that, under this head the expenditure in Telangana was much higher than it would be if the proportion was 1 : 2 between the two regions. On the basis of this fact, it was urged by the representatives of Telangana region that the allocation of the expenditure on police by Shri Kumar Lalit has not been correct. We have checked up the figures and we have found that, except under the head of 'purchase of clothing and equipment for police' all other allocation has been made on correct principles. There is special armed police consisting of 6 Battalions; 4 of them are in Andhra region and 2 in Telangana region. Then there is other Reserve police under Reserve Inspectors attached to each District. The expenditure on all this police has been allocated to the region where that police is posted. In Hyderabad, there is a separate Commandant of special Reserve Police whose jurisdiction is confined to Telangana Districts and whose establishment charges have been debited to Telangana. It also appears that the expenditure on police in Telangana region has been higher because of larger requirements of police in the twin cities of Hyderabad and Secunderabad for local administration. This largely explains why the expenditure in Telangana region on police is not one-half of that in Andhra region. In respect of purchase of clothing and equipment, it appears that, since the price was paid at Headquarters, the entire expenditure has been debited to Telangana, even though the clothing and equipment were needed for policemen who were posted in the Andhra region also. From statistics gathered by us it appears that the strength of the police in the two regions of Andhra and Telangana is in the proportion of 22 : 19. We have, therefore, allocated the expenditure on purchase of clothing and equipment in this proportion.

Another point arising out of maintenance of police force by the State that was raised before us on behalf of the Andhra region was that some police forces were lent to other States and the receipts from those States relating to those police forces have all been credited to Telangana as they were deposited at Headquarters, while some of the members of the police force so deputed outside came from the Andhra region. On checking up the manner of crediting the receipts from other States, we have found that in almost all cases receipts in respect of police sent out of the State have been credited to the same region to which the expenditure on that police has been debited and wherever this was not done, we have made alterations to give effect to this principle.

(21) **Compensation for Zamindari Abolition :** Shri Kumar Lalit in his calculations took into account compensation which was paid during the years in question to Zamindars in Andhra whose rights were acquired on abolition of Zamindari rights. The representative of the Andhra region urged before us that the abolition of the Zamindari rights took place prior to the merger of the two states in 1956 and, consequently, whatever payments have been made to the Zamindars should be treated as payments towards loans incurred prior to 1956, and should not, therefore, be treated as development expenditure at all. There can be no doubt that abolition of Zamindari rigths is beneficial to more successful carrying on of agricultural operations by the cultivators and that step taken is one leading to development. It may be true that the development actually took place in Andhra region before 1956 by abolishing the Zamindari rights at that time, but the expenditure towards that development is being incurred in the years to which our calculations relate. Those payments are, thus, directly towards development activity already carried out and cannot, therefore, be treated otherwise than as development expenditure incurred in the years in which the amounts have been paid to the Zamindars.

(22) **Items to be included in calculating amounts spent on development in the two regions :** For purposes of making the computations, Shri Kumar Lalit prepared for each year a statement showing capital expenditure of that year and its allocation between the two regions. We have already indicated earlier that the figures that are really required to give effect to the agreement of 1956 must relate to the development expenditure and not capital outlay. In the statements prepared by Shri Kumar Lalit there are included certain items which, though they may be treated as capital expenditure, are obviously not in the nature of development expenditure. The items which are of this character are indicated hereafter.

Payments made in respect of commuted value of pensions to retired Government servants cannot in any way bring about development of the region where the pensioners may be residing and receiving payments. Capital outlay on State Trading Schemes which we have dealt with already at item number (12) cannot be included as development expenditure for the reason we have already given at that stage. Repayments of debts, loans and advances are obviously not expenditure on a development activity and must be excluded even though the debts, loans or advances may be the sources from which the money is made available for such expenditure. If repayments are to be included, there would be double inclusion of same amounts—once when the money actually spent is accounted for and a second time when there is repayment to the source from which the money is drawn. Further, appropriations to the contingency fund have no bearing on development in any region.

At the same time there has been a very significant omission because Shri Kumar Lalit confined himself at this stage to computation of capital expenditure and did not realise that what needed to be computed was expenditure on development. Even part of the revenue expenditure can result in development and, on the face of it, all expenditure incurred under plan schemes approved by the Planning Commission must be held to be expenditure on development, because the Planning Commission does not sanction any expenditure in its Plan schemes except for the purpose of development. Revenue expenditure thus incurred on Plan schemes has to be included in the head of 'expenditure on development', even though it may not be capital outlay. Such revenue expenditure on Plan schemes was included by Shri Kumar Lalit at the stage of calculating the surplus of income over expenditure of Telangana region. These statements thus prepared by him require modifications so as to exclude from that stage of calculation of surplus the revenue expenditure on Plan schemes and that amount has to be transferred to the second stage of calculation of expenditure on development. This will apply to the Plan revenue expenditure in each of the two regions. A consequential alteration that necessarily follows is that all Plan grants which are intended for development, received from the Central Government, cannot be treated as revenue income of the State or the region. Such grants received can only be taken into account when considering the development expenditure and the sources from which money was drawn for that purpose. Consequently, in any calculation of the surplus, the Plan grants on the expenditure side have to be excluded and both these items are to be taken into account only when working out the development expenditure. In making the calculations, we have given effect to these principles on the basis of the figures available in the accounts of the State.

(23) **Revenue Deficit of Andhra Region**: The last point we need deal with relates to the claim put forward on behalf of the Telangana region that, in making the computations of the unspent surplus of Telangana, we should work out a share for Telangana in the revenue deficit of Andhra and add that share to the unspent surplus. The point raised, in our opinion, does not arise at all and is not relevant to the determination to be made by us which is clear from the principles we have indicated earlier for making the calculations. The surplus of income of Telangana over its expenditure is in no way dependent on whether Andhra had a surplus or a deficit in its income over expenditure. As regards amounts spent on development of the two regions, the principles adopted by us will show that the sources from which amounts were derived for development expenditure have no material bearing. The calculations are based on the actual amounts found available for development expenditure in each year for the two regions together and on the proportion in which those amounts were spent in the two regions. As we have already indicated earlier, the terms of the "Gentlemen's Agreement" of 1956, properly interpreted only required that the revenue surplus of Telangana should be spent on developments of Telangana in addition to the fair share out of the sums actually available for development of the State as a whole in each year. The fair share of Telangana in the amount available for expenditure on development has already been allowed for by us, so that no question can arise of taking into account the revenue deficit of Andhra in making the computations.

Unspent Surplus

We have had tables prepared on the basis of the principles settled by us above showing the revenue receipts of Telangana, the revenue expenditure of Telangana and the expenditure on development of the State with details showing separately the development expenditure in Andhra and Telangana regions. These Annexures give year-wise figures covering the entire period with which we are concerned. Annexures D-1 to D-12 contain the details of the receipts of Telangana under each Head of Account while Annexures E-1 to E-12 contain similar details of expenditure in that region. Annexure F-1 to F-12 give, year-wise, the amounts spent on development of the whole of the State under each head with separate figures for each region. From these figures we have worked out the year-wise surplus of income over expenditure of Telangana, the fair share of Telangana in the development expenditure, and the amount actually spent on development in Telangana. These figures are contained in Annexures G-1 to G-12 which also show the unspent surplus of Telangana in each year. The figures of the unspent surplus of Telangana are, for convenience, reproduced below :

(Rs. in lakhs)

Year	Amount
1956-57	633.01
1957-58	378.04
1958-59	516.71
1959-60	697.27
1960-61	142.13
1961-62	79.69
1962-63	466.93
1963-64	764.23
1964-65	191.13
1965-66	113.53
1966-67	(—)360.01
1967-68	(—)788.35

The unspent surplus so worked out totals to a figure of Rs. 2,834.31 lakhs.

A question has, however, been raised whether it would be correct for us to state that this amount of Rs. 2,834.31 lakhs is the sum which ought to have been spent on the development of the Telangana region in accordance with the "Gentlemen's Agreement" but remained unspent on the 31st March, 1968. It, no doubt, represents the total of the amounts found unspent in each of the twelve years in respect of which we had to make our determination but two aspects have been brought to our notice which require consideration. The first one is that, if the amounts of surplus found which remained unspent in any year had actually been spent in that very year or in the year succeeding, the amount of development which could have been brought about by such amount would have been much larger than would be possible on 31st March, 1968 or thereafter. The obvious reason is that there has been a continuous rise in the price level. The result of this rise in prices is that, for doing the same amount of development work which could have been done earlier, the amount that will have to be spent after 31st March, 1968 would be very much larger. On this basis, it was urged by the representatives of the Telangana region as well as the Head of the Economics Department of the Osmania University that it would be fair to revalue the amount of unspent surplus of each year in proportion to the rise in price index of that year and the price index prevailing on the 31st March, 1968. The second aspect that pressed before us was that, if these amounts had been spent in those very years when they were available for development, the prompt execution of the works of development would have given its own return and that return would have further accelerated the pace of development. It was argued that in any case, this aspect should justify a claim for interest at a reasonable rate being added to the unspent amounts of surplus in lieu of that anticipated return in the form of accelerated development.

There is considerable force in both these points. At the same time, we have in our view the purpose of the "Gentlemen's Agreement" of 1956 and the circumstance that, when that agreement was arrived at in the meeting of the leaders of the two regions, one of the decisions arrived at was that the provision relating to reservation of unspent surpluses for development of Telangana would be limited to a period of five years and would be extended for another five years in case the legislators from Telangana so desired. As we have indicated earlier, the object of this Agreement was to ensure that Telangana, which was a backward region, received special treatment in order that the standards of education, living etc., in that region may rise so as to enable the residents of Telangana to come up to the standards attained in the Andhra region. The minutes of the meeting drawn up at the time when the Agreement was arrived at appear to indicate that the Parties to that Agreement envisaged that the special treatment for a period of five years or ten years would serve the purpose sought to be achieved by this reservation of unspent surplus for development. The figures contained in the Annexures G-1 to G-12 show that in almost all the years during this period, the expenditure on development is Telangana has been in excess of its proportionate share and that, in fact, a large portion of the revenue surplus arising in Telangana has been utilised in accordance with the "Gentlemen's Agreement". The amounts that have remained unspent have not been very large. In the last two years 1966-67 and 1967-68 the development expenditure in Telangana was so much higher than its due proportion that a sum exceeding Rs. 11 crores out of the previously unspent surplus was utilised. In spite of all this, the object has not yet been achieved. This appears to be the reason why the provision for limiting the reservation to a period of five or ten years has not been given effect to. Already, the period with which we have dealt covers twelve years, and our terms of reference themselves envisage that this Agreement is to be acted upon in future also. This step that has been taken was obviously called for because the spirit of the Agreement of 1956 required the adoption of such a course. Now that this course is being adopted of continuing reservation of the unspent surplus for future we do not think that there is any necessity for us to alter the figure of unspent surpluses by accepting the two suggestions made on behalf of the Telanagana region which we have discussed above. We are, however, doubtful whether this provision of reservation of Telangana surplus, even in addition to its fair share in the development expenditure of the State can, by itself, fully achieve the purpose of the "Gentlemen's Agreement" which, as we have indicated earlier, is that Telangana region should be able to catch up with Andhra region. We, therefore, except that, apart from complying with the terms of the "Gentlemen's Agreement", the State Government will keep in view the object of that Agreement and take appropriate measures in future to ensure that Telangana is allocated adequate funds to speed up its development so as to enable it to make up the deficiency.

For future, to the extent that the terms of the "Gentlmen's Agreement" of 1956 are to be carried out, we can see no reason for laying down principles for calculation of unspent surplus different from those which we have applied in making our calculations for the past period. These principles are contained in the documents of 1959 and 1969 but are to be applied subject to the interpretation and variations which have been laid down by us in our decisions in Chapter III. We may, however, add that allocation of revenue expenditure and revenue income to two different regions within a single State is a complicated mattar because accounts are normally maintained for the State as a whole. It appears that, in view of the "Gentlemen's Agreement" of 1966, special measures were adopted by the Government of Andhra Pradesh to ensure that in the accounts region-wise figures should be available and the Accountant General also maintained separate figures in respect of a number of Heads of Account for the Districts of the two regions. Even then, difficulty arose because there was no such regionwise separation for all the items which required allocation, e.g., separate figures regionwise were not kept for Sales Tax receipts after taking into account tax paid by dealers having places of business in both regions. It was also difficult to discover which particular works carried out in each region were of developmental nature and which were not. It will, therefore, be necessary that in furure, the State Government, its Departments and the Accountant General make suitable alterations in the method of keeping accounts so that the figures needed in order to give effect to these principles are readily available. This can be ensured if the principles laid down by us are carefully studied and suitable instructions issued. Further, if the real object of the Agreement is to be achieved, it will be desirable to compile data which would show the regionwise per capita income etc., so that appopriate indices are readily available which would enable proper assessment of the stage of development of the two regions and the progress made in the more backward region. It will then be easier for the Government to adopt adequate measures for giving effect to the spirit of the "Gentlemen's Agreement".

Annexure B

Gentlemen's Agreement

A. **Regional Standing Committee.** (1) There will be one legislature for the whole of the Andhra Pradesh State which will be the sole law-making body for the entire State and there will be one Governor for the State aided and advised by a Council of Ministration.

(2) For the more convenient transaction of the business of Government with regard to some specified matters, the Telangana area will be treated as a region.

(3) For the Telangana region there will be a Regional Standing Committee of the State Assembly consisting of the members of the State Assembly belonging to that Region including the Ministers from that region but not including the Chief Minister.

(4) Legislation relating to specified matters will be referred to the Regional Committee. In respect of specified matters proposals may also be made by the Regional Committee to the State Government for legislation or with regard to questions of general policy not involving any financial commitment other than expenditure of a routine and incidental character.

(5) The advice tendered by the Regional Committee will normally be accepted by the Government and the State Legislature. In case of difference of opinion reference will be made to the Governor whose decision will be final and binding.

(6) The Regional Committee will deal with the following matters :

(i) Development and economic planning within the framework of the general development plans and policies formulated by the State Legislature ;

(ii) Local Self-Government, that is to say, the constitutional powers of Municipal Corporations, Improvement Trusts, District Boards, and other district authorities for the purpose of Local self-government or village administration ;

(iii) Public health and sanitation, local hospitals and dispensaries ;

(iv) Primary and Secondary Education :

(v) Regulation of admissions to the educational institutions in the Telangana region ;

(vi) Prohibition ;

(vii) Sale of agricultural lands ;

(viii) Cottage and small-scale industries ; and

(ix) Agriculture, Co-operative Societies, Markets and Fairs.

Unless revised by agreement earlier this arrangement will be reviewed after ten years.

B. **Domicile rules.** A temporary provision will be made to ensure that far a period of five years. Telangana is regarded as a unit as far as recruitment to subordinate services in the area is concerned ; posts borne on the cadre of these services may be reserved for being filled by persons who satisfy the domicile conditions as prescribed under the existing Hyderabad rules.

C. The position of Urdu. The Government of India would advise the State Government to take appropriate steps to ensure that the existing position of Urdu in the administrative and judicial structure of the State is maintained for a period of five years.

D. Retrenchment of surplus personnel in the new State. The Government of India do not anticipate any retrenchment. The intention is that so far as possible, the service personnel from the Hyderabad State should be automatically integrated into the services of the Andhra Pradesh without any process of screening. Should, however, any retrenchment be found necessary, the entire personnel of the services of the enlarged State will be treated on an equal footing.

E. Distribution of expenditure between Telangana and Andhra Regions. Allocation of expenditure within the resources of the State is a matter which falls within the purview of the State Government and the State Legislature. Since, however, it has been agreed to between the representatives of Andhra and Telangana that the expenditure of the new State on central and general administration should be borne proportionately by the two regions and the balance of income from Telengana should be reserved for expenditure on the development of Telangana area, it is open to the State Government to act in accordance with the terms of this agreement in making budgetary allocations. The Government of India propose to invite the attention of the Chief Minister of Andhra to this particular understanding and to express the hope that it would be implemented.

STUDY GROUP-I OF POWER ECONOMY COMMITTEE—POWER GENERATING STATIONS, 1969—REPORT

Delhi, Manager of Publications, 1973, 2 vols.

Convener : Shri M.W. Goklany.
Members : Shri B.V. Deshmukh ; Shri B.N. Ojha ; Shri B.N. Banerjee ; Shri K.A. Dave : Shri K.L. Vij ; Shri S.N. Vinze.

APPOINTMENT

The resolution setting up the Power Economy Committee states that the cost of electricity supply in the country has been rising despite large scale technological development and points to the need for detailed review of the measures for better utilisation of existing generating facilities as an urgent need for utilising the limited resources of the country efficiently. The study Group I has been set up by the Power Economy Committee for the purpose of carrying out this review. The Government of India set up a High Powered Committee consisting of experts in the field of electricity development vide Resolution No. E.L.I. 32 (84)/68 dated May, 27th 1969.

TERMS OF REFERENCE

"To review the pattern of utilisation of available plant capacity during the past 5 years and their operational efficiency and fuel consumption, to consider the scope of improving economy in power generation together with specific measures for attaining them."

CONTENTS

Scope ; Power Plant Availability and Utilisation ; Hydro-Electric Power Stations ; Steam Power Stations ; Common Problems; Conclusions and Recommendations; List of Tables; List of Figures; List of Annexures.

RECOMMENDATIONS

Power Plant Availability and Utilisation

There is an urgent need to improve power plant availability and utilisation. For this integrated operation of the power systems in every region as well as improvement in availability of thermal power plants are necessary.

Modern methods of scientific management, particularly operation analysis should be introduced immed ately and utilised increasingly for improving the quality of preventive maintenance and reducing the plant outage time for maintenance.

Separate technical cells for quality control in operation and maintenance, improving fuel efficiency etc., should be set up in each organisation directly under the Chief Engineer and in the case of Electricity Boards directly under Technical Members.

Continuous monitoring of the plant availability (including partial availability) should be introduced immediately.

There should be system of studying the plant availability causes of outages and statistical analysis of availability outages on a nationwide basis. This may be done through Central Board of Irrigation and Power. The system evolved by Edison Electric Institute of U.S.A. may be adopted for the purpose with certain modifications.

A system of voluntary reporting in respect of technical problems of equipment failures and operating difficulties should be instituted immediately. The systems already developed in India as well as in U.K. and U.S.A. should be studied and common modern system of reporting and analysis should be evolved, for All-India application. The data collection may be at the level of individual systems or regions, but the analysis of incidence and sharing of this valuable technical experience should be on an All-India basis. This should be organised through the Central Water and Power Commission.

If the above system of voluntary reporting of problems does not work satisfactorily, statutory regulations making compilation and supply of such information obligatory should be made.

Hydro-Electric Power Stations

Each Hydro-electric Project should be designed for flexibility of operation and the capability to assist optimisation of power system performance should be built into it.

All new projects should permit (i) substantial additions to installed capacity for enabling low load factor operation and (ii) addition of governing and excitation equipment for remote monitoring and control and better system performance.

Design capability for planning engineering and designing of hydro-electric projects needs to be built up in a big way.

Each hydro-electric power station must be operated to utilise fully the energy potential available at the site from year to year and season to season.

Periodical expert inspection and preventive maintenance must be arranged for all the different components of hydro-electric projects.

Every effort must be made to maintain the instrumentation, control, protection and alarm devices in the hydro-power stations fully operative at all times.

Communication facilities between different portions of hydro-electric project should be watched and improved wherever necessary from time to time.

In all power stations, special facilities as well as equipment and tools and tackles required for efficient and rapid maintenance operations should be kept available.

The maintenance and overhaul of hydro-electric plants should be carefully scheduled to ensure full plant availability and utilisation.

Projects older than about 20 years should be reviewed from time to time to see how the benefits from these could be improved by modernisation.

The performance of hydro-electric plant and the water conductor system etc. should be checked every 2-3 years by index methods. The necessary calibration for the index methods should be provided during the initial commissioning tests.

A service organisation for the safety of water storage structures should be set up immediately. Its scope should preferably cover water conveyance structures as well, in the case of hydro-electric works.

Steam Power Stations

Efficiency of energy generation : The causes of decrease in efficiency with increase in energy generation in some of the large power stations mentioned in Section 6, para 4.3 should be investigated.

Studies should be undertaken to see if the power station listed in section 6, para 4.5 could not be backed down and the energy requirements supplied from higher efficiency plants in the region.

Concerted efforts should be made to improve the efficiencies of the plants listed in section 6, para 4.3 or to reduce their energy generation in favour of generation at higher efficiency plants in the region.

Coal Prices: Pit head Coal Prices need to be rationalised on the basis of heat contents of the coals.

Long term coal contracts should be drawn up on the basis of standard form to be developed by the Regional Electricity Boards. These should cover the question of prices as well as the quality of the fuel.

Utilisation of By-products from Coal Washeries : The working of existing coal washeries should be modified to reduce the ash content to 28-32 per cent and also to ensure removal of stones and other abrasive material from the by-products supplied to the power station as fuel. A practical time schedule should be drawn up for this immediately. Studies and designs for the additional equipment and any changes required in the processes for the above purpose should be started immediately jointly by National Coal Development Corporation, Hindustan Steel Ltd., Central Fuel Research Institute etc.

The future coal washeries should be 3 stage ones

and the ash content of the middlings should be restricted to 28-32 per cent, and adequate arrangements for removal of abrasive material should be made.

The factors responsible for erosion damage to the boiler plant and equipment should be identified by careful and intensive research through the Central Fuel Research Institute and other appropriate bodies. Apart from identification of these factors, this should lead to improved supply of fuels and also include design and construction of boiler plant and appurtenant equipment for minimising the maintenance outage costs.

Design, construction and materials in the boiler plant and its auxiliaries require considerable further work for devising ways and means of operating satisfactorily with washery by-product fuel. The existing installations should be utilised for making field trials of different new innovations or designs of equipment for this purpose.

The equipment requiring particular attention is the coal mills, I.D. Fans, layout and arrangements of super-heater and economiser tubes, design and arrangement of burners and ash handling and disposal systems. It is recommended that indigenous boiler plant manufacturers and manufacturers of appurtenant equipment should be asked to tackle this problem in collaboration with the organisations owning and operating the existing power stations.

Transportation of coal to thermal stations—unit train : Considering the volume of coal traffic for individual large power stations, the time is now ripe for the introduction of new innovations such as unit trains in the matter of transport of coal by rail. A study in death should be undertaken for this purpose immediately by the Railways jointly with the coal and power station authorities.

Rationalisation of freight structure over short distances. The freight structure for transport of coal by rail over short distances under 50 k.m. should be reviewed and rationalised.

Petroleum fuels : The pricing of by-product petroleum fuels should be based on the costs of Indian crudes instead of on the basis of import parity.

Wherever there is possibility of obtaining supplies of petroleum, firm long term contracts should be made between the suppliers of petroleum fuels and the power station authorities.

In the years to come, the by-products of refineries will mostly be required as industrial raw-material. No large power stations should, therefore, be based on petroleum fuels alone. Unless the petroleum authorities assure supply of petroleum on long term contract basis, the siting of the power stations should be decided primarily on the basis of these being coal burning power stations.

Commitments made regarding supply of petroleum fuels to power stations should be honoured fully in future also. In case of 100 per cent petroleum fuel based power stations if petroleum fuels are not likely to be available in future, these power stations should be given a warning sufficiently in advance to enable their making alternative arrangements. The Power stations should be compensated for the additional costs involved on this account.

Oil is essential for supporting for all pulverized fuel fixed installations and its availability in adequate quantities at economic price must be ensured for such installations.

Problems of operation and maintenance : The thermal power plant equipment should be matched closely to the type of fuel, cooling water temperature and other site conditions.

The working of each power plant installation should be continuously watched for removing any stage at the incipient stage and improving the operation and maintenance. Full use should be made of the experience on similar power plants in other parts of the country.

A number of common problems in operation of steam power stations discussed in the report should particularly be avoided by proper action in planning, design and operation of the plant.

Relaxation of boiler act provisions : The provisions of Boiler Act should be modified to permit biennial inspection of boilers instead of annual. In fact it may be worthwhile to have a separate set of rules and regulations drawn up for large project installations of modern steam power stations with unit sizes of say over 30 MW.

Ash disposal : Representatives of the Electricity Supply Industry and Central Water and Power Commission should be invited to participate in formulation of regulations regarding pollution of air and water courses.

Intensive research and development work as well as promotional work should be undertaken for utilisation of the ash produced by-product in the steam power stations. Organisations like Central Building Research Institute, Central Road Research Institute, National Building Organisation, Cement Research Institute, as well as Indian Standards Institute and Central Water and Power Commission should be brought together for devising ways and means for utilisation of the fly-ash and bottom ash.

Utilisation of ash should be entrusted to a non-profit corporation to be established cooperatively by the different power station authorities in each region. This corporation, financed mainly from sale of ash, should organise the development and promotional work applied research work (in different appropriate institutes) and the work of marketing and disposal of ash from thermal power stations.

Common Problems

Staffing for power plants : The pattern of staffing of the large power stations and their appurtenant works such as stores etc. should be standardized on the basis of parameters of the generating sets, their number, type of fuel etc. The standardized patterns should be got approved from the Government as well as representatives of the management and labour. The scope of work and the responsibility of each person should be laid down clearly in the standardized staffing patterns.

The exact requirement of staff for any installation in the context of the standardized pattern mentioned above, should be specified by the designers of the installation.

The staff required for operation and maintenance should be sanctioned with the finalisation of the design and start of construction and in any case at least 18 months before the expected date of commissioning of the first unit. The sanctioned strength should be fully recruited at the earliest, for purposes of training on similar installations during the year preceding the commissioning of the power plant. The full sanctioned strength of the technical personnel should be in position for gaining an understanding of the plant by assisting during the Acceptance and Commissioning Tests and installation of the major plant sub-assemblies.

A Separate Generation Cadre should be instituted to ensure that adequately trained staff is available at generating stations. A system of incentives or special pay etc. should be introduced for the Generation Cadre to attract and keep suitable persons.

Training of personnel: There should be a requirement preferably statutory that the O&M staff must be qualified by proper training and experience preferably through some recognized training institutes before being given the full and independent charge of the costly and intricate modern power station equipment. A system of certification of the O&M staff similar to that in vogue in the Civil Aviation Industry could be adopted.

Refresher Training Courses should be arranged for all the technical staff in a phased manner so that each person has to go through a course at the interval of 5-7 years. Even the O&M staff at the technical level should be routed through other similar systems.

Existing facilties for training of personnel for operation and maintenance of steam power stations are grossly inadequate.

Training of personnel for operation and maintenance of power stations should be the responsibility of the Regional Electricity Boards. They should assess the requirements and organise adequate training facilities including in-plant training to suit the requirements peculiar to the respective regions.

For the purpose of certification of competency in operation and maintenance the Central Electricity Authority should formulate the minimum requirements on a nation-wide basis.

Instrumentation for Power Plants : Special attention should be given to the adequacy of control protection and instrumentation systems in every installation. Proper operation and maintenance of these systems is of the highest importance for minimising forced outages. Well equipped instrument laboratories should be provided for each large installation or group of installations. Special Instrumentation Cells should be manned by highly competent trained personnel who should ensure proper functioning of the instrumentation system throughout.

Documentation : Detailed completion drawings and reports should be available at each project, so that all changes adopted during construction are properly recorded.

Comprehensive manuals and instructions complete with drawing photographs, descriptions etc. must be available for each element of power plant installations. These must cover operation, maintenance and instructions for abnormal conditions. Sufficient number of copies must be available for all concerned and these must be reviewed and brought up-to-date every year.

Manufacturing and designing Capability of indigenous manufacturers : There is an urgent need to develop the design capability in the manufacturing units, so that the technology acquired for plant and equipment is fully utilised in a manner suiting the Indian conditions.

At the time of commissioning any hydro-electric project, detailed guidelines for water management, most appropriate for the project, should be laid down.

The high cost of plant and equipment from indigenous sources causes an undue burden on the power systems in the country. Equitable methods should be evolved for apportioning the heavy cost of acquiring new technology among the present and future projects. The cost of social benefits like new housing colonies, schools, hospitals and other facilities need not be a change on the cost of plant and equipment for new power stations but should be borne by respectives States in which the factories are situated.

Import of spares : The following should be done to streamline the procedure for import of spares for operation and maintenance of power systems and to eliminate the procedural delays and difficulties.

The clearance of applications from indigenous angle should be done by Central Water & Power Commissions itself. For this purpose, the Directorate General of Technical Development should equip the Central Water and Power Commission with all the information about indigenous availability of spare parts, anciliaries etc. The Electricity Boards/ Project authorities should adopt modern methods of inventory control for dealing with their replacement of spares. In any case the position regarding spares should be reviewed by them at least every quarter and anticipatory action taken, so that the time normally required for release of foreign exchange, issue of import licence etc. does not come in the way of proper operation of the power installations or execution of projects. A special cell should be created in the Central Water and Power Commission and the concerned officer should be provided proper facilities for conveyance etc.

Where a number of identical Power plants have been installed in the country, some additional emergency spares, such as a spare thrust bearing may be obtained and kept in common reserve. Such common pool of spares, financed cooperatively by the different power station authorities may go a long way in reducing the loss of energy generation due to forced outages.

The Chief Controller of Imports and Exports should give necessary facilities to the Liaison Officer of the Central Water and Power Commission for expediting the cases of issue of import licence for spares. This can be done by placing an officer of the Central Water & Power Commission in the Office of the Chief Controller of Imports and Exports for carrying out liaison work. After release of foreign exchange and indigenous clearance Regional Joint Chief Controller of Imports and Exports should be authorised to issue import licences.

Revalidation of import licences in cases on which Project authorities have entered into commitments, after clearance of the Directorate General of Technical Development, should be done as a matter of routine by the Chief Controller of Imports and Exports within a week. Any back reference by the Chief Controller of Imports and Exports should be addressed to the Central Water and Power Commission and not to the project authorities.

Paragraphs mentioned in the Recommendations Section 6, Para 4.3

It is seen that the energy generation at practically all the large high efficiency stations, viz.. Trombay, Neyveli, Chandrapura, Durgapur and Bandel has increased substantially in the year 1968-69. In this process, however, the efficiency of some of these power stations has been reduced. Such reduction in efficiency with increased energy production is not what would normally be expected and it would be worthwhile to investigate these happenings. In the case of Chandrapura, it is understood that the coal mill rejects had increased in 1968-69 owing to poorer quality of washery by-products being supplied.

Section 6, para 4.3.

In the following power stations which are relatively small and also rather old, scope for improvement in working may be limited but the gain by eliminating these in due course may be worthwhile from the viewpoint of economy and resources conservation :

(1) DESU Rajghat.
(2) Kandla.
(3) Porbandar.
(4) Nepa Nagar.
(5) Gouripur.
(6) Ramagundam (old plant).
(7) Sijna—Jharriah.
(8) Benares.
(9) Gorakhpur.
(10) Dishergarh.
(11) Old Cossipore.
(12) Mau.
(13) Mainpuri
(14) Indore
(15) Sikka.

STUDY GROUP-III OF POWER ECONOMY COMMITTEE, 1969—REPORT

Delhi, Controller of Publications, 1973. 46p.+iip.

Convener : Shri Ipe Mathai.
Members : Shri K.B. Rao ; Shri B.V. Deshmukh; Shri K.M. Chinnappa ; Shri B.N. Ojha; Shri M.N. Chakravarty ; Shri H.V. Narayana Rao ; Dr. K. Venugopal.
Secretary : Shri C.K. Chandran.

APPOINTMENT

The Resolution setting up the Power Economy Committee states that the cost of electricity supply in India has been rising "despite large scale technological development", and stresses that in order to efficiently utilise the limited resources of the country it is now necessary to implement measures for bringing down costs.

The Government of India set up a High Powered Committee consisting of experts in the field of electricity development vide Resolution No. E.L.I. 32 (84)/ 68 dated May, 27th 1969.

TERMS OF REFERENCE

(a) to review, under prevailing conditions the economics of electricity generation from different sources—hydro-thermal and nuclear.

(b) to review their future trends ; and

(c) to suggest factors, which must prevail in the choice of alternative schemes in each region of the country.

CONTENTS

Outline of Work of Study Group-III; Costs of Generation and Supply under Prevailing Conditions; Future Cost Trends; The Time Factor; Basic Energy Resources; Implications of Regional Development and Perspective Approach for Power Supply; Problems of Matching Indigenous Manufacture of Heavy Electrical Equipment to the Economic Dictates and the Power Supply Industry; Conclusions and Suggestions; Annexures I to XII.

RECOMMENDATIONS

Relative costs of energy generation—hydro, thermal and nuclear alternatives : In this respect, "certain conclusions leap to the eye" to borrow an expression from the Energy Survey Committee. Under existing conditions, and according to expected trends in the near future of the three main alternatives—hydro-thermal (coal fixed) and nuclear, conventional thermal schemes involve, by far, the highest costs of energy generation in this country, which during 1968-69 varied from 6-10 paise per unit even at relatively new and large power stations. In terms of capital outlays, they cost nothing less than Rs. 1800/kw installed today or about Rs. 2500 per kw of firm capacity on purely thermal systems—allowing for the usual margins to cover scheduled maintenance, spinning reserves, etc. Even the resort to unit sizes of the order, of 200 mw—may not help bring down costs of future thermal generation appreciably under conditions of indigenous manufacture and rising costs of coal.

The costs of generation at nuclear stations, existing and under construction on a comparable basis are estimated at about 5 paise to 6 paise per kwh. With the adoption of large units of the order of 500 to 600 mw, it has been estimated by A.E.C. that the cost of generation will reduce significantly. More detailed studies are required to establish a realistic picture of cost of nuclear power from stations with bigger units and adopting advanced reactor concepts. Nevertheless, it has to be noted that even the cost of energy generation from 200 mw CANDU type reactors at about 6 paise per unit would be competitive, with prevailing cost of thermal generation at most of our thermal stations which are remote from collieries, even after allowing for the necessary standby provisions. We are therefore, undoubtedly on the right path of low cost generation in depending on nuclear power stations as the cheaper of these two alternatives, at most sites which are remote from the collieries. But to accept this as a major policy decision, we must have better assurances of figures of capital and running costs on the basis of the actual operating performance of these stations for a few years.

Hydel schemes have established themselves as undoubtedly the cheapest source of electricity generation in India involving in the past decade comparable and in many cases even lower capital outlays per kilowatt of effective capacity. Their energy generation costs range from 1 to 3 P/kwh, 2P being the overall average (not representative in all regions). Besides these obvious and great economic benefits, the Working Group on Power (1968) recognised the fact that non-utilisation of hydel resources represented a colossal irrecoverable loss of valuable natural resources. Hydel developments over the next 2/3 decades are expected to be about the same levels of intrinsic economy as prevailing at present, and it has been indicated that our river systems are capable of providing 80-100 million kw of hydel capacity at favourable sites compared to the 7 million kw installed today.

It would be noted that maximum utilisation of capacity is possible at thermal installations which operate on the base of the load curves of the respective mixed hydro-thermal systems having adequate hydel capacities to operate complementarily to take the low-load-factor peaks. Examples are Neyveli (5800 kwh/kw installed) and Trombay (5640 kwh/kw installed). On the other hand, the average energy output of power stations of our purely thermal systems during 1968-69 was generally less than 4,000 kwh per kw installed as a system average—one or two new stations in a system may have exhibited better figures—pointing to the conclusion that even in areas proximate to our collieries, it would have been decided by more economic to rely on mixed hydro-thermal power systems with their potential for full utilisation of generating capacities and other great economies, rather than on purely thermal installation as at present. Providing these primarily thermal systems also with complementary hydro peaking stations to improve their utilisation is one of utmost priority for the 4th and 5th Plans.

Relative Priorities For Development Of Different Alternatives, Hydro-Thermal And Nuclear

In regard to the relative priorities for development of different alternatives hydro, thermal and nuclear power, in view of what is stated above, there is little to add to the conclusion of Dr. H.J. Bhabha in 1965 viz.,

"The obvious conclusion is that, wherever power is needed and it is feasible to generate it by water power, this should be done in preference to other methods.",
the recommendations in CW & PC's perspective plans (1962) viz.

"In view of the above capital cost comparisons, the far lower foreign exchange components required for hydro schemes, their much lower costs of generation, and the fact that there is no depletion of natural resources, it is obvious that, on purely economic considerations, hydro power should be resorted to whereever feasible and thermal (including nuclear) resources developed to a complementary extent to meet the expected deficits. This therefore has to from the basic principle for a perspective plan for future power development during the next two decades,"
the recommendations of the Energy Survey Committee (1965), viz.

"In the light of these estimates, it seems clear that India will be well advised to continue to exploit hydro resources wherever there are suitable sites available".
and the recommendations of the Working Group on Power for the Fourth Plan (1968) viz.

"As power generation has to be planned on the basis of the most economic schemes, both in capital investment and in recurring costs, it is inevitable that a greater part of the additional capacity (required in the Fourth Plan) would have to come from hydro schemes."

The above conclusions have been derived from an analysis of the direct costs to the power supply industry. The actual costs of generation during 1968-69 represents the true costs of power generation to the industry, as accounted. We may benefit from a more comprehensive analysis including present worth analysis etc. Typical studies of this sort on selected power projects in this country are being carried out by Dr. Venugopal, Member of the Power Economy Committee in consultation with the Member-Secretary. The results of these studies may be awaited to consider whether the above conclusions need to be modified on any account. However, as the time factor of actual construction remains practically the same in all these alternatives, and the capital costs of hydro schemes are either comparable to or lower than the other alternatives, it does not appear, prima facie, that the conclusions above would be altered. On the other hand, a fuller economic analysis of the total investments required for different alternatives not only in the power supply industry, but also in the associated mining and fuel processing industries and those associated with transport and disposal of fossil and fissile fuels would tend to increase the margin of differences between the hydro costs and its alternatives in its favour.

An economic factor, which requires further analysis is regarding the relative foreign exchange components of these alternatives under existing conditions. At the stage when all heavy plant and equipment was being imported, the preference lay with hydro-electric schemes as their capital investment had the highest indigenous content. With recent trends of indigenous manufacture, the position has become somewhat different and complex. During earlier stages of manufacture the information given by our manufacturers to Parliament's "Committee on Public Undertakings" indicated that manufacture of hydro units had already developed to a stage where it involved relatively lower import content than manufacture of steam sets. We have separately recommended that the PEC may obtain information in this regard. The exact position may be reviewed when this information is received.

Both CWPC's perspective plan for most economic development of power supply and the Energy Survey

Committee's Report (1965) had recommended—with indications of exact sites to be developed—that 52 per cent of the total capacity during 1969-74, should be of hydel installations. Actually, they account, instead, for just 40 per cent of the total now. Failure to develop the country's hydel resources at a faster pace during the past decade and the resort instead to large-scale thermal generation, especially in areas within economic reach of hydel potential and remote from our collieries, thus saddling our power systems with energy generation costs 5-6 P higher than necessary, emerges as the most important contributing factor to current high prices for power supply. If the admittedly more economic path of lowest cost developments suggested earlier had been followed, at prevailing tariffs, the power supply industry would be generating additional Revenue surpluses of the order of Rs. 180 crores during the 4th plan. This figure of cost benefit would increase during the 5th Plan it steps are not immediately taken to put the country's power development plans back on the path of lowest cost developments. The main reasons for our inability to ensure choice of schemes for expansion of power generation and supply following the path of lowest cost developments in the pare are (i) delay in adopting the regional approach to power development—which alone would have provided the necessary wide canvas for choice of the most economic alternatives, (ii) a consistent lack, in the final stages of planning, of a perspective approach designed to secure lowest cost developments, (iii) expectations of large surpluses (subsequently behind) of by-product fuels from coal washeries, (iv) and a general prevailing impression about large and decisive differences in the "construction time" factor in favour of conventional thermal generation. Other reasons, less important, are the large-scale dependence during the past decade on foreign aid and hence on alternatives which inevitably involved choices with higher import contents, and the orientation of our public sector heavy electrical equipment factories towards manufacturing steam generation units. Now that the reasons for higher power supply costs are apparent, and it is desired that they should be reduced, remedial measures must be taken and rational considerations allowed to prevail in the future in the choice of schemes for expansion of power generation and supply.

Costs of energy generation and supply in this country have now to be drastically controlled and reduced ; fuel utilisation of generating facilities already built up has to be ensured; and we have also to ensure that limited capital allocations to the power supply industry go the farthest distance in meeting our estimated deficits. To achieve these objectives; it is inescapable that, during the Fifth and Sixth Plans, the bulk (about two-thirds) of new generating capacity to be added must be derived from hydro sources, both of the energy intensive and peaking categories, as laid down most recently by the Inter-ministerial Working Group on Power for the Fourth Plan (1968) which took into account the requirements of the Fifth Plan, For, this above can arrest the steady increases in costs of power supply. The balance of new generating capacity should be derived from super-steam power stations, employing the largest possible unit sizes, and located at the coal washeries/coal mines, since this alternative is bound to be cheaper in the immediate future, and in the long run than locating the thermal stations far away from the collieries. Nuclear power generation would have to be resorted to preferentially at all points which are remote from collieries and involve long haulage of coal in steadily increasing measure. The above provides the broad guidelines for future power policy to ensure utmost economy in power generation and supply for the foreseeable future accordingly the current costs and trends in the fields of hydro, thermal and nuclear generation. It has to be noted, however, that a predominantly hydro based power plan involves considerably greater effort at the stages of investigation and planning, and the institutional apparatus for this has to be arranged.

Industrial changes necessary to ensure that economic plans are drawn up, implemented and that the power stations are operated for optimum economy.

The Study Group noted that in the past high cost power stations have to be developed at several places and on an extensive scale, in preference to cheaper alternatives. The impact of these departures from the economic plans drawn up by the perspective plan and Energy Survey Committee during the Fourth Plan has been estimated as high as Rs. 180 crores of additional costs of power supply. This has largely been the result of the lack of adherence to the perspective plan for power development and advance action thereon at the appropriate time. It was the unanimous conclusion of all members that it is imperative now that a perspective plan aimed at securing the lowest cost paths of development should immediately be drawn up at the Central level and its adherence ensured. All necessary efforts should be made for progressing investigations on a country-wide basis and an preparation of proper reports. The Study Group considered that the main weaknesses lie in the institutional arrangements and that binding up adequate machinery to improve the present state of affairs is the paramount need. The objectives and the work involved has first to be spelt out.

The work involved in ensuring economy in power

supply could be considered broadly in three categories; (a) investigations and planning, covering the entire process from the station or project concept, its preliminary and detailed investigations in the field, project designs, fitting the scheme into perspective plans, and extending right upto the stage of initiation of construction; (b) actual construction; and (c) coordination of operation of the station into state/regional power systems. It is a highly complex technical function, which also involves extensive coordination of the activities of a number of organisations at state/regional and Central levels. The Study Group felt that, as at present situated, it would have to be tackled from two points of view, one, the long term (when the desired institutional re-modelling is completed); and the other, to meet the immediate short-term requirement of suitably orienting the Fifth Plan programme, which would have to be done within the existing frame-work.

The long-term economic perspective plan, it was felt, would have to be drawn up independently for the power sector and co-related and fitted into the overall economic plans. As future power development cannot be organised rationally and economically on a state basis, the study group felt that the perspective plan should be prepared on a Regional basis. The Fourth Plan recognises this as a basic feature of future planning which has been accepted by the National Development Council.

The Study Group felt that perspective plans could easily be made on the basis of regional demands for power, projected from historical trends. These demands for power could be adjusted for any departures that would be seen to be necessary, on a comparison with overall perspective projections, which, it is understood, are made from time to time by the Planning Commission. The long-term plan would have to be reviewed at regular intervals, which may correspond with the periods for which the perspective plans of the Planning Commission are prepared, and in any case should be reviewed every year, on the basis of up-to-date information available. The Study Group felt that the long term perspective plan must provide sufficient flexibility for changes which may be required to meet short-term requirements of the overall economy but must always be such as to ensure power supply ahead of demand. Once finalised, there should be a firm commitment to implementation of this perspective plan at the desired rate, at the Central/State levels. No uneconomic shemes should be considered as individual additions thereafter.

Planning at central level : The Study Group reviewed the present position of responsibility for planning for power at the Central level, and found that it is at present divided between the Planning Commission, the CW & PC (Power Wing), the Technical Advisory Committee (now the Ad hoc Committee). The Ministries of Irrigation and Power and Finance : The Study Group considered that this division of responsibility was not conducive to a unified and purposeful approach which is so essential now for economic planning in the power supply industry. It felt that the entire work preparing long-term perspective plans should be entrusted to a single centralised agency which is competent to carry it out, and ensure that the above objectives are achieved. The work involved being primarily of a technical nature, the main question to be decided is whether this central responsibility should be discharged by the CW and PC (Power Wing) or the Central Electricity Authority.

The CW & PC has been set up primarily as a high level Consultant body to function at the request of State and other organisations. It has no statutory authority for carrying out investigations and this seems to be the biggest bottleneck in implementation of economic plans. Notwithstanding major contributions e.g, national hydro-electric surveys (1953-60), preparation of the first perspective plan for power development (1962) and other important contributions to planning and designs of power projects, it would be noted that the CW & PC was not entrusted by the Central Government with the work of investigations of 62 hydel sites. Its coordinating role in this regard has not been effective, judged by results. The position is best summarised by Dr. Bhagvantam, Chairman of the CW & PC Reorganisation Committee in March 1969, in his letter of transmittal of the Committee's report :

"By and large, the CW & PC had during the course of its existence over the last two decades discharged its functions satisfactorily, commensurate with the status given to the organisation, and the responsibility devolving on those at the top level. Nevertheless the Committee feels that it could have done much better had it been given adequate powers to deal with the problems at a national level."

The Central Electricity Authority, on the other hand, even now enjoys statutory status and has the responsibility inter alia to develop a sound, adequate and uniform national power policy, and to coordinate the activities of the various planning agencies in the country, to carry out such investigations as are necessary and to collect and record all data concerning generation, distribution and utilisation of power and the development of power resources. These powers, it may be noted were vested in the CEA on the basis of the recommendations of the Select Committee appointed by the Constituent Assembly to consider the Electricity Supply Bill—which ultimately became the Electricity (Supply) Act, 1948—which deliberately widened the scope and functions of the Authority. They had felt even then that non-statutory institutions would not serve the purpose even of discharging the duties of the Electricity (Supply) Act of 1948. The Indian Atomic Energy Act, 1962, while empowering the Central Government "to develop a sound and adequate national policy in regard to atomic power", also lays down that the Central Government should "coordinate such policy with the CEA". This Act further directs (a) that the Central Government should "fix rates for and regulate the supply of electricity from atomic power stations with the concurrence of the CEA", and (b) that "differences of opinion between the Central Government and any State Electricity Board in regard to construction of necessary transmission lines (for inter-State supply of power from nuclear power stations), the matter shall be referred to the Central Electricity Authority whose decision shall be binding on the parties concerned". It is clear from the above that the required status to ensure that the work of planning for power development is carried out unimpeded, already vests in the CEA, in principle.

It was noted that the Bhagvantam Committee has recommended, though not unanimously, that the Central Electricity Authority should concern itself in future only with arbitration work and that its functions other than arbitration shall be added on to the Power Wing of the CW & PC, "after undertaking such legislation as may be necessary".

No particular reason has been advanced by the Bhagvantam Committee beyond the statement : "This Committee also feels that the CEA should concern itself with arbitration work only and nothing else". In his dissenting note Shri H.R. Bhatia, recalls the views of the Government of India on the Gokhale Committee's recommendations regarding the CEA :

"The Central Electricity Authority is charged inter-alia with the development of a sound, adequate and uniform national power policy and particularly with the coordination of the activities of the planning agencies in relation to the control and utilisation of national power resources. In view of the heavy programme of power development in the country, any change in the constitution of the Central Electricity Authority, and reduction of its functions to a mere Arbitration Board would be a retrograde step."

This was the view then indicated by the Ministry of I & P to the Estimates Committee of Parliament in 1963. Shri Bhatia has argued that the present situation calls for greater concentration of effort and strengthening of CEA rather than weakening it. It is noted that the present position is that a final decision on the question has yet to be taken by the Government of India.

In this connection, the Study Group feels that, when a statutory authority like the Central Electricity Authority is already in existence, is fully invested with powers to undertake all the work required on rational considerations, and it is admitted on all hands that it is lack of this statutory status which has been inhibiting the work of the CW&PC. It is obviously not necessary to look for any other agency to carry out this task. As Shri Bhatia has stated, there is no point in introducing or attempting fresh legislation merely for taking away functions from the Central Electricity Authority and entrusting it to another Commission. The Study Group, therefore, came to the conclusion that the overall responsibility for planning for power, including investigations, and processing of schemes right upto the point of initiation of construction, should be centralised clearly, as required by existing legislation with the Central Electricity Authority. This will, in effect, mean activisation of the Central Electricity Authority which has never been set up as a full-time body, and is, therefore, not adequately equipped now to discharge this responsibility. The CW&PC has been carrying out these responsibilities on a de facto basis. In fact, there appears to be no reason why the CW&PC (Power Wing) or the units thereof which are engaged on this work, should not be reconstituted as the Central Electricity Authority, and the Authority further strengthened on a technical and administrative plane to discharge these and other centralised functions indicated in the Bhagwantam Committee report, effectively.

The Study Group realised that the implementation of schemes included by the Central Electricity Authority in the perspective plans would always depend on the availability of funds, and that the Planning Commission are essentially concerned with this aspect. It would be necessary for the CEA to ascertain the position of availability of funds from the Planning Commission and to adjust their programmes accordingly. The study Group felt that the Planning Commission may be requested to advise the CEA of the extent of funds available in a particular 5-year plan or a particular year for the development of power and the CEA may then communicate sanction to schemes within the limits of available funds. It would improve matters further, if a representative of the Planning Commission functions on a part time basis on the Authority. The ministries of Irrigation and Power, Finance and Law are already represented on the C.E.A., in that capacity. On the basis of these sanctions of the CEA, the regional authorities, the State Government and Electricity Boards may then proceed to issue final sanctions and execute projects.

The Study Group considered in some detail the mechanics of preparation of the perspective plan and of ensuring, on short-term and long-term basis, that investigations of power projects are actually carried out on an adequate basis. The time has clearly come when the original jurisdiction of the CEA for carrying out investigations and overall planning in the best regional and national interests, should be invoked to remedy the prevailing ills. For long-term regional planning, the Study Group felt that advantage should be taken of existing institutions at Regional/State levels for they would be in the best position to evaluate new schemes for expansion of power generation and supply in the best interests of the region as a whole. They should be encouraged to take the help of CW&PC/other consultants in preparing feasibility reports should be forwarded to the Central Electricity Authority who would fit them into their overall perspective plan. After the inclusion of schemes in the perspective plan detailed designs for projects selected on regional basis may be arranged. In this, again, either the help of CW&PC's design organisation, or of consultants already working in this field may be utilised when needed.

The Study Group felt that the immediate problem concerns the selection of schemes for meeting demands during the Fifth Plan period as it may be some time before the CEA is fully constituted and activised. For this purpose, it was agreed that the Planning Commission would immediately address all Electricity Boards and State Governments asking them to forward to the Central authorities concerned a list of all proposals for expansion of power generation and supply on the most economic lines, along with feasibility reports prepared on the basis of investigations carried out. The Planning Commission would make it clear to the State Governments that the object to locate all economically beneficial schemes and that these schemes will be considered irrespective of the availability of demands for power in the respective States or of financial resources within the State Plans. It would also have to indicate that in future following decisions taken at the National Development Council, priorities for schemes of power generation and supply would be based on choosing the most economically beneficial ones in each Region, The schemes proposed by the State Governments will be scrutinised in these lines by the CW&PC (Power Wing) and thereafter the State Governments/Electricity Boards would be requested to prepare and forward detailed project reports in respect of those schemes which are approved in principle. The Study Group felt that if this position is made clear to various States, on the basis of investigations carried out so far, sufficient project proposals/feasibility reports/detailed project reports would be forthcoming to choose the most economical schemes for the Fifth Plan. It will also act as a great incentive to the States well endowed with natural resources to investigate them quickly and prepare schemes for their development to meet regional requirements. The further programme of investigations can be reviewed by the CW&PC/CEA after the response to this approach is known.

Construction of projects : The question of the agency for construction of schemes chosen essentially on regional basis was considered by the Study Group. They felt that at times and in certain cases such as nuclear power stations it may be more appropriate for the Centre to directly undertake the construction and maintenance of some of these stations. In other cases, the alternative of the States themselves implementing these projects on a joint venture, perhaps with central assistance cannot be ruled out, as in this manner, it would be possible to utilise local enthusiasm to the maximum possible extent. It is also entirely possible that certain States would have built up adequate technical capacity, though not endowed with all the financial resources to implement large schemes of regional importance, entirely by themselves. In such cases, with an adequate assurance that the States concerned would implement the scheme in time according to the requirements of the entire region, even this alternative of entrusting the implementation of regional projects to such well-equipped individual States should be considered. The Study Group was of the view that a pragmatic approach to the problem of construction of power schemes selected on a regional basis, which would keep all these alternatives open, would be preferable. They felt that the institution of Control Boards which has developed to meet the pattern of requirements of constructing large multi-State, multi-purpose projects and has been extended even to single-purpose power projects located in one State, can be usefully followed. In regard to the composition of the Boards, their accountability to the authorities, financing etc. the Study Group suggested that it should follow closely the pattern of financing of the projects.

Regional electricity boards : The regional organisations would be primarily concerned with ensuring maximum economy at the stage of operation of the power systems. In each region, they would have to be adequately organised and equipped to ensure that the State power systems are operated in an integrated manner, i.e., as if the entire power facilities were under a common ownership. The relationship of the Regional Electricity Boards to the Central Electricity Authority requires to be clarified either the Electricity (Supply) Act, 1948 which creates the Central Electricity Authority, nor the resolutions of the Government which create the Regional Electricity Boards, clarifies the assumption, made in some quarters, that the Regional

Electricity Boards function under the Central Electricity Authority. Actually, they are at present only voluntary associations of State Electricity Boards, who have given their consent to the national policy of integrated operation of power systems of contiguous States, for mutual advantage. According to the resolution, the Boards are supposed to function in an advisory capacity, but constituted as they are of powerful executive bodies, there is nothing to prevent decisions taken by them in concert, from being immediately implemented. Regional load despatch centres are to be set up under the Fourth Plan for ensuring the necessary coordination of State-Central power stations/systems for integrated operation. In this connection, the question of the authority for operation of the Regional centres becomes important. This is essentially an operational function and it is obvious that necessary authority for the purpose would have to be relegated to the regional organisation by the state organisations, who own most of the facilities in their respective areas. It is considered however that the regional organisations would have to be considerably strengthened on the technical side, and given statutory recognition—the difference from statutory authority—should be noted. The relationship between the CEA and the Regional Electricity Boards should also be clearly spelt out.

The Study Group felt that once the Central Electricity Authority is constituted as recommended by them, and the Regional Electricity Boards are also duly strengthened they will be in an advantageous position to assist the Central Electricity Authority in planning for expansion of power supply in each region according to the best economic interest and the interest of the region as a whole.

Special situations: With the suggestions made above, the Study Group felt that it would he possible to deal with problems of the Fifth Plan, and, on building up of the Regional Electricity Boards and the Central Electricity Authority, the problem on a long-term basis also can be effectively tackled. However they recognised that there would be certain areas of the country, such as the Indus Valley, Godavari Basin etc. where the magnitude of the schemes, geographical locations etc. are such that the above institutional arrangements may not be adequate. In such cases, separate River Valley authorities may be more conducive both for conducting of the investigations in their respective valleys and for executing the projects as individual schemes find a place in the overall perspective plan. These are, however, special cases which should be dealt on their merits.

Indigenous manufacturing capacity of heavy electrical equipment.

At present the requirements of different kinds of heavy electrical equipment—hydro, thermal, nuclear etc.—for maximum economy of the power supply industry, and actual capacity built-up in the equipment manufacturing industry, are unfortunately opposite to each other. The industry ostensibly has surplus capacity to meet requirements to thermal units, but is woefully short on capacity to supply hydro units, and consequently strongly prefers the former to be utilised in greater measure on our power system. For every 1000 MW of conventional thermal capacity which is substituted for hydel installations at prevailing investment and operating costs, the power supply industry would have to incur additional working expenses of order of Rs. 25 crores every year besides arranging for the additional initial investments required, which would vary with the actual costs of the hydel schemes so postponed. It can ill afford to pay this price for the failure of the heavy electrical equipment manufacturing industry to organise itself for manufacture of hydro units, on the originally targeted scale (1.8 million KW annually, plus converted capacity at Ranipur) and at conventional pace. The Study Group recommends that an appropriate resolution on the subject may be immediately forwarded by the PEC to the Government in view of its importance.

Central assistance: The inability of the various States to provide adequate financial resources for expansion of power supply on the scales required even to maintain historical rates of growth has often been set out as one of the reasons for the low allocations to power in the Fourth Plan. Central involvement would obviously have to be on a more generous scale than in the past to correct this situation, but it would have to be judiciously oriented towards those solutions which represent the most economic ones for the States, the regions and the country as whole. At present, there are no clear principles guiding the indirect central assistance which accompanies decisions to construct certain projects e.g. Neyveli, Damodar Valley Power stations and nuclear power stations, either wholly or partly in the Central sector. Undoubtedly, these decisions are regarded by the States as major forms of Central assistance, and often lead other states to clamour for them even when the solution are prima facie unattractive on a techno-economic basis. The immediate interest of Kerala in a nuclear station illustrates the point. The study Group might like to suggest that in a choice of schemes on a regional basis, and particularly for deciding on the scope of Central assistance to these projects, a set of financial principles which clearly put a premium on the most economic alternatives would have to be laid down and followed uniformlly to avoid uneconomic solutions and avoidable friction.

Collection and publication of data: The Study Group

noted that the collection and publication of data particularly of actual data regarding investment costs, operating performance of power stations and power systems of different categories is not being discharged. In fact the information collected by Member (Comml.), CW & PC was found to the only data regarding actual costs which is available to us on some acceptable and uniform basis. The great value of this data in introducing a sense of practical economies was accepted by members who felt that collection and publication of relevant cost and economic data regarding generation and operation of power systems would go a long way towards introducing the necessary cost consciousness in the power supply industry and the country as a whole. This is a statutory function of CEA, which it has not been able to discharge so far. It should be organised to do so without delay.

Economic Factors For Power Development In Each Region.

The main economic factors which must prevail in the choice of appropriate sources of power supply in each region in the country can now be considered. Future expansions of capacity must be planned not merely on a calculation of the deficit between maximum demands and the firm capacity of individual State systems as at present but after assessing the full energy potential of each Regional Grid and the firm capacity of the Regional Grid as a whole. The effect of diversities in demand in the Region must also be taken into account to arrive at the regional maximum demand, and the regional energy requirements. The most economical paths for meeting the deficits in these two categories during the 5th Plan, for which options are still open, have then to be laid down on a long-term basis. Owing to shortage of time, schemes/sites of development are not being suggested in this paper in complete detail. Such details can easily be worked out once the approach indicated below is generally approved by the Study Group.

Northern region: In the Northern Region, at the end of the 4th Plan the aggregate installed capacity would be 6000 MW, of which 3000 MW will be hydro, 2600 MW thermal, and 400 MW nuclear. To reduce the cost of power in this region, the bulk of its power supply can and must be derived from the hydro electric resources, with initiation of large-scale nuclear generation to meet demands of the early eighties. That the main sources of hydro power in H.P. and J&K are not unfabourably located and are ample enough to meet the combined requirements of all these States and Punjab, Haryana, Delhi, Northern Rajasthan and perhaps the western most part of U.P. for the foreseeable future is beyond doubt. Unfortunately U.P. does not have major economic hydel located within its boundaries and this is the main reason why during the past decade they have resorted in increasing measures to high cost thermal alternatives. Consideration of development of the colossal hydro resources of the Sarda and Karnali rivers on the basis of international cooperation is therefore, an urgent economic necessity and would provide very large blocks of power, at the lowest possible costs, and with an area of reticulation spreading up to Delhi, Rajasthan and stretching well into the Eastern Region of the country. The economic imperatives of hydel development in this region are so great that the setting up special "Indus Valley" and "Ghagra Valley" authorities, charged with full responsibilities for this work to be done on time-bound schedules, should be considered.

Eastern region: This is a region of large coal reserves, which has relied, almost exclusively, on thermal generation in the past. The aggregate capacity in the region by 1973-74 would be 4600 MW, of which only 900 MW is hydel, the balance being conventional steam units. The Region thus has ample "energy" potential for meeting even 5th Plan needs, and what it needs most urgently is low investment "peaking" hydro units which would enable fuller utilisation of these thermal installations, and bring them up to the levels of performance actually attained at Neyveli and Trombay. The 1000 MW Koel Karo project and pumped storage installations, e.g. 200 MW Konar scheme are examples which must be considered for urgent implementation by the end of the Fourth Plan or early in the Fifth Plan. Others can be planned and worked out as required. Thereafter, the relative economics of developing the Himalayan hydro resources just beyond the Northern border of the region and conventional thermal/nuclear alternatives would need to be studied in the context of reducing costs of supply in the region.

In the Southern part of the Region, Orissa, with its untapped hydel potential, can adequately provide all the low cost power it needs during the Fifth and Sixth Plan periods. There are attractive schemes like Upper Indravati 600 MW, Upper Lokab (180 MW), Tikkarpara etc. which the States has already investigated and can be taken up to meet the requirements of the States as well as the region.

Southern region: This region, with an aggregate capacity of 5000 MW by 1973-74 of which 3600 MW would be derived from hydro resources has a good mix of different sources. For meeting future demands, Kerala and Mysore have a number hydel sites which can adequately meet the requirements of the Fifth and Sixth Plans. Mysore State in particular, has a wealth of hydel resources, as yet untapped, which can not only meet its requirements during the Fifth and Sixth Plan periods but also leave adequate surpluses for meeting the requirements of Tamil Nadu in the most economic manner. The hydel resources of Andhra Pradesh are located to the far North of the Region on inter-State stretches of the Godavari and its tributaries and requires a comprehensive basin-wise approach for their implementation. It is unlikely that coal-based thermal generation at Singareni could provide an economic source of power supply to resource scarce Tamil Nadu, competitive either with local nuclear generation or imported hydro power from Kerala and Mysore. Development of the seasonal potentialities of the Cauveri river on the inter-State stretch between Sivasamudram and Mettur through installation of reversible pump-turbines, offers a spectacular possibility of large scale seasonal energy generation combined with firm peaking capacity located at the centre of gravity of the entire Southern Region, with major possibilities of all round economy. In the Southern Region, with the range of alternatives presented on a regional canvas, available resources can easily sustain a programme of predominant hydro generation to meet the total demand, through schemes involving the lowest investment and energy costs.

Western region : Gujarat and Maharashtra have little untapped water power potential and they are located far away from the collieries. The Narmada, river, which has a limited potential of about 2000 MW at 3 or 4 sites below Punassa, is the source of importance in the western portion of the State. Madhya Pradesh has a number of hydel sites on its northern and southern peripheries—viz. the southern tributaries of Ganga, and the Indravati river (Godavari valley), which it could usefully exploit to bring down prevailing high costs of generation. The basic problem in the Western Region would be to provide energy at the lowest cost levels at the western fringe of this area viz. the coastal stretch between Bombay, Ahmedabad and Surat. Located as it is, the nuclear alternatives are prima facie the only answer for low cost energy supply in this area. However, to operate the nuclear stations at base load, it would be desirable to provide complementary hydro peaking alternatives, and intensive surveys would have to be carried out to ensure that straight hydro peaking schemes and pumped storage developments are developed in time.

North-eastern region : This is a region, where there is a natural abundance of hydro power. Demands even by 1980 would not utilise more than a small fraction of the firm power resources based largely on run-of-the-river developments. It can, without doubt, sustain all its industries on water power alone at the lowest cost levels. This region has such abundant resources of cheap power that special efforts would in fact be called for to utilise these hydel resources by relying on them for various electricity-intensive alternatives such as production of fertilizer and enrichment of uranium, if considered necessary.

STUDY GROUP-IV OF POWER ECONOMY COMMITTEE—RURAL ELECTRIFICATION, 1969—REPORT

Delhi, Controller of Publications, 1974. 117p.+vp.

Convener : Shri B.N. Ojha.

Members : Shri L.B. Dudhane; Shri N. Tata Rao; Shri A.C. Bandyopadhyay; Shri P.A. Raman; Shri A.P. Seethapathy; Mr. Lyle M. Robinson; Shri K.B. Mathur; Shri B.M. Safiulla; Shri K.L. Vij; Shri S.N. Vinze.

APPOINTMENT

The Government of India set up a High Powered Committee consisting of experts in the field of electricity development vide Resolution No. EL.I. 32 (84)/68 dated May 27th, 1969. Study Group IV was formed to consider and examine the above task in detail.

TERMS OF REFERENCE

"To review and examine the technical and economical aspects of rural electrification, particularly with a view to enabling the State Electricity Boards and Electricity Authorities to undertake a massive programme of rural electrification and making electricity available at an economical rate."

CONTENTS

General Review; Perspective Planning for Rural Electrification in India and Magnitude of the Task; Under-ground Water Resources in India; Financing; Economy in Designs of Lines and Sub-Stations; Standardisation of Designs, Specifications of Materials and Equipments and Construction Practices; Tariff and Incentives for Rural Electrification; Summary of Conclusions and Recommendations; Annexures I to XII Appendix.

RECOMMENDATIONS

Electricity has now become a necessity rather than an amenity and must be recognised as an important factor in economic progress even in rural areas. The higher production of foodgrains required to meet the minimum demand of 1975-76 can be achieved economically only through extensive irrigation electrification of pump sets and by using modern electric equipment on the farmsteads.

There is considerable scope for effecting economy in the equipment, construction practices, designs etc. for rural electrification and also in the basic cost of power as discussed in the different Study Group Reports already.

The N.C.A.E.R. studies on Punjab and Kerala have conclusively established the socio-techno-economic benefits from rural electrification.

The N.C.A.E.R. study shows larger benefit/cost ratio for smaller villages. This indicates desirability of extension of rural electrification to cover smaller villages notwithstanding the lower percentage of return on the capital employed.

PEC Estimate Of Progress

Availability of underground water and absence of salinity should be checked before any scheme for electrification of tube-wells is sanctioned. A survey of ground water resources should be conducted in the potential scheme areas and data in this respect kept ready by the State Electricity Boards. This work could perhaps, be carried out by the Department of Agriculture or the Underground Water Organisation in the State. Assistance could also be obtained from the Geological Survey of India and Exploratory Tube-well Organisation of the Union Ministry of Agriculture.

Cooperative use of the tube-wells should be encouraged. This would help in pooling up of the resources for taking tube-well connection. Cooperative use of tube-wells and selling of tube-well water would increase the load factor and improve the economics of rural electrification.

Finances

Investment upto 1968-69 provided by ear-marked Central assistance was Rs. 254.00 crores. An estimate of financial resources for the 4th Plan is as follows :

(In crores of Rs.)

(i) Fourth Plan outlay by the State/Union Territories etc.	294.50
(ii) Rural Electrification Corporation	150.00
(iii) Financial Institutions comprising	75 00

(a) Land Development Banks.
(b) Agricultural Refinance Corporation.
(c) Commercial Banks.
(d) Agricultural Finance Corporation.
(e) Life Insurance Corporation.

	As on 31-3-69	During 1969-74	During 1980-81
No. of villages	71,410	53,590	1,40,000
Pump sets	10,88,696	15,00,000	28,11,000
Investment (Rs. crores). . . .		520	1,850

Rural Electrification in India can spread rapidly if it takes the shape of a people's movement. As pilot projects, the Government have set up five rural electric Cooperatives—one in each of the States of Andhra Pradesh, Gujarat, Maharashtra, Mysore and U.P. The Cooperatives will enthuse the spirit of ownership in the villages and would also facilitate cooperative use of pump sets, electric appliances such as threshing machines, drying facilities for fruit, cold storage facilities etc. This will not only help the poor farmer to use such costly appliances but would also result in the improvement of the load factor in the rural areas.

It is felt that, in order to accelerate the development of rural areas, the easiest and quickest way would be to integrate rural electrification programmes with the programme of agricultural and other rural industrial development schemes. It is recommended that Co-ordination Committees should be set up (1) at the level of the State Electricity Boards and (2) at the District level, as suggested in the meeting in Planning Commission in July, 1970.

The work of rural electrification through voluminous and involving considerable expenditure, is of repetitive nature. Therefore, there is a very large scope for achieving economy by standardized designs, manufacture and construction practices in the field of rural electrification.

A special Technical standards Committee should be formed for simplifying and standardising materials and Code of construction practices for rural electrification works. This Committee should have a permanent Secretariat and should work in coordination with the CWPC, ISI, REC, manufacturers and Research Organisations.

Single phase power distribution is inherently cheaper than 3-phase power distribution and deserves consideration. This system is very effective for villages with small loads, especially those with a population of upto 500 (which number about 3.67 lakhs).

Breakdowns in power supply are mostly (60—90%) on account of failures of distribution lines and substations. Standardized plans for operation and maintenance of these should be evolved.

Minimum consumption guarantee for agricultural consumers should be reduced to a reasonable figure.

There is considerable scope for increasing the load factor in the rural areas.

Suitable incentives are required to be provided to encourage the farmers to go in for the use of electric power.

Rural electrification could be viable and successful if the integrated development of the rural area be done on an intensive basis by Agriculture, Irrigation Industries Departments etc. of the State Government in conjunction with the Electricity Board.

STUDY GROUP-V OF POWER ECONOMY COMMITTEE— IMPLEMENTATION OF POWER PROJECTS, 1969—REPORT

Delhi, Controller of Publications, 1973. 91p.+iiip.

Convener : Shri B. V. Deshmukh.

Members : Shri M. W. Goklany; Shri K. M. Chinnappa; Shri M. N. Chakravarti; Shri B. N. Baliga; Shri K. C. Krishnamurthi; Shri K. L. Vij; Shri S. N. Vinze.

APPOINTMENT

The Resolution setting up the Power Economy Committee States that "in order to efficiently utilise the limited resources of the country to take up required schemes for generation, transmission and distribution of power, which are largely capital intensive in nature, it is necessary to implement measures for bringing down costs of power development. This would require a detailed review of measures taken by Government to ensure utmost expediency in the construction of power projects . . . ." The Study Group-V has been set up by the Power Economy Committee for carrying out this review.

The Government of India set up a High Powered Committee consisting of experts in the field of electricity development vide Resolution No. E. L. I. 32 (84)/68 dated May 27th, 1969.

TERMS OF REFERENCE

"To review the causes of delay in the execution of the power projects, to suggest measures for improving the manner of implementation of power projects and reducing construction periods".

CONTENTS

Scope; Survey of Present Position; Magnitude of the task; Committee on shortfall in Generation during the Third Five Year Plan; Principal Causes of Delays; Planning; Investigation; Project Preparation; Financing Procurement; Manufacture of Equipment; Transport Facilities; Shortages and Breakages in Equipment, Construction Equipment and Plant; Construction Contracts; Miscellaneous Bottlenecks; Project Organisation and Management; Marshalling of Resources; Future Pattern of Project Execution; Summary of Conclusions and Recommendations; Tables; Figures; Appendices 1 to 9; Annexures.

RECOMMENDATIONS

Present Position

There are serious shortfalls in achieving the targets for installation of generating capacity and transmission system in the country, year after year. If this trend continues there are grim prospects of wide-spread and serious shortages of electric power. Further, an account of inadequacy of advance planning and investigations, there is likelihood of serious power shortage in the 5th and 6th Plans also, leading to grave consequences in retardation of industrial and agricultural activity and economic progress. Concerted action on a wide front is essential for correcting this position and making up for the lost ground.

Causes of Delays

Causes of delays in the projects taken up for implementation have been identified and are listed in Section 5 of the report.

Planning

A fairly large programme of construction has to be in hand all the time in order to keep up with the normal load growth. This in consonance with experience in other countries also.

The perspective plant for the next 15 years should be available at any point of time and, every year, such plan should be up-dated and extended to cover the future 15 years. Advance action in respect of preliminary investigations and designs and estimates should proceed in a continuous manner. The proposals for the next 10 years should indicate details of the specific projects to be undertaken and their time-table of the major stages. The plans for the first 5-7 years should be very definite at anytime and should be already under implementation.

Planning for electric power should be organised on a nation-wide basis. The overall responsibility for planning, including investigations and processing of schemes right upto the point of execution should be centralised with the Central Electricity Authority. The existing legislation is adequate for this.

Each State Electricity Board should have a Planning Cell which will be capable of taking into account the long range needs for electric energy as well as utilisation of the resources in the best possible manner.

Similar long-range Planning Cells should also be created in the Regional Electricity Boards. These should be able to coordinate and correlate the plans prepared by the State Cells so as to make the best utilisation of the available resources in the Region.

At the Centre, the Planning Commission and the CWPC should keep in constant touch with the work and progress of these Planning Cells at the Regional and State levels and a long-term power plan should be evolved continuously.

There is an urgent need for strengthening the Civil Engineering Organisation in each Electricity Board in order to cope with the large programme of investigations, planning and construction required for hydro projects. An experienced Chief Engineer (Civil) should be appointed for each Board. Among other things, he should be in overall charge of a whole time planning and investigation circle.

The indigenous manufacturers should plan the manufacture of further larger sizes of generating units so that these are available in time when the power systems require these shortly.

Investigations

A massive and continuous programme of field investigations is needed immediately in each Region of the country, so that the needs of the Fifth and Sixth Plan periods for investigated projects can be fulfilled.

The CWPC should keep in close touch with these investigations so that these proceed on fruitful lines, technically, throughout.

The finances for project investigations should be provided in the initial stages as "on account grants" in the nature of promotional expenses. These expenses can be reimbursed to the common fund from the project estimate when a project is taken up for execution.

Detailed investigations should be entrusted to well organised Survey and Investigation Units (in each State) equipped for geological as well as other investigations. Services of the Research Stations such as CWPRS, CSMRS etc. should be utilised for arriving at adequate scientific data. Keeping the design engineers associated with the investigation work also proves valuable in ensuring proper orientation of the investigations and avoiding fruitless efforts.

Where inter-State development of a resource is indicated, the Regional Electricity Boards should take up the work Formation of a River Valley Authority to take responsibility for further detailed project investigations and subsequent execution of individual schemes in the River Valley (according to a time-table prescribed by the perspective plan) may also be considered.

After the feasibility of a hydro-electric project is established. construction of the minimum access road facilities should be taken up immediately from the 'investigation funds'. This will enable expeditious detailed investigations.

When a project is sanctioned, the construction of the access roads should be undertaken and completed at the earliest. This will expedite the execution and completion of the project.

Project Preparation

The model proforma circulated by the Planning Commission should be followed strictly for the preparation of project report. This will eliminate protracted correspondence and resultant delays in sanctioning of the projects.

Financing

In order that the Project Authorities can plan and execute the construction programme according to the plan schedule, the finances should be made available as per the phased requirements of the project.

Power Projects sometimes suffer due to diversion of funds to other purposes by the State Government. This could be discouraged by the Planning Commission by "earmarking" the funds for specific projects at the time of formulation of plan provisions.

In the past there has been a great deal of excess expenditure as well as slippages in achievements of targets in the case of both generation and transmission. This is on account of two reasons, viz.

(i) Under estimation of cost at the time of preparation and sanction of the project report; and

(ii) Rising costs of materials, labour and other services like transport etc. in the course of project execution.

The under-estimation of the cost is mostly due to lack of adequate investigations and inadequate or incompetent design and engineering. It is, therefore, very essential to have thorough and detailed investigations and sufficient preliminary designs as the basis for realistic estimates of the time and the cost of project execution.

The CWPC should be charged with the responsibility for the accuracy of the estimates of time and cost of project execution. The CWPC should organise and equip itself for such work without any delay.

Procurement

Tender specifications should be as detailed as possible and should include listing of all the information (such as technical data, requirements of firm deliveries, contractual and financial requirements, etc.) required of a tenderer.

M/s. HE and M/s. BHE should make their quotations thoroughly business like by furnishing detailed lists of all equipment and accessories they would supply and the supplementary equipment that the project is expected to procure from elsewhere to make the supply complete.

A good many items of plant, their ancillaries and other items have been standardized, the purchase specifications should be based on these as far as possible.

A model "general conditions of contract" applicable to public sector and, if possible, to private sector manufacturers, binding on all the parties, would reduce the time between the receipt of the tenders and placing of the orders, and should be prepared and adopted.

The manufacturing capacity presently available in the two manufacturing units, viz., M/s. HE & M/s. BHE is not sufficient to meet the requirements of the country fully. There is, therefore, no need at present for competitive biddings between them and their energies should not be so diverted.

The model technical specifications (prepared by CBI & P Working Group) for each type of hydro-electric turbo-generator set based on each of the technologies adopted by M/s. HE and M/s. BHE should be adopted for ordering of the hydro-electric generating units. Considerable saving of time and effort can thus be effected.

It is possible to secure overall economic advantage by grouping the orders placed on the two manufacturing units for different projects rationally, so as to obtain optimum benefits regarding development and designs. This matter is complex and requires a cautious and informed approach. The planning of the orders may, therefore, be done in consultation with CWPC.

Manufacture Of Equipment

The manufacturer should indicate his need of foreign exchange (source as well as the amount) at the time of tender. The concerned Ministries should ensure the release of adequate foreign exchange.

The manufacturer should indicate all factors and assumptions on which their promise of delivery period is based. It would be desirable as a contractual obligation for the manufacturers of major items to furnish the project authorities with their PERT network chart for items of their supply including exchange of drawings and data.

Manufacturers should attempt to reduce the erection work at site to a minimum by adopting shop assemblies in as large a measure as possible. For this purpose, special wagons/transporters may be devised, if necessary for transport to site.

The Ministry of Irrigation and Power should be responsible for assigning priorities and programmes for the manufacture of equipment for various projects in consultation with all concerned.

There is much scope for standardisation and rationalisation of manufacture of a number of sophisticated items like automatic voltage regulators, excitation equipment, governors for generating sets etc. The Manufacturing Units and CWPC should work jointly to achieve this.

In view of the monopoly of M/s. HE and M/s. BHE in respect of generating plant and equipment, it is imperative to devise a mechanism whereby it can be ensured that the Manufacturing Units will strive towards attaining better efficiencies and producing increasingly superior machines. A Standing Advisory

Committee comprised of representatives of the two manufacturers, CWPC and are two academicians should be set up to decide the targets and coordinate the action in this regard.

Transport Facilities

The Design Organisation of CWCP should survey and catalogue the special transporters available with the various organisations so that the different projects can draw upon these when required.

In view of the increasingly large sizes of generating units and other equipment, special transport equipment presently available will not meet all future needs. The CWPC in consultation with M/s. HE and M/s. BHE should take up the matter with the Railways for design and construction of special wagons, mobile cranes etc.

Shortages And Breakages In Equipment

Whenever any shortages or breakages are revealed, the project manager should have these inspected on his own and should proceed with ordering of the replacement. The process for making the insurance claim and necessary inspection etc., therefore can proceed separately simultaneously. The procedure of ordering the replacement should be initiated immediately after damage or shortage comes to notice, without waiting for acceptance of the claim by the Insurance Company.

Construction Equipment And Plant

The engineer incharge of the project should decide the extent of mechanisation at the design/planning stage after taking the various factors into consideration. The procurement of construction equipment and plant should be initiated well before the start of the execution of the project so that it is available in time.

Construction Contracts

For timely execution of the project, it is necessary to draw the overall project schedule as well as the schedules for the construction jobs proposed to be handled on contract before inviting tenders, or in any case, before awarding the contract. Such schedules should define the required date for any significant point of communication or transfer of responsibility between the contractor and other participants on the project.

The ability to control a construction project, most elements of which are given on contract, depends largely on the soundness of the contract documents. A loosely defined contract may create considerable dissensions between the contractors and the project management due to individual interpretations of the intent as well as contents of the contract.

During the course of execution of the contract, the Project Management should retain full authority under the terms of contract to request any measures that may be necessary for the proper and timely execution of the work. The projet personnel should constantly watch the project and evaluate the effect of slippage on the part of any contractor, on the rest of the project.

Most of the needs of generating plant are going to be met from the indigenous manufacturers M/s. HE and M/s. BHE, who are not sufficiently equipped to undertake erection work of their own equipment. The Electricity Boards should, therefore, build up suitable teams for undertaking the work of installation and commissioning of plant and equipment. Such teams will be of great value to the organisation in arranging overhaul and proper maintenance work also.

In the absence of free exchange of ideas between the contractors and project officers, there are considerable difficulties regarding measurement or assessment of work done, contractual obligations and responsibility of different parties etc. These difficulties are increasing with the increasing complexity and volume of project construction work. Some organisation like the Institution of Engineers (India) should bring together the contractor firms and project execution people to evolve a common understanding of the problems and to work out possible solutions.

The accounting proformae and procedures prescribed for the project works of complexity, particularly the electrical works, do not suit the work involving complex technology. The Ministry of I & P should appoint an Expert Committee to go into the methods, detailed rules and performae and suggest changes for simplifying and rationalising the work in the projects including methods of recording measurements.

The consultancy organisations should build up the expertise and capacity for undertaking inspection during manufacture and witnessing of tests on behalf of the projects.

The CWPC should make a comprehensive survey of the facilities available in the country for undertaking quality control "type" and other proving tests and catalogue these for the use of Project Authorities.

Miscellaneous Bottlenecks

The project authorities should be aware of the various possible serious bottlenecks such as land acquisition, rehabilitation, labour strikes, clearances of Local/State Authorities, etc. and timely action should be taken for tackling these matters at the appropriate level.

Project Organisation And Management

It is essential that every project should be organised

from the beginning under a suitable qualified and experienced project manager who is vested with adequate financial and administrative powers including placement of contracts.

Modern Management methods need to be adopted for efficient and timely execution of the projects. "Systems" approach to the question of project management and control should be adopted. Proper planning of the project work at all stages, marshalling of all the resources (material as well as human) in appropriate combinations at every stage, proper intermeshing of the vast number of different activities by different agencies and monitoring and control of the project by watching the progress of physical achievements as well as spending of funds in a rational manner are the main techniques by which an optimum efficiency and speed can be achieved.

PERT/CPM network techniques should be introduced from the earliest possible stages of the project and preferably even to cover the planning stages also. Establishment of a PERT Cell to cover all the projects of an organisation as well as individual PERT cells for each project or even its major elements are very desirable.

These network techniques have to be integrated in a comprehensive management information and control system. The objectives of this management information system should be primarily based on achieving on time and on cost completion of each phase of the power project.

Where the project organisations are not adequately equipped it is advisable to retain the services of an experienced consulting engineer organisation such as the Specialised Engineering Organisation of CW & PC or other consulting Engineers available in each specialised field.

The system of "performance budgeting" should be adopted as an important management tool for monitoring and control of a project.

Marshalling of Resources

Nation-wide survey and planning is necessary to ensure adequate resources for construction projects in respect of construction materials, equipment manufacture, construction machinery and design and engineering capability.

There should be a panel of experts who may be available in the State Electricity Boards, Universities and other Organisations in the country. Standing arrangements should be made so that the CW & PC or the projects can avail of the expertise of these persons whenever required, at short notice.

In view of the ever increasing scale of project-execution in the field of power, there is an urgent need of expansion of the design units in the Electricity Boards/Undertakings, the Specialised Engineering Organisation of CW & PC and Consulting Engineer Firms.

The CW & PC has the dual role of being Consulting Engineers to the power projects and Technical Advisers to the Central Government. There is an urgent necessity to undertake a deliberate programme for building up of the specialised Engineering Organisation of CW & PC in order to ensure that the design and engineering capability in specific areas of complexity is available.

There is an urgent need for developing technical manpower resources to remove scarcity of adequately trained and experienced personnel for manning technical jobs at all levels. This will also help reduce growing unemployment among persons passing through technical institutes.

Every effort should be made to accelerate the growth of the capabilities of M/s. HE and M/s. BHE and their feeder projects so that the future requirement of plant and equipment for power projects can mostly be met by these.

Where M/s. HE and BHE cannot cope up with the needs of the power supply industry for enabling it to meet the needs of growth of industry and agriculture, import of plant and equipment to the extent necessary for uninhibited growth of the power sector should be approved.

Close collaboration of the Design and Research Organisations in the country should be established for developing designs to get around problems of scarcities of certain materials arising from time to time.

Each State Electricity Board should form a pool of construction plant and machinery for all its construction projects. Each project should draw upon this pool in respect of equipment, spares as well as operation and maintenance personnel according to needs. The Regional Electricity Boards should assist by keeping consolidated inventories of the equipment and spares available at different places or with different Electricity Boards in the region facilitating better utilisation of the equipment and reduction of down time for want of spares. At the national level, the CWPC should take a census of the plant and machinery and its current condition periodically and make this information available to the Electricity Boards/Construction Projects.

Future Pattern of Project Execution

In view of the ever increasing tempo of project execution in the field of power, the Centre will have to play an increasingly active role. The Centre should take immediate steps to review and strengthen the Central Electricity Authority.

For a number of reasons discussed in the report, it would be desirable for the large or Inter-State projects to be taken up for execution by the Regional Boards or by the Centre.

Presently, the State Electricity Boards are engaged in multifarious activities and adequate attention cannot be given to the problems of long-term planning etc. The top management should, therefore, be strengthened and organised by having the State Electricity Boards headed by an experienced power engineer as the Chairman and by putting all technical work directly under the charge of two technical members heading two Wings of the Board.

Section 5 mentioned in the Recommendations.

Section 5

Causes of Delays

The principal causes of delays have been listed by the shortfall Committee in their report as follows :

"Thermal

1. Lack of adequate project data.
2. Inadequate investigation before finalising technical project report.
3. Major change in scope of work.
4. Delay in site selection and land acquisition.
5. Delay in issue of authorisation by Central and/ or State Authorities.
6. Delay in foreign exchange tie up.
7. Deficiency in organisation for planning and engineering the project.
8. Delay in appointment of consultants wherever required.
9. Lack of local organisation of consultants resulting in delay in communicating decision.
10. Delay in procurement of equipment due to :

(a) late issue and late finalisation of tenders;

(b) procedural delays in processing through DGS & D;

(c) processing of foreign exchange release by Government of India.

11. Delay in levelling and dressing at site due to :

(a) inaccessible nature of site;

(b) delay in procurement of construction equipment.

12. Late receipt of erection drawings.
13. Delay in procurement of construction equipment like tower crane, Gantry crane etc.
14. Shortage of Cement and Steel, welding rods, explosives, etc.
15. Late arrival of erection specialists.
16. Delay in delivery of equipment due to :

(a) failure of supplier to keep up schedule;

(b) lack of ships, port strikes etc.;

(c) overcarriage of equipment;

(d) impounding of equipment in Pakistan.

17. Difficulties in transporting equipment to site :

(a) in moving overdimensional packages on railway due to restrictions imposed bridges, tunnels etc.;

(b) due to lack of suitable rolling stock etc.;

(c) due to difficult terrain and lack of proper access routes.

18. Delays in getting replacement for items of equipment damaged or lost in transit.
19. Lack of proper planning and coordination of various construction schedules and failure to anticipate delay in case of critical phase of construction activity in advance.
20. Labour strikes and civil disturbances.
21. Unprecedented rains and floods.
22. Difficulties experienced due to change in the course of lean water flow in river.
23. Change in top personnel in the course of implementation of project.
24. Stoppage of work due to enemy action.

Hydro

1. Inadequate investigation before finalising technical project report.
2. Major change in the scope of work like :

(a) change in the location of dam;

(b) change in design of dam foundation;

(c) change in design of Water Conductor System;

(d) change in location of power station and switch yard;

(e) change in generator capacity.

3. Delay due to inter-State aspects.
4. Delay in issue of authorisation by Central and/ or State authorities.
5. Delay in foreign exchange tie-ups.
6. Change in key personnel in the course of advance planning and execution.
7. Delay in procurement of equipment due to :

(a) late issue and late finalisation of tenders;

(b) procedural delays in processing through D.G.S. & D;

(c) processing of foreign exchange release by Government of India.

8. Delay in procurement of construction equipment.
9. Shortage of Cement and Steel, welding rods, explosives, etc.

10. Shortage of spare parts for construction equipment.

11. Late arrival of erection specialists.

12. Delay in delivery of equipment due to failure of supplier to keep up schedule.

13. Difficulties in transporting equipments to site :

(a) in moving overdimensional packages on railway due to restrictions imposed by bridges, tunnels, etc.;

(b) due to difficult terrain and lack of access roads.

14. Unprecedented rains and floods.

15. Land acquisition and rehabilitation."

Nuclear

In addition to the causes of delays listed under thermal, due to the special features of atomic power stations certain additional causes of delays exist. These are :

1. Protracted negotiations have been generally necessary before finalising the various agreements.

2. Long delivery period in the supply of equipment and machinery, both by the Indian and Foreign suppliers.

3. Locating Indian suppliers of the equipment to meet standards and other requirements in the fabrication of the various equipments to achieve maximum indigenisation.

4. Technical improvements which had become necessary during the construction phase.

Besides, these, the much larger scale of activities and complete dependence on indigenous manufacture of power plant and equipment have introduced some further difficulties. The larger scale and complexity make it necessary now to adopt the modern management techniques developed recently and to remove or reduce the Administrative difficulties. In the following Sections, the different factors influencing the execution of Projects from conception to commissioning, are discussed.

COMMITTEE ON GOVERNANCE OF UNIVERSITY AND COLLEGES, 1969—REPORT

New Delhi, University Grants Commission, 1973. 20p.

Part III. Teachers; Conditions of Service, Emoluments, Responsibilities and other matters relating to University and Colleges teachers.

Chairman : Dr. S.N. Sen

Members : Prof. R.P. Bambah; Rev. Mother Mary Braganza; Dr. L. Bullaya; Dr. M.M. Chakravarty; Dr. Kamla Chaudhuri; Dr. Chandran D.S. Devanesen; Dr. S.N. Ghosal; Prof. Tapas Majumdar; Prof. M.V. Mathur; Dr. Sukumar Mitra; Shri J.P. Naik; Shri D.P. Nayar; Prof. T.S. Sadasivan; Sardar Bishan Singh Samundri; Shri J.B. Sandil; Shri Hridya Narain Singh; Shri Ram Swarup Narain Singh; Dr. L.S. Chandrakant; Prof. M.N. Srinivas.

Member-Secretary : Shri R.K. Chhabra.

APPOINTMENT

On the recommendations of the Conference of Vice-Chancellors convened by the Ministry of Education and Youth Services and the University Grants Commission held in April 1969, the University Grants Commission appointed two Committees to consider issues relating to Governance of Universities and Colleges respectively in June, 1969.

TERMS OF REFERENCE

Committee on Governance of Universities

To consider the structure of universities; functions, responsibilities and powers of the statutory bodies; conditions of service of staff, student participation, and related matters.

Committee on Governance of Colleges

Relationship of Colleges with the Universities, conditions of affiliation, procedure of selection and conditions of service of teachers, constitution and powers of governing bodies, university representation, student participation, and related matters.

Subsequently, the two Committees were amalgamated into one.

CONTENTS

Introduction; Terms of Reference; General Observance; The Need to Attract the Best Talents; The Need to Improve the Functions and professional Competence of Teachers; Pay Scale and Their Rationale; University Teachers; College Teachers; Evaluation of Teachers; Principals of Colleges; Tutors and Demonstrators; Basis of Fixation of Pay; Scales of Pay of Library Staff and Physical Instructors/Directors of Physical Education; The Need for a National Wage Policy; Recruitment of Teachers in Affiliated Colleges; Conditions of Service; Code of Conduct; Acknowledgement.

RECOMMENDATIONS

The scales of pay of university teachers should not be inferior to the scales of pay available to the members of all-India services so that a reasonably good proportion of the most talented students are attracted to the teaching profession.

During the early part of a teacher's career, he should be exposed to some training in methods of teaching, human psychology, problem of students, organisation and management of higher education and its role in contemporary society. The UGC in collaboration with the universities may make arrangements for such courses for research student and young teachers.

A single running grade to cover all categories of teachers would curb initiative. The teaching service at the university level should be divided into a small number of groups in which there would be no artificial barriers preventing persons doing outstanding work from moving from lower to higher grades.

There should be three-tiers of posts in the universities —lecturers, readers and professors with the following scales of pay :

1. Lecturer Rs. 400—40—800—50—1250.
2. Reader Rs. 900—50—1250—60—1550—75—1700.
3. Professor Rs. 1300—75—1600—100—2000.

The scales are exclusive of the usual allowances as are available in the Government Services. These will have to be readjusted if basic scales are revised in Government Services and similar professions.

The improvement of salary scales should be linked with the improvement of qualifications.

There should be provisions for outstanding teachers to get higher rank and scale through assessment after lapse of a particular period.

For the appointment of teachers in the universities, the selection should be on merit to inspire confidence.

Eminent professors in the country ought to be given scales of pay applicable to Directors of National Laboratories.

The scale of pay of a lecturer in an Undergraduate College should be 400—40—800—50—950 assessment—50—1250. There should be provision for a lecturer to get higher rank and scale after assessment of his work when he has reached Rs. 950.

Posts of Reader/Professor may be sanctioned in selected affiliated Colleges both undergraduate and Postgraduate on the basis of prescribed criteria. Persons appointed to these posts should have the same qualifications and same facilities for assessment to a higher grade as are available to university teachers and they should be subject to the same selection procedure.

There should be provision for evaluation of teachers.

The scales of pay of Principals of affiliated Colleges should be either of the following :

(i) Rs. 900—50—1250—60—1550—75—1700.

(ii) Rs. 1300—75—1600—100—2000.

There is no need for demonstrators in universities and colleges. The scale of pay of the existing incumbents should be revised to Rs. 300—600.

For the recruitment of teachers in affiliated colleges, the following alternatives have been suggested :

(i) Joint Universities Commission for recruiting teachers of all affiliated colleges in a State;

(ii) University Committee(s) for recruiting teachers of colleges affiliated to that University;

(iii) College based selection committee.

The universities should make provision for framing statutes with regard to security of service. The statutes should provide for a contract between the university and every teacher. Provision should also be made for the settlement of disputes. The State Governments should make provisions for the security of service of teachers in the affiliated colleges through appropriate legislation.

The scheme of pension-cum-gratuity-cum-general provident fund and contributory provident fund-cum-gratuity introduced in the Central Universities may be extended to other universities and affiliated colleges.

The period of probation should not exceed 24 months.

The work-load of all university and college teachers should be the same and not less than 40 hours a week. This will include preparation for teaching, actual classroom teaching, correction and examination work (including invigilation), research, tutorials and guidance to students, extra-curricular activities, and administrative and professional work.

The age of superannuation should be 60 years. Thereafter, if necessary, a teacher may be appointed on contract not exceeding five years.

Medical and housing facilities for teachers in universities and colleges should be provided.

The proposed revision of salary scales will involve additional expenditure. It may be mentioned that when in 1966, the scales of pay of teachers were revised by the Government of India on the recommendations of the U.G.C., the additional expenditure involved was shared between the Government of India and the State Governments concerned on 80 : 20 basis for a period of five years after which the entire expenditure was to be borne by the State Governments. In the case of the Central Universities, the additional expenditure involved was provided through the maintenance grant payable to the universities. If the proposals for further revision are now accepted, the Government of India will have to decide the pattern of assistance before recommending the scales to the State Governments for implementation.

The report of the Committee on Governance of the Colleges is likely to be submitted by the Committee by the end of June 1973.

The Vice-Chancellor, Delhi University, had sent a copy of the resolution of the Academic Council passed on December 9, 1968 regarding the merger of the lecturers and readers grade along with a brief note stating the reasons which prompted the Academic Council in passing such a resolution. A copy each of the resolution and the brief note sent by the Vice-Chancellor, Delhi University, are attached (Appendices II and III). The Vice-Chancellor, Delhi University, requested that these be placed before the Committee on Government of Universities and colleges. The Committee considered this matter at its meeting held on 31st March and 1st April, 1973. The Committee noted that the scale of pay of the lecturers in the affiliated colleges of the Delhi University is the same as of the university appointed lecturers and that 25 per cent of the lecturers in the selection grade of Rs. 700—1250 the same as for the readers in the university departments. The Committee also noted that the scales of pay of the lecturers in the affiliated colleges of other universities were lower than that of the lecturers of an affiliated college of the Delhi University. In view of the recommendation of the Committee that the salary scale of a lecturer in an affiliated college be Rs. 400—950—assessment—1250, the Committee felt that no further consideration of the reference of the Vice-Chancellor, Delhi University, was necessary. The Committee was also not in fovour of 25 per cent of the posts of lecturer in the affiliated colleges of the Delhi University being in the selection grade of Rs. 700—1250.

The matter is placed before the Commission for consideration.

The Committee* on Governance of Universities and Colleges considered the question of the service conditions of teachers in Universities and Colleges. The Committee took into account the suggestions made by various teachers' organisations and individuals in this regard. The Committee noted that the University Grants Commission had recommended the scales of pay for teachers in universities and colleges indicated in Annexure II to be effective from 1-4-1966. The Committee also noted that the Education Commission (1964-66) had expressed the view that the disparity in the salary scales of university and college teachers should be reduced. The scales recommended by the University Grants Commission earlier were a step in this direction.

(1) General Observations

The development of higher education is very vital for the economic and social development of the country. If higher education is to play the role which is expected of it, the crucial importance of the teacher has to be recognised. It is most important that a fair proportion of the most talented people should go into the field of education and research. The scales of pay should signify the high priority given to education, especially higher education. The level of scales provided to teachers in universities and colleges should take note of all these points.

Scales of pay of Library Staff and Physical Instructors/Directors of Physical Education

The Committee is not making any recommendations regarding the revision of scales of pay of Librarian and other staff in the Libraries and Physical Instructors in Universities and Colleges and suggests that may be considered along with the revision of scales of pay of non-teaching staff. However, when teachers are appointed in the Universities/Colleges for teaching in the Departments of Library Science and Physical Education, they should be treated on par with other teachers provided they fulfil the qualifications.

The need for a National Wage Policy

We are of the view that the basic problem facing the country in education—or any other walk of life—cannot be solved unless an appropriate national wage policy is evolved and enforced. We have, however, assumed the

*Constitution of the Committee is at Annexure I.

present pattern of remuneration of the employees of the Government of India as valid, and, relative to that pattern indicated what the scales of pay of teachers in higher education should be if university education is to have its due share of talent. But we agree in principle that there should be a national wage policy covering all sectors of life. The teachers of all categories should be given their due place within this over-all frame; and we expect the teachers of the country will not hesitate to support the proposals even if, in terms of the national wage policy, it may imply a reduction of remuneration in monetary terms.

Code of Conduct

While making these recommendations we have assumed that the teachers in general will not misuse their responsibilities and privileges. We venture to suggest that the following lapses would constitute improper conduct on the part of a University/College teacher :

(i) Failure to perform his academic duties such as preparation/lectures, demonstrations, assessment, guidance, invigilation, etc.

(ii) Gross partiality in assessment of students, deliberately over-making/under-marking or attempts at victimization on any grounds.

(iii) Inciting students against other students, colleagues or administration (This does not interfere with the right of a teacher to express his difference on principles in seminars or other places where students are present).

(iv) Raising questions of caste, creed, religion, race or sex in his relationships with his colleagues and trying to use the above considerations for improvement of his prospects.

(v) Refusal to carry out the decisions by appropriate administrative and academic bodies and/or functionaries of the universities. This will not inhibit his right to express his differences with their policies or decision.

COMMITTEE ON GOVERNANCE OF UNIVERSITIES, 1969—REPORT

New Delhi, University Grants Commission, 1971. Part I—96p.

Chairman : Dr. P.B. Gajendragadkar.

Members : Prof. R.P. Bambah; Shri G.K. Chandiramani; Dr. Kamla Chaudhuri; Prof. S. Nurul Hasan; Prof. M.V. Mathur; Shri D.P. Nayar; Prof. T.S. Sadasivan; Dr. S.N. Sen; Prof. M.N. Srinivas; Dr. R. Satyanarayan.

Secretary : Dr. P.J. Philip.

The Committee on Governance of Universities was amalgamated with the Committee on Governance of Colleges and reconstituted as under:

Chairman : Dr. P.B. Gajendragadkar.

Members : Prof. A. Aiyappan; Prof. R.P. Bambah; Mother Mary Briganza; Dr. L. Bullaya; Dr. M.M. Chakravarty; Shri G.K. Chandiramani; Dr. Kamla Chaudhuri; Dr. Chandran D.S. Devanesen; Dr. S.N. Ghosal; Prof. S. Nurul Hasan; Prof. Tapas Majumdar; Prof. M.V. Mathur; Dr. Sukumar Mitra; Shri J.P. Naik; Shri D.P. Nayar; Dr. R. Satyanarayan; Prof. T.S. Sadasivan; Sardar Bishan Singh Samundri; Shri J.B. Sandil; Dr. S.N. Sen; Shri Hridya Narain Singh; Shri Ram Swarup Narain Sinha; Prof. M.N. Srinivas; Dr. P.J. Philip.

Secretary : Shri R.K. Chhabra.

APPOINTMENT

The Committee on Governance of Universities was constituted under the University Grants Commission in June 1969 to consider the issues relating to governance of universities.

TERMS OF REFERENCE

To consider the structure of universities; functions, responsibilities and powers of the statutory bodies; conditions of service of staff, student participation, and related matters.

CONTENTS

Our Approach to the Problem; Acts, Statutes,

Ordinances and Regulations; The Visitor and the Universities; Authorities of the Universities; Other University Bodies; Organization of Teaching Departments; University Administrators; Student Participation; Miscellaneous; Appendices I to III.

RECOMMENDATIONS

Acts, Statutes, Ordinances and Regulations

The universities in India are established or incorporated by Acts of Legislature. Legislatures have sovereign authority to deal with university education, subject to the limitations to which reference has already been made. We have pointed out that in order that the universities may perform their functions properly, their autonomy should be scrupulously respected by the legislatures and the executive, though there would be some spheres in which the State may exercise supervisory authority over the administration of the universities, and that should only be through the Visitor, as indicated later. In the scheme which we recommend, the President will be the Visitor of the Central universities, and the Governor will be the Visitor of the State universities.

Act

The Act under which a University is established may provide for the following : definitions; objects; powers; jurisdiction of the University; visitation; officers of the University; authorities of the University and their powers; audit of the accounts of the University; provision for correspondence courses; private candidates; and autonomous colleges/departments. The Act should make it obligatory for the University that its teachers (including Colleges) shall be appointed on a written contract, and that there should be a provision for arbitration in case of any dispute arising out of such contract; further, that every employee or student of the University (including colleges admitted to its privileges) should have the right to appeal to the Executive Council of the University, in case he feels aggrieved by the action of any officer or authority of the University/College. It may also provide that the Statutes adopted under the Act shall prescribe conditions under which colleges and other institutions may be admitted to the privileges of the University and the withdrawal of such privileges; conditions of service of staff (including the manner of termination of their service) and pension; insurance and provident fund. The Act may indicate the items which may be provided through Statutes and Ordinances, and the procedure for the framing of Statutes and Ordinances and Regulations. The Act may provide that Statutes shall be framed for establishing "student Unions" in the universities and colleges, and for the participation or representation of students in the functioning of the university college. Similarly, it may provide that the statutes may be framed for 'teachers associations' and 'non-academic staff associations'.

The Act may further provide that the proceedings of any of the authorities shall not be rendered invalid merely because of any vacancy not filled up or any 'formal defect' in the composition of the authorities; that there will be no civil liability in respect of action taken by the officers or employees of the university in good faith; the power of the Registrar or other person authorised by the University to enter into agreements and to sign documents, authenticate records, etc.; delegation of powers by the authorities or officers of the University to individuals or committees. Provision should also be made to enable the Vice-Chancellor to exercise the powers of the statutory bodies of the university, and pass appropriate orders, if in his opinion the relevant matter is so urgent that an immediate decision in respect of this is necessary. Such action of the Vice-Chancellor should in due course be reported to the appropriate authority whose power he has exercised. In view of our recommendation regarding delegation of powers, the occasions for the exercise of such power by the Vice-Chancellor, in respect of urgent matters, may not frequently arise.

A provision may also be made that no member of the university (teacher, student or non-academic staff) shall engage in any activity instigating or involving violences including threat of violence, likely to disrupt teaching or study or research or the administration of the University or the proceedings of any of its bodies, or obstruct any teacher or officer of the University in the performance of his duties, damage or deface any property in the University or any colleges admitted to its privileges, or occupy or use the same otherwise than in accordance with the rules or other provisions made therefore by the University or College authority concerned. In defining the powers of the University, the Act should give specific authority to the University to cooperate or collaborate with other Universities, learned bodies or associations in such a manner as may be prescribed in the Ordinances.

Statutes

Though the first Statute of a University may be framed under the authority of the legislature, they should be authorised subsequently to amend, repeal or add to the said Statutes. However, no change in the Statutes thus made should come into operation without the previous approval of the Visitor. The Executive Council may, from time to time, make new or additional Statutes or may amend or repeal Statutes, provided that the Executive Council shall not make any Statute or any amendment of the Statute affecting the status, powers or constitution of any existing authority of the University until such authority has been given an opportunity of expressing an opinion on the proposal, which shall be stated in writing, and shall be considered by the Executive Council.

Every Statute or addition to the Statute or any amendment or repeal of the Statute shall require the approval of the Visitor, who may give his assent thereto or withold his assent or remit the same to the Executive Council for re-consideration. A new Statute or Statute amending or repealing an existing Statute shall not come into operation unless it has received the assent of the Visitor.

The Statutes may provide for the following :

(a) The composition, powers and duties of the Court, Executive Council, Academic Council, Student Council, Selection Committee, Faculties/Schools, Finance Committee, and such other bodies as may be deemed necessary to be constituted from time to time; the establishment and recognition of Students Union, Teachers Association and non-academic Staff Association; the mode of appointment of the Vice-Chancellor, and Pro-Vice-Chancellor, the terms and conditions of their service, and their powers; the mode of appointment and powers of the Registrar, Finance officer, Librarian, Principals of the University-maintained Colleges, Deans of Faculties; principles governing seniority; conditions of service of staff, the manner of termination of service of staff and disciplinary action; and the provision of pension, insurance and provident fund for the benefit of the employees of the University.

Statutes may also provide for the following matters:

Discipline of students, classification of the emoluments and manner of appointment of teachers; conferment of honorary degrees and other distinctions; withdrawal of degrees, diplomas, certificates and other academic distinctions; establishment and abolition of faculties/schools, departments, halls/hostels, colleges and institutions; procedure for admitting colleges and other institutions to the privileges of the University and for the withdrawal of such privileges; alumni associations and/or conditions of registration of old students. In these matters the Executive Council should be obliged to obtain the views of the Academic Council before modifying the Statutes.

Ordinances

The Executive Council should be given the power to make, amend, repeal and add to the Ordinances of the University. All Ordinances made by the Executive Council should come into effect immediately (unless the Council itself decides otherwise to await the directions, if any, from the Visitor within the period indicated in the following paragraph).

Every addition, amendment or repeal of Ordinances should be submitted to the Visitor within a specified time, say a fortnight. The Visitor should have the power to direct the University, within a specified time thereafter not exceeding four weeks, that the operation of any such Ordinance be suspended. The operation of such Ordinance shall thereupon be suspended on receipt of the above mentioned order of the Visitor. The Visitor shall as soon as possible inform the Executive Council about the objection that he has to the proposed Ordinance, and ask the Executive Council for its comments. After receiving the comments of the University, the Visitor may either withdraw the order suspending the Ordinance or disallow the Ordinance. The decision of the Visitor shall be final. It may be mentioned that there are a few universities where according to their present Acts no reference to the Chancellor (Visitor recommended here) is required for additions or amendments to ordinance. This practice may continue.

The Ordinances may provide for the following :

(a) The establishment and constitution of Centres of Study, Boards of Study, Inter-disciplinary Committees, Special Centres, Special Laboratories, Committees for Advanced Study and Research, Committees of Departments/Centres, Admission Committee, Examination Committee, Boards of Residence and Halls, Student Advisory Committee of Colleges. Hostels/Halls, Faculties, Departments, manner of cooperation and collaboration with other universities, learned bodies or associations or among the institutions admitted to the privileges of the university, etc.;

(b) Such other terms and conditions or service of teachers as may be prescribed in accordance with the Statutes;

(c) The qualifications of teachers;

(d) Student participation in University/College affairs and governance;

(e) Management of colleges and other institutions founded or maintained by the University and the supervision and inspection of colleges and other institutions admitted to the privileges of the University;

(f) Degrees, diplomas, certificates and other academic distinctions to be awarded by the University, qualifications for the same, the duration of the courses of study and other essential features of such courses and the type and nature of examination for such degrees, diplomas or certificates;

(g) The conduct of examinations including the terms of office and the manner of appointment and the duties of examining bodies, examiners and moderators;

(h) The admission of the students to the University and their enrolment, the maintenance of discipline among the students, the conditions regarding residence of students;

(i) The conditions of award of fellowships, scholarships, studentships, exhibitions, medals and prizes;

(j) The fees to be charged for courses of study and for admission to the examinations, degrees and diplomas of the University;

(k) Remuneration to be paid to examiners, moderators and tabulators, etc.

(l) Creation, composition and functions of other bodies, committees, or boards necessary or desirable for improving the academic life of the University;

(m) Special arrangements, if any, for the residence, discipline and teaching of women students; and

(n) Terms and conditions of service of the academic non-teaching and of the non-academic staff of the University.

The Act should provide that in framing Ordinances relating to matters enumerated above except (b) and (n), the Executive Council shall act on the recommendation of the Academic Council. The Executive Council should not have the power to amend the draft as prepared by the Academic Council, but it may either reject the proposal or return the draft to the Academic Council for reconsideration, either in whole or in part, together with any amendments which the Executive Council may suggest. In such a case the Academic Council may consider the question afresh, and if it reaffirms its original draft by a majority of not less than two-thirds of the members present and voting, and more than half the total number of members of the Academic Council, the same will be sent back to the Executive Council which shall then either adopt it or refer it to the Visitor, whose decision shall be final.

It should also be provided that the Academic Council shall consult the Student Council before proposing the draft of an Ordinance in respect of the constitution of Student Advisory Committees and matters indicated under items (d), (h), (i) and (m) above.

It would be advisable for the Universities not to bring into the Ordinance, the details of the number or title of papers or the marks allotted to each paper prescribed for the various examinations. Doing so would prevent changes being introduced from time to time, hamper innovation and experimentation, and lead to a rigid uniformity which would not be in keeping with the present-day requirements of academic life.

Regulations

The authorities of the University and other statutory bodies may make regulations consistent with the Acts, Statutes and the Ordinances for :

(a) Laying down the procedure to be followed at their respective meetings and the number of persons required to form a quorum; providing for the giving of notice to the members of such authority of the dates of meetings and the business to be considered, and for the keeping of record of the proceedings of the meetings. They may also provide for all other matters solely within their jurisdiction and not provided for in the Act, Statutes or the Ordinances.

(b) Travelling allowance rules, leave rules, financial procedures, etc.

(c) A provision should be made in the Act that the Executive Council may direct any authority or committee of the University, other than the Court, to cancel or amend in such form as may be specified any regulation made by such authority or such body, and such authority or body shall cancel or amend the regulation, as directed.

The Visitor And The Universities

In dealing with the question of autonomy of the universities, we have already indicated, that the concept of university autonomy does not exclude the broad supervisory function of the State over the administration of the university. We recommend that the Visitor should have such supervisory powers. We would like to indicate that in our view it would be convenient hereafter, if according to the Acts of the Central Universities which describes the President of India as the Visitor of the Central Universities, the State Governors are similarly described as Visitors of the universities in the respective States. Apart from the advantage of having a uniform nomenclature for the Central and State Universities, the powers that we propose to recommend for the Visitor are really such as are essentially the supervisory powers of the State, and are not the powers that ought to be exercised by the head of a university. At the same time, we would not like the Government to interfere directly with the functioning of a university. By making it essential that the authority of the State is exercised through the President or the Governor in his capacity as the Visitor, the possibility of direct intervention by Government officials in the functioning of the university would be eliminated.

As our recommendations will show, we contemplate the appointment of a Chancellor, and recommend that the Chancellor should have the privilege of presiding over the convocations of the university, but he would not be saddled with any administrative responsibility or authority. In other words, the idea in making this recommendation is to associate some distinguished citizens in the State with the universities.

The important power which the Visitor should have is the right, whenever he is satisfied that it is necessary to use it, to cause an "inspection" to be made by such person or persons as he may direct, of the university or any institution maintained by the university, or of a college/institution admitted to the privileges of the university, including the buildings, laboratories, record and equipment thereof, and also of the conduct of examinations teaching and other work conducted or done by it, or to cause an inquiry to be made in a like manner in respect of any matter connected with the administration and finance of the university or the institutions maintained by it. In the Acts of the universities where similar provision has already been made, it has been provided that the university or the institution, in whose case an inspection or an inquiry is to be made, shall be entitled to appoint a representative, who shall have the right to be present and be heard at such inspection or inquiry. We are, however, of the view that while full liberty should be given to the university/institution concerned to be heard by the Committee that may be appointed by the Visitor, it should be left to the Committee to decide whether or not, having regard to the nature of the subject matter of the inquiry, the representative of the university and of other parties interested in the inquiry should be allowed to be present during the hearings of the inquiry. It is, however, necessary that before the Visitor issues a directive to the university, in pursuance of the report received by him as a result of the said inquiry, he shall give an opportunity to the Executive Council or the Committee of management of the College to make its comments on the findings of the inquiry or inspection and the recommendations made. The Visitor may after considering the comments of the university or college decide what action, if any, and the manner in which it should be taken in respect of the recommendations made in the report.

The Visitor should also have the right to annul any proceedings of the university which are inconsistent with the Act, Statutes or the Ordinances. A provision may, however, be made that before making any such order the Visitor shall call upon the university to show cause why such an order should not be issued, and if any cause is shown within reasonable time, he should consider the same before giving the final order.

We would recommend to the Government of India that before the Visitor exercises his power in regard to the Central Universities, he may consult the University Grants Commission. We also recommend to the State Governments that where important questions of academic policy are involved, they might also take advantage of the advice of the University Grants Commission, or advise the Visitor of a State University to obtain the advice of the University Grants Commission.

We recommend that the Visitor should have the power to nominate persons on some of the statutory authorities or bodies of the university. Specific suggestions in this regard will be made when we deal with different bodies and authorities of the university in the course of this report. At this stage, we want to emphasise the fact that as an integral part of this recommendation, we also recommend that in exercising his power of nomination, the Visitor should choose a person from out of a panel of names drawn up by a committee consisting of his own nominee, who will be the chairman of the committee, a nominee of the Chairman, University Grants Commission, and a nominee of the Vice-Chancellor of the university concerned. This process will apply in the case of every recommendation that we have made about the Visitor's power to nominate, except in the special cases where we have indicated to the contrary. It is important that persons nominated to various bodies of the university are able to give adequate time to the work of these bodies.

We recommend that a provision should be made in the Act that the Visitor should appoint a committee at regular intervals (say every five years) to determine the annual maintenance grant of a university in the form of "block grants". On such a committee there should be at least one representative of the university, one educationist not in the service of the university nominated by the Visitor, a nominee of the University Grants Commission, and one person each representating the Finance and Education Ministries/Departments of the State. In the case of the Central universities it is not necessary for the Visitor to appoint representatives of the Finance and Education Ministries, since both these Ministries are represented on the University Grants Commission. The recommendations of this committee in relation to State universities should be considered by the appropriate State Governments and the University Grants Commission, and the decisions reached after such consideration should be given effect to. Similar recommendations in regard to the central universities may be considered by the University Grants Commission, and thereafter given effect to by the Central Government.

The block grant should take into account the normal expenditure of the university, the increase resulting from periodical increments in emoluments etc., and the need to provide some financial "cushion" for the normal development of a university, in respect of items not covered by the development grant from the University Grants Commission, and the committed expenditure arising out of the development grants. It should also be ensured that if the Government approves any revision of pay scales/allowances of its own staff, which would have its effect on the staff of the university, the Government should provide additional grants to meet such additional financial expenditure outside the annual block grant.

The block grant will give flexibility to the university administration, only if the university is permitted to accumulate the unspent balance of a financial year, to be spent in the subsequent years of the period, for which the block grant has been fixed. This would, it is hoped, avoid wasteful expenditure during the closing months of each financial year. It would also enable the universities to plan their expenditure more judiciously.

In respect of development grants, we feel that there should be a machinery for consultant between the university, the University Grants Commission, and the State Government. We endorse the existing practice followed by the University Grants Commission in appointing visiting committees of experts to indicate the fields and priorities for development. It is necessary that a high-powered independent body of academics, who can take a detached view, should assess the needs and requirements of the universities. Furthermore, the developmental needs of the universities should be judged in the wider national perspective, and in accordance with a rational and effective use of the resources of a State. But once the proposals made by the said committee receive the approval of the University Grants Commission, the State Governments are expected to and should normally accept the proposals as approved by the University Grants Commission.

As we have already observed, the autonomy of a university would be meaningless if it is not accompanied by adequate financial resources, but at the same time a certain measure of financial control is essential, since the universities use public funds provided by the State Governments or the University Grants Commission. Such control should be more in the nature of general supervision rather than an examination so detailed as to leave little room for innovation or operational flexibility, and should be exercised with restraint, imagination and understanding.

In recent times there has been a tendency on the part of some State Governments to require universities to conform to the financial rules of the Government. This is not always in the best interest of the functioning of universities and their academic development, and in some cases may involve elaborate procedures, neither necessary nor suited to the working of universities. Also if all such rules and procedures were to be observed, universities may need setting up an auditing and accounting machinery which may involve substantial expenditure, without any corresponding advantage. We recommend that the University Grants Commission should, in consultation with the Comptroller and Auditor General of India, suggest simplified financial procedure and rules for the guidance of the universities.

Authorities of the Universities

We recommend that the three principal authorities of the universities already in existence in most universities, namely the Court/Senate, the Executive Council/ Syndicate and the Academic Council be continued, and where anyone of these does not exist, it should be provided. We also recommend the introduction of two new authorities, namely the Faculties/Schools and the Student Council.

We also recommend that the State Governments may take note of the variations between the different types of universities in their respective States, and may consult the University Grants Commission in accordance with Section 12 of the UGC Act, before they decide upon formal legislation for the universities.

However, we feel that the powers and functions of the authorities which we recommend may be suitably provided in the Acts of all types of universities.

Court

Powers and functions : The Court/Senate of a university performs a vital role in the life of a university. It provides a forum where a cross-section of the academic community (including those responsible for formulating the academic policies of the university teachers and students) and representatives of different sections of the general community meet together periodically, generally once a year, to discuss and review the broad policies and programmes of the university, to suggest measures for its improvement and development, and to express its views on the annual report and the annual accounts of the university. Discussion of basic issues by the Court would make the university responsive to the needs and requirements of society, and provide an opportunity to the wider community to understand its policies and problems. The Court should, therefore, remain essentially a 'deliberative' body, and should not be saddled with the authority to over-rule decisions of the Executive and Academic Councils, or the other academic bodies of the university. Consequently, the word "supreme authority" or "supreme governing body" used to describe the Court in the Acts of many universities may be dropped. Since we are visualising a division of functions between the university authorities rather than a hierarchical structure, the concept of a "supreme authority" or "supreme governing body" would be out of place. On the other hand, the views of such an important body, regarding the broad policies and programmes of the university, will naturally carry a great deal of weight with different university bodies, as well as with the Government, without compromising the academic autonomy of the university.

The Act may, therefore, provide for the court in the following terms :

1. There shall be a Court and its constitution and the terms of office of its members shall be as prescribed by the statutes.

2. Subject to the provisions of this Act, the Court shall have the following powers and functions, namely :

(i) to review from time to time the broad policies and programmes of the university and to suggest measures for the improvement and development of the university;

(ii) to consider and pass resolutions on the annual report and the annual accounts, together with audited report of the university; and

(iii) perform such other functions as may be prescribed by the Statutes.

Composition : The numerical strength of the Court may range between 100 and 150, depending upon the size and the type of the university, and the number of its departments and colleges. We recommend a definite proportion of the total membership for each category of the constituents; it would not be desirable to provide for a category of membership which would keep on increasing and thus upset the ratio.

Forty per cent of the members of the Court should be drawn from outside, while the remaining 60 per cent should be internal (including students).

Outside members : This 40 per cent of the external representation may be distributed as follows :

1. Alumni elected by registered graduates or by the Association of former students, by proportional representation.	10%
2. Members of the Legislature/Legislatures nominated by the Presiding Officer/Officers.	5%
3. Representatives of learned professions and special interests including representatives of industry, commerce, trade unions, banking and agriculture to be nominated by the Visitor, in the manner described in Chapter III, the remaining members of the Executive Council, representatives of the civic body or bodies, Ministry/Department of Education, etc.	25%
Total	40%

Having regard to the principle of associating the representatives of the community outside the university no member of the Court in the above-mentioned categories should be an employee or a student of the university or a college or an institution admitted to its privileges.

We have deliberately recommended the elimination of the donor's constituency from the membership of the Court. It is also not necessary that the Vice-Chancellors of sister universities in a State as well as the Ex-Vice-Chancellors be ex-officio members of the Court. Experience shows that such a provision rarely serves any useful purpose.

Internal members : The members of the Court from within the university community may be appointed, nominated or elected in the following manner :

1. Ex-officio members
   - Vice Chancellor
   - Pro-Vice-Chancellor/Rector
   - Deans of Faculties/Schools
   - Dean of Students Welfare
   - Chairman, Student Council

2. Heads of Departments of Studies and Principals of Colleges (maintained by the university or affiliated to it)	20%
3. Teachers other than Heads of Departments and Principals	15%
4. Students	10-15%

It is obvious that the Vice-Chancellor, the Pro-Vice-Chancellor or Pro-Vice-Chancellors, the Deans of Faculties, the Dean of Students Welfare and the chairman of the Student Council should be ex-officio members, and their number should not be restricted.

The situation we would like to see is that in a university, the head of every teaching department and the Principal of every college maintained by or admitted to the privileges of the university, is a member of the Court. However, where this cannot be achieved, and if the number of departments and colleges is very large, the heads of departments and Principals of colleges will have to serve on the Court by rotation (according to seniority). In those universities which have a large number of teaching departments and also a very large number of colleges, not more than half of the members under this category may be from among the Principals. We realise a large majority of colleges at any given time would not be represented in the Court in many of the universities. This may not be desirable, but we feel the remedy lies in restricting the number of colleges affiliated to a university as strongly urged by us earlier, rather than making the Court unwieldy.

In the next category, i.e. of teacher other than heads of departments and Principals, we suggest a suitable ratio may be fixed as between Professors, Readers and Lecturers in the case of university-appointed teachers, and also as between university-appointed teachers and college-appointed teachers. In the latter category, it may be desirable to have a further sub-division between those having a standing of ten years and above, and those with a standing below ten years, so that the association of the younger teachers with the Court may be ensured.

As already discussed by us in Chapter I, we recommend that where the number of teachers in a particular category is not large, as in the case of unitary universities, positions may be filled on the Court by the method of rotation. In the case of affiliating universities, where the number of colleges is large, these positions may be filled by election in the manner suggested by us earlier.

Student members : We do not think it necessary to spell out in detail the manner of student representation. It will have to vary from university to university, depending upon the type of the university and the stage of its development. We, however, recommend that :

(i) one-third of the student members of the Court should represent the University Students' Union and the Student Council recommended by us. The President of the University Students' Union and the Secretary of the Student Council may be made ex-officio members of the Court. The rest may be elected by the Executive Committee of the Students' Union and the Student Council. Where there is no University Students' Union, an electoral college consisting of the presidents and secretaries of the college students' unions may elect such student members of the Court, just as in the other universities members are elected, by the University Students' Union;

(ii) one-third of the student members of the Court may be elected by an electoral college consisting of those students who have demonstrated their academic merit. Suitable provision may be made to secure the representation of the different faculties. In this category one seat may be reserved for a student elected by the research students (excluding teachers registered for research) of the university from among themselves; and

(iii) the rest of the one-third members may be elected by an electoral college/colleges consisting of the University Games Committee, University Cultural Programmes Committee and the University Social Service Committee (whose creation is being recommended by us). Where for some reason such committees have not been formed, an electoral college or colleges of college students, who represent extra-curricular and co-curricular activities, may be set up.

In the matter of student representation, it would be desirable to adopt the following regulations :

1. No student who passed the High School Examination more than eight years earlier, or a Pre-University or equivalent examination more than seven years earlier, or who has taken more than one year in excess of the period prescribed for the course of which he is the student, would be eligible to be a member of the Court.

2. He must have been a student of the university for at least one year previous to his becoming member of the University Court.

3. He shall cease to be a member of the Court on his ceasing to be a student of the university or holding the office which entitles him to become a member of the Court.

Term of membership : The term of the members of the Court, except ex-officio members, should be three years provided that in the case of student members, it should be one year.

Executive Council : The Executive Council/Syndicate of a university, while being the principal executive body of the university, should not be deemed to be a governing council in a hierarchical sense. The powers of the university should be shared between the different authorities. Apart from the fact that this is in accordance with the principle of checks and balances, an authoritarian body would hardly be the most suitable executive authority in a university.

Composition : The Executive Council should be a body of about 20 persons with the Vice-Chancellor as the ex-officio Chairman, and the Pro-Vice-Chancellor/Rector as ex-officio members. A majority of its members should consist of teachers of the university (including colleges), while the rest may be persons elected by the Court and nominated by the Visitor. We suggest that three persons may be elected by the Court from among its own members by a system of proportional representation, none of whom should be an employee or a student of the university or a college/institution admitted to its privileges.

Four persons may be nominated by the Visitor out of a panel to be drawn up in the manner recommended in Chapter I. Not more than one of these four persons may be an official of the Government.

Among the teacher members, there may be three to four Deans of Faculties appointed by rotation according to seniority as Professors; two to three Principals of college maintained by or admitted to the privileges of the university, by rotation according to seniority; one Professor by rotation according to seniority; and three teachers elected by the Academic Council from among its own members by a system of proportional representation, of whom at least one shall be a Lecturer.

For the purpose of appointing Deans and Principals by rotation, it may be desirable in universities having a large number of Faculties/Schools and Colleges, to group the Faculties/Schools or Colleges so as to ensure their optimum representation.

Term of members : The term of elected and nominated members of the Executive Council should be three years. Such members may be eligible for re-election or re-nomination.

Powers and functions : Most of the powers and functions of the Executive Council have already been discussed in Chapter II, in connection with the framing of the Statutes and the Ordinances. In addition to those powers, the Executive Council should have control over the finances and properties of the university, the creation and abolition of posts, appointments, control over the staff welfare, and discipline of the staff and students, the power to deal with representations made by staff and students and to redress their grievances, affiliation to colleges and their inspection, and of ensuring that affiliated colleges conform to the Statutes and the Ordinances of the university, arrangements for the management and the general supervision of the university-maintained institutions, colleges, halls of residence and hostels, appointment of examiners, moderators, tabulators, etc.

The Executive Council may exercise its powers regarding the affiliation and inspection of colleges and the residence of students, and student discipline and welfare after obtaining the views of the Academic Council. However, in respect of rules affecting student welfare and discipline, sports. literacy and departmental societies, management of hostels, canteens, student study centres, library, students health, national service scheme, N.C.C., extension work, national sports organisation programmes, cultural activities and social work programmes, the Executive Council shall ordinarily consult the Student Council before taking any decision. Further, the Executive Council shall exercise its powers regarding appointment of examiners, moderators, tabulators etc., after ascertaining the view of the Faculties/Schools.

Academic Council : The Academic Council should be the principal academic body of the university, with power to coordinate and exercise general supervision over the academic policies of the university.

Composition : The Academic Council may consist of the following :

(i) Vice-Chancellor
(ii) Pro-Vice-Chancellor/Rector
(iii) Deans of Faculties
(iv) Two persons from among the Dean of Students Welfare/Warden/Proctor
(v) Librarian
(vi) Heads of Departments of Studies
(vii) Twenty Principals/Heads of Institutions, ten with less than ten years of service and ten with more than ten years of service
(viii) Five Professors other than the Heads of Departments
(ix) Five Readers other than the Heads of Departments, suitably distributed between Faculties
(x) Five University-appointed Lecturers—two from among those with more than ten years of service, and three with less than ten years of service
(xi) Fifteen college-appointed teachers
(xii) Five persons not being in the service of the university, coopted by the Academic Council for their special knowledge, provided that not more than two persons will be coopted from subjects assigned to any one faculty.

In unitary or city universities where the number of affiliated colleges is small, all Principals and Heads of Institutions shall be ex-officio members, and the number of university-appointed lecturers may be raised to 10 while proportionately reducing the number of college-appointed teachers.

In the case of large affiliating universities, the representation of the college-appointed teachers may be by election as suggested in Chapter I. For the categories mentioned under clauses (7) to (10) appointment may be by rotation according to seniority. The term of members other than ex-officio members may be two years

Powers and functions : We recommend that the area of functioning of the Academic Council be considerably reduced, as compared to the prevailing practice in most of the universities today. The Academic Council should have the power of policy-making, or proposing Ordinances and framing regulations and rules, the power to bring about inter-faculty coordination, to give broad directives for ensuring academic standards, and for taking up matters of general academic interest to the university. Matters such as approving the syllabus, the names of the examiners, moderators and tabulators. or reports of examiners of research theses, etc., need not go before the Academic Council. In its composition, all sections of teachers are associated, and so it is appropriate that only academic matters of general importance should be its concern. In addition to the powers and functions suggested for the Academic Council in Chapter II in connection with the framing of Statutes and Ordinances, the Academic Council should have powers :

(a) to exercise general supervision over the academic policies of the university, and to give directives regarding methods of instruction, cooperative teaching among colleges, evaluation of research or improvements in academic standards;

(b) to bring about inter-faculty coordination to establish or appoint committees or Boards, for taking up projects on an inter-faculty basis ;

(c) to consider matters of general academic interest

either at its own initiative or referred to by a Faculty or, Executive Council to the university and to take appropriate action thereon ; and

(d) to frame regulations and rules in consonance with statutes and ordinances regarding the academic functioning of the university discipline, residence, admissions, award of fellowships and studentships, fee concessions, corporate life, attendance, etc.

The Academic Council may ordinarily meet twice a year.

Faculties/Schools : In view of the fact that there has been an evergrowing expansion in the activities of most universities, and large number of disciplines and specialities are being provided for to meet the needs of the society, and to keep abreast with the explosion in knowledge, the Academic Council cannot usefully devote its attention to the accademic problems of all the disciplines. It is, therefore, necessary that the Faculties/Schools comprising of related or cognate departments and subjects should be given a large measure of autonomy. While the Faculties must respect the expert views of Boards of Studies and of Departments etc., they should also ensure coordination of teaching and research activities, and the fostering of inter-disciplinary courses, as well as projects of research.

The grouping of departments in faculties in many of the universities is not rational. While some faculties consist of a very large number of departments, there are some single department faculties. Similarly, the growing needs of subjects cannot be properly attended to on the basis of the existing groupings. For example, instead of the usual single faculty of science, it may be worthwhile having a faculty of Physical Sciences, another of Biological Sciences, and a third of Earth Sciences, and another of Mathematical Sciences. If there is a more meaningful constitution of faculties or schools, it would be possible for a department to be associated with more than one faculty or school. We recommend that the universities may apply their minds to the reorganisation of faculties or the setting up of schools. It is on the basis of reorganisation of faculties or schools that we are recommending the composition of the Faculties/Schools.

Composition : The Faculty may comprise the following :

(i) Dean of Faculty/School ... ... Chairman

(ii) All University Professors in the Faculty

(iii) All Heads of University Departments assigned to the Faculty who are not Professors

(iv) One Reader per Department

(v) Two Lecturers per Department (One above ten years of service and one below ten years)

(vi) Four persons nominated by the Academic Council from other Faculties of the University

(vii) Five persons not in the service of the university coopted by the Board for their special knowledge of any subject assigned to the faculty ; provided that not more than one person may be coopted in respect of a subject assigned to a single Department

(viii) One teacher from each College teaching subjects assigned to the Faculty, provided that the number of such teachers should not exceed 50% of the total number of members mentioned under (ii) to (v).

As we have stated earlier, the representatives of college teachers on the Faculties may be elected in accordance with the principles stated in Chapter I, while the Readers and Lecturers of university departments may serve on the Faculties by rotation, according to seniority.

The term of members other than *ex-officio* members may be two years.

Powers and functions : In addition to the powers and functions of the faculties, prescribed under the Statutes and Ordinances, they should have powers :

(a) to coordinate teaching and research activities of Departments/Centres assigned to the Faculty, and to promote and provide for inter-disciplinary teaching and research ; and to arrange for examinations and periodical tests in subjects falling within the purview of the Faculty ;

(b) to appoint Boards of Studies or Committees or to undertake research projects common to more than one Department ;

(c) to approve courses of study proposed by the Departments ;

(d) to recommend to the Executive Council the recommendations of the Board of Studies or Committees for Advanced Studies and Research ;

(e) to propose the draft of Ordinances for the examinations for courses conducted by the Faculty/School ;

(f) to recommend proposals for the creation and abolition of teaching posts ; and

(g) to carry out such other duties as the Executive Council and Academic Council may prescribe.

In a subsequent Chapter, we visualise that some of the universities would establish Centres of Study in addition to or in lieu of Departments of Studies. There should be a general provision that for purposes of the composition of the university authorities, the word "Department" would include a "Centre".

Student Council : We have recommended that the

Statutes of each University should provide for the establishment of a Student Council. The functions of this Council may be as follows :

(i) to make recommendations to the Executive and Academic Councils in matters affecting the academic work of the students such as the structure of courses, pattern of instruction, etc., the corporate life of the university in so far as it concerns the students, and the co-curricular and extra-curricular activities in the university,

(ii) ordinarily, all rules affecting discipline, welfare, sports, literary, and departmental societies, management of hostels, student homes, non-resident student centres, extension work, social work, students health, National Service Scheme, N.C.C. etc., shall be placed before the Student Council for obtaining its views, which will then be communicated to the Academic and the Executive Councils for decision, and

(iii) the Council shall have the right to communicate its views, observations and recommendations to the Vice-Chancellor or any authority of the university, in respect of any matter which concerns the students. The Chairman of the Student Council will be authority to decide whether a matter does or does not concern the students.

The meetings of the Council shall ordinarily be held at least three times every year, and not more than six months shall elapse between two meetings. Extraordinary meetings may be held either at the instance of the Chairman, or at the request of not less than half of the members of the Council.

The composition of the Student Council may be as follows :

(i) President, Vice-President, and Secretary of the University Students' Union

(ii) The Secretary of the Students Advisory Committee of each Faculty

(iii) Ten persons elected by an electoral college consisting of one student representative of each College Student Council (or of Students Advisory Committees of Hostels, in case of unitary universities) in accordance with the system of proportional representation

(iv) Five students nominated by the Vice-Chancellor from among outstanding students or sportsmen or those who have distinguished themselves in any field of student activity, giving due consideration to the representation of special interests.

We recommend that it would be desirable to have a teacher nominated by the Vice-Chancellor to be the Chairman of the Council.

The Secretary of the Student Council shall be elected by it from among its own members.

It is hardly necessary to mention that, as members of an authority of the university, they will be entitled to the normal TA/DA for attending the meetings or for travel necessary in the performance of their duties. It should be legitimate for the Executive Council to provide certain funds, if it so desires, where sanction for expenditure may be given by the Student Council, without reference to the Executive Council, in accordance with rules for expenditure framed by the latter in this behalf, for such purposes as the Executive Council may specify from time to time, in connection with the organisation of corporate life, curricular, extra-curricular and welfare activities etc. At this stage we may mention in anticipation that we propose to make a similar recommendation in respect of colleges/institutions admitted to the privileges of a university.

Other University Bodies

Finance Committee : As stated elsewhere, the Treasurer or the Finance Officer of the university should be subject to the authority of the Executive Council. In the same way the Finance Committee should be a sub-committee of the Executive Council. Presumably to protect the financial interest of the universities, the constitution of some universities provides for an elected treasurer or an elected finance committee. While it is necessary to provide safeguards against wastage, and to secure careful and well considered utilisation of university resources, it is not useful to have an independent Treasurer or a Finance Committee. Each university should have a Finance Committee which should consider the budget prepared by the office of the university, and scrutinise the proposals—new and old—keeping in view the resources available, and recommend to the Executive Council the financial ceiling within which the university could incur expenditure. The office in preparing the budget will take account into the proposals/budgets submitted by the departments/institutions of the university, and any proposal or views expressed by the Academic Council with regard to the academic work and progress of the university. It shall place before the Finance Committee a statement containing all proposals submitted by the departments/institutions. The Finance Committee should be treated as an advisory authority, and the final decision should be taken by the Executive Council. It is necessary that the Executive Council would keep in view the resources available to it, before it takes any decision on the financial commitments. The Executive Council should also see that it does not go beyond its resources. The constitution of the Finance Committee may be as follows :

(i) Vice Chancellor ... ... Chairman

(ii) Pro-Vice-Chancellor

(iii) Two Deans of the Faculties, to be nominated by the Executive Council

(iv) One person nominated by the Executive Council from amongst its members other than those in the service of the university or college/institution admitted to the privileges of the university,

(v) Three persons nominated by the visitor (in accordance with the procedure suggested in Chapter I).

Wherever there is a Finance Officer, he should serve as Secretary of the Cemmittee, but need not be a member thereof. The Registrar of the university should be a permanent invitee, and have the right to participate in the discussions of the Finance Committee but may not be a member thereof. However, where the university has no Finance Officer, and the Registrar is in the overall charge of the university administration, he should act as the Secretary of the Finance Committee.

It is clear that the nominees of the Visitor, who may be officials or non-officials, would serve on the Finance Committee in their individual capacity, and would not represent any organisation.

Selection Committee : We feel that no appointment for a period exceeding two years (including any period of ad hoc or temporary appointment made earlier) should be made by the Executive Council, except on the recommendation by duly constituted Selection Committee, which should be provided by the Statutes. The same should apply to part-time appointments of fellows or any other category of appointments against permanent or quasi-permanent posts.

The statutes should provide that there shall be a Selection Committee for making recommendations to the Executive Council for appointment to the posts of Professor, Reader, Lecturer, Registrar, Finance Officer, Librarian, and Principal of a University-maintained college/institution.

Every Selection Committee shall consist of the Vice-Chancellor, who shall be the chairman thereof, and a person nominated by the Visitor ; and, in addition, the Selection Committee (for making recommendations for appointment to a post specified in column 1 of the following Table) shall include as its members the persons specified in the corresponding entry in column 2 of the said Table :

Table

1	2
Professor	(i) The Head of the Department* concerned, if he is a Professor. (ii) One Professor of the Department to be nominated by the Vice-Chancellor.** (iii) Three persons not in the service of the university, nominated by the Executive Council, out of a panel of names recommended by the Academic Council for their special knowledge of or interest in the subject with which the Professor will be concerned.
Reader/ Lecturer	(i) The Head of the Department concerned.* (ii) One Professor of the Department to be nominated by the Vice-Chancellor.* (iii) Two persons not in the service of the university, nominated by the Executive Council, out of a panel of names recommended by the Academic Council for their special knowledge of or interest in the subject with which the Reader or Lecturer will be concerned.
Registrar/ Finance Officer	(i) Two members of the Executive Council nominated by it. (ii) One person, not connected with the University, nominated by the Executive Council.
Librarian	(i) Two persons not in the service of the university, who have special knowledge of the subject of Library Science/Library Administration to be nominated by the Executive Council. (ii) One person, not in the service of the university, nominated by the Executive Council.
Principal of a college/institution maintained by the University	Three persons not in the service of the university of whom two to be nominated by the Executive Council and one by the Academic Council for their special knowledge of or interest in a subject in which instruction is being provided by the college/institution.

*The statutes may provide that where the appointment is being made for an inter-disciplinary project, the Head of the project may be deemed to be the Head of the Department concerned.

**It is presumed that the Professor will be concerned with the speciality for which the selection is being made and that the Vice-Chancellor will consult the Head of the Department and the Dean of Faculty before nominating the Professor.

The procedure to be followed by a Selection Committee in making recommendations, and the quorum required for its meeting, may be prescribed by the Ordinances.

If the Executive Council is unable to accept any recommendations made by the Selection Committee, it may remit the same to the Selection Committee for reconsideration, and if the difference is not resolved, the Executive Council shall record its reasons and submit the case to the Visitor for orders.

The constitution of the Selection Committees for the purpose of recognising teachers may be provided for by the Ordinances.

In case of newly established university or universities, or newly established faculties in older universities, the Selection Committee may consist of the following :

(i) Vice-Chancellor ... ... Chairman

(ii) One person nominated by the Visitor

(iii) Three persons, not in the service of the university, nominated by the Executive Council, for their special knowledge of or interest in the subject, with which the professor will be concerned.

The Ordinances may provide for temporary appointments for Lecturers, in some cases for Readers but not Professors, for a period not exceeding one year at a time, but in no case exceeding two years, to be made by the Executive Council on the recommendations of a Selection Committee, consisting of the head of the department (Chairman) and two Professors or Readers concerned with the subject for which the teacher is to be appointed, and another teacher not belonging to that department. The Committee may be nominated by the Vice-Chancellor and should have a term of two years. The Executive Council may delegate to the Vice-Chancellor the authority to appoint a teacher on a temporary basis on the recommendations of such a Selection Committee.

It should, however, be provided in the statutes that the period of service as temporary teachers appointed in the above manner shall not count for purposes of seniority, though it may count for other benefits.

Committee for advanced study and research : It would be desirable for every faculty or school to constitute a Committee of Advanced Study and Research to examine the suitability of topics for research theses, as recommended by the departments or centres or joint committees, appoint one or more supervisors for research degree students, prescribe conditions under which work done jointly by a number of scholars could be assessed for purposes of the Ph. D. degree, recommend the appointment of examiners for research degree, consider the recommendations of such examiners, and examine proposals for research received from departments or to initiate proposals for research, and promote inter-disciplinary and cooperative research. The Committee should be presided over by the dean. It may have three 'Core' members, one professor, one reader and one lecturer, elected by the Faculties/In addition to these 'Core' members, the Head of the department, the matter concerning whose department is on the agenda of a meeting, should be a full-fledged member for the purpose of that meeting. It should be the duty of the Dean to invite the Professor in charge of a Section, or a speciality of a department, or the chairman or convenor of a joint committee (of departments) concerned with the proposal on the agenda of the meeting to attend such a meeting of the committee. Such invited members should have the right to participate in the deliberations of the committee.

The term of the elected members of the committee may be two years. It would be desirable for the Faculties Schools to appoint one or two experts from outside the university to serve on the Committees of Advanced Study and Research.

It should also be possible for two or more Faculties/ Schools, to establish jointly a Committee of Advanced Study and Research to promote a deal with inter-disciplinary research. The constitution of such a committee may be suitably modified.

Admission committee : In view of the fact that admission procedures have been the cause of a great deal of public dissatisfaction it would be advisable for the universities imparting instruction directly, to appoint, through an Ordinance, an Admission Committee/Committees to lay down the principles governing the policy of admission in the colleges or faculties, and to appoint such number of committees as may be desirable for supervising the actual admissions or for consulting students rendering admission policy, where the number is very large and the seats limited. The Admission Committee should have the power to designate a person or a sub-committee as the admitting authority in respect of each category of students. The Admission Committee should function under the general supervision and guidance of the Academic Council.

The Admission Committee should invariably be presided over by the Vice-Chancellor, and the Registrar should be its Secretary. It should include a few Dean, a few Principal as well as a few other teachers

(Professors, Readers, Lecturers) nominated by the Vice-Chancellor.

It is important to ensure that admission procedures enjoy the full confidence of all concerned for their fairness, impartiality and integrity, and no consideration, whatsoever, is given to "influence" or "favouritism" of any kind.

Examination committee : Every university should set up through an Ordinance an Examination Committee which should, subject to the general control and guidance of the Academic Council, exercise the following functions :

(a) General supervision of the examinations conducted by the Faculties/schools or by the Registrar, including moderation and tabulation.

(b) Recommendations to the Academic Council rules concerning examinations.

(c) Review from time to time of the results of university examinations and submission of reports thereon to the Academic Council.

(d) Discussion of the pattern of examinations and recommendations for the improvement of the examination system.

The Examination Committee should have the power to appoint as many sub-committees as it may deem necessary, including a committee to deal with cases relating to the use of unfair means by the examinees.

The Examination Committee should be presided over by the Vice-Chancellor or in his absence by the Pro-Vice-Chancellor. It should have as its members a few Deans, a few Principals and a few teachers nominated by the Vice-Chancellor. The Registrar/Controller of Examinations should be the Member-Secretary of this Committee.

Building committee : It would be advisable for the Executive Council to appoint a Committee to look after building projects of the university. It may have besides the Vice-Chancellor a few technical experts, including at least one from outside the university. With such a committee teachers who are concerned with the construction of a particular building may also be associated.

Grievances of employees other than teachers : It is hardly necessary to point out that in the smooth functioning of the university and its general efficiency the administrative staff plays an important role. It is, therefore, of utmost importance that the problems of the non-academic staff should always be solved by mutual consultation and discussion. In our view it would be prudent on the part of the Vice-Chancellor as well as the Registrar and other higher authorities of the administrative staff to keep in touch with the subordinate members of the administrative staff, meet them frequently, and try to understand their difficulties and problems. The adoption of human touch will enable the higher authorities to secure from all the members of the administrative staff the best cooperation. That is a matter which the university administration must always keep in mind.

As regards the question of the constitution of a Joint Consultative Committee, we do not propose to examine it here. That is a matter which each university will have to examine for itself in the light of its special needs and circumstances. In any case, there should be a continuous dialogue between the administrative staff and the authorities, conducted in a spirit of sympathy and informality. At the same time, there should be, in our opinion, a formal procedure for redressing genuine grievances. This may be done through a mandatory provision for arbitration in the case of individual grievances, and through a committee which would deal with the grievances of the employees, as well as the conditions of their work.

Grievances of students : We have already suggested in chapter II that the Act should give the power to a university student who has a grievance to go in appeal to the Executive Council. Where the grievance has been on the ground that a legal right of the student has been infringed, it could be desirable for the Executive Council to set up a tribunal to enquire into the complaint of the student, the constitution of which may be determined in consultation with the Academic Council and the Student Council. The finding of the tribunal should be binding on both parties. Such a procedure is likely to reduce litigation and dissatisfaction with the administration of the university.

Organisation Of Teaching Departments

Where the university conducts teaching, the most important problem which will confront it in the coming decade, is the balancing of the need for upgrading the quality of teaching and research and the pressure of expanding enrolment, and the balancing of the needs of an individual discipline with the requirements of inter-disciplinary teaching and research. We, therefore, feel that while departments of studies should cater to the requirements of individual disciplines, this has to be accompanied by a development of teaching and research programmes on an inter-disciplinary basis ; and this should be encouraged and facilitated by providing for the establishment of a suitable organisation, through Ordinances, having powers to recommend creation of posts, syllabi and courses, enrolment of research scholars, appointment of examiners etc.

Some universities may set up (besides the usual departments) a few centres of study, essentially multi-disciplinary in character, having the same powers as "departments". We can also envisage an organisation of the entire academic programme on the basis of multidisciplinary "centres" or "schools". A discipline may of course find a place in more than one centre. We feel that innovation and flexibility should be permitted, so that national needs and the growing academic requirements may be fully taken into account.

While providing for opportunity to different specialities of a subject or discipline, undue proliferation of specialities in a department should be discouraged. Sufficient autonomy should be given to each specialised section within a department. In particular, the professor in charge of a speciality within a department should be associated with the selection of teachers and researchers in that speciality, in addition to the head of the department.

The primary academic unit, be it a department or a centre, should have sufficient autonomy as well as internal democracy in its functioning. Autonomy can be ensured if the basic academic decisions are initiated at the departmental level, and some administrative authority is delegated to the departments. For internal democracy, it would be necessary to appoint broad-based committees of teachers (with a measure of student participation) to deal with the specific problems, permitting them as much initiative as possible for innovation and experimentation. However, a continuity of policy is essential for the functioning of a department. There would be need for a degree of direction and coordination, to ensure that the interests of students as regards teaching and research have the first priority and claim, in relation to the department's resources and activities. The procedure should be such as to give no occasion or opportunity for the growth of factionalism.

Departments/Boards of studies and departmental committees : It is essential to ensure that in all academic decisions, such as the framing of courses of studies, the allocation of teaching work, the appointment of examiners, approval of subjects for research for various degrees, and other requirements of research degrees, appointment of supervisors of research, creation and abolition of teaching posts or upgrading the posts, determination of the field of study of each post at the time of recruitment, and the general academic programme and functioning of the department, the teachers in the department have a full sense of participation.

Where the number of teachers in a department, including those teaching the subject in affiliated colleges, does not exceed, say 20 the functions listed above may be performed by the entire department, subject to general guidance and approval by the higher bodies as indicated elsewhere. It would be desirable to arrange for the participation of a suitable number of teachers belonging to allied and cognate subjects in a university, to be assigned by the Academic Council, and two experts of the subjects not in the service of the university, coopted by the Department. All the teachers of the Department and teachers from other departments and experts as mentioned above would constitute the Board. However, if it is considered desirable to have a Board, it may be on the general lines indicated below for postgraduate studies, but it would be responsible for both postgraduate and undergraduate work.

Where, however, the number of teachers (including those teaching the subject in affiliated colleges) is large, it may be desirable to appoint two Boards of Studies per Department (one for undergraduate and the other for post-graduate studies), and one Committee of the Department.

Board of undergraduate studies : The functions of the Boards of Studies for undergraduate studies shall be :

(a) to recommend courses of study and appointment of examiners for the undergraduate (including Honours) degrees :

(b) to suggest measures for period assessment ;

(c) to suggest measures for the improvement of the standard of under-graduate studies.

The composition of the Board may be as follows :

(i) The Head of the University Department teaching the subject. . . . . . . Chairman (ex-officio)

(ii) Professors in the Department.

(iii) Two Readers in the Department, engaged in teaching undergraduate classes.

(iv) Two Lecturers engaged in teaching undergraduate classes in the university.

(v) Five teachers from affiliated colleges, engaged in teaching undergraduate classes, nominated by the Faculty.

(vi) Two outside experts nominated by the Vice-Chancellor on the recommendation of the Head of the Department.

If a university department is not undertaking instruction at the under-graduate level, only one Reader may serve as a member of the Board. On the other hand, in a unitary university where bulk of the undergraduate teaching is done in the department itself, the number of Lecturers may proportionately be increased. The general principle of rotation according to seniority should be applied in the case of appointments under categories (iii) and (iv).

Board of postgraduate studies : The functions of the Board of Postgraduate studies should be :

(a) to recommend courses of studies and appointment of Examiners for postgraduate courses, but excluding research degrees ;

(b) to approve subjects for research for various degrees and other requirements of research degrees ;

(c) to recommend the appointment of Supervisors of research ; and

(d) to suggest measures for the improvement of the standard of postgraduate teaching and research.

The composition of the Board may be as follows :

(i) Head of the Department ...... Chairman

(ii) Professors in the Department

(iii) Two Readers in the Department

(iv) Two Lecturers in the Department, one with more than seven years of service and the other less than this period

(v) Two Heads of Postgraduate Departments of affiliated colleges.

(vi) One Lecturer teaching postgraduate classes in affiliated colleges

(vii) Two persons teaching allied or cognate subjects in the university assigned by the Academic Council.

(viii) Two experts not in the service of the university appointed by the Vice-Chancellor on the recommendation of the Head of the Department.

The general principle of rotation according to seniority should be applied in the case of appointments under categories (iii) to (vi).

The term of appointment of members other than ex-officio may be two years.

In some of the universities the Boards of Studies are prescribed over by outsiders, while in others the Head of the Department is not the ex-officio Chairman of the Board of Studies. It is recommended that the Chairmanship of the Board must always be with the Head of the University Department.

The Head of the Department should be well advised to hold one joint meeting of the two Boards every year, so that there may be extensive consultation on academic policies before detailed recommendations are made by the respective Boards. Regulations may also provide that joint sub-committee of the two Boards may be set up for any specific or general purposes.

We have recommended earlier that it may not be desirable to have separate departments responsible for the different specialities of a single broad discipline. It is hoped that this recommendation would find favour with the universities. If, however; for any reason the different specialities of a discipline continue to remain in the charge of separate departments in some of the universities, it would be desirable to have at least one common Board of Undergraduate Studies, and its constitution may be suitably modified in such cases. We also recommend that in such universities, the Faculties or Schools might hold periodic joint meetings of the Board of Postgraduate Studies so as to ensure greater coordination and cooperations.

Departmental committee : Each university teaching department, having a large number of teachers, should associate the teachers in teaching, research and administration of the department through a Departmental Committee. This Departmental Committee should allocate teaching work, recommended the creation or abolition of teaching posts or their upgrading, make recommendations regarding the field of study of each post at the time of recruitment, and consider matters of general and academic interest to the department, and of its functioning.

The Departmental Committee may consist of :

(1) Head of the Department ... Chairman

(2) Professors in the Department

(3) Two Readers

(4) Two Lecturers

The Readers and Lecturers may be appointed by rotation according to seniority for a period of two years.

This committee should meet regularly and the minutes of its meetings should be submitted to the Vice-Chancellor. It is hoped that this committee will not normally take any formal vote and arrive at decisions on the basis of general consensus.

Each subject may be divided into its natural and normal subdivisions which we shall call are as—for example, in Physics the areas will be mathematical physics, solid state physics, nuclear physics, electronics and so on. All the teachers, teaching courses in a particular area and having competence in it, will form an area committee, which may meet frequently—at least once a quarter— to review the teaching and research programme and to make suitable recommendations.

However, ia addition to the Departmental Committee and the Boards of Studies, the Head of the Department, should occasionally convene meetings of the entire Department and obtain advice regarding the academic work of the Department.

Joint teachers student committee of departments : In view of the fact that a close association of the students with the functioning of the department would be conducive to the raising of academic standards, and would provide an opportunity to the students to receive proper initiation in shouldering academic responsibilities, we recommend the constitution of a Joint Teacher Student Committee in each department of a university. The function of the Joint Committee shall be to discuss matters affecting the academic work of the students in the departments, or any other matter which affects them in so far as it relates to the functioning of the Departments.

The Joint Committee may consist of the following :

(i) Head of the Department ... Chairman

(ii) One Professor

(iii) Two Readers

(iv) Three Lecturers

(v) Two research students elected by themselves

(vi) Four students of the department elected by the Executive Committee of the Departmental Society.

University Administrators

Chancellor : We recommend that all the universities should have a Chancellor. The Chancellor may be a high dignitary of the State or the Union of India or an eminent scholar or an eminent person in the public life of the State, nominated by the Visitor on the recommendation of the Executive Council, for a period of three years. He should be eligible for re-appointment. The Chancellor should have the right to preside over the Convocations of the University. It may not be appropriate to assign to him any administrative responsibility or authority.

Vice-Chancellor : Let us quote what the Committee on 'Model Act for Universities' has said on the position, functions and responsibilities of the Vice-Chancellor :

"The Vice-Chancellor is by far the most important functionary in a university, not only on the administrative side but also for securing the right atmosphere for the teachers and the students to do their work effectively and in the right spirit. His duties and responsibilities and the qualities needed for bearing them have been described as follows in the Report by the Committee on Higher Education appointed by Prime Minister under the chairmanship of Lord Robbins in the United Kingdom :

"This leads us to the position of the Vice-Chancellor or Principal. His is a role which, probably unfortunately, is seldom precisely spelt out in written constitutions. Yet it would be difficult to overstate its importance, particularly in a period of expansions, which calls for imagination and continuous initiative. There is a grave danger that the needs of expansion and the increasingly complex relations between institutions of higher education and Government will impose upon the heads of universities a quite insupportable burden. There are certain duties of which the Vice-Chancellor cannot divest himself. He is atonce a member of the governing body and the chairman of the main academic councils. He must therefore be at the centre of all discussions involving broad questions of internal policy or relations with the outside world. He must represent his institution in all formal or informal relations with the University Grants Committee ; he must be present at meeting of the Committee of Vice-Chancellors and Principals; he must keep in touch with potential benefactors, and he must be aware, in general, of developments in t e various branches of learning. No other enterprise would impose on its chairman the variety and burden of work that the modern university requires of its Vice-Chancellor.

The selection of a Vice-Chancellor or a Principal is perhaps the most important single decision that the governing body of a university may be called upon to make; and arrangements for doing so are not made easier by the fact that such a decision may arise only once in ten to twenty years".

The Committee on Model Act further stated :

"The responsibilities of a Vice-Chancellor are not less heavy in this country than in the United Kingdom or anywhere else. in certain respects the burden of a Vice-Chancellor in Indian Universities is even greater. Among other things, he is the chairman not only of the academic body which determines the courses of study but he is also chairman of the executive body. He also presides at the meetings of the court. One of the most important questions to be determined in the light of past experience is with regard to the mode of appointment of the Vice-Chancellor."

We are in general agreement with these observations.

The Vice-Chancellor is the principal executive and academic officer of the university, and should exercise general supervision and control over the affairs of the university, and give effect to the decisions of all its authorities. He shall be the ex-officio chairman of the Court, Executive Council, the Academic Council, the Finance Committee and the Selection Committee, and shall in the absence of the Chancellor, preside at any convocation of the university for conferring degrees; he shall be entitled to be present at and to address any meetings of any authority or board or committee of the university, but may not be entitled to vote there at, unless he is a member of such authority or board or committee. It shall also be the duty of the Vice-Chancellor to see that the provisions of the Act, the Statutes and Ordinances and Regulations are fully observed, and he should have the power necessary for the discharge of this duty. He shall peform such other acts as would be necessary to carry out the provisions of the Act, Statutes and Ordinances.

If in the opinion of the Vice-Chancellor an emergency has arisen which requires immediate action to be taken he shall take such action as he deems necessary, and shall report the same at the next meeting to the authority, which in the ordinary course would have dealt with the matter, provided that where any such action taken by the Vice-Chancellor affects any person in the service of the university, such person shall be entitled to prefer an appeal to the Executive Council, within the specified time from the date on which he receives notice of such action.

All powers relating to the proper maintenance of discipline in the university should be vested in the Vice-Chancellor.

In addition to the above, the Vice-Chancellor shall

exercise such other powers as may be prescribed by the Statutes, Ordinances or the Regulations.

Mode of appointment of vice-chancellor : We have given considerable thought to the mode of appointment of the Vice-Chancellor. We are of the view that the best system of appointment of the Vice-Chancellor would be for the Visitor to appoint the Vice-Chancellor from amongst a panel of names submitted to him by a committee. We feel that in the composition of this Committee the appropriate Government should, to some extent, be involved. That is why we have recommended a provision in the three patterns proposed by us for a nominee of the Visitor on the said Committee.

It has also been stressed that wherever a committee is appointed to suggest a panel of names, it should prepare the panel, arrange it in an alphabetical order and need not indicate any preference. We agree with this suggestion. If the panel is so prepared and submitted to the visitor, the visitor will be entitled to select any one of the persons nominated in the panel. In case the visitor is unable to accept any of the names included in the panel, he may call upon the committee to submit a fresh panel of names.

We considered several alternatives for constituting a committee which would recommend the panel for consideration of the Visitor for the appointment of Vice-Chancellor. We are aware that it may not be possible to have a uniform system in all the universities. We suggest the following alternatives, on the assumption that in the case of smaller universities a committee of three persons may be regarded as appropriate, whereas in the case of other universities a committee of five persons would be appropriate :

Pattern I (a) A nominee of the Visitor
(b) Two nominees of the Executive Council*

Pattern II (a) A nominee of the Visitor
(b) A nominee of the Chairman, UGC
(c) A nominee of the Executive Council*

Pattern III (a) A nominee of the Visitor.
(b) A nominee of the Chairman, UGC.
(c) Three nominees of the University, one of whom may be nominated by the Academic Council and the other two by the Executive Council. Alternatively, one to be nominated by the Executive Council and the other two by the Academic Council.*

---

*The person/persons to be nominated by the Executive Council or the university may not be employees of the university or the members of the Executive Council/Academic Council.

We also suggest that in the case of the new universities, the first Vice-Chancellor should be appointed by the Visitor. Further, this authority may be exercised by the Visitor for appointment of the Vice-Chancellor during the first five years of the life of a university.

Term of Appointment of the Vice-Chancellor : The Vice-Chancellor should hold office for a term of five years. He may be reappointed for another term in the same university.

Every effort should be made that a new Vice-Chancellor is designated before the expiry of the term of an existing Vice-Chancellor.

We recommend that in the event of a teacher of a particular university being appointed as a Vice-Cancellor of that University or any other university, provision should be made to give him leave to take up this appointment. This provision would enable experienced and youthful teachers being appointed as Vice-Chancellors of the universities, who after completing their tenure of office as Vice-Chancellor, would revert to their original teaching appointments. The leave rules should be liberalised so as to take into account the period spent as Vice-Chancellor for purposes of pension, terminal benefits, increments, leave, etc. Besides, we propose to make a similar recommendation, in a different section, in respect of teachers who may have to be granted leave for a period exceeding three years.

In regard to the question of prescribing on age limit of retirement for Vice-Chancellors, it may be observed that where the post of the Vice-Chancellor is honorary, and the Vice-Chancellor is expected and required to work voluntarily, it may not be realistic to lay down any age limit. Besides, we may add that some of the distinguished full-time salaried Vice-Chancellors who at the time of their appointment or during their tenure had crossed the age of 65 years, are known to have rendered signal service to their respective universities. Nevertheless, we think in view of the arduous duties, the office of the Vice-Chancellor should retire on completing the age of 65 years.

There should not normally be much of a difference between the salary of a Vice-Chancellor and that of a Professor The Vice-Chancellor may be paid a salary of Rs. 3,000 per month. He should be provided with a furnished house for which he would pay rent at the normal rates. For facilities to a Vice Chancellor, except those for official use, the Vice-Chancellor should pay. We recommend that a provision be made for a suitable pension to a Vice-Chancellor retiring after completing five years. The amount of the pension may be the same as for a member of the Union Public Service

Commission whose salary is analogous.

It may be provided that if the office of the Vice-Chancellor becomes vacant due to his death, resignation or otherwise, the Pro-Vice-Chancellor, or the Rector or senior-most Professor or any other person nominated by the Visitor for that purpose shall act as Vice-Chancellor, until the date on which the new Vice-Chancellor is appointed and assumes office.

Pro-Vice-chancellor : The following is quoted from the Report on "Model Act for Universities" :

"The Vice-Chancellor is concerned, inevitably with almost every part of the work of the university. This in itself is an exceedingly heavy responsibility, and it becomes still more so if the university is an affiliating one with a large number of colleges and departments and students. It sometimes happens that he is unable to attend adequately to the more important work of policy making and development because of the need to attend to routine work and administration. It is, therefore, very important that the Vice-Chancellor where necessary, is provided with a deputy, that is a Rector or a Pro-Vice-Chancellor. Ability to delegate and yet to keep a general overall control is difficult art. It is important that relief is given to the Vice-Chancellor; but the manner in which it is done sometimes creates difficulties and complications. It may happen that if the Pro-Vice-Chancellor, or Rector, or other officer intended to provide relief to the Vice-Chancellor is chosen in the same manner as the Vice-Chancellor, it may not be possible to ensure that there is between them the complete understanding that is essential if the Pro-Vice-Chancellor is a real help to the Vice-Chancellor. One of the simplest ways in which the Pro-Vice-Chancellor can be chosen is for the Executive Council to fix the salary and other conditions of service, and leave it entirely to the Vice-Chancellor to choose the Pro-Vice-Chancellor for the duration of his own term or for a shorter period if he so desires, It will work most satisfactorily if the person so chosen is one of the Professors with some flair for administration. The next Vice-Chancellor may re-appoint the same person, but if he prefers somebody else, the last Pro-Vice-Chancellor can revert to his department."

We concur with these observations. We recommend that the age of superannuation for the Pro-Vice-Chancellor, as in the case of the Vice-Chancellor, should be 65 years and he should be paid a salary of Rs. 2,500 plus the allowances admissible to the teachers of the university. Though a house may be provided for him, he would be expected to pay rent for the same, on the usual basis. No other free facility would be provided to him. In certain cases, the Executive Council may authorise the Vice-Chancellor to appoint more than one Pro-Vice-Chancellor, and the Act that Statutes should contain the necessary enabling clauses. It should also be possible for the Vice-Chancellor to appoint a Professor to discharge the duties of the Pro-Vice-Chancellor, in addition to his own duties as Professor. In such cases, the Executive Council may sanction a suitable allowance not exceeding Rs. 500 per mensem.

Deans: The Dean of the Faculty should be appointed from amongst the University-appointed Professors, by rotation, according to seniority for a period of two years. However, in Faculties where there is no University-appointed whole-time Professsor, the Dean may be appointed in accordance with the same principles, from amongst the Professors recognised by the universities. The Dean should perform his duties in addition to his normal duties as a Professor and should not be paid any additional allowance. He should preside over the meetings of the Faculty and the Committee for Advanced Study and Research, and should assist the Vice-Chancellor in his administrative duties. He should have the right to be present and to speak at any meeting of the Board or Committee in the Faculty or school, but should not have a right to vote at the meeting unless he is a member thereof. He may also perform such duties and exercise such powers as may be delegated to him by the Admission Committee, the Examination Committee or by any authority of the University. He should, however, not be saddled with too many administrative functions, since we have recommended that administrative responsibility should devolve on the departments.

It would not be desirable to treat the Dean as the executive head of Faculty or the school. Recommendations of the departments to the Executive Council or the Vice-Chancellor in administrative matters need not be routed through the Dean, but he should have sufficient power to implement the decisions of the Faculties in respect of the organisation of common teaching programme, or inter-departmental or inter-disciplinary research and teaching. In the absence of the Dean, the Vice-Chancellor may nominate the next senior-most Professor to act in his place. However, in certain cases, specially of new universities, the Vice-Chancellor may be authorised to appoint the Dean from amongst the Professors of a Faculty or School.

In the case of certain professional faculties, specially where the faculty is comprised of a single or more than one college which are not maintained by the university, the Dean may be appointed by rotation from amongst the Principals of such colleges.

Head of the department : We are not in favour of appointing the senior-most professor in the department as the Head of the Department, automatically, as a matter of course. The proper procedure that may be followed for appointment of Heads of Departments, as also the term of appointment, would need careful consideration, and may vary from university to university, depending upon the needs and the stage of development of the university. Considering the important role and functions of heads of departments, it is essential that the selection procedure inspires general confidence.

We have already recommended that the Head of the Department should perform his duties in consultation with the Departmental Committee. He should ordinarily delegate and distribute the administrative functions amongst his colleagues, both to allow himself adequate time for teaching and research, and to promote a sense of participation among the members of the Department.

We have already recommended that there may be a provision for a Professor other than the Head of the Department also to serve on the Selection Committee. It would be advisable for the Vice-Chancellor to invariably associate the Professor-in-Charge of a particular field of specialisation with the Selection Committee recommending appointments in that field.

The administration of a university should take care to ensure that the equality of all Professors and the autonomy of teachers in academic matters is respected, and that no teacher is "forced" to make certain recommendations concerning his speciality through the Head of the Department. The Vice-Chancellor may, where necessary, direct that the recommendation of the Head of the Department may be accompanied by the minutes of the Department/Departmental Committee on that matter.

Chairman of student council: The Chairman of Student Council should be appointed by the Vice-Chancellor from among the teachers and should hold office during the Vice-Chancellor's pleasure. He should be paid a suitable honorarium and be provided with such facilities as the Executive Council may determine. The Chairman should make available to the secretary of the Council adequate facilities by way of office accommodation and staff etc., to enable him to discharge the responsibilities of the office he holds.

The Chairman of the Student Council should not be burdened with the responsibility of looking after discipline, halls/hostels, welfare programme; etc. He should be readily accessible to the students, inspire confidence among them, and act as a friend, philosopher and guide. He should be kept informed of the major decisions of the University in regard to matters likely to be raised in the Student Council, and should have access to all information necessary for the discharge of his duties. He has to perform the dual role of explaining to the students the point of view of the authorities and the Vice-Chancellor, and of conveying to the Vice-Chancellor and the administration of the university the point of view or reaction of the students.

Dean of students welfare, wardens and proctor: We do not propose to go in detail regarding the appointment of Deans of Student Welfare, Proctors, and the Wardens of Halls/Hostels. We feel that there should be sufficient flexibility in these matters. However, the statutes may provide that the Dean of Students Welfare, the Proctor or the Warden shall be appointed by the Executive Council on the recommendation of Vice-Chancellor. Their term may be three years and they should be eligible for re-appointment. They should perform such duties as may be prescribed in the Ordinances or by the authorities of the University or by the Vice-Chancellor. The Executive Council may fix a suitable honorarium to be paid to them. There should also be a provision that the Dean of Students Welfare may be appointed by the Executive Council, on the recommendation of the Vice-Chancellor, on a whole-time basis. In such a case, he should draw a salary in the scale of his substantive appointment, and in addition, he may be paid a suitable allowance. But even where a Dean of Students Welfare is appointed on a whole-time basis, the period of appointment should not exceed three years at a time, and he should continue to be associated with his parent department. He may even continue to do some teaching work without detriment to the discharge of his duties as Dean of Students Welfare.

Registrar: In dealing with the position of the Registrar in relation to the administration of the university, it would be useful to refer to the pertinent observations made in the Report of the Commission on Inquiry of the Oxford University which has analysed the role of civil service in a university. The relevant part of the report is reproduced below:

"The value of an efficient civil service in a university is that it makes it possible, even with a complicated structure, to practise democratic control by academics of the policies that shape their environment".

"Officials, of the sort we are discussing, should do more than the basic secretarial duties of keeping the minutes and helping to form an agenda. They should be expected to inform and to advise in the course of the meetings they attend. But they should not vote; nor is the responsibility for decision theirs. We are also certain that some of the business which at present goes for decision to committees should not go there at all. We would think it proper for committees to decide what rules they want to have, for instance, for sabbatical leave or for the payment on non-academic staff, but we think that the decision of where a particular case fits under such schemes should not go to a Committee but should be decided by officials. In case of doubt, the official would be expected to consult the chairman of his committee, who, unless the case falls outside the rules, should decide, reporting his decision, if of sufficient importance, at the next meeting of the committee. The secretary of a committee supported by his chairman, can usually deal with most of the detail, thereby savings academics from acting as clerks; they waste less time because at their meetings they can address themselves to the important points".

"As the senior university official and head of the secretariat, the Registrar has important duties. Working under and with the Vice-Chancellor, he is his confidential adviser ; in his capacity he can exercise initiative. The Vice-Chancellor, speaking for council, told us Oral Evidence, Part 79, (p. 60) : Under the present regime most of the initiative for conducting the business and br nging it up and dealing with it at this stage comes from the Registrar. This arises from the fact that the Registrar is head of the machine which is getting it ready and bringing it up . . . . The Advisory—initiative side is very much developed, and is essential. 'He is the Secretary of Council, but he has also become its continuing adviser, expected to offer an opinion or to make a suggestion, though not to decide or vote. He has also come to be recognised as the regular adviser of people in the university holding responsible academic positions : they have come to turn to him first on their problems (Oral Evidence, Part 79, pp. 59-65)'.

The Registrar has, of course, many other duties, but it is in these ways that, to use the words of the Vice-Chancellor quoted in the preceding paragraph, he behaves as a Principal. We recommend that such behaviour should be recognised as proper to the post of the Registrar in Oxford, and should be expected of its holder. We also recommend that similar behaviour should be expected of the other officials of this unified secretariat : they should become advisers of the chairman of the committees they serve; they should exercise initiative, working with their chairman, in the preparation and conduct of business; they should act as advisers, free to speak and suggest, but not to vote, on the committees".

We wish to add with respect that this passage generally brings out the nature of the position, functions and duties of the Registrar vis-a-vis the university administration in India as much as in the United Kingdom.

While we are dealing with the Registrar, his duties and functions, we should also like to quote with approval the following passage from the report of the Committee on 'Model Act for Universities' :

"The office of the Registrar is also an important one. In many cases, universities find it difficult to secure a person of the right type to fill this office. Two areas from which Registrars can be recruited are :

(1) The university office : the most competent among the Deputy Registrars or Assistant Registrars can be chosen.

(2) The teaching staff : Occasionally special talent for administration and organisation is discovered in some one of the status of a Reader, who could in course of time become a Professor. But all things considered it would perhaps not be a loss to academic life if he is taken away from the department and asked to become a Registrar.

The Registrar represents the permanent part of the university executive. Vice-Chancellors hold office for a limited period in the best of circumstances, even if legislation does not impose a maximum limit to the tenure of a Vice-Chancellor. The Registrar is therefore the custodian of the traditions of the university, of its efficiency and integrity. It is also necessary that his entire loyalty should be to the university. Sometimes conflicts arise between the Registrar and one or other of the teachers or all of them together. The Registrar must, therefore, exercise his powers with discretion and understanding. His practices should always be responsive to the academic traditions of the university he serves. The Registrar should be appointed by the Executive Council. The terms and conditions of service should be clearly determined by Statutes. It is not likely to do universities much good, if officers are borrowed from outside the universities to serve for a limited period, as such an arrangement has all the disadvantages of an interim arrangement. In exceptional situations, however, in order to rectify serious errors or corruption into which a university may have fallen, it will certainly be in order, as a temporary measure, to secure the services, on deputation, of an outstanding administrative officer."

We agree with the view taken by the committee on 'Model Act for Universities' and reccommend that the Registrar should be the secretary of the different authorities, and not a member of any of them, except where deemed necessary and advisable. Even if the Registrar is not a member of any of the statutory bodies of the university, he will be entitled to participate in the debates of the said bodies if authorised by the Vice-Cnancellor or the Chairman of the authority or the Committee.

In regard to the question as to whether the Registrar should be an ex-officio member of the Court/Senate, we wish to make some observations. The Vice-Chancellor presides at the meetings of the Court/Senate and as such functions as the Chairman of the meetings. If any points are made against the administration at the meetings of the Court/Senate, the Vice-Chancellor does not and is not ordinarily expected to answer them. Answers to the points made against the administration of the university will, therefore, have to be given either by the members of the Executive Council/Syndicate or on many occasions by the Registrar himself, who always acts as the permanent secretary of the authorities and bodies of the university. This aspect of the matter will assume greater significance in future when we take into account the recommendations we have made in regard to the composition of the Court/Senate. According to the scheme recommended by us for the composition of the Court/Senate, representatives of the general public would take a larger share in the deliberations of the Court/Senate, and may legitimately be expected to raise questions pertaining to the administration of the university, which they would feel are important from the point of view of the general community. In such a case it would, we think on the whole, be desirable to recommend that the Registrar should be an ex-officio member of the Court/Senate.

Treasurer/Finance officer : The following is quoted from the Report of the Committee on 'Model Act for Universities':

"The Committee is of the view that with the expansion of university work and activities, honorary (or paid) Treasurers independently elected by the Court or the Executive Council is not in general a satisfactory arrangement. The Committee recommends that the Treasurer or Finance Officer should be whole-time salaried officer appointed by the Executive Council specially charged with the responsibility of looking after the finances of the university. The officer should be designated as Finance Officer rather than Treasurer. It would be his duty to attend to proper investment of the university's funds, watch the expenditure, and to deal generally with matters connected with the finances of the university. He should not operate as a brake or as an instrument for delaying progress. This, however, should not be understood to mean that the importance of keeping correct accounts and following the budgetary laws is under-estimated."

We endorse the above recommendation. In some of the universities, the Finance Officer and the Registrar have the same status, and are in the same scale of pay, and the Finance Officer is responsible directly to the Pro-Vice-Chancellor/Vice-Chancellor. We do not propose to recommend any fixed pattern for the working of these two officers i.e. the Registrar and the Finance Officer, as we feel that each university may have to determine its own procedure, keeping in view the stage of development of the university, the work-load on the Registrar and the Finance Officer, and the tradition of the university. It may be left open to the university to decide whether the Finance Officer should work under the Vice-Chancellor through the Registrar or should work directly under the Vice-Chancellor.

Student Participation

One of the important terms of reference of this Committee relates to the questions of the participation of students in the administration of the university, both in academic and non-academic matters. We have earlier stated that, in our view, the participation of students in the academic life and affairs of the university is an essential part of the functioning of a university, and the concept of university autonomy has been discussed in a previous chapter. We believe that this participation would be of vital importance if the universities are to play a major role in national development. Student participation is not a static concept. It is an evolving concept and is intimately related to the progress of universities, improvement of academic standards and university reform generally. Whereas every university in our view should make a constructive and deliberate effort to promote student participation, the level of effectiveness and intensity of such participation would obviously depend on a variety of factors, specially the stage of development of the university and tone of its academic life. In other words, it is an academic concept, and is based on the assumption that the process of learning in the university is a joint adventure or quest of the teachers and students, a partnership in the acquisition of knowledge, and as such, it is not a unilateral process in which the teachers teach or instruct, and the students learn or receive knowledge. Considered purely as an academic concept, the participation of students in the academic life of the university involves a continuous dialogue between the teachers and the taught. It is a serious inadequacy in our university system today that in respect of matters pertaining to education or instruction, the system does not seem to provide a channel of communication, either formal or informal, between the teachers and the students, or between the administrative wing of the university and the students. Absence of such communication creates a feeling in the mind of the students that they do not have any share in the management of the affairs of the university. They do not, therefore, develop a sense of belonging to it, which is very essential for the successful working of the university.

The process of learning and the training of the student's mind involves his active participation, rather than passive assimilation. Similarly, his participation should be sought in matters relating to the organisation of learning and in academic administration. Such participation would create among the students a greater sense of responsibility, help in developing their personality, enable teachers to benefit from the fresh ideas of the youth and also serve to make the educational system responsive to the urges and challenges of the society.

Throughout the world young people, specially university, students, are feeling restive. The unrest in Indian Universities is a part of this world-wide phenomenon, although in many important respects, the nature of this unrest differs from that in the western, particularly affluent, countries. We, however, do not propose to discuss the nature of the student movement outside India. In our country the origin of the present day unrest is to be found partly in the social and political factors outside the academic system, and partly in the situation prevailing within the universities.

Broadly speaking, the student movement acquires political overtones when it is motivated by a dissatisfaction with the established order. Occasionally, it leads to a desire to destroy the existing social order and to create a new one in its place. This dissatisfaction with the entire establishment is negative and nihilistic in character. It seeks to destroy without determining what new social order has to be constructed and how. We do not propose to deal with this trend in our report We however, must refer to other factors which are relevant for our discussion.

In our country, the main problem facing an overwhelming majority of students is the desire that their social status be raised as quickly as possible. Their parents had been denied the benefits of higher education, and had to live a life of backwardness with hardly any hope of betterment. They are now anxious that their children should derive the maximum benefit from university education. Since the higher rungs of the social ladder appear to be reserved almost entirely for the highly educated, there is a wide-spread desire among the masses, and specially among the weaker sections, to receive higher education. The attempt of some universities to restrict admission only on the basis of merit or academic achievement does not appeal to the backward sections of society, who consider such criteria to be weighted against them. No attempt to curb the expansion of higher education is, therefore, likely to be successful under the circumstances.

Although higher education has in fact, been expanding at a rate of about 13 per cent per annum, the per capita expenditure on education, in terms of constant prices, has actually declined. Consequently, schemes of academic reform have been thwarted, and this has adversely affected the student community. The pupil-teacher ratio has become unsatisfactory, resulting in a lack of contact between the teachers and students in and/outside the universities. For the same reason, various schemes of academic reorganisation have not been implemented. Students cannot be blamed for falling standards when laboratory and library facilities are inadequate and buildings unsuitable. The condition in which students live and work are in most cases very unsatisfactory. There are neither enough scholarships nor hostels, nor opportunities to develop a healthy personality, and to spend leasure time gainfully.

Financial allocations made at the Centre and in the States show that higher education has not been given the high priority it deserves. Critics of the university system may be justified in referring to the failure of the universities to meet the challenge of the time, and to satisfy the requirements and expectations of the community at large, but it should not be forgotten that proper development and restructuring of university education on modern lines involves large expenditure. Lack of adequate financial resources is an insuperable difficulty. We wish to emphasise this aspect of the matter because it is of vital importance.

Dissatisfaction has become particularly acute among students because of unemployment among the educated youth, particularly the growing unemployment of the technically trained personnel. The present system of education appears to lack any concrete aim or purpose, and to be a mere ritual devoid of inner strength and reality.

The ivory-tower concept of universities is now widely questioned. Many teachers and students wants education to be more closely related to the problems of life and society. There is, hence, a demand for a change in the syllabus, the structure of courses, the system of examinations, and methods of teaching.

The universities have not always done their best to improve academic standards, and the system of instruction and examination, even within the resources available to them. This is specially to be seen in respect of out-moded and old-fashioned syllabuses or courses which do not appeal to the students. These courses are neither satisfactory in developing the intellect of the student, nor in equipping him for the needs of society.

The dissatisfaction of the students with society in general, and with the existing academic opportunities in particular, can easily be exploited by interested faction leaders within the academic community, as well as those without, and this leads to the eruption of agitations based on regional, linguistic or communal demands.

Unfortunately, in our country there is a section of society which has, it seems, come to believe, that no grievance, however justified or legitimate, receives proper consideration or redress, unless it is enforced by aggressive pressure, militant agitation or even violence. The students being the most impressionable part of the community, quite frequently, adopt this view. Consequently, the resentment and frustration of students occasionally lead to unfortunate cases of violence and destruction of property. This is another aspect of the matter which we cannot ignore.

Sometimes a disturbing feature of student agitation witnessed on some university campuses has been a demand made by representatives of students, and at times even by large groups of students, which could not conceivably be regarded as academically desirable or sound and, which if conceded, would irrevocably jeopardise the educational standards. In making this observation, we have in mind demands such as those for lowering the percentage of pass marks or cancellation of question papers on the ground that some of the questions were "unexpected". We hope that this is merely a passing phase. We may again emphasize, that our approach to the question of the participation of students in university administration, is based on the assumption that the students desire such participation; with the object of making education received by them richer, deeper, more meaningful and significant; in other words, the students desire for participation is founded on academic and not political considerations.

While these general factors are extremely important it cannot be disputed that in most universities and colleges there is no machinery for continuous exchange of ideas between the students and teachers, and between students or teachers and the authorities. As a result, dissatisfaction unnecessarily mounts up where the cause of irrigation can easily be removed, and misunderstanding persists though in some cases the removal of alleged grievances is beyond the competence of the academic authorities. This is specially so in cases where the case of student unrest lies outside the campus.

It is our considered opinion that in addition to a constant dialogue between teacher and students in respect of all aspects of university activity, an institutional machinery for consultation of student opinion and ensuring student participation should be established in each university.

While examining the question of the participation of the student in the administration of universities and colleges, the following aspects deserve careful consideration :

(a) What should be the level of participation? Should it be advisory and consultative, or decisive? Should students be full members of the authorities of the university?

(b) On what aspects of administration should there be participation at the various levels mentioned in (a) above?

(c) What should be the nature of student representation (faculty-wise, college-wise, nominated or elected, role of Student Union, etc.)?

Student should have the opportunity to play a leading role in the organisation of corporate life, extra and co-curricular activities. The teachers may guide and advise them in such matters, but the decision-making should, as far as possible, be the responsibility of students. The head of the institution should have, in all such cases, emergency powers to over-ride the decision of the students; but obviously these powers should be exercised, if at all, only for compelling reasons, and the action should later be reported to the appropriate university bodies.

The students should also be encouraged to give their thought to important academic questions like the structure of courses, the content of syllabus, pattern of instruction, and of examination. Through a suitable machinery of consultation, they should also be made aware of the broad administrative problems facing the university, including its budget and finances, by giving them representation in the court. If the students are given the opportunity to discuss with their teachers these important academic and administrative matters, they would understand and appreciate better how a university functions. It is in the interest of the universities as well as of the nation that tomorrow's leaders should adequately understand the problems of the management of universities.

The nature of student representation would naturally depend upon the aspects of university activity in which student participation is to be provided. For example, if questions concerning matters which are essentially within the purview of a faculty are to be discussed, there should be a Faculty Committee. Similarly, for hostel affairs or college affairs, Hostel or College Committees should be set up. When matters concerning the entire university are to be considered, there should be representatives of the various student bodies of the university as well as some representatives of the university Students Union on the committee concerned. We are of the view that to secure the maximum participation of the best students, there should be a blending of the principle of direct election, and of indirect election and election through various sports and cultural organisations of students, as well as nomination of some students by the head of the institution on the basis of outstanding performance.

We recommend the principle of decentralisation of authority in all spheres of university activity. It is, therefore, logical that all matters of interest to the students should not be dealt with only at one level, as for example solely by the representatives of the Students Union. At the same time, we wish to encourage the Students' union to play a responsible role in the life of the academic community.

Court : We have already recommended an effective participation of students in the Court. The token representation of students which has sometimes been suggested is, in our opinion, hardly desirable, nor is it in the circumstances of today, appropriate. Unless the student representatives feel that they can put forward their point of view effectively, they will not get a real sense of participation. As members of the Court, they will have the opportunity to express their views on all aspects of university activity. Their voice will also carry a great deal of weight in electing the members of the Executive Council from the Court, because under the system of proportional representation, 10 to 15 per cent student members of the Court can, under certain circumstances, play a decisive part in such election.

Executive Council and Academic Council: We have considered carefully the suggestion made by the Education Commission (1964-66) regarding the participation of students in the Academic Council. On the other hand, we have also given due weight to the view, nearly unanimous, expressed by the Members of Parliament, teachers and student representatives whom we met, that at present it would not be desirable to give students any representation on the Executive Council.

The Executive Council's functions include inter alia, the appointment of teachers and examiners according to the procedure prescribed, and we are inclined to take the view that it would be wiser to take the first step in a fairly big way, watch how it works, and then take the other steps in the same direction, so as to reach ultimately the ideal of full participation of students in the university administration.

We also feel that at the present moment no useful purpose would be served by giving representation to the students on the Academic Council. Instead, we have recommended the setting up of a Student Council which would enable the students to make their recommendations to the Executive and the Academic Councils. Their suggestions, we are confident, will be given due consideration by the Executive and the Academic Councils.

Faculty and department: We have recommended elsewhere that the time has come for greater decentralisation of academic authority in every university. We have, therefore, recommended that more power be vested in Faculties. This would mean that the Faculties would be the decision-making authority in many vital spheres, such as courses of study, and recommendatory authority in respect of the appointment of examiners, and the creation and abolition of teaching posts, etc. Similarly, we have recommended that Departments/Boards of Studies/Departmental Committees should have the power to initiate particularly all academic proposals. It would not be desirable in the interest of maintaining academic standards to give representation to students on the Faculties or on Departments/Boards of Studies/Departmental Committees. But we feel that it would be necessary to provide for the establishment of Student Advisory Committees in the Faculties, and for joint Teacher-Student Committees in the Departments.

Student advisory committee of faculties: We recommend that there should be a Student Advisory Committee for each Faculty. It should have the right to express its views on important academic questions like the structure of courses, the content of syllabus pattern of instruction and of examinations, and should also have the power to voice the grievances of the students and to make suggestions for the better working of the Faculty. Not less than two ordinary meetings of the Committee may be held in each academic year, and there should be a provision for meetings requisitioned by the student members of the Committee.

The Student Advisory Committee of the Faculty should be established by an Ordinance of the University. We recommend that its composition may be as follows:

(a) The Dean of the Faculty... ... Chairman

(b) The Head of each Department of Study in the faculty or a teacher nominated by him.

(c) One student to be elected by the postgraduate and research students of each department.

(d) Not more than half the number of students mentioned in (c) above, to be nominated by the Dean from among the academically outstanding students.

The Secretary of the Committee may be elected by its student members from among themselves.

In the case of the universities where postgraduate education is also provided in colleges admitted to the privileges of the university, provision may be made to associate some of the students from the colleges.

The primary academic unit of the university, be it a Department or a Centre of Study, should ensure that there is a continuous exchange of ideas between its students and teachers including the Head of the Department or the Centre. We have, therefore, recommended the desirability of setting up Joint Teacher-Student Committees of Departments.

While we recommend close and frequent consultation between teachers and students at all levels, we are not in favour of students being members of any of the academic bodies. The reason for this comparatively restricted role of students in academic decision-making, as distinct from consultation, is the urgent need to modernise and upgrade courses of instruction, and to bring them into line with the developments in the most advanced countries. Unfortunately, even postgraduate students are not yet fully aware of the major changes taking place in universities outside India ; nor are they fully conversant with the academic needs and requirements of the country.

Halls of residence/hostel committee : In every Hall of Residence/Hostel, Students Advisory Committees should be set up to aid and advise the authorities of the universities in the management of the Hall/Hostel including mess, the maintenance of discipline, and organisation of extra-curricular and corporate activities.

Organisation for co-curricular and extra-curricular activities : We recommend that every university should ordinarily establish three committees—one for games, another for social service, and the third for cultural activities. Each of these committees should comprise representatives of clubs or societies devoted to different activities, and these should be established in accordance with the principle of student self-government. Teachers may be associated to guide or advise, but should not ordinarily exercise any authority. However, the Head of the Institution may himself or through a teacher nominated by him exercise the power to over-see the financial affairs of these committees, and should also have the power to override decision in an emergency. All these clubs and committees should be represented on the Executive Committee/General Council of the Students' Union.

Student welfare : We recommend, with all the emphasis we can command, that resources be placed at the disposal of the universities and colleges to provide basic amenities to the students ; these should include adequate provision for hostels, day-students homes, adequate library seats, text-books libraries and book banks, scholarships and fee concessions, provision of cheap but wholesome meals, play-grounds, and accommodation for taking up corporate activities etc.

In addition to these physical facilities it would be desirable to entrust every teacher with the responsibility of looking after about 20 students (the present national average of pupil-teacher ratio is about 20 :1), These teachers should try to win the confidence of their students, give them advice and guidance, help to solve their difficulties to the extent possible, and remain in close touch with them. It would be desirable for each teacher to meet each of these students at least once a month, Where the number of teachers is small the services of senior students may be utilised for the purpose.

Teachers should also be persuaded to devote some of their time to act as advisers in the various corporate activities of the students mentioned above.

It is extremely important that teachers put in charge of hostels should get to know each of their wards personally. Therefore, we are of the view that the number in each hostel should not preferably exceed 50 to 70,

Similarly, some teachers should be entrusted with the responsibility of assisting in the organisation of corporate activities of non-resident students.

The activities of the various teachers looking after the welfare of the students should be suitably coordinated, and the Principal/Vice-Chancellor should give his special attention to the establishment of a suitable organisational machinery for this purpose.

Student Union : We are broadly in agreement with the recommendations of Education Commission (1964-66) regarding student Unions. The Education Commission had recommended as follows :

"Student unions represent an important way of providing student participation in university life outside the classroom. Properly organised, they help in self-government and self-discipline, provide a healthy outlet for students' energies and give the students useful training in the use of democratic methods.

It is for each university to decide how its students' union will function and would welcome a good deal of experimentation. But some broad principles can be indicated.

(1) Membership of the students' unions should be automatic in the sense that every student should be presumed to be its member. But every student should be expected to choose at least one activity organised in the institution, e.g., arts society, football club, drama association, etc., and pay the required subscription. There should be no separate payment for the membership of the Students' Union as such. Each of the activities will thus have funds of its own and these would be handled by appropriate committees. The funds of the central union—to the extent they are needed—would be formed by contributions from each activity committee. The University or College should also give aid to the central union as well as to the different activities.

(2) It may be desirable to elect the office-bearers, not directly by the large body of students (many of whom are freshmen), but indirectly by the different students' societies in the university who would send selected representatives to the union executives.

(3) There should be some disqualification for office-bearers. For instance, persons who have spent two or more years in the same class should be disqualified.

(4) The successful working of student unions depends to a large extent upon the mutual trust and confidence between the teachers and the students. Greater teacher involvement in union activities should, therefore, be ensured. We would strongly commend the establishment of a university or college union in which all teachers and students automatically become members. All committees of the union and various activity groups

should have teachers on them and it should be their responsibility to guide the students tactfully on right lines without curbing their freedom to decide for themselves."

We feel that each university should continue to have a union, the membership of which should be automatic, for every student.

The number of students in every university is so large that direct democracy can hardly be effective, and hence, as has been stated by another committee, caste, regional, communal and other undemocratic factors seem to exercise an undue influence. We are, therefore of the opinion that the ultimate power of the university union should be vested in a General Council (or a Parliament of the students in a particular university prefer this form). Such a council may consist of about 100 members. About three-fourths of the total membership of the Central Council may comprise of elected representatives of departmental societies and/or elected representatives of faculties and/or colleges. We do not suggest any rigid or uniform pattern because this will differ according to the type of each university.

One-quarter of the membershiy of the General Council should consist of representatives of Games Committee, Committee for Cultural Activities and Social Service Committee, etc.

The General Council may elect the office bearers and the executive committee.

The University may either fix lumpsum as Union fee which may then be distributed among different clubs and departmental societies in consultation with the students, or there may be no Union fee as such but a club or society fee of which a share may be paid to the Union for its activities,

It should be the duty of the university to arrange for the auditing of the accounts of the Union and other students societies, whose funds are collected through the university every year. Where there has been a misappropriation or misuse of funds, it should be the duty of the university to take suitable action in order to protect the rights of its students.

We feel that the condition recommended by us for a student to be a member of the Court may also be prescribed for a student to be member of the General Council of the student union or its office-bearer.

Miscellaneous

Autonomous Colleges/Departments : The Education Commission (1964-66) has stressed the importance of setting up autonomous colleges. The University Grants Commission has also given considerable thought to this question, and has encouraged the idea of initiating this experiment in some selected colleges, It has, however, not been possible to make any headway in the matter, as in the legislative enactments governing most of the universities no provision has been made to provide for autonomous colleges.

We recommend that in the Acts which may be drafted hereafter, not only a provision for autonomous colleges should be made, but provision may also be made to give certain autonomy to the teaching departments or the units of the departments, in particular the Centres of Advanced Study. We recommend that in the Acts of the Universities, the following provision as already exists in the Himachal Pradesh University Act may be made :

"The University may grant, in the manner and after following the procedure prescribed in the relevant statutes, to a college, department or unit, which satisfies the conditions laid down in the said Statutes in this behalf, the privileges of modifying or changing for its students the courses of study prescribed by the university and of holding examination in the course so modified and such college, department or unit shall be declared in the manner prescribed in the statutes to be an Autonomous College.

"The extent to which the courses may be varied and the manner of holding examinations conducted by such college or department as the case may be shall be determined in each case by the University."

Grants committees in the states : The Education Commission (1964-66) had observed in its report as follows :

"The Model Act Committee raised the question of University Grants Commission or committees being set up by the State Governments for universities within a State, but made no specific recommendation. The Standing Committee of the I.U.B. was strongly against the establishment of such committees in the State holding that if the State Government required any advice, it should consult the UGC. We agree with this view. In giving grants to universities, the question of finance and standards, and collaboration between universities outside a given State, are all intimately linked. It may lead to confusion if the responsibility for coordinations standards was distributed amongst a number of bodies such as the Central UGC and the State UGCs. It would also hinder the existing direct relationship between the UGC and the universities."

We concur with the observations of the Education Commission. We would, however, suggest that each State should have a Coordinating Committee of the Vice-Chancellors of the Universities in the State to discuss problems of mutual interest. The Committee should be of an advisory nature, and not an additional authority in the hierarchy for the development of the universities.

Collegiate education committee : In some States where the number of colleges is large and where these colleges are affiliated to a number of universities, it may be useful to have a Collegiate Education Committee to advise the State Government on all policy matters affecting the colleges. This would enable the State Government to take long-term decisions on the development of collegiate education, and to decide on matters related to different disciplines taught in different colleges, at widely different levels. It would also enable the Governments to maintain a reasonable continuity of policy in regard to collegiate education. Such a committee might consist of Vice-Chancellors of the universities in the State, Director of Education, the Secretaries of the Education and Finance Departments of a State, and a few eminent educationists. The State Government could, perhaps, request the Chairman of the University Grants Commission to nominate a representative to serve on such a committee.

Annual Report : We recommend that a provision may be made in the Acts of the Universities requiring that the annual report of the university shall be prepared under the direction of the Executive Council, and it shall be submitted to the Court on or before such date as may be prescribed by the statutes, and this report would be considered by the Court at its annual meeting. As recommended earlier, the Court may only communicate its comments thereon to the Executive Council.

Audited Accounts : In the case of the central universities, the accounts of the universities are audited at regular intervals by the Accountant General concerned or a person authorised by the Comptroller and Auditor General. In some of the State Universities, the accounts are audited by the Examiner, Local Fund, and in others by the Accountant General and in few cases by Chartered Accountants.

We recommend that the Acts of the Universities may provide for the audit of the accounts of the universities at regular intervals, but the agency or the person who may audit their accounts may be left to be determined by the appropriate Government. The audited accounts along with the Audit Report should be submitted to the Court/Senate, with the observations of the Executive Council thereon, and a copy sent to the Visitor. Any observation of the Visitor, should also be brought to the notice of the Court. Similarly, the observation of the Court, after being considered by the Executive Council, should be communicated to the visitor.

Delegation of powers : We recommend that for an efficient working of the universities, it is desirable that the provision for delegation of powers should not only be made in the case of the Vice-Chancellor, Pro-Vice-Chancellor/Rector, Registrar or other administrative officers of the university, but it should include delegation of powers to the teaching departments. Our intention in making this recommendation is that not only should the relevant powers be delegated to the heads of the departments, but the heads of the departments in turn should further delegate such powers as are appropriate to their colleagues in the departments, so that they are able to assist the head in the administration of the department. It should, however, be understood that the delegation of powers does not result in a divorce between powers and responsibilities, and that both go together.

Administrative/Financial Procedure : In the universities at present the heads of the departments and other academic persons have to undertake considerable work relating to administration and finance of the department concerned. We are of the view that there is need to relieve the academic staff of as much administrative/financial routine as possible, without creating a bureaucratic machinery. We have not gone into the details of this question but we recommend that the UGC may set up a committee to study in depth this matter as well as the staffing pattern for administration of the departments and the faculties ; relationship of the heads of departments and deans with the administrative staff, and the administrative and financial procedures and rules.

STUDY GROUP ON ROAD SAFETY, 1969—REPORT

Delhi, Manager of Publications, 1973, 272p.

Chairman : Prof. K. T. Merchant (Resigned, replaced by Shri Tulsidas Jadhav).

Members : Shri Himatlal V. Gandhi; Shri B. N. Lahiri; Shri Indrakant Patel; Shri Dilip K. Sen; Dr. N. S. Srinivasan; Shri C. L. N. Iyengar.

Deputy Secretary : Shri Inder Jit Murgai.

Honorary Secretary : Shri K. G. Subramanian.

APPOINTMENT

The ever increasing number of road accidents in the country in recent years, has posed the need for appropriate remedial measures being taken for promoting safety on the roads. In order that the problem might be examined in detail, and suitable remedial measures chalked out, the Government of India, in the Ministry of Shipping and Transport, by their Resolution No. 19-T(14)/68 dated 3rd June, 1969 appointed for this purpose a Study Group with headquarters in Bombay.

TERMS OF REFERENCE

(a) to enquire into the incidence of road accidents in urban areas and on highways in India, ascertain the causes of such accidents and suggest a suitable organisational set-up for collection and analysis of data/ statistics relating to such road accidents;

(b) to suggest measures for education of road users in road safety and better enforcement of traffic laws and regulations and recommend improvements in roads as may be necessary to ensure the maximum possible safety on roads, and

(c) to suggest such other measures as may be germane to (a) and (b) above.

CONTENTS

Introduction; A Review of the Road Safety Problem; Causative Factors in Highway Accidents; Role of Different Agencies in Highway Safety; Accident Records, their collection and Analysis Suggested Remedial Measures; Road Accidents in Hill Areas; Summary of Conclusions and Recommendations; Annexures 1 to 16.

RECOMMENDATIONS

Causative Factors In Highway Accidents

In order that oncoming vehicles are not handicapped by the dazzle of headlights, it should be obligatory that as the two vehicles approach from opposite directions, the main beam is switched off and dipper used instead to enable them to pass each other in safety.

Driving licences should not be renewed automatically. After a certain age, the applicants should be subjected to tests regarding their vision, reaction time, colour blindness and hearing. Only on passing these, their licences should be renewed.

The hours of work prescribed by law applicable to drivers of commercial vehicles are seldom observed or enforced. The rules in this connection should be respected both by the person in charge of the vehicle as well as by its owner. The authorities, on their part, should see to it that the relevant provisions are strictly enforced.

Overspeeding by commercial transport vehicles for any reason whatsoever should not be condoned; on the contrary, it should be put down with a stern hand.

The manufacturers of motor vehicles should be required to equip their vehicles with safety fittings like seat belts, collapsible steering columns, padded dash boards without any protruding knobs, wing mirrors and safety glass wind shields. They should improve the quality of the vehicles which should conform to accepted standards in countries where the industry is highly developed. The accessories and fittings used should be of high class material to give a reasonably long life and good performance.

Adequate facilities for repair and maintenance of motor vehicles should be available to ensure their roadworthiness.

A significant reduction in the severity and frequency of road accidents can be effected only if the roads and regulations for their use are made to fit in with the traffic conditions and the known patterns of human behaviour. The other requirements are a detailed analysis of every accident to establish its causative factors followed up by a collective analysis for improvement of design standards, maintenance practices, traffic regulations and control, besides correction of local conditions.

The geometric design standards of the Indian Roads Congress would require to be enlarged to account for traffic types and volumes as determinants for varying the standards for different classes of roads. Since the up-grading of the roads to these design standards fully, would take a long time at the current rate of spending, there is also a case for developing tolerable standards for meeting the immediate needs of traffic. In this connection, the accident data for different roads should also be one of the considerations.

The minimum requirement for safe operation of traffic along the main rural highways is a paved width of 7 metres for two lanes. Since a very large length of these roads is still of a single lane width of 3.5 m and sometimes even less, it is very necessary in such cases that the condition of the shoulders should be improved to make them firm so that even during the rainy weather, vehicles which have to use them may do so safely. Such firm shoulders should be of a minimum width of 1 m on either side.

In the case of roads with paved widths widened in stages to non-standard widths of 5-6 m, a centre line marking should be provided to keep the opposing directions of traffic to their proper side.

Wherever isolated short curves exist along main highways without limited sight distances, realignment of the road to avoid them should be taken up. Where this is not possible, speed restrictions should be imposed and such locations should be marked with over-sized warning signs well ahead of them. They should also have central line markings preferably with a reflecting type of markers.

For road junctions along rural roads, particularly those occurring at long intervals, measures should be taken to maintain proper sight distances, if necessary by flaring the width of the side-roads and clearing off all sight obstructions. In addition, proper warning signs should be posted on both the main and the side roads. Where there is heavy night traffic, the junction should be either illuminated or have blinkers.

Locations along main road surface is likely to be slippery either through wear or other causes would be identified and adequate warning signs posted ahead with a recommended safe speed.

Under the existing conditions, a liberal use of road signs is the easiest way to encourage safe road use. Such signs should be made uniform throughout the country by adopting those standardized by the Indian Roads Congress. These signs being symbolic are easily understood. Wide publicity should be given to these signs to improve their effectiveness.

Rural highways on their approach to urban areas, should be widened up to a reasonable length to permit of segregation of different types of traffic including pedestrians. Such approaches should also be provided with street lighting.

All unmanned railway level-crossings should be provided with gates and manned. Where the number of trains at such crossing is more than 12 per day or where the road traffic exceeds 500 vehicles per day, either over or under-bridges should be provided. Where rail crossings cannot be seen from a reasonable distance, warning signs should be provided well ahead of them. The road surface at such crossings should be kept in good condition.

Where narrow bridges occur, advance warning signs should be prominently located and the ends of the parapets should be painted preferably with reflectorised paint for good visibility at night.

Since the presence of stray cattle or cattle herds being driven along main rural highways constitute a serious hazard to fast moving traffic, measures, should be taken where accidents from this cause are frequent, to keep them away from the main road. Where the need for leading large herds is essential, separate tracks should be provided on the roadsides for them.

For maximum utilisation of urban road space, the roadway surface should be properly paved from kerb to kerb and lane markings provided for guidance of slow and fast moving traffic. Strict enforcement should be combined with the above to ensure segregation of mixed traffic. Where found impracticable, measures should be taken to restrict the use of the road to fast moving traffic in peak hours and for the gradual elimination of slow moving traffic.

Footpaths should be freed of all encroachments and provided with a good surface to encourage their use by pedestrians and prevent them from straying on to the road. They should be of adequate widths to meet pedestrian demands and should not be cut into for widening of the roadway indiscriminately. The illumination of the road should also cover the entire footpath.

Pedestrian crossings should be properly located and marked, and regularly spaced to encourage their voluntary use. On minor streets also such pedestrian crossings should be better illuminated than the rest of the road.

Under the conditions of high volumes of mixed traffic separate routes for different types of traffic, restricted time regulations, and diversion of obsolete forms of transport to mofussil areas have all to be resorted to, to reduce accident hazards and provide for efficient movement.

Standards should be formulated by the Indian Standards Institution for the road traffic signals, their location and operation, their components, their degree of illumination as well as for the types and sizes of their reflectors. Signal heads of turning arrows should not be avoided, from considerations of cost. Where the turning movements are heavy these have to be regulated by these turning arrows.

Parking along main roads in urban areas should

be regulated by proper markings, time restrictions, and use of parking meters. Where parking leads to undue congestion of moving traffic, it should be prohibited and recourse should be had to off-street parking either in separate lots or multistoreyed garages. The location of these facilities should provide for easy access to them from the main road. They should also be within reasonable walking distance of the destinations of the users thereof.

Bus stops and loading and unloading zones should be so located along urban roads as not to interfere unduly with traffic movement. Wherever possible, suitable lay-byes should be created by the roadside for them. Appropriate regulations to restrict the use of loading and unloading zones to accommodate peak hour traffic should also be enforced.

Big traffic generators like cinemas, theatres, supermarkets etc. should not be authorised along roads without prior investigation of the possibility of satisfactory traffic movement on the adjoining road system following their construction. A feasibility study of traffic factors should precede the preparation of such projects.

In single lane rural roads carrying large volumes of traffic in opposing direction, till such time as their widening is taken up, passing zones of 30 to 40 m length by widening them to two lanes should be created at intervals of every 500 m or so, so that most of the drivers use such widened areas for crossing and overtaking.

Roadside trees and other vertical obstructions should be gradually removed over widths of 10 m from the pavement edge along heavily trafficked sections of national and state highways and substituted by plantings beyond the above widths. In addition, the slopes of the embankment should be eased to 1 in 6 or more to act as a recovery area for vehicles straying off the carriageway. Like the roadside trees, utility poles, sign posts and milestones should also be kept away from the road by similar clearances. Construction equipment, storage of road construction material, etc. have also got to be avoided over hazard areas and removed to the roadsides beyond 10 m.

An Indian standard for kerbs should be developed so that those of proper sizes and shapes are used at the required places. For good night visibility they should be properly painted or made of the reflecting type.

Channelising islands should be designed by qualified traffic engineers to reduce the area of conflict at intersections. Where, in public interest, large traffic islands are used for other purposes, warning signs for them should be put up on the approach streets. Experimental arrangement should also be made with portable lightweight kerbs so that they reflect correctly the efficiency of the final arrangement.

Medians should be as wide as possible. They should not be used for very narrow roads. Where narrow medians are used, the lengths of gaps should be such as to permit the turning vehicles to stop in them without conflict with through movement.

Role of Different Agencies in Highway Safety

The Police personnel investigating accidents should be fully trained and adequately equipped for an analysis of their causes. The traffic police should keep a continuous record of accidents and mark their locations on a map to identify the black spots and take suitable remedial measures. Their final report in any particular case should mention in sufficient detail all contributory causes such as the condition of the road or of the vehicle or of the driver responsible for the accident.

It is necessary for all States to emphasize the Highway Safety aspect of police work by providing adequate personnel for it, apart from improving the quality of their training, equipping them suitably for better mobility and providing them with more sophisticated instruments for the detection of speeding etc. Their working with reference to road safety should be reorganised to make it more thorough and expeditious. They should have sustained road safety programmes with adequate financial support.

Inspectors General of police in their fortnightly crime reports to their respective State Governments should include a paragraph on road accidents and the measures taken to combat them. There should be a similar mention made by Chief Engineers of Public Works Department, in their periodic reports to State Governments.

Through a more rigorous system of inspection of all motor vehicles and driver licensing procedure, the Motor Vehicles Department must ensure a traffic condition in which accidents arising from defective vehicles and the faults of drivers are minimised.

Road construction and maintenance agencies should initiate special programmes for eliminating the causes of road accidents. They should make a proper investigation of the flow of traffic and the incidence of road accidents with a view to suitable preventive measures being taken.

Since a vast number of variables covering all the fields of planning, designing, construction and maintenance of highways enter into the picture of highway safety, highway engineers should be put through a special course of training to enable them to identify such factors and make the highways more safe for traffic.

In large metropolitan areas, where the problem of

increasing the available road space is beset with difficulties, effective traffic engineering remedies are required to supplement the enforcement measures for ensuring a reasonable amount of traffic safety. These engineering facilities should be provided in all cities having a population of over 1,00,000. Besides discharging their responsibility for the construction and maintenance of roads our municipalities and corporations should control the unlawful activities of pedlars, hawkers and others who indulge in the wrongful use of road space and its adjoining lands.

The economic loss to the community due to traffic accidents should be evaluated properly and brought into a correct perspective if the influence of vested interest who pressurize the public authorities into allowing the misuses of road space is to be checked.

Since much of the character of traffic on the highways is influenced by the types of land use, the Town Planning Department should ensure bigger land use divisions to reduce frequency of cross-roads, elimination of frontage of properties and side walks along arterial roads and, locations of inter-zonal activities in the outskirts of the zones to eliminate through traffic from the interior roads.

These departments can function effectively, if besides being safety minded at the time of preparation of their plans, they are equally watchful that their original plans are not altered without thought at the time of redevelopment.

The Education Department can educate the future generations in the proper use of the road by introducing highway safety lessons for different classes in schools.

Road user groups, like the Automobile Associations, Transport Undertakings, Safety First Organisations, the Lions Clubs, the Rotary Clubs and the Junior Chambers of Commerce, among others, can play a big part by their efforts to encourage safety on the roads. A sustained message of highway safety can be very effectively transmitted to the public through the Press, the Advertising Agencies, the Film Industry and Television. The media of these agencies should be employed more and more for educating the public in road safety and creating a proper road sense in them.

Remedial Measures

Children below 12 years of age should not be allowed to ride a bicycle or drive any vehicle on public roads in Municipal areas.

Applicants for a driving licence for a motor vehicle should possess a minimum educational qualification of fifth standard.

Professional drivers should undergo successfully a course of training in a recognised driving school for a minimum period of at least six weeks.

Wherever possible Government should run such driving schools.

The instructors should be not only skilled drivers but must also be well-versed in teaching traffic rules and regulations, besides possessing a knowledge of motor mechanism and maintenance. They should be able to impart a sense of defensive and sportsmanlike driving to all the trainees.

The driving test should be more rigorous. There should be an oral or written test, preferably both, to test the applicant's knowledge and awareness of road signs, road signals, road markings, common traffic rules, basic knowledge of motor mechanism and the safety factors including reaction time and braking distances.

The road test should be conducted over a distance of at least two and a half kilometres and a duration of 25 to 30 minutes. It should embrace in its scope varying traffic and road conditions to bring out the driving skill and knowledge of traffic rules of the applicant.

The driving test must also size up human personality in its physical and psychological aspects. The testing procedure should be phased. The determination of the physical capability of a driver should be followed by a reaction time test.

The driver must be tested to judge his ability to attend to sound and light emerging from behind. He should be capable of receiving and reacting to movements within a range of 180°.

The applicant should be examined to judge his ability to anticipate the relative size of a near and a distant object.

A glare recovery test should be carried out to gauge the applicant's ability in this direction.

The application form for obtaining driving licence should contain a page listing the items for test. An applicant who fails in the test should be furnished with a statement of his shortcomings.

The Union Ministry of Transport should bring out a detailed driving Manual, in English, Hindi and the regional languages.

A "pass" in the driving test should entitle an applicant to a provisional driving licence only, valid for 3 years. If, during this period, the holder is involved in a serious accident and convicted, his licence should be revoked and he should be given a fresh provisional licence only on his passing a fresh test. If, however, he has a clean record, the provisional licence should automatically get confirmed and he should be eligible to have it renewed under the normal rules.

Photographs of all licence holders together with their signatures (both duly attested) should be affixed to their driving licences.

Processing for the issue of a driving licence should be done in two stages. The applicant should first obtain a competence certificate of driving from the Transport Authorities. He should then present it to the Police Authorities for issue of the driving licence after such verification as may be called for. The renewal of a driving licence should also be done by the Police who, if the record of the person concerned is poor, may refer him to the Transport Authorities for a repeat driving test.

Motor cyclists and scooterists holding learner licences should learn their driving only in open grounds and by-lanes, instead of along main road.

The point system for dealing with traffic offenders should be introduced, to start with, in the large metropolitan areas of the country.

A limit of blood alcohol content of 0.05 per cent should be fixed and a person exceeding this limit should be deemed as drunk. Action should be taken against a driver found having taken alcohol in excess of the limit by way of an endorsement in his licence, court fine, revocation of licence, as may be necessary, depending upon whether it is his first or repeated offence. Large-scale manufacture of an equipment similar to an alcohol meter of balloon type and its distribution among the Police Officers throughout the country, should be taken up to enable the Police to launch a determined drive against drunken drivers.

The driver's skill in driving and physical fitness to drive, should be subjected to tests once in six years or more frequently. If at the time of obtaining his licence, he wore glasses or used hearing aids or other devices, the validity of the licence should be conditional on the use of such aids by the holder while driving unless he satisfies the Licencing Authority that he no longer requires such aids.

To promote good and safe driving, careful drivers should be encouraged. One with a clean record over a continuous period of six years should be issued a distinctive de luxe licence which he will forfeit the moment he gets convicted for a traffic accident.

The employment of computer technique for maintaining records of drivers will enable enquiries about applicants for driving licences being dealt with promptly.

In the case of all drivers of motor vehicles involved in serious traffic violations, resulting in Court convictions, such information should be recorded in a National Driver Register.

There is an urgent need for examining all the traffic regulations framed in the country and arriving at a set of basic uniform ones so that uniformity of their application throughout the country is achieved.

Supplementing the basic uniform traffic regulations, a set of model ones for urban areas, covering the requirements of all modes of traffic, has to be formulated.

Provisions of the basic uniform traffic regulations and the model traffic regulations for cities should be condensed in the form of a Highway Code and brought out in several regional languages in addition to Hindi and English.

Separate Traffic Courts should be set up to try traffic and road accident cases, composed of Magistrates with a working knowledge of the automobile and a driving experience of at least five years.

The Traffic Courts should be manned by full time Magistrates and they should have trained traffic prosecutors assigned to them for dealing with violation cases. Persons charged with 'moving violations' should be required to appear before such courts in person.

Traffic Courts should arrange to record the evidence deposed by witnesses on the very day they appear before them. The Courts should have summary power. The right of more than one appeal against their verdict should be disallowed.

The Traffic Courts should give directions for a copy of the order of conviction being sent to a Central Licences Record Office to ensure completeness of its records.

The persons accused of petty traffic offences should be given an option to plead guilty by a registered letter addressed to the Court and to remit to it such sum as may be specified in the summons, instead of having to appear before the Court.

Accident Investigating Squads, consisting of high ranking officers conversant with the traffic laws and regulations, should scrutinize the facts of each accident reported and institute proceedings against those found to be at fault. Where such squads are not available each Police Circle/Division, particularly in urban areas, having a high density of traffic, should have at least one Traffic Inspector conversant with the traffic laws and regulations.

Mobile Courts assisted by Mobile Traffic Patrols should bring about effective enforcement of traffic regulations by dispensing on-the-spot justice to erring traffic offenders. They can thus reduce the work load on the regular courts and leave them free to hear cases involving serious offences while disposing of the minor ones themselves.

The law should prescribe in addition to a maximum punishment, a minimum punishment as well, in the case of all endorseable offences mentioned in the Fifth Schedule of the Motor Vehicles Act of 1939. The minimum punishment should be at least 50 per cent of the maximum laid down.

Since the condition of a vehicle and its proper upkeep are essential to accident prevention, there should be a periodic inspection by the registering authority of the mechanical condition of all types of automobiles on the road and unfit vehicles should be kept off the road, till they are made road-worthy.

Fitness tokens valid over prescribed periods should be issued and their display made compulsory to prevent vehicles in unsafe condition from operating on the road.

For transport motor vehicles, the vehicle inspection should be made at intervals not exceeding a year and should also cover compulsory equipments such as horns, wipers, rear view mirrors, brakes, steering connections and suspension.

For motor cars and motor cycles, the vehicle inspection should be performed and fitness certificate issued for periods ranging from 1 to 3 years depending upon the condition of the vehicle.

A motor vehicle inspection code should be framed stating minimum standards of safety including braking performance. This should be supplemented by an inspection manual setting down standard procedures for the operation of vehicle testing stations.

Vehicle inspection or testing stations should be established by the Government to work on a self-supporting basis by charging a fee. Where it is not possible to locate such stations at reasonable distances, mobile testing stations should be introduced.

Spot inspection of vehicles considered unsafe should be carried out by a motor Vehicle Inspector or by a police officer of a rank not below an Inspector. In the case of vehicles found unsafe, a written order should be given to the owner/driver to obtain a fresh certificate of road worthiness within a week from the registering authority. The written order should indicate the extent of the inspection made.

Compulsory periodic inspection should be applicable to all motor vehicles when they are three years old and above.

Vehicles found defective at vehicle inspection should be given time to have the necessary repairs and adjustments effected before re-submission of the vehicle for further inspection.

There should be a regular programme for checking the registrations of motor vehicles using the road.

Uniformity in the display of registration marks facilitates identification of the vehicles. When registration marks are assigned, it should be obligatory for the owners of motor vehicles to obtain and display registration number plates, conforming to the prescribed regulations. Such number plates should be supplied either by the authorities themselves, or by an agency approved by them.

When a motor vehicle changes hands, the transfer of ownership should be promptly entered in the records of the registering authorities.

The responsibility for having the change of ownership entered within the specified period should be laid on both the purchaser and the seller of the vehicle.

There is a need for standardising the height of head lamps from the ground level to minimise the glare effect on on-coming vehicles. In addition, the equipment should be immunised against operating the main and dipper filaments together.

The Indian Standards Institution should take up standardisation of head lamps and accessory light fittings so that the degree of illumination and the types of reflectors are adhered to by the manufacturers. In addition, there should be a total ban on other lighting accessories such as triangular illuminated red lamps on the rear wind screen and miniature signal heads.

A fixed standard for the colour, size, and level of illumination of amber lamps should be developed so that they are effective for operation under foggy conditions.

Use of safety helmets should be encouraged for the drivers as well as pillion riders of scooters and motorcycles by allowing a higher rate of insurance compensation for such of them as were wearing such equipment at the time they were involved in an accident. Gradually their use should be made compulsory. Likewise, wearing of goggles protecting the drivers of motor cycles and scooters should be encouraged to prevent disturbances to vision from dust and insects. Rear wheels of motor cycles should be properly covered to prevent loose garments of pillion riders being entangled in the spokes of these wheels. Roll-over bars should be provided for all scooters and motor cycles to prevent body injuries in the case of over-turning, Rear view mirrors, stop lamps, and illuminated direction indicators should be made compulsory equipment for such vehicles. Riding by more than two persons or the transport of bulky goods should be disallowed on them. The feasibility of increasing the diameter of the scooter wheels should be examined to reduce their proneness to overturning.

For school buses, metal bodies with low entrance and exit steps, grade handles and guard rails, separate driver's cabins seats facing the front and emergency doors should all be made compulsory.

Illuminated direction indicators and rear view mirrors should be fitted compulsorily on all tempos and three wheeler rickshaws.

Cat's eye reflectors and the use of lights during dark hours should be made compulsory for slow moving vehicles such as tongas, bullock carts and bicycles. Also where such vehicles ply on steep grades, they should be provided with suitable brakes.

Zebra markings should be adopted for all pedestrian crossings. In addition, safety zones of about 20 metres length on either side of such crossings should be marked, where parking, halting and overtaking of vehicles should be prohibited. Where vehicular traffic is heavy mid-block pedestrian crossings should be provided with push button signals, pedestrians should be forced to observe traffic regulations and in case of flagrant breaches suitable fines should be imposed. On-the-spot action should be taken by mobile courts for traffic violations by pedestrians.

All the requirements of road safety should be provided for, as far as possible, in the construction stage itself. During the course of construction also, safety measures such as the lighting of barriers, the provision of signs and good surfaces for diversions should be properly enforced.

Prompt maintenance operations should take care of (1) all road surfaces including their shoulders, (2) repainting of the traffic lines and signs, (3) clearance of all obstructions to movement of traffic such as fallen trees and boulders, (4) removal of sight obstructions at junctions and curves and (5) timely warning of hazardous road conditions. Requirements of emergency maintenance under conditions of flood and land slides, should be planned in advance and adequate equipment and personnel made readily available for them.

Street lighting in urban areas and other locations should be improved by augmentation of the resources for such schemes and by working out long term and short term plans for their implementation in a systematic manner.

Wayside amenities along roads should be given early attention and the needed facilities provided. Telephones should be installed along busy highways at intervals of 15 to 20 km.

For prevention of ribbon development alongside the national highways a Central legislation should be passed. For this purpose, the provisions of Articles 252(1) of the Constitution should be invoked whereunder the States concerned should pass necessary resolutions authorising the Centre to pass necessary legislation. The States also should make similar legislation following the pattern of the Central legislation for ribbon developments alongside the States highways.

Bye-passes diverting the main highway traffic outside built-up areas should be provided and strict measures taken along such bye-passes to regulate road-side developments so that they do not interfere with the case of traffic movement and also endanger safety.

Ring roads should be planned and constructed for urban areas to divert inter-city traffic to peripheral areas. Their location and design should be based on a proper traffic survey allowing for future requirements of traffic.

Truck termini with adequate arrangements for storage and handling of goods should be provided at the out skirts of large urban areas to eliminate the movement of heavy transport vehicles inside them.

Well-planned programmes of education in road safety covering all road users should be drawn up and implemented.

Road safety education of children should start right from the primary classes. In the initial stages, simple rules relating to the correct use of the road and the possible consequences of not observing them, should be pictorially represented to make a deep impression on their minds. This should be followed up by more difficult rules, assisted by educational aids like posters, cinema slides, cinema shots, slogans, models, comics and stories with road safety as their underlying theme. In the secondary stage a practical bias to the instruction can be given by a scheme of Roads Safety Patrols to make the youngsters disciplined road users.

The establishment of Traffic Training Parks for children is a necessity. Such parks should be provided in all cities for children from all the schools in the neighbourhood to play traffic games.

National propaganda through the Press and the Radio should also be aimed at parents to prevent children from using the road except in the company of responsible persons. Such a campaign should be supplemented by propaganda by the local unofficial organisations devoted to road safety.

The Government of India should enunciate a national policy in regard to road safety education in schools. It should appoint a national Committee on Road Safety Education, comprising traffic experts, educationist and representatives of the general public and entrust it with the task of (a) defining the basic Road Safety Code which is to be taught to children in schools; and (b) preparing the blue print for a scheme of Road Safety Education in primary and secondary schools for adoption all over India. The scheme should be immediately implemented and become part of the educational curriculum under Social Studies.

Road Safety education should be given to the adult road users in the garb of entertainment or through media like posters, slogans, cinema slides and television which convey at a glance the requisite message. This should be supplemented by the use of mobile police vans, equipped with amplifiers and loud speakers, to exhort the public to observe the rules of the road. The holding of essay competitions, safety slogan and poster contests, among students as well as the general public, will arouse interest in road safety.

Motor sports, like reliability trials and rallies, should be encouraged to promote, safer driving and careful maintenance of motor vehicles.

Road Safety Congresses, Seminars, Symposia, Study Weeks, Safety Weeks and Safety Talks should be organised to foster exchange of ideas and experience on problems of road safety and their solutions.

Safety awards to drivers of public service vehicles and conferment of the distinction of "Driver of the year" on drivers with outstanding records will stimulate good driving.

Newspapers should mobilise public opinion in favour of measures for promoting road safety by publishing pictures, slogans, feature articles and safety supplements conducive to such a cause.

Since the present accident report form A-1 is not comprehensive for proper analysis of accidents, a revised form is suggested. This should be introduced for use uniformly throughout the country. All accidents, whether minor or major, should be directly recorded on this form and the present practice of entering some accidents in the Police daily diaries only should be discarded. Personnel should be trained to fill up the form as accurately as possible.

The summary accident record form-4 as revised in conformity with the proposed form A-1 should be used for preparation of summaries.

In all cities, accident investigation squads with trained men should be set up. For this purpose a city should be divided into zones, each zone being headed by an officer not lower in rank than a Deputy Superintendent of Police who should have all the accidents occurring in his particular zone reported to him.

Fatal accidents on a sample basis should be occasionally studied by a team of experts, including a police officer, a doctor, a traffic engineer, an automobile engineer and a psychologist, to find out the cause and to make concrete suggestions for better road safety.

There should also be a statistical cell attached to the traffic branch of the police for compilation and analysis of accident data. A traffic Research Supervisory Committee should be established to assist the work of the Statistical Cell.

A Traffic Enforcement Division should be set up at the State level in the Police department for the investigation of accidents on rural roads and planning of enforcement measures.

For planning and directing road safety activities on a sustained basis throughout the country, a National Road Safety Council should be constituted as a statutory body through an enactment in the Parliament on the lines approved by the Transport Development Council at its meeting held on 30-4-1963, together with a few modifications as suggested by the Study Group.

State Road Safety Councils should be created as counterparts of the National Road Safety Council for coordinating the activities of various departments as are related to road safety.

District Road Safety Councils should be constituted to coordinate the activities of official and non-official bodies concerned with road safety in the districts.

A Road Safety Fund of non-lapsing nature should be created for the working of the National Road Safety Council and its resources built up from various collections as stated in the draft constitution on the said Council and further supplemented by diversion of an additional 20 per cent of the Central Road Fund exclusively for its use and a contribution of 10 per cent of the insurance premia on the motor vehicles.

Traffic Engineering Divisions should be set up in all State PWDs and Municipal Corporations with functions as detailed in the report.

Wireless Traffic Aid Posts should be set up all over the country along the National Highways.

Overloaded vehicles should be checked and relieved of their excess loads at regular weigh bridges located at points of entry into and exit from main highways near big cities.

Decisions in regard to speed limits should be taken on the expert advice of traffic engineers and based upon a scientific assessment of the different factors involved. The 'prudent speeds' of vehicles should be observed and analysed in relation to the character of the road and the accident rate thereon.

Existing speed limits should be reviewed and, after due modifications and lapse of a period of warning, they should be strictly enforced. The effect of these restrictions on the flow of traffic and the accident rate should be watched carefully and the limits modified from time to time on the basis of experience gained.

In some areas of sufficient size, to yield reliable results, highly trained mobile police patrols should be employed in large numbers to ensure effective supervision. They should be provided with motor cycles so that they can readily thread their way through traffic. They should also be equipped with portable 'wheel weighers'. There should be special Traffic Squads in fast moving automobiles to check speed violations, hit and run cases, over-loading of vehicles and other such violations of the law.

Traffic Wardens selected from the general public should be appointed in urban areas with a population of more than 4 lakhs and invested with some minor powers of the traffic police. They should report to the traffic authorities, violations of the rules by any driver or bus conductor or other road user, for appropriate follow-up action. Besides, they should render assistance to the victims of road accidents.

A few ambulance vehicles, adequately staffed for first-aid, should be made available to the police, so that prompt assistance can be rendered to the victims of accidents.

Advertising signs on the roadside should be controlled by the adoption of a code on a voluntary basis by the trade and also through legislative and administrative action.

UNECONOMIC BRANCH LINES COMMITTEE, 1969—REPORT

New Delhi, Ministry of Railways, 1970. 105p+iip.

Chairman : Shri Rohan Lal Chaturvedi
Members : Shri S.C. Samanta; Shri T.K. Patel; Shri N.P.C. Naidu; Shri G.C. Baveja; Shri K. Narayanan.
Secretary : Shri J.B. Rao.

APPOINTMENT

On 18th March 1969, during the course of the debate on the Railway Budget for the year 1969-70, the then Minister for Railways, Shri Ram Subhag Singh, made the following statement in Lok Sabha :

"There has been a unanimous feeling in the House, both in this House as well as in Rajya Sabha, that in respect of the Railways which are being called uneconomical lines and which are supposed to be dismantled, we should reconsider and give a second thought to that idea. Having regard to the unanimous feelings that have been expressed in the House—Shri Deven Sen who is a great union leader also made a mention of it—I feel that we should try to increase our earnings by introducing better coaches and strengthening the lines. Shri Sonavane also said about Pandharpur. He is conversant with that place. That is a very famous place of pilgrimage and it is a fact—I have some idea about it—that the pilgrims who go there to offer puja at Pandharpur have to undergo a good deal of difficulty while travelling in trains. Though the policy so far has been not to improve that line, having regard to the opinions expressed in this House as well as in the other House, I propose not to dismantle any Railway line wherever it may exist".

He further stated,

"Wherever it is possible, we would try to convert the Narrow Gauge Railway into the gauge of that area. If there is a Metre Gauge, we shall try—I do not know how far our resources will permit but as a policy I say that there would not be any dismantling and as far as possible we will keep on strengthening those lines and also converting them into the gauge of that area, be it Metre Gauge or Broad Gauge".

During the course of the debate, a suggestion was made by a member—Shri N.P.C. Naidu—that a small Committee should be appointed, to go into the working of those branch lines. This suggestion was accepted by the Minister for Railways.

As a result a committee called "The uneconomic Branch Lines Committee, 1969" was constituted under Railway Board Resolutions No. E(RB)1/69/CO1/27 dated 28th April, 1969 and No. E (RB)1/69/CO 1/27 dated 12th June, 1969.

TERMS OF REFERENCE

"To review the existing procedure and policy regarding identification of uneconomic branch lines and measures taken to improve their working and keeping in view the recommendations made by the Committee on transport policy and coordination, the Estimates Committees (1967-1968), Tenth Report (Fourth Lok Sabha) and Public Accounts Committee (1968-69) 49th Report, to suggest ways and means of improving the working of the uneconomic branch lines so as to make them economically viable and recommend suitable measures to reduce or eliminate the burden on the Indian Railways of the recurring financial loss of working these uneconomic lines".

CONTENTS

Introduction; Historical Background; Identification of uneconomic Branch Lines; Review of Policy in regard to uneconomic Branch Lines; General Suggestions; Review of Specific Lines; Summary of Conclusions and Recommendations; Annexures 1 to 15.

RECOMMENDATIONS

For the purpose of examination of viability, only the following should be treated as Branch lines :

(1) A line of any gauge, joined to the main system at one end only, and

(2) All Narrow Gauge lines.

Chord lines or parts of chord lines—other than Narrow Gauge lines—need not be considered from the point of view of economic viability.

A branch line should be considered as a whole. Only if the whole branch line is found to be uneconomic, should an end section of such a branch be considered separately.

In making estimates of loss, the interest element should not be taken into account, as laid down in para 846 of the Railways General Code.

The formula adopted by certain Railways in estimating main line earnings, does not bear scrutiny.

In the division of goods earnings between main line and a branch line, the procedure should allow for a credit for terminals to the end Railways.

In arriving at the expenses at a branch line, by pro rata calculations, expenditure not relevant to branch lines, should be excluded, as far as possible.

In estimating the share of joint expenditure to be attributed to a branch line, a percentage only of the expenditure should be taken, as under—

Head of account		Percentage
A-II	...	40 per cent
B-II	...	80 per cent
C-II	...	60 per cent
C-III	...	60 per cent

No part of expenditure falling under General Administration should be apportioned to a branch, unless the "branch" is an extensive system.

The instructions in Paras 844, 845 and 846 of the General Code, should be elaborated, so that a correct and uniform procedure is followed by all Railways in estimating losses.

We suggest trained Cost Accountants being attached to the Costing Cell of the Railway Board.

Branch lines should not be looked at in isolation but as part of an integrated Railway system.

Even though a line may be losing, we must look at the economic purposes it is serving to an area.

The postponement of proper maintenance and replacement of stock have themselves resulted in deterioration of service, which, in turn, has contributed to loss of revenue.

We observe that sometimes conversion of crossing stations into halt stations is opposed, as this involves loss of Telegraph facilities.

The directive that Railways should encourage development of road transport service on routes parallel to unremunerative lines should be cancelled.

An examination should be made whether the charges for goods traffic on Narrow Gauge lines can be appropriately enhanced.

State Governments who feel strongly on the closure of Branch lines should take a more active part in ensuring better rail-road coordination.

Wagon stock should be augmented and timely supply of adequate number of wagons ensured.

Supply of matching stock at transhipment points should be arranged on a preferential basis, to avoid delays in transhipment.

Attention should be paid to adjusting train timings to suit local needs and to ensure proper connections with main line trains.

Passenger services should be frequent and for this purpose diesel car units, developed by the Eastern Railway, are most suitable, for the Narrow Gauge.

Dieselization of motive power should be considered, particularly for sections far removed from coal-fields.

A study should be made whether mechanical maintenance of track, even for lightly worked sections, can give economies.

The scope of economies by power operation of points and signals should be examined.

Possibilities of Centralized Traffic Control over lightly worked sections, giving economies by way of staff reduction, should be examined.

Greater attention should be paid to the provision of facilities at stations on the uneconomic lines.

Where there are a number of trains running each way, at least one of them should be made into a fast train.

When possible, all available trains should not be run as mixed trains and at least one of the trains should run as a fast passenger train.

All trains are scheduled at 10 per cent less than the maximum permissible speed. Feasibility of either eliminating this or reducing this should be examined.

As far as possible booking of passenger by Guards of trains should be discontinued and this work arranged through Halt Agents.

There should be no distinction between rural and other areas in respect of Commission to Halt Agent. It should be ensured that even in rural areas the rate of commission yields about Rs. 150 per mensem.

To ensure that tickets for distant places are stocked by Agents, a suitable scheme should be evolved to enable them return unsold tickets.

Stricter and more constant ticket checking should be enforced.

On uneconomic sections; provision of halts, even if an existing station is less than 5 kilometres away, should be considered.

Attractive special rates should be quoted on uneconomic branches to recreate a travel-by-rail habit.

There should be a vigorous drive by contacting rail users to attract goods traffic.

Possibility of letting out rest houses to outsiders on a fairly high rent should be considered.

Surplus land should be rented out.

Divisional officers should carry out frequent and surprise inspections of Branch lines.

The public and State Governments should appreciate that Railway finances are subject to a very heavy strain and should cooperate in making the branch lines viable. The State Government should play a more active role by asking the Regional Transport Authorities to regulate not only route permits but also timings of buses etc.

The State Governments can make a positive contribution by using the Railways to transport their own traffic.

There should be committees at the Railways Zonal and Divisional levels to review periodically the problems of uneconomic lines. The Railway Board should annually review the working of these committees and place copies of such reviews on the Table of both Houses of the Parliament.

Special attention should be paid to the following eight lines as they account for the major portion of the losses :—

(i) Gwalior-Shivpur,
(ii) Gwalior-Shivpur Kalan.
(iii) Barasat-Hasnabad.
(iv) Darjeeling-Himalayan.
(v) Tezpur-Rangapara North.
(vi) Metupalaiyam-Ootacamund.
(vii) Bangalore City-Bangarapet.
(viii) Satpura Railway.

(1) Gwalior-Shivpuri, (2) Gwalior-Sheopur Kalan and (3) Gwalior-Bhind : The track should be improved and the rolling stock replaced urgently.

Dholpur-Tantpur-Sirmuttra : (i) The track and rolling stock should be ronovated.

(ii) Diesel Car units should be introduced.

(iii) Special attention should be paid to check ticketless travel.

Extension of Dholpur—Tantpur to Band Bareta should be surveyed.

Pachora-Jamner : (i) Conversion of the line to Broad Gauge and extension to Bodwad should be surveyed.

(ii) Diesel Car units should be introduced.

Neral-Matheran : (i) Rolling stock should be renovated.

(ii) Traction should be completely dieselized

Barasat-Hasnabad : (i) Through services from Hasnabad or Basirhat to Sealdah should be introduced,

(ii) The following stations should be converted to halt stations :—

Kedambagadri.
Beliaghata Road.
Madhyampur.

Bakhtiyarpur-Rajgir : The State Government must be persuaded to provide feeder roads to the stations.

The passenger stock used on the line should be properly maintained.

Extension of the line to Nawada should be surveyed.

Shantipur-Nabadwipghat : Survey should be made of dismantling the Krisnanagar City-Nabadwipghat and simultaneously converting Krishnanagar City-Shantipur to Broad Gauge.

(ii) The Narrow Gauge line should be brought upto standard.

(iii) The sections should be open only for passenger traffic.

(iv) The service should be run by Diesel Car units.

Rohtak-Gohana : (i) Restoration of the Gohana-Panipat link should be surveyed.

(ii) Track should be properly ballasted and trains run at faster speeds.

Barhen-Etah : (i) Track should be ballasted and brought upto standard.

(ii) Trains should be run faster.

(iii) Diesel Car services should be introduced.

Approach road at Jalesar and Awagarh should be improved.

(i) Extension of the line to Kasganj is recommended.

(ii) Linking Barhan with Agra should be surveyed.

Akbarpur-Tanda : (i) Time of rail travel should be substantially reduced.

(ii) Extension of the line to bring it nearer to Tanda Town should be surveyed.

Pathankot-Joginder Nagar : Dieselization of the traction should be considered.

An out-agency at Jawalamukhi Temple should be established.

Batala-Qadian : Possibility of curtailing the train service should be examined.

Kalka-Simla : Steam traction should be completely replaced by Diesel traction.

The Rail Cars should be replaced by new ones.

Speed should be improved.

Mathura-Vrindaban : (i) Timings of trains should be reexamined.

(ii) A through train from Achnera to Vrindaban should be introduced.

The facilities at Vrindaban Road station on the Central Railway should be improved.

Mariani-Jorhat-Neamati : The section from Jorhat to Neamati is not serving any useful purpose.

The service on the Mariani-Jorhat section should be improved.

Lataguri-Ramshai : This line serves no purpose.

Rangapara North-Tezpur : Feasibility of easing the curves should be examined,

Extension of the line to Bhumraguri should be surveyed.

Darjeeling-Himalayan Railway : (i) Every effort should be made to attract tea traffic to the Railway.

(ii) Railways should organize their own road service for carrying some of the up traffic.

(iii) Steam locomotives should be replaced by diesels.

Sagara-Talguppa : Extension to Honavar should be reexamined.

Nanjangud-Chamarajanagar : Track should be brought upto standard.

Extension of the line to Satyamangalam and from there to Coimbatore should be surveyed.

Mettupalaiyam-Ootacamund : (i) Timings of trains should be adjusted and trains should be speeded up.

(ii) Diesel traction should be introduced.

Reduced rates for 1st class should be quoted in the off season.

Possibility of carrying all goods traffic by trucks owned by the Railway, should be examined.

Shoranur-Nilambur : The line should be properly maintained.

Bangalore City-Bangarapet : There should be stricter checking against ticketless travel.

Diesel car units should be introduced for catering to passenger traffic.

Stations between Bangalore City and Kolar should be closed down for goods traffic.

Conversion of the line to Metre Gauge with a link between Srinivaspuri and Madanapale Road should be surveyed.

Madurai-Bodinayakkanur : (i) Cardamom traffic from Bodinayakkanur should be canvassed.

(ii) There should be stricter check over ticketless travel.

Tamil Nadu Government may be approached again regarding closing down the line.

Chikjajur-Chitradurg : The line should be kept open for passenger traffic only and diesel cars should be run.

Extension of the line to Rayadurg should be surveyed.

Mayuram-Tranquebar, Peralam-Karaikkal : Diesel car services should be introduced over these two lines.

Nidamangalam-Mannargudi : Track should be strengthened so that the axle-load restriction can be removed.

Walajah Road-Ranippettai : The firm at Ranippettai should be persuaded to use the Railway. If not, there is no alternative to closing the line.

Villupuram-Pondichery : Diesel car service should be introduced.

Salem-Metur Dam : There should be vigorous canvassing for the traffic from Metur Dam.

Dhond-Baramati : The track should be improved.

Possibility of inducing Walchand Industries to improve their tram line to Bhigwan should be examined.

Latur-Kurduwadi-Miraj : The section Kurduwadi-Pandharpur should be converted to Broad Gauge.

Converted goods stock should not be used for passenger traffic in normal times.

Conversion of Kurduwadi-Latur section to Broad Gauge with extension to Latur Road should be surveyed.

(i) The necessity for speed restriction to the Kurduwadi-Barsi section should be examined.

(ii) The Maharashtra Government should be persuaded to widen the road.

Existing rolling stock should be immediately replaced.

Mudkhed-Adilabad : A through bogie between Secunderabad and Adilabad should be introduced.

Satpura Railway : A departmental committee should examine the economies of the Satpura Railway section by section.

A study should be made of the economies achieved by the introduction of diesels.

Trains over the Parasia-Seoni section should be speeded up.

A survey should be conducted for the gradual conversion of the northern section to Broad Gauge.

Raipur-Dhamtari : Goods traffic has been diverted to road due to non-availability of wagons.

Conversion of the line to Broad Gauge should be surveyed.

Naupada-Gunupur : Hardly anything has been done to improve the line after taking it over from the Maharajah of Parlakimidi.

Passenger traffic will improve, if speeds are improved.

Orissa Government should be requested to correct a misapprehension that foodgrains traffic cannot move from one part of Orissa to another part because such movement is over Andnra Pradesh.

Extension of the line to Rayagada should be examined along with agencies concerned with development of tribal areas.

Track and rolling stock should be rehabilitated.

Rupsa-Talband : Goods traffic can be attracted by provision of better services.

(i) Track between Baripada and Bangriposi should be made fit for heavy type of engines.

(ii) Passenger trains should be provided with vacuum.

Conversion of the line to Broad Gauge should be surveyed.

(i) Bangriposi to Talband should be reopened for traffic.

(ii) Provision of a link between Budamara and Chakulia or Rajluka and Kokpara should be surveyed.

(iii) Extension to Rairangpur may be examined along with agencies concerned with development of tribal areas.

Track should be made fit for speeds of 50 km.p.h.

Purulia-Kotshila : Conversion of the line to Broad Gauge should be examined.

If conversion is not justified, diesel car units should be introduced to cater for passenger traffic.

Ranchi-Lohardaga : Efforts should be made to attract vegetable traffic.

Western Railway—Narrow Gauge lines

Conversion of Chhota-Udaipur to Pratapnagar. together with the branch Chhuchhapura-Tankhala to Broad Gauge should be surveyed.

(i) On the other lines, track should be maintained properly and trains should run faster.

(ii) It should be examined whether Jambusar Town requires three stations to serve it.

Nadiad-Kapadvanj and Nadiad Bhadran sections should be closed down for goods traffic.

Godhra-Lunavada section should be closed down for goods traffic and diesel car units introduced to cater- to the passenger traffic.

If the manganese ore traffic over the Champanere—Pani Mines dries up completely, the section should be closed for goods traffic and passenger traffic should be catered to by diesel car units.

(i) If the Nawagaon Dam construction comes up early, conversion of Ankleswar-Rajpipla line to Borad Gauge should be surveyed.

(ii) Otherwise, this line, along with the branch Jhagadia-Netrang should be brought upto standard.

The track on the Kosamba-Umarpada section should be brought upto standard and speeds of trains improved. If possible, an additional train should be run.

Conversion of Bhavnagar-Mahowa line to Metre Gauge should be surveyed.

The locomotives on the section and the track should be renovated urgently.

Joravarnagar-Sayla section should be closed for goods traffic and diesel car units introduced for passenger service.

Morvi-Ghantila section should be closed for goods traffic and diesel car units should be run for passenger service.

Piplad-Dengadhbaria section should be closed for goods traffic and should be catered for by diesel car units.

Ujjain-Agar section should be closed for goods traffic and diesel car service introduced for passenger traffic.

Conversion of Billimoria-Waghai line to Broad Gauge should be surveyed.

Western Railway—Metre Gauge Sections

Kunkavav-Derdi section can be closed down without any public inconvenience.

Prachi Road-Kodinar section can be closed down for goods traffic and diesel car units introduced to cater for passenger traffic.

Ningala-Gahada-Swaminarayan section can be closed down for goods traffic.

Extension of Botad-Jasdan line upto Rajkot should be surveyed.

If the section Okha-Viramgam is converted to Broad Gauge, the Than-Chotila section should be closed down.

If Okha to Viramgam is converted to Broad Gauge, Hadmatia-Jodia section can be closed down.

The stations on the Fatehpur-Shekhawati-Churu section can be closed down for goods traffic.

A city booking office should be established at the Shree Kalyanji Temple near Diggi on the Sanganer Town-Toda Rai Singh line.

Possibility of extending the line upto Bundi should be surveyed along with the survey of Kotah-Chittor line which is in hand.

Specific sums should be set aside for carrying out the projects and improvements suggested by us.

STUDY GROUP ON RESOURCES MOBILISATION FOR EDUCATION, 1969—REPORT

New Delhi, Asian Institute of Educational Planning and Administration, 1970. 67p.

Convenor : Dr. S.N. Mehrotra.

Members : Prof. M.V. Mathur ; Shri S. Krishnaswamy; Shri J.S. Mehta; Shri P.C. Pande (relinquished the post of Education Secretary, UP, and Shri G.P. Pande became member); Shri J.C. Sen-Gupta; Shri J.L. Azad; Shri A.K.N. Nambiar.

Co-opted Member : Prof. D.T. Lakdawala

APPOINTMENT

The Study Group on Resources Mobilization set up by the Ministry of Education and Youth Services vide D.O. Letter No. F 21-2/69 IV dated 14th July, 1969.

TERMS OF REFERENCE

(1) To review the existing measures adopted by the State Governments for raising resources for educational development programmes, such as levy of educational cess, betterment fund, popular contribution etc.

(2) To suggest concrete measures for adoption by the State Governments (i) for raising additional financial resources either through legislation or otherwise for educational development programme, (ii) for increasing community support to educational development such as the School Improvement projects of Tamil Nadu, and (iii) for optimum use of existing physical facilities like introduction of Shift-System, intensive utilization of existing buildings and other facilities like laboratories, libraries, and

(3) To make broad estimate of existing resources available for educational development programmes and the additional resources likely as a result of the various measures suggested by the Group and the need for earmarking such resources for these programmes.

CONTENTS

Introduction; Existing Resources—a Review; Educational Expenditure by sources—an Analysis; Proposals for Raising Additional Resources; Optimum Utilisation of Resources; Summary of Recommendations; Annexures I to VII.

RECOMMENDATIONS

Trends of educational expenditure by sources over the three plan periods indicate that the responsibility for financing of education at all stages will have to be increasingly shouldered by Government.

While the major responsibility for financing education must necessarily lie on the States, education being primarily a State subject, the Centre must also assume increasing financial responsibility in the spheres of technical education, higher education and research. It must also play a stimulative, innovative, consultative and promotional role in the educational development of the country.

The States should progressively increase their investment in education to the extent of at least 25 per cent of their budget by the end of the Fourth Plan period and strive to reach the mark of 30 per cent within a period of ten years. The Centre should also progressively raise its allocation for education to at least 8 per cent of its budget.

Educational cess may be levied both in rural and urban areas, for the specific purpose of expeditiously fulfilling the Constitutional directive for providing free and compulsory education to children upto the age of 14 in the manner suggested below :

(a) In rural areas, educational cess may be levied by the local bodies in the form of surcharge at a minimum rate of 20 paise per rupee on land revenue and utilised by them within their own jurisdiction. They may also be authorised to raise voluntarily the surcharge rate beyond the prescribed minimum upto the maximum of 50 paise per rupee. In order to stimulate the use of this authority, a grant-in-aid proportionate to the additional revenues thus raised should be guaranteed by the State on the principle of equalization from area, i.e. proportionately larger grants to the poor and backward areas.

(b) In urban areas, educational cess may be levied by the local body on rented property at some minimum obligatory rate with provision of matching grant for additional cess raised voluntarily minimum but within the prescribed maximum. The minimum and maximum rates should be laid down by the State Governments in the light of local circumstances. The matching grant may be on the principle of equalization from area to area.

(c) In those areas where education is not administered by local bodies, education cess may be in the manner suggested in (a) and (b) above and the proceeds utilized for construction and repairs of elementary school buildings.

The practice of permitting educational institutions to charge more than the standard tuition fee within the prescribed limits, which is in vogue in some of the States, may be adopted by other States also. However, in order that this may not entail any burden may be raised from 17-1/2 to 33-1/2 per cent.

The option to charge development/better fee, within the ceiling laid down by the Education Department, may be left to institutions beyond the compulsory stage, i.e., at the secondary and college stages.

The practice of raising and accepting voluntary donations and contributions for the development of education which is so far confined to private educational institutions should be extended to Government institutions also.

The institutions may adopt one or more ways of augmenting their resources, namely, by charging higher tuition fee and optional development betterment fee within the prescribed ceilings and by voluntary donations. The proceeds from the sources should form part of the School Fund.

Government may permit the creation of a School Fund for each educational institution—Government as well as non-Government. The essential features of the School Fund should be as follows :

(i) The contributions to the School Fund shall in no way be linked with admissions and examinations.

(ii) The proceeds will be utilised for the improvement of Educational facilities in the institution concerned and not for the payment of teachers salaries and allowances.

(iii) The Fund will be managed by a Committee consisting of the parents, teachers and students with the Head of the institution as its Chairman. The specific purpose in terms of the institutional plan for which the funds may be collected and utilised will be indicated by this Committee.

(iv) The amount collected will be kept separately by the institution. It will not be creditable to the treasury, nor will it adversely affect the grant-in-aid of the institution.

(v) The School Fund will be subject to regular departmental audit and the accounts would be published along with the names of the donors.

(vi) In order to stimulate contributions to this Fund, the State Government may provide some matching grants based on the principle of equalization from area to area.

The good offices of voluntary organization engaged in the task of education should be fully utilised for mobilising public opinion for raising voluntary donations for development of education.

The rules of recognition by the State Department of Education and affiliation of the university should be clearly defined and rigorously implemented.

The programme of School Improvement Conference, successfully implemented by the State of Tamil Nadu should be made a people's programme throughout the length and breadth of India.

Systematic accounts be maintained of voluntary donations made by the community for (a) establishing new schools and fulfilling statutory and regulatory requirements of recognition and affiliation and (b) for improvement of existing institutions.

Some existing financial corporation may be authorised or an autonomous organisation in the form of a State Educational Buildings Corporation be set up to give loans for construction of school buildings. All grants earmarked for the construction of educational buildings should be diverted to this fund. A total corpus of Rs. 50 crores may be created for the purpose. Educational institutions in the State should be made shareholders of the corporation. The State Government should guarantee the repayment of the loan granted by the Corporation and other financing agencies and should permit secondary schools and colleges to charge building fee for a specified period at a specified rate so as to enable them to pay back the loan.

Determined efforts should be made towards economising building costs. Specifications on the basis of minimum cost and maximum space, with permissible flexibility within the minimum cost, should be evolved through research, keeping in view the regional variations. The Building Development Groups in the States should play a useful role in this programme.

The existing educational facilities and resources should be utilised to the maximum possible extent.

As a part of the strategy to overcome the present educational crisis created by explosion of numbers and implosion of finances, the following measures, among others, may be tried :

(i) Use of shift system in schools and colleges (with full staff complement for each shift) be tried to secure optimum utilization of the existing school plant i.e. the building, equipment, laboratory, playground etc.;

(ii) Organisation of part-time and correspondence courses on a large scale for workers and other who cannot be placed in full-time institutions. Most of the States are in favour of the programme. Some universities have already made a beginning in this direction. The University Grants Commission may promote this programme in a big way in the Fourth Plan period;

(iii) New institutions in unserved areas may be started only if they can be of a viable size;

(iv) Reduction in the cost of building, equipment and apparatus by better designing, large scale production, improvisation, careful handling and proper maintenance;

(v) Modernizing educational administration by introducing flexibility in administrative and financial procedures and provision of adequate decentralisation of authority to avoid wasteful expenditure;

(vi) Longer working days and increase in their number : proper utilization of vacation which may better be called 'vacation term; and

(vii) Greater emphasis on programme which need more of human talent, dedication and hard work such as modernizing curricula, preparation of taxtbooks, teaching and learning aids, etc. rather than those involving large financial investment.

Utilization in depth may be undertaken in selected areas to assess the efficiency of the utilization of educational expenditure and physical facilities in educational institutions at different levels. The Indian Council for Social Science Research may undertake such utilisation studies in collaboration with the universities in different parts of the country.

The State Government may undertake case studies of their own educational finances in depth with a view to maximising the utilisation of existing resources and exploring the possibilities of mobilising additional resources in the light of the recommendations made above.

COMMITTEE ON AUTOMATION, 1969—REPORT

Delhi, Manager of Publications, 1972. 164p+vp,

Chairman : Shri R. Venkataraman (Resigned. Replaced by Prof. V.M. Dandekar).

Members . Shri G. Ramanujam; Shri Begaram Tulpule (resigned, replaced by Shri Ram Desai); Shri Satish Loomba; Shri B.D. Somani; Shri Balubhai M. Chinai; Shri Naval H. Tata; Prof. V.R. Rao; Brig. B.J. Shahaney; Dr. B.S. Garud.

Secretary : Shri M A.M. Rao.

APPOINTMENT

In pursuance of the suggestion made at the ILC meeting (July, 1968) for condition of a tripartite subcommiitee on automation, the Government of India, in the Ministry of Labour, Employment and Rehabilitation decided to constitute a committee with an adequate number of experts on it. The central organisations of employers and employees were requested to nominate their representatives. The Committee on Automation was set up vide Resolution No. 31/7/68 LRIV, dated 19th July, 1969 of the Ministry of Labour, Employment and Rehabilitation.

TERMS OF REFERENCE

(1) To review the total effects of the operation of automation in the enterprises in the public and private sectors in which it has been already introduced.

(2) To recommend criteria for the determination of any specific areas and fields in which introduction of automation including computers, may be permitted or restricted with due regard to :

(i) The need for raising efficiency and productivity in industry and trade, and in particular industries which are export-oriented;

(ii) the requirements of scientific research and development;

(iii) the need for the timely tabulation, analysis, study, etc. of the large masses of data that arise in modern industry, trade, transport, etc.; and

(iv) the need for restricting the import of foreign equipment for automation and for encouraging the use of such equipment manufactured in the country.

(3) To recommend safeguards for avoiding or minimising any harmful social effects of the introduction of automation.

(4) To consider and make recommendations on any other related matters.

CONTENTS

Introductory; Scope and Present Position; Impact of computers; A Policy for Computors—Recommendations; Explanatory Notes; Appendices I to XVI.

RECOMMENDATIONS

For purposes of laying down any general criteria

determining specific areas or fields in which use of computers may be permitted or restricted, it seems appropriate to make a distinction between use of computers by (a) educational, scientific and research institutions, statistical organisations of the Central and State Governments and defence establishments, and (b) commercial and industrial establishments (whether in the private or public sector) including consultancy services. The need and desirability of the use of computers in category (a) are generally agreed to subject to reasonable provisions to protect employment and working conditions. We, therefore, recommended that subject to reasonable provisions to protect the existing employment and ensuring proper working conditions, the use of computers by educational, research and scientific institutions (non-profit making), statistical organisations of the Central and State Governments and defence establishments should be permitted. We should make it clear that we do not include in these categories the research and development divisions of business and industrial establishments, whether in the private or public sector, and also consultancy firms where research is done primarily for the use of managements of particular commercial and industrial establishments.

The use of computers in category (b), namely by commercial and industrial establishments whether in the public or private sector, including consultancy services has to be treated differently and several additional considerations must be taken into account. We have carefully considered whether we could lay down general criteria determining specific applications for which the use of computers by such establishments may be permitted or restricted and have come to the conclusion that this would not be possible. Factors favouring and not favouring the use of computers for particular applications differ greatly between different establishments. Therefore, rather than laying down general criteria for this purpose, we suggest that the case for the use of computers by commercial and industrial establishments should be examined and scrutinized for each establishment separately by a panel of experts taking into account all relevant considerations.

In our opinion, the legitimate and proper use of computers in commercial and industrial establishments is as an aid to management for improving its efficiency which could not be achieved otherwise. Though there is a general agreement on this point, evidence before us shows that, in a number of cases, the computers are currently being used mainly for routine jobs which could as well be done manually or with mechanical aids including unit-card system. Alternatively, the computer installations have remained under-utilized. It is possible that this is because the use of computers in our country is still new and the management of many establishments are not yet equipped and experienced to make full and proper use of the computers for this legitimate purpose. It is also possible that use of computers for management decisions requires the data to be brought in a form which makes it inevitable that certain operations or jobs which could as well be otherwise performed have to be computerised. This is a matter which will require close scrutiny of each case separately. But it seems to us that in many cases the present underutilisation or improper use of existing computers is mainly due to the fact that computers have been installed without sufficient justification, thought and adequate preparation and planning for their legitimate use. We emphasise that in future this practice will have to be prevented.

One method to ensure full and proper use of computer installations as an aid to management, is to provide computer facilities in computer service centres accessible to commercial and industrial establishments, both public and private, including consultancy firms for legitimate applications. Creation of such facilities will (a) ensure full utilisation of computer installations as such computer service centres will execute approved jobs received from numerous establishments, (b) avoid installation of in-house computers in small firms where there is not enough work-load for a computer and thus will prevent under-utilisation or misuse of computer installations, (c) enable larger establishments to use computer on an experimental basis, to explore its full potentiality as management aid, (d) provide facility to professional computer scientists engaged in consultancy work and development of software, and (e) provide facilities for training and education in computer technology. We, therefore, recommend that adequate computer service facilities in appropriately located computer service centres should be created to meet the demands for approved uses.

As we have conceived it, a computer facility is in the nature of a public utility or an infra-structure facility and hence we feel that, as far as possible, it should be created in the public sector. However, if for any reason it does not become possible to provide adequate computer facility in the public sector, computer service centres in the joint sector, failing which in the private sector, may be allowed subject to appropriate licencing and regulation regarding their use.

Even after adequate computer service facilities are created, there may be cases where individual commercial and industrial establishments may need in-house computers of their own. The justification of such in-house computers will have to be (a) operational difficulties in the way of these establishments using the available facilities of the computer centres, and/or

(b) because of the volume of work of approved use, the ability of these establishments to make full and proper use of the in-house computers. Such cases will have to be carefully examined and scrutinized individually by a panel of experts.

Whether the commercial and industrial establishments use the computer centre facilities or instal in-house computers, the possibility of its adversely affecting the employment has to be kept in mind as a governing consideration. After a careful examination of this question, we have come to the conclusion that the question must be examined at two levels, namely, (a) effect an employment in relation to the whole economy and (b) effect on employment in concerned establishments and particularly in the relevant departments of the establishments. As for (a) namely the effect on employment in relation to the whole economy, it seems to us that the considerations here are similar to those involved in the use of mechanisation, rationalisation and in general in the progressive use of advanced and capital intensive technology. This is a matter which must obviously be covered by a general policy on technology. So far as the use of computers is concerned, we think that, within the general framework of the policy on technology, the necessary decisions must be taken on the basis of relevant considerations at the level of individual establishments concerned. As for (b) namely the effect on employment in the concerned establishments and particularly in the relevant departments, we think that, besides the examination and scrutiny of the question by a panel of experts; it is essential that the concerned workers are satisfied that their employment and working conditions will not be adversely affected. We therefore recommend that all use of computers by commercial and industrial establishments, whether by resort to the computer centre facilities or by installation of in-house computers should be subject to a prior agreement with the workers.

We may thus summarise the criteria and considerations which, in our opinion, should govern the use of computers by commercial and industrial establishments : (a) all such proposals should be examined and scrutinised, case by case, by two experts who will take into account all relevant considerations; (b) use of computers for unapproved purposes and under-utilization of computer installations should be prevented; (c) as far as possible, the needs of computer use should be met from computer centre facilities to be created preferably in the public sector; and (d) in all cases, the use of computers should be subject to a prior agreement with the workers.

In order to meet the above considerations, we recommend that in all future uses of computers by commercial and industrial establishments whether in public or private sector, the following procedure should be adopted.

If the management of a commercial and/or industrial establishment desires to use computer for an application which is of a casual or non-repetitive nature, it may send the job directly to an approved computer centre and inform the workers accordingly. If the workers have any objections, they may raise them with the management. If a dispute arises, either party may take the matter to the National Bipartite Machinery.

If the management of a commercial and/or industrial establishment desires to use computer for applications which may be of repetitive nature, the management should prepare a Justification Report giving justification for the use of the computer and making clear whether resort to a computer centre facility or installation of an in-house computer is desired.

Where resort to a computer centre is desired, the Justification Report to be prepared by the management should detail the following :

(i) the broad types of data from the establishment which will be sent to the computer centre;

(ii) the kind of analyses to which the data will be subjected;

(iii) the periodicity of each type of application whether occasional daily, weekly, monthly, quarterly or annual;

(iv) the reasons why the jobs cannot be done without resort to a computer.

Where installation of an in-house computer is desired, the Justification Report to be prepared by the management should detail the following :

(i) the reasons why the same could not be done through existing computer centre facilities;

(ii) specifications and estimated prices (or rentals) of the machines proposed to be installed;

(iii) the types of applications, with their periodicity, which will be handled by the proposed computer installations;

(iv) the benefits to be expected as regards improvement in efficiency, quality, cost reduction, economy, etc.;

(v) likely effects on the employment in the establishment and particularly in the relevant departments;

(vi) likely effects on conditions of employment, promotion prospects, working conditions, wages, etc. of the concerned workers;

(vii) methods of adjusting employees rendered surplus, if any; and

(viii) safeguards to protect the workers' interests, including the method of sharing possible benefits.

The Justification Report by the management should be referred to a panel of two experts for evaluation, assessment and comments. The experts should be selected, jointly by the management and the workers, from a panel of experts having sufficient knowledge of computer technology, maintained by the government for this purpose. The experts, either on their own or at the instance of the parties, may call for any additional information. The report of the experts should be advisory and should not have the effect of arbitration,

The Justification Report by the management together with the experts' report on the same should form the basis of the negotiations between the management and the workers. Whoever may represent the workers in general in such negotiations, cares should be taken to ensure that the workers likely to be affected by computerisation are also appropriately associated.

If, as a result of these negotiations, an agreement is reached between the management and the workers on the use of computers, the same should be permitted according to the terms of the agreement. If the agreement is for the use of the facilities of a computer centre, it should be the responsibility of the computer centre to ensure that the particular data and applications sent to it by the management from time to time are in accordance with the agreement. It will be obligatory on the part of the centre to furnish, at the request of the workers, information in regard to the types of jobs being done. In case of violation of any agreement and failure to agree mutually, the dispute may be referred by either party, to the National Bipartite Machinery.

In case, no agreement is reached between the management and the workers, the matter should be referred to a Bipartite Machinery at the national level, comprising representatives of the employers and trade unions. The National Bipartite Machinery should be composed of equal number of members representing employers and employees, to be nominated by the All-India Organisations of employers and trade unions represented in the Indian Labour Conference. The Justification Report prepared by the management and the experts' report on the same will form the basis for the consideration of the Machinery. It shall here the parties concerned and may take the opinion of other experts, if considered necessary. The recommendations, if unanimous, will be binding. In cases where there is no unanimity. the matter must return to the establishment level.

We have so far considered how new computer installations may be regulated. In the light of our recommendations, we have to consider an appropriate policy in regard to the existing computer installations. As we have mentioned, in some cases, the computers have been installed after appropriate consultation and agreement with the workers. By and large, these installations have been working smoothly. In other cases, disputes have arisen and while in some cases, these have been settled satisfactorily, some of the disputes are still active. It is obvious that these disputes as also any which may arise in future should be resolved satisfactorily. We think that the National Bipartite Machinery is the appropriate agency to settle such disputes. We, therefore, recommend that all present and future disputes in relation to the working of the existing and future computer establishments would be referred to the National Bipartite Machinery.

From our recommendations for future computer installations, it follows logically that all expansion of capacity of the existing installation should be governed by similar considerations and procedures. We, therefore, recommend that all future expansion of capacity of the existing computer installations whether by installation of additional computers or by replacement of the old computers by improved ones, should be subject to the same procedure as recommended earlier for future computer installations.

In conclusion, we should say that our approach to the problem of the use of computers is positive: while we have emphasised the need for appropriate regulation of the use of computers in the present stage of socio-economic development of the country and safeguards to prevent its adverse effects, we do recognize certain legitimate uses of computers in education, science, research, statistics and defence as also in commercial and industrial establishments. Consistent with this approach, we recommend that steps should be taken to ensure that the legitimate needs of the country in this field, both in hardware and software, be met as far as possible from indigenous sources. This will not only help in reducing imports and thus saving of foreign exchange but, by creating fresh avenues of employment, will also help to offset, at least partly, any possible adverse effects of computerisation on employment. It will also make possible development of research and training of skilled manpower in the field of computer technology and more generally in the field of electronics. We understand that the Department of Electronics is seized of the matter of ensuring self-reliance in this vital field.

EXPERT COMMITTEE ON COMPENSATION CLAIMS, 1969—REPORT

New Delhi, Railway Board (Ministry of Railways), 1970. 635p. (Memiographed)

One-man Committee : Shri R.B. Lal.
Secretary : Shri M.S. Bhandari.

APPOINTMENT

The Committee was appointed by the Railway Board (Ministry of Railways), vide letter No. ERBI-69/Col/51 dated August 1st, 1969 to go into the question of loss of and damage to consignments booked by Railways and the compensation claims arising therefrom.

TERMS OF REFERENCE

To go into the problem from the following three angles :

(i) Preventive measures which may reduce the incidence of losses and damages;

(ii) Prompt ard efficient handling of claims cases; and

(iii) Streamlining of the arrangements for contesting the claims cases.

CONTENTS

Introductory; **Part I**—Prevention of Claims—The Nature and Magnitude of the Problem; Claims Consciousness; Commercial and Claims Organisations; Unconnected Goods and Parcels; Addressing and Marketing; Labelling, Sealing and Riveting of Wagons; Staff Responsibility; Pilferage through Panel Cuts; Damage by Wet, Railway Protection Force; Bagged Consignments; Parcels; Perishables; Betel Leaves; Tea; Iron and Steel; Piece Goods; Detentions to Wagons; Stationery and Forms; Rule and Reference Books; Damage and Deficiency Messages; Claims Statistics; Miscellaneous; **Part II**—Settlement of Claims—Main Complaints of Public; Opening of Cases and Issue of Acknowledgements; Missing Goods Reports; Assessment and Shortage Certificates; Summary Disposal of Claims of Small Valuation; Enquiries in High Valuation Claims; Financial Concurrence; Procedure for Payment; Strengthening of the Claims Settlement Organisation of Eastern Railway; Repudiation of Claims; Statistical Disposal and Reopening of Claims; Time Limit for Settlement; Quantum of Compensation; Inter-Railway Liability; Demand for Change in System; Port Railways; Public Cooperation; **Part III**—Rationalisation of Legal Work—Prevention of Litigation; Causes of Suits; Results of Contested Suits; Technical Pleas; Preventive Measures; Pleadings and Evidence; Jurisdiction; Satisfaction of Decrees; Railway Advocates; **Part IV**—Organisational Matters—Separation of Commercial Cadre; Organisation to Implement Recommendations; Inspectors and Tracers; Staff at Loading, Unloading and Transhipment Points; **Part V**—Summary of Observations and Recommendations; Annexures I to VII.

RECOMMENDATIONS

Introductory : This report naturally highlights the weak spots in railway work which need strengthening. Much of it is devoted to a recountal of defects and shortcomings resulting in loss of or damage to goods and parcels. But it would be wrong to infer from this that our railways are not running efficiently. Claims represent a negative and small, though important, side of railway work, and do not in any way detract from the devoted service railways render to the nation, the high standards of efficiency they maintain and the impressive progress they have made in many directions.

This does not mean that there is no room for improvement. What this report does, within this Committee's terms of reference, is to indicate the directions in which improvement is necessary and possible and the ways of achieving it.

Nature And Magnitude Of The Problem

Loss, damage or deterioration of goods in transit is nothing but an accident or mishap to the particular consignment. To prevent claims is to ensure greater "safety" of goods and parcels.

Safety when applied to commodities should be understood to means not only that the consignment does not suffer any loss or damage but also that it reaches its correct destination. Both these aspects have to be attended to by railway staff, since goods and parcels cannot take care of themselves.

Compared to the train kilometres, the number of accidents is negligible. The same is true when the number and amount of claims are viewed in relation to the total value of goods, or even the net tonne kilometres carried.

Nevertheless close and constant attention must be paid to the safety of traffic; and this is no less necessary for goods and parcels than for passenger traffic.

Very little has been done so far for the safety of goods and parcels. Since goods and parcels account for 67 per cent of railway revenue, since goods traffic is more remunerative than passenger traffic and since the movement of goods is well recognised to be essential for the development of a country, the "safety" of goods and parcels certainly deserves a better deal from railways than it has received so far.

A claim arises when goods are lost, delayed or damaged. Therefore, every claim is a complaint against the railway and not simply a demand for compensation.

To the owners a claim may mean much inconvenience, stoppage of a factory, holding up of an important construction, breach of contract with another party, loss of business, locking up of valuable capital, etc.

The Railway Freight Structure Committee (1957) observed, " . . . what the consignors and consignees are most anxious about is not so much the rate of freight charge as the timely and safe arrival of goods at destination."

To the railways, every claim means loss of goodwill. When railways pay Rs. 10 crores as compensation, their total loss may well be put down at Rs. 100 crores in view of the loss of goodwill and the resulting diversion of high rated traffic. Undoubtedly this is one of the major factors responsible for driving away traffic from the railways.

In 1968-69 railways received 7,20,000 claims, and if in each claim five persons were interested, railways lost the goodwill of 36 lakhs of their customers. With so many railway users losing confidence in the ability of railways to carry the goods safely or to settle the claims gracefully, it may, well be imagined what an uphill task the Marketing and Sales and the Public Relations Organisations of railways have in retrieving either lost goodwill or lost traffic.

Claims are an important index of Railway efficiency. It is not sufficient for railways to increase the tonnage and earnings of goods and parcels traffic; they must also speed up the movement of the latter and at the same time ensure their greater 'safety'.

The prevention and settlement of claims must be given the same importance by railway administrations as is given to the safety of trains and the disposal of accident cases.

Statistics show that both in absolute terms and in relation to earnings claims have been going up. The rate of increase has become rather steep during recent years.

Even when an allowance is made for the increase in traffic and the general rise in prices, the index of increase in compensation indicates 59 per cent deterioration in the last two years. This deteriorating trend has continued in 1969-70, with a 12 per cent increase in the gross amount of compensation paid during April-September, 1969 as compared with the same period of 1968.

Available statistics show that one out of every 21 consignments becomes a casuality in transit. There is an obvious need for improving the safety factor of goods and parcels on railways.

Compared to Canadian, German and Japanese Railways, the position of Indian Government Railways in respect of claims is much worse. A better picture emerges in comparison to the figures of American Rail Roads. But while making this comparison, the following facts should also be kept in view—

(a) On American Rail Roads, 91 per cent of claims are paid ; the corresponding figure on Indian Government Railways is 53 per cent.

(b) On American Rail Roads, loss of entire packages accounts for 2.6 per cent of the entire amount paid ; the corresponding figure on Indian Government Railways is 31 per cent.

(c) Most of the claims an American Rail Roads are due to improper handling of goods, train accident and concealed damage.

When some of our officers go to foreign countries, it will be useful if they study and report on the efforts railways in those countries make for the prevention and speedy settlement of claims and how their claims organisations stand in public estimation.

If we compare the claims on goods and parcels traffic, it is seen that parcel traffic is more vulnerable to loss and damage, even though most of it is being handed from guard to guard, and the mode of transport is faster.

For every rupee earned as freight the compensation paid on parcels is thrice as much as on goods. Among parcels, perishables are more susceptible to loss and damage than non-perishables.

Most of the claims preferred and paid are on consignments of 'smalls' (less than wagon loads) whether booked as parcels or goods, though their earnings is much less. Taking all goods and parcels together 71% of the claims are on smalls, though parcels and goods smalls contribute only about 13% of the earnings.

Preventive effort has, therefore, to be specially directed to perishables, parcels and to goods in small lots.

Articles of food account for 55 per cent of the number and 47 per cent of the amount of claims paid.

Special studies of some of the important commodities like betal leaves, tea and piece goods have been made by this Committee and the results are given in separate chapters. These studies are only given as illustrations of what claims offices themselves should do every now and then in order to determine the direction of their preventive effort.

For appreciating the problem of claims, one should look not merely at the amount of compensation paid but at the total value of the claims received. In 1968-69, the gross amount of compensation paid was Rs. 10.2 crores. But the total value of claims received in the same year was about Rs. 55 crores.

The sharp rise in claims is partly due to the general deterioration in law and order position, soaring prices and scarcity of many articles of daily use, abnormal rains and floods and may to that extent be regarded as beyond the control of the Railways.

But a substantial part of the claims arises from causes well within the control of Railways, and it is to the eradication of these causes that Railways efforts should be directed with greater vigour.

The numerous memoranda this Committee received from railway users are unanimous in their criticism of lack of care in the transport of goods and parcels and of apathy in the disposal of claims by railways.

I was also struck by the fact that many of the observations made in these memoranda show remarkable insight in the working of railways in general and of claims offices in particular. It is clear, therefore, that railways will not be able to put off much longer the various reforms which are self-evident to the public and are necessary to ensure greater "safety" of goods and parcels and more efficient handling of claims.

Fortunately there is greater scope for improving the safety of goods than the safety of trains. Greater human care given to goods will be handsomely rewarded in the form of improved safety of consignments.

Another bright side to the picture is that claims prevention offers a great opportunity for producing results. Because so little was done in the past, much can be done now—with more effort and determination. "Safety" of goods and parcels is practically a new field only waiting to be exploited by the railways.

Claims Consciousness

If any scheme for the prevention of claims is to be successful it must begin by arousing the interest of all officers and staff in the safety of goods and by educating them in the various ways in which they can assist in preventing loss and damage.

The safety of goods requires the concerted efforts of staff of all departments—R.P.F., Transportation, Mechanical, Engineering, stores, etc. claims consciousness has therefore, to be instilled in the officers and staff of all departments.

It is necessary for the Railway Board to give a lead in the matter and for General Managers to take keen and sustained interest in the safety of goods and the efficient disposal of claims. Only in this way can concern for the safety of goods filter down to Goods Clerks, Trains Clerks, Train Examiners etc.

General Managers at their periodical meetings with their Heads of Departments should scrutinise the general position regarding the incidence and settlement of claims and matters of inter-departmental coordination having a bearing on claims.

General Managers should also regard the high value claims, which are sent to their office for sanction, as the pulse of the claims office and as indications of the weak spots which may need strengthening.

General Managers can galvanise the working of the claims organizations and improve the safety of goods, if they devote two minutes per day, or one hour every month, to matters connected with the prevention and settlement of claims.

The large numbers of staff who are actually responsible for the safety of goods, should be educated and got interested in various aspects of claims prevention and settlement. One way of doing this is for railways to issue frequent claims bulletins in their fortnightly Gazette or separately, if so desired.

Every issue of the Railway's Gazette should have some pages devoted to claims matters. The write-ups should be easy to understand and also as attractive, instructive and varied as possible. Some of the matters which can be profitably brought home to staff are listed in the report.

Commercial And Claims Organization

As the claims branch is responsible not only for the settlement but also prevention of claims, a weak claims organization itself becomes a major cause of increase in claims.

No one would think of making or maintaining 100 engines with the manpower or material sanctioned for 10. No one would think of maintaining 100 or even 40 kilometres of track with the staff sanctioned for 10. But when it comes to commercial work there seems to be a general feeling that whatever the increase in workload, the existing officers and staff will always be able to manage it somehow.

Railways are carrying ever increasing loads of traffic and all other departments have been suitably strengthened. But all these years very little or nothing has been done to augment the outdoor commercial staff who actually deal with the traffic, the Commercial Officers and Inspectors who supervise their work or those who deal with claims in the Claims Offices.

In such circumstances, a progressive deterioration in the efficiency of commercial work, with a consequent increase in claims and public dissatisfactions is inevitable.

Compared with 1950-51 the number of claims registered annually has more than doubled and the amount paid has more than trebled. But nothing has been done to strengthen the claims Organization on Railways. This is undoubtedly one of the major contributory causes of the increase in claims. For when a claims organization is weak not only is settlement work done in a dilatory and slipshod manner but the preventive side is largely neglected. Thus a vicious circle is set up; as the quality of work goes down, the number of claims goes up and with every rise in claims, the quality goes down fur ther.

In the last two years, the amount paid by Eastern Railway shot up from Rs. 98 lakhs to Rs. 167 and Rs. 262 lakhs. What has happened on Eastern Railway is by no means a strange or unexpected phenomenon. It may well be taken as a warning of what is going to be repeated, sooner rather than later, on the other railways unless energetic steps are taken to arrest the deterioration.

While prevention and settlement of claims are inter-related and inter-dependent, of the two, prevention is the more fundamental and more fruitful. Unless the major sources of claims are plugged, the number of claims goes on increasing unendingly, completely throwing out of gear the machinery that deals with claims as well as the resulting litigation. Therefore effective prevention holds the key to the entire problem of claims.

Whether judged from the view point of railways' good name, public satisfaction or retention or development of high rated traffic, prevention of claims should be considered an essential work and given very high priority. And this requires a strong claims organization and effective supervision of Commercial work at stations on all railways.

Unconnected Goods and Parcels

In the cause-wise analysis of claims paid a distinction is made between theft of complete packages or consignments and loss of complete packages or consignments. In 1968-69, the number and amount of claims paid on account of thefts of complete packages or consignments were 992 and Rs. 8 lakhs respectively, while the number and amount of claims paid on account of loss of complete packages or consignments were 104,609 and 315 lakhs respectively.

Since packages or consignments shown under "Loss" were not stolen, the obvious question is what happened to them and how they were lost on the railways.

My conclusions are that while some of these 'Lost' cases should have been classified under the head of thefts, the vast majority would fall under the following categories :—

(i) Goods mislaid and lying unconnected on the railways;

(ii) Surreptitions removals from sheds by consignees or their agents;

(iii) Goods wrongly delivered to private sidings or out-agencies though not belonging to them; and

(iv) Small packages disappearing from the custody of railway staff such as guards, travelling Goods or Parcel Clerks.

A thing mislaid is a thing lost and there is no doubt that in many claims paid for loss of packages or consignments the goods are actually lying unconnected at other stations—perhaps hundreds of kilometres away. Striking confirmation of this explanation is seen in the wagon load and smalls consignments lying unconnected or railways, whose numbers run into hundreds and thousands respectively.

Figures furnished by railways show that on 1.9.'69, 1295 unconnected wagon load consignments (excluding coal) were lying on the Indian Railways, some of them for even 3 or 4 years. In addition, the number of unconnected coal wagons on the railways must run into hundreds.

A physical check made by a couple of Inspectors at Mughalsarai between 15.12.'69 and 27.12.'69 showed 489 unconnected wagons standing underload in that yard for long periods. Of these the arrival particulars of 336 wagons could not be traced and the other 153 wagons, whose arrival particulars could be traced, had been received at Mughalsarai during the period June 1969 to November 1969.

The problem of connecting wagons found without labels at Mughalsarai is formidable. In the 11 day period from 21.12.'69 to 31-12.'69, 1103 wagons were either received without labels or lost their labels in the yard. Many of these wagons remain in Mughalsarai yard for months awaiting connections and despatch.

When a wagon becomes unconnected, it is detained underload while efforts are made to ascertain its correct destination. Detentions to unconnected wagons mean diminished wagon availability and loss of valuable space in yards. And such detained wagons are liable to be lost sight of completely and the older they become the more difficult becomes the task of connecting them. The detentions to unconnected wagons may vary from a few days to a few weeks or even months. Old dated unconnected wagons may be found in most of the large yards. This is another aspect of unconnected wagons which railways will do well to bear in mind.

Lists of unconnected wagon loads compiled by railways are by no means complete. There is every reason to believe that the actual numbers of unconnected wagon loads on railways would be much more than what are reported by stations.

In addition to these wagon load consignments, there are large numbers of small packages lying in the various Lost Property Office, goods sheds and parcel offices. Many of these packages are very costly.

Unconnected consignments—wagon loads and smalls—present a gold mine for claims prevention as the goods are still in the custody of railways when claims are paid.

Many of the unconnected consignments undergo deterioration and pilferage while they lie with the railways for months together. Most of these goods are eventually sold at throw away prices.

The usual approach to the problem of unconnected packages/consignments is to try to connect them. But railways should not be content merely with efforts to connect up the goods which have become unconnected. They should go down to the root of the matter and do all they can to prevent the goods from becoming unconnected.

The consignments of goods loose or in bulk, such as minerals, coal, fire-wood, sand, etc. become unconnected if the labels on the wagons containing them get detached or are intentionally removed. Therefore, the way to tackle this part of the problem is to take steps to ensure that wagon labels are correctly prepared and properly secured and in case of deliberate removal of labels, people responsible are taken to task.

Packed goods become unconnected if—

(i) wagons containing them lose labels and if in addition,

(ii) the packages do not show the railway marks and senders' and consignees' addresses.

The way to prevent such goods becoming unconnected is to insist on a meticulous compliance with the rules for marking of goods and for labelling and guidancing of wagons.

When packed goods lie unconnected for months, it shows four-fold failures, viz.,

(i) The seal cards and bracket labels somehow disappeared;

(ii) None of the packages were marked or addressed;

(iii) No guidance or invoice was placed inside the wagon; and

(iv) No paste on labels were affixed inside the wagon.

Railways do organise P.L.M. (Packing, Labelling and Marking) Campaigns from time to time but the station staff do not take these campaigns seriously. If the problem of unconnected goods is to be solved Railways cannot afford to be satisfied with even 99.9% compliance with the rules: the target for the station staff must be 110% compliance with the rules which are very simple to carry out. There is no reason why, for example, a bale of piece goods, a case of machine parts or of medicine should not bear the mark or address on two sides.

A post office would not accept even a bundle of old newspapers unless it bears sender's as well as consignee's full address, but on the railways even packages worth thousands of rupees are accepted for booking without proper documentation. An examination of the packages passing over the railways shows that contrary to rules many of them, especially parcels of perishables, are marked and addressed very inadequately.

Rule 1537 of the Commercial Manual requires that (a) covered wagons will carry seal card or tie on labels in addition to bracket labels and (b) open wagons will have tie on labels in addition to bracket labels. But it is very rare to find a wagon carrying four labels. Usually they carry either bracket labels or seal card/tie on labels but not both. Tie on labels are very rarely used on wagons. Labels are often written out illegibly. Contrary to the Rules, code initials of station names are used. Some labels are of brown colour on which the blue pencil does not show off well. Many are written with black pencil or in ink which fades away or is washed down.

Out of Rs. 3.15 crores that railways paid under this head in 1968-69, they could easily have saved at least Rs. 1.5 crores if their arrangements for the documentation of wagons, goods and parcels had been satisfactory.

To every unconnected consignment or package on which a claim is paid, there are several unconnected packages which are eventually taken to the correct destination and do not result in actual payment. Even the latter type of goods, for which no statistics are readily available but whose number must be large, throw a good deal of strain on the railways and at the same time cause loss and inconvenience to the public.

The problem of unconnected goods is a major one to be tackled by railways in right earnest, quite apart from its large financial implications to the railways themselves.

Unconnected goods are potentially a very rich field for claims prevention and one which will respond quickly to determined and concerted effort, seeing that though claims are paid, the goods are still in the custody of the railways and are eventually auctioned for trifling sums after suffering damage, deterioration and pilferage.

I.R.C.A. Office near New Delhi station maintains a daily account of all wagons interchanged between Railways. These records are very useful for connecting up unconnected wagons, but full use is not being made of them. Railways should notify all concerned staff about the availability and utility of the records maintained in I.R.C.A., which should be consulted as soon as wagons become unconnected without waiting for claims or complaints from the public.

I.R.C.A. Office also receives transhipment particulars of wagon load consignments at some break of gauge tranship points. But no use is being made of these records. Railways should give wide publicity to their availability and utility through circulars and notifications. I.R.C.A. should also ensure that the returns are received from the break-of-gauge points regularly. Copies of these returns should also be sent to the adjoining Railways/Divisions for ready reference.

It will be helpful if the work of connecting unconnecting wagons can be computerised. In the same process, over-due wagons can be traced—as what is an unconnected wagon at one station will be an over-due wagon at another station.

While the Railways paid Rs. 3.15 crores in 1968-69 on account of loss of complete packages, the amount recovered from the sale of both unconnected and unclaimed goods was only Rs. 63.6 lakhs.

The value of unconnected goods realised during 1968-69 works out to Rs. 46.40 lakhs or about one sixth of the total compensation paid on loss of entire packages. It is obvious that Railways are not able to get a fair price for the unconnected goods in auctions. This confirms the conclusion of the Committee that if we can bring down the number of wagons/packages becoming unconnected, a substantial reduction can be made in the Railways' claims bill.

The economics of the working of the existing Lost Property Offices deserve examination. If the annual rental value of buildings and godowns occupied by the above-mentioned Lost Property Offices and the other miscellaneous expenses, such as cost of transport of goods from the stations to the L.P.O., cost of auction-notices, amounts paid to professional auctioners, value of stationery, etc. are added to the staff costs, expenditure on L.P.Os. may perhaps work out to be even more than the sale-proceeds of goods.

Thus, the gains from the auction sales of unconnected goods seem to be largely illusory, if not altogether negative. This is another fact that underlines the necessity of preventing goods and parcels from becoming unconnected.

As far as possible unconnected goods should be set off against 'missing' consignments or delivered on valuation. And this should be done as soon as possible after the goods are found to be unconnected.

Auctioning of unclaimed and unconnected goods should be decentralised. As far as possible, goods should be auctioned at the station where they are found or at the nearest marketing centre, with the least possible delay. Some Railways are already arranging local auctions and this should be encouraged. At the same time the work-load in the existing L.P.Os. should be reviewed and staff adjustments made.

Railways should consider the desirability of conducting auctions departmentally instead of through professional auctioneers.

Addressing And Marking

Addressing and marking of packages are essential in order to identify them, to take them to their correct destinations and to correlate them with particular bookings.

Goods of a non-perishable nature can be kept on hand for some time while efforts to connect them with their specific bookings are being made. But perishable articles become a dead loss if they are so detained.

Though railways may succeed in connecting up at a great cost of time and labour a percentage of unconnected articles of a non-perishable nature, there is no chance of such success in case perishable goods become unconnected. Therefore it is extremely important—in fact indispensable—that all cosignments of perishables whether in smalls or full wagon loads, be marked in a fool proof manner and wagons or vans containing them be provided with proper seal cards, bracket and perishable labels.

Tie-on labels used on perishable bags or brackets are not very suitable. The writings in ink on them may be washed away, then may easily get torn or detached or may be intentionally removed or detached in order to make them unconnected and available for memo-delivery or auction.

When tie-on labels are attached to baskets containing perishables, consignee's address be also shown on the basket itself, and when the basket is of such a make that the consignee's name and address cannot be shown on it, it should either be enclosed in gunny or at least have a gunny patch spread and attached on to it for writing both sender's and railway marks, and the gunny patch should be large enough to accommodate all this. Such gunny patches are already in use on some railways. Separate clauses should be added in order to bring this out in Rule 705 of Coaching Tariff and Rule 121 of Goods Tariff.

It will be better if the headings of the rules in the Goods and Coaching Tariff are changed so as to read "Addressing and Marking of Goods/Parcels" instead of simply "Marking of Goods or Parcels" as at present.

This change is necessary in order to emphasise the fact that addressing—and not merely marking—of consignments is an essential condition for safe transport.

Rule 705 of I.R.C.A. Coaching Tariff Pt. I should be amended so as to make it obligatory for the sender to show the consignee's name and full address on all packages which are not booked to self. In case of Parcels booked to self, the sender should also show "Self" and full name of destination station together with an identifying private mark on each so as to distinguish the packages booked to different consignees from one another as a safeguard against exchange, cross delivery and possible claims.

It should also be clarified in the Goods and Coaching Tariffs that perishables cannot be booked to self. Consignee's full name should invariably be shown on each package containing perishables.

Senders should be prohibited from using Code abbreviations of either the forwarding or the destination station. They must show the full name of the station in all cases and as a further precaution they must also show after the destination station name (except in case of large and well known stations like Calcutta, Allahabad, Madras) either the state or the Railway where it is located.

Railway staff should also be prohibited from using Code abbreviations of station names in railway marks, in railway receipts and in wagon labels. This will go a long way in reducing the high incidence of losses of entire packages or consignments.

It should be clarified in Rule 705 (1) of I.R.C.A. Coaching Tariff and Rule 121 (1) of Goods Tariff (Part I) whether packages in full wagon loads and not requiring transhipment should be marked by the sender in full or only 10 per cent. It is also necessary to add a new clause in both the Rules in order to clarify that whenever transhipment enroute is involved the sender must mark every package even in case of consignments in full wagon loads.

In case of marking by railway also, it is necessary to add a new clause under Rule 705 (2) of the Coaching Tariff (Part I) and Rule 121 of Goods Tariff (Part I) so as to leave no room for doubt that when goods are consigned in full wagon loads but require transhipment, the Railway marks are to be given on each and every package by railway staff.

Many kinds of goods which can be easily marked are not being marked. Railways should make all out efforts to train their staff and persuade the despatchers to mark all the goods which can be marked. Special arrangements in this connection are required to be made with big despatchers.

For quick connection of consignments reaching destination station without a copy of Invoice, with the help of the machine abstracts of railway receipts, it would be advantageous to adopt the system of marking railway receipt number on the Packages at all stations. Any Railway who envisages difficulty in changing over to this system should study the working at Wadi Bunder and other stations of the Central Railway where this method of marking is already in vogue.

Labelling, Sealing And Riveting Of Wagons

If the labels on a wagon are not affixed or lost or torn or deficient or illegible, the wagon is liable to become unconnected as it would not then be known at what station the wagon was loaded and to what station it is booked.

Large stations usually have several big consumers of coal, such as Power House, Loco Foreman, Textile Mill, etc. It should be ensured that collieries show the consignee's name on all wagons.

Railways should make para 1537 of Indian Railways Commercial Manual known to all staff and take steps for its rigid compliance.

Wagon labels should all be made of white card board so that the writing on them will stand out clearly against the white background. The seal and tie-on labels should have at least two holes through which tape may be passed. The eyelets on seal and tie-on labels should be suitably reinforced with paper, cloth or tin, so that the labels will not easily tear away at the holes. These labels are required to be tied to handles or other suitable places on the wagon by means of cotton tape and the use of sootlie for this purpose is prohibited.

In actual practice the supply and use of wagon labels are seen to be far from satisfactory in several respects as enumerated in this report.

Correctly prepared and firmly secured labels are the key to the correct transport of wagons.

The Committee does not recommend the use of paste-on labels outside wagons at present.

The existing rules, which are being carried out half-heartedly and partially, should be implemented in their entirety.

Railways should collect information about the practice in vogue in other advanced countries in regard to the labelling of open and covered wagons.

Railways should see that the use of code initials on wagon labels is completely stopped.

Names of selected pairs of stations (from and to stations) between which traffic is fairly heavy (say, 20 wagons or more per month) should be got printed on both sides of the 'bracket' labels and 'tie-on' labels and seal card labels in bold letters as is done in the case of printed card tickets. This would eliminate the problem of illegible labels. An alternative suggestion is the use of a 'Bradma' machine at large goods depots and transhipment points for printing of 'Station From, and 'Station To' on the labels at the time of loading.

Marshalling yards should exercise proper checks on wagon labels. Where label on one side is found missing it should be replaced by the Trains Clerk taking the particulars from the label on the other side of the wagon. When both sides labels are missing, fresh labels should be put in on the basis of the incoming guard's vehicle guidance. Similar action should be taken by guards at stations where trains have long halts.

In case of loaded bogie wagons, there should be two brackets labels and are tie-on label on each side.

Rule 1536 of the Commercial Manual requires that 'Paste-on' labels should be pasted on inside panels of the doors on both sides of the wagons This rule should be enforced.

The pasting of labels and their subsequent removal both present difficulties. Some wagons have pockets on the inside panel for keeping such labels. A more extensive provision of such pockets inside covered wagons preferably on the doors, will be useful.

For various reasons about 90 per cent of the wagons found with defective seals are allowed to go through without checking of the seal defective wagons whose contents are checked only a small percentage is found with shortages.

Railways should consider whether a change is required in their outlook towards seals and seal checking. The practice obtaining on railways in some foreign countries may be ascertained to see if we can profit by their experience in this respect.

So long as the rules stand as they are, sealing wax of good quality, seal card labels of strong and standard design and tape should be regularly supplied to stations in adequate quantity, so that seal card labels may be firmly tied to wagons.

Railways may also consider the relative merits of lac seals and lead seals.

Rules 1551 (b) of the Commercial Manual should be made known to all staff and should be enforced.

The Committee examined many wagons during its tours and observed that only one rivet on a door is generally used though there are four places for it.

Method of riveting has also been explained in the Manual with a diagram. In several cases found that the riveting had not been done properly and the rivet could be easily taken out.

In the case of wagons loaded with valuable commodities, I recommend that (i) nut and bolt type of rivet of ordinary size may be used in the latch of the vertical bar—one end of the rivet has to be hammered and flushed, (ii) thicker type of nut and bolt rivet may be fixed at the place where seal cards are now tied. Some stations have already started using these types of rivets for better security of goods, (iii) on some wagons, the vertical bar used as locking bolt has a riveting hole near the top. Staff should put a rivet through this hole on wagons where it is provided and which are loaded with valuable goods. On account of its height thieves will find it very difficult to remove this rivet.

I would emphasise the necessity for taking stringent measures to ensure proper locking of brake-vans, luggage vans, and parcels vans. Many big thefts are reported from time to time from brake-vans of Mail and Express trains and it is essential that their luggage compartments be kept properly locked at all times.

Staff Responsibility

The usual custom in dealing with cases of damage, loss, etc. is that responsibility of staff is fixed and disciplinary proceedings are started, if at all, only when a claim has been paid. This practice is untenable. It is contrary to the universally accepted principle that punishment should follow default with as little delay as possible. Moreover, the longer an investigation is deferred the greater the difficulty in bringing the charge home to the defaulter—and in the meantime he goes on committing similar offences either willingly or unwillingly.

The present system has done much harm to the railways as staff are very rarely taken to task for carelessness and even wilful negligence resulting in claims; and whatever punishments are inflicted are generally very mild and delayed and, therefore, quite ineffective. This is undoubtedly one of the major causes of the increase in claims.

The Committee examined a number of claim files on different railways and found that except in a very few cases enquiries to fix staff responsibility, even if started, were not completed and this is even more true of through traffic than of local traffic. Even in cases where packages worth thousands of rupees disappeared from the custody of staff files did not show that any vigorous action was taken either to trace the missing goods or to fix the responsibility of the staff.

Statistics furnished by railways show that the number of staff penalised for loss, damage, etc. is insignificant compared to the total number of claims attributable to their default and the punishments awarded are generally very light.

Statistics furnished by railways show that disciplinary action was taken in barely one case out of every 100 in which it was due. Stated differently, it means that the chances of being caught and punished for causing loss or damage to goods are one in a hundred; that is to say, a man can safely commit 50 or 80 irregularities resulting in loss of goods without running any serious risk of being penalised.

On the Western Railway, there is a system according to which Railway Protection Force fixes responsibility on staff in cases of shortages found from seal intact wagons, but Divisions only issue warnings to staff in such cases. Such warnings in stereotyped form act as an encouragement rather than a deterrent to staff.

In case of a detention to a train, engine failure, accident or fraud, no one would wait for a complaint before starting investigations with a view to disciplinary and preventive action. Yet this is precisely what is happening in dealing with cases of loss or damage to goods.

That the claims bill is not more than what it actually is, inspite of a permissive system of supervision, is a reflection of the high sense of duty of the vast majority of railwaymen. Nevertheless, the few staff who wittingly or unwittingly cause loss or pilferage, cannot be allowed to have their own way as their example will prove infections.

This Committee recommends that in order to arrest the alarming pace of increase in claims railways must resort to a system of taking prompt and deterrent action against all staff found responsible for thefts and losses.

Enquiries should be started to trace a missing package or localise the loss and fix responsibility as soon as loss or damage or pilferage comes to notice and without waiting for the claim. In other words, action should be initiated promptly on the basis of damage and deficiency advices issued by transhipment and destination stations or the Missing Goods Reports submitted by destination stations.

The work of enquiries may be suitably apportioned between Claims Offices and Divisions, avoiding duplication and keeping in mind the fact that enquiries under Disciplinary Rules are properly the function of Divisions.

Whenever the loss or damage is heavy, say Rs. 3,000 or more, it should be arranged that the Divisional Commercial Superintendent or Assistant Commercial Superintendent will personally witness it as far as possible and in any case order immediate enquiries to localise the loss, fix responsibility and suggest preventive measures.

Commercial Officers/Inspectors should regularly scrutinise inward D.D. messages of their stations or transhipment sheds (i.e. the reports of loss and damage on the goods or parcels despatched) and take immediate action where the responsibility of staff of their Division is clearly established e.g. shortage from seals intact wagon, mis-despatches wrong or inadequate marking, non-provision of dunnage, non-compliance with compulsory packing or loading conditions, etc.

During the course of regular as well as surprise inspections, Commercial Officers and Inspectors should check up whether the discrepancy reported in the outward D.D. messages tallies with the goods unloaded and whether wagons have been correctly loaded. Staff responsible for any irregularity detected during the course of such inspections should be taken to task as a regular practice.

In heavy claims, an Inspector should trace the movement of the consignment right from the booking station to the destination station. He should record statements of the staff concerned and fix responsibility for loss, damage or delays.

In order to ensure quick tracing of valuable packages and the prompt fixation of responsibility, the different railways will have to function in these matters as zones of one and the same organization and not as separate and independent railway systems. There should, therefore, be no objection to a senior Inspector of one Railway making enquiries on another Railway or his report being sent by our Railway to a Divisional Superintendent of another Railway for disciplinary action.

A copy of the enquiry report should be sent to the Division or Railway concerned to take up with the staff responsible and intimate the action taken to the claims office of the destination railway.

Heavy claims deserve the same importance and attention as the Operating Department gives to accident cases.

Chief Commercial Superintendents should treat it as their personal responsibility to watch that in all cases of heavy loss or damage due to irregular working on the part of railway staff, the defaulters are brought to book promptly and the penalty imposed is adequate.

Demi-official letters should be written and meetings held at various levels from time to time in order to ensure that prompt and adequate action is taken against defaulting staff—even those working on foreign railway—in all outstanding cases where the loss was heavy.

Enquiries will have to be instituted not only promptly but also in a much larger number of cases. Where responsibility is fixed in one case at present, it will have to be done in 100 cases. For this purpose the organization in claims offices and on Divisions will have to be adequately strengthened. This is an indispensable requirement.

Exemplary punishment in proved cases will have a widespread salutary effect and the number of cases of heavy loss and the work load on the claims offices will both decline. Earlier completion of enquiries in advance of receipt of claims will also go a long way to speed up the settlement of claims and help in the tracing of missing packages.

Pilferage Through Panel Cuts

Rs. 106 lakhs or nearly 1/4th of the total compensation was paid due to pilferage through body holes or panel cuts. The corresponding amount in 1966-67 was Rs. 31 lakhs only.

Incidence of payment due to panel cuts is very high on the Eastern, Southern, North-East Frontier, South Eastern and Central Railways.

The main commodities pilfered are foodgrains, sugar, oilseeds, spices, jeera and turmeric on which some payments in individual cases have been very heavy.

Sometimes as many as 20 to 90 bags (along with coverings) were reported stolen through panel cuts of a wagon with forwarding station seals intact.

A sample check made by the Southern Railway for a week at Raichur disclosed that 42 per cent of the covered stock handed over at this inter-change point had body holes or panel cuts. It indicates that a large number of such wagons are in circulation. North-East Frontier Railway has been compelled to make an arrangement under which contents of panel cut wagons are transhipped into good wagons at Katihar.

It is not clear why thieves should take the trouble of cutting panels of wagons and extracting large quantities of goods through them, which must be a slow process, when they can more easily remove the rivets of the doors of the wagons and take away entire bags.

Security Department should collect information as to how these thefts are being committed and where.

While the incidence of shortage found per victimised wagon is very heavy on certain Railways like Eastern, North-East Frontier and North Eastern it is not so heavy on other Railways like Southern and Central. It is quite possible that in certain cases the shortages are being exaggerated by staff in collusion with the consignees.

Trains/wagons loaded with foodgrains, sugar, oil seeds etc. should be shadowed by Railway Protection Force Staff in order to detect the modus operandi of such crimes and the areas where they are common and to arrest the criminals.

Machinery should be created for more large scale and widespread repairs of panel cut wagons not only in workshops and Sick Lines, but also in Goods sheds and yards in order to restrict the circulation of the damaged wagons.

I found three methods being used for the repair of panel cuts—namely welding, riveting and patching with a plastic compound. Even the last method is quite effective as a temporary expedient.

The lower portion of the wagon panel upto, say 60 cms., above the floor level may be strengthened and thicker plates used over this portion in new constructions.

To minimise the possibility of fraudulent claims being preferred under this head, Commercial Officers and Inspectors should make spot checks to ascertain :

(i) The number of packages actually found loaded in a wagon compared with the number shown in railway receipt/guidance.

(ii) Number of packages actually unloaded and their condition compared with the shortages shown in the station records, vig. Damage and Deficiency Advice. There should be instructions to all stations which are in the habit of reporting heavy shortages from panel cut wagons that all such wagons should be unloaded in presence of an officer or an Inspector or the senior most staff present at the station.

The loading of bagged and valuable consignments in wagons having body holes or panel cuts should be completely banned.

Where a full wagon load of broad gauge is transhipped into full metre gauge wagons or where one wagon load of metre gauge is transhipped into one full broad gauge wagon, the bags should be loaded in the middle of the wagon, leaving about 30 to 60 cm. of empty space near the walls all around.

Section Controller should advise Sub-Inspector, Railway Protection Force, as soon as a goods train with loaded Wagon is stabled at a roadside station. Sub-Inspector, Railway Protection Force should promptly despatch at least 2 rakshaks to guard the stabled loads at road-side stations. Commercial Controllers and Officers should also watch and ensure this.

Damage By Wet

Claims paid in 1968-69 on account of damage by wet numbered 35,021 and the amount paid was Rs. 1·12 crores. Numerically they represent 8.3% of all the claims paid and monetarily 11% of the total amount paid.

The chief commodities, on which claims for damage were paid, were foodgrains, spices, sugar, piecegoods, tea and cement. They accounted for Rs. 83 lakhs or 74 per cent of the amount paid for damage by wet.

Foodgrains are often carried in open wagons even during the monsoon months on account of the imperative necessity of moving the grains soon after harvesting and shortage of covered stock. Though railways have issued instructions that foodgrains loaded in open wagons must be covered with tarpaulins, this precaution, even when it is carried out, does not afford enough protection to the grains. Railways should see that the movement of foodgrains in open stock is totally stopped.

Railways set up a special organization for repairs

of leaky roofs of wagons during the monsoon months, viz., June to October. But these arrangements do not adequately meet the needs of even the monsoon months, not to speak of other months of the year.

Whatever the arrangements for making wagons water tight, either many non-water tight wagons have perforce to be used for loading damageable goods or the wagons are made water tight in such a way that their roofs are unable to withstand heavy showers. The Mechanical department should look into the adequacy of the existing arrangements for making wagons water tight, especially the durability of the waterproofing plastic components or compounds used at present.

As high rated traffic, which railways are anxious to develop and retain, is all susceptible to damage by wet, water tightness of wagons deserves much greater attention.

Though the recognised monsoon period is from June to October, cases of damage by wet are reported at some stations all the year round. Obviously water tight wagons are neeeded even during the so called dry months.

The organization which railways set up temporarily during monsoon months for making the wagon water tight should be retained, on a suitable scale, all the year round for patching up both roofs and panels of wagons.

During the monsoon period arrangements for making wagons water tight should be made not only in sick lines but also in goods sheds and sidings where there is heavy loading of sugar; grains and pulses, c.p. goods, spices, tea and cement.

For commodities like cement which are worthless after becoming wet, the damaged stuff should be segregated and weighed to arrive at the extent of damage, instead of giving ad hoc percentage assessment. Use of this method has resulted in considerable reduction of claims.

Railway Protection Force

The various memoranda sent by the public have voiced great concern at the working of the Railway Protection Force.

Many railway officials too, from Heads of Departments and Divisional Superintendents down to Commercial Clerks, have complained bitterly of indifferent working and aggressiveness on the part of R.P.F.

Though R.P.F. has on the whole done good work, it could have done better, and not all the criticism levelled against it is unjustified.

The present difficulties stem primarily from the fact that in recent years the R.P.F. has sought to grow up as an altogether independent organization. Some of the officers drawn from the Police have in the past been liabilities rather than assets to the railways. They started with the initial handicap of being unfamiliar with the details of railway work and did not identify themselves with the great organization which they were called upon to serve.

This department has shown some evil tendencies : for example reluctance to cooperate with other departments, departmentalism and even aggressiveness. The weaknesses of the R P.F. arise chiefly from these causes. Even though I have drawn pointed attention to them, it is not with the intention of implying that they are universal or wide spread, but merely to emphasise the necessity for early remedial measures so that they may be checked before they have spread too far.

Railways should adopt firm measures to inculcate a spirit of service and cooperation among the personnel of the R.P.F. As the largest organized enterprise in the country, railway cannot function for a moment unless a spirit of mutual cooperation permeates the working of all their departments. The R.P.F. cannot be allowed to be an exception to this general principle.

Railways spent Rs. 13.30 crores in 1968-69 on R.P.F. and if they are to get full value for the money spent, the R.P.F.—more particularly the Police Officers in it —will have to identify itself whole heartedly and completely with all the other departments of railways especially with the Commercial Department.

So far as keeping watch on goods and parcels is concerned, the R.P.F. staff deployed on such duties must be trained to regard themselves for all practical purposes as members of the Commercial Department and not its masters.

Efficiency, cooperation and esprit de corps have to be built into the organizational pattern itself so that no one will be left in any doubt as to what is expected of him, particularly in regard to his responsibilities to other departments.

For this purpose, the recent trend to develop the R.P.F. as an entirely independent organization should be reversed and steps should be taken to secure its emotional and organizational integration with the other departments of the railway.

At the Divisional level, the Security Organization should be placed under the Divisional Superintendent, like Engineering, Transportation and other branches. At present, Assistant Security Officers are left more or less to themselves without adequate supervision by the Chief Security Officer or the Security Officer who have extensive jurisdictions and multifarious pre-occupations.

The R.P.F. when it is placed under the Divisional Superintendent, will itself reap the benefits of the Divisional system.

The recruitment of Rakshaks is at present done by a committee of Assistant Security Officers. This, I was told, has resulted in many complaints and Vigilance cases.

The recruitment of Rakshaks should be made in the same way as for other Class IV staff on the railways. In other words, the Selection Committee, should include the Assistant Security Officer and at least two other officers of other departments

At present, training in goods and parcel work is given to Sub-Inspectors as well as Rakshaks by R.P.F. Inspectors. Instructors in Commercial work for R.P.F. schools and college should be drawn from the rank of senior and competent commercial hands as is done in the case of Transportation Schools on the railways.

I understand there is a rule that only Police Officers can bacome Chief Security Officers. Owing to the difficulty of getting really first class officers from the Police Department and in view of past experience, this policy should be changed.

Railways should develop their own officer cadre for R.P.F. In course of time, the posts of Security Officers and Chief Security Officers will have to be thrown open to these officers. But even at present, there is no reason why competent officers, whether from the Security or Traffic Department, should not be selected to fill some of the posts of Chief Security Officers.

It is recommended that one-third to one-half of the C.S.Os posts may be filled by promotion from within the railway. For this purpose, due consideration may be given to ex-Army Officers already serving on the railways in J.A. and I.A. grade.

The utmost care should be exercised in selecting officers from the Police for R.P.F. Railway Board should not go merely by the confidential reports but should also have a personal interview with the proposed candidates and if possible make independent enquiries before arriving at a decision.

I understand that under the existing rules, appeals against the orders of C.S.O, are disposed of not by the General Manager, but by the Director, Security Force. This, again, is a wrong arrangement indicative of a spirit of departmentalisn.

For the Armed Wing, Training School and the Intelligence Branch, posts may be reserved for Police Officers. But there is no compelling necessity to employ Police Officers for general posts in R.P.F.

Promotion to Class II in R.P.F. is also done at present on a purely departmental basis inasmuch as the Selection Committee consists of R.P.F. officers. For the reasons already mentioned earlier, selection for promotion as A.S.O. should be made railwaywise and the Selection Committee should include the Chief Commercial Superintendent and the Chief Operating Superintendent or any other Head of Department in lieu of the Chief Operating Superintendent.

One retired Chairman, Railway Board, expressed the view that as the Security Department exists on railways primarily for the Security of packages, the C.S.O. should be under the C.C.S. There is much force in this suggestion, especially because General Managers, under whom the C.S.Os. are nominally placed at present, have really no time to exercise any supervision check on the working of the R.P.F.

As a first step I recommend that (a) the Security Department be placed under the General Manager for all purposes like Operating, Mechanical or Engineering department and (b) General Managers should see to it that the Chief Security Officers give the fullest co-operation to other departments, especially the commercial department.

R.P.F. have been doing good work in combating crime with the help of the Railway Property Unlawful Possession Act. When they have gained more experience of this work and placed it on a proper footing, it will be advantageous to extend their powers so that they can deal with all cases of theft within railway premises even when the stolen property has not been recovered. Eventually the best arrangement for railways from every point of view would be to have their own Railway Protection Police by taking over the G.R.P. and merging it with the R.P.F.

It is recommended that the post of Assistant Security Officer be upgraded to senior scale in the heavier Divisions, particularly at the major State capitals such as Lucknow, Patna and Jaipur, where the Security Branch is often required to liaise with Senior Police Officers.

It will be better to have Divisional Security Officers in direct control of the Divisional Security forces, in replacement of the existing Security Officers, whose work is more or less of an administrative nature.

To arrest the rising trend of crime, railways should consider strengthening the Intelligence branch of R.P.F.

The Intelligence branch should work in close co-operation with claims offices and assist not only in checking thefts but also fraudulent and exaggerated claims.

Places like Mughalsarai, Garhara, Chitpur, Farakka and Kalyan, which are infested with thieves, pose a challenge to the R.P.F. and should receive special attention.

Shortages of entire packages from open wagons, seal defective and seal intact wagons should be classified as 'theft'. Participation of the R.P.F. in the investigation of such cases will be helpful.

I suggest that in their crime Reports, the Security department should show two sets of figures in juxtaposition—(1) No. of Reports received and (2) No. of cases registered. The station staff must docket a copy of D.D. message, wherever they suspect any criminal interference, to the concerned official in charge of the R.P.F. post. The Commercial officers and the Security officers should check whether these docket copies have been received by official-in-charge of R.P.F. and whether it has been duly included in 'No. of Reports received' by the R.P.F.

Principal of the R.P.F. College at Lucknow mentioned that he was not able to get good instructors because of non-availability of quarters for them. There are no private houses nearly and people are reluctant to come on deputation without living accommodation. The allowances given to these Instructors are also not at par with those given to the teaching staff of the other Area Schools of the Railways. These matters deserve onsideration.

There is a need for more equipment in the Model Room of the College for practical and visual demonstrations in regard to the working of goods sheds, tranship sheds and parcel offices.

The trainees should also be taken to the field for mock trials of thefts.

The College should invite Security and Claims Prevention Officers and Inspectors from different Zonal Railways to give lectures on the general and specific problems connected with loss and theft of goods.

Facilities should also be developed in the training college for giving proper coaching in the art of detection or intelligence.

To facilitate surprise inspections it will be useful to provide a jeep to the A.S.Os or S.Os at large Commercial centres like Bangalore and Ahmedabad where there are several important depots to be inspected.

Bagged Consignments

The commodities which are packed in bags contribute most to the claims bill. These commodities are—grains and pulses, sugár, oil-seeds, spices, cement, chemical manures and salt.

Among these, the more important commodities from the claims prevention point of view are (i) Foodgrains, (ii) Sugar, and (iii) Oil seeds, which accounted for 35% of the total amount of compensation paid in 1968-69.

The incidence of loss and damage on foodgrains and sugar has more than doubled in two years, although the traffic has dropped.

Statistics show that (i) the relative incidence of claims paid on foodgrains is very high on N.F., S.C., Central, Eastern and Southern Railways; (ii) the incidence on sugar and jagree is abnormally high on Eastern and quite high on N.F. Railway; and (iii) that incidence on oil seeds is abnormally high on Eastern and quite high on Central, South Eastern and South Central Railways. As paying Railways, these Railways will have to make greater efforts to bring down the claims on these commodities, even though the causes of some of the claims may actually lie on other Railways.

The standard of bagging, particularly in the case of imported foodgrains loaded by the Food Corporation of India, needs to be improved.

Railways should (i) insist on the sender to give clear and specific remarks as to how the packing is defective in the Forwarding Note—such as, bags with hook-holes, mouth corners open, stitching weak bags not of prescribed tare weight and size, etc.; these remarks should be reproduced on the railway receipt in toto; and (ii) when the shortage in a bag is due to wastage and if sweepings, are collected from the wagon floor, it should be invariably mentioned in the deficiency message.

Use of hooks for lifting of bags is prohibited. The Railways should persuade the trade to ensure that bags are provided with ears or lifts to facilitate their lifting at the time of loading and unloading. The R.P.F. staff should be given instructions to seize the iron-hooks. In the agreements with the labour contractors, use of iron hooks should be prohibited with a clause for penalty.

To meet any sudden influx of traffic at certain specific points in a short span of time, it is desirable that the Food Corporation of India builds enough storage capacity at the producing centres. This would facilitate despatch of consignments on a programmed basis spread over the whole year instead of rushing the railway loading during a few weeks.

Every Railway should have a mobile squad of commercial clerks to be deployed at different stations during rush of seasonal traffic. In any case railways should collect prior information and make advance arrangements for heavy rush of goods traffic just as they do in case of heavy passenger traffic at the time of holidays or Melas.

Covered wagons loaded by Food Corporation of India (Senders) should also be sealed by them, and if these seals are intact, the railways should have no liability for short receipt of full bags or shortage from torn bags found in the middle of the stack.

It would also be worthwhile to post a representative of F.C.I., at important transhipment points to supervise loading and unloading of their consignments at these places and to affix their seals on the transhipped wagon. The seal to be used by the senders should be of a type which will not give way under the usual strains of transit. S.C. Railway has prepared a design of an aluminium tape seal, which could be tried for the purpose.

For preventing pilferage through flap-door crevices, it was decided as far back as 1926 to fit plates or angle irons at the doors of covered wagons. But many wagons are still without this device.

The Railway Board must lay down the target time for completing this work on all wagons, so that the recurring loss arising due to pilferage through flap door crevices can be checked. It must also be ensured that in new wagons, this device is invariably fitted.

Examination of a number of wagons loaded with foodgrains, sugar, etc, has convinced the Committee that provision of dunnage, as per condition S/27 of the Goods Tariff is a fairly effective precaution against bleeding through flap door crevices.

While railways should make every effort to fit all covered wagons with anti-bleeding device, they should also (a) insist on provision of dunnage as required in the rules, and (b) make this condition S/27 applicable to other pilferable commodities such as zeera, turmeric, pepper, cloves, dhania and other spices, as also milk powder in bags.

In regard to the use of dunnage there are several points which require clarification by the Board. These points have been detailed.

When the claims for pilferage through flap door crevices are not payable under specific agreement, the Food Department or the F.C.I. would do well not to prefer such claims, so as to avoid unnecessary clerical work at both ends. The number of such claims now preferred and repudiated is by no means small.

Cases have come to notice where consignments are loaded by the F.C.I. but consigned to a private traders who insists on the claim being paid, despite dunnage not being provided by F.C.I. In such cases, the Railway Board should clarify its policy.

Railway staff should see before booking that the bags have not already been damaged by water either in the godown of the consigner or in the truck/cart or in the course of handling. If so, necessary remarks must be obtained in the Forwarding Note and reproduced in the Railway Receipt.

At unloading points, damageable consignments should be stacked in covered sheds and protected by tarpaulins. Supervision at the loading and unloading stations has to be tightened up.

Parcels

Railways should compile (i) separate statistics of number of claims and amount paid on parcels traffic—which should be further divided into perishables and non-perishables and (ii) the figures of total tonnage of parcels traffic carried.

One would expect that as parcel traffic is fast and is usually passed from hand to hand, it would enjoy a high safety factor like registered postal parcels. But as a matter of fact the incidence of claims is even higher on parcels than on goods.

Though parcel earnings are about 5 per cent of the total freight receipts for goods and parcels, the amount of compensations paid on parcels is about 16 per cent of the total amount paid and the number of claims received on parcels is about 30 per cent of the total number of claims received.

There is a very strong case for parcel traffic being given much better attention than at present.

Many consignments of parcels are being detained in transit. Some examples of this are given.

At Mughalsarai whenever there is a rush of traffic parcel vans are detained for want of room in the siding. Parcels for Gomoh and Dhanbad are sent via Danapur and Asansol in four-wheelers, because there is a shortage of bogie parcel vans which alone are permitted as passenger trains on the Grand Chord.

With better programming, the movement of parcels can be rationalised, eliminating unnecessary delays and handling en route.

Many parcel vans, luggage vans and brake vans move without being locked. In fact, some of the staff are under the impression that sealed compartments of luggage vans or brake vans need not be locked.

Railways should make an adequate supply of locks to Guards and Brakesmen and should arrange for frequent surprise checks to ensure full compliance with the rules.

No packing conditions have been prescribed for parcels, although all kinds of valuable things are being carried by passenger trains. Suitable packing conditions should be prescribed for parcels on the same lines as for goods.

Fresh fish is required to be packed with ice, but the proportion of fish and ice has not been specified.

The railways should pay special attention to the eradication of the causes that give rise to claims on parcels, specially perishables.

Insufficient accommodation for parcels in trains is unquestionably one of the biggest causes of malpractices, complaints and claims.

Due to inadequate room on trains (a) many packages are left behind at loading and transit points and (b) loading is done in a haphazard, uncheckable or mixed up condition with the result that difficulties arise at the time of unloading and many parcels are either overcarried or unloaded short of destination. Lack of proper marks on the packages, insufficient stoppage of some trains and shortage of staff are also partly responsible for these irregularities.

Railways should provide adequate transport capacity for parcels—at least for perishables—and as far as possible such additional capacity should be developed on Mail, Express or long distance fast passenger trains, so that both transit time and transhipments enroute are reduced to the minimum. This matter deserves the highest priority.

I recommend that as soon as possible selected unimportant or less popular Express trains should be dieselised and their loads should be augmented with adequate parcels vans for clearance of parcels between important points like Calcutta-Delhi, Madras-Bombay, Delhi-Bombay, Ahmedabad-Delhi, Bombay Central-Dehra Dun, Pathankot-Sealdah. In this way, not only will parcel earnings be increased but claims on parcels will also be reduced.

The public, I feel, would even be willing to pay a small surcharge on the parcels carried by direct Mail or Express trains.

Many parcel offices have a shortage of staff-particularly at stations where booking of perishables is heavy. Shortage of staff results in short cut methods of work and inevitably takes its toll in the form of claims. Acceptance, marking, counting, weighment and loading or unloading of parcels are altogether ignored or left to merchants or to porters.

One serious flaw, well known to railway administrations, is that there is no proper system of taking over and making over of parcels between station staff and guards; parcels, far from being tallied with summaries, are not even counted at the time of taking over and making over because neither time nor staff are available.

Since trains are run in order to carry traffic, adequate stoppages should be provided on passenger trains to permit of loading and unloading in a proper manner; and there should also be adequate staff for this purpose on trains and adequate labour and staff at stations.

Railways should keep under constant review the requirements of labour and staff in parcel offices, Luggage Guards or Parcel Delivery clerks on trains and the stoppages of passenger, Mail and Express trains.

Provision of staff and labour should not be based on the average number of parcels handled but should take full account of the conditions prevailing at the time of grouping of passenger trains.

As railways have lost and are still losing high rated traffic and are making serious efforts to recapture it, it is worthwhile for railways to make a determined effort to get back high rated traffic in the form of parcels rather than goods.

Parcel traffic bears high freight. Even the traffic carried at half parcel rates earns as much freight as the so-called high rated traffic (piece goods, tea, leather goods) when carried by goods trains. And the cost of parcels carried by regular passenger trains is only marginal.

Perishables

It is necessary to draw special attention to the claims on perishables, as one out of every four claims is a claim on perishables.

In recent years there has been a sharp increase in the number of claims as well as amount paid on perishables.

Rules regarding marking of perishable baskets will have to be revised and strictly followed. There cannot be any substitute for or short cut to the 'correct address' on a package which has to travel hundreds of kilometres, and requires to be handled at junction points and delivered to the right consignee at the destination station.

The present state of marking on perishables is anything but satisfactory.

It is essential that the consignee's full name and address and the destination name in full be shown on all packages containing perishables because generally their delivery has to be given on General Indemnity notes in absence of the Parcel Way Bills, and the only authority by which the rightful owner can be identified is the address on the package itself. Delivery of perishables cannot be deffered even for a day in order to make enquiries about the correct destination or consignee.

One of the chief causes of loss of packages is loading in a mixed up condition due to insufficient space in the luggage compartment of brake vans.

The Committee checked unloading of parcels from 17 Dn Madras-Delhi Janata Express at Jhansi on 24-12-69 and found that 8 packages of Bina and 15 of Bhopal had been over-carried to Jhansi while 7 packages of Gwalior, 51 of Agra and 44 of Mathura had been unloaded short of destination. This happened because of haphazard loading at Madras making it impossible to sort out the packages during the scheduled halts at the stations en route.

Railways must study the flow of perishable traffic destination-wise, and rationalise their loading programme at each important booking station.

It would be helpful if the vans are suitably compartmentalised, with movable or immovable partitions, so that packages meant for each big destination or junction are loaded in separate compartments. Ample parcel room should be provided on trains, so that parcels can be stacked there in separate and checkable lots.

For destination stations, with less traffic, the suggestion to provide big coir-containers to accommodate 5 to 10 packages in each could be considered and tried out.

Southern Railway should consider the running of a regular Parcel Van between Madras and Lucknow, containing parcels for Jhansi, Kanpur and Lucknow.

Another peculiar feature of perishable traffic is that large numbers of baskets are tendered at the station for booking in the nick of time, that is, just before train time. In consequence, enough time is not available for checking the condition and weight of packages, writing of railway marks and preparation of railway receipts and loading summary. Sometimes, booking is done after despatch.

The problem of 'Memo-deliveries' at large stations like Howrah, Bombay V.T., Delhi, Ahmedabad, Kanpur and Nagpur has assumed such large proportions that unless booking, weighment, marking and loading of perishables are set on a proper footing Railways would continue to pay heavy claims. The problem should be tackled in two ways.

Every effort should be made by railways to persuade trade to bring their packages to the station for booking as early as possible.

The number of railway staff and labour should be enough for completing all the work—including issue of railway receipts and loading—within the time available before the departure of the train. This is a matter which should receive attention at fairly high levels.

Delay in transit is undoubtedly one of the main causes of deterioration of perishables. Movement of perishables by the fastest available trains, without any detention at junctions en route is an obvious necessity.

Because of its perishable nature, it is necessary to consider the condition of the consignment at the time of booking. The fruits or vegetables or betel-leaves may be over-ripe or even in partly rotten condition at the time of booking ; if so, they may get damaged even within the normal transit time.

During the course of my examination on one railway, I found that claims on perishable parcels —even those where heavy amounts and long hauls are involved —are being paid whenever the time taken in transit exceeds the normal or minimum transit time by a day or more and the cosignment is found deteriorated at destination.

According to the law, Railways are not responsible for deterioration of such goods if the detentions to them were unavoidable or if the goods when tendered for despatch were already in a ripe or over-ripe condition and therefore unable to stand the normal duration of transit.

In dealing with petty claims on perishables, whose number is large, the use of a rough and ready formula based on the normal transit time is inescapable. But in case of heavy claims or when a large number of small consignments arc received by the same train or wagon in a deteriorated condition, thorough enquiries should be made right from the booking station upto the destination station to determine—(a) the location and causes of detentions, and (b) the condition of the consignment at different points during the course of its transit.

Even when the detentions are found to have been due to carelessness on the part of railway staff, the Railway is liable only for the extent of deterioration attributable to the delay that occurred on the Railway and not necessarily for the full amount of damage assessed at destination.

It would be useful to get studies made of the deterioration of perishables within the normal transit time and circulate expert opinions to the assessing officials and the mercantile community.

Betel Leaves

One single commodity amongst perishables which accounts for the largest number of claims is 'betel-leaves'. On the Northern Railway, the number of claims received on betel leaves has been 38 to 43 per cent of all claims on perishables during the last three years.

On the Central Railway, 25% to 30% of the amount paid on perishables is paid on betel leaves traffic alone.

North Eastern Railway made a test analysis of 200 cases paid on betel leaf consignments in March, 1969 and found that 83% of the claims were for non-receipt, 13 per cent for pilferage and 4 per cent for damage.

A similar study made by Varanasi Claims Office showed that claims on betel leaves are substantial; it details the main irregularities responsible for them.

Special study of the booking of betel leaves at Tirur was made by the Committee. Nearly 1000 Parcel Way Bills are issued and 3000 baskets of betel leaves are despatched per day from Tirur during the busy season. A large number of these packages are destined for Delhi and via.

Consignee's name is nowhere shown—instead, some code marks are given, which do not convey anything to the Railway staff.

Even in Parcels Way Bills, railway staff have been showing only the code of the consignee's name. The rules require the consignee's name and address to be shown on each parcel and this is inescapable if the parcels are to reach the correct persons.

To reduce the high incidence of claims the following system should be adopted in regard to private marks : (1) In all Forwarding Notes full name of the consignee should be shown by the sender, (2) on the card label attached to each basket senders should show the full name of the consignee and the destination station as in the Forwarding Note, and (3) on the body of each basket the consignee's name in brief and the code initials of the destination station will be shown.

Tie-on labels for baskets are always in short supply. Indents placed in 1967 had not been met till November, 1969. Thereafter only 700 labels were received from Stores, although the daily consumption is 3000 labels. The railway should fix the scale of supply and ensure that the supply is made regularly.

To cope with the rush of traffic, Tirur station has devised its own system of railway marks. For each basket the serial number of acceptances (called the Forwarding Note Number) is shown on the sender's label instead of the Parcel Way Bill number.

The Forwarding Note numbers are also shown on the Parcel Way Bills, but as many way bills do not reach the destination and as the consignee's name is shown in codes, the staff at destination have no means of knowing to which merchant any particular basket belongs which has arrived without way-bill. This is a major cause of the high incidence of memo deliveries at destination stations and also of claims.

To enable P.W. Bill number to be shown in railway marks, the merchants should make out a separate Despatch list of consignments corresponding to each money value book. Thus, all consignments for one and the same Money Value will be already sorted out and booking staff will be readily able to allot Parcel Way Bill numbers to them in serial order.

Many parcels have to be despatched before their Parcel Way Bills have been prepared. At present, the acceptance time is from 6 to 10 hours and all the parcels have to be despatched by 14 hours. During this period about 3000 baskets have to be weighed, marked and loaded and about 1000 Parcel Way Bills have to be prepared. The manpower available is not sufficient to complete all the work within the time available. The despatch of hundreds of perishable parcels before their Parcel Way Bills have even been prepared is a major cause of claims.

Southern Railway should review the arrangements for the handling of this traffic. Earlier timings may be fixed for the acceptance of betel leaves : some of the merchants were agreeable to bring their baskets even at 2 or 3 A.M., if railway work is facilitated thereby.

Adequate staff should be provided at this station so that all Parcel Way Bills and guidances can be prepared well before the departure of the train, that is, 14 hours.

I would like to stress that saving of a few Parcel clerks at the cost of efficiency is bad economy; for much more is being paid in claims than what the additional staff would cost,

To facilitate weighment of such a large number of baskets in a short time the existing weighing machines should be replaced with Dial type or automatic weighing machines.

Provision of automatic weighing machines should be considered for all stations where booking of parcels is heavy.

In the past, failures in the daily supply of parcel van have been frequent. During the summer season, there is an increased demand for movement of mango traffic, and as such the parcel van, on its return trip, is sometimes detached either at Madras or some other station depriving Tirur of its regular traffic. It is recommended that there should be an adequate number of Parcel Vans so that the requirements of all stations at the peak of the 'Perishables' season may be met properly. A close watch should also be kept on the movement of Parcel Vans both loaded and empty.

In loading baskets of betel leaves running lines have to be crossed. If possible, this should be avoided by providing the loading platform and parcel office in the same place.

Southern Railway should make efforts to persuade trade to dispatch betel leaves in baskets of 10 kgs. each. If this can be arranged, the magnitude of all the problems connected with marking, weighment, booking and loading, etc. will be reduced.

Last minute disturbance of the original packing in order to reduce weight is one of the potential causes of further loss in transit. Such last minute disturbance of the packing should not be allowed and the trade should be persuaded to pay freight as per weight originally offered.

Tea

4.55 per cent of the total compensation paid is on tea. There was a phenomenal increase of 119% in the amount paid on this commodity in a period of two years.

The ratio of amount of compensation paid to goods earnings from tea was 5.97 in 1966-67, 9.76 in 1967-68 and 14.29 in 1968-69.

The Eastern Railway pays more than two-third of the total tea claims. About one-third of the the payment is on account of damage by wet and about two-third on account of partial shortage due to breakage or pilferage or both.

The packing condition for tea as per I.S.I. specification should be brought up-to-date and its basic requirements should be notified to staff.

It is necessary for North-East Frontier and Eastern Railways, where most of the tea is booked, to have periodical checks made to satisfy themselves that the plywood chests used by trade satisfy the prescribed specifications.

Investigations show that the amount paid per claim is much less when tea is packed in wooden cases than when it is packed in chests.

Even when tea is packed in chests, but if it is covered with gunny, the incidence of breakage and pilferage is much reduced.

I am of the opinion that to cover with gunny the tea chests booked to long distances would be a distinct advantage, and the additional cost of packing involved would be comparatively insignificant. The important point to be borne in mind is that if some dispatchers can voluntarily cover their tea chests with gunny, why cannot the others do likewise ?

It is of utmost importance that tea is loaded in good water tight wagons and there is adequate covered area at stations and in the sidings for protection against rain at the time of loading. It is not enough merely to see 'WT' mark on the wagon. Water-tightness of the wagons supplied for tea loading should be carefully examined by the Station Master personally.

The assessment of damage allowed by Tea Brokers on consignments of tea booked to Calcutta area is very much higher than that allowed by the claims Inspectors/Senior Subordinates at other stations. There is no reason for the Eastern Railway to depend on a third party in case of consignments of tea booked to Calcutta area. The matter needs taking up in consultation with the Tea Board in order to have a better control.

The incidence of breakage/pilferage on consignments booked to Calcutta Port Commissioners' area has been found to be on the high side. There is a strong presumption that shortages are being exaggerated in the Port Commissioners' area. It is, therefore, necessary for railways to take suitable remedial action.

Efforts should be intensified to divert tea traffic from stations on C.P.C. Railway to stations on the Eastern Railway such as Sealdah and Kalighat. This has also been suggested by the Indian Tea Association.

For the greater safety of the goods, trade should be encouraged to book their export tea by the all metre gauge route from Assam to Kandla Port. I was told that some block rakes sent in this manner some time back reached destination with their contents in very good condition.

As claims on the consignments are paid by Eastern Railway, that Railway should exercise some supervision over the deliveries and assessments made at Calcutta Port Commissioners. A suitable working arrangement should be arrived at in consultation with the Port Trust.

The present practice in regard to tea consignments received in Calcutta area is that the quantitative assessment of damage or shortage is made at the time of delivery, but the determination of its monetary value is done only after the individual packages affected have actually been sold. Such auctions are usually held two months after the arrival of goods. Claimants, therefore, prefer their claims in instalments.

The Eastern Railway should come to an arrangement with the Tea Association so that the monetary value of the loss or damage is determined at the time of delivery on the basis of the prices then prevailing, as is done in the case of other commodities. Truly speaking, the prices prevailing on the date of delivery are more relevant than those prevailing two or three months later.

Iron And Steel

A sum of Rs. 39.75 lakhs was paid as compensation on iron and steel consignments in 1968-69. This formed 4 per cent of the total amount paid and 0.60 per cent of the total earnings from this commodity.

One of the major difficulties in regard to steel structurals is that of marking, addressing and labelling. It has been reported to the Committee that structurals despatched by steel plants bear neither any private marks nor railway marks and as a result they often go astray.

Somehow the thinking hitherto has been that marking by the railway is not feasible, but steel plants should do their own marking and steel plants have been resisting it on one ground or another. So the present position is that neither railways nor steel factories do any marking. To break the ice, railways should take the initiative and give a practical demonstration as to how the marking can be done at the time of loading.

In my opinion, it should be quite easy for railways to mark not only the name of the destination station, but even the invoice or Railway Receipt number on the packages at the time of loading.

Another difficulty pointed out in this connection is that sometimes owing to the imposition of movement restrictions the destination station is required to be changed after the wagon has been loaded. As a matter of fact, such occasions should not arise.

It is suggested that the steel plant stations should send a daily list of all wagons loaded with iron and steel structurals, showing full booking particulars, to the Head Office of each Railway, for the purpose of ready reference. This will be helpful in connecting unconnected wagons and preventing mis-delivery or fraudulent delivery.

There are complaints of heavy shortages of pig iron from open wagons in which it is generally loaded. Pig iron is an expensive material and has to be treated with more care than coal. As far as possible, pig iron should be loaded in covered wagons, which should be riveted.

The Security Branch should use its detective forces to find out the foundries which use such stolen goods and break the racket.

When there is an apparent heavy shortage in the contents of a wagon, it would be only fair to allow re-weighment, of course, on recovery of re-weighment charges.

It is recommended that facility of a free escort already granted by railway in case of wagons loaded with livestock be extended to tractors, motor vehicles and heavy machinery loaded in open wagons.

Piece-goods

In 1968-69, Railways paid Rs. 65.77 lakhs as compensation for loss and damage in 18,329 claims on piece-goods. This was 6·5 per cent of the total amount paid in 1968-69.

Compared with 1966-67 there was a 17 per cent increase in the number of claims paid and about 40 per cent increase in the amount paid in 1968-69.

Statistics show that in relation to terminating traffic, the payment is very high on the North-East Frontier, North Eastern, South Central, Eastern and Northern Railways. Eastern Railway has to pay particular attention to losses from seals intact wagons, N.F. Railway to pilferage and damage by wet, N.E Railway to unlocalised loss of entire bales and pilferages and Western Railway to loss of entire packages from the possession of the guards/van clerks.

Many claims are being paid for damage to cloth due to rubbing of corners. Railways, particularly Northern Railway should examine whether it is due to mishandling at the forwarding and destination stations, or due to oscillation in transit or due to defective packing or it is fictitious.

Northern Railway should get the damages in a number of such cases inspected personally by a responsible officer so that suitable remedial action may be taken.

The study also confirms the belief that repacking or handling of goods in transit and carriage thereof in road-vans is largely responsible for loss and pilferage of packages. This brings out the necessity for a thorough investigation of the shortages reported by guards. Prompt fixation of staff responsibility should go a long way in reducing such cases.

P-14 is the packing condition prescribed for bales of piece-goods. An inner lining of polythene is compulsory. There is a prohibition against chatai being used in contact with polythene. This prohibition is not known to most of the despatchers with the result that they continue to use chatai alongside the polythene. Some railways have been repudiating their claims for damage by wet on this ground. The prohibition against the use of chatai in contact with polythene needs to be brought to the notice of all despatchers of piece-goods as also of railway staff. Further, as trade apparently finds chatai useful, it is advisable to legislate that a layer of gunny be interposed between the polythene lining and the chatai.

According to a study made by N.E. Railway many thefts are occurring on Varanasi-Mughalsarai section where according to newspaper reports, many shops are flourishing on stolen goods only. This is a field in which the Intelligence Wing of R.P.F. should be able to suggest effective remedies.

More strict supervision is required at booking stations like Wadi Bunder, Carnac Bridge and Kankaria in the matter of correct weighment. During the investigations made by the Commitee, several types of irregularities in the booking and loading of bales of piece-goods came to light.

Seeing that each bale of piecegoods costs thousands of rupees and in the aggregate railways paid Rs. 65 lakhs in one year in claims on this commodity, it is worthwhile for railways to post a senior man in the Piecegoods Loading shed to double check the work of the Goods clerks who accept, weigh and load the bales.

Detention To Wagons

Detention to a loaded wagon/van en route is a prolific cause of loss, theft, damage, pilferage and deterioration of goods and parcels booked. The longer a wagon is detained, the greater the chances of its victimisation by thieves.

While detentions to goods trains and stock from the movement point of view are the special responsibility of the Operating Department, it is necessary for Commercial Officers, Inspectors and Controllers to watch the delays to loaded wagons from the claims point of view—specially the types of loaded wagons which are liable to be overlooked.

'Stabling of trains' of loaded wagons should be watched daily and arrangements made for temporary posting of Railway Protection Force staff at such stations for guarding and checking of seals/cutting of panels.

Commercial Controllers should be picked men of adequate experience and status.

Stationery And Forms

The supply of stationery, forms and books to stations is generally unsatisfactory on the railways. The shortages appear to be chronic.

There is a general complaint of the shortage of carbon paper, whose scale of supply, it is said, was curtailed sometime back as a measure of economy.

Standing orders require that only tape and not twine or sootlie is to be used for preparing Seal Card Labels. Nowadays, one rarely finds tape used on any wagon. Sootlie is useless for the purpose as it gives way easily, resulting in loss of the labels and wagon becoming unconnected.

There is no doubt that shortage of essential stationery and stores is one of the contributory causes of the alarming increase in claims. It is, therefore, necessary that the supply of such essential stores to stations be placed on a proper footing—not only in regard to the regularity but also the quantity and quality of the articles supplied.

The scale of supply and the period and system of distribution should be reviewed and it should be ensured that under normal circumstances every station will have an ample stock of all items of stationery, forms and books, etc. to meet its day-to-day requirements.

On several Railways it was suggested that their powers for emergency purchase of stationery items should be doubled, that is to say they should be authorised to make emergency purchase of six months consumption, instead of 3 months permitted at present. I endorse this suggestion.

Commercial Officers and Commercial Controllers on Divisions should have an arrangement whereby shortages of stationery, stores, forms, etc. will be brought to their notice in good time for necessary action. They should view these shortages more seriously and take vigorous and urgent action to make good the deficiencies.

Divisional Superintendents should exercise their powers of emergency purchase whenever necessary and it should also be considered whether these powers should be increased.

A list of the most essential items of stores, stationery and forms should be furnished by the Commercial Department to the Stores Department, so that the latter may give them priority in order to keep their ample stocks for regular supply to stations.

Shortages of forms are generally due to the Railway Printing Press being over loaded. Where such is the case there should be no hesitation in off-loading some of the work to private presses. On each railway the Commercial and Stores Departments should make a joint examination of the existing capacity, to what extent shortages are occurring at present, and how the printing work may be rationalised in order to ensure regular and ample supplies of all forms and money value books.

Rules And Reference Books

Many officers and Inspectors have not seen the Commercial Manual published by Board and are unaware even of its existence. The Area Training Schools have got a few copies but are not able even to lend a copy to each of the trainees for study. Copies of the Commercial Manual should be supplied liberally to stations, goods and transhipment sheds etc. and to each Commercial Clerk. Everyone, who attends a training or refresher course in an Area School, should be given a personal copy—unless he already has one. All, who have been given a copy, will be responsible for keeping it posted up-to-date with correction slips.

During their inspections of stations, officers and Inspectors should make it a point to test some of the staff in their knowledge of the rules of daily application and record the result in their Inspection Notes.

The Alphabetical List of stations was out of stock for several years. The new edition just brought out should be brought up-to-date. Alphabetical List of stations and Junctions Distance Tables which are basic documents should be revised every alternate year at the most.

Damage And Deficiency Messages

D.D. messages are not properly issued by stations. The common defects found in D.D. messages have been detailed. Railways should instruct station staff about the correct procedure of issuing D.D. messages.

It should be the duty of Commercial Officers and Inspectors during their visits at stations to test and educate the staff on the point of correct issue of D.D. messages.

It should be the personal responsibility of the Station Master/Goods Inspector/Chief Transhipment Clerk/Chief Parcel Clerk to ensure that all messages received are serially numbered and entered in the register, to call for explanations from staff and to initiate such other actions as may be necessary.

Some staff, particularly of transhipment sheds, have a tendency to issue unnecessary D.D. message or report inflated shortages to save themselves from being held responsible for further shortages. If any, this should be discouraged.

As the D.D. messages are specialised types of messages which are valuable records for settlement of claims and fixation of staff responsibility, it would be better to evolve and print a separate type of D. D. message from instead of using the ordinary telegram form as is now done.

To keep the workload on telegraph offices to the minimum, telegraph codes should be used in D.D. messages as far as possible. A list of relevant telegraph codes of the phrases generally used in the D.D. messages should be got printed separately and a copy supplied to each station/goods shed/parcel offices and also to the claims office.

D.D. messages should be treated by the Commercial Department as accident messages are treated by the Operating Department. On the Western Railway, there is a system of classifying D.D. messages on the basis of the value of loss involved. It would be useful to adopt a similar system on other railways so that due attention may be paid according to the importance of each message.

I suggest that it should be made compulsory for each Divisional Commercial Officer and each Assistant Commercial Officer to check, study, analyse and take up D.D. messages of one large station and one small station his Division every month.

Claims Statistics

Very little use is being made of claims statistics for preventive action, because most of the claims organizations are short handed and barely able to do justice even to settlement work.

Claims offices could make special statistical analyses of claims from time to time in order to spotlight the weak spots on which preventive effort could be focussed.

Cause-wise statistics are now compiled for 'claims paid' only. Railways should direct their efforts to prevent even those claims which are repudiated and settled otherwise. It is, therefore, recommended that cause-wise statistics of 'repudiated and otherwise settled claims' should also be compiled.

Railways' requirements will be adequately met by having detailed statistics on 'settled basis' only, and those on 'received basis' can be dispensed with.

It is necessary that R.P.F. be made responsible to a greater extent for the investigation of cases of loss. It is, therefore, recommended that the shortage of complete packages from seal intact wagons, seal defective wagons and open wagons be classified as "Thefts" and not as" Loss".

'Loss of complete packages' from seal intact wagons should be further sub-classified.

For claims on parcels and luggage, separate cause-wise statistics should be maintained on the same lines as for all claims. The mode of transport of parcels and luggage is different from that of goods and, therefore, preventive action for the former has to be different from the preventive measures for the latter.

Completeness in compilation of statistics needs to be improved. Enquiries should be made for promptly and in a much larger number of cases than at present in order that they may be correctly classified under their appropriate heads and a fuller picture of the causes may be available for remedial action.

While going through cause-wise and commodity wise statistics of the Zonal Railways, the Committee noted some obvious mistakes. There is need for greater care in compiling these statistics, as wrong statistics are liable to put preventive actions on a wrong trail.

At present, monthly claims statistics are reported by the Zonal Railways in one set of proforma to the Commercial Directorate of the Railway Board and in another set of proforma to the Statistical Directorate of the Railway Board. Several items included in these two statements are common. This duplication of work is available. It would be better if these two statements could be combined and dealt with in the Commercial Directorate only.

Each railway has its own computer and use thereof could be made for disclosing the fields on which preventive action should be directed. I must, however, utter a warning. A costly system for compilation of detailed statistics will be a waste, unless a suitable organization exists to make use of them.

Miscellaneous

Packing conditions : Some of the packing conditions are very difficult to understand. They should be reviewed and simplified.

Pamphlets should be issued explaining details of the packing prescribed for different types of commodities for the guidance of the staff as well as the consignors.

Railways should consider the following suggestions which have been made to this Committee : (1) that the packing of general merchandise consignments booked by military authorities is generally of a poor standard and should be improved ; (2) that the packing of cigarettes, Godrej locks, electric bulbs and cycle and machine parts is generally weak; (3) that zeera, cloves and pepper should be required to be packed in cases and not in double gunny as at present; (4) that dunnage be made compulsory for turmeric; (5) that provision of polythene lining be made compulsory for bags of turmeric.

In the case of regular customers, the use of defective packing should be stopped by persuasion and personal contacts. The officer in the Division should take more interest and initiative in this matter.

Out-of-course transhipment : Wagon loads detached en route due to hot axle, accident, over-weight or any other cause should be quickly transhipped or repaired and dispatched. Further it should be ensured that particulars of such transhipment are communicated by the transhipping station to the destination station without fail. The Commercial Controller should maintain a separate list in duplicate showing booking particulars, commodity, number of the wagon from which contents unloaded and number of the wagon to which contents reloaded, and send one copy every month to the claims office for reference in case of claims or for connecting unconnected wagons.

To ensure greater security of costly goods, rationalization of delivery points in big cities like Culcutta and Bombay should be considered. Some points of destination are more vulnerable to thefts while others are comparatively safe. It would be only prudent to concentrate highly costly items of goods traffic on safer stations and the less costly or less amenable to theft or pilferage on those stations where thefts are regular and systematic. For instance, thefts of oil-seeds booked to Chitpur and sugar booked to Kantapukar (c p.c. Railway) are common, damage and pilferage of tea booked to Tea Warehouse (c.p.c.) are more than that booked to other stations in the Calcutta area. Diversion of such traffic to safer stations should be tried.

Newspapers and magazines : The traffic of newspapers and magazines is very sensitive and important. Railways should give it the same urgent and careful attention as suggested for perishables.

Destination station should be written or printed in bold and conspicuous letters on the top of each bundle of newspapers/magazines so that the guard makes no mistake.

Special arrangements should be made for sorting out the bundles of newspapers/magazines at train changing points and despatching them by first available train.

All Station Masters should be authorised to grant shortage delivery, as newspapers cannot await arrival of Inspectors.

Advance booking of periodicals and magazines from the publishing centres should be permitted so that issue of Railway Receipts is not delayed. Its necessity and arrangements required for the purpose would depend on the local conditions of each place.

There is no need for calling of 'Beejuck' for ascertaining the price of newspapers and magazines which are well known.

Magazines are of topical value. Agents refuse delivery of delayed consignments which are returned to the publishers who prefer claims. Such claims should be entertained if the monthly magazines are not delivered within 30 days, fortnightly magazines in 15 days and weekly magazines in 7 days, subject to the minimum of normal transit time.

If the system is to send the Railway Receipt along with the bundles, production of original Railway Receipt should not be insisted on in the case of claim for non-delivery of the entire consignment.

Liquid consignments : The cater for the growing petroleum traffic, Railways should pay special attention to the maintenance of tank wagons. While many claims were repudiated, a sum of Rs. 23 lakhs was paid on account of leakage in 1968-69. Apart from the question of payment or repudiation, it should be realised that the POL traffic is a high-rated traffic which should receive more careful treatment.

All base stations for POL traffic should be well equipped with staff and material so that tank wagons are thoroughly examined and all deficiencies of equipment rectified before the tanks are supplied for loading.

Breakage : To minimise breakage due to handling, better handling facilities, such as, rubber tyred hand barrows, loading and unloading mats, dunnage bags, etc, should be provided and maintained in good order at the stations. For lifting heavy packages, the railways should also go in for 'Forklifts' to be provided at selected places.

The labour should be taken to task for carelessness in handling. The penal clause in the labour contract should be invoked, if the labour provided by the contractor is responsible for rough handling.

Transhipment and repacking sheds should have arrangements for repairing packages and bags which may be found torn, damaged or broken.

Frauds : Care should be taken to accept parcels and goods in regard to items where on the face of it, it would appear that the senders are sending "Ice to Iceland" or "coal to New Castle" or using any particular booking station which in the usual course is not the convenient station of booking for the particular party and particularly where goods are found covered by Insurance.

Excepted Articles

It would be advisable to add the following articles to the list of Excepted articles published in the I. R. C. A. Goods Traffic—(1) Terylene, (2) Nylon, (3) Terycot, (4) Terywool, (5) Woollen fabrics and (6) Medicines.

Protection works : There should be adequate covered and closed accommodation in the goods sheds, transhipment sheds, repacking sheds and parcel offices for protection of goods and parcels against rains.

There should also be enough accommodation for keeping the transit parcels and wherever necessary additional cages or rooms on or near the platforms should be constructed.

The following suggestions made by the High Powered Committee on Security and Policing on the Railway (1966-68) should be implemented on a programme basis :

(i) there should be proper lighting arrangements in all goods sheds and transhipment sheds, apart from all other arrangements for their basic security ; (ii) all big and important yards should be protected by perimeter wall or fencing ; (iii) watch towers should be erected at focal points of the yards fitted with flood lights; and (iv) there should be no built-up habitation either permanent or temporary in yards.

Main Complaints Of The Public

The various memoranda received by the Committee

have all complained bitterly about the manner in which Railways dispose of claims, the following being the principal points emphasised—

(i) that settlement of claims, particularly of heavier amounts, is inordinately delayed;

(ii) that delays occur in verification, fixation of inter-railway liability, accounts concurrence and issue of pay orders and cheques;

(iii) that claims notices are seldom acknowledged; reminders and appeals remain unattended for long periods;

(iv) that the amount of claim paid is insufficient and less than that payable under law; and

(v) that claims are repudiated on flimsy and unjustifiable grounds.

The committee examined a number of cases on different Railways and found that the complaints made by the public are not baseless.

A large number of appeals and complaints are received by the Railway Minister and Railway Board every day, the average for one fortnight being 19 per working day.

Suits are being filed against railways even by Government departments and public sector undertakings.

The number of claims lying unsettled with the railways has also been on the increase even according to official statistics.

Opening Of Cases And Issue Of Acknowledgments

In many Claims Offices, there are serious delays in opening a file on receipt of a fresh claim. It is necessary for all claims offices to rationalise the handling of fresh claim letters in the receipt and index sections and ensure that all new claims files are opened and are ready for dealing within 72 hours of the receipt of letters in the claims office.

While the zonal Railways may adopt any system which suits them most to reach this target, they may consider decentralisation of section (Case opening section). Within the existing claim dealing sections divided on a geographical basis, claims pertaining to each destination station should be marked to one or more dealers; the Index register cards should be maintained in each claim dealing section instead of in a separate centralised section.

If decentralisation of Index section is not considered feasible, an alternative arrangement would be to locate Index and Acknowledgment clerks of all sections in the Receipt section itself where they can sort out the incoming letters, give numbers to new claims, issue acknowledgments then and there, and thereafter pass on the files to the respective dealing sections.

It is essential that acknowledgments bearing proper references are issued simultaneously with the opening of the file.

The form of printed acknowledgment card for use by claim offices, as per sample at Annexure II, is recommended. The general hints given on this card for the information of the claimants will be useful in obtaining the relevant information and documents.

Missing Goods Report

Delay in the submission of Missing Goods Reports by stations, contrary to standing instructions, is a general cause of delay in the settlement of claims.

The whole attitude of the station staff to damage to goods and parcels should be brought on par with their attitude to accidents, and the prevention and settlement of claims should receive the same urgent and careful attention at the hands of Commercial Officers as is given to the prevention and disposal of accident cases by the Operating Officers.

It is essential that the rules regarding timely submission of MGR'S be rigidly enforced; and enquiries on them be started within a week of their receipt with the triple object of —

(a) Settling the claim expeditiously when received;

(b) taking up with the staff responsible irrespective of the claim; and

(c) taking other preventive action as warranted.

Different Railways have different types of forms of MGRs and some of them are very lengthy covering four pages with as many as 50 to 80 entries. Railways should consider adoption of a combined form of simplified M.G.R. and shortage certificate. A draft is suggested at Annexure III.

Normally a case should be opened according to the booking particulars on receipt of the advance Missing Goods Report and there should be no necessity to allot any separate or new number to the letter of claim received subsequently. If this procedure is followed, the general complaint of the station staff that advance M.G.R.'s are not properly connected in the claims offices will be removed.

Assessment And Shortage Certificates

Several Chambers of Commerce have complained that heavy delays occur in getting damages assessed by claims Inspectors, etc.

As the number of consignments requiring assessment delivery has increased, the railways should examine the workload of Claims Inspectors and should take such steps as are necessary to ensure that assessments are made by Claims Inspectors within two or three days of the receipt of a consignment at destination.

While there may be some excuse for consignments getting damaged in transit, there can be none for allowing that damage to get worse owing to delay in assessment.

There is a common cnmplaint that when consignments of machinery are received in a damaged or deficient condition, heavy delays occur in getting the damages assessed.

Whenever a Station Master receives a request for assessment of damages on a consignment of machinery, he should report the matter immediately by telephone to the D.C.S. or A.C.S. who will make the necessary arrangements in consultation with his colleagues of the Electrical and Mechanical Departments. If there is any hitch, the D.C.S. or A.C.S. should bring the matter to the notice of the D.S. or Dy. C.C. S. claims to ensure that the assessment is made promptly.

In respect of packed consignments, the assessment or open delivery report should specifically state the source of breakage or leakage of tins or barrels en route.

It is also complained that in many cases considerable delay takes place in issuing shortage certificates without which claims cannot be preferred.

Railways have already framed rules according to which shortage certificates are issued at the time of granting delivery. Railways must insist on strict compliance with these rules. It is understood that on some Railways shortage assessment certificates are issued only on applications from the consignees. While an application from the consignee for granting of open/assessment delivery is necessary, issue of shortage/assessment certificates should automatically follow open/ assessment delivery and no separate application need be insisted upon for the purpose.

Summary Disposal Of Claims Of Small Valuation

56 per cent of claims are for the values upto Rs. 200 and about 15 percent for value between Rs. 201 and Rs. 500.

Once a Missing Goods Report is available in claims office, which should be received in advance of the claim, it should be possible to dispose of most of the petty claims cases (e. g, those of partial shortage, damage and non-delivery of small consignments of perishables) without further enquiry.

Settlement of petty claims is often prolonged for various reasons.

Selling rates of articles on common use should be available with all claims offices and should be made up-to-date from time to time. They should be used as a guide for determining the amount of compensation payable and it should not be necessary to get the price verified by Claims Inspectors in individual cases of small valuation.

In the low valuation claims for damage, it should not ordinarily be necessary to verify the actual loss suffered by the claimant from his account books.

Settlement of claims should not be deferred for fixation of staff responsibility.

Railways will have to make an all out effort to establish traditions of settling claims in a business like, graceful and efficient manner. Promptitude in disposal will have to be given top priority and for this purpose, the first and indispensable step is to concentrate on the prompt settlement of all claims which are either of small valuation or easy to dispose of.

Twice or thrice every month all claims offices should turn up their pending files to make sure that no case of small valuation or partial shortage and damage has been lost sight of.

Petty claims of the station where a claims office is situated should be disposed of within 7 days and should not in any case take more than 15 days even in the case of other stations on any railway system.

Several claims are kept pending for confirmation of bookings from the forwarding stations when the destination stations do not receive copies of invoices. As a consequence of mechanisation, each station is now receiving monthly abstracts of all consignments booked from all stations to that station and normally an entry in these abstracts should be enough to confirm booking.

Enquiries In High Valuation Claims

In heavy claims, the officer should personally direct all enquiries at the earliest possible stage and all foreseeable action should be taken simultaneously. The senior officers should apply their minds to the facts of the case right from the beginning and take full responsibility for prompt disposal. This might necessitate an increase in the number of senior officers in claims offices.

Enquiries are often made piece-meal or claimants are required to furnish certain documents or information piece-meal. This tendency to get rid of a file anyhow without giving it proper attention is a prolific cause of delays and multiplication of work. One of its effects is the tendency to repudiate any claim in the first instance, hoping to arrange payment if pressed to do subsequently.

ı or quick determination of the amount payable and verification of the Beejuck, all claims offices should be equipped with market reports. In addition, they should maintain a rates diary recording rates of original trade invoices and rates verified by Inspectors in individual files for future reference in similar cases.

In case of big customers a customer-wise list of claims preferred/pending for non-delivery of full wagon loads should be maintained. If the wagon remains untraced inspite of reasonable enquiries, the claims of officers should be authorised to dispose of a claim b delivery of unconnected materials.

Enquiries should be instituted as soon as the consignment becomes overdue so that the settlement of claims, when subsequently received, is not held up for tracing the missing goods.

Financial Concurrence

Having noticed abnormal delays in obtaining financial concurrence and arranging payment of Rs. 1,000 and above, I sent a special report recommending that the lower limit for financial concurrence be raised from Rs. 1,000 to Rs. 2,000. This recommendation was accepted by the Railway Board.

This recommendation was only on interim measure designed to meet the immediate needs of the situation. But going deeper into the matter it is necessary to reassess the gains achieved by Railways in getting proposals for payment vested by the Account Department in other words, the advantages of pre-audit over post audit which was in force formerly.

Pre-auditing of claims cases means divisions of responsibility and duplication of work which in my opinion, is not a healthy system to follow. With pre-auditing, higher officers, who have ultimately to sanction the amount, take things for granted and over-burdened with work as they are, do not apply their minds fully; thus claims work is largely deprived of their guidance. Unless the higher officers are made to study the claims, which they alone are empowered to sanction and accept full responsibility for their own actions, neither the delays and deficiencies of dealing will be taken up nor will preventive action be initiated.

Most of the claims are concurred in as proposed, and only a few cases are returned without concurrence or with minor modifications in the amount proposed.

On one Railway, the Committee found that the objections or suggestions made by the accounts department were not always reasonable.

The Railway Board should give serious thought to the question whether Railways cannot revert to the old practice of post-audit, instead of pre-audit, even when the payment involved is over Rs. 2,000. In any case, further raising of the limit will have to be considered if the present enhancement does not give adequate relief to the Accounts Department and delays still persist.

From clause (13) of para 2248 of Accounts Code Part II, it is apparent that this Rule only gives details of the checks to be exercised at the time of post audit. As there is no separate Rule regarding the checks to be made at the time of pre-audit, Accounts Department has been applying this very rule, with varying degrees of rigidity, before giving financial concurrence; and necessarily there is delay in doing so because of the numerous details required to be scrutinised in each case.

I, therefore, recommend that there should be a separate rule for pre-audit of claim cases. This new Rule should simply require the Accounts Officer to see before giving financial concurrence that (a) the claim is one for payment, and (b) the amount proposed to be paid has been correctly arrived at. It should also be clarified that the existing Rule 2248A-II applies only to post audit.

Procedure For Payment

Even after the sanction of the amount by the competent authority, inordinate delays take place in arranging actual payment—in issue of pay orders as well as cheques.

The railways should issue station pay orders up to Rs. 1,000 on selected and specified stations and upto Rs. 500 on all other stations.

On most railways, there are delays in the preparation and despatch of Pay Orders. Railways should take steps to ensure that stations pay orders as well as accounts pay orders are despatched within 3 days of the date of sanction. The Committee is of the view that decentralisation of pay order section would obviate unnecessary transfer of files, enable better supervision and expedite preparation of pay orders.

The tendency to accumulate cases for disposal at the end of each month resulting in bunching of work in pay order and despatch sections should be avoided by evenly spacing out the work of out-door staff throughout the month.

The practice either to back-date the pay order or to count the date of sanction and not the date of pay order as the date of disposal to show better statistics is deprecated. Falsification of figures should not be permitted under any circumstances.

To obviate back references for issue of fresh pay orders involving unnecessary additional work and harassment to claimants, the currency of station pay order should be three months.

The arrangement for issue of cheques should be streamlined. The railways may examine the suggestions of dispensing with issue of accounts pay orders, isssue of cheque at the same time when the Accounts concurrence is given and authorising commercial officers to issue cheques on behalf of the F.A. & C.A.O.

Regardless of the amount, payment may be made by cheque to those who specially ask for it or reside at a station other than the destination station of the consignment in question.

Delays in despatch of cheques or pay orders by registered post should be eliminated by making suitable arrangements with the Post Offices.

To avoid unnecessary clerical work, pay order and pay order advice (sent to the claimants) can be combined as is done in the case of railway receipts and invoices.

All pay orders sent to the Chief Accounts Officer on any one day should be forwarded under a single covering letter and not under a separate covering letter for each, as is the practice on some railways.

On Western Railway, the station is required first to acknowledge receipt of pay order and then to intimate the fact of encashment to the claims office. This procedure is unnecessary and may be discontinued.

On some Railways each Pay Order Clerk prepares 15 Pay Orders daily. The out-put of Pay Order Clerks on North Eastern Railway and North-East Frontier Railway should be brought at par with South Central, Central and Western Railways where each Pay Order Clerk prepares 25 to 30 Pay Orders daily.

Whenever the amount paid is less than the amount claimed, the covering letter should contain a brief explanation as to how the payable amount has been arrived at.

To curtail the work-load involved in writing as well as in adding of amount paid, the total amount of compensation paid should be rounded off to the nearest rupee.

Claims of higher valuation need close scrutiny by senior, experienced and more mature officers. At the moment such attention is largely lacking on most of the railways and the inevitable result is slipshod disposal of claims and neglect of preventive effort. It is a well known principle of administration that responsibilities should be commensurate with status and pay and what claims offices need now is not further enhancement of the powers of A.C.Os and S.C.Os but the posting of additional officers of senior and administrative rank according to requirements.

The decision taken by the Food Corporation of India not to prefer claims of less than Rs. 10 is a wise step and other large customers should be persuaded to do likewise.

Strengthening Of The Claims Settlement Organization Of Eastern Railway

A study of the claims compensation on Eastern Railway revealed that that railway needed immediate assistance in order to cope with the increasing intake and arrears of claims. An interim special report was, therefore, sent to the Railway Board on 20.11.1969 for strengthening the claims settlement organization of Eastern Railway which has since been partially accepted.

Repudiation Of Claims

Normally one would expect that after assumption of common carrier liability railways would be admitting a larger proportion of the claims, but statistics do not show that this is so.

It has been stressed in several of the memoranda received by the Committee that the policies followed by Claims Office, in dealing with claims are not in conformity with the law and many of the repudiations are unjustified. I have found, after studying a number of claims files on railways, that this complaint is not without some justification.

Non-compliance with packing conditions does not protect the railway against pilferage (as distinct from wastage), and yet several claims of this nature are rejected on that plea.

Even when the Railway Receipt bears remarks that dunnage bags have been provided, some claims for pilferage through flapdoor crevices are rejected on the plea that bags were not found at the destination station (wagon having passed transhipment point) or the dunnage bags were of substandard size.

Number of claims for damage by wet were repudiated by railways on the plea of non-provision of dunnage.

There is also a complaint that claims have been repudiated on ground of non-provision of dunnage, though shortage was found in the middle of the wagon.

Repudiation of claims on the ground of non-provision of dunnage bags or provision of sub-standard dunnage bags is being indiscriminately resorted to by the Southern Railway and it was noticed that the repudiated cases, when taken to court, are compromised and paid. This is not a healthy practice as it gives rise to the widespread feeling that railway claims offices do the right thing only under extreme pressure.

Even when the liability of the railways was that of a bailee, they had to bear responsibility for theft and loss of entire packages from open wagon. Under Section 75A of the Railways Act, railways' responsibility has in no way diminished and the railways are responsible for theft and loss from open wagons even where open wagons are used at sender's own request. But there is a complaint that claims are being repudiated on ground of shortage found from open wagons.

One complaint made by many public bodies is that railway staff posted in Private Sidings and sometimes even those working at railway stations do not count the number of packages/bags and make such remarks on the railway receipts as 'loading and unloading by owner', 'Loading not supervised by railway staff', 'one wagon said to contain . . . . . bags'. Such remarks are prejudicial to the interests of the owners of the goods, especially the consignees who when they pay for a railway receipt do not know what remarks it bears.

It should be made clear to staff that even though a

consignment is required to be loaded or unloaded by owners, still railway staff are responsible for supervising the loading and unloading operations.

I consider that in the case of 'said to contain' railway receipts, if a consignment is transhipped en route from a wagon with forwarding station seals intact, enquiries at the transhipment point should be made. The owners would be responsible for the number of bags found short at the transhipment point and railways would be responsible for any further shortage found at destination. Railway Board should issue an authoritative ruling on this point for the guidance of railways as to how such claims are to be disposed of.

Statistical Disposal and Reopening of Claims

If there is any delay on the part of the claimant in furnishing material information or documents, such as original railway receipt, Beejuck, letter of authority, etc., the claims are statistically closed till the receipt of such documents. This type of disposal has been permitted by the Railway Board under certain specified conditions.

This Committee found that on Central Eastern, South Central and South Eastern Railways, number of claims closed due to non-receipt of documents from the parties as compared to the total disposal is very high.

It was also observed that in several cases, railways are not fully following Board's Orders of serving two registered notices to the claimants.

In some claims, the railways close the cases simultaneously with the writing of a letter to the claimant calling for certain documents but the claimant is not advised that the case had been closed. Nor are such letters always sent by registered post.

The Committee also observed that once a claim is treated as statistically closed, the actual settlement of that case even after receipt of requisite documents, is delayed for months and on one Railway for years.

I recommend that the claims office must wait for at least two months from the date of the first letter calling for documents before closing the case, and that the party must invariably be advised about such closing.

Cases which are statistically closed, pending receipt of requisite documents from the claimants, should continue to be kept with the dealing clerk and should not be sent to the Record section so that letters received from the claimants may be quickly attached to the file and dealt with further.

Statistics of disposal should separately indicate the number of cases closed on account of delay in receipt of documents from the claimants; large incidence of this type of disposal should be a matter for the management to investigate.

Efforts should be made to educate the people as to what documents should accompany the claim application.

Printed standardised application forms indicating all requisite entries should be made available at every station to be handed over to the merchants at the time of granting open/assessment delivery.

By strict supervision over the work of receipt of letters and attaching thereof to the files in the claims offices, a sense of trust should be cultivated in the minds of the claimants that their documents will be properly linked in the claims offices and the original documents would be returned, if the claimant needs them for other purposes.

There should be no hesitation in re-opening and paying a claim if it is found on review or appeal that the same had been earlier repudiated on insufficient grounds. What is undesirable is the repudiation of or closing of cases merely to complete the fixed quota or just to get rid of a file. Unfortunately this has become quite a common practice.

According to the Statistical Manual, the time taken for the disposal of a reopened case should be reckoned from the date of receipt of the communication which caused reconsideration leading to amendment of the previous decision But in practice, the average time for disposal of reopened cases is counted from the day of order of reopening and is generally taken as one day only.

Statistics of reopened cases should be compiled strictly according to the instructions.

Time Limit for Settlement

One of the pressing demands of the Chambers of Commerce as well as individual members of public is that there should be a time limit for verification of facts and settlement of a claim by the Railway—in the same way as there is a time limit of six months for lodging a claim.

The Railway Board have constantly stressed the need for expeditious disposal of claims, and have also prescribed average time limits within which claims should be disposed of. The overall average time for disposal of a claim laid down by the Board is 30 days. The Railways have also been told that no claim should remain outstanding for more than one year and six months old cases should not exceed 50 on each Railway. But these targets are nowhere being observed.

As the number of claims has increased, the arrears of pending claims—specially old cases—have been mounting up. Obviously there is need for taking effective measures to speed up the settlement of claims—inspite of the erroneous belief held in some quarters that the faster the claims are settled, the more will they increase.

Quantum of Compensation

The High Courts have generally taken the view that the claimant is entitled to the market price of the goods prevalent at the destination station at the time when the goods were damaged or should have reasonably reached the destination. This view has been accepted by the Supreme Court as a settled law.

In claims offices, the general practice at present is that if a claim is preferred by the consignee, payment is made at the price of the Sender's Sale Invoice (Beejuck) and if the claim is preferred by the Sender, payment is made at 5 to 10 per cent less than the Beejuck price. When Beejuck is not available or goods are known to be despatched for sale on commission basis, compensation is allowed on the basis of market value, deducting 10 to 15 per cent toward the element of profit.

This practice of setting compensation claims at Beejuck value only and sometimes even less than the Beejuck value has been the subject matter of criticism by a large number of claimants and it has been represented that the person who orders his goods from the suppliers obviously gets his capital locked up and expects to make a reasonable profit in the transaction of sale of his goods and therefore, payment of compensation at Beejuck value is causing hardship to the trade and is not in accordance with the law. It has also been represented that the Railways policy of settlement of compensation claims has forced the mercantile community either to seek the assistance of a court of law or to look for alternative modes of transport.

The Committee recommends that it should be made clear to all claims officers that to repudiate a claim which is actually fit for payment or to pay Rs. 9 where Rs. 10 is due is not prevention of claim but only harassment of the public. Claim prevention requires that a claim should not arise; in other words, that the goods should be delivered to the consignee in a safe and sound condition. But when damage has occurred and a claim has arisen, the compensation paid should be such as would be considered fair and reasonable by any disinterested observer; it should be neither more nor less than the due amount.

After considering all the aspects of the problem, the Committee recommends that the following principles may be laid down for the guidance of claims officers for determining the quantum of compensation—(1) If the claim is preferred by the sender (who holds the title) or any of his agents, compensation should be paid at the market price of the forwarding station at the time of booking which will be reflected in the Sale-invoice or Beejuck, i.e. replacement cost at the forwarding station. Freight paid should be added. (2) If the claim is preferred by the consignee, compensation should be paid at the whole-sale market price prevailing at the destination station at the time when the damage occurred or when the consignment ought to have reached the destination, i.e. replacement price at the destination station on the probable date of delivery. "To Pay" freight, if not already paid, should be deducted if compensation is allowed at the destination selling rate. (3) If the claimant is not a trader but a consumer, compensation should be paid at the price at which goods were purchased, i.e., purchase price plus proportionate freight, if already paid by the claimant. In any case, the quantum of compensation should not exceed the value of the goods at the destination station market rate.

Item 6 of Para 2248 of Accounts Code Part II should be amended.

Inter-Railway Liability

A study of files and discussions with the claims officers of the zonal Railways have convinced the Committee that the fixation of inter-railway liability is a time consuming and largely fruitless process and the notices exchanged between the zonal railways do not lead to any positive preventive action in most of the cases.

The fixation of inter-railway liability was a matter of necessity when different railways were owned by different agencies. With the major railways all coming under state ownership, this aspect has lost all practical utility and its main purpose is the maintenance of a separate account for each railway.

For making minor adjustments of this nature in each Railway's accounts, it is not necessary to fix inter-railway liability in each individual case. This can be done by some ad hoc formula based on past experience or on study of sample cases or any other suitable method.

Under the present system claims on through traffic which accounts for 86 per cent of the amount of compensation paid not only take longer to settle but also receive less attention from the preventive angle. While in the case of local claims, Railways do sometimes try to locate the loss, fix staff responsibility and take remedial measures, in the case of claims on through traffic, the anxiety for strict compliance with Conference Rules tends to throw all preventive action into the background.

The man-power now employed in apportioning inter-railway liability on claims is costing the Railways Rs. 36 lakhs. But most of the work done in this connection is purely of a routine nature and confined to opening of cases, writing of letters to the stations, transhipment points and inter-change points for furnishing the particulars of transit and closing of the files on receipt of payment advice received from the settling Railway.

An increasing number of claims on inter-changed traffic are being paid under 'suspense' head, as increase in claims has put the machinery for fixing inter-railway liability completely out of gear.

Technical sharing of liability among the Government Railways is doing more harm than good. I, therefore, recommend that the present system of fixing inter-railway liability as between Government railways should be abolished.

Abolition of inter-railway liability would result in abolition of Outward and Cross-Sections, substantial reduction in the clerical work of the dealing and despatch sections of inward claims sections, curtailment of clerical work of the accounts sections as a result of a large reduction in the number of transfer certificates and bills, and above all, expedite settlement of claims.

The staff withdrawn from this work would be utilised more profitably on settlement and prevention work. But eventually when the prevention drive has got into a stride, I do expect that clerical work in claims offices would be reduced and some clerk's posts would become surplus.

Experience has shown that railways do not give proper attention to their outward and cross-traffic claims. It is, therefore, necessary that the paying railway, which is usually the destination railway, should be made entirely, responsible for the efficient handling of all claims on through traffic. For this purpose all railways should regard themselves not as separate entities but as zones of one big railway system. The settling railway should deal with through claims just like its own local claims.

Apart from taking up individual cases for investigation/fixation of staff responsibility, the paying railway should also have a regular system of analysing the claims paid on through traffic, to pin point not only the commodities affected and causes of claims but also the places where thefts are occurring or the working is irregular, negligent or deficient. This analysis, supported by facts and figures, should be forwarded to the Chief Commercial Superintendents of sister railways for remedial actions.

Demand for Change in System

The dissatisfaction voiced in the memoranda sent to the Committee has expressed itself in a general demand for a change in the present system and for this purpose the following concrete proposals have been made by various Chambers of Commerce and other railway users—(1) that railways should hold periodical meetings with their larger customers like Steel Plants, Food Corporation of India, Tea Association, Oil Companies, etc. to discuss problems relating to claims; (2) that claims work should be decentralised; (3) that the system of mobile claims offices should be adopted more extensively; (4) that instead of litigation railways should permit joint arbitration by railway officers and representatives of the larger concerns; and (5) that Claims Tribunal should be established on the same lines as there are tribunals for suits under the Motor Vehicle Acts.

Periodical meetings with the bigger undertakings, Chambers of Commerce, State Governments will certainly be useful not only for more expeditious settlement of claims but also in clearing doubts and misunderstandings. Such meetings should be held quarterly or six-monthly, as a regular measure. At such meetings railways should not merely acquaint themselves with the complaints and suggestions of their major constituents but also seek their cooperation in regard to various measures of claims prevention.

The Commiteee feels that to start with it will be useful to delegate powers to settle claims upto a specified amount to the Area Superintendents, Divisional/Assistant Commercial Superintendents in the Divisions, in respect of claims pertaining to their Headquarters stations. Each Railway may take such action as it deems fit, keeping in view the special requirements of its own system.

It is necessary to add that a large number of public bodies and rail users, and one retired Chairman of the Railway Board, have stressed the need for divisionalisation of claims work. This demand largely voices their feeling of dissatisfaction with the way claims are generally handled and is based on the hope that a change in the system would somehow remove the present difficulties.

After an exhaustive study of the problem of claims, I have come to the conclusion that the present difficulties arise not because there is over-centralisation but because the Commercial department of railways is very weak. In the circumstances mere decentralisation of claims work will only transfer the problems from claims Offices to Divisions without effecting any genuine improvement. What the railways need is a strong and efficient Commercial organisation at stations, on the Divisions and in Claims Offices so that both prevention and settlement of claims may receive due attention.

I am confident that if my recommendations are fully implemented, including a measure of delegation to Divisions, Area Superintendents and large stations, Railways will be well set to dispose of claims in a business like way and to retrieve both public goodwill and a good deal of the high rated traffic lost to road transport.

The Committee commends the scheme of mobile Claims Office introduced on South Central Railway for adoption by all the zonal railways with such modifications and refinements as they may deem fit.

Station Masters of certain important stations and Commercial/Claims Inspectors were authorised to settle claims upto Rs. 50 in 1948. This limit was enhanced to Rs. 100 in 1958.

The Committee has found that claims upto Rs. 100 continue to be dealt within the Claims Offices in large numbers, because (i) Station Masters/Inspectors, are generally reluctant to exercise their powers; (ii) Small claims are mostly either on perishable consignments which Station Masters/Inspectors are barred from settling under Clause (ii) and (iv) of Rule 2149 of the Commercial Manual or on bagged consignments (Pilferage) with remarks of 'Packing condition not complied with' which Station Masters/Inspectors are not empowered to settle under Clause (v) of the Rule ibid; and (iii) Claims upto Rs. 100 are to be preferred either to the C.C.S. or to the Station Master depending on the conditions of booking. As the claimants find it difficult to decide the authority to whom claim is to be lodged, to be on the safe side, they generally send their claims to the C.C.S.

I have examined these aspects and recommend that the powers of Station Masters/Inspectors should be unfettered within the pecuniary limit of Rs. 100 and the prohibitory clauses (ii) to (v) of Rule 2149 of the Commercial Manual should be deleted.

The demand for arbitration or claims tribunal has arisen, in my opinion, largely out of a feeling of frustration and desperation. There is no reason why the railways themselves should not do what the public expect to get through arbitration or claims tribunals. If the railways make their Commercial department in general and the Claims Offices in particular, strong and efficient, the safety of goods can certainly be improved, the rising trend in claims can be controlled, their sattlement can be made prompt and business like, and public confidence can be restored.

Port Railways

Claims cannot be settled by Eastern and South Eastern Railways on behalf of Calcutta Port Commissioners without specific written authority of the Traffic Manager of the C.P.C., even though their liability is correctly established according to the Conference Rules. Such written consents are not received even after prolonged correspondence. According to the agreement, if the authority to pay is not received within a month from the receipt of the Missing Goods Report, the C.P.C. Railway may be called upon to arrange settlement in direct communication with the claimant. If this method is adopted, claimants will be put to great inconvenience. It has not been possible to act according to these terms and as a result on the Eastern Railway alone, a huge amount to the tune of Rs. 34,80,000 was outstanding on 30-9-69 against C.P.C. Railway.

There is a chronic problem of delays in submission of Missing Goods Reports by the C.P.C. Railway resulting in wastage of outdoor staff for chasing them and abnormal delays in disposal of claims.

Not only the contiguous Railways (Eastern and South Eastern) but also other zonal Railways are facing difficulties in settlement of claims on outward traffic of C.P.C. Railway.

The Committee has been informed that there are chronic delays in issue of railway receipts by C.P.C. Railway Stations, due to centralisation of documentation for all loading points at one place. This should not be allowed to continue.

In cases of consignments of imported machinery which arrived at destination stations in damaged condition survey reports were called for by the Northern Railway from the C.P.C. Railway but the latter refused to supply the same.

Heavy thefts and pilferages are taking place in the port area. Kantapukur is the most favourite spot for pilferage of sugar and Tea Warehouse for pliferage of tea. Special security and claims prevention measures are necessary, but Indian Government Railways have no control over this area.

The marking of goods, particularly of machinery consignments booked by C.P.C. is not at all satisfactory.

Though a claim on through traffic is paid by Bombay Port Trust Railway, the entire amount is debited to Central Railway who has to fix inter-railway liability by further correspondence. It apparently causes duplication of work.

It may be mentioned that Port Railways are also members of the Indian Railways Conference Association. One would expect the zonal Railways to take full advantage of this position by referring their disputed claims to the Commercial Committee.

The ideal solution would be for the contiguous Government Railways to take over the working of the railway in the ports which have very small rail kilometrage and cannot by themselves provide the expert and high level supervision which prevails on the Indian Government Railways. While railways may not be able to take any initiative in this matter, it is obviously necessary for them to have a close look at the arrangements in vogue on Calcutta, Madras and Bombay Port Trust Railways and to take suitable steps to protect their own interests in connection with the traffic coming from or booked to these Ports.

Public Cooperation

Both prevention and settlement of claims are dependent on public cooperation. Therefore, the Railway administration must communicate again and again to the public—its customers—through the medium of newspapers, bulletins, pamphlets, posters, seminars and meetings—

(1) How they can help in prevention of loss and damage to consignments?

(2) What information and what documents are necessary to be sent with the claim application?

(3) In what way the claimants can help the administration in expeditious and fair settlement of claims?

(4) Under what circumstances the railway administration is not liable for loss and damage and the rationale behind these protective provisions?

(5) Facts and figures of what the railway is doing in the direction of prevention and expeditious disposal of claims, so that the good work done by the administration does not remain unknown and unrecognised.

Every Officer in the Commercial Department must cultivate the aptitude of a public relations officer and devote some time and energy to this aspect of work. The administration must recognise this role of Commercial Officers and see that they are fully equipped for it.

Prevention Of Litigation

More than 17,000 suits are filed per annum—against the railway by its customers, and what is even more telling, against the State by its subjects.

In 97 out of 100 cases, the decisions of railway officers are accepted by claimants. This indeed is not a mean achievement. But handling of 17,000 new suits per annum; which keep on accumulating as disposal by courts cannot keep pace with the institution, is a gigantic task. Efficient conducting of such a large number of suits in the various courts spread all over the country requires man-power totally incommensurate with the financial gains expected.

The total cost incurred by railways on litigation includes (i) cost awarded to the plaintiff in suits decreed or compromised, i.e., court-fee paid in the court and plaintiff's lawyer's fee; (ii) fees paid to railway lawyers; (iii) miscellaneous expenses such as stamps on applications, adjournment costs, etc., (iv) cost of staff engaged in court section and (v) cost of adducing evidence in the court. The total direct cost of litigation regarding compensation claims on Indian Railways may be placed at Rs. 50 lakhs per annum. With 14,127 suits disposed of in 1968-69, the average cost of litigation per suit comes to Rs. 3500. The average value of a suit comes to Rs. 680. These statistics disclose that when a claim is paid after a legal suit, Railways have to pay about 50 per cent over and above the original value of claims as litigation expenses.

More than 60 per cent of all the suits are compromised. On Central Railway, the percentage of suits compromised to total disposed of was as high as 86 per cent in 1968-69. These figures of compromised suits, represent unwarranted and unnecessary litigation, which deserves serious notice by the top management. Railways must have a machinery to ensure that those claims which are admitted by not good for contest are not allowed to be taken to court.

Another striking feature is that a large number of suits are for petty amounts. More than 5000 suits filed every year are for recovery of Rs. 200 or less, whereas the average litigation cost per suit is Rs. 350. Legal battles for such small claims can neither benefit the claimant nor the Railway.

Claims of petty amounts should not be allowed to go to the court, unless some important general principle is involved and the legal stand of the railways is very strong.

Causes of Suits

Incidence of suits for want of decision is very high on the North Eastern, North East Frontier and South Central Railways. Incidence of suits on the allegation of short-payment is very high on the Central and Northern Railways. Incidence on account of repudiation at claim stage is very high on the Western, Eastern, Southern, South Eastern and North East Frontier Railways. Northern, Eastern, Central, South Eastern and North East Frontier Railway should also further analyse as to how suits shown under 'others' were caused, as this is sure to unfold some incorrect or irregular method of working or counting.

It is necessary to draw special attention to a prolific but avoidable source of litigation; namely the tendency on the part of some claims offices to stick to old policies in spite of adverse decisions in courts.

Railways should have a regular system of scrutinising all adverse judgments of courts.

When the rulings given by courts are found to be just and reasonable, officers should be given strict instructions to follow them in all subsequent cases so as to prevent unnecessary litigation.

It is not a wise policy to force claimants to go to court in order to get the benefit of court rulings.

Results Of Contested Suits

52 to 54 per cent of contested suits are lost by the railway. The majority of cases are lost either due to decision to contest being wrong or due to failure in

adducing the evidence.

There are also some suits which are contested only on the ground of quantum of compensation and decreed after substantial reduction in the amount claimed. It is much better for railways to arrive at such settlements through their own agency rather than through courts of law.

Technical Pleas

Among the suits dismissed, a sizable number are won on technical grounds. A sample study on all the zonal railways revealed that 40 per cent were won on technical grounds and 60 per cent were won on merits. This shows that mere fact of dismissal of suit should not make the administration complacent.

My opinion is that the railway administration, as a limb of the Government of India, and as the largest public undertaking in the country should confirm to the highest standards of business morality and should admit all just and valid claims. I have no objection, if technical pleas are also taken when claims are otherwise fit for repudiation on merits. But it does not serve the larger interests of the administration, not even in its capacity as a commercial concern, to take the help of technical pleas to defeat rightful claims. The Railways are now facing keen competition from road transport and if they are serious about promotion of their sales, they can ill afford to displease their customers by legal quibblings.

Preventive Measures

The present annual figure of about 17,000 new suits can easily be brought down to 4000 or at the most 5000 if railways have a strong and efficient organization for the settlement of claims.

When the number of suits is brought down to this figure, the expenses would be reduced by at least Rs. 20 lakhs per annum and the Court sections of railways will be able to give individual attention to the suits and contest them successfully.

Claims offices should be made thoroughly familiar with the Railway's liability under the amended Act. They should follow a fair and equitable policy of payment. They should not only be just and fair in their disposal of claims but must also build up a reputation of being so. Only in this way can they inspire public confidence.

It should be remembered that to repudiate a claim which is fit for payment or to pay less than the amount due under the law, is not claim prevention; it is only harassment of the public which must have undesirable repercussions sooner or later.

At present officers are only concerned that there should no unjustified or excess payment but it is no worry to them if some one is deprived of his just dues. Very often cases are marked closed only to meet the requirements of statistics or repudiated without any justification. To stop such practices it is necessary to make officers accountable for wrong repudiations and short payments. Senior officers should also be made alive to their responsibility to see that the officers under them decide claims in a just and reasonable manner.

Even when the claims are rejected on sufficient grounds, letters of repudiation sent to the claimants should be made as convincing as possible by giving full facts and points of law. This would minimise the chances of the claimants going to court.

The railways on which institution of suits for want of decision and for short-payment is very high, should make detailed investigations to find out why the position on their systems is worse than on other railways and tighten up their weak links.

In all claims offices there should be a proper system of dealing with reminders and appeals. Some senior person or persons should be detailed to keep a special watch on them and ensure that they receive prompt attention and are not lost sight of. Effective arrangements to call for and review each case on receipt of a reminder or appeal would go a long way to prevent unnecessary litigation.

Appeals against wrong repudiation or short payment should not be allowed to be disposed of by the officer who passed the original order, as is the practice on some railways, but should be put up to a higher officer who should use his independent and unbiased judgement to decide the appeal.

It is essential that all cases are thoroughly and critically reviewed on receipt of a notice of suit under section 80 CPC. Railways may consider the establishment of a special section in their claims offices to deal with all notices of suit. Its main functions would be as detailed in the report.

On one Railway, it was noticed that delays take place in sending notices of suit from the office of the General Manager to the claims offices. This needs to be watched.

Decision whether to admit a claim or to contest it in a court should be taken on receipt of suit notice under section 80 CPC and not after insitution of a suit.

The decision to contest a suit should not be allowed to be taken by ACOs or SCOs as at present but should be taken only by Dy. CCS or CCS. The time spent by an administrative officer at this stage will pay rich dividends as it will reduce unnecessary work later on, avoid irrelevant and untenable pleas and make the defence more precise, meaningful and effective.

Pleadings And Evidence

The main causes of adverse decision, even when the railway has a good case, are—(i) delay in completion of enquiries resulting in delay in the submission of the written statement; (ii) delay in filing documentary evidence, (iii) non-attendance of witnesses; and (iv) improper pleadings.

Railways generally take a number of adjournments before filing the written statement. Where the court refuses to grant further adjournments even on the payment of costs to the opposite party, the Railway advocate is instructed to file a provisional written statement on general denial.

The system of obtaining repeated lengthy adjournments and filing irrelevant written statements on general denial is not in keeping with the prestige of an institution like Railway. Radical steps will have to be taken to stop these methods, as they have become almost customary.

The administration should ensure that necessary enquiries are completed in time and proper pleadings are framed after careful verification of the facts alleged in the plaint. It would be possible to do so, if the claims are thoroughly scrutinised and facts marshalled immediately on receipt of the notice under section 80 CPC. and the file is complete by the time of the receipt of the summons from the court.

The officer who decides to contest a suit should be fully conscious of the expenditure and inconvenience involved in arranging evidence of staff from the forwarding transhipment, junction and destination station.

The terms and utility of section 139 of the Indian Railways Act should be thoroughly explained to the station and office staff all over the railways so that they may learn how certified copies of relevant entries in railway record should be prepared, signed and sent. In many cases attendance of staff with original records can be obviated by invoking this provision.

As soon as a decision is taken to contest a suit, a list of evidence necessary for defence should be prepared and certified copies of the requisite documents should be called for from the stations concerned so that all material is kept ready for framing the written statement.

A list of names of the witnesses along with the names and addresses of the supervisory officials under whom they work should be made available to the Railway Lawyers and they should be authorised to intimate the date of hearing directly to the official incharge as well as the Divisional Commercial Superintendent or Divisional Superintendent under whom such witnesses are working even on foreign railways. There should be a direct channel of correspondence between the lawyers on one hand and the Divisional Superintendent/Divisional Commercial Superintendent and the official in-charge of the witnesses.

For journeys undertaken for giving evidence on behalf of the railway, free duty passes given to the staff should be of the next higher class than what he is generally entitled to. So also he should be paid daily allowance at the next higher rate than what he is generally entitled to.

In sanctioning the strength of the relieving staff at the larger depots, particularly transhipment points and also of Claims or Law Inspectors, man-days lost due to court attendance should also be taken into account.

Letters sent to Station Masters, Yard Masters, etc. for arranging witnesses should clearly spell out the facts required to be proved so that the right individual man can be sent with the right documents. Supervisory officials will also have to be told that it is their personal responsibility to relieve the correct person for attendance in court.

One Railway Advocate has mentioned that as the period of limitation for filing suits has been increased from one to three years, the difficulty of records not being available has been felt in certain cases. It is suggested that the period for which commercial records are required to be maintained by stations should be correspondingly increased.

Copies of necessary commercial rules books should be supplied to all Railway Advocates.

Jurisdiction

One of the main reasons for contesting suits on inadequate grounds is non-receipt of instructions from sister Railways. A sample study indicated that about 21 per cent of the total number of suits have to be conducted by Railways other than those who disposed of the claims. These suits are generally neglected.

Railways may consider an amendment of Section 80 of Indian Railways Act on the following lines :—

(i) Suit for compensation can be filed either in a court having jurisdiction over the booking station or in a court having jurisdiction over the destination station; and

(ii) Suit for compensation should be filed against the Union of India which should be represented either by the General Manager of the booking railway, if the suit is filed in a court with jurisdiction over the booking station or by the General Manager of the destination Railway, if the suit is filed in a court having jurisdiction over the destination station.

In any case, it is necessary for all railways to look upon themselves as one entity and to conduct suits filed against other railways with the same interest and care as suits filed against themselves. The railway where the trial court is situated should handle all suits as its own, should be responsible for their success and should bear all costs. The destination Railway should send its complete claim file to the Railway which is conducting the suit instead of merely sending a letter of instructions, and the final decision to contest should be taken by the conducting Railway.

Satisfaction Of Decrees

There should be no delay in satisfaction of decrees. The statistics of cases in which decrees remain outstanding at the end of each month are mostly incorrect. There are serious delays in satisfaction of decrees on some Railways.

A decree register should be maintained in the proforma given in the report for watching satisfaction of decrees. This register should be put up to Dy. Chief Commercial Superintendent/Claims, periodically.

There have been some stray cases in the past where the courts ordered attachment of station property on account of non-satisfaction of decrees. Such cases get wide publicity and damage the reputation of the railways. Severe disciplinary action should be taken against the staff responsible for such serious delays.

Railway Advocates

As Railway Advocates have to deal mainly with claims cases, it is only right that their selection and appointment are made by the Chief Commercial Superintendent in consultation with the Divisional Superintendent. The Railways which are following a different procedure should be advised to act on the principles already laid down by the Railway Board with which the Committee agrees.

Most Railways have an arrangement to watch the performance of individual lawyers. This should be done in a regular systematic manner and at least once every quarter Dy. Chief Commercial Superintendent/ Chief Commercial Superintendent should go through the registers in which the proceedings of cases compromised, won and lost by each lawyer are recorded. If any lawyer's performance is consistently below the mark, Chief Commercial Superintendent may terminate his services.

Railway Lawyers are not employees of the Railways but their counsels and as such should be treated with greater dignity and respect; issue of written warning letters to them is not in keeping with the relationship of a litigant and his counsel.

The Railway standing counsels at places where there are more than 50 suits pending should particularly be lawyers of tested ability and integrity and their work should be carefully watched. The Zonal Railways must also make suitable arrangement, such as posting of Law Assistants at these places, for remaining in day-to-day touch with the Railway Advocates and doing all that a common litigant has to do in pursuing his own case.

The minimum fee for railway lawyers should be fixed at Rs. 25 per contested case and Rs. 20 per settled case. The fee of the clerk of the lawyer should be fixed at 10% of the pleader's fee subject to a minimum of Rs. 5 in contested cases, Rs. 2 in cases settled out of court and maximum of Rs. 25 per case.

The Committee would stress the need for streamlining the procedure for passing bills of lawyers and suggest to the railways to work to the target of passing every bill within a month. A note indicating the reasons for deduction from the Bill, if any, should also be sent to the Advocate.

The system of sending advance of Rs. 10 or Rs. 20 for miscellaneous litigation expenses in each individual case by a separate cheque may perhaps be advantageously replaced by the system of keeping a permanent imprest or advance of fixed amount with every lawyer, depending on the number of suits handled by him. There should be an arrangement for the automatic recoupment of the imprest as bills in individual cases are paid from time to time. This will not only ensure timely action on the part of Railway lawyers but will also reduce the clerical work.

Separation Of Commercial Cadre

During my tours on different railways, the one thing that struck me most was the general feeling of frustration and inferiority that pervades all ranks of commercial officers and staff.

Any operating officer who is considered not upto the mark is transferred to the Commercial department. This practice is so common that there seems to be a stigma attached to the entire Commercial department and any posting to the Commercial department is taken to imply condemnation.

In the joint cadre of Commercial and Operating Officers, an Operating Officer can get promotion in the Commercial department even if he has never worked in the Commercial department but Commercial Officers are hardly ever promoted to senior posts in the Operating department or to general posts such as General Managers or even Divisional Superintendents. Generally speaking, there is only one way traffic between Operating and Commercial departments, namely, from the Operating to Commercial.

After a few years experience, Operating Officers should be given a thorough grounding in the actual work done and situations handled by Operating Officers in Divisions and at Headquarters. At such refresher courses and seminars, lectures on the day-to-day duties of Operating Officers of various levels should be delivered by senior and experienced officers.

The raising of a corps of able and dedicated officers is one of the major responsibilities of all administrators, and this is a matter to which railway administrations—particularly their Operating and Commercial departments—should give special attention. All officers should regard it as their inherent obligation to build up the requisite qualities among those working under them.

The atmosphere in the Operating department is predominantly one of insecurity and in the Commercial department one of frustration. So neither department can give of its best to the Railway. But the conditions in the Commercial department are simply pathetic. Many distinguished Committees before me were well aware of this and strongly recommended the rehabilitation of the Commercial department.

I endorse the recommendation of the Administrative Reforms Commission that "the image of the Commercial Department should be refurnished and due importance should be given to it." Implementation of this recommendation would require, among other things, that some important functions connected with the sale of transport should be entrusted to the Commercial department, for example, allotment of wagons, arranging of special trains, creation of additional capacity for clearance of parcels, running of Parcel vans, introduction of additional passenger trains or extension of existing trains, attachment of extra coaches to clear long waiting lists.

In my considered opinion, if the rehabilitation of the Commercial department is still a dream despite the recommendations of so many important Committees in the past, it is largely because the Commercial department is generally regarded as just an appendage to, or dumping ground for the Operating department. If railways wish to maintain public goodwill as well as their own fair name, if they wish to get more traffic and earnings, they will have to be more customer oriented and more Commercial minded; and this will require a Commercial department strong and capable enough to manage the functions which properly belong to it. But this cannot be achieved until the present position is radically altered. I, therefore, strongly support the recommendation of the Administrative Reforms Commission that a separate cadre be constituted for the Commercial Department.

Right from the level of Assistant Officers the working of the Transportation and Commercial departments is completely separate. So there should be no difficulty in separating the cadres.

The separation of cadres will have to be effected even in Class II. Some categories of Class III staff will be declared as purely Transportation and some as purely commercial and they will be eligible for promotion only in their respective departments. Some other posts, for example, those of Station Masters, who do both Transportation and Commercial work, will be eligible to be considered for promotion to Class II on both Commercial and Transportation sides.

Organisation To Implement Recommendations

Implementation of suggestions made in this report would require intensified supervision, constant chasing of station staff and closer scrutiny of work.

As the claims started mounting up, the claims Prevention Officers had to be deployed for settlement work and now they are Prevention Officers only in name.

As a matter of fact, the very idea that a small organization attached to the claims office can effectively prevent claims on a railway is fundamentally wrong. Although the claims office is entrusted with the responsibility of settling claims and initiating preventive measures, it is well to remember that claims are not born in the claims office, but at stations, in yards and sheds.

Preventive work to be successful will have to be done on a railway wide scale, and for this purpose a suitable organization with adequate authority must exist on each Division as well as at the Railway headquarters.

With increased passenger, goods and parcels traffic and new types of problems coming up, the work load of Divisional Commercial Superintendents has increased several times during recent years. The strength of Commercial Officers on Divisions was fixed many years ago and has remained unchanged in spite of the heavy increase in the volume and complexities of their work.

Having thoughtfully considered the matter and after discussing it in detail with Chief Commercial Superintendents and a number of Divisional Superintendents and Commercial Officers in the Division, I recommend the creation of (a) an additional post of Dy. D.S. (Com.) for ten of the most important and Commercially most heavy Divisions; and (b) an additional post of D.C.S. in each of the other Divisions (except that for Asansol and Dhanbad Divisions taken together one additional D.C.S. would be sufficient).

The important items of Commercial work in the Division which at present are either neglected or are not done at all because of the inability of the existing D.C.S. to carry the entire lead and for which an additional D.C.S. is justified.

For many years, the workload of the C.C.S. has been increasing not only due to more traffic and more terminals but also due to changes in the economic, social and political structure of the country. Public and staff grievances demand full attention. Public complaints, Parliament Questions, Parliamentary Committees, meetings with customers and trade unions, etc., appeals, departmental catering, reservations, ticketless travel, ticket printing and passenger amenities have assumed much importance and keep the C.C.S. very busy, leaving him little or no time for problems connected with Goods and Parcels traffic. Claims work receives the lowest priority, because it has no immediate or direct repercussions.

The present system under which S.P.E./Vigilance keep pursuing non-corruption mistakes is very demoralising for the staff, subversive of discipline and creates a good deal of unnecessary work for senior railway officers. While fully endorsing the views of Wanchoo Committee on this subject, I also recommend that there should be an arrangement whereby it should be left entirely to railways to deal, as they deem fit, with non-corruption irregularities which SPE/Vigilance may come across during the course of their investigations. There should be no need for the railways to review and justify again and again the punishments awarded for non-corruption mistakes, simply because they were brought to light by S.P.E. or Vigilance.

Apart from intensified supervision, preventive effort will require continuous research into the methods of packing goods; methods of loading damageable goods, a review of the arrangements made by the railways for the handling of the main streams of traffic most susceptible to claims and publication of literature on claim prevention.

After examining the workload of the existing C.C.S. and the time they are able to devote to claims work, I have come to the conclusion that they are already over worked and will not be able to pilot the preventive measures suggested by me: I, therefore, recommend creation of an additional post of Chief Claims Manager on each Railway. He should be in Senior Administrative grade (Rs. 1800-2250) in the case of the Eastern, Northern, Central, Western and South Eastern Railways and in the grade Rs. 1800—2000 in the case of the remaining four railways.

The officers selected for these newly created posts of Chief Claims Managers should be men of proved ability with a flair for getting things done not only by their own subordinates but also by other departments as well as outsiders. They should have the energy and the enthusiasm to spend 15 to 20 days on the line every month meeting officers, staff and the public and explaining to them what is required to be done and why, and making surprise checks on various aspects of railway work having a bearing on the safe and correct transport of goods and parcels.

It is also necessary to post one additional senior scale officer in the head office on each railway for claims settlement work, so that the S. C. O. or A. C. O./Claims Prevention may be utilised for his own proper work of prevention of claims.

One of the non-claims Dy. C. C. S, be upgraded to Inter-Administrative grade, so that with greater authority, he can dispose of some of the work at present handled by the C.C.S. It will also remove another source of weakness in the Commercial department of the Railways, namely, the absence of an Inter-Administrative grade post in the Headquarters organisation, in consequence of which there is a tendency for officers of merit drifting away from the Commercial department thus depriving the department of continuity of tenure, maturity of experience and a second line of command in the organisational chain.

I recommend that the yardstick of 650 claims per month for each A. C. S. (claims settlement) should be adopted.

For outward and cross-traffic work, one A. C. S. may be provided for every 1300 cases. If the Outward and Cross-Traffic sections are abolished, as recommended by me, the yardstick of 650 cases for each A. C. S. (claims) would probably be found to be on the high side, as in that case he would have to devote more time to claims on through traffic.

Railway Board should also take continuous interest in the prevention and settlement of claims and exercise adequate supervision. For this purpose I recommend that the Board should have an additional Member Claims instead of a Director, so that he will have the requisite authority to give directions to railways on all matters pertaining to the speedy and safe movement of consignments. He should be essentially an outdoor man with a capacity to galvanise the working not only of claims offices but of all departments in so far as they cover the safety of goods and parcels. His principal functions will be the same as outlined for the Chief Claims Manager, except that his jurisdiction will cover all railways and he will be specially charged with the responsibility of directing and coordinating preventive effort on through traffic, which no railway can manage effectively by itself.

When my recommendations are implemented, benefits should appear in several forms. There will be a toning up of the entire Commercial department. With intensified supervision on the work of stations there should be a large reduction in the number of wagon load and small consignments lying unconnected at stations and in the Lost Property Offices. The confidence of the public in the capacity of the railways to carry goods safely and their ability to settle claims quickly and efficiently will be restored, resulting in the retention and capturing of high-rated traffic by the railways.

Normally, measures calculated to increase the safety of transport are justified, not on the basis of their financial return, but on the ground of their essentiality. But there is, in addition, ample financial justification for it. The actual savings effected through prevention of claims should be about Rs. 1.5 crores under the head "Loss of entire consignments or packages and Rupees one crore under the head "Pilferage" adding up to Rs. 2.5 crores per annum besides the savings under other heads. The savings are quite feasible and these should be the target set for the claims organisation.

The total saving in staff and litigation costs, as a result of the implementation of my recommendations, should be Rs. 56 lakhs in addition to Rs. 2.5 crores in the shape of savings in loss and damage.

I would urge that the new organisation recommended above should be set up as soon as possible in order to improve the deteriorating position of claims on railways, and I am sure that the addition expenses will be justified many time sover.

Inspectors And Tracers

The Claims and the Commercial Inspectors on the Railways are generally in lower grades of pay in relation to their worth of charge as well as in comparison to their counterparts in the other Railway Departments.

Statistics show that there is no uniformity in the number and grades of Commercial Inspectors sanctioned on the different railways.

The posts of the Commercial Inspectors, and particularly of the Claims Inspectors, in the higher grades are very few, which is brought out conspicuously when compared with the number of Inspectors in each grade in the Transportation Department. There is a strong case for upgrading some posts of Claims and other Commercial Inspectors.

In fact, not only the Inspectors but also the other categories of senior supervisory staff in the Commercial Department have been denied the higher grades. Statistics show that the percentage of higher paid staff to the total class III staff is 0.1 in the Commercial Department, which is not only the lowest of all the Departments but several times lower—4 times lower than that on Transportation, 12 times lower than that on Engineering, 22 times lower than that on Accounts and 45 times lower than that on Medical. These figures bear glaring testimony to the complaint that the Commercial Department of the Indian Railways has been relegated to the inferior most position.

The Northern Railway should consider absorbing the staff of the Task Team in the cadre of claims Tracers.

Staff At Loading, Unloading And Transhipment Points

In sufficiency of staff at loading, unloading and transhipment points is one of the major contributory causes of increase in the Railways' Claims bill.

It is suggested that a quick survey be made of the utilisation and sufficiency of staff at all the larger goods sheds, Transhipment Sheds, parcel offices and private sidings and early steps taken to make such adjustments or additional appointments as may be necessary for full compliance with the rules regarding acceptance, booking, loading, unloading and transhipment of goods and parcels.

There is a need for the raising of the grades of the supervisors at the larger goods sheds, parcel offices and transhipment sheds. The Committee considers that even the posting of a Gazetted Officer would be more than justified to hold overall charge of the large depots.

The staff posted to transhipment sheds have to work under very hard conditions. They are responsible for many claims and occupy a key position in the transit of smalls as well as of all traffic involving change of gauge. For the prevention of claims it is very necessary to make Transhipment Clerks interested in their work. For this purpose, I recommend the grant of a special allowance of Rs. 50 and Rs. 30 to each Class III and Class IV staff respectively posted at Transhipment sheds.

In addition, I consider that a system of rewards be introduced for all Transhipment sheds—and also large goods sheds and parcel sheds. Suitable norms should be laid down for the purpose and rewards may be given only to those sheds which after an annual review, are found to have passed the minimum qualifying standard.

Office clerks as well as Law Assistants of the Claims Offices should be given short duration training in Goods and Parcel work as well as the basic procedures followed in the settlement of claims, tracing of missing goods, fixing staff responsibility, etc.

Short duration refresher courses for Commercial staff should be arranged at important stations in each Division.

ANNEXURE II

Acknowledgement Card

——————————Railway

No.——————————

Chief Commercial Supdt's Office.

Dated, the-————19———

Dear Sir/ Madam,

From——————————————————To——————————————————

Inv.————————————————R/R PWB CT————————————Dated————

I beg to acknowledge receipt of your letter No.——————————of——————————. Such action as may be considere l necessary will be taken.

Yours faithfully,
for Chief Commercial Supdt.

Important Hints For The Information Of The Claimants

To facilitate disposal of your claim the following should be complied with :—

1. Furnish details showing how the amount claimed has been arrived at and submit the sender's Sale Invoice in original in support of the same and also the following :

2. Short Certificate, Assessment memo, letter from the firm who paid freight and effected delivery authorising you to receive payment.

3. As far as possible, either the original or at least a true copy to the original Railway Receipt should be submitted along with the letter of claim.

4. In the case of missing luggage a full description of the missing package (such as wooden box, steel trunk, suitcase, hat box, or bundle, with or without padlocks, gunny covering any label, address or distinguishing mark) should be furnished along with its size, shape, colour as well as details of contents of each individual package along with the respective values of each item contained therein,

ANNEXURE III

Shortage/Damage Certificate

No.——————————————Date——————— | Station Stamp |

From——————————To——————————Via——————————
Inv. No.——————————R/R——————————Date——————————
PWB

Consignment of——————————Mark——————————Wagon No.——————————
Sender——————————————————————————
Consignee——————————————————————————
Remarks on the R/R——————————————————————————
Packing condition applicable——————————————————————————
——————————————————————————————————

Actual condition of packing found at the time of survey :

Delivery Remarks

It is without prejudice I agree to the above
Consignee SM/GI/CI

(FOR OFFICIAL USE ONLY—MISSING GOODS REPORT)—B

Unloading Details :

1. Train, Wagon No., Date, Time of arrival of train.
2. Date and time of unloading.
3. Condition of seals and rivets.
4. Where unloaded at Goods Sheds or at Private Siding ?
5. Was unloading supervised by a Commercial Staff or R.P.F. ?
6. Cause of shortage/damage/pilferage.
7. Other Remarks.

Enclosures :

1. O.R.R.
2. D.D. Message
3. Seals
4. Copy of Beejuck
5. TXR Certificates

Station Master

Note :—In case where monetary value of claim is likely to exceed Rs. 1000, a special report giving detailed facts of the case, fixing staff responsibility to the extent possible and suggesting preventive measures should be prepared by the Station Master/Inspector personally and attached to this Report.

STUDY GROUP ON BANKING COSTS, 1969—REPORT

Delhi, Manager of Publications, 1972. 321p

Chairman : Shri Rameshwar Thakur.

Members : Shri N. Ramanand Rao; Shri Kantilal F. Ghiya; Shri S.R. Mohindroo; Shri R.K. Datta; Shri H.B. Dhondy; Shri L. Swaminathan.

Convener : Shri A.V. Ramanathan.

APPOINTMENT

The Study Group on Banking Costs was constituted under the Banking Commission vide their office Order No. BC/S-Costs-1/69-70 dated September 17, 1969.

TERMS OF REFERENCE

(i) To examine the manner in which cost accounting techniques can be used in the Banking industry—both commercial and cooperative—and to examine the applicability of programmes on this subject developed elsewhere;

(ii) To collect and analyse the data for cost accounting in the Indian banking industry, if necessary on a representative basis;

(iii) To develop methods for estimating the net costs of the various services rendered by banks in India;

(iv) To make recommendations on the extent to which costs in this industry are amenable to control and the manner in which they may be controlled; and

(v) To make any recommendations on any other related subject matter as the Study Group may consider germane to the subject of enquiry or any related matter which may specifically be referred to the Group by the Commission.

CONTENTS

Introduction; Brief Survey of Cost Analysis Studies in other Countries and in India; Cost Analysis—Methodology Used; Result of the Survey; Analysis of Profitability of Bank Activities and of Branch Level Profitability; Variation in Costs in Relation to Size of Physical Output; Cost Structure of the Foreign Exchange Business of Banks; Cost Structure of the Apex and Central Cooperative Banks; Profit Planning, Bank Charges and Interest Rates; Management Accounting for the Indian Banking System; Extent and the Manner of Using Cost Control Techniques in Banking; Summary of Findings and Recommendations; Annexure A to F.

RECOMMENDATIONS

Now that the major sector of the banking industry has to follow the same overall policy objectives while competing with each other in the same market for deposits and advances, the banks should adopt a practice in regard to transfer prices which is suitably designed to the needs of the times.

The Study Group recommends that in evolving a method for profitability analysis of bank branches, care should be taken to ensure that the method truly and fairly measures the profit performance of a branch against the background of the policies of the bank.

In the context of transfer price mechanism in respect of funds transferred to and from branches to Head Office, the Study Group recommends the adoption of the concept of "Central Pooling" of all funds. This system which is simpler to work with than others assumes that each branch lends the whole of its deposits and other funds to the Head Office which is regarded as constituting a Central Pool for funds of the banks and borrows the entire requirements for its advances from out of this Central Pool. To this Central Pool are added the owned funds of the banks, i.e., capital and reserves, and the funds obtained by the Head Office by borrowing. The Central Pool meets the statutory requirements, lends funds to branches for their advances, and invests the balances in the money market; treasury bills and other Government Securities.

The Study Group feels that "market rate" as the transfer price rates is not suitable for the Indian Commercial banks. It would recommend a cost-based transfer price rate which should include also an element of profit margin. The profit margin may be related to the actual profit made by the bank on its funds activity.

There should be two separate rates—one for funds lend to Central Pool and the other for funds borrowed from it.

No differentiation in rates according to the category of deposits needs be made. There should be only one single rate for all deposits. This is not however the case in respect of advances for the different activities. It is necessary that instead of adopting one common rate for all advances, a weightage system to indicate priorities should be worked out and separate rates for priority sector, other advances and deposits should be computed.

The calculation of rates to be charged for transfer price mechanism should be done at quarterly intervals. If, however, there is a major change affecting either the level of the interest rates or their pattern, it will be necessary to revise the transfer price immediately such a change occurs.

The use of transfer price mechanism on the lines discussed in this Report will assist banks in making their branches conform to their overall policies. The Group therefore recommends that the Head Office of the banks should advise their branches at the beginning of each quarter the transfer prices that would be in force for that quarter.

The Group recommends that the work done so far, which marks the beginning of a systematic attempt to evolve methods of cost and profitability analysis appropriate to the conditions under which banks have to function in India, should be developed further and studies of this type continued in a regular manner, so that the banking system works in an efficient manner in the pursuit of the overall objectives of national policy.

It is possible to gain much greater insight into the relationship between output and costs. Through Statistical analysis of the data and further research on various aspects of these relationships. The Group recommends that such research should be carried out bank-wise in order to find out the scope for increasing banks profitability by increasing the business of their branches. For this purpose, historical data are necessary giving the total outputs of the branches and their costs at various points of time. These can be combined for branches doing similar type of business and the relationships worked out.

The Group's study indicates that there is a need for banks to examine carefully their existing procedures and methods of handling foreign exchange transactions and also for developing methods of cost and profitability analysis in this field. The Group recommends further work in this matter by bankers who have the necessary expertise.

Profitability of cooperative apex and central banks can be improved by (a) bringing down excess cash reserves for which the authority should 'notify' the scheduled banks with whom balances are maintained to facilitate remittances and other operations and the cooperative banks giving attention to better management of resources and (b) by efficient management of liquid assets by diversifying activities and improving the absorbing capacity of primary societies.

The validity of policies being pursued now to strengthen the capital base of cooperative banks through members' contribution as well as Government participation has to be re-examined to ensure a reasonable return on capital.

The Group recognises that evolving an optimal price structure for the banking industry is no mean task. This has to satisfy not only the profit requirements of the industry but has also to fulfil the overall objectives of the Government in regard to deposit mobilisation, pattern of bank credit and the general development of banking facilities and banking habit. Considerable research is needed to ascertain the effects of the changes in interest rates and service charges on the demand for banks' services. The Group feels that, with the major part of the banking industry in India in the public sector, a restructuring of the prices with due attention to the cost element will help the authorities significantly in the realization of their broader objectives. The Group is of the opinion that there is scope for modifying the pricing system, so that, in fixing charges levied on the different customers, the use they make of the banking system is taken into account.

An important first step in restructuring the price for banks' services, in the Group's view, is to define the profit objective which the banks should have. In the case of nationalised banks, a reasonable return on this investment would be expected by the Government. As to what this should be is a matter for the Government to decide. The method of cost control and pricing policy in such cases should be such as to ensure this rate of return.

The Group recommends that there should be a common policy for all the public sector banks in regard to size of equity funds, which would lay down that the banks must provide to the full extent towards their fixed capital requirements and the bad and doubtful debts classified as such by an appropriate authority and also make an additional provision to be decided on by the appropriate authorities.

From the point of view of maximum deposit mobilisation, the deposit interest rate structure has to conform to the expectations of the public about the appropriate rates for deposits of different terms. One method of achieving this is to let banks complete freely for deposits, so that market forces determine the rate structure. In the absence of market determination of rates, a considerable amount of research will have to be undertaken to determine which rates need revision and in what direction. The Group recommends that this should be done.

The effects on Servicing Costs because of shifts in the distribution of deposits between current, savings and fixed consequent on changes in interest rates for deposits is also an area in which research is needed to ascertain the direction and the magnitude of such effects.

Banks could improve their profitability and also have a more equitable system of charges by adopting for deposits, the Measured Service Charge Method described in paragraph 9·6 of the Report. The Complete Analysis System, though theoretically still more equitable, would be very difficult to apply in practice except for very large accounts because of the detailed calculations it involves. The Group therefore recommends the adoption of a simple method, the main elements of which should be (i) minimum balances to be prescribed for each type of account; (ii) the extent of free facilities should be dependent on the size of the account; (iii) a charge should be made per transaction if the balance in the account is below the minimum, or the total number of transactions in a period exceeds the maximum allowed for the account; and (iv) consideration should be given to the need to encourage the banking habit particularly amongst the small account holders. The manner in which such a system can be evolved by using cost and profitability analysis on the lines of Chapters IV and V is illustrated from paragraphs 9.30 onwards.

The Group would like to emphasize that the actual details of the schedule of charges given from paragraphs 9.30 onwards are only of an illustrative nature. They could and indeed should be improved upon in the light of more comprehensive data on costs such as would be obtained when the arrangements recommended for collecting such data are brought into effect. It needs also to be pointed out that the suggestions made are on the basis of the averages for all banks. A more correct way would be to fix the charges according to the size groups of the banks.

It is very important to keep a watch on how the revision of charges actually works out in practice. If for instance, they result in over-fulfilling the profit objectives, suitable adjustments should be made to lower the schedule in the interests of the broader objective of spreading the banking habit

The Group would like to suggest that Indian commercial banks, especially after nationalisation of the larger units, should study the Management Information Systems employed by banks in the U.S.A. and the Federal Republic of Germany and initiate active attempts at formulation of comprehensive Management Information Systems for their respective banks with a view to achieving improved performance, productivity and profitability.

The Group recommends that the re-orientation of the Accounting System of banks in India should not proceed on the lines of the super-imposition of a separate departmentalised costing system on the existing reporting systems of such banks; on the other hand, the present reporting system should be gradually replaced by the blending of the cost and financial accounting into an integrated Management Information System which combines and correlates the collection, analysis reporting and interpretation.

The Group wishes to emphasize that, between the two Managerial levels of Branches and Head Office, it is essential that the flow of information and communication should be in both directions, so that there is a constant inter-change of information making for better discharge of responsibilities at each level.

To know how efficiently his branch is working, the branch manager should be able to analyse his costs and income and compare them with those of branches comparable to his in terms of overall size and character of business, location and so on. This can be done if a system of costs and income analysis, and assessment of branches profitability is developed.

Operational Efficiency, i.e., maximum income at optimum cost has to be necessarily achieved by every bank. This can be effectively done through the proper planning of the year's activities sufficiently in advance and fixing targets for performance, income and expenditure. This would require a system of Budgetary Control to be established.

The basis on which the budget should be built-up will be the annual "Business Survey Report" sent by branches to their Head Offices. This report would generally cover the business trend noticeable at the time as well as anticipated to be developed during the budget period in the area served by the branch. Branches should also be encouraged to make suggestions for the formulation of the future policy of the bank and highlight those factors which are likely to affect the expansion of their own activities.

Based on the monetary policy and the business survey report the Head Office should formulate its overall performance targets for the year, and invite each branch to fix its own share of the overall targets through a budget. The target should be so fixed as to inspire in the branch a spirit of challenge and a confidence of attainability.

Cash management in banks is akin to inventory management in industries. The Group feels that greater attention has to be paid to develop techniques of cash management, to study in particular, the consequences of a branch not having adequate cash to meet its obligations or having locked-up cash in excess of its requirements.

The main object of any reporting system under the scheme of budgetary control should be to initiate action where needed so as to obtain the desired result. It is advisable that each bank should develop a uniform system of reporting which all its branches should follow. The branches should include in their reports their own reactions to the variations from the targets and point out precisely whether any of the targets would require to be revised.

In order to emphasize the importance of working to the budget and to make all concerned cost-conscious, the Board of Directors should review each month the consolidated Budget Report in addition to noting the actual working results.

In the preparation of a budget, the previous statistical behaviour of both deposits and advances have to be taken note of, as also the fact that a higher growth rate has to be assumed as people get more bank minded. The assumption of a constant growth rate may be not only misleading but also over-rate the performance of a branch.

The Group wishes to emphasize that the budget system has to be used as a means for setting standards of performance, for measuring actual results and for guiding management to satisfactory achievement and not as a "pressure device" to good people to greater effort.

For any reduction in staff cost, or its control, a bank management has to examine how best the effort required to do a particular job can be reduced to a workable minimum. The establishment of an Organization and Methods Department will be a step in the right direction.

The requirements of cost analysis at the branch and Head Office levels can be met by: (a) requiring all branches to maintain a regular record of all physical outputs, in addition to the record of monetary outputs, and (b) organising a sample survey on a regular basis to obtain detailed estimates of unit costs and income for the different types of outputs for representative types of branches. Such estimates of unit costs and income can then be used in conjunction with the record of physical and the monetary outputs and of the earnings and expenses maintained by the branches to evaluate their efficiency and profitability in the manner described in Chapter V.

Based on the experience gained from the sample survey conducted by the Group, it is recommended that the following arrangements for continuous sample survey should be organised for the analysis of bank costs and income:

(i) The sample survey should be conducted by a Central Agency which should have the necessary expertise, facilities (like computers) and the status to secure cooperation from all banks.

(ii) This agency should prepare the "sampling frame" for all the banks which will need to be updated from time to time.

(iii) The Agency should conduct pilot studies on the sampling frame to decide which of these particulars could be used for selecting the sample units, i.e., the branches. (The sample selected should be such that it will enable bank-wise estimates to be made for a large and medium sized banks with a satisfactory degree of accuracy).

(iv) As the survey is to be a continuing one, it is necessary to change the selected branches from time to time.

(v) The Agency should advise each bank of the cost and income for representative types of branches and also the average cost and income for each of the large and medium sized banks, taking into account the datails of their branch network.

(vi) The Agency should calculate all-India averages for the various cost and income so as to help the authorities in framing their policies in regard to interest rates on deposits and advances, and the various charges levied by the banks.

Based upon the figures of costs and income as worked out by the Central Agency, each branch should compare its own actual cost with the average costs for a comparable unit and develop a cost index to measure its relative efficiency.

In comparing inter-branch or inter-bank efficiency merely the amount of profit or size of deposits will not give a true measure of profitability. This can only be ascertained through certain management/financial ratios. At the branch level, the useful ratios to be worked out should be operating ratios, efficiency ratios and profitability ratios; at the bank level, the ratios which should be worked out will be stability ratios, liquidity ratios and capital ratios.

The management/financial ratios taken collectively will be indicative of the branch efficiency and the branches should be ranked according to the efficiency thus revealed. To facilitate measurement, branches should be ranked by allocating to them marks either in descending or in the ascending order and a comparative tabulation should be made of the ranks as expressed in marks. In such valuations it may perhaps be necessary to give weightage to the relative importance of each ratio in the measurement of the overall branch efficiency. The exact basis to be followed for giving this weightage to any ratio, is a matter of policy which each bank should be free to decide, depending upon the extent to which these are directly controllable by the branch managers.

The ratio of man-hours employed to man-hours required both at the branch and bank levels would be a useful comparison. In the case of inter-branch efficiency, the comparison should be related to the banks' own target of the man-hours required whereas for inter-banks efficiency the target should be related to the overall average for the industry as compiled by the Central Agency referred to earlier.

BANKING COMMISSION STUDY GROUP REVIEW LEGISLATION AFFECTING BANKING, 1969—REPORT

First Report on Banking Legislation. Delhi, Manager of Publications, 1971. 326p

Chairman : Dr. P. V. Rajamannar.
Member : Shri C.R. Pattabhi Raman; Shri Mukund R. Mody; Shri R.M. Halasyam; Shri K.J. Natarajan; Shri R. Krishnan (Convener); Shri R.K. Gandhi.
Member-Secretary : Shri V.G. Pendharkar

APPOINTMENT

The Banking Commission was set up by the Government of India in February 1969 to review the working of the banking system as a whole and that of the non-banking financial intermediaries including indegenous bankers. The Commission has also been specifically asked to review the existing legislative enactments relating to commercial and cooperative Banking. In the broader perspective of the terms of reference of the Commission and with particular reference to the review of the enactments relating to Commercial and Co-operative Banking, the Banking Commission constituted a Study Group on October, 13th 1969.

TERMS OF REFERENCE :

The terms of the Reference of the Group are as follows :

(i) To make a study of the various enactments by the Centre and the States which have an impact on the working of the banking system;

(ii) To consider, in particular, the problems that arise in the working of the banking systems as a result of its being subject to the Companies Act, 1956 and the rules made thereunder;

(iii) To examine the special legislation relating to banks and Cooperative Credit institutions;

(iv) To examine the existing legislation in respect of non-banking financial intermediaries; and

(v) To make recommendations in respect of (i) to (iv) above taking into account the future needs of the country in the matter of a flexible and adaptable system of Banking institutions and non-banking financial intermediaries.

CONTENTS

Introductory; Banking Definition, Annexure 'A', Annexure 'B', Banks, Banking institutions and banking regulations; Banks and Secrecy; Credit information; Repayment of deposits and release of assets by Banks; other laws affecting 'Banking'; Summary of Conclusions and Recommendations; Appendix I. Terms of Reference of the Banking Compression; Appendix II. Questionnaire (Parts1-21), Appendix III. List of persons who have answered parts 1-4 of the questionnaire; Appendix IV. Replies of Mr. Carl W. Funk to parts 1-4 of the questionnaire; Appendix V. Replies of Mr. Maurice Megrah to parts 1-4 of the questionnaire. Appendix VI. Foreign Offices who gave information materials relating to the position in other countries; Tables of Cases; Index.

RECOMMENDATIONS

Summary Of Conclusions And Recommendations

While giving a summary of our conclusions and recommendations made in the earlier chapters, we do not want to restate the full context in which they are made, as that would be an unnecessary repetition of the arguments. So, we have avoided this. But we are indicating the number of the relevant paragraph of the chapter relating to the conclusion/recommendation, to facilitate the same being understood in the context in which it is made.

Banking Definition

"Banking" has to be defined in India, for the purpose of banking regulation, on the one hand having regard to what is understood as "banking" in other countries, and so far in India, and on the other hand having regard to the objectives of banking regulation. The objectives of banking regulation are:

(i) to safeguard the interests of the depositors;

(ii) to ensure that the deposits are utilised having regard to public interest; and

(iii) to ensure the effective implementation of the monetary policy and credit policy.

The definition should also have regard to the division of powers between the Union and the States under the federal set-up of our country.

The narrowing down of the scope of the definition to taking of only demand deposits would not serve to further the objectives of banking legislation. The definition of "banking" should not also be confined to cover only deposits withdrawable by cheque or other negotiable instrument.

"Banking" should be defined to include also the business of accepting deposits by a person for the purpose of investment in his own business such as manufacture or trade.

The expression "from the public" in the definition of "banking" should be clarified as covering also the acceptance of deposits by a body from its member or shareholders.

There is no reason for applying the English Common Law distinction between "loans"and "deposits" while dealing with banking regulation in India. This distinction can be avoided by a statutory definition of "deposit".

It is necessary to define "deposit" in the context of the definition of "banking", and "deposit" for this purpose should include also borrowings by way of loans, but should exclude the following :

(i) borrowings by companies or other corporate bodies by way of debentures; and

(ii) borrowin gs from banks, or other financial institutions they may be notified by the Central Government.

In the light of our earlier recommendations, "banking" definition, for the purpose of banking regulation, should cover all forms of acceptance of deposits from the public.

Banks, Banking Institutions and Banking Regulation

Banking undertakings may be classified having regard the form of banking business undertaken, the purpose for which deposits are obtained by them and their legal status.

The expression "cheque" found in Section 49A of the Banking Regulation Act, 1949, should not be understood and confined only to instruments which would satisfy the definition given for their expression in the Negotiable Instruments Act, 1881. Such an understanding would stultify the effectiveness of ths provision. Moreover, having regard to the economic significance of deposits withdrawable on demand against a negotiable instrument, there should be no differentiation in law between deposits withdrawable by "cheque" and other kinds of deposits repayable on demand against any negotiable instrument. The expressions "deposit" and "from the public" in Section 49A of the Banking Regulation Act, 1949, have to be understood in the sense in which they are understood for the purpose of "banking" definition.

The acceptance of chequeable deposits is a particularly important form of banking business and those undertaking such business have to conform, in the interest of the national economy, to certain strict standards.

It is only institutions which are authorised to carry on all forms of banking, that is, the accepting of all kinds of deposits including chequeable deposits, that should be required and permitted to use as part of their business names as the expression "bank", "banker" or "banking". Others, including other banking undertakings, should be precluded from using such expression as part of their business names.

The business of accepting chequeable deposits, that is, deposits withdrawable on demand against cheque or other kinds of negotiable instruments (e.g., deposits withdrawable against hundis), should be allowed to be carried on only by corporate bodies. Firms and individuals who are not having the business of accepting chequeable deposi ts should be required to have their undertakings incorporated within a reasonable time, or eschew the acceptance of such deposits.

The directives issued by the Reserve Bank under Chapter III-B of the Reserve Bank of India Act, 1934, aim to confine the acceptance of demand, and demand, deposits only to banks. Such restrictions may have to be there for the effective implementation of the regulation relating to the business of accepting chequeable deposits.

Institutions authorised to accept chequeable deposits could be classified into "national banks", "Co-operative banks" and "other banks". By "national banks" we refer to the State Bank, the Subsidiaries and the "new banks", that is, the banks owned by the Central Government directly or indirectly. They form a class by themselves. By "Co-operative banks" we refer to the Co-operative credit societies carrying on the business of accepting chequeable deposits. By "other banks" we refer to banks which are not either national banks or Co-operative banks.

Co-operative credit institutions carrying on banking

and subject to banking regulation are to comply with certain provisions of the Banking Regulation Act, 1949 (a Central enactment) administered by the Reserve Bank. They have also to comply with the provisions of the Co-operative Societies Act (States' enactment) administered by the Registrars of Co-operative Societies. The best way of reconciling the schemes of these two jurisdictions would be to make such co-operative societies subject to banking regulation in such matters as will not encroach on the States' jurisdiction.

The present classification of banks as scheduled banks and non-scheduled banks need not be continued.

Of the "other banks", the present non-licensed ones are those which have applied for licence on or before the 16th September 1949. The continuance of non-licensed banks for such a long time is an anomaly.

When companies accepting chequeable deposits or demand deposits which are not now subjecting themselves to banking regulation (e.g., such Nidhis as are accepting demands deposits from their members) are brought within the scope of banking regulation, they would fall within the category of "non-licensed banks", since they have to be allowed to carry on such business till they are either licensed or refused a licence.

Section 6 of the Banking Regulation Act, 1949, may be amended to authorise banks :

(i) to engage themselves in the business of equipment leasing;

(ii) and also to undertake any form of business which the Reserve Bank may notify with the prior approval of the Central Government.

Section 19 of the Banking Regulation Act, 1949, may be amended to provide that banks may form subsidiaries :

(i) for carrying on any business which they are permitted to do under Section 6 of the Banking Regulation Act, 1949; and

(ii) for carrying on any other business considered by the Central Government in consultation with the Reserve Bank, as conducive to the spread of banking or otherwise useful or necessary in public interest.

It may also be clarified in this context that in such circumstances it would be in order also for the national banks to form subsidiaries.

There is some difficulty in applying the principle underlying Section 20 of the Banking Regulation Act, 1949, with reference to persons nominated by Government or financial institutions on the boards of Government companies or statutory corporations, and for their nomination on the boards of the national banks. At present, in such cases, Government is issuing separate notifications exempting the application of Section 20 in respect of transactions relating to loans and advances that may be entered into between a national bank and a Government company or statutory corporation. It is desirable to add a proviso to Section 20 ibid giving a general exemption for such cases.

The proviso to Section 42 (1) of the Reserve Bank of India Act, 1934, enables the Reserve Bank to vary the cash reserves to be maintained by the scheduled banks within a range of 3 per cent to 15 per cent of the total of the demand and time liabilities. Provision somewhat on similar lines is necessary for the maintenance of liquid assets under Section 24 of the Banking Regulation Act, 1949.

Concerns accepting non-chequeable deposits could be classified into those accepting deposit liabilities (i) for the purpose of lending or investment, and (ii) for the purpose of financing their own business such as manufacture or trade. For the purpose of banking regulation, the former could be termed "financial institutions" and the later as "deposit-receiving institution". Though financial institutions, which are "companies", are even now "banking companies", banking regulation has not been effectively applied to them. Consistent with our recommendations on the definition of "banking", financial institutions and deposit-receiving institutions accepting non-chequeable deposits from the public should be regulated as a class of banking concerns.

Private limited companies accepting non-chequeable deposits from their shareholders, companies taking such deposits from their directors, and firms accepting such deposits from their partners need not be brought within the scheme of banking regulation. This exclusion is justified having regard to the limitations as to the number of persons from whom such deposits could be taken and the presumption that people so depositing would be familiar with the financial position and standing of the concerns accepting such deposits.

It may be that financial institutions which accept deposits from the public for the purpose of their lending or investment activities could be further classified having regard to the nature of their lending or investment activities. While regulating them as institutions carrying on banking business, further classification may be made, if necessary, on appropriate lines. There is also the question of applying the scheme of regulation as set out in the Banking Regulation Act, 1949, to "companies" and others accepting non-chequeable deposits for the purpose of lending or investment. We could go into these matters only after considering the Report of the Banking Commission's Study Group on "Non-Banking Financial Intermediaries".

The distinction between a person doing banking and a person doing moneylending really rests on the presence or absence, as part of such person's business, of the acceptance of deposits from the public. While a person doing "banking" relies on the deposits accepted by him from the public, wholly or partially, for carrying on his lending activity, the person doing "money-lending" does not seek or accept deposits from the public for his lending.

The expression "indigenous bankers" would comprise different classes of persons. Of them, only those who accept deposits from a public may be regarded as doing banking and the others only moneylenders.

Under our Constitution, it is only the Union that could legislate for the regulation of firms and individuals carrying on the business of banking. While as regards moneylending, the States have enacted moneylending legislation, as regards firms and individuals doing "banking", there is at present no regulation. It is necessary for the Union to frame, with reference to them, a scheme of regulation by legislation.

For the effective enforcement of banking regulation, it is desirable that concerns accepting non-chequeable deposits from the public for the purpose of lending or investment have their undertakings incorporated. But, we do not consider it necessary that firms and individuals carrying on such business should be compelled immediately to incorporate their undertakings. However, in any scheme of regulation, it would be appropriate to differentiate between corporate bodies carrying on such business, and firms and individuals doing it. In prescribing the conditions to be complied with by concerns or inducement, incorporation can be made one of the conditions. Subject to this, all the provisions that apply to corporate undertakings carrying on this form of banking should also apply to firms and individuals doing this business, with such necessary modifications as may be necessary, or considered desirable, having regard to the difference in their legal status.

The provisions of the Pennsylvania Banking Code (1965) can be considered while framing a scheme of regulation for firms and individuals carrying on the business of accepting non-chequeable deposits for lending or investment.

The directives issued by the Reserve Bank under Chapter III-B of the Reserve Bank of India Act, 1934, regular the deposit-taking business of concerns accepting non-chequeable deposits for financing their own business such as manufacture or trade "(deposit-receiving institutions)". They may be regulated as banking concerns. But with reference to them, the objectives of the regulation would be met if the regulation deals with the terms (including the terms relating to period of repayment, payment of interest, etc.) subject to which the deposits could be accepted, and contains necessary provisions to ensure that the borrowing concerns have adequate repaying capacity. Having regard to public interest, the provisions may enable the authorities to restrict, regulate or prohibit the acceptance of deposits. The regulating authorities should also be given the necessary powers to enforce the observance of the requirements of the regulation by the "deposit-receiving institutions". But, the licensing of such institutions should not be necessary for the purpose of banking regulation.

It is desirable to have separate licensing/regulating authorities entrusted with statutory powers to administer the provisions of the banking regulation applicable to concerns accepting non-chequeable deposits from the public. Such authorities may be set up at the State level with an apex body at the all-India level. While the authorities at the State level should be invested with statutory powers to deal with concerns accepting non-chequeable deposits (for the purpose of lending or investment or merely for the purpose of investment in their own business such as manufacture or trade), the apex body should act as a supervisory authority over the State level authorities. The apex body should mainly concern itself with questions of policy and should be the authority to take decisions on matters of all-India importance. The State level authorities should deal with the administration of the regulatory/licensing provisions of the banking regulation applicable to concerns accepting non-chequeable deposits from the public. This arrangement would be conducive to the effective implementation of banking regulation with reference to such forms of banking. The Registrars of Companies at the State level and the Company Law Board at the Centre may serve as an analogy. The Reserve Bank has to be actively associated in the functioning, and it may also have to take the initiative for setting up such machinery to deal with all types of banking concerns other than banks. It would also be necessary to ensure co-ordination between the Reserve Bank and such a body to ensure effective implementation of the scheme of banking regulation.

There is need for bringing the different pieces of legislation governing the carrying on of the business of banking in one form or another, under one comprehensive scheme. It would be conducive to the objectives of banking regulation if all the categories of persons accepting deposits from the public are dealt within a comprehensive scheme of banking regulation. This would ensure that there is a proper perspective over the control that is exercised in regard to the different categories of banking institutions, having regard to certain common objectives, such as the protection of the interests of the depositors, the safeguarding of public interest and the effective implementation of monetary policy and credit policy.

In the light of the above, a banking code may be enacted which would classify and regulate all forms of banking. The classification could be as shown in the chart (given at page 86 of this report). The banking code would contain the scheme of the Banking Regulation Act, 1949 (with suitable modifications) in its application to institutions taking chequeable deposits. The present enactments governing the national banks could be repealed and the provisions that are considered appropriate for them could be introduced as a separate Part in the banking code. Chapter III-B of the Reserve Bank of India Act, 1934, may be repealed; instead, the provisions that should govern the concerns accepting non-chequeable deposits for lending or investment and those accepting non-chequeable deposits for their business such as manufacture or trade may be included as separate parts of the banking code. A scheme of regulation which is considered appropriate for private bankers (non-corporate private bankers) may form another part of the code. Our recommendations for a comprehensive banking code should not be the cause for any delay in promoting any scheme of regulation governing any category of banks or banking institutions. If necessary, legislation can deal separately with the different categories of banking institutions. But eventually there should be one comprehensive banking code relating to all forms of banking business.

National Banks

The State Bank, its seven subsidiaries and the 14 "new banks" are practically owned by the Central Government. They could be appropriately described as "national banks". The national banks form a class by themselves.

The provisions governing the State Bank, the subsidiaries and the "new banks" are not uniform. There is no justification for continuing the differences in the schemes governing all the national banks, as they are attributable mostly to historical reasons. If the national banks are to have a common programme of functions and responsibilities in the development of the banking/credit system of the country, it is necessary that they are governed by a uniform scheme. In evolving such a uniform scheme, such features as have more a historical, rather than any present day value, may be discarded. Though there are similar provisions with reference to many matters, the constitution, functions, powers and duties of the national banks are not, in essential features, uniform; the relevant provisions of the State Bank are not on the same lines as those applicable to the subsidiaries, and the pattern of both differs from that of the "new banks". The schemes governing all the national banks should be uniform. Similarities in the nature of legal provisions governing the national banks are to be expected; but the provisions which differentiate between them inter se need to be explained.

It is not appropriate to have rigid provisions as to ceiling as regards the capital requirements. The statute may provide for the capital of the national banks being raised or revised by them in consultation with the Reserve Bank and with the approval of the Central Government.

The future ownership pattern of the national banks should be uniform with reference to all of them.

On principle, it is not appropriate that the Reserve Bank, which is a body entrusted with supervisory jurisdiction, inter alia, over the national banks, should also hold the whole or a substantial portion of their capital.

So long as the State Bank is made responsible for the running of the subsidiaries, its links with the subsidiaries may have to continue. 0owever, if, in any future restructuring of the national banks, their number is to be reduced, the subsidiaries could be merged with the State Bank.

In public interest, shareholdings of the outside shareholders in the paid-up capital of the State Bank and its subsidiaries (only four of the subsidiaries have such-shareholdings) may be acquired by the Central Government by legislation.

As the intention is that the "new banks" should also transfer a portion of their net profits to their general reserves, and thus build up adequate reserves, it may be specifically provided that the transfer of the surplus to the Central Government would be only the balance of net profits remaining after transfer to the general reserve fund.

Consequent on the implementation of our recommendation for the acquisition of the individual shareholdings in the State Bank and four of its subsidiaries, there may be no need to continue the Integration and Development Fund.

In the discharge of their functions, the Boards of the State Bank and the subsidiaries are required to act "on business principles, regard being had to public interest". There is no such provision applicable with reference to the "new banks". Similar guidelines should be laid down also for the "new banks".

Uniformity in pattern is necessary as regards the provisions dealing with the porsons who should head the Boards of Directors of the national banks vis-a-vis the persons entrusted with powers to act as their Chief Executives.

The same persons should not occupy the office of the Chairman of the Board of a national bank and also be its Chief Executive to facilitate the objective appraisal by the Board of the performance of the administration headed by the Chief Executive. It would also enable the Chairman to bestow his attention mainly to questions of policy, and not details of administration.

There is no provision for a Vice-Chairman in the

case of the subsidiaries and the "new banks". The necessity for the same may be considered.

Appropriate provisions may be made in the enactments applicable to the national banks to enable the appointment of, and payment of remuneration to, the Chairman/Vice-Chairman on a whole-time or part-time basis.

The principle of giving representation to persons of particular occupations on the Boards of the national banks has gained Parliamentary recognition in the Act of the "new banks". This principle should also be recognised while determining the composition of the Boards of the State Bank and the subsidiaries.

aving regard to the cost, time and trouble involved in the following an elective process for selecting representatives of the specified classes of persons like depositors, farmers, workers and artisans, the reference in the Act of the "new banks" to the election of such representatives may be deleted. owever, in the case of selecting the representatives of employees, the provision which enables as elective process to be followed may remain.

Section 10A of the Banking Regulation Act, 1949, provides for the majority of the Board of Directors consisting of persons who have special knowledge or practical experience in respect of matters specified therein. The principle underlying Section 10A ibid has validity with reference to all banks. Provisions on similar lines may be made with reference to the national banks as well.

It is not desirable to provide for the Reserve Bank having its representatives on the Boards of the national banks. If, however, it is considered necessary that the Reserve Bank should be closely in touch with the developments in the national banks and the decisions of their Boards, it would be sufficient to provide for the Reserve Bank appointing observers on the Boards of these banks.

It should be in order for the Central Government to nominate, as its representatives on the Boards of the national banks, either officials or non officials.

The provisions applicable with reference to the State Bank and the subsidiaries preclude a Member of Parliament or a Member of State Legislature from continuing also as a director of any of these banks. However, no such prohibition applies with reference to the "new banks". Either the prohibition found in the enactments governing the State Bank and the Subidiaries should be applied also with reference to the "new banks" or such prohibition should be removed.

The General Manager of a subsidiary may be made a member of its Board and designated as its Managing Director.

While there are adequate provisions in the Acts of the State Bank and the subsidiaries, dealing with the set-up, functions and powers of the Committee of the Central Board, the provisions regarding such Committees for the "new banks" are not adequate. Adequate provisions may be made in the statute with reference to the "new banks" also.

Provision may be made in their statute itself, instead of leaving the matter to subsidiary legislation, for the up of an Executive Committee for the "new banks" and the entrustment of powers of its.

Following the pattern of the State Bank and the subsidiaries, it may be provided that any director (including the whole-time director) of a national bank, though he is not named as a member of the Managing Committee, may participate in the meetings of the Executive Committee as a member provided he is able to attend its meetings.

Provision for the setting up of other Committees and the power to associate outsiders, with such Committees may be made in the enactments of the national banks.

The Chief Executives of all the national banks may be vested with the same, or similar, powers. The Chief Executive should be the administrative head of the bank and should be entrusted with all necessary powers.

Provision may be made in the statutes governing the national banks for the appointment of their Chief Executives and for the remuneration payable to them, and such provision may be on uniform lines with reference to all the national banks.

Having regard to the size, extent and area of operation and such other relevant factors, the desirability of providing for deputy chief executives (e.g., Managing Directors in the State Bank) for all the national banks may be considered.

There are no provisions in respect of the "new banks" for the setting up of regional Boards with statutory powers and responsibilities to carry on their business independently, as in the case of the State Bank. Provision may be made to enable the constitution, in the "new banks", of such regional Boards with statutory powers and responsibilities to carry on their business independently, wherever necessary.

In the matter of the composition of the Local Boards for the national banks, it is necessary to include also at the local level, representatives of the specified classes of the persons and persons with special knowledge or experience, having regard to the purpose for which such persons are included in the Boards of the "new banks". Provision may be made to provide also for such representation in the composition of the Local Boards.

In the case of the "new banks" also, provision may be made for constituting Committees of Local Boards, having regard to relevant factors, such as their size, area of operation, etc.

The State Bank Act empowers its Central Board to constitute Local Committees for any area to exercise such powers and perform such functions as the Central Board may confer on, or assign to, such Committees. Such enabling provision may be made with reference to the other national banks as well.

Appropriate statutory provisions may be made for the "new banks" also having regional chief executives on the pattern of the provisions applicable to the Secretary and Treasurer of the State Bank.

The Act of the "new banks" does not, but it is only their scheme that does, provide for the constitution of the Regional Consultative Committees. Since the Committee's function is to review the banking development in the region and make appropriate recommendations, the Committees have to take note of the developments not only of the "new banks" but also of other banks and the interests of the public. Hence, the provisions relating to the set-up and functions of the Regional Consultative Committees may be embodied in a separate Chapter of the Banking Code.

The State Bank and the subsidiaries may also be given representation on the Regional Consultative Committees. Similar representation may also be given to the non-national banks including the Co-operative banks.

The fetters in the State Bank Act, on the bank entering into all types of banking and allied transactions should be removed thereby giving that bank the same powers for the carrying on of business as are at present available to the "new banks" and subsidiaries.

In relation to the transaction of Central Government business, all the national banks should be treated on par. Section 45 of the Reserve Bank of India Act, 1934, may be suitably amended for this purpose.

The mechanism of the Currency Chests, it is reported, enables the State Bank to operate with slender cash balances. The "new banks" may also be given similar privileges.

It may be provided statutorily that any of the national banks may be entrusted with State Government business.

Government may modify suitably its administrative instructions issued earlier to enable all the national banks being entrusted with the banking business of Local Bodies and statutory corporations.

The statutory and other applicable provision in, or under, other Central or State enactments should be suitably modified so as to provide for the business of Trusts and other statutory bodies being given to any national banks.

The references in Sections 18 and 24 of the Banking Regulation Act, 1949, and Section 42 of the Reserve Bank of India Act, 1934, to the State Bank may be substituted by a reference to the "national banks."

The annual accounts of all the national banks may be placed before the Parliament for consideration. There should also be uniformity as regards the persons who should sign the accounts and the time for the completion and submission of accounts of all the national banks.

A specific statutory provision may be made that by reason of the statutory form of declaration of secrecy provided for the officials of the national banks, the banks are not disabled from disclosing information relating to their affairs as distinct from those of their individual customers.

There are some minor differences in the provisions applicable to the national banks in relation to the appointment of their auditors, the carrying out of special audit, the remuneration of auditors, the form of the auditors' certificate, and submission and verification of the auditors' report. The provisions relating to audit should be uniform for all the national banks.

The auditors of the national banks have felt certain difficulties in following the formula prescribed under the Companies Act for the audit of the branches of national banks. It is desirable to provide specifically for the branch audit of the national banks on the pattern of the provisions applicable to companies.

While in the case of the "new banks" the Central Government may directly give them directions on matter of policy involving public interest, with reference to the State Bank and the subsidiaries, the Central Government is required to act through the Reserve Bank. There should be a uniform rule with reference to all the national banks.

While with reference to the "new banks" the Central Government has powers, by framing a scheme, to alter suitably their capital structure, the constitution of their Boards and to reconstitute, amalgamate or transfer their undertakings (wholly or in part), it has no such power under the enactments governing the State Bank and the subsidiaries. Since it would facilitate the restructuring of all the national banks, if the Central Government has similar powers with reference to all the national banks, including the State Bank and the subsidiaries, their statute may provide for this.

While the Central Government has powers to make Rules to give effect to the provisions of the State Bank and the Subsidiaries Acts, it has no such powers with reference to the "new banks" Act. It is desirable that such power is vested in the Government.

Section 35 of the State Bank Act and Section 38 of the Subsidiaries Act enable these banks to acquire other banking undertakings pursuant to a Scheme framed by the Central Government. These provisions also exhaustively set out matters that could be dealt with under such schemes. Provision on similar lines may be made for the "new banks" as well.

Provisions that should apply to the new corporations that may come into existence by reason of the break-up or amalgamation of any of the "new banks" may be laid down in the statute itself.

The pattern of the provisions found with reference to the schemes that could be framed under the Banking Regulation Act, the State Bank Act and the Subsidiaries Act may be adopted with reference to the provisions to govern the schemes that could be framed under the "new banks" Act.

There are specific provisions in the enactments governing the State Bank and the subsidiaries, providing that in the event of the transfer of the services of the, staff, pursuant to any scheme, the employees will have no claim for compensation (like that payable under the Industrial Disputes Act 1947). There is no such provision applicable with reference to the schemes framed under the "new banks" Act. Statutory provision may be made to this effect.

The State Bank and the Subsidiaries Acts, as also the Banking Regulation Act, 1949, containing enabling provisions specifying in detail the matters that can be provided for in the schemes framed thereunder. Such enabling provisions help to decide whether or not the scheme could deal with a particular matter. They reduce the scope for disputes regarding the validity of such scheme provisions. The act of the "new banks" does not specify expressly matters that could be provided for in the scheme. Similar provisions could be made in respect of the schemes under the "new banks" Act.

The differences in the provisions relating to the set-up, powers and functions of the different classes of national banks have to be reconciled and a uniform pattern evolved. This could be achieved by the separate Acts now governing these banks being repealed and all these banks brought within one statutory framework. This could find place as a part of the comprehensive Banking Code which we envisage.

Banks and Secrecy

The obligation of banks to maintain in confidence the affairs of their customers should continue in order to encourage the spread of the use of the bank facilities and instill in the public mind confidence in banks. But this obligation should be subject to recognised exceptions and qualifications.

The obligation of a bank to observe secrecy regarding the affairs of its customers should not affect in any manner the banks furnishing information of a general nature relating to the affairs of their customers without revealing the identity of the individual constituents. This position may be statutorily so clarified.

A statutory provision may be made in the Bankers' Books Evidence Act to the effect that during police investigations it should be sufficient for banks to produce before the police authorities certified copies of the relevant extracts from the books of banks, unless the production of the copies is considered by the authorities as not adequate for proving the crime.

When the books or other records are destroyed by banks, in the regular course of business, and the documents have been microfilmed before such destruction, the relative positives of the films are admissible as evidences provided they are properly produced and proved in court. A statutory amendment to the Bankers' Books Evidence Act may expressly clarify the position.

The position regarding the preservation of records by banks required to be clarified having regard to public interest and the development of banking. Section 209 of the Companies Act, 1956, is inadequate for this purpose, as this provision does not as such apply to the national banks and to the Co-operative banks. A statutory provision may be made for this purpose. The minimum period for which the banks should preserve their several records should be fixed, for each type of record, having regard to—

(i) the period for which it would be desirable for banks to maintain them for their own needs;

(ii) the period up to which such records could be usefully required in connection with tax or other regulatory proceedings; and

(iii) the practical difficulties the banks may face in preserving their records beyond a reasonable length of time.

Provision for such preservation of records should also apply to all State Co-operative Banks, Central Co-operative banks and Urban Co-operative banks. However, it may be neither desirable nor feasible to apply such requirements to Primary Co-operative credit societies carrying on banking business, in view of their limited administrative and other resources. The statutory provision that should be made for the preservation of various bank records being prescribed from time to time by the Central Government in consultation with the Reserve Bank.

Having regard to all the circumstances, a statutory provision may be made fixing the period of preservation by banks of paid instruments. When for valid reasons, customers require the return of the paid instruments before the period specified for their preservation, the relevant instruments may be returned only after being microfilmed. The cost of microfilming shall be borne by the customer. This provision may be applied also to the return of paid instruments drawn by Governments and statutory corporations.

Just as for the purpose of collection of Central taxes (including income-tax) the information available with banks is made use of by the tax authorities, so also it would be in order for the State laws to provide for the relevant and material information with banks being disclosed to authorities to check evasion of State taxes, like Sales Tax. While making such provisions, State Governments may act after consultation with the Reserve Bank.

There is need for clarifying one of the qualifications for the Bank's obligation to observe secrecy regarding the affairs of its customers, i.e., "duty to the public to disclose", by enumerating certain instances attracting such qualification.

In the following instances it should be statutorily laid down that the bank is under a duty to disclose the relevant information in public interest :

(a) When a bank is asked for information by a Government official concerning the commission of a crime and the bank has reasonable cause to believe that a crime has been committed and that the information in the bank's possession may lead to the apprehension of the culprit;

(b) When the bank considers that the customer is involved in activities prejudicial to the interests of the country;

(c) Where the bank's books reveal that the customer is contravening the provisions of any law; and

(d) Where sizeable funds are received from foreign countries by constituents.

It may also be statutorily clarified that if and when a bank bona fide forms an impression that it owes a duty to the public to disclose, it is relieved of its obligation to maintain secrecy if it discloses the relevant information to the concerned authorities.

If public interest, a statutory provision may be made permitting the disclosure of information by banks, for research purposes, regarding the affairs of their constituents, provided the information furnished relates to a period interior to twenty years.

A statutory provision may be made to the effect that with reference to any Commission or Committee appointed by Government, though not under the Commissions of Enquiry Act, the Government is empowered to declare that banks are obliged to disclose to such Commission or Committee, in public interest, such information as may be required from them by such Commission or Committee.

There is not much justification for the national banks being allowed to maintain undisclosed reserves or "secret reserves". It is also not desirable to differentiate in this regard between the national banks and the other banks. The present forms of balance sheet and profit and loss account of banks, specified in the Banking Regulation Act, 1949, may have to be amended suitably when the provision requiring 'full disclosure' becomes effective.

The undisclosed reserves, or "secret reserves", of banks, existing as on the date on which the requirements as to full disclosure becomes effective, should be statutorily required to be transferred to their general reserves (which are now disclosed). There should also be a provision (taking effect thereafter) for banks transferring to their general reserves a larger percentage of their net profits. The exact percentage may be left to be laid down by the Central Government in consultation with the Reserve Bank.

Credit Information

It is necessary that there should be adequate provisions for banks and financial institutions giving and receiving of credit information; and for the fairly accurate credit rating of persons seeking financial assistance from such institutions.

Statutory provision may be made giving protection for banks and financial institutions freely exchanging credit information on the affairs of their customers. The law should also provide that the concern or the bank receiving such information shall keep it in confidence and shall not disclose it except to those to whom such information could be legally given.

The statute governing the national banks should also, expressly provide for full, free and frank communication of credit information among national banks inter se.

Specialised agency, or agencies, for collecting, collating, processing and furnishing credit information to banks and financial institutions may have to be set up in India, by legislation.

The credit Information Bureau set up in the Reserve Bank is not adequate to meet the needs of banks and financial institutions.

It may not be desirable for the central bank of the country to undertake the responsibility of collecting and furnishing on a large scale, to banks and financing institutions, credit information useful and necessary to assess the creditworthiness of numerous persons, big and small. It is necessary to provide by legislation for the setting up of separate specialised agencies, on the lines of the institutions in U.K. and U.S.A. for this purpose.

A statutory provision making it obligatory for banks and financial institutions to furnish the credit information bureaux with such information and in such form, as the bureaux may require, would safeguard the banks from any action by their constituents.

While providing for credit reporting agencies collecting and furnishing credit information to banks and financial institutions, there should be provision for such agencies adopting reasonable procedures in a manner which is fair and equitable. There should also be opportunity given to the reported person to ask for correction of any error in the report on him.

A statutory provision may be made for the credit reporting agencies being indemnified from any action for damages or other losses which may be suffered by any person consequent on the credit information being given on, or for the use of, such person, so long as such agencies exercise their powers and perform their function bona fide. Such protection should also be available to banks when they furnish credit information on their constituents.

Simultaneously with the taking up of measures to set up specialised agencies for furnishing adequate and reliable credit information to banks and other financial institutions, legislative measures may also be taken for providing that the financial statements furnished to such institutions by their borrowers (including prospective borrowers) shall be true and correct, and that any wilful breach of this obligation is punishable.

Repayment Of Balances And Release Of Assets By Banks

On the lines of the provisions found in the banking codes of the States of the United States of America e.g. Pennsylvania Banking Code (1965) and the District of Columbia Code, for the repayment by banks of deposits held in accounts opened in the names of more than one individual, express statutory provisions may be made.

Statutory provisions may be made on the lines of the provisions found in the banking codes of the States of the United States of America, to facilitate banks dealing with adverse or conflicting claims to deposits held in bank accounts.

Statutory provision may be made for giving nomination facility in relation to deposits by individuals with banks.

The effect of a nomination in relation to bank deposits should be statutorily provided for on the lines of the provisions contained in the public Debt Act, 1944, and banks should be required to make payment to the nominee(s) unless restrained by an order of a competent court.

A statutory provision may be made for an individual borrower availing of credit facilities from a bank nominating a person(s) who could be allowed in the event of the death of the borrower, to repay the debt and obtain redemption of the assets charged to the bank by the borrower. While such redemption should give a good discharge to the bank, it should not affect the rights and claims of other parties to the assets of the deceased. It may also be provided that the nominee obtaining release of the charged assets will have a prior claim for getting himself reimbursed of the amounts expended by him to obtain the release of the charged assets. Such a nomination should not also affect any other rights the bank may have for realising any of its other dues recoverable from the estate of the deceased.

In relation to immovable properties mortgaged to banks, it may be provided that on the death of the mortgagor, a nominee indicated by him would have the right to redeem the mortgage by repaying the amount due to the bank in respect of such mortgage. Such a provision could also be made by way of an amendment to the Transfer of Property Act. It may also be provided that the nominee so redeeming the property will be subrogated to the rights of the bank vis-a-vis other persons who may have claims on the property. Such a nomination should not, however, affect the rights inter se of individual parties claiming under the mortgagor. Statutory provisions may be made accordingly.

Statutory provision may be made for enabling banks to return the articles kept in safe custody with them to the nominees of the depositors. The form for acceptance of valuable and securities for safe custody may provide for a depositor nominating a person to whom the valuable and securities may be handed over in the event of the death of the depositor. The effect of the provision should be to relieve the bank from any obligation in relation to such asset, but should not affect the rights inter se of the nominee and others claiming under the deceased depositor.

Statutory provision may be made for those renting safety lockers from banks indicating the persons to whom access may be allowed to the lockers on their death, or on the death of any one jointly renting the lockers, and when any such access is allowed on the death of the person(s), a responsible bank official or a representative of the taxing authority should be present and an inventory should be taken of the contents of the locker(s) in his/their presence.

It is necessary in public interest that there should be some similarity in the treatment meted out to all cash lenders.

There is the need for co-ordination of the regulation relating to lending by moneylenders on the one hand and the banks and financial institutions on the other. For this purpose, there should be a review of the moneylending legislation of the States.

A model legislation may be framed for the consideration of the States regarding the regulation of the business of lending against hundis which would only be a form of money-lending.

With the increasing reliance on the banking system for the development of the country, it is essential to ensure that the laws, both relating to and affecting banking, of the Union and of the States are rational, devoid of complications and complexities and are conducive to the spread and effective functioning of the banking system. This could be achieved only by a constant review of such laws. The approach should be not merely to review the laws from the perspective of banks, but essentially having regard to public interest. There is an imperative need for such constant review when we compare the pace at which the laws relating to and affecting banking have been reviewed and suitable remedial measures taken elsewhere and in India.

For the purpose of such review, there should be a special body constituted by the Central Government. This should be presided over by a jurist. Its members should be drawn from the legal profession, from legal experts who have worked with or working with banks, and from experienced bankers and others possessing expert knowledge or experienced considered necessary or useful for such review. The Reserve Bank may be asked to meet the expenses of, and give such assistance as may be required by, the reviewing body.

STUDY GROUP ON INDIGENOVS BANKERS, 1969–REPORT

Delhi, Manager of Publications, 1972. 139p+vip

Chairman : Shri H.T. Parekh.

Members : Shri V.C. Patel; Shri G. Lakshminarayanan; Shri H.L. Narang; Shri Premanand Ochiram; Shri Mohanlal A. Parikh.

Convener : Kum. (Dr.) C.J. Batliwala.

APPOINTMENT

The Study Group on Indigenons Bankers was constituted under the Banking Commission vide their Office Order No. BC.S/IB-1/69 dated November 24th, 1969.

TERMS OF REFERENCE

(i) To review the working of the various classes of indigenous banking agencies such as multanis and shroffs, evaluate their utility in the money market complex;

(ii) To examine whether indigenous bankers can in course of time usefully extend their activities to provide specialised services in the money and capital markets other than what they are providing at present;

(iii) To consider what steps are necessary to develop the link between indigenous bankers and the organised financial system; and

(iv) To make any recommendations on any other related subject matter as the Study Group may consider germane to the subject of enquiry or any related matter which may specifically be referred to the Group by the Commission.

CONTENTS

Introductory; Evolution and Growth of Indigenous Banking; Structure; Functions and Methods of Operation of Indigenous Banking Agencies; Instruments of Credit of Indigenous Financial Agencies; Financial Operations of Multani Bankers; Relation of Indigenous Banking Agencies with the Commercial Banks and the Link with the Organized Money Market; An Approach to Regulation and Control; Future of Indigenous Banking System—Suggestions and Recommendations; Statements I to VII; Annexures I to VI; Exhibits 1 to 15.

SUGGESTIONS AND RECOMMENDATIONS

The broad conclusion of the Study Group's enquiry is that the system of indigenous banking is an institution worthy of notice, its roots firmly established in the soil, its evolution and growth a striking measure of its popularity and superiority over other financial institutions, at least in regard to some specific financial needs. Oral evidence given by a cross-section of the borrowers supports the belief that indigenous bankers have fulfilled their limited role rather well.

The hundi is the oldest surviving credit instrument, the merits of which cannot be denied. For instance, the case with which a darshani hundi can be endorsed and the widespread use of this instrument for transfer of funds suggests that this indigenous instrument has a close kinship with the more sophisticated demand draft. Likewise, the usance hundi has essentially the characteristics of a usance bill of exchange; it is a short-term paper, highly liquid in character. The evolution and growth of hundis has been prompted by convention, custom and usage of the mercantile community in different parts of the country and is not an instrument born out of law. It has thus proved to be a convenient instrument for financing trade and investment.

In many ways the indigenous bankers constitute an indispensable link between the organised banking system and the class of small borrowers who may not be in a position to obtain funds at the right time and in the right quantum from the organised banking system. True, the organised and the unorganised markets are largely separate, but the indigenous bankers who are the organised groups in the unorganised sector, provide a vital link. For instance, the discounting shroffs (the multanis) act as the intermediary between the commercial banks and the small borrowers about whose creditworthiness the bank would not usually have adequate information. To some extent, a link is also provided by the Gujarati Shroffs who maintain accounts with the commercial banks and the Marwari kayas and chettiars who also enjoy discounting facilities with commercial banks.

At one time these arrangements could have been made the basis for the growth of an integrated money market through a direct link with the Reserve Bank. Hundis supported by the endorsement of a commercial bank could theoretically speaking be accepted by the Reserve Bank for rediscounting as eligible paper. In the view of the Study Group, the hundi could have provided an appropriate basis for the development of a truly integrated bill market adapted to the needs of the local environment. The hardening of attitudes on both sides, however, rendered any direct link or integration with the organised sector difficult. The indigenous bankers were reluctant to segregate their banking and non-banking activities. Another major difficulty was that the authorities were sceptical of regarding the hundi as emanating from a particular trade transaction and therefore as a genuine trade bill. In their opinion the advances were more often in the nature of accommodation paper and in the absence of documentary evidence to back the paper, it was difficult to say that the credit was in all cases used to support a genuine productive activity.

In any event, with the nationalisation of major commercial banks and the emphasis of policy on the expansion of branches and direct financing of priority sectors like small-scale industry and agriculture, the urgency for link between the two sectors appears to have receded into the background. The orientation of the commercial bank lending policy to cover a wider area of the previously unsatisfied or partially satisfied borrowers and meeting their needs at a lower cost, no doubt poses a potential threat to the traditional business of indigenous bankers. Although the Central Banking Enquiry Committee recommended that the indigenous bankers be linked directly with the Reserve Bank of India and although the indigenous bankers were keen on such a link in the first half of this century, the Study Group is of the opinion that it is not now necessary or feasible to establish such a direct link.

In some quarters the extreme view is held that indigenous bankers make no contribution to development and should be eliminated. The Study Group does not subscribe to this view; in their opinion the indigenous bankers continue to play an important role in the Indian financial system, in that they look after the credit needs of numerous small industrialists and retail traders. Their services will, therefore, be needed for a long time to come, more so in view of the rapid growth in the economy. With the growing credit requirements of the small-scale industries and retail trade sectors and various constraints on bank resources, it is necessary that some other financial intermediary should be there to fill in the credit gaps.

The system no doubt suffers from a number of shortcomings but these are not incapable of correction. Nothing should therefore be done to make indigenous bankers lose their individuality add identity or to deprive them of their special characteristics. Because they remain outside the rigid cast-iron framework of rules and regulations they are able to operate with a certain degree of flexibility which is what attracts the small borrower. This is not to suggest that regulation and control of their activities is inherently undesirable and they should be allowed to operate in an unrestrained manner. The proper course would be for the Reserve Bank to exercise indirect influence over the business of indigenous bankers through the medium of commercial banks. There are various ways in which this may be accomplished and these are outlined in the recommendations.

What is needed is that the methods of operation of indigenous bankers should be systematised and some element of discipline and regulation introduced into their operations. At the same time their operations should not be unduly hampered by excessive legislation and straitlacing. It would merely drive the indigenous bankers out of business and create a void.

Bearing this in mind, the Study Group has sought in its recommendations to suggest ways and means to enhance the effective role of the indigenous banker rather than suggest ways which would ultimately result in the disintegration of these financial intermediaries. What is needed is a positive approach to increase the volume of finance from this source and create conditions in which they can evolve to meet the future needs of the economy.

The Group believes, however, that a number of steps must be taken to ensure the development of indigenous banking along sound lines. Our recommendations do not involve new departures as much as the adoption of measures which are calculated to improve the working of the system.

Earlier discussions in the Report have brought to light the areas where latent weaknesses exist, e.g,, improper accounting, inadequacy of supervisory and inspection arrangements, legal loopholes, the problem of inadequacy and continuity of discounting facilities and high interest and other charges. In each case our aim is to strengthen the indigenous banking agencies so that their financial condition and accountability may fully justify the confidence reposed in them by the community.

The growth of indigenous banking agencies has stagnated in the recent past but the Group expects that with some measure of self-regulation and discipline, it could be revived and agencies with sound management traditions could become useful adjuncts of the organised banking system. However, the hundi business must work under arrangements which enable it to respond effectively and quickly to the needs of the borrowers depending upon this market. Raising the value and status of the hundi, bringing new borrowers into the hundi market, introducing new financing techniques and accepting new types of business should help to achieve this objective and further enhance the usefulness and responsiveness of the hundi business.

The focus of the recommendations is how best to institutionalise the lending and financial operations of indigenous bankers, thereby extending the area of operations of the banking system and harnessing some extra resources for meeting the credit needs of smaller people in industry and trade alike. With this as the ultimate objective, the recommendations aim at introducing a certain measure of financial and social discipline into their activities. It may be pointed out that it is not the idea of the Study Group to discriminate in favour of multanis or against the other agencies. The facilities suggested by the Group would be available to all indigenous bankers whose business is banking and who are prepared to accept the discipline demanded of them and observe the code of conduct required of them in today's social context.

With this as the emerging picture of the financial system, the following are the suggestions and recommendations of the Group with regard to these financial intermediaries.

Definition Of Indigenous Bankers

Constructive recommendations with regard to indigenous bankers would require a more clear definition of this group of bankers. The Study Group has defined indigenous bankers as those individuals or firms who accept deposits or rely on bank credit for the conduct of their business and are close to or on the periphery of the organised money markets and are professional dealers in short-term credit instruments (hundis) for financing the production and distribution of goods and services. The effect of this definition is clearly to exclude money lenders.

Regulation

Organisationally, indigenous bankers are sole proprietary or partnership concerns and the provisions of the Banking Regulation Act, 1949 do not apply to them. The constraints imposed by the moneylenders Acts prevailing in the various States are, as we have seen, inadequate to guard fully the interests of the public in relation to the indigenous bankers.

The result is that the present form of regulation over the institutions doing banking business is neither uniform nor adequate. For instance, the activities of indigenous bankers are subject to hardly any regulation. In order to plug the regulatory gap, the Group recommends that some form of uniform regulation be applied preferably through Reserve Bank of India to a wider group of institutions doing the banking business. This would mean that these institutions should obtain a licence for starting the business and it should be made incumbent upon them to supply information about deposit and advances.

The essential feature of banking regulation must be good supervision and inspection of the various institutions doing banking business. However, regulation in the form of detailed administrative supervision and periodic inspection as in the case of commercial banks would not be a practical proposition. The best approach to the problem would be for the regulating authority to stimulate the financial institutions to create their own internal regulation. The authorities should rely on such self-regulation and on external audit, once satisfactory standards have been developed. Such an approach is both effective and more economical than building up a large and costly inspection machinery. To this end, the Group recommends that the Reserve Bank should have powers to call for regular returns from the indigenous bankers and to require that they maintain adequate internal inspection procedures and be subject to regular outside audit, the auditors being recognised chartered accountant firms. It is also suggested that the nature of the supervision should be free of rigid rules and regulations.

Licensing Of Indigenous Bankers—Terms And Conditions

A system of licensing needs to be introduced which may provide for recognition by the Reserve Bank of the various Associations of indigenous bankers with details of each individual member's qualifications. While the Reserve Bank should encourage the formation of Associations, membership of such Associations need not be a precondition for licensing of an indigenous bankers. Direct licensing of indigenous bankers could also be considered for areas where no Associations are in existence on their satisfying the basic conditions.

Any scheme of licensing presupposes that certain terms and conditions would have to be adhered to by members seeking the licence. The scheme of licensing should aim at introducing certain minimum financial discipline in the activities of this sector. The requirements which indigenous banker should fulfil in order to get licensed and be entitled to discounting facilities are :

(a) Indigenous bankers—Gujarati shroffs, multani shroffs, chettiars and kayas—should preferably be members of an Association recognised by the Reserve Bank. They should principally be engaged in banking and should not be engaged in trading activity other than commission agency business.

(b) As in the case of the banking companies, some minimum capital requirements should be prescribed. The minimum paid-up capital for commercial banks is Rs. 5 lakhs. For the indigenous bankers, the Group would suggest Rs. 1 lakh as the minimum owned resources which an indigenous bankers should have to qualify for a licence. In turn, discounting limits should be fixed as a multiple of owned funds of each banker at the maximum of 5 times. This can be established by the indigenous banker declaring his limits with other banks in the return he submits to commercial bank when applying for a credit limit. This will act as an inducement to add to his own funds in business.

(c) Indigenous bankers should evolve for themselves a self-imposed convention in regard to the relationship between their own funds and outside commitments. No licensed indigenous banker should hold at any one time risk assets in excess of seven times the amount of his own capital invested in the business.

(d) The indigenous banker will have to agree to maintain books of account in the usual recognised manner and have them annually audited and certified by a recognised firm of auditors.

(e) A summary statement of the volume and nature of business (in the form indicated in Annexure VI) should be furnished annually by each indigenous banker to the Reserve Bank. The commercial banks and the Reserve Bank after due consultation with the associations will review annually the activity of indigenous bankers to assess if advances granted by them are for socially desirable purposes and not detrimental to the interests of the depositors.

Nature Of The Link With The Organised Banking Sector

Hitherto the link between the organised sector and this part of the indigenous financial system has been tenuous. Although successive attempts were made in the past by the indigenous bankers to establish a direct link with the Reserve Bank, in the changed circumstances, the Study Group is of the view that it is neither necessary nor practicable to link them directly with the Reserve Bank. From the administrative aspect it is felt that the refinancing will involve considerable labour (disproportionate to the amounts of refinance) both for the banks and the Reserve Bank as the hundis are for small amounts and the day-to-day turnover in them (receipts and deliveries) will be large. The Reserve Bank will also have to watch repayments of a larger number of hundis on their due dates.

To simplify the procedure, the Group feels that the requirements of the situation can be met to an adequate extent, if the Reserve Bank would allow a certain quantum of refinancing facilities to commercial banks financing the indigenous bankers. The financial discipline sought to be fostered on the indigenous bankers and their greater utility in financing the productive requirements of the weaker sections of the community will reach a greater compulsion, if the indigenous bankers were to be linked with the Reserve Bank through the commercial banks by a system of refinance of commercial banks' holdings of indigenous bankers' papers. One reason for the high interest rate charged to the end-user of credit appears to be the incidence of the high cost of funds to the indigenous banker.

The Group is, therefore, of the view that the Reserve Bank could well introduce a system of refinance at Bank Rate to the commercial banks against their holdings of indigenous banker's papers, on condition that commercial banks in turn charge concessional interest to the indigenous bankers, and the indigenous bankers in turn make the cost of credit to the end-user reasonable. There are in operation at present several schemes of concessional lending to priority sectors such as exports, small-scale industry and agriculture. Since this finance is also intended for the small man, a scheme along similar lines could be formulated for the indigenous bankers. The Reserve Bank may issue necessary guide-lines depending upon structure of interest rates from time to time. This scheme of finance to the end-user at reasonable cost should induce indigenous bankers to reduce the interest rates on their own lendings outside the Reserve Bank's refinance as well. The benefit that accrues to indigenous bankers by virtue of concessional refinance through the Reserve Bank should enable indigenous bankers to make up for reduced level of earnings on their lendings.

Such an arrangement could become the nucleus of a genuine bill market. People are accustomed to the hundi, but the present bill market schemes makes no provision for the inclusion of bills of the indigenous agencies. This recommendation contains the seeds for the growth and development of a genuine bill market.

Regulation Of Interest Rates And Other Charges Levied By Indigenous Bankers

It is suggested that some understanding should be reached between the Reserve Bank and the indigenous bankers regarding the level of interest that such bankers should charge on advances to their customers. The normal spread between the deposit and advances rates of the commercial banks is 4.5 per cent; in rare circumstances it exceeds 6 per cent. In the case of Commercial banks the higher spread is due to the cost of many other services. In the case of the cooperative banks the spread between the borrowing rate from the Reserve Bank and the ultimate rate charged by the primaries to the borrowers is 5-6 per cent. However, when cooperatives are loaning Reserve Bank funds there is a mark-up of only 1-1/2 to 2 per cent as between two consecutive agencies. On the other hand, the spread between the borrowing and lending rates of the indigenous banks have tended on an average to be much wider than those prevalent in the commercial or cooperative banking sectors though in recent months with the sharp increase in the commercial banks' discount rates for the hundi, the margin between the borrowing and lending rates of the indigenous bankers have tended on an average to be much wider than those prevalent in the commercial or cooperative banking sectors though in recent months with the sharp increase in the commercial banks' discount rates for the hundi, the margin between the borrowing and lending rates has narrowed considerably. True, in the content of the organised money market rates indigenous lending rates appear usurious, but the business involves risky lending and lack of security. Experience shows that on an average bad debt record is not too heavy but that does not imply that it is always so; there are some years in which bad debts are larger and it is in those years that the wider margin helps in covering up the losses. Although the Moneylenders Act in the different States specify ceilings on the interest rates that can be charged, the Group is aware that ceilings have been and are being evaded by making cash deductions to cover higher loan servicing charges at the time of executing a promissory note. The Reserve Bank should periodically indicate as a guideline the interest spread which is considered adequate for this business and which should broadly be the same as the spread allowed to commercial banks and cooperative banks. In other words, the Reserve Bank should rediscount hundis of the indigenous bankers at the Bank Rate, and should fix the discount rate as in the case of export bills or advances to small-scale industries which the commercial banks availing of the rediscount facilities could charge to the indigenous banker. Further, the commercial banks availing of the rediscounting facilities should make every effort to verify on a random basis the rates charged by the indigenous bankers to the ultimate borrowers. Indigenous bankers found to be consistently indulging in malpractices should be debarred from further bank accommodation. While the business methods of indigenous bankers appear to be sound, nonetheless a code of conduct should be formulated for their operations.

At present, indigenous bankers and moneylenders are regulated by Registrars of Cooperatives under the Moneylenders Acts which in the case of indigenous bankers set limits on the interest charges they may levy on secured and unsecured advances. The Group recommends that it should be mandatory to disclose the terms of the loan transactions to the customer. In addition to indicating the rupee amount of loan and the interest, the indigenous banker/broker should be required to express them in terms of the effective rate of charge per year. Also legislation should impose penalties for excessive charges or failure to disclose; and in cases of flagrant violation, the authorities should have the power to suspend the licences of indigenous bankers.

Besides the steep interest charges there are some unstandardised incidental charges such as brokerage and charity, which vary from region to region. For a realistic approach to the cost problem the Group suggests that these charges be periodically reviewed by the Associations.

Reserve Bank To Formulate Broad Guidelines In Respect Of Hundi Business

The Group recommends that the Reserve Bank should from time to time in consultation with the Indigenous Bankers Associations, lay down some broad guidelines with regard to this business, e.g., the type of hundis to be selected, the overall quantum of limits to be sanctioned, the amount per maker and some formula for sanctioning individual limits. At present the limits sanctioned have little meaning because the utilisation of the limits is restricted; in fact, in the recent past, the banks have been known to cut back the limits without any forewarning.

Need For Better Screening Procedures And Credit Analysis By Commercial Banks In Respect Of Hundi Business

The observations of the Group with regard to this

segment of the credit market are that commercial banks have paid little attention to building up this line of business on systematic or scientific lines. The Group recommends that systematic evaluation of the financial statements of indigenous bankers be undertaken by the commercial banks. In granting limits to indigenous bankers, commercial banks should not lay stress on the personal factors only; all factors, personal, financial and economic, should be given due weight. Despite the practical difficulty, the commercial banks should make some attempt at independent, evaluation of drawer's financial status, and should satisfy themselves even on a random basis that the credit used is for the purpose for which money had been given. In other words, the screening process with respect to this business should be more rigorous. This would induce the indigenous bankers to lend for productive purposes and remove the doubt that indigenous lending is for unproductive purposes.

Enlarged Commercial Bank Assistance To Indigenous Bankers In The Form Of Larger Discounting Facilities

The proposal for introducing discipline among the indigenous bankers is dependent upon their getting larger credit facilities from commercial banks who in turn will have the facility of rediscounting with the Reserve Bank of India at the bank rate. The Group recommends that once the present approach of the commercial banks to credit analysis of indigenous hundi business is replaced by a systematic credit analysis process, the flow of assistance from the commercial banks to the indigenous bankers should, not only be enlarged to the extent required from time to time but it should be steady and uninterrupted. At present, although from the commercial banks' point of view, it is a highly remunerative business, it has received the lowest priority from the banks. When banks are flush with funds, the multani bankers who avail of commercial bank's discounting facilities have no difficulty in securing accommodation, but in periods of credit stringency, the requirements of these bankers are the first to be slashed. It is like giving the umbrella when it has stopped raining. Furthermore, even when bill discounting limits were sanctioned by the banks, utilisation of limits were not assured or automatic as in the case of other bank borrowers, for it is within the discretion of the bank to accept or reject the contract, without assigning any reasons for its rejection. Yet another practice prevalent with some banks was to bring all outstandings to nil balance at a stated time in the year. All these practices seem to militate against the multani banker and the irregularity in the availability of funds has introduced an element of uncertainty in the hundi business and rendered difficult the exercise of planning his financial resources. In the view of the Group, since no special advantages are known to accrue from such practices, the Group recommends that practices of this nature be given up. Further enlarged discounting facilities should be made available by banks to the indigenous bankers, particularly in the context of the emphasis to finance small businesses and industries on a priority basis. Most important is that the flow of funds to this sector should be sustained and regular, not spasmodic and intermittent which in turn would help in some reduction in the costs to the ultimate borrowers.

Inclusion Of Hundis Within The Scope Of 'Liquid Assets'

The Group has considered the request made by the multanis themselves that Reserve Bank should include within the scope of 'liquid assets' under Section 24 of the Banking Regulation Act all multani bills discounted by the Scheduled banks. It is certainly true that multani hundis have proved to be extremely good liquid assests. But on exploring the possibility of including them within the meaning of liquid assets under Section 24 of the Banking Regulation Act—the object of which is to ensure that a certain proportion of the deposit resources of the banking system is made available for gilt-edged paper—it was found that this object would suffer if multani bills were accorded liquidity status. Further. inclusion of multani bills in liquid assets would mean demand for inclusion of other kind of assets, e.g., export bills. In view of this, the Group has not pressed for its inclusion within the meaning of liquid assets .

Raising The Value Of Hundi

Although the practice has been to restrict the value of a multani hundi to Rs. 5,000 in order to spread the risk, the Group feels that it would be desirable gradually to raise the value of the hundi from Rs. 5,000 to Rs. 10,000 and in the case of credit worthy borrowers to, say, Rs. 25,000, in view of the fact that increasing amount of indigenous banking funds are channelled to meet the working capital requirements of small-scale industry.

Status Of The Hundi

The view has been expressed in some quarters for the discontinuance of indigenous negotiable instruments not coming within the scope of the Negotiable Instruments Act. The Group does not favour the discontinuance of indigenous negotiable instruments not coming within the scope of the Negotiable Instruments Act, but suggests codifications of the peculiar incidents and usages and bringing them within the Negotiable Instruments Act. The Group also suggests that a standard form of the Darshani (sight) and Muddati (usance) types of hundis could be evolved. The Study Group to review legislation affecting banking could suggest which of the usages and incidents applicable to the different types of indigenous negotiable instruments could be given legal recognition and which are beyond the pale of legal sanction.

Darshani Hundi

For reasons outlined in Chapter III, the Study Group recommends that Darshani hundis be exempted from provisions of section 40 (A) (3) of the Income-Tax Act which requires that all payments exceeding Rs. 2,500 which are claimed as deductions in expenditure should be made by crossed cheque or draft.

Public Relations

To increase private indigenous banking and make these relationships more productive, it is necessary to organise better channels of communications between the indigenous banker and the entrepreneur. Indigenous bankers must recognise the need for some amount of public relations work. Hitherto there have been considerable misunderstanding and apprehensions on the part of the public regarding the activities of indigenous banking agencies. There is a feeling that these agencies operate as a closed system where trading in mixed with lending and there is no proper financial accounting; there is, thus, the fear that assistance rendered to these agencies may be misused. Perhaps this may be due to indigenous bankers not being aware of the need in the modern world of providing appropriate information about themselves and their methods of working to the rest of the economy.

The justification for the proposed liberalisation of Commercial bank facilities lies ultimately in the ability of the indigenous bankers to grant credit to the small man at reasonable rates. The indigenous banker should do everything possible to improve his image before the business community by doing everything possible to serve this purpose.

Report With Commercial Banks

In their relationship with Commercial banks they should aim at creating a better 'rapport' so that they could avail of some of the information and expertise available with Commercial banks as is the case in a number of other countries.

On the other hand with an adequate and regular supply of funds being made available to commercial banks for the hundi trade, the commercial banks should take such effective steps as may be necessary to put this business on a more scientific basis.

Liaison With Brokers

Since the multanis, even the Gujarati shroffs, rely on the brokers there should be a proper liaison between the shroffs and the brokers. Multanis normally operate through professional hundi brokers who bring business to them and also keep them informed about the activities of trade. As far as the brokers are concerned, their activities should be systematised. The Multani and the Gujarati Shroffs Associations should have a list of approved hundi brokers and issue regular licences to them. This would prevent too many from entering the field, crowding the market and lowering the standards. The duty of the approved brokers would be to get correct information on the financial standing of the borrower. Each approved broker should undertake to keep the Association well informed about the total commitments of various drawers. This would enable the Association to know, through the agency of the brokers, the aggregate commitments for any one drawer at a given point of time.

Future Role Of Indigenous Bankers

In the view of the Group the future course of indigenous banking seems to be in their considering other ways of linking themselves with the organised financial system. For instance, indigenous banking agencies could take on some of the activities of ancillary non-banking financial intermediaries such as dealings in short-term paper. Despite the sophisticated state of the German economy and its banking industry, a flourishing private banking sector continues to co-exist there along with organised banking. The West German private bankers, both the purely unlimited liability type and the mixed type, handle a variety of business such as issuing securities, industrial finance, financing foreign trade, real estate, executing wills and administering properties. Their number has declined considerably in the post-war period. However, they are still regarded as an important sector in German banking particularly because of their expertise in those sectors of the economy where individual knowledge, flair and judgement are decisive. The German private banks are very similar to our indigenous bankers; their importance is largely local and confined to cities. Their survival depends on the continuing importance of their local knowledge and the continued growth of the economy. With foresight, they have gradually evolved from proprietorships to partnership concerns. There is also a rather peculiar group called "Kommanditgesselschaft and Aktien (KGaA)" which combines the limited liability and the partnership forms of organisation.

In the U.S.A. and U.K. such institutions like small

loan finance companies and merchant bankers, perform functions similar to indigenous bankers. France too has private bankers. These bankers generally perform two types of useful functions. In the first place, because of their small size and low administrative costs they are able to give better attention to the needs of smaller businessmen—whether industrialists or traders. Secondly, they are able to go in for special types of business, which commercial banks either have no time to think about or develop.

The accent of official policy has been on discouraging non-corporate entities and favouring corporate ventures. It might probably be worthwhile for indigenous bankers to think along these lines and consider setting up joint stock ventures or limited liability concerns. Indigenous banking agencies, if they are to survive, should envisage the possibility of evolution and be ready to combine themselves on joint stock principles of pooling their capital resources to form the nucleus of indigenous joint stock banks.

As the economy grows, more sophisticated financial institutions would be required to meet the ever growing credit needs of the community and discount and acceptance houses might become necessary. With their banking acumen and traditional skills the more efficient of the indigenous bankers could transform themselves into discount and acceptance houses for they would be the appropriate agency for undertaking these functions, provided they see the writing on the wall clearly and their adaptability proves equal to consummate banking skill in accepting organisational, structural and functional chargesr equired for such an evolution. In fact, discount houses could provide a specialised market in commercial bills. Rather than banks themselves holding the bills, the banks could evolve a system of lending a portion of their funds to bill brokers (indigenous bankers could act as bill brokers) and the latter could use these funds to buy bills on their own account and the bills so acquired could be used as collateral and deposited with the lending banker. Occupying an intermediary position between the central bank and the commercial banks, the discount houses could become the channel through which the central bank directs its operations to implement its credit control. In this manner the discount houses could render valuable service to bankers borrowing funds surplus to immediate cash requirements and to the mercantile community by discounting of bills to provide finance for trade.

To assist development of the credit structure the indigenous bankers could also consider transforming themselves into acceptance houses. An acceptance house is a firm or company, an important part of whose business consists of accepting Commercial bills. A large number of these financial firms in the city of London are loosely described as merchant bankers. They originally did the function of ordinary buying and selling of goods but in course of time a variety of other services were added for purposes of business conventions. All of them do banking in some form, that is to say, they keep money in current and other accounts for their customers, keep securities in safe custody for account of customers and attend to the investment of their funds. Some acceptance houses also act as trustees for trust funds and act as investment advisers to the manager of the pension and other-endowments. In fact, the business of the acceptance houses is not standardised or homogeneous. Each house has its own characteristics and specialities on which it is regarded as an authority, but granting of acceptance credits to finance trade of others is a business which they all have in common. Generally the acceptance business of these 'houses' account for 20 to 25 per cent of all bills outstanding. For its services the acceptance houses charges a commission to its customers which varies according to the standing of the customer and the terms of the credit arrangement between the customer and the acceptance house. In Germany too there is a specialised institution called the Prime Acceptance Company which deals in acceptances for financing imports, exports and third country trade.

The future of the indigenous bankers would thus lie in their evolving as discount or acceptance houses or as mini merchant banks oriented towards financing small scale industry. To begin with, they might not be in a position to provide the more sophisticated merchant banking services being offered today by the merchant banks in the West. But they could perform a similar role on a much smaller scale, for instance, in assisting small-scale industry by providing their services as issuing house to tap institutional and other sources of capital finance. And in time they could develop considerable expertise and good will in their role as negotiators in fund raising operations for new and developing small-scale industries. At a later stage they could also consider offering 'nersery finance' to some industries and thereby 'groom' these industries to enter the capital market at a later date. Evolution and growth of the kind envisaged here would be accelerated when the croporate form of organisation is increasingly resorted to.

In effect, it is the conclusion of the Study Group that the indigenous banking business, of the multanis in particular, needs to be resuscitated. This can be achieved by the Reserve Bank of India extending credit facilities for rediscounting of the hundis at the Bank Rate under the Bill Market scheme in order that the commercial banks may finance the hundi business in larger amounts at reasonable rates of interest and in a regular manner and uninterruptedly throughout the year. Once the indigenous banking business is sustained in this manner, it is the Study Group's hope that indigenous bankers will evolve new procedures and organisational patterns to develop further their role to suit the changing requirements of the economy. In this process of evolution, qualitative change in the functions of the indigenous bankers should play a vital role, for instance, it would be desirable for them to take up functions of acceptance credits, etc. Quantitatively, the magnitude of each transaction—the value of the hundi should be increased so as to bring about a decline in the unit cost of their operations, which in turn would help to bring about the long desired decline in the cost of credit to the ultimate borrower. Once the directions in which the indigenous bankers are to move is accepted by them and understood by society, it would be comparatively easy to bring about the necessary organisational changes such as conversion of partnership firms into corporate enterprises without which the indigenous bankers themselves would find it difficult to assume their rightful place in the changing economic milieu of the country.

STUDY TEAM ON LEAKAGE OF FOREIGN EXCHANGE THROUGH INVOICE MANIPULATION 1969—REPORT

Delhi, Ministry of Finance, 1971. 129p

Chairman : Shri M.G. Kaul.
Members : Shri Jasjit Singh; Shri M.G. Abrol; Shri K.G. Wagh; Shri J. Banerjee; Shri M.P. Singh; Shri R.P. Chatterjee.
Secretary : Shri R.C. Misra.

APPOINTMENT

The Study Team on Leakage of Foreign Exchange Through Iovoice Manipulation was constituted under the Ministry of Finance vide their letter No. F. 8/24/69-Cus. VI dated December 12, 1967.

TERMS OF REFERENCE

The terms of reference of the Study Team were as follows :

(i) The team will examine the problem of leakage of foreign exchange through over-invoicing and under-invoicing of imports and exports and will, for this purpose, locate the possible avenues now existing because of organisational deficiencies or policies of various departments, particularly, the Customs Department, Directorate, of Enforcement Reserve Bank of India and the Directorate of Export Assistance and suggest suitable changes in organisational policy and procedures.

(ii) The team will also examine the legal and administrative set-up relating to imports and exports and the role of the respective agencies in implementation of the relevant procedures, for suggesting suitable remedial measures.

CONTENTS

Introductory; The Problem; Areas Vulnerable to Manipulation; Imports; Export Valuation; Special Valuation Cell; Exchange Control on Repatriation of the Value of the Goods Exported; Some Remedial Measures of General Nature; Other Administrative and Legal Measures; Problems Relating to Bilateral Account Trade; Perspective; Summary of Recommendations; Annexure.

RECOMMENDATIONS

Areas Vulnerable To Invoice Manipulation

A systematic and continuous study is called for to identify areas where the scope or the possibility for manipulation of values is greater.

Import or export transactions between parties closely associated over a period of time should be scrutinised more closely to ensure that the values are not unduly low.

Where the same party is operating at the two ends as importer and exporter under different names, apart from a careful scrutiny of documents and comparison values, the concerned agencies must rely on systematic collection of intelligence to detect manipulation.

Transactions between parties financially linked need specialised examination.

In cases of technical collaboration between the importer and the exporter, apart from the need for exercise of great care in approving the rates of royalties, the values should be examined with particular care to be sure that a part of the consideration for the goods is not being adjusted against payment of royalties.

The special valuation cell, proposed to be set up should also collect data regarding the prevailing international trade practices in respect of agency commissions for different commodities and supply that information to the Reserve Bank. Reserve Bank should have proper coordination with this cell.

The Export Special Branch should, while examining the books of accounts, also keep in view the possibility of manipulations in respect of agency commissions.

While permitting a remittance on account of 'overprice', the Reserve Bank should ensure that it is a genuine case of overpricing and the exporters has not inducted his own man abroad for the purpose of sending remittance in the guise of over price.

Trade with countries where there are no currency restrictions or exchange control is not strict, being more susceptible to invoice manipulation, needs to be watched carefully.

Under-Invoicing Of Exports

The procedure for advance registration of contracts of jute goods should be compulsory and there should follow-up action to relate contracts to actual shipments.

There should be a more rationalised system of physical examination of jute goods at the manufacturing or packaging stage in, coordination with the export inspection Council authorities, with a view to reducing the scope of manipulation of export values by misdeclaration of construction, yardage or weightage of such goods.

As regards garden tea shipped on consignment basis and sold in London auction :

(i) We should send observers to watch that the auctions take place under open and competitive conditions;

(ii) Our staffed abroad should check that the auction prices are correctly reflected in the brokers' publications, and

(iii) The auction prices should be properly correlated with the sale prices mentioned in the account sales furnished to the Reserve Bank.

As for tea purchased in Calcutta auction and then exported, some supervision should be exercised from the auction stage onwards to help in the proper correlation between the auction prices and export prices.

To reduce the possibility of manipulation of values in the export of unmanufactured tobacco, the following measures could be usefully considered :

(i) Improvement in gradation to bring about standardisation to the extent possible so as to facilitate comparison and check of values;

(ii) fixation of realistic floor prices;

(iii) the feasibility of introducing the system of auctions akin to tea trade and failing that on the pattern of the system in vogue in the coffee trade;

(iv) examination of books of account of the exporters by Export Special Branch to find out the true nature of the relationship between the exporters and the foreign buyers; and

(v) where final price is not settled prior to export, the goods should be exported on consignment basis.

It should be insisted upon the exporters that they declare the size, colour, cut and perfection of the diamond in invoice.

In the shipping bill, in addition to the export value, the exporter should be asked to declare the local market value of the diamonds.

In the case of exports of handicrafts and art ware of standard varieties, sufficient expertise with the Customs authorities is necessary. In case of need, assistance of the all-India Handicrafts Board may be sought.

Valuation check with regard to hides and skins (undressed) imported into India should be more rigorous.

Values of goods imported under open general licences need to be carefully checked from ever-invoicing angle.

The Scheme Of Exchange Control In Relation To Imports

In case where the imports documents are directly received by the importer and not through banking channels, the Reserve Bank should ensure that the exchange control copy of the bill of entry is submitted to it and there is no lapse in this regard, and where the bill of entry is not produced by the importer within the stipulated period without proper justification, suitable action is taken against such importer.

Steps should also be taken to ensure that the import licences are issued strictly in terms of the Registered Exporters Scheme.

In fraudulent cases, besides the action which may be taken against the exporter under the F.E.R.A for non-rapatriation of the export proceeds, action should also be taken under the Imports and Exports (Control) Act for contravention of Clause 10(d) of the Imports (Control) Order.

Imports and Exports (Control) Act may be amended empowering the Import Trade Control Authorities to impose fines and penalties in departmental adjudications in cases of misutilisation of the goods imported against Actual User's licenses.

The Customs authorities should introduce a system of regular scrutiny of the manifest of every vessel with a view to taking follow-up action in respect of imported worthless goods which are abandoned.

The Customs officers should insist on the production of the bank attested invoice before finalising the bill of entry.

The D.G.T.D. should exercise some valuation check while recommending issue of licenses for machinery and capital goods.

Appropriate statutory provision should be made to make over-invoicing of imports an offence.

Export Valuation

Valuation check in exports should be exercised even at the primary level by an appraiser.

It is of utmost importance that Customs Officers should examine all the terms of the contract with meticulous care and then take a view about the correctness of the declared value.

Customs requirements of examination goods, where possible, should be detailed with the inspection by the Council. Steps will also have to be taken to ensure that there is no substitution of goods after the inspection by the Council.

The Reserve Bank machinery for checking the final sale values of consignment exports should be considerably strengthened.

Variations in price on account of post-export factors should continue to be dealt with by the Reserve Bank and in specified areas by the authorised dealers.

R.B.I. should take the help of the officers to be posted abroad for ascertaining whether the post-export reduction in price has been claimed on a genuine ground or not.

Special Valuation Cell

For the purpose of collection of valuation data, its collation and dissemination to the customs appraising officers, a special Valuation Cell in the Customs organisation may be set up.

The Special Valuation Cell should have subsidiary cells at four major ports, namely, Bombay, Calcutta, Madras and Cochin, each cell dealing with the commodities mainly exported through that port.

In order to provide coordination of the work of these cells at four places, there should be a Director of Valuation at headquarters unit at Delhi.

Exchange Control On Repatriation Of The Value Of The Goods Exported

The Customs authorities should take particular care to see that there is no delay in forwarding shortshipment intimations to the R.B.I.

The system of security numbers introduced at Bombay should be introduced at all ports immediately.

To guard against leakage of foreign exchange through exports by bogus parties, there should be a verification of the identity and antecedents of the exporter before he is assigned a code number by the Reserve Bank.

The Custom House Clearing agents also should, to some extent, be made responsible for verifying the status of his principal before taking the agency functions.

Some Remedial Measures Of General Nature

From the point of view of the problem of leakage of foreign exchange through trade channels, feasibility of canalising the trade in the commodities which are particularly vulnerable to invoice manipulation, should be considered by the Government. For instance, canalisation of export of films, mica and shellac may be considered.

Where canalisation is effected, it should be in reality and not merely inform.—

Floor prices should be fixed realistically.

Floor prices should be kept under constant review and revised in time.

Customs authorities should be careful in checking the values even in respect of commodities for which floor prices are fixed.

Other Administrative And Legal Measures

The existing system and machinery for collection of intelligence, in respect of under-invoicing and over-invoicing and about the activities of specific exporters and importers, from sources in India and abroad, needs to be suitably strengthened and improved.

As for internal intelligence, a planned direction and closer coordination of the activities of the existing internal agencies concerned with fiscal and exchange matters are necessary.

Greater attention should be paid by the intelligence agencies to gathering information and intelligence with regard to under invoicing and over-invoicing.

The strength of the appraising investigation units in the Custom Houses should be augmented to cope with the anticipated increase in the investigation work.

It would be desirable that the Economic Wing of C.B.I. should have on its staff some officers who have adequate expert grounding in technical valuation work.

The Enforcement Directorate should have the wherewithal to deal with the majority of prosecution cases.

The words in section 12(2) "no person entitled to sell or procure the sale of" should be replaced by a more appropriate expression.

Sections 337, 338, 339 and 339A of the Criminal

Procedure Code may be amended to provide for tendering pardon to accomplices in cases relating to contravention of Customs and Foreign Exchange Laws.

Problems Relating To Bilateral Account Trade

There should be as strict a check in the valuation of the goods exported to or imported from N.C.R. countries as that in the case of the goods exported to or imported from free foreign exchange area.

Market intelligence with regard to the value of goods exported by the N.C.R. countries to other countries who are not covered by bilateral agreements should be collected.

A better assessment of the genuine requirements of the countries covered by bilateral agreements is necessary.

In respect of commodities where diversion is strongly suspected, the quota ceiling fixed for the commodity in the bilateral agreements with the country should be reduced to a realistic level and be strictly adhered to.

Perspective

To the extent possible, policy measures for reducing pressures in some of the areas of demand, without too much cost to the economy, are worth exploring.

Stronger preventive and enforcement measures are necessary against smuggling and other areas of consumption of unauthorised foreign exchange.

Public opinion should be educated against the ill effects of the foreign exchange offences on the economy of the country.

BANARAS HINDU UNIVERSITY INQUIRY COMMITTEE, 1969—REPORT

New Delhi, Ministry of Education and Youth Services, 1969. 238p

Chairman : Dr. P.B. Gajendragadkar.
Members : Mr. Justice V.S. Desai; Prof. K.S. Bose; Prof. R.C. Mehrotra.
Secretary : Mr. R.K. Chhabra.

APPOINTMENT

In exercise of the powers conferred by Sub-section(2) of Section 5 of the Banaras Hindu University Act (hereafter called "The Act"), the President, in his capacity as the Visitor of the Banaras Hindu University (hereafter called "the University"), appointed the present Committee to inquire into the recent state of unrest and agitation in the University. Intimation about the Constitution of the Committee was duly communicated to the University vide Government of India, Ministry of Education Letter No. F.1-40/68-U2 dated December 31, 1968.

TERMS OF REFERENCE

The terms of reference of the Committee are as under :—

(i) To inquire into the recent state of unrest and agitation in the university, and

(ii) To make such recommendations as may be considered necessary or expedient for remedying the situation and for improving the general tone of discipline and law and order in the University.

CONTENTS

Committee at Work; Our Inquiry; Causes of Recent Unrest and Agitation in the University: Remedies; Annexures I to XVIII.

RECOMMENDATIONS

Having regard to the conclusions which have recorded at the end of the last chapter, our first recommendation for immediate implementation is that the Act under which the Banaras Hindu University at present administered should be amended. If and after the Visitor is pleased to accept this recommendation should be implemented, if possible, before the University re-opens after summer vacation. In other words, what we have suggested that the Act and Statutes of the University may be amended. The present bodies including the standing committee of the Academic Council responsible for the administration of the University should be dissolved and appropriate steps taken to provide for a "nominated" Executive Council and a Court and a new Vice-Chancellor. We are conscious that this is a drastic recommendation, but we ought to add that having considered the evidence placed before us, we have no hesitation in suggesting that the administration of the University under the provisions of the present Act cannot possibly restore normalcy on the campus without which University life in the ordinary sense would be impossible. The term of the nominated authorities should be as brief as possible and not more than three years. In making the recommendation we ought to repeat what we have already said in the previous chapter, that for several reasons indicated by us the present administration, including the Vice-Chancellor, has lost confidence of an overwhelmingly large proportion of the University Community. We ought to explain that we are impressed by the view that the nominated Executive Council which we are recommending would have a measure of coherence and commitment and would be able to take expeditious decisions so necessary to restore normalcy and win the confidence of the academic community. In support of our recommendation we may be permitted to say that a large number of witnesses who gave evidence before us themselves suggested the immediate replacements as a temporary measure, of the present Executive Council and Court by nominated bodies of relatively, small size and of persons enjoying the esteem and confidence of the University. We would like to refer to the witnesses who gave evidence before us on behalf of the Citizen's Committee. Their evidence appeared to us to be impartial, fair and reasonable. They suggested to us in categorical terms that unless the present administration was removed, it would be impossible to restore peace and harmony on the university campus.

In constituting the appropriate bodies by nomination, we would recommend to the Visitor that in nominating on them educationists and other eminent persons on an all-India basis, it should be ensured that they should make it a point to attend meetings of the bodies on which they are nominated. We would also recommend that teachers of repute working in the Banaras Hindu University should find a place in these bodies. What should be proportion of these different elements is a matter for the Visitor to decide.

The second set of recommendations will cover two different aspects. The first will be in relation to the academic structure of the University and the second will be in relation to the composition of the different bodies which will manage the affairs of the University. We shall first deal with the academic structure of the university.

Before we make our specific recommendation about the academic structure of the University, we ought to make some preliminary observations. Though the evidence given by witnesses in matters relating to the causes of recent unrest and agitation differed, fortunately all the witnesses agreed before us that the all-India character of the University and even more the goal of quality and excellence which inspired Malaviyaji in establishing the University should be sustained and re-inforced, and our recommendations in regard to the academic structure of the University are based primarily on this consideration.

While considering this recommendation, it is necessary to face the facts as they exist today. The University enrolment, specially in the undergraduate level is drawn largely and not un-expectedly, from the neighbouring areas, mainly the eastern U.P. and Western Bihar. Also, why students from distant areas do not seek admission at the undergraduate stage is that in almost all regions new universities in recent years have been established catering to the needs of the local undergraduate students.

Further, if an overwhelmingly large number of students at the undergraduate level come from neighbouring areas, it would follow without anybody's fault that even at the postgraduate stage, proportion of local students will be unduly large.

We are, therefore, satisfied that if the all-India character of this University is to be maintained and strengthened and if the quality of education imparted at the University is to substantially improve, the student body or at any rate the bulk of it should be more mature, more carefully selected to ensure a higher level of ability and instruction than is the case at present. Also some steps should be taken to secure a more equitable distribution of seats at the university in respect of different regions of the country. That is why in our opinion it is desirable that the University should confine its teaching activities mainly to postgraduate courses and to technical and professional courses. We would, therefore, recommend that ordinarily for admission to the Banaras Hindu University the age of entry should be 19 plus and a basic qualification of first degree in arts and science. What selection procedure should be followed in order to achieve this end is a matter which may be worked out by the University in consultation with the University Grants Commission in due course.

We would like to stress that the Benaras Hindu University is very fortunately placed in having a large number of faculties on its campus and it should, we think, be its special privilege to develop an inter-disciplinary approach amongst these various faculties such as faculties of science, agriculture, medicine and engineering. Besides these, a number of border-line courses can be developed in the teaching of which all these faculties can contribute without resorting to duplication of efforts in individual units. Apart from this, there is a considerable need for interaction between modern scientific subjects and Indian philosophy. These are some of the special sphere of higher educational activities in which the Banaras Hindu University can and should take a lead.

We feel that there is an immediate need for the reorganisation of engineering and technical education at the University. The existing facilities at the university no doubt need to be strengthened but also there should be a much closer association than at present between the several engineering and technological departments of the existing faculties of engineering and technology and faculty of science. We think that the present engineering and technology faculties of the University should be brought together and made to function in an integrated and coordinated manner within the broad framework of the University. Many witnesses who appeared before us accepted this concept as also that of university entry at the age of 19 plus. A very welcome and desirable result of this proposal would be that the campus will gradually have mature and better qualified students from all over the country, which would help to make the University a truly all-India university. When we refer to technical and professional courses, a point may arise whether admission to these courses should be after the first degree or earlier. Two views are possible on this subject. So far as law and teacher education are concerned, admission is after graduation. As regards engineering, agriculture and medicine, some academics, but certainly not all, hold the view that if not the entire admissions, at least a substantial proportion should be of students who have taken their first degree in science. The Central Universities would be the obvious choice for providing professional courses with a first degree as the entry qualification. This will be in conformity with our recommendations made earlier with regard to the age of entry at the university level. The entire matter would need further examination and we would suggest it be considered by the Union Education Ministry in consultation with the University Grants Commission.

Flowing from this conclusion, it follows that we are of the opinion that the University should not be concerned with pre-University, B.A., B.Sc., and B.Com. courses. This would also mean the closing of the Women's College, which only provides teaching at the undergraduate level.

The University also runs to high schools, one for boys and the other for girls. It may be that due to sentimental reasons, this has been continued for all these years. We strongly feel that the two schools should not be run by the University and the Faculty of Education should take advantage of the faculties available in other schools in Varanasi for practical training.

The University has also some affiliated colleges providing for undergraduate education in Varanasi. There are other colleges also in Varanasi which are affiliated to the Gorakhpur University. We see no reason why, particularly in view of the fact that we have recommended that there should be no undergraduate courses in the University, the University should continue to affiliate these colleges, over which its control is rather remote. The University may make recommendations for academic development, but the funds required for such development, are to be obtained by these colleges from the State Government. This dual control is not conducive to the maintenance of proper standards.

If the University stops providing teaching facilities for undergraduate courses, it may be necessary for the State Government or private agencies to start a few more colleges in Varanasi. We can appreciate the sentiments of the people of Varanasi of having these colleges affiliated so far to the Banaras Hindu University. We would suggest that apart from the affiliation of these colleges to the Gorakhpur University, the possibility of reorganising and affiliating these to the Kashi Vidyapith, which is a deemed University, or to the Varanaseya Sanskrit Vishvavidyalaya may be explored.

We have taken cognizance of the fact that if the above recommendations of the committee are accepted, a considerable number of staff would become surplus. In any case, this closure of the pre-university and undergraduate courses will have to be done over a period of four years. It may be that by that time some of the teachers would retire and also with the expansion in the postgraduate wing, which we envisage, it may be possible to absorb some of them, but this a matter of detail and, as suggested above, could be looked into by the University Grants Commission.

Further, to attract students from States other than UP, the University may consider the possibility of providing some scholarships for such students and also travel grants.

The conference considered the question of the place of regional languages in higher education and affirmed its conviction that energetic development of Indian languages and literature is vital for the promotion of higher education and of national culture generally. The subject of change-over of medium of education to regional languages, the conference stressed, could only be considered as an integral part of a deliberate policy and plan with a view to improving the quality of education, promoting creativity and national integration and bringing education closer to the needs and aspirations of the community.

The conference was in general agreement with the recommendations of the Education Commission with regard to change-over in the medium of education.

But, higher education is a closely integrated system and any modification such as a change in the medium of education. would have a direct effect on other parts of the system. The conference recognised that the change-over in the medium of education, if properly carried out, would be a major step towards improvement of higher education and towards strengthening of its roots in our soil. The programme should be pursued in a sustained and systematic manner. The conference endorsed the statement of the Education Minister that "the programme of change-over to regional languages as media of education will have to vary from university to university, from subject te subject, and even from institution to institution, in the same university. The criteria in each case should be that the change-over helps, at every stage, to raise standards". The manner and speed of the change-over should be left to the university system. This was in acoordance with the recommendation of the Education Commission and was reiterated by the Education Minister in his address to the conference.

The conference felt that at the undergraduate stage, the change-over in medium of education to regional languages could be carried through in about five to ten years, depending on the degree of preparatory work already done, on the nature of subject and other relevant factors. In the programme of change-over the importance of English should be fully recognised and adequate arrangements for its study made at the undergraduate level.

At the postgraduate and research level the question of "medium of education" loses its usual meaning as students will have to depend, for instance, in science, medicine and technology, on books and journals in English and other important world languages because of the university and rapid growth of knowledge.

In the case of all-India institutions, the present arrangements regarding the medium of education may continue, as recommended by the Education Commission.

In the case of large cities, with multilingual population, the medium of education may continue to be English, in addition to the regional languages which the university would provide.

We may add that in regard to the medium of instruction in law and in medicine, different considerations will have to be taken into account. The language of the High Courts and the Supreme Court will determine the medium of instruction in law and the medium of instruction in medicine will be influenced by the decision which the Medical Council of India may take in that behalf.

We understand that the University Grants Commission, on the advice of the Vice-Chancellors' Conference held in April, 1969, have appointed a committee to consider the general question of the structure of universities and composition of and representation on the various university bodies i.e., executive council, academic council, court etc., and the question of student participation in the statutory bodies of the universities. The recommendations made by this committee should be available in the near future and would be useful for framing the revised Act of the University, We however venture to suggest some points for consideration for the preparation of the new Act.

Court

In the Acts of the Central Universities, the Court has been decided as the 'supreme authority/governing body' of university. Unfortunately, the members of the Court have construed this description somewhat liberally and literally when they seek to exercise their authority as members of the Court in relation to questions pertaining to the framing of policies and programmes of the University and suggesting general measures for the improvement of the University which fall within the purview of the Academic Council or Executive Council.

It appears to be the general feeling of the members that the Court could cover rule or impose its views on the other bodies of the University, in matters both academic and others. In view of this, it would perhaps be desirable not to define the Court as the 'supreme authority' and a policy-making and a reviewing body. Even the review should be generally in such a way that it does not infringe the powers given to the Executive Council and the Academic Council.

The strength of the Court should not exceed 100 and preferably it should be about 80. Further about 50 per cent membership should be from outside the University. We have not gone into the character of different categories but we strongly feel that the representation of the registered graduates should be kept to the minimum. In this connection, we would like to quote from the Report of the Committee on "Model Act for Universities" :

"The older pattern did not include the Academic Council particularly at the stage when the University's main responsibility consisted largely of examining and very little of teaching. It is necessary clearly to demarcate the functions of these bodies, each having specified authority as confusion can arise by each body trying to advise the other with regard to its functions. At one time when there was no academic Council it was usual to describe the Court as the supreme governing body. But in some of the newer Acts, this has been advisedly omitted. In general, the Court is intended to bring into the university the lay element and this has the advantage of bringing the university into contact with eminent men in public life, in industry and trade, and those who provide finances for it. The 'lay representatives' in the Court (and any other authority) can render great service to the university by their greater knowledge of the world and their ability to represent the general desires and aspirations of society. The committee recommends that in general the authority to be given to the Court should be firstly for framing the budget, as it would be necessary to have a larger body than the Executive Council to take responsibility for this. Secondly the Court should have the authority to indicate broadly what courses a university should have no power to interfere with the decisions of other authorities acting within the powers given to them by law; the Court is not to be regarded as a superior body to revise the decisions of the Executive Council or the Academic Council. Legislation by the Executive Council or by the Academic Council need not require confirmation by the Court. It should operate as a body concerned with general policy and the well-being of the university."

Generally, a provision in the University Acts is made that persons are elected from the Court to the Executive Council and in such elections the teachers of the universities are debarred. We feel that this is not a healthy practice. The teachers should have equal opportunities as other members in seeking election to the Executive Council. The only point to be kept in view is that the Executive Council is not dominated entirely by teachers. With regard to the nomination of the Members of Parliament on the Court, we would quote the following paragraph from Report of the Committee on "Model Act for Universities" ;

"It is left that Parliament or State Legislatures or other local bodies need not be separately represented, but members of these bodies may be nominated by the Visitor in their personal capacity".

in our view, this would meet the need of the association of the Parliament with a Central University.

We also feel that to enable the University to move forward in changing times, the Statutes after approval by the Executive Council should be referred direct to the Visitor and not through the Court which meets once or twice a year.

Executive Council

The Committee on "Model Act for Universities" has suggested the composition of the Executive Council as follows :

Vice-Chancellor	1
Pro-Vice Chancellor or Rector of University	1
Deans (who should be full-time teachers) of faculties	4
Principals of Colleges	4
Persons elected by the Court from among its members	3
Persons nominated by the Visitor (which may include Government representatives).	4
	17

It may be an advantage to have on the Council two professors, other than deans, and also one or two persons nominated by the Chancellor.

We would, however, suggest that the constitution of the Executive Council of the Banaras Hindu University may be as follows :

Vice-Chancellor	1
Rector(s)	1
Deans of Faculties	3
Four members elected by the Academic Council. Three from amongst themselves; (one Professor, one Reader and one Lecturer); one woman teacher not necessarily a member of Academic Council.	4
Persons selected from the Court from its members provided not more than one teacher is included in this category	3
Persons nominated by the Visitor.	5
	17

Academic Council

The present constitution of the Academic Council could continue, but we feel that to make this more compact body the number of professors other than the heads of the departments in the University may not exceed five.

Standing Committee Of The Academic Council

As already explained, we would recommend, that the standing committee of the Academic Council should be abolished. The functions at present specified by the relevant statutes of the University have been divided between the Academic Council and the standing committee of the Academic Council. We feel that the entire functions covered by the said statutes should rest with the Academic Council. It would be, however, open to the Academic Council to appoint committees or sub-committees to deal with subject-matters but the decision taken on all academic matters should be subject to the approval of the Academic Council. It may also be desirable to have a Board of Research Studies.

Selection Committee

The present statute provides for making recommencation for appointment to the posts of Professors, Readers, Lecturers, Registrar, Finance Officer, and Librarian. This may remain as at present, but we feel that the statute should provide also for the constitution of the selection committee for heads of academic institutions which may not be working on a faculty basis. In this connection, we quote the following from the Estimates Committee Report (1965-66;—Banaras Hindu University :

"The Committee note the observations made by the Enquiry Committee regarding selection of teachers. They also note that since then the procedure for selection of teachers has been streamlined. The Committee, however, regret that even then the same has not been uniformly and properly followed. Selections have been made of readers and lecturers even when the requisite number of experts were not present in the meeting, even though it was in violation of the rules. The Committee note that during the last three years, there were four cases where conflicting views were expressed by the Executive Council and the Selection Committee over the choice of some teaching staff. The Committee would stress that greatest possible care should be exercised in the recruitment of teaching staff, as this has got a direct bearing on the standards of teaching in the University and maintenance of discipline. The Committee note that in the Banaras Hindu University (Amendment) Bill, which is now pending before the Lok Sabha, a provision has been made for associating the Visitor's nominee with every Selection Committee".

A provision should be made that no recommendations of a selection committee would be treated valid unless at least two experts in the case of professor and at least one each in the case of reader and lecturer attend the meetings. We also suggest that in view of the large number of meetings of the selection committee, the work for presiding over the selection committees may be distributed between the Vice-Chancellor and the Rector by appropriate provision in the statutes.

Finance Committee

We would suggest the constitution of the Finance Committee as follows :

Vice-Chancellor	1
Deans of Faculties to be nominated by Executive Council (out of Deans who are the members of the Executive Council).	2
Nominees of the Visitor	3
Person who is not an employee of the University nominated by the Court.	1
	7

Finance Officer should act as the secretary of the Committee.

Vice-Chancellor

The present system of appointing the Vice-Chancellor may continue, but we would suggest that the two nominees of the University on the committee which recommends the panel should be the nominees of the Executive Council and should not be nominated by the Court, or in the alternative the committee may consist of the following :

(i) A person nominated by the visitor.
(ii) A person nominated by the Chairman, U.G.C.
(iii) A person nominated by the Executive Council.

The person nominated by the Visitor will be the chairman. The present rules provide that the Vice-Chancellor shall hold office for a term of five years and shall not be eligible for re-appointment. We feel that ineligibility clauses should be omitted, but no one should hold office for more than two consecutive terms.

Rector

We would again like to quote the following from the Report of the Committee on "Model Act for Universities" with regard to the appointment of Pro-Vice-Chancellor or Rector :

"The Vice-Chancellor is concerned, inevitably, with almost every part of the work of the university. This in itself is an exceedingly heavy responsibility, and it becomes, still more so if the university is an affiliating one with large number of colleges and departments and students. It sometimes happens that a Vice-Chancellor is unable to attend adequately to the more important work of policy-making and development because of the need to attend to routine work and administration. It is therefore very important that Vice-Chancellor, where necessary, is provided with a deputy, that is, a Rector or a Pro-Vice-Chancellor. Ability to delegate and yet to keep a general over-all control is a difficult art. It is important that relief is given to the Vice-Chancellor; but the manner in which it is done sometimes creates difficulties and complications. It may happen that if the Pro-Vice-Chancellor, or Rector, or other officer intended to provide relief to the Vice-Chancellor is chosen in the same manner as the Vice-Chancellor, it may not be possible to ensure that there is between them the complete understanding that is essential if the Pro-Vice-Chancellor is a real help to the Vice-Chancellor. One of the simplest ways in which the Pro-Vice-Chancellor can be chosen is for the Executive Council to fix the salary and other conditions of service, and leave it entirely to the Vice-Chancellor to choose the Pro-Vice-Chancellor for the duration of his own term or for a shorter period if he so desires. It will work most satisfactorily if the persons so chosen is one of the professors with some flair for administration. The next Vice-Chancellor may reappoint the same person, but if he prefers somebody else, the last Pro-Vice-Chancellor can revert to his department.

During the time that a professor or other member of the University staff works as Pro-Vice-Chancellor an additional allowance may be given to him. The age of superannuation and other terms and conditions of service of the Pro-Vice-Chancellor should be the same as for the professor of the University".

We endorse these views but feel that the designation of the post should be 'Recot'. We also suggest that in view of the complexity of work in the University, particularly in the light of its big campus, it may be desirable to provide for more than one Rector in case of necessity. This should, however, be made clear that this is not a decorative office, but the incumbent should take full responsibility in sharing the burden of the Vice-Chancellor.

Heads Of Departments

We feel that in view of the fact that the University would have more than one professor, particularly in all the major departments, it would be desirable that the hardship in the departments should go by rotation amongst the professors. The term of the head of the department may be two to three years. Each department should have a small advisory committee consisting of the junior and senior teachers. This Committee should look into the development needs and facilities for staff and research needs. The committee should meet regularly and keep minutes of the meetings which may be submitted to the Vice-Chancellor. This would provide a sense of sharing of responsibility and participation in the life of the department. In this connection, we may quote the following extract from the Report of the Estimates Committee (1965-66)—Banaras Hindu University :

"The Committee feel that there is an urgent need for relieving the heads of departments of routine administrative work so that they can devote more time for the planning and direction of research and teaching".

Deans Of Faculties

In view of the suggestions made regarding appointment of heads of departments, we are not suggesting any change in the present system of appointment of deans by rotation from amongst the heads of the departments. However, where both the offices of the principals and deans of faculties exist, the powers, functions and duties of the deans in such cases may be clearly defined.

Delegation of Powers

In the efficient working of the university, it is desirable that the provision of delegation of powers should not only be made in the case of the Vice-Chancellor, Rector, Registrar, or other administrative wings of the University, it is essential that there should also be delegation of powers to the teaching departments. Our intention is that not only also the relevant powers be delegated to the heads of the departments, but the heads of the departments in their turn should further delegate such powers as are appropriate, to their colleagues in the department so that they are able to assist the head in the administration of the department. It should be understood that delegation of powers does not result in a divorce between powers and responsibilities. Both should do together.

Extension Of Service Of Teachers

Another cause which according to some witnesses leads to discontent amongst the teachers has been the procedure followed by the University in giving extension to teachers beyond the age of 60 years. We recommend that some guidelines should be drawn by the Executive Council in this regard so that extension of service would not seem arbitrary or dependent on extraneous considerations. In fact it would be a healthy practice if every case of a teacher nearing the age of retirement is placed before the Executive Council (say, a year in advance of the expected date of retirement), or preferably, before a committee of the Executive Council, and then put to the Executive Council with the recommendations of the committee.

Although there is an elaborate system of proctorial board and dean of student welfare and wardens in various hostels of the University, the arrangements for looking after the discipline of the students needs considerable planning and coordination. The duties, responsibilities and spheres of activities of these various agencies which look after the discipline and welfare of the student community should be coordinated and defined to avoid confusion and ambiguity.

The Chief Proctor as well as the other members of the Proctorial Board should be the senior teachers commanding the respect of the teaching as well as the student community and should not be overloaded with other duties such as those of warden, etc. Senior students should also be associated with the Proctorial Board. There should be sufficient delegation of authority to the proctors and others so that they can deal with minor acts of indiscipline but in case the aggrieved party is not satisfied, an arrangement should be made for a court of appeal by an independent organization in which teachers as well as students should be represented. The Vice-Chancellor should act as a final court of appeal so that the students feel satisfied that they have had sufficient opportunity of their cases being reviewed within the University and they have not to resort to outside agencies, like court, for redress.

In this connection, we reproduce below the two important recommendations made in the Report of the Committee on Relations with Junior Members set up by the Oxford Universities under the chairmanship of Professor H.L.A. Hart :

1. A short clause should be included in the university statutes saying : "No junior member shall (i) engage in conduct likely to disrupt teaching or study or research or the administration of the university or to obstruct any officer or servant of the university in the performance of his duties"; (ii) "damage or deface any property of the university or of any college, or occupy or use the same otherwise than in accordance with the rules or other provision made therefor by the university or college authority concerned".

2. "Other disciplinary rules (apart from library and dress regulations and rules for conduct in examinations) should be made by a Rules Committee consisting of six Senior Members (Comprising : one Proctor, who shall act as Chairman; two Proctors elect; two college Deans elected by the Committee of Deans; and one member of congregation appointed by the Hebdomandal Council) and six Junior Members (comprising : three appointed by the Student Representative Council from its members; two presidents of Junior Common Rooms elected by the Committee of J.C.R. Presidents; and one president of a Middle Common Room elected by the Conference of M.C.R. Presidents)."

We feel that the above recommendations could appropriately be adopted by the Banaras Hindu University with suitable modifications, taking into account the local needs and conditions.

Student Participation

As regards student participation in the affairs of the University, there could be no question that they should have a measure of participation but what needs examination is the degree and level of such participation and how it is to be brought about and promoted. In that areas students should be invited to participate and what form that participation should take, are matters which need to be carefully considered, but in our opinion, one thing is clear that without a sense of participation, a sense of commitment to academic values will not be achieved. In dealing with this question, the level of degree of maturity of the students will have to be taken into account. In some areas, the students can be left to manage their own affairs and these areas would be those pertaining to extra curricular activities which have become an essential part of modern education; for instance, such areas are covered by the management of hostels, running of youth welfare boards, and other cultural and physical activities. In some areas, their views may be ascertained and taken into account by decision-making authority, but in identifying these areas and determining the manner of participation of students, we must never forget that the main object of associating students with the university administration is to emphasise the academic significance of such participation which would make education richer and meaningful in every way; it is not intended to enable the students to introduce political overtones in university matters. In addition, all departments should set up Council of Students Affairs or Students Advisory Councils consisting of students and teachers. As we have just observed a committee appointed by the University Grants Commission will soon go into this question exhaustively and what the committee recommends will have relevance to what should be done in regard to the Banaras Hindu University.

Student Union

In view of the existing position in the Banaras Hindu University, we feel that the University should continue to have a Union and the membership of the same should be obligatory. However, the student population is not too large for direct democracy to function and hence caste, regional, communal and other unacademic factors seem to have exercised an inordinate influence. It would, therefore, be desirable that a general council of about 60 to 80 members be elected on faculty basis. The council may elect office-bearers and the executive committee. A provision should also be made to co-opt some members on the general council who have special interest in the extra curricular activities such as dramas, debates, photography and games etc. It would be of real value if the student unions issued annual reports describing their activities and achievements of the year. An audited statement of accounts should be issued every year. This is essential.

It is desirable that some qualifications are prescribed for the persons being eligible to be elected as office-bearers or the members of the General Council as suggested above. Many of the universities in India which have such unions or associations have prescribed such qualifications. We suggest that no person who passed the high school examination more than 8 years earlier or a pre-university or equivalent examination more than 7 years earlier or who has taken more than one year in excess of the period prescribed for the course of which he is the student would be eligible to be a member of the Council or to be elected as an office-bearer. In this connection we may usefully quote some of the relevant recommendations made by the Education Commission. Said the Comission :

Student Unions

"Student unions represent an important way of providing student participation in university life outside the classroom. Properly organised, they help in self-government and self-discipline, provide a healthy outlet for students' energies and give the students useful training in the use of democratic methods.

It is for each university to decide how its students' union will function and would welcome a good deal of experimentation. But some broad principles can be indicated.

(1) Membership of the student unions should be automatic in the sense that every student should be presumed to be its member. But every student should be expected to choose at least one activity organised in the institution. e.g., arts society, football club, drama association, etc. and pay the required subscription. There should be no separate payment for the membership of the students' union as such. Each of the activities will thus have funds of its own and these would be handled by appropriate committees. The funds of the central union -to the extent they are needed—would be formed by contributions from each activity committee. The university or college should also give aid to the central unions as well as should also different activities.

(2) It may be desirable to elect the office-bearers, not directly by the large body of students (many of whom are freshmen), but indirectly by the different students' societies in the university who would send selected representatives to the union executive.

(3) There should be some disqualification for office-bearers. For instance, persons who have spent two or more years in the same class should be disqualified.

(4) The successful working of student unions depends to a large extent upon the mutual trust and confidence between the teachers and the students. Greater teacher involvement in union activities should, therefore, be ensured. We would strongly commend the establishment of a university or college union in which all teachers and students automatically become members. All committees of the union and various activities groups should have teachers on them and it should be their responsibility to guide the students tactfully on right lines with curbing their freedom to decide for themselves."

Hostels

We regret that though a large number of hostels have been provided in the University, it does not have adequate amenities except in the case of the hostels constructed in the recent past. The present provision for dining and kitchen is far from satisfactory and needs considerable improvement. The size of the hostels is too large and would need reorganization on a smaller unit. At present the deans of faculties/principals are also the wardens of the hostels. We feel that the present system of allotting hostels either faculty-wise or college-wise is a very undesirable practice. The students of all the faculties should be mixed together and no hostel should be earmarked for a particular type of students. Of course, the University will have to provide for separate hostel for women. Apart from meetings the problem of discipline, this gives the feeling of oneness to the students, inter-change of academic ideas and it may also be a strong source of national integration, particularly when we are pressing that the University should maintain its all-India character. The present system of appointment of wardens desires to be looked into. There should be no ex-officio appointment to the post of wardens. Only suitable presons who have time and have a flair for administration and are interested in the welfare of the students should be appointed as wardens. The wardens should be provided with residential accommodation in the hostel itself. Similarly, it may be desirable to appoint preferects from the students in the hostels, who would look after the cultural and welfare activities. Management of the hostels should also be entrusted to the students as much as possible under the guidance of the wardens.

University Administration

We quote from the Estimates Committee Report (1965-66)—Banaras Hindu University :

"The Committee have been told that since the Report of the Enquiry Committee, the office of the Banaras Hindu University has been reorganized, in the light of the recommendations contained therein. They need hardly stress that since the organizational set-up of a university has to play a pivotal role in the smooth and efficient working of the University, the working of the administration should be kept under constant review so as to avoid recurrence of similar situation and to effect improvements as and when necessary".

We regret to say that from our experience and the statement made by the Vice-Chancellor, we have no doubt that working of the administration is not what it should be, and we recommend that an expert committee should review this and suggest measures to streamline the office administration. In this connection we would like to cite the following view expressed by the Vice-Chancellor :

"An office in Banaras Hindu University that needs immediate attention is that of the Registrar. It is in a state of confusion. Not only there is indiscipline but also a great deal of inefficiency. Even the Vice-Chancellor has found it difficult to get files and several reminders have to be issued. Files are often incomplete and records have been found to be missing. Instances have also come to the notice of the Vice-Chancellor and the Executive Council of the mutilation of files. The rules of promotion of the ministerial staff have been changed repeatedly. So there is a great deal of discontent in the office. It is necessary to take promptly some effective steps to bring the university office into proper shape. Many students' agitations spring from the office delays and inefficiency".

RSS Building

There is another point which remains to be considered and that is in regard to a two-room building which is allowed to be used by the RSS ever since Malaviyaji's time. When Malaviyaji gave permission to the RSS to use this building, it was not surrounded by any University buildings. But after the new building of the Law Faculty was constructed, the situation has completely altered. As it stands in front of the new building of the Law Faculty, it looks entirely out of place. This is one important factor which must be considered in dealing with the question as to whether the RSS should be allowed to use this building in future. From a purely aesthetic and architectural point of view, this building needs to be demolished.

It is however, true that except during the period in 1948 when it was declared an illegal organisation, ever since 1941 RSS has been allowed to use this building and that too with the permission of Malaviyaji. RSS attaches sentimental importance to the facility given to them by Malaviyaji. But the continuance of the use of the building by RSS raises one important question as to whether an outside institution, though it may be cultural, should be allowed to have a building on the University campus, whether or not RSS is a purely cultural association at present, is a question on which we wish to express no opinion. But even on the basis that RSS is a cultural association, if it is allowed to use a building on the University campus, a similar claim made by other cultural associations cannot be resisted. When we put this aspect of the matter to the office-bearers of RSS at Varanasi, they fairly conceded the strength of the above argument.

It was, however, urged on their behalf that having regard to the long association of RSS with the building in question, some other plot should be allotted to them where they would be able to construct a building for their use. But even this request does not meet the main objection that allowing one inevitably lead to similar claims by similar cultural organizations. On principle, we are inclined to take the view that on the University campus no outside organization should be allowed to have a building of its own. Considered from this point of view, it seems to us somewhat inappropriate that RSS should be allowed to hold its Shakha meetings on the campus of the University and use the building in relation to the said activities. We wish that the University would soon take action in the matter so as to avoid any controversy in future.

An Appeal To Political Parties

The question as to whether university students should take part in politics or not has agitated the minds of educationists all over the country for some years past. No one can, seriously dispute the fact that university students many of whom are voters are entitled to study social, political, economic issues and form opinions of their own. No one can dispute that in this process as a part of extra-curricular activity, all views whether social, political or economic should be allowed to be expressed before the students and should form the subject-matter of debates in the University Students' Union from time to time. In fact, it is desirable that teachers and students themselves should discuss all current social, political and economic issues without any fear or inhibitions. Indeed, fear of ideas is completely foreign to the spirit of inquiry which inspires all academic work on a university campus. But it is necessary to bear in mind that to be informed about all ideas pertaining to several issues is not the same thing as to be actively involved in them. At present, different political parties owing allegiance to different political power by democratic means; that no doubt is a legitimate part of the democratic way of life. Therefore, agitations and protests are bound to find a place in the public life of our country; but where agitations and protests are started in support of partisan political causes, the University students should not be involved in them. We would, therefore, earnestly appeal to all the political parties not to induce the students to take part in partisan political agitations, whilst they are continuing their studies on the University campus. We trust that all political parties will recognise the validity of the view that non-involvement of students in partisan political causes will be in the interest of the country as a whole.

We would like to recommend that students should avoid enrolling themselves as active members of the political parties whilst they are studying on the University campus. If a student becomes an active member of any political party, he may often have to face conflict of loyalties, his loyalty to the political party to which he belongs may not always be reconciled with his loyalty to the University to which he belongs. We, therefore, feel that students who are entitled to play their legitimate part in the affairs of the University should not be actively associated with the day-to-day work of the political parties.

What we say about the students applies in equal force to the teachers. In fact, if teachers become active members of political parties and introduce political philosophies of their respective parties while teaching in the class room or even outside, that may introduce an element of indoctrination which is bound to lead to conflict and disharmony and that in turn would disturb the peace of the University.

It should be noticed that throughout our report, we have refrained from commenting on any political party as such and we have confined our inquiry only to the question as to what were the causes that led to the recent unrest and agitation on the University campus. For reasons which we have already set out in describing our approach (we do not propose to pronounce any verdict as to whether any political party or parties was or were concerned with any of the major incidents what in our view led to the recent unrest and agitation in the University campus. That is a matter which we have thought is outside the purview of our inquiry.

Entry To Campus

Even though the campus of the Banaras Hindu University is one of the very few compact campuses in India, it appears that the University has not been able to control the flow of visitors to the University. The main reason for this is the location of the temple in the campus and also the provision of a service hospital. We understand that with the extension of the hospital which the University now proposes to undertake, the entry to the hospital could be so arranged as to avoid the use of the main gate. Similarly, the University should explore the possibility of providing separate entrance to the temple which we understand is possible. If this is done, it should be possible to have effective control on the entry of the persons to the University campus.

Central Universities—UGC—Government Of India Relations

The President of India, as the Visitor of the Banaras Hindu University exercises his powers on the advice of the Union Minister of Education. We feel that since with the setting up of the University Grants Commission under an Act of Parliament, the responsibility for the coordination and maintenance of standardness of higher education has been vested in it, and it is also the responsibility of the Commission to determine the maintenance grants of the Central Universities, a convention may be developed that where the Visitor exercises his powers under the relevant provision of the Acts of the Central Universities, the advice of the University Grants Commission should be obtained by the Minister before advising the Visitor.

Procedure For The Consideration Of The Report : A Suggestion

There is one more point to which we wish to refer, though not without reluctance. Section 5(4) of the Act provides that "The Visitor may address the Vice-Chancellor with reference to the result of such inspection and inquiry, and the Vice-Chancellor shall communicate to the Executive Council the views of the Visitor with such advice as the Visitor may offer upon the action to be taken thereon." This shows that after our report is received by the Visitor, he will have it examined and result of the recommendations made by us in our report. The views which the visitor may form in respect of this advice are required to be communicated to the Vice-Chancellor, by section 5(4), Section 5(5) deals with the next stage. It provides : "The Executive Council shall communicate through the Vice-Chancellor to the Visitor such action, if any, as it is proposed to take or has been taken upon the result of such inspection or inquiry". This sub-section means that the Executive Council in substance accepts the advice of the Visitor and communicates to the Visitor that the advice is being given effect to. Section 5(6) deals with a case where the Executive Council does not wish to give effect to the Visitor's advice and wants to give an explanation in support of its attitude. It provides : "where the Executive Council does not, within a reasonable time, take action to the satisfaction of the Visitor, the Visitor may, after considering any explanation furnished or representation made by the Executive Council issue such directions as he may think fit and the Executive Council shall be bound to comply with such directions." Having regard to the fact that we are recommending, as an interim measure, the abolition of some of the bodies entrusted with the task of administering the University affairs, it would, we think, be inappropriate to give to the Executive Council an opportunity under Section 5(6) to say why this recommendation should not be accepted.

It is obvious that our recommendations will have to be examined by the Visitor before he reaches any conclusion as to which of them, if any, should be given effect to. But we venture to suggest to the Visitor to consider whether, having regard to the fact that as an interim measure we are recommending the abolition of the relevant bodies of the University, including the Executive Council, it would be expedient or reasonable to give the said Executive Council an opportunity to offer an explanation why our recommendation for its abolition should not be implemented. We would also suggest that the Visitor should have this recommendation fully examined and, if he comes to the conclusion that it should be implemented, he should ask the Union Government to implement it without reference to the present Executive Council. We ought to add that if the Visitor is pleased to adopt this course, he may take such steps as he deems reasonable and fair to consult the new nominated Executive Council in regard to the other recommendations we have made about the future set-up of the University, both in the academic and administrative spheres. We may incidentally mention that a similar request was made by the Mudaliar Committee to the Visitor in its report.

Before we conclude, we would like to say that in making our recommendations for remedying the situation, we have borne in mind the spirit of idealism which inspired Malaviyaji in founding this institution. In this connection, we would also like to emphasise what we have discussed before that the Central Universities have to play a significant role in helping the development of higher education in the country and in that behalf, they have to strike a path which may be different from the path which the State Universities would normally take. We are keen as were indeed all the witnesses who appeared before us, that the all-India character of this institution should become a reality; and towards this end every effort should be made. Our recommendations have been based primarily on this consideration. With a magnificent campus and a glorious past, this institution must, we think, take a place of pride in the academic world of Indian course of time. It is unfortunate that it has had to face periods of crisis in the past. But we feel confident that the spirit of its great founder, whom all of us proudly and justly called "Mahamana Malaviya" will guide its destinies in future. We have tried to consider the evidence and judge the merits of respective points dispassionately, objectively and fairly and have made our recommendations in the confident hope that, if they are implemented, the object of the Visitor in appointing the committee may be served.

EXPERTS' COMMITTEE TO STUDY AND REPORT ON THE TECHNO-ECONOMIC FEASIBILITY OF LOCATING ADDITIONAL REFINING CAPACITY IN ASSAM, 1969—REPORT

Dehra Dun, Government of India, 1969, 80p

Convener : Shri B.S. Negi
Members : Shri M.G. Krishna; Shri S.D.Bhambri; Shri A.K. Ghosh; Shri Hari Narain.

APPOINTMENT

The Government of India in the Ministry of Petroleum and Chemicals and Mines and Minerals Constituted the Experts Committee to Study and Report the Techno-Economic Feasibility of Locating Additional Refining Capacity in Assam vide its Resolution No. 25 (1)/68-OR dated April, 2, 1969.

TERMS OF REFERENCE

(i) Crude Oil resources of Assam, yearly rate of production from the various fields and the quantities that will remain available after meeting fully the requirements of the existing refineries quantities that will remain available after meeting fully the requirements of the existing refineries at Digboi, Gauhati and Barauni operating to their optimum design capacities.

(ii) The nature and extent of demand for petroleum products within the State of Assam existing and in future, and the area of economic distribution for marketing the additional production.

(iii) Techno-economic feasibility and comparative economics of establishing a new refinery or expansion of one or more of the existing plants, taking also into account the means of transport available or proposed.

(iv) Other relevant factors which may have a bearing on the establishment of the additional refining capacity in Assam.

CONTENTS

Acknowledgements; Introduction; Crude Oil Resources

of Assam; Yearly Rate of Production from Various Fields and the Quantities that will Remain Available after Meeting fully the Requirement of the Existing Refineries at Digboi, Gauhati and Barauni; Processing Scheme and Refining Costs; Demand for Petroleum Products within the State of Assam existing and in future; Areas of Economic Distribution for Marketing Additional Production and Comparative Costs of Transportation of Crude Oil and Petroleum Products pertaining to different Locations for Additional Refining Capacity; Total Costs of Refining and Transportation of Crude Oil and Petroleum Products; Possibilities of producing Aromatics and Ammonia from Assam crude oil; Conclusions; Annexures I to XV.

RECOMMENDATIONS

The known crude oil reserves in Assam are likely to sustain production rate of about 4.1 million tonnes per year from 1971 onwards upto 1977 and a decreasing rate thereafter. However, the maximum possible rate of production on the basis of established reserves could be as follows :—

1971	4.6263	million tonnes
1972	4.6167	,, ,,
1973	4.6060	,, ,,
1974	4.5955	,, ,,
1975	4.5865	,, ,,
1976	4·5780	,, ,,
1977	4.5700	,, ,,
1978	4.2630	,, ,,
1979	4.0570	,, ,,

The three refineries operating on crude oil produced in Assam have the following design capacities :—

Digboi	0.525	million tonnes/year
Gauhati	0.75	million tonnes/year
Barauni	3.00	million tonnes/year
Total	4.275	million tonnes/year

With marginal additional investment the built-in capacities of these refineries can be utilised to operate as follows ;—

Digboi	0.525	mtpa
Gauhati	1.1	mtpa
Barauni	3.4	mtpa
Total	5.025	mtpa

These refineries are disigned specifically to process the low-sulphur crude oils from the Naharkatiya-Moran fields. It is not possible to process imported high-sulphur crude oil in these refineries without extensive modifications, which may involve, in addition to the provision of new lining in the fractionating towers and transfer lines, the installation of secondary processing units like Reformer, Desulphurisation Unit and Visbreaker, at considerable capital cost. Since it is to the economic advantage of the country to operate these refineries at their optimum capacities, crude oil produced from the Assam oil fields upto 5.025 million tonnes should be supplied to these refineries on a first priority basis, subject to the suitability of economic processing of the crude oil likely to become available from the new Assam fields as per para 7.10 below.

Since the rate of crude oil production from the Assam oil fields in the foreseeable future will be considerably less than the optimum capacities of the refineries at Digboi, Gauhati and Barauni, it is not considered necessary to create additional refining capacity of the conventional type for processing the crude oil presently estimated to be avilable in Assam.

The prospecting operations of ONGC and OIL may in the future establish the presence of additional reserves of crude oil. Based on this hypothesis, a techno-economic study of the feasibility of installing additional refining capacity at alternative comparative costs of transportation and refining in establishing additional refining capacity at alternative location, namely Galeki-Nazira, Gauhati, Dhubri, Barauni and Kanpur have been studied on the basis of :

(i) one million tonne per annum, and

(ii) two million tonnes per annum,

of crude oil production being available over and above the 5 million tonnes per annum required for the existing refineries at their optimum capacities.

The total comsumption of major petroleum products in Assam is estimated to be 1.09 million tonnes during 1975 and 1.66 million tonnes by 1980. The present refining capacity of 1.625 million tonnes in Assam will be enough to meet the local requirements of all major products except kerosene upto 1980. Since the additional requirements of kerosene can be met economically by movement from outside, it is seen that there is no need to increase the refining capacity in Assam to meet the local requirements of refined products.

A study of the pattern of demand for petroleum products and of the economies of transportation of products from alternative refineries to the various consuming centres has shown that the market for the products from any additional refining capacity will by and large be in the area west of Kanpur.

The cost of movement of crude oil and refined products (by pipeline for white products upto Delhi) calculated on the basis of actual pipeline costs and railway freight rates, and the refining costs for 1 mpta and 2 mpta additional refining capacity with cocking operation are estimated as follows :—

(Rs. lakhs)

Impta	Galeki-Nazira	Gauhati	Dhubri	Barauni	Kanpur.
Cost of transportation of crude oil	—	200	360	440	780
Cost of transportation of products	1255	934	878	680	253
Cost of refining	362	332	357	278	349
Total cost	1617	1466	1595	1398	1382
Cost of transportation of crude oil	—	280	440	700	1080
Cost of transportation of products	1719	1448	1403	974	395
cost of refining	608	560	596	473	586
Total cost	2327	2288	2439	2147	2061

These calculations show that for a throughput of either one million or two million tonnes per year, the total costs will be the lowest if additional refining capacity is located at Kanpur. However, the advantage to Kanpur would be modified if calculations could be based on costs of rail haul rather than railway freight rates. A refinery too far to the west also impinge on the economies of supply of crude by the procedure of crude oil. If the choice is limited to the first-four locations, Barauni is the most economical choice for an additional throughput of 2 mtpa and Barauni and Gauhati are more or less comparable if the additional refining capacity is only 1 mtpa, since the slight advantage to Barauni may be modified by the difference between railway freight rates and railway costs. Thus, if the additional finds crude oil in Assam are of the order of one million tonne per annum and if the resources can be found by the railways to cope with the additional requirements of rolling stock, etc. the feasibility of creating additional refining capacity of the conventional type for 1 million tonne throughput at Gauhati or Barauni could be considered, subject to the consideration that in the context of the substantial deficit of petroleum products appearing in the north-western region by 1973-1974 creation of additional refining capacity there might also be necessary.

It is considered that the refining of crude oil for production of coventional petroleum products is not the only optimum way of utilising crude oil. Processing of crude oil as a chemical feed-stock for the production of automatics, ammonia and ethylene-based petrochemicals also presents attractive economic possibilities. In the context, in particular, of utilising additional crude oil from Assam oil-fields, these possibilities appear all the more attractive since,

(a) the market for petroleum products from additional crude oil finds will by and large lie in far-off areas viz. western Uttar Pradesh and beyond resulting in expensive transportation;

(b) there will be considerable unsatisfied demand for ammonia in West Bengal, North Bihar and Uttar Pradesh in the years to come;

(c) Aromatics, especially after conversion to high-priced DMT, cyclohexane, synthetic fibres, etc. will command good market and bear long haulage costs; and

(d) Aromatics and ethylene-based chemicals can become the nucleus for the development of economic activity for the ultimate production of consumer products; a conventional refinery by itself cannot generate economic activity and increase employment potential.

The present knowledge about the characteristics of the initial production of crude oils from Lakwa and Rudrasagar is not adequate and it is not known whether these crude oils will be suitable for economic processing at Barauni, in particular for the production of certain high-price products. No information is available about the quality of any new crude oil finds. The quality of these crude oils will not, however, affect their suitability as a feed-stock for the production of chemicals. An integrated complex for the production of chemicals and kerosene is worthy of serious consideration, when additional crude oil production of either one or two million tonnes is established. In the limited time available to the Committee it has not been possible to establish the economics of such a chemical complex. This matter needs to be studied further by a separate technical group.

As stated above, the present knowledge of the characteristics of the Lakwa and Rudrasagar crude oils is not adequate; regarding the characteristics of the crude oil from any new finds, there is presently no information whatsoever. If the characteristics of the aforesaid crude oils should warrant employing a more sophisticated technology compared to what has been envisaged in Chapter III, the cost of refining will increase. In such an event, the comparative economies of pressing the aforesaid crude oils at Barauni and using a suitable imported crude oil to supplement the Naharkatiya and Moran crude oils for processing at

Barauni (along with the economies of using the existing Haldia-Barauni pipeline for crude oil transportation and of the consequential movement of refined products from the refinery at Haldia by rail) will need to be examined. If the economies of the alternatives available justifies the importation of crude oil of the order of 1.4 mtpa for processing at Barauni, only about 2 mtpa will need to be supplied from Assam to Barauni. The total requirements of the three refineries for Assam crude oils will then be 2.0+1.1+0.525 i.e. 3.625 mtpa. Thus in the above situation, even with the normal crude oil production rate of 4.1 mtpa of the maximum possible production rate of 4.6 mtpa, there will be surplus of 0.5 to 1.0 mtpa of crude oil in Assam for utilisation in the above-mentioned chemical complex.

KRISHNA WATER DISPUTES TRIBUNAL, 1969—REPORT

Delhi, Controller of Publications, 1974—76. 4 Volt (including further reports.)

Chairman : Shri R S. Bachawat
Members : Shri Shamsher Bahadur; Shri D.M. Bhandari.
Member-Secretary : Shri M. Prasad.

APPOINTMENT :

The Government of India, Ministry of Irrigation and Power Constituted the Krishna Water Disputes Tribunal vide Notification No. S.O. 1419 dated April 10, 1969.

TERMS OF REFERENCE :

"For adjudication the water dispute regarding the Inter-State river Krishna and the river valley thereof" and

"Certain matters connected with and relevant to the said water dispute."

CONTENTS

Volume I : Letter of Transmital; Representatives of the State Governments; Genesis of the Dispute; References and Subsequent Proceedings; The Krishna River and River Basin; Inter-State Conference and Disputed Agreement of July 1951; Disputes Concerning the Tungabhadra; Claims arising out of the States Reorganisation Act, 1956; Diversion of the Godavari Waters to the Krishna; Ground Water; Determination of dependable flow Return Flow; Inter-State Water Disputes Act, 1956; and law relating to Equitable Appointment of the Benefits of an Inter-State River; Protection of existing uses. **Volume II :** Diversion of the Krishna Waters outside the Krishna Basin; Appointment of the Waters of River Krishna; Concluding Observations; Final order of the Tribunal. **Volume III :** Appendices from A to U. **Further report :** Letter of transmital; Representatives of the Government of India and the State Governments; Preliminary; Reference No. I of 1974 by the Government of India, Reference No. II of 1974 by the State of Andhra Pradesh; Reference No. III of 1974 by the State of Karnataka; Reference No. IV of 1974 by the State of Maharashtra; Modifications in the Report of the Tribunal (except in the Final Order); The Final order of the Tribunal modified as a result of the explanations given by theTribunal under section 5(3) of the Inter-State Water Disputes Act, 1956.

CONCLUSIONS :

The Governments of Maharashtra, Karnataka and Andhra Pradesh shall bear their own costs to appearing before the Tribunal. The expenses of the Tribunal shall be borne and paid by the three States in equal shares. This is in accordance with the practice followed in America as well as the precedent of the Indus Commission Report. The expenses could be assessed only after the final dissolution of the Tribunal.

On April 19, 1971, the Tribunal passed an order in terms of agreed minutes filed by the parties regarding diversion of The Godavari waters. It was stated by the parties that each of the concerned States "will be at liberty to divert any part of the share of the Godavari waters which may be allocated to it by the Godavari Tribunal from the Godavari Basin to any other Basin". None of the States thereafter asked for a mandatory order from the Tribunal for diversion of the Godavari waters into the Krishna Basin. With effect from that date, the Krishna and Godavari cases got separated from each other. In cosequence of the order passed by the Tribunal on 19th April, 1971, the

States of Madhya Pradesh and Orissa were discharged from the record of Krishna case and were no longer parties. In our order of 19th April, 1971 we directed the States of Madhya Pradesh and Orissa to pay their own costs.

In order to inform ourselves fully about the projects of the different States, as also to assess their relative importance in the general scheme of allocation and above all to comprehend objectively the site problems presented to us by the different States by having a close look at them, we inspected many places in the Krishna Basin. Though this tour took little more than four weeks of the Tribunal's time, the experience and the result were very rewarding. The visits to Koyna Nagar, Narayanpur, Alamatti, Nagarjunasagar, Vijayawada, Srisailam, Tungabhadra Dam and Suneksela amongst the many places we saw unfolded at a glance the manifold facets of the problems of the projects and structures located there and left little scope for explanation and elaboration which would have been necessary if arguments before the Tribunal had been addressed without the usual aid provided by these inspections. The State of Maharashtra, Karnataka and Andhra Pradesh extended to us the utmost courtesy and spared no efforts to make our visit extremely useful and instructive. The officials deputed to look after the inspection arrangements of the Tribunal and its staff made a commendable work of it and we give our need of praise for the unobstructive efficiency displayed by them.

We would be failing in sincerety and no less in our duty if we fail to acknowledge our debt of gratitude for the active co-operation extended to us by the eminent counsel of the States and the assistance derived by them as also by us from their respective engineers, scientists and technicians. These experts had to put in hours of hard work and industry and we genuinely felt that sometimes we were a little too exacting in asking for details and technical information on special problems at a very short notice. Not once was their active support or co-operation withheld or delayed. The State Governments were equally keen to render the utmost assistance to the Tribunal in the expeditious disposal of its task in hand. The respective Governments placed the services of two stenographers each at the disposal of the Tribunal during the period when the oral evidence was recorded and arguments heard. These officials did not take long to make themselves familiar with their work and became quite at ease in the shortest possible time with the scientific terms, phrases and formulae used by the witnesses. To them we owe a great deal for saving the time of the Tribunal and the maintenance of a satisfactory record by the Tribunal's officials.

We would add that without the active willingness of the State Governments and their specialist advisers, our task would have assumed stupendous proportions. The Tribunal was called upon to decide on questions involving technical and engineering matters of utmost complexity. At the very beginning we were asked by the counsel for the different States to get along with our work without the assessors whose technical assistance could be made available to us under the Inter-State River Disputes Act. We acceded to the request jointly made by the counsel for all the States. We can now say at the end of our labours that it would have been difficult to arrive at conclusive results unless the willingness of the State Governments, their counsel and engineers to reach the maximum possible agreements on complex technical points of dispute, was readily forthcoming. We have already made reference to such matters in our report and need not advert to these again. We hope earnestly that the equally important task of implementation of the decisions at which we have reached would receive the ready support and co-operation by the concerned States. For reasons, which we have explained in our report, we are not immediately setting up an authority to maintain watch and supervision over the work of implementation. The amity and goodwill displayed by the parties in the conduct of this long trial lead us to hope that our expectations will be amply fulfilled.

To our own staff, we are indebted for the unstinted efforts and the conscientious discharge of duties in performance of the Tribunal's work at all hours of the day. Mr. M. Prasad, the secretary of the Tribunal, has been conspicuous in the discharge of his duties with zeal and devotion. It would be invidious to mention individuals from amongst members of the staff but it would be true to say that one and all they have done excellent work in which they evinced great interest and assiduity.

Final Order Of The Tribunal

The Tribunal hereby passes the following order :—

Clause I : This order shall come into operation on the date of publication of the decision of this Tribunal in the Official Gazette under Section 6 of the Inter-State Water Disputes Act, 1956.

Clause II : The Tribunal herebv declares that the States of Maharashtra, Karnataka and Andhra Pradesh will be free to make use of underground water within their respective State territories in the Krishna river basin.

This declaration shall not be taken to alter in any way the rights; if any, under the law for the time being in force of private individuals/'bodies'/authorities.

Use of underground water by any State shall not be

reckoned as use of the water of the river Krishna.

Clause III : The Tribunal hereby determines that, for the purpose of this case, the 75 percent dependable flow of the river Krishna upto Vijayawada is 2,060 T.M.C.

The Tribunal considers that the entire 2,060 T.M.C. is available for distribution between the States of Maharashtra, Karnataka and Andhra Pradesh.

The Tribunal further considers that the additional quantities of water as mentioned in sub-clause A(ii), A(iii), A(iv), B(ii), B(iii) B(iv), C(ii), C(iii) and C(iv) of clause V will be added to the 75 percent dependable of flow of the river Krishna upto Vijayawada on account of return flows and will be available for distribution between the States of Maharashtra, Karnataka and Andhra Pradesh.

Clause IV : The Tribunal hereby orders that the waters of the river Krishna be allocated to the three States of Maharashtra, Karnataka and Andhra Pradesh for their beneficial use to the extent provided in clause V and subject to such conditions and restrictions as are mentioned hereinafter.

Clause V : (A) The State of Maharashtra shall not use in any water year more than the quantity of water of the river Krishna specified hereunder :—

(i) as from the water year commencing on the 1st June next after the date of lhe publication of the decision of the Tribunal in the official gazette upto the water year 1982-83—565 T.M.C.

(ii) as from the water year 1983-84 upto the water year 1989-90—565 T.M.C. plus
a quantity of water equivalent to seven and a half per cent of the excess of the average of the annual utilisation for irrigation in the Krishna river basin during the water years 1975-76, 1976-77 and 1977-78 from its own projects using 3 T M.C. or more annually over the utilisations for such irrigation in the water year 1968-69 from such projects.

(iii) as from the water year 1990-91 upto the water year 1997-98.
a quantity of water equivalent to seven and a half percent of the excess of the average of the annual utilisations for irrigation in the Krishna river basin during the water years 1982-83, 1983-84 and 1984-85 from its own projects using 3 T.M.C. or more annually over the utilisations for such irrigation in the water year 1968-69 from such projects.

(iv) as from the water year 1998-99
onwards—565 T.M.C. plus.
a quantity of water equivalent to seven and a half percent of the excess of the average of the annual utilisations for irrigation in the Krishna river basin during the waters years 1990-91, 1991-92 and 1992-93 from its own projects using 3 T.M.C. or more annually over the utilisations for such irrigation in the water years 1968-69 from such projects.

(B) The State of Karnataka shall not use in any water year more than the quantity of water of the river Krishna specified hereunder :—

(i) as from the water year commencing on the 1st June next after the date of the publication of the decision of the Tribunal in the official gazette upto the water year 1982-83—695 T.M.C.,

(ii) as from the water year 1983-84 up to the water year 1989-90—695 T.M.C. plus
a quantity of water equivalent to seven and a half per cent of the excess of the average of the annual utilisations for irrigation in the Krishna river basin during the water years 1975-76, 1976-77 and 1977-78 from its own projects using 3 T.M.C. or more annually over the utilisations for such irrigation in the water year 1968-69 from such projects.

(iii) as from the water year 1990-91 up to the water year 1997-98—695 T.M.C. plus.,
a quantity of water equivalent to seven and a half per cent of the excess of the average of the annual utilisations for irrigation in the Krishna river basin during the water years 1982-83, 1983-84 and 1984-85 from its own projects using 3 T.M.C. or more annually over the utilisations for such irrigations in the water year 1968-69 from such projects.

(iv) as from the water year 1998-99 onwards a quantity of water equivalent to seven and a half per cent of the excess of the average of the annual utilisations for irrigation in the Krishna river basin during the water years 1990-91, 1991-92 and 1992-93 from its own projects using 3 T.M.C. or more annually over the utilisations for such irrigation in the water year 1968-69 from such projects.

(C) The State of Andhra Pradesh will be at liberty to use in any water year the remaining water that may be flowing in the River Krishna but thereby it shall not acquire any right whatsoever to use in any water year nor be deemed to have been allocated in any water year water of the river Krishna in excess of the quantity specified hereunder :

(i) as from the water year commencing on the 1st June next after the date of the publication of the decision of the Tribunal in the official gazette up to the water year 1982-83—800 T.M.C.,

(ii) as from the water year 1983-84 up to the water year 1989-90—800 T.M.C.,
a quantity of water equivalent to seven and a half per cent of the excess of the average of the annual utilisations for irrigation in the Krishna river basin during the water years 1975-76, 1976-77 and 1977-78 from its own projects using 3 T.M.C. or more annually over the utilisations for such irrigation in the water year 1968-69

from such projects.

(iii) as from the water year 1990-91 up to the water year 1997-98—800 T.M.C. plus
a quantity of water equivalent to seven and a half per cent of the excess of the average of the annual utilisations for irrigation in the Krishna river basin during the water years 1982-83, 1983-84 and 1984-85 from its own projects using 3 T.M.C. or more annually over the utilisations for such irrigation in the water year 1968-69 from such projects.

(iv) as from the water year 1998-99
onwards—800 T.M.C. plus
a quantity of water equivalent to seven and a half per cent of the excess of the average of the annual utilisations for irrigation in the Krishna river basin during the water years 1990-91, 1991-92 and 1992-93 from its own projects using 3 T.M.C. or more annually over the utilisations for such irrigation in the water year 1968-69 from such projects.

(D) For the limited purpose of this clause, it is declared that:

(i) the utilisations for irrigation in the Krishna river basin in the water year 1968-69 from projects using 3 T.M.C. or more annually were as follows:

From projects of the
State of Maharashtra—61.45 T.M.C.
From projects of the
State of Karnataka—176.05 T.M.C.
From projects of the
State of Andhra Pradesh—170.00 T.M.C.

(ii) annual utilisations for irrigation in the Krishna river basin in each water year after this order comes into operation from the projects of any State using 3 T.M.C. or more annually shall be computed on the basis of the records prepared and maintained by that State under Clause XIII.

Clause VI. Beneficial use shall include any use made by any State of the waters of the river Krishna for domestic, municipal, irrigation, industrial, production of power, navigation, pisciculture, wild life protection and recreation purposes.

Clause VII. (A) Except as provided hereunder a use shall be measured by the extent of depletion of the waters of the river Krishna in any manner whatsoever including losses of water by evaporation and other natural causes from man-made reservoirs and other works without deducting in the case of use for irrigation the quantity of water that may return after such use of the river.

The water stored in any reservoir across any stream of the Krishna river system shall not of itself be reckoned as depletion of the water of the stream except to the extent of the losses of water from evaporation and other natural causes from such reservoir. The water diverted from such reservoir by any State for its own use in any water year shall be reckoned as use by that State in that water year.

The uses mentioned in column No. 1 below shall be measured in the manner indicated in column No. 2.

Use	Measurement
Domestic municipal water supply	By 20 per cent of the quantity of water diverted or lifted from the river or any of its tributaries or from any reservoir, storage or canal.
Industrial use	By 2.5 per cent of the quantity of water diverted or lifted from the river or any of its tributaries or from any reservoir, storage or canal.

(B) Division of the waters of the river Krishna by one State for the benefit of another State shall be treated as diversion by the State for whose benefit the diversion is made.

Clause VIII. (A) If in any water year any State is not able to use any portion of the water allotted to it during that year on account of the non-development of its projects or damage to any of its projects or does not use it for any reason whatsoever, the State will not be entitled to claim the unutilised water in any subsequent water year.

(B) Failure of any State to make use of any position of the water allocated to it during any water year shall not constitute forfeiture or abandonment of its share of water in any subsequent water year nor shall it increase the share of any other State in any subsequent water year even if such State may have used such water.

Clause IX. As from the 1st June next after the date of the publication of the decision of the Tribunal in the official gazette.

(A) Out of the water allocated to it, the State of Maharashtra shall not use in any water year:

(i) more than 7 T.M.C. from the Ghataprabha (K-3) sub-basin.

(ii) more than 90 T.M.C. from the main stream of the river Bhima.

(B) Out of the water allocated to it, the State of Karnataka shall not use in any water year:

(i) more than 295 T.M.C. from the Tungabhadra (K-8) sub-basin and more than 42 T.M.C. from the Vedavathi (K-9) sub-basin.

(ii) more than 15 T.M.C. from the main stream of the river Bhima.

(c) Out of the water allocated to it, the State of Andhra Pradesh shall not use in any water year:

(i) more than 127.5 T.M.C. from the Tungabhadra (K-8) sub-basin and more than 12.5 T.M.C. from the

Vedavathi (K-9) sub-basin.

(ii) more than 15 T.M.C. from the main stream of the river Bhima.

(C) Out of the water allocated to it, the State of Andhra Pradesh shall not use in any water year :

(i) more than 127.5 T.M.C. from the Tungabhadra (K-8) sub-basin and more than 12.5 T.M.C. from the Vedavathi (K-9) sub-basin.

(ii) more than 6 T.M.C. from the catchment of the river Kagna in the State of Andhra Pradesh.

(D) (i) The uses mentioned in sub-clauses (A), (B), and (C) aforesaid include evaporation losses.

(ii) The use mentioned in sub-clauses (C) (i) does not include use of the water flowing from the Tungabhadra into the river Krishna.

Clause X : The State of Maharashtra shall not out of the water allocated to it divert or permit the diversion of more than 67.5 T.M.C. of water outside the Krishna river basin in any water year from the river supplies in the Upper Krishna (K-1) sub-basin for the Koyna Hydel Project or any other project.

Provided that the State of Maharashtra will be at liberty to divert outside the Krishna river basin for the Koyna Hydel Project water to the extent of 97 T.M.C. annually during the period of 10 years commencing on the 1st June, 1974 and water to the extent of 87 T.M.C. annually during the next period of 5 years commencing on the 1st June, 1984 and water to the extent of 78 T.M.C. annually during the next succeeding period of 5 years commencing on the 1st June, 1989.

(2) The State of Maharashtra shall not out of the water allocated to it divert or permit diversion outside the Krishna river basin from the river supplies in Upper Bhima (K-5) sub-basin for the projects collectively known as Tata Hydel Works or any other project or more than 54.5 T.M.C. annually in any one water year and more than 212 T.M.C. in any period of five consecutive water years commencing on the 1st June, 1974.

(3) Except to the extent mentioned above the State of Maharashtra shall not divert or permit diversion of any water out of the Krishna river basin.

Clause XI : (A) This order will supersede :

(i) the agreement of 1892 between Madras and Mysore so far as it related to the Krishna river system.

(ii) the agreement of 1933 between Madras and Mysore so far as it related to the Krishna river system;

(iii) the agreement of June, 1944 between Madras and Hyderabad;

(iv) the agreement of July, 1944 between Madras and Mysore, in so far as it related to the Krishna river system;

(v) the supplemental agreement of December, 1945 among Madras, Mysore and Hyderabad ;

(vi) the supplemental agreement of 1946 among Madras, Mysore and Hyderabad.

Copies of the aforesaid agreements are appended to the report of the Tribunal.

(B) The regulations set forth in Annexure 'A' to this order regarding protection to the irrigation works in the respective territories of the State of Karnataka and Andhra Pradesh in Vedavathi sub-basin be observed and carried out.

(C) The benefits of utilisations under the Rajolibunda Diversion Scheme be shared between the States of Karnataka and Andhra Pradesh as mentioned herein below :

Karnataka	...	12 T.M.C.
Andhra Pradesh	...	15.9 T.M.C.

(D) The reservoir loss of Tungabhadra reservoir shall be shared equally by the works of the State of Karnataka on the left side and the works on the right side of the reservoir. The half share of the right side in the reservoir loss shall be shared by the States of Andhra Pradesh and Karnataka in the ratio of 5.5 to 3.5.

Clause XII. The regulations set forth in Annexure 'B' to this Order regarding gauging and gauging sites in the Krishna river system be observed and carried out.

Clause XIII. (A) Each State shall prepare and maintain annually for each water year complete detailed and accurate records of :

(a) The annual water diversions outside the Krishna river basin.

(b) annual uses for irrigation from irrigation works using less than 1 T.M.C. annually.

(c) annual uses for irrigation from all other projects and works.

(d) annual uses for domestic and municipal water supply.

(e) annual uses for industrial purposes.

(f) annual uses for irrigation with the Krishna river basin from projects using 3 T. M. C. or more annually.

(g) areas irrigated and duties adopted for irrigation from irrigation works using less than 1 T. M. C. annually.

(h) estimated annual evaporation losses from reservoir and storages.

(i) formulae used co-efficient adopted for measuring discharges at project sites.

Each State shall send annually to the other States a summary abstract of the said records.

The said records shall be open to inspection of the other State through their accredited representatives at all reasonable times and at a reasonable place or places.

(B) The records of gaugings mentioned in Annexure 'B' to this order shall be open to inspection of all the

States through their accredited representatives at all reasonable times and at a reasonable place or places.

Clause XIV. (A) At any time after the 31st May, 2000 this Order may be reviewed or rivised by a competent authority or Tribunal, but such review or revision shall not as far as possible disturb any utilisation that may have been undertaken by any State within the limits of the allocations made to it under the foregoing clauses.

(B) In the event of the augmentation of the waters of the river Krishna by the diversion of the waters of any other river, no State shall be debarred from claiming before the aforesaid reviewing authority or Tribunal that it is entitled to greater share in the waters of the river Krishna on account of such augmentation nor shall any State be debarred from disputing such claim.

Clause XV. Nothing in the Order of this Tribunal shall impair the right or power or authority of any State to regulate within its boundaries the use of water or to enjoy the benefit of waters within that State in a manner not inconsistent with the Order of this Tribunal.

Clause XVI. In this Order :

(a) Use of the water of the river Krishna by any person or entity of any nature what soever within the territories of a State shall be reckoned as used by that State.

(b) The expression "water year" shall mean the year commencing on 1st June and ending on 31st May.

(c) The expression "Krishna river" includes the main stream of the Krishna river, all its tributaries and all other stream contributing water directly or indirectly to the Krishna river.

(d) The expression "T.M.C." means thousand million cubic feet of water.

Clause XVII. Nothing contained herein shall prevent the alternation, amendment or modification of all or any of the foregoing clauses by agreement between the parties or by legislation by Parliament.

Clause XVIII. The Government of Maharashtra, Karnataka and Andhra Pradesh shall bear their own costs of appearing before the Tribunal. The expenses of the Tribunal shall be borne and paid by the aforesaid three States in equal shares.

Annexure A

Regulations regarding protection to irrigation works in the respective territories of the States of Karnataka and Andhra Pradesh in Vedavathy sub-basin.

The State of Karnataka will not put up any new work on the streams mentioned in Schedule I within the limits shown in the map* appended here with, without the previous consent of Andhra Pradesh to protect the irrigation interests under the existing irrigation works in Andhra Pradesh and similarly the State of Andhra Pradesh will not put up any new work on the Streams mentioned in Schedule II within the limits shown in the said Schedule and marked in the map* appended herewith, without the previous consent of the State of Karnataka to protect the irrigation interests under the existing irrigation works in the State of Karnataka.

This State of Karnataka will not put up any new construction on Suvarnamukhi river so as to affect the supply of Agali tank in Andhra Pradesh for the irrigation of an ayacut of 884 acres, the supplies for which are drawn from the Agali Anicut in the State of Karnataka.

Schedule I

List of streams on which no new construction should be undertaken by the State of Karnataka without the previous consent of Andhra Pradesh.

Sl.No.	Name of the stream or catchment	Location in the Map	Limits within which no new construction should be undertaken by Karnataka without Map the previous consent of Andhra Pradesh.
1.	Hagari (Vedavathy)	A	From Vanivilas Sagar in Karnataka upto Bhairavanithippa Dam in Andhra Pradesh.
2	Dodderi tank Halla (Garanihalla)	B	4-1/2 miles up stream of confluence with Hagari.
3.	Talak tank Halla (Garanihalla)	C	From the Salem-Bellary road bridge over this stream upto confluence with Hagari.
4.	Chinnahagari	D	Upto 16 miles upstream from Karnataka-Andhra Pradesh boundary.
5.	Amarapuram tank catchment	E	Catchment of Amarapuram tank in the State of Karnataka.
6.	Virapasamudram tank catchment	F	Catchment of Virapasamudram tank in the State of Karnataka.
7.	Yeradkere tank catchment	G	Catchment of Yeradkere tank in the State of Karnataka
8.	Rangasamudram tank catchment	H	Catchment of Rangasamudram tank in the State of Karnataka.

*See Map II in Volume IV of the Report.

9. Nagalapuram tank catchment	I Catchment of Nagalapuram tank in the State of Karnataka.

Schedule 2

List of streams on which no new constructions should be undertaken by the State of Andhra Pradesh, without the previous consent of Karnataka.

Sl. No.	Name of the stream	Location in the Map	Limits within which no new construction should be undertaken by Andhra Pradesh without the previous consent of the State of Karnataka.
1	2	3	4
1.	Madalur Doddakere nala	J	Entire catchment of the nala in Andhra Pradesh.
2.	Madalur Gidaganahalli Kattenala	K	Entire catchment of the nala in Andhra Pradesh
3.	Doddabanagere Doddakere nala	L	Entire catchment of the nala in Andhra Pradesh.
4.	Dharmapur tank nala	M	Entire catchment of the nala in Andhra Pradesh
5.	Parasurampur Doddakere nala	N	Entire catchment of the nala in Andhra Pradesh
6.	Kadehoda Achuvalikere nala	O	Entire catchment of the nala in Andhra Pradesh.
7.	Parasurampur tank nala	P	Entire catchment of the nala in Andhra Pradesh.
8.	Gowripura Palydakere nala	Q	Entire catchment of the nala in Andhra Pradesh.
9.	Jajur tank nala	R	Entire catchment of the nala in Andhra Pradesh.
10.	Thippareddihalley Kyatanakere nala	S	Entire catchment of the nala in Andhra Pradesh.
11.	Oblapur tank nala	T	Entire catchment of the nala in Andhra Pradesh.
12.	Hagari (Vedavathy)	U	Below Bhairavanithippa Dam upto Andhra Pradesh-Karnataka border.
13.	Chinnahagari	V	From Karnataka-Andhra Pradesh border upto its confluence with Vedavathy (Hagari)

Annexure B

Regulations regarding gaugings and gaugings sites in the Krisha River System.

The river Krishna and its tributaries should be gauged at the following sites :

1. At all the dam and weir sites-existing, under construction and future projects-utilising annually—1 T.M.C. or more :

At all such sites the following measurements will be made and recorded three times a day—6 A.M. in the evening :

(a) Diversions into canals, penstocks, tunnels etc.

(b) Water let down through the various sluices in the dam, weir or barrage.

(c) Overflow over waste weir or spillways.

(d) Estimated evaporation losses.

(e) water lifted from the river or reservoirs for irrigation, water supply and for any other purpose. These measurements will be made by the States in which the dams and weirs are situated.

The cost of such measurements will be borne by the States concerned.

II. Gauging on Inter-State Streams

Three times daily at 6 A.M.. 12 Noon and 6 P.M.

A. Inter-State streams between Karnataka and Andhra Pradesh

1. The Krishna river near	Deosugar (at present a CW & PC gauging site)
2. The Bhima River near	Yadgir (CW & PC gauging site).
3. The Tungabhadra River	Madhawaram bridge site.
4. (a) The Vedavathy River near	Bhariavanithippa.
(b) The Vedavathy River near	Rampur (at present a CW & PC site)
5. The Kagna River near	Jiwargi
6. The Chikkahagari River near	Amkundi Bridge or Aqueduct site on High Level Canal.

The location of these stations may be changed from time to time as the river channels and flow conditions of the rivers may require. The river gauging at Deosugar, Yadgir, and Rampur will be continued to be done by the CW & PC as at present, the States bearing the cost as being done now. The river gauging at Madhawaram, Bhairanithippa, Jiwargi and Amkundi Bridge will be done jointly by the States of Karnataka and Andhra Pradesh or by the CW & PC if willing to do so, and the cost will be shared between all the three States equally.

B. Inter-State streams between Maharashtra and Karnataka :

1. The Krishna river near	Shirti (at present a CW & PC gauging site)
2. The Bhima river near	Takali (at present a CW & PC gauging site),

3. The Ghataprabha river near	Daddi
4. The Vedganga river near	Bastawad
5. The Dudhganga river near	Kagal at the bridge site on IV Highway.
6. The Panchaganga river near	Tewad (at present a CW & PC gauging site)
7. The Agrani river near	Pendagaon
8. The Hiranyakeshi river near	Gotur weir
9. The Bornala river near	Konkangaon
10. The Borinala near	Diksanga site or Railway bridge near Rudewadi
11. The Doddahalla near	Shivadhan
12. The Benithora river near	Diggi

The location of the said stations may be changed from time to time as the river channels and water flow conditions of the rivers may require.

The river gauging at Shirti, Takali and Terwad will be continued to be done by the CW & PC as at present, the States bearing the cost [as being done now. The river gauging at Daddi, Bastawad, Kagal, Pendagaon, Gotur, Kankangaon, Diksanga or Rudewadi, Shivadhan, and Diggi will be done jointly by the States of Maharashtra and Karnataka or the CW & PC if willing to do so, and the cost of gauging at these sites will be shared between all the three States equally.

C. CW & PC Gauging Sites :

In addition to the CW & PC gauging sites as mentioned in A and B above, the CW & PC will continue to do the river gauging as at present at the following sites, the cost being borne by the three States as at present.

(a) On the Krishna river at :
- (1) Karad (in Maharashtra)
- (2) Almatti (in Karnataka)
- (3) Dhannur (in Karnataka)
- (4) Yaparala (in Andhra Pradesh)
- (5) Moravakonda (in Andhra Pradesh)
- (6) Srisailam (in Andhra Pradesh)
- (7) Damerapadu (in Andhra Pradesh)
- (8) Wadenpalli (in Andhra Pradesh)
- (9) Vijayawada (in Andhra Pradesh)

(b) On the Koyna river at
- (10) Koyna dam (Maharashtra)
- (11) Warunji (-do-)

(c) On the Warna river at
- (12) Samdoli (Maharashtra)

(d) On the Dudhganga river at
- (13) Sadalgi (Maharashtra)

(e) On the Ghaatprabha river at
- (14) Dhupdal weir (in Karnataka)
- (15) Bagalkot (-do-)

(f) On the Malaprabha river at
- (16) Haranur (in Karnataka)

(g) On the Bhima river at
- (17) Dhond (in Maharashtra)
- (18) Narsingpur (-do-)

(h) On the Nira river at
- (19) Sarati (in Maharashtra)

(i) On the Sina river at
- (20) Wadakbal (in Maharashtra)

(j) On the Tungabhadra river at
- (21) Harlahalli (in Karnataka)
- (22) Manuru (-do-)
- (23) Mantralayam (-do-)
- (24) Banapuram (in Andhra Pradesh)

(k) On the Tunga river at
- (25) Shimoga (in Karnataka)

(l) On the Bhadra river at
- (26) Lakkavali (in Karnataka)

(m) On the Varada river at
- (27) Marol (in Karnataka)

(n) On the Musi river at
- (28) Damercherla (in Andhra Pradesh)

(o) On the Palleru river at
- (29) Palleru bridge (in Andhra Pradesh)

(p) On the Munneru river at
- (30) Keesra (in Andhra Pradesh)

The Final Order set forth in Chapter XVI of the Original Report Vol. II pages 226-233 modified in accordance with the explanations given by the Tribunal under section 5(3) of the Inter-State Water Disputes Act, 1956 is given below :

Final Order of Tribunal

The Tribunal hereby passes the following order :

Clause I : This Order shall come into operation on the date of the publication of the decision of this Tribunal in the Official Gazette under section 6 of the Inter-State Water Disputes Act, 1956.

Clause II : The Tribunal hereby declares that the States of Maharashtra, Karnataka and Andhra Pradesh will be free to make use of underground water within their respective State territories in the Krishna river basin.

This declaration shall not be taken to alter in any way the rights, if any, under the law for the time being in force of private individuals, bodies or authorities.

Use of underground water by any shall not be reckoned as use of the water of the river Krishna.

Clause III : The Tribunal hereby determines that,

for the purpose of this case, the 75 per cent dependable, flow of the river Krishna upto Vijayawada is 2060 T.M.C. is available for distribution between the States of Maharashtra, Karnataka and Andhra Pradesh.

The Tribunal further considers that additional quantities of water as mentioned in sub-clauses A(ii), A(iii), A(iv), B(ii), B(iii), B(iv), C(ii), C(iii), and C(iv) of Clause V will be added to the 75 per cent dependable flow of the river Krishna up to Vijayawada on account of return flows and will be available for distribution between the States of Maharashtra, Karnataka, and Andhra Pradesh.

Clause IV : The Tribunal hereby orders that the waters of the river Krishna be allocated to the three States of Maharashtra, Karnataka and Andhra Pradesh for their beneficial use to the extent provided in Clause V and subject to such conditions and restrictions as are mentioned hereinafter.

Clause V: (A) (i) The State of Maharashtra shall not use in any water year more than the quantity of water of the river Krishna specified hereunder :

As from the water year commencing on the 1st June next after the date of publication of the decision of the Tribunal in the Official Gazette up to the water year 1982-83.

(ii) as from the water year 1983-84 upto the water year 1989-90.—560 T.M.C. plus
a quantity of water equivalent to 10 per cent of the excess of the average of annual utilisation for irrigation in the Krishna river basin during the water years 1975-76, 1976-77 and 1977-78 from its own projects using 3 T.M.C. or more annually over the utilisations for such irrigation in the water year 1968-69 from such projects.

(iii) as from the water year 1990-91 up to the water year 1997-98—560 T.M.C. plus
a quantity of water equivalent to 10 per cent of the excess of the average of the annual utilisations for irrigation in the Krishna river basin during the water years 1982-83, 1983-84 and 1984-85 from its own projects using 3 T.M.C. or more annually over the utilisations for such irrigation in the water year 1968-69 from such projects.

(iv) as from the water year 1998-99 onwards .
—560 T.M C. plus.
a quantity of water equivalent to 10 per cent of the excess of the average of the annual utilisations for irrigation in the Krishna river basin during the water years 1990-91, 1991-92 and 1992-93 from its own projects using 3 T.M.C. or more annually over the utilisations for such irrigation in the water year 1968-69 from such projects.

(B) The State of Karnataka shall not use in any water year more than the quantity of water of the river Krishna specified hereunder :

(i) as from the water year commencing on the 1st June next after the date of the publication of the decision of the Tribunal in the Official Gazette up to the water year 1982-83.—700 T.M.C.

(ii) as from the water year 1983-84 up to the water year 1989-90.—700 T.M.C.
a quantity of water equivalent to 10 per cent of the excess of the average of the annual utilisations for irrigation in the Krishna river basin during the water years 1975-76, 1976-77 and 1977-78 from its own projects using 3 T.M.C. or more annually over the utilisations for such irrigation in the water year 1997-98
—700 T.M.C. plus
a quantity of water equivalent to 10 per cent of the excess of the average of the annual utilisations for irrigation of the annual utilisations for irrigation in the Krishna river basin during the water years 1982-83, 1983-84 and 1984-85 from its own projects using 3 T.M.C. or more annually over the utilisation for such irrigation in the water year 1968-69 from such projects.

(iv) As from the water year 1998-99 onwards.
—700 T.M.C. plus
a quantity of water equivalent to 10 per cent of the excess of the average of the annual utilisations in the Krishna river basin during the water years 1990-91, 1991-92 and 1992-93 from its own projects using 3 T.M.C. or more annually over the utilisation for such irrigation in the water year 1968-69 from such projects.

(C) The State of Andhra Pradesh will be at liberty to use in any water year the remaining water that may be flowing in the river Krishna but thereby it shall not acquire any right, whatsoever, to use in any water year water of the river Krishna in excess of the quantity specified hereunder :

(i) As from the water year commencing on the 1st June next after the date of the publication of the decision of the Tribunal in the Official Gazette up to the water year 1982-83.—800 T.M.C.

(ii) As from the water year 1983-84 up to the water year 1989-90.—800 T.M.C. plus
a quantity of water equivalent to 10 per cent of the excess of the average of the annual utilisations for irrigations in the Krishna river basin during the water years 1975-76, 1976-77 and 1977-78 from its own projects using 3 T.M.C. or more annually over the utilisations for such irrigation in the water year 1968-69 from such projects.

(iii) As from the water year 1990-91 up to the water year 1997-98.—800 T.M.C. plus
a quantity of water equivalent to 10 per cent of the excess of the average of the annual utilisations for irrigation in the Krishna river basin during the water years 1982-83, 1983-84 and 1984-85 from its own projects

using 3 T.M.C. or more annually over the utilisations for such irrigation in the water year 1968-69 from such projects.

(iv) As from the water year 1998-99 onwards —800 T.M.C. plus a quantity of water equivalent to 10 per cent of the excess of the average of the annual utilisations for irrigation in the Krishna river basin during the water years 1990-91, 1991-92 and 1992-93 from its own projects using 3 T.M.C or more annually over the utilisations for such irrigation in the water year 1968-69 from such projects.

(D) For the limited purpose of this clause, it is declared that—

(i) the utilisations for irrigations in the Krishna river basin in the water year 1968-69 from projects using 3 T.M.C. or more annually were as follows :

From projects of the State of Maharashtra—61.45 T.M.C.

From projects of the State of Karnataka—176.05 T.M.C.

From projects of the State of Andhra Pradesh—170.00 T.M.C.

(ii) annual utilisations for irrigations in Krishna river basin in each water year after this order comes into operation from the projects of any State using 3 T.M.C. or more annually shall be computed on the basis of the records prepared and maintained by that State under clause XIII.

(iii) evaporation losses from reservoirs of Projects using 3 T.M.C. or more annually shall be excluded in computing the 10 per cent figure of the average annual utilisations mentioned in sub-clauses A (ii), A (iii), A (iv), B (ii), B (iii), B (iv), C (ii), C (iii), and C (iv) of this clause.

Clause VI : Beneficial use shall include any use made by any State of the waters of the river Krishna for domestic, municipal, irrigation, industrial, production of power, navigation, pisciculture, wild life protection and recreation purposes.

Clause VII : (A). Except as provided hereunder a use shall be measured by the extent of depletion of the waters of the river Krishna in any manner whatsoever including losses of water by evaporation and other natural causes from man-made reservoirs and other works without deducting in the case of use for irrigation the quantity of water that may return after such use to the river.

The water stored in any reservoir across any stream of the Krishna river system shall not of itself be reckoned as depletion of the water of the stream except to the extent of the losses of water from evaporation and other natural causes from such reservoir. The water diverted from such reservoir by any State for its own use in any water year shall be reckoned as use by that State in that water year.

The uses mentioned in column No. 1 below shall be measured in the manner indicated in column No. 2

Use	Measurement
Domestic and Municipal water supply.	By 20 per cent of the quantity of water diverted or lifted from the river or any of its tributaries or from any reservoir, storage or canal.
Industrial use	By 2.5 per cent of the quantity of water diverted or lifted from the river or any of its tributaries or from any reservoir, storage or canal

(B) Diversion of the waters of the river Krishna by one State for the benefit of another State shall be treated as diversion by the State for whose benefit the diversion is made.

Clause VIII. (A) If in any water year any state is not able to use any portion of the water allocated to it during that year on account of the non-development of its projects or damage to any of its projects or does not use it for any reason whatsoever, that State will rot be entitled to claim the unutilised water in any subsequent water year

(B) Failure of any State to make use of any portion of the water allocated to it during any water year shall not constitute forefeiture or abandonment of its share of water in any subsequent water year nor shall it increase the share of any other State in any subsequent water year even if such State may have used such water.

Clause IX. As from the 1st June next after the date of the publication of the decision of the Tribunal in the official Gazette.

(A) Out of water allocated to it, the State of Maharashtra shall not use in any water year :

(i) more than 7 T.M.C. from the Ghataprabha (K-3) sub-basin.

(ii) more than the quantity of water specified hereunder from the main stream of the river Bhima.

(a) as from the water year commencing on the 1st June next after the date of the publication of the decision of the Tribunal in the Official Gazette up to the water year 1989-90—90 T.M.C.

(b) as from the water year 1990-91—95 T.M.C.

(B) out of the water allocated to it, the State of Karnataka shall not use in any water year :

(i) more than the quantity of water specified hereunder from the Tungabhadra (K-8) sub-basin.

(a) as from the water year commencing on the 1st June next after the date of the publication of the decision of the Tribunal in the Official Gazette up to the water year 1982-83.—295 T.M.C.

(b) as from the water year 1983-84 up to the water year 1989-90.—295 T.M.C. plus

a quantity of water equivalent to seven and a half per cent of the excess of the average of the annual utilisations for irrigation in the Krishna river basin during the water year 1975-76, 1976-77 and 1977-78 from its own projects using 3 T.M.C. or more annually over the utilisations for such irrigation the water year 1968-69 from such projects

(c) as from the water year 1990-91 up to the water year 1997-98.—295 T.M.C. plus

a quantity of water equivalent to 7 and a half per cent of the excess of the average of the annual utilisations for irrigation in the Krishna river basin during the water years 1982-83, 1983-84 and 1984-85 from its own projects using 3 T.M.C. or more annually over the utilisations for such irrigation in the water year 1968-69 from such projects.

(d) as from the water year 1998-99 onwards—295 T.M.C. plus

a quantity of water equivalent to seven and a half per cent of the excess of the average of the annual utilisations for irrigation in the Krishna river basin during the water years 1990-91, 1991-92 and 1992-93 from its own projects using 3 T.M.C. or more annually over the utilisations for such irrigation in the water year 1968-69 from such projects. For the limited purpose of this Sub-clause, it is declared that:

the utilisations for irrigation in the Krishna river basin in the water year 1968-69 from projects of the State of Karnataka using 3 T.M.C. or more annually shall be taken to be 176·05 T.M.C.;

annual utilisations for irrigation in the Krishna river basin in each water year after this order comes into operation from the projects of the State of Karnataka using 3 T.M.C. or more annually shall be computed on the basis of the records prepared and maintained by that state under clause XIII.

evaporation losses from reservoirs of projects using 3 T.M.C. or more annually shall be excluded in computing the seven and a half per cent figure of the average annual utilisations mentioned above.

(ii) more than 42 T.M.C. from the Vedavathi (K-9) sub-basin, and

(iii) more than 15 T.M.C. from the main stream of the river Bhima.

(C) Out of the water allocated to it, the State of Andhra Pradesh shall not use in any water year :

(i) more than 127.5 T.M.C. from the Tungabhadra (K-8) sub-basin and more than 12.5 T.M.C. from the Vedavathi (K-9) sub-basin.

(ii) more than 6 T.M.C. from the catchment of the river Kagna in the State of Andhra Pradesh.

(D) (i) The uses mentioned in sub-clauses (A), (B) and (C) aforesaid include evaporation losses,

(ii) The use mentioned in sub-clauses (C)(i) does not include use of the water flowing from the Tungabhadra into the river Krishna.

(E) (i) The following directions shall be observed for the use of the water available for utilisation in the Tungabhadra Dam in a water year :

(a) The water available for utilisation in a water year in the Tungabhadra Dam shall be so utilised that the demands of water for the following projects to the extent mentioned below may be met :

(i) Tungabhadra Right Bank Low level canal.—52.00 T.M.C.

water available for Tungabhadra Right Bank low level canal shall be shared by the States of Karnataka and Andhra Pradesh in the following proportion :

State of Karnataka	22.50
State of Andhra Pradesh	29.50

(ii) Tungabhadra Right Bank Highlevel canal—Stages I and II—50.00 T.M.C

water available for Tungabhadra Right Bank High level canal shall be shared by the States of Karnataka and Andhra Pradesh in the following proportions :

State of Karnataka	17.50
State of Andhra Pradesh	32.50

(iii) Tungabhadra Left Bank low level and high level canals—102.00 T.M.C.

(iv) Raya and Basavanna channels of the State of Karnataka—7.00 T.M.C.

(v) Assistance by way of regulated discharges to Vijayanagar channels other than Raya and Basavanna channels of the State of Karnataka.

(vi) Assistance by way of regulated discharges to the Rajolibunda Diversion Scheme for use by the State of Karnataka and Andhra Pradesh in the proportion mentioned in clause XI (c) —7.00 T.M.C.

(vii) Assistance by way of regulated discharges to the Kurnool-Cuddapah canal of the State of Andhra Pradesh—10.00 T.M.C.

230.00 T.M.C.

The utilisations of the projects mentioned in Sub-clauses (a) (i), (ii) and (iii) above include the evaporation losses in the Tungabhadra Dam which will be shared in accordance with clause XI (D).

(b) If, in any water year, water available for utilisation in the Tungabhadra Dam is less than the total quantity of water required for all the projects as mentioned above, the deficiency shall be shared by all the projects proportionately. The proportions shall be worked out after excluding the evaporation losses.

(c) If, in any water year, water available for utilisation is more than the total quantity of water required for all the projects as mentioned above, the requirements for all the projects for the month of June in the succeeding water year as estimated by the Tungabhadra Board or any authority established in its place shall be kept in reserve and the State of Karnataka shall have the right to utilise the remaining water in excess of such reserve in the Tungabhadra Dam for its projects mentioned in sub-clauses (a)(i), (ii) and (iii) above drawing water from that dam even though thereby it may cross in any water year the limit on the utilisation of water from Tungabhadra (K-8) sub-basin placed under clause IX(B) of the final order but in no case such utilisation shall exceed 320 T.M.C.

(d) the balance water, if any, shall be kept stored in the dam for use in the next year.

(2) The working tables for the utilisation of the water in the Tungabhadra Dam shall be prepared as hithertofore by the Tungabhadra Board or any other authority established in its place so as to enable the States of Karnataka and Andhra Pradesh to utilise the water available for utilisation in the Tungabhadra Dam as aforesaid.

(3) If, in any water year either of the two States of Karnataka and Andhra Pradesh find it expedient to divert the water available to it in the Tungabhadra Dam for any one of its projects to any other of its project or projects mentioned above for use therein, it may give notice thereof to the Tungabhadra Board or any other authority established in its place and the said Board or authority may, if it is feasible to do so, prepare or modify the working table accordingly.

(4) T e States of Karnataka and Andhra Pradesh may use the water available in the Tungabhadra Dam in accordance with the aforesaid provisions and nothing contained in clause V shall be construed as overriding the provisions of clause IX(E) in the matter of utilisation of the water available in the Tungabhadra Dam nor shall anything contained in clause IX(E) be construed as enlarging the total allocation to the State of Karnataka or as enlarging the limit of acquisition of any right by the State of Andhra Pradesh in the waters of the river Krishna.

(5) The States of Karnataka and Andhra Pradesh may by agreement, without reference to the State of Maharashtra, alter or modify any of the provisions for the utilisation of the water available in the Tungabhadra Dam mentioned above in any manner.

Clause X. (i) The State of Maharashtra shall not out of the water allocated to it divert or permit the diversion of more than 67.5 T.M.C. of water outside the Krishna river basin in any water year from the river supplies in the upper-Krishna (K-1) sub-basin for the Koyna Hydel project or any other project.

Provided that the State of Maharashtra will be at liberty to divert outside the Krishna river basin for the Koyna Hydel Project water to the extent of 97 T.M.C. annually during the next period of 5 years commencing on the 1st June, 1984 and water to the extent of 78 T.M.C. annually during the next succeeding period of 5 years commencing on the 1st June, 1989.

(2) The State of Maharashtra shall not out of the water allocated to it divert or permit diversion outside the Krishna river basin from the river supplies in the upper Bhima (K-5) sub-basin for the projects collectively known as the Tata Hydel Works or any other project of more than 54.5 T.M.C. annually in any one water year and more than 213 T.M.C. in any period of five consecutive water years commencing on the 1st June, 1974.

(3) Except to the extent mentioned above, the State of Maharashtra shall not divert or permit diversion of any water out of the Krishna river basin.

Clause XI (A). This order will supersede—

(i) the agreement of 1892 between Madras and Mysore so far as it related to the Krishna system;

(ii) the agreement of 1933 between Madras and Mysore so far as it related to the Krishna river system;

(iii) the agreement of June, 1944 between Madras and Hyderabad;

(iv) the agreement of July, 1944 between Madras and Mysore so far as it is related to the Krishna river system;

(v) the supplemental agreement of December, 1945 among Madras, Mysore and Hyderabad;

(vi) the supplemental agreement of 1946 among Madras, Mysore and Hyderabad.

Copies of the aforesaid agreements are appended to the Report of the Tribunal.

(B) The regulations set forth in Annexure 'A' to this order regarding protection to the irrigation works in the respective territories of the States of Karnataka and Andhra Pradesh in the Vedavathy sub-basin be observed and carried out.

(C) The benefits of utilisations under the Rajolibunda Diversion Scheme be shared between the States of Karnataka and Andhra Pradesh as mentioned herein below :—

Karnataka—1.2 T.M.C.

Andhra Pradesh—15.9 T.M.C.

(D) The reservoir loss of Tungabhadra reservoir shall be shared equally by the works of the State of Karnataka on the left side and the works on the right side of the reservoir. The half share of the right side in the reservoir loss shall be shared by the States of Andhra Pradesh and Karnataka in the ratio of 5.5 to 3.5.

Clause XII. The regulations set forth in Annexure

'B' to this order regarding gauging and gauging sites in the Krishna river system be observed and carried out.

Clause XIII (A). Each State shall prepare and maintain annually for each water year complete detailed and accurate records of—

(a) annual water diversions outside the Krishna river basin.

(b) annual uses for irrigation from works using less than 1 T.M.C. annually

(c) annual uses for irrigation from all other projects and works.

(d) annual uses for domestic and municipal water supply.

(e) annual uses for industrial purposes.

(f) annual uses for irrigation within the Krishna river basin from projects using 3 T.M.C. or more annually.

(g) areas irrigated and duties adopted for irrigation from irrigation works using less than 1 T.M.C. annually.

(h) estimated annual evaporation losses from reservoirs and storages using 1 T.M.C. or more annually.

(i) formula used and co-efficient adopted for measuring discharges at project sites.

Each State shall send annually to the other States a summary abstract of the said records.

The said records shall be open to inspection of the other States through their accredited representatives at all reasonable times and at a reasonable place or places.

(B) The records of gauging mentioned in Annexure 'B' to this order shall be open to inspection of all the States through their accredited representatives at all reasonable times and at a reasonable place or places.

Clause XIV (A). At any time after the 31st May, 2000, this order may be reviewed or revised by a competent authority or Tribunal, but such review or revision shall not as far as possible distuıb any utilisation that may have been undertaken by any State within the limits of the allocation made to it under the foregoing clauses.

(B) In the event of the augmentation of the waters of the river Krishna by the diversion of the waters of any other river, no State shall be debarred from claiming before any authority or Tribunal even before the 31st May, 2000 that it is entitled to a greater share in the waters of the river Krishna on account of such augmentation nor shall any State be debarred from disputing such claim.

Clause XV. Nothing in the order of this Tribunal shall impair the right or power or authority of any State to regulate within its boundaries the use of water or to enjoy the benefit of waters within the State in a manner not inconsistent with the order of this Tribunal.

Clause XVI. In this order :

(a) Use of the water of the river Krishna by any person or entity of any nature whatsoever with the territories of a State shall be reckoned as used by that State.

(b) The expression "water year" shall mean the year commencing on 1st June and ending on 31st May.

(c) The expression "Krishna river" includes the main stream of the Krishna river, all its tributaries and all other streams contributing water directly or indirectly to the Krishna river.

(d) The expression "T.M.C." means thousand million cubic feet of water.

Clause XVII. Nothing contained herein shall prevent the alteration, amendment or modification of all or any of the foregoing clauses by agreement between the parties or by legislation by Parliament.

Clause XVIII (A). The Government of Maharashtra, Karnataka and Andhra Pradesh shall bear their own costs of appearing before the tribunal. The expenses of the Tribunal shall be borne and paid by the Governments of Maharashtra, Karnataka and Andhra Pradesh in equal shares. These directions relate to the reference under Section 5(1) of the Inter-State water Disputes Act, 1956.

(B) The Government of India and the Governments of Maharashtra, Karnataka and Andhra Pradesh shall bear their own costs of appearing before the Tribunal in the references under Section 5 (3) of the said Act. The expenses of the Tribunal in respect of the aforesaid references shall be borne and paid by the Governments of Maharashtra, Karnataka and Andhra Pradesh in equal shares.

POWER ECONOMY COMMITTEE, 1969—REPORT

Delhi, Manager of Publications, 1972. 89p.

Chairman : Shri K. L. Vij.

Members : Shri H.V. Narayana Rao; Shri Ipe Mathai succeeded by Shri P.P. Gangadharan; Shri B.N. Ojha; Shri K.B. Rao; Shri K.M. Chinnappa; Shri M.W. Goklany; Dr. K. Venugopal; Shri B.V. Deshmukh; Shri M.N. Chakravarti.

Member-Secretary : Shri S.N. Vinze.

APPOINTMENT

Under Section 18 of the Electrical (Supply) Act, 1948, the State Electricity Boards are charged with the general duty of promoting the co-ordinated development of the generation, supply and distribution of electricity within the State in the most efficient and economical manner. Power demand has outstripped its supply in the country and has been rising despite large scale technological development.

In order to efficiently utilise the limited resources of the country to take up required schemes for generation, transmission and distribution of power which are largely capital intensive in nature, it is necessary to implement measures for bringing down costs of power development. This would require a detailed review of measures taken by Government to ensure utmost expediency in the construction of power projects, better utilisation of existing generating facilities, planning of future schemes to utilise the most economic energy sources in each region and reduction in transmission losses.

Thus the Government of India, Ministry of Irrigation and Power appointed the Power Economy Committee vide its Resolution No. EL. I. 32(84)/68 dated May, 27, 1969.

TERMS OF REFERENCE

(i) To review the pattern of utilisation of available plant capacity during the past 5 years and their operational efficiency and fuel consumption, to consider the scope of improving economy in power generation together with specific measure for attaining them;

(ii) A review of economies of power generation from different sources, hydro, thermal and nuclear sources under prevailing conditions and expected future trends to indicate the factors which must prevail in the choice of schemes for expansion of generation and supply in each region of the country in future;

(iii) To review the conditions of power supply including reliability, voltage fluctuations and the extent of transmission losses, to be followed by specific suggestions to improve the conditions of supply and reduce transmission losses to the minimum extent possible;

(iv) To review the causes of delay in the execution of the power projects, to suggest measures for improving the manner of implementation of power projects and reducing construction periods;

(v) To review and examine the technical and economical aspects of rural electrification, particularly with a view to enable the State Electricity Boards and Electricity Authorities to undertake a massive programme of rural electrification and making electricity available at an economical rate.

CONTENTS

Appointment of Committee and Terms of Reference; Introduction; Cost of Electric Power; Energy Resources and Utilisation; Planning for Future; Regional Operation of Power Systems; Inter-Regional and Inter-State Exchanges of Power; Transmission and Distribution Losses; Delays in Construction of Projects; Hydro-Electric Power Stations—Utilisation and Availability of Plants; Thermal Power Stations—Utilisation and Availability of Plants; Selection of Next Higher Steam Generating Unit Sizes; Nuclear Power Stations—Scope, Operations and Costs; Rural Electrification; Research and Development; Summary of Conclusions and Recommendations.

RECOMMENDATIONS

Cost of Electric Power

1. During the last six years the cost of electric energy has, generally, been rising. If the element of increase in the cost of energy owing to unrealistically low older rates is discounted, the increase in the cost of energy is substantially less than the general rise of price levels in the country.

2. In some countries like U.S.A. and Canada the cost of electricity has been decreasing due to economies secured by operation on increasingly larger scale and economies due to technological advances. In order to keep the cost of power supply as low as possible, India also has to plan, construct and operate the power systems in the economic manner.

Plant Availability And Utilisation

3. There is an urgent need to improve power plant availability and utilisation. For this itegrated operation of the power systems in every region as well as improvement in availability of thermal power plants are necessary.

4. Modern methods of scientific management, particularly operation analysis should be introduced immediately and utilised increasingly for improving the quality of preventive maintenance and reducing the plant outage time for maintenance.

5. Separate technical cells for quality control in operation and maintenance, improving fuel efficiency etc., should be set up in each organisation directly under the Chief Engineer and in the case of Electricity Boards directly under Technical Members.

6. Continuous monitoring of the plant availability (including partial availability) should be introduced immediately.

7. There should be a system of studying the plant availability, causes of outages and statistical analysis of availability outages on a nationwide basis. This may be done through Central Board of Irrigation and Power. The system evolved by Edison Electric Institute of U.S.A. may be adopted for the purpose with certain modifications.

8. A system on voluntary reporting in respect of technical problems of equipment failures, loss of efficiency and operating difficulties should be instituted immediately. The systems already developed in India as well as in U.K. and U.S.A. should be studied and common modern system of reporting and analysis should be evolved, for all-India application. The data collection may be at the level of individual systems or regions, but the analysis of incident and sharing of this valuable technical experience should be on an all-India basis. This should be organised through the Central Water and Power Commission.

If the above system of voluntary reporting of problems does not work satisfactorily, statutory regulations making compilation and supply of such information obligatory should be made.

Hydro-electric Power Stations

9. Each Hydro-electric Project should be designed for flexibility of operation and the capability to assist optimisation of power system performance should be built into it.

10. All new projects should permit (i) substantial additions to installed capacity for enabling low load factor operation and (ii) addition of governing and excitation equipment for remote monitoring and control and better system of performance.

11. Design capability for planning engineering and designing of hydro-electric projects need to be built up in a big way.

12. Each hydro-electric power station must be operated to utilise fully the energy potential available at the site from year to year and season to season.

13. Periodical expert inspection and preventive maintenance must be arranged for all the different components of hydro-electric projects.

14. Every effort must be made to maintain the instrumentation, control, protection and alarm devices in the hydro-power stations fully operative at all times.

15. Communication facilities between different portions of hydro-electric project should be watched and improved wherever necessary from time to time.

16. In all power stations, special facilities as well as equipment and tolls and tackles required for efficient and rapid maintenance operations should be kept available.

17. The maintenance and overhaul of hydro-electric plants should be carefully scheduled to ensure full plants availability and utilisation.

18. Projects older than about 20 years should be reviewed from time to time to see how the benefits from these could be improved by modernisation.

19. The performance of hydro-electric plant and the water conductor system etc. should be checked every 2-3 years by index methods. The necessary calibration for the index methods should be provided during the initial commissioning tests.

20. A service organisation for the safety of water storage structures should be set up immediately. It should preferably cover water conveyance structures as well, in the case of hydro-electric works.

Steam Power Stations

Efficiency of Energy Generation : 21. The causes of decrease in efficiency with increase in energy generation where occurring should be investigated.

22. There is a need for improvement in efficiency of operation and maintenance of thermal power plants.

23. Studies should be undertaken to see if the power station listed in Section 6, of the Rport of Study Group No. 1 could not be backed down and the energy requirements supplied from higher efficiency plants in the region.

24. Concerted efforts should be made to improve the efficiencies of the plants listed in Section 6 of the Rport of Study Group No. 1 or to reduce their energy generation in favour of generation at higher efficiency plants in the region.

Coal and Washery By-product Prices : 25. Pit head coal prices need to be rationalised on the basis of heat content of the coals.

26. Long-term coal contracts should be drawn up on the basis of standard form to be developed by the Regional Electricity Boards. These should cover the question of prices as well as the quality of the fuel.

27. The Energy Survey Committee of India which submitted its report in 1965 had considered the washery by-products as zero cost fuels for planning purposes. There is, therefore, a clear case for a lower price for these. This can be worked out taking into account the loss of efficiency, plant availability and plant capability in power stations using such fuels. For middlings having ash content less than 32 per cent, it may be reasonable to fix the price at a rate equivalent to that for coal of the same heat value less Rs. 2·5 per tonne.

28. In order to improve the operation of the thermal generating units it is considered that the ash content of the fuel burnt in the boilers should not exceed 32 per cent. For this purpose blending will be required to be done when either coal or washery by-products with ash content of more than 32 per cent have to be utilised, When, therefore, washery by-products with ash content of more than 32 per cent are supplied by the washeries further necessary adjustments in price will need to be made to cover the expenses on account of blending arrangements.

29. It is also recommended that the cess on middlings by-products should be waived.

Utilisation of By-products from Coal Washeries : 30. The working of existing coal washeries should be modified to reduce the ash content to 32 per cent and also to ensure removal of stones and other abrasive material from the by-products supplied to the power stations as fuel. A practical time schedule should be drawn up for this immediately. Studies and designs for the additional equipment and any changes required in the process for the above purpose should be started immediately jointly by National Coal Development Corporation, Hindustan Steel Ltd, Central Fuel Research Institute etc.

31. The future coal washeries should be 3 stage ones and the ash content of the middlings should be restricted to 32 per cent, and adequate arrangements for removal of abrasive material should be made.

32. The factors responsible for erosion damage to the boiler plant and equipment should be identified by careful and intensive research through the Central Fuel Research Institute and other appropriate bodies. Apart from identification of these factories, this should lead to improved supply of fuels and also include design and construction of boiler plant and appurtenant equipment for minimising the maintenance outage costs.

33. Design, construction and materials in the boiler plant and its auxiliaries require considerable further work for devising ways and means of operating satisfactorily with washery by-products fuel. The existing installation should be utilised for making field trials of different new innovations or designs of equipment for this purpose.

The equipment requiring particular attention is the coal mills, I.D fans, layout and arrangements of superheater and economiser tubes, design and arrangement of burners and ash handling and disposal systems. It is recommended that indigenous boiler plant manufactures and manufacturers of appurtenant equipment should be asked to tackle this problem in collaboration with the organisations owning and operating the existing power stations.

Transportation Of Coal To Thermal Stations : 34. Considering the volume of coal traffic for individual large power stations, the time is now ripe for the introduction of new innovations such as unit trains in the matter of transport of coal by rail. A study in depth should be undertaken for this purpose immediately by the Railways jointly with the coal and power stations authorities.

Rationalisation Of Freight Structure Over Short Distance : 35. The freight structure for transport of coal by rail over short distance under 50 km should be reviewed and rationalised.

Petroleum Fuels : 36. The pricing of by-product petroleum fuels should be based on the costs of Indian crudes instead of on the basis of import parity.

37. Wherever there is possibility of obtaining supplies of petroleum, firm long-term contracts should be made between the suppliers of petroleum fuels and the power station authorities.

38. In the years to come, the by-products of refineries will mostly be required as industrial raw material. No large power stations should, therefore, be based on petroleum fuels alone, unless the petroleum authorities assure supply of petroleum on long-term contract basis, the siting of the power stations should be decided primarily on the basis of these being coal burning power stations.

39. Commitments made regarding supply of petroleum fuels to power stations should be honoured fully in future also. In case of 100 per cent petroleum fuel based power stations if petroleum fuels are not likely to be available in future, these power stations should be given a warning sufficiently in advance to enable their making alternative arrangements. The power stations should be compensated for the additional costs involved on this account.

40. Oil is essential for supporting for all pulverised fuel fired installation and its availability in adequate quantities at economic price must be ensured for such installations.

Problems of Operation and Maintenance : 41. The thermal power plant equipment should be matched closely to the type of fuel, cooling water temperature and other site conditions.

42. The working of each power plant installation should be continuously watched for removing any snag at the incipient stage and improving the operation and maintenance. Full use should be made of the experience on similar power plants in other parts of the country,

43. A number of common problems in operation of steam power stations discussed in the report of Study Group I should particularly be avoided by proper action in planning, design and operation of the plant.

Relaxation of Boiler Act Provisions : 44. The provisions of Boiler Act should be modified to permit biennial inspection of boilers instead of annual. In fact, it may be worthwhile to have a separate set of rules and regulations drawn up for large installations of modern steam power stations with unit sizes of say over 50 MW.

Ash Disposal : US. Representatives of the Electricity Supply Industry and Central Water and Power Commission should be invited to participate in formulation of regulations regarding pollution of air and water courses.

46. Intensive research and development work as well as promotional work should be undertaken for utilisation of the ash produced as by-product in the steam power stations. Organisation like Central Steam Power. Building Research Institute, Central Road Research Institute, National Building Organisation, Cement Research Institute, as well as Indian Standards Institution and Central Water and Power Commission should be brought together for devising ways and means for utilisation of the fly-ash and bottom ash.

47. Utilisation of ash should be entrusted to a non-profit corporation to be established co-operatively by the different power station authorities in each region. This corporation, financed mainly from the sale of ash, should organise the development and promotional work applied research work (in different appropriate institutes) and the work of marketing and disposal of ash from thermal power stations.

Common Problems

Staffing for Power Plants : 48. The pattern of staffing of the large power stations (Hydro-Thermal or nuclear) and their appurtenant works such as storages (hydro plants) etc. should be standardized on the basis of parameters of the generating sets, their number, type of fuel etc. The standardized patterns should be got approved from the Government as well as representatives of both Management and Labour. The scope of work and the responsibility of each person should be laid down clearly in the standardized staffing patterns.

49. The exact requirement of staff for any installation in the context of the standardized pattern mentioned above, should be specified by the designers of the installation.

50. The staff required for operation and maintenance should be sanctioned with the finalisation of the design and start of construction and in any case at least 18 months before the expected date of commissioning of the first unit. The sanctioned strength should be fully recruited at the earliest, for purposes of training on similar installations during the year preceding the commissioning of the power plant. The full sanctioned strength of the technical personnel should be in position for gaining an understanding of the plant by assisting during the acceptance and Commissioning Tests and installation of the major plant sub-assemblies.

51. A separate Generation Cadre should be instituted to ensure that adequately trained staff is available at generation stations. A system of incentives or special pay etc. should be introduced for the Generation Cadre to attract and keep suitable persons.

Training of Personnel : 52. There should be a requirement preferably statutory that the O and M staff must be qualified by proper training and experience preferably through some recognized training institutes before being given the full and independent charge of the costly and intricate modern power station equipment. A system of certification of the O and M staff similar to that in vogue in the Civil Aviation Industry could be adopted.

53. Refreshed Training Courses should be arranged for all the technical staff in a phased manner so that each person has to go through a course at the interval of 5.7 years. Even the O and M staff at the technical level should be routed through other similar systems.

54. Existing facilities for training of personnel for operation and maintenance of steam power stations are grossly inadequate.

55. Training of personnel for operation and maintenance of power stations should be the responsibility of the Regional Electricity Boards. They should assess the requirements and organise adequate training facilities including in-plant training to suit the requirements peculiar to the respective regions.

56. For the purpose of certification of competency in operation and maintenance, the Central Electricity Authority should formulate the minimum requirements on a nation-wide basis.

Instrumentation of Power Plants : 57. Special attention should be given to the adequacy of control protection and instrumentation systems in every installation. Proper operation and maintenance of these systems is of the highest importance for minimising forced outages. Well-equipped instrument laboratories should be provided for each large installation or group of installations. Special Instrumentation Cells should be manned by highly competent trained personnel who should ensure proper functioning of the instrumentation system throughout.

Documentation : 58. Details of completion drawings and reports should be available at each project, so that all changes adopted during construction are properly recorded.

59. Comprehensive manuals and instructions complete with drawings, photographs, descriptions etc. must be available for each element of power plant installations. These must cover operation, maintenance and instructions for abnormal conditions. Sufficient number of copies must be available for all concerned and these must be reviewed and brought up-to-date every year.

Manufacturing and Design Capability of Indigenous Manufacturers : 60. There is an urgent need to develop the design capability in the manufacturing units, so that the technology acquired for plant and equipment is fully utilised in a manner suiting the Indian conditions.

61. At the time of commissioning any hydro-electric project, detailed guidelines for water management, most appropriate for the project, should be laid down.

62. The high cost of plant and equipment from indigenous sources causes an undue burden on the power systems in the country. Equitable methods should be evolved for apportioning the heavy cost of acquiring new technology among the present and future projects. The cost of social benefits like new housing colonies, schooling, hospitals and other facilities need not be a charge on the cost of plant and equipment for new power stations but should be borne by respective States in which the factories are situated or by the Central Government.

Import of Spares : 63. The following should be done to streamline the procedure for import of spares for operation and maintenance of power systems and to eliminate the procedural delays and difficulties.

63.1. The clearance of applications from indigenous angle should be done by Central Water and Power Commission itself. For this purpose, the Directorate General of Technical Development should equip the Central Water and Power Commission with all the information about indigenous availability of spare parts auxiliaries etc. The Electricity Boards/Project Authorities should adopt modern methods of inventory control for dealing with their replacement of spares. In any case, the position regarding spares should be reviewed by them at least every quarter and anticipatory action taken so that the time normally required for release of foreign exchange, issue of import licence etc., does not come in the way of proper operation of the power installations or execution of projects. A special cell should be created in the Central Water and Power Commission and the concerned officer should be provided proper facilities for conveyance etc.

63.2. Where a number of identical power plants have been installed in the country, some additional emergency spares, such as a spare thrust bearing may be obtained and kept in common reserve. Such common pool of spares, financed co-operatively by the different power station authorities may go a long way in reducing the loss of energy generation due to forced outages.

63.3. The Chief Controller of Imports and Exports should give necessary facilities to the liaison Officer of the Central Water and Power Commission for expediting the cases of issue of import licence for spares. This can be done by placing an Office of the Central Water and Power Commission in the Office of the Chief Controller of Imports and Exports for carrying out liaison work. After release of foreign exchange and indigenous clearance, Regional Joint Chief Controller of Imports and Exports should be authorised to issue import licences.

63.4. Revalidation of import licences in cases on which project authorities have entered into commitments after clearance of the Directorate General of Technical Development, should be done as a matter of within a week. Any back reference by the Chief Controller of Imports and Exports should be addressed to the Central Water and Power Commission and not to the project authorities.

64. Adequate attention should be paid to the selected installation and operation of electrical equipment as discussed in Section 4 of the Report of Study Group No. 1.

Measures to Promote Integrated Development and Operation of Power Systems in India : 65. Power shortage conditions prevail today in many parts of the country. This position is likely to continue in the next few years or so and the available generating capacity would not be able to meet the anticipated load demand. It is, therefore, important to derive optimum benefits from the generating capacity available. This can be done only through integrated regional power systems. Substantial economies in the cost of power generation can also be achieved by developing well-integrated regional power grids, leading to the evolution of national power grid. There is an urgent need to devise measures which would promote development of such grids. As a first step a phased perspective plan of development of power systems leading to the National grid should be formulated.

66. Greatest economies in the cost of power production can be achieved through planning which looks far beyond the needs and requirements of small indivi-

dual systems. The planning should, therefore, be done on a regional basis and the power projects should be chosen on regional considerations and on the basis of minimum cost and the operation should be planned with a view to optimising the use of national wealth.

67. The review of existing and proposed inter-State and inter-regional transmission lines in the country has brought out that the transmission capacity has been utterly inadequate in the past to permit efficient use of resources. It has also revealed that the proposed additions up to 1973- 4 would not remedy this situation to any large extent. There is need for a complete change in the strategy of planning of inter-system tie lines and need for allocation of more investments for this purpose.

68. The transmission and distribution network has to be strengthened. There has been an imbalance in the investments in the electric power supply industry in favour of generation. The allocation of funds for transmission and distribution should be separately made and it should be ensured that these funds are not diverted for other purposes.

69. One of the main reasons for low availability and utilisation of power plants in India is lack of inter-connections and integrated operation between the small power systems obtaining in our country.

70. The capacity of the inter-State/Regional ties should be about 10 per cent of the size of the systems which are tied together so that they may take care of a load slip of at least one year which is inescapable in a developing economy like that of India.

71. A case study for the Southern Region indicates that Rs. 8.27 crores could have been saved in the fuel charge alone in 1968-69 if principles of economic generation scheduling were applied to all resources. Similar study for the anticipated operating conditions in 1973-74 also shows that savings of Rs. 8.33 crores can be achieved if coordinated generation scheduling is, therefore, essential for effecting economies and securing optimum benefits.

72. The large range planning strategy should be based on the fact that in the next 10 years or so, not only the State system should completely integrate to form regional grids, but also that the regional grids should get adequately interconnected to form a National Grid.

73. In the next 5 years, it is easy to conceive power transfers between the regions of the order of 500/700 MW over distance up to 1000 km in the interests of economic utilisation of resources. For this purpose, a higher voltage in the range of 400/500 kV would be necessary. A Study Group should be set up to evaluate the needs of the country over the next 10 to 15 years and recommend the suitable voltage level above 220 kV.

74. There are instance where integrated operation of power is not taking place though transmission capacities exist. One of the reasons for this is lack of a commercial agreement between the two systems. The tariff principles should provide the necessary incentives to both the seller and the buyer. If economy interchanges the position of seller and buyer is inter-changeable and hence the tariff structure should be reversible.

75. It is desirable to spell out all the objectives of interconnected or integrated operation in unambiguous terms in the agreements between parties should necessarily precede construction so that all issues subsequently can be judged with these criteria.

76. U.S.A. has shown that independent utilities voluntarily surrender their individual authorities to a common pool for economic advantages. Similar conditions should be created in India.

77. Central Electricity Authority should take a lead and help various systems in the country to evolve and conclude agreements based on sound operating and costing principles.

78. In order to achieve optimum utilisation of resources and at the same time ensure reliability and continuity of power supply, proper institutional and technical set-up has to be created. This function is known as system operation management.

79. In an efficient operation management, the flow of decisions and the information between the participatin organisations should be free and unrestricted to evolve a final dynamic operation policy and its execution.

80. Philosophy of interconnected operation should be evolved for each region by their technical coordination committee to ensure safety security of the regional power system and coordination. Digital computer studies should be made to evaluate future operating costs. Long range operation plans evolved should be cleared through the various policy-making bodies in each region.

81. State and Regional Local Despatch Stations (Pool Centres) should be set up at a very early date to enable integrated operation.

82. In operational planning, efforts should be made to optimise and conserve fossil fuel resources in the larger interests of the country and increase the utilisation of available nuclear and hydro resources.

83. In operational planning, a number of major and far reaching policy decisions are required to be taken. This function should be performed by the Regional Electricity Boards comprising representatives of various constituents of the regions having major generating capacities at the level of Chairman. This Board should be assisted by a full time Member-Secretary and by a Technical Co-ordination Committee

and a number of groups consisting of specialists in various fields.

84. Execution of the operational plans and targets laid down by the operating Committee should be executed in day-to-day operations by multi-tier load despatch organisations.

85. Load Despatch Stations should be equipped with the required communication facilities, instrumentation, controls inter-connection manuals, safety manuals, operational planning computer etc. There is need to provide effective inter-system coordination and to provide the various load despatch centres with adequate modern tools for monitoring and control of power system.

Reliability of Power Supply : 86 The reliability of power supply can be improved by careful application of the well-known principles of power system planning, operation and maintenance. Due to rapid development in power supply facilities, the standards of operation and maintenance have tended to be lowered in many systems. This tendency must be reversed by vigorous administrative measures.

87. There should be sufficient generation reserve, adequate transmission capacity and protection of various equipment and transmission lines should be suitably coordinated.

88. A well-organised load despatch centre is necessary for ensuring high system reliability. Restoration of a system to normalcy after a disturbance requires centralised decision-making mechanism.

89. There should be (a) written operating instructions for all elements in the system for the operating staff covering switching procedures and other precautions; (b) adequate number of recording instruments at all major nodal points; and (c) disturbance recorders which can record a sufficient number of quantities simultaneously etc.

90. On long transmission lines, on-line fault locating equipment which can indicate faulty sections within a few seconds and save patrolling time should be provided.

91. Frequency of trippings can be reduced by adopting the practice of periodic inspection of lines and inspection after every trip-out. Comprehensive preventive maintenance procedures should be drafted and issued for the guidance of the maintenance staff.

92. All disturbances on the distribution network should also be fully reported and properly analysed and classified. It is only by keeping good records and carrying out an analysis of the causes that steps to improve reliability can be devised continuously and economically.

93. Spares and special T & P and expert team for quick restoration of normalcy in each part of the power system, i.e. different types of generating plant, substations, transmission and distribution.

94. O & M procedures and difficulties should be reviewed by expert teams periodically.

Transmission and Distribution Losses : 95. The losses in the transmission and distribution systems in India are on the high side and have shown a tendency to increase further. Optimum performance of the power system is necessary for achieving economy. The principal lines of action are indicated below —

(i) Improvements in the transmission and distribution system designs by :

(a) Selection of transformers with reference to expected load cycle so as to obtain minimum total fixed and variable losses.

(b) Use of flow iron loss transformers, particularly for rural areas and areas of low load factor.

(c) Reduction in the number of power transformation stages.

(d) Improvement of power factor—installation of capacitors etc. at appropriate locations.

(e) Selection of appropriate sizes of low tension feeders keeping in view their lengths and load required to be carried.

(ii) Introduction of proper instrumentation and information collection system at all levels for monitoring of system performance.

(iii) Integrated operation of power systems including reactive scheduling.

(iv) Elimination of theft of energy.

(v) Elimination of miscellaneous losses by improved operation and maintenance.

(vi) Continuous monitoring of system performance and introduction of corrective action at the divisional level.

Factories in the Choice of Power Generation Schemes : 96. In 1967 the effective consumption of energy in India was nearly 600 kg. of coal equivalent per head against 9830 in U.S.A., 8090 in Canada, 3960 in U.S.S.R., 2270 in Japan and the total world average of 1640. The per capita energy consumption will have to be considerably increased to better the economic lot of the people. In view of the lack of adequate oil and gas resources, the country would have to rely on electricity more and more to reach a reasonable figure of energy consumption. In this context, the nuclear energy has an important role in our future energy economy.

97. Under the existing conditions in the country, the hydel schemes costitute the most economic sources of electricity production. The estimated cost of power from the Atomic Power Stations based on heavy water reactor technology under construction indicate that atomic power would be competitive with prevailing cost of power from thermal stations located remote from

the collieries. Conventional thermal stations based on coal located away from the collieries (600 Kms) involve the highest cost of energy generation in the country. Apart from their intrinsic economy, hydro schemes designed for complementary peaking with thermal/nuclear stations enable better utilisation of available generating capacity and energy potential.

98. The fact that hydro electric resources constitute the most economic sources of power generation in the country was recognised as early as 1956. Both the perspective plan for power development prepared by the CW & PC in 1962 and the report of the Energy Survey of Indian Committee (1965) emphasised the need for greater reliance on hydro power for economic power supply. During the last decade, the country's hydel resources have not been developed at the pace recommended and large scale thermal generation, especially in areas within economic reach of hydel potential and remote from the collieries, has been resorted to resulting in higher energy generation cost. It is estimated that if the economic path of power development indicated earlier had been adhered to the power supply industry would be generating additional revenue surplus of the order of Rs. 180 crores at prevailing tariffs during the Fourth Plan,

99. The main reason for our inability to ensure choice of schemes for expansion of power generation and supply following the path of lowest cost of development in the past are :

(a) Delay in adopting the regional approach to power development ;

(b) consistent lack in the final stages of planning of a perspective approach designed to secure the lowest cost development;

(c) expectations of large surplus of by-product fuels from coal washeries, which have subsequently been belied;

(d) a general prevailing impression about large and decisive differences in the "construction time" factor in favour of conventional thermal generation; and

(e) longer plant delivery periods for hydro due to inadequate manufacturing capacity.

Now that reasons for higher power supply costs are apparent and it is desired that they should be reduced, remedial measures must be taken and rational considerations allowed to prevail in the future in the choice of schemes for expansion of power generation and supply.

100. To control and reduce the cost of energy generation and a supply in the country, to enable full utilisation of generating facilities already built up and to ensure that the limited capital allocations to the power supply industry go the farthest in meeting the country's estimated deficits, the bulk of new generating capacity to be added during the 5th and 6th Plans should be derived from hydro sources, both of energy intensive and peaking categories. The balance of new generating capacity should be derived from super-steam power station employing the largest possible unit sizes and located at the coal washeries/coal mines. Nuclear power generation would have to be resorted to preferentially in areas with limited hydro resources and which are remote from collieries. Region-wise optimal would, of course, need to be made. The above provides the broad guidelines for future power policy to ensure utmost economy in power generation and supply for the foreseeable future.

101. It is also essential that a perspective plan for power development covering a period of 15 to 20 years should be drawn up for the entire country on a regional basis purely on economic consideration, irrespective of location of the resources and this plan adhered to in actual implementation.

102. The main economic factors which must prevail in the choice of appropriate sources of power supply in the various regions have been discussed in the Report of Study Group No. III. Suggestions for new schemes regionwise for deriving benefits in the Fifth Plan and early Sixth Plan have been made in consultation with CW and PC after taking into consideration all relevant problems.

103. The programme for indigenous manufacture of heavy electrical equipment is at present based on consideration other than the needs of economic power development in the country. This should be altered and the manufacturing programme revised to suit the needs of the power supply industry.

104. The inability of the various States to provide adequate financial resources has been one of the main reasons for the low allocation to power in the 4th Plan, which cannot even sustain expansion of our power-supply on the scale required to maintain past rates of growth during the 4th Plan. To avoid critical power supply position in the future, central involvement would have to be on a much larger scale. Such increased central participation should be decided upon on purely techno-economic considerations and judiciously oriented towards providing economic power supply on regional and national considerations. A set of principles for deciding on the scope of central assistance in the various regions should also be evolved.

Institutional Arrangements : 105. Some changes in the institutional arrangements are considered necessary to enable power development in a rational and coordinated manner throughout the country and faster pace of hydro-electric development which involves considerably greater efforts at the stages of investigation and planning. These are :

(a) The Central Electricity Authority, which has statutory recognition, should be set up on a full time basis and should be charged with the responsibility for preparing the national perspective plan for power development, carrying out necessary investigations of schemes and processing them up to the point of construction. In drawing up such a plan, it may seek the help of Regional and State Electricity Boards which are familiar with the conditions in their respective areas.

(b) As preparation of perspective plan for power development has to be coordinated with plans for development of the other sectors of the economy and take into account the availability of financial resources, it is essential that the Central Electricity Authority works in close coordination with the Planning Commission. It would, therefore, be desirable to associate a representative of the Planning Commission as a part time member of the Central Electricity Authority to ensure proper coordination between the two organisations.

(c) The agency for construction of power projects would have to be decided on the basis of type of scheme, its location with respect to the areas where output is to be consumed, type of financing etc. The institution of Control Board, which is already being adopted for implementation of many of our projects, may be followed for projects taken up on regional considerations.

(d) The Regional Electricity Boards should continue to concern themselves primarily with ensuring maximum economy by integrated operation of constituent power systems in the respective regions. In view of their knowledge of the local conditions, the Central Electricity Authority may utilise their services for the purposes of drawing up perspective plans for power development in their respective regions. The position of Regional Electricity Boards with respect to the CEA is not clearly defined at present. This anomaly should be removed by giving the Regional Electricity Boards statutory recognition and clearly defining its relationship with other State and Central organisations. The Regional Boards should also be strengthened to discharge their responsibilities.

(e) While the above suggestions, if adopted, would by and large make it possible to deal with the problems of short-term and long-term power development, it is recognised that there would be certain areas such as the Indus Valley and the Godavari basin, where the magnitude of the schemes, geographic location etc. are such that the above institutional arrangements may not be adequate. In such cases, separate river valley authorities may be more conducive both for conducting of investigation and execution of the project. These are, however, special cases which would have to be dealt with on their merits.

(f) A proper analysis of power supply industry is extremely difficult at present because of paucity of data regarding actual investment costs, operating performance of power stations and power system etc. The CEA should be organised to collect and publish this data regularly.

Rural Electrification : 106. Electricity has now become a necessity rather than an amenity and must be recognised as an important factor in economic progress even in rural areas. The higher production of foodgrains required to meet the minimum demand of 1975-76 can be achieved economically only through extensive irrigation, electrification of pump sets and by using modern electric equipment on the farmsteads.

107. There is considerable scope for effecting economy in the equipment, construction practices, designs etc. for rural electrification.

108. The N.C.A.E.R. studies on Punjab and Kerala have conclusively established substantial economic benefits from rural electrification.

109. The N.C.A.E.R. study shows larger benefit/cost ratio for smaller villages. This indicates desirability of extension of rural electrification to cover smaller villages notwithstanding the lower percentage of return on the capital employed.

Estimate of Progress

	As on 31-3-69	During 1969-74	During 1974-81
No. of Villages	71,410	53,590	1,40,000
Pump sets	10,88,696	15,00,000	28,11,000
Investment		Rs. 520 crores	Rs. 1,850 crores

110. Availability of underground water and absence of salinity should be checked before any scheme for electrification of tube-wells is sanctioned. A survey of groundwater resources should be conducted in the potential scheme areas and data in this respect kept ready by the State Electricity Boards. This work, could, perhaps, be carried out by the Department of Agriculture or the Underground Water Organisation in the State. Assistance could also be obtained from the Geological Survey of India and Exploratory Tube-well Organisation of the Union Ministry of Agriculture.

111. Co-operative use of tube-wells should be encouraged. This would help in pooling up of the resources for taking tube-well connections. Co-operative use of tube-wells and selling of tube-well water could increase the load factor and improve the economies of rural electrification.

112. Finances : Investment up to 1968-69 provided

by earmarked central assistance was Rs. 254,000 crores. An estimate of financial resources for the 4th Plan is as follows :

	(In crores of rupees)
(i) Fourth Plan outlay by the States/ Union Territories etc.	294.50
(ii) Rural Electrification Corporation.	150.00
(iii) Financial Institutions comprising:	75.00
(a) Land Development Banks.	
(b) Agriculture Refinance Corporation.	
(c) Commercial Banks	
(d) Agricultural Finance Corporation.	
(e) Life Insurance Corporation.	

113. Backward areas should be given due consideration in rural electrification programme.

114. State Governments should give loans on easy terms to State Electricity Boards for Rural Electrification.

115. Rural Electrification in India can spread rapidly if it takes the shape of a people's movement. As pilot projects, the Government have set up five rural electric co-operatives—one in each of the States of Andhra Pradesh, Gujarat, Maharashtra, Mysore and U.P. The co-operative will enthuse the spirit of ownership in the villages and would also facilitate co-operative use of pump sets, electric appliances such as threshing machines, drying facilities for fruit, cold storage facilities etc. This will not only help the poor farmer to use such costly appliances but would also result in the improvement of the load factor in the rural areas.

116. It is felt that, in order to accelerate the development of rural areas, the easiest and quickest way would be to integrate rural electrification programme with the programme of agricultural and other rural industrial development schemes. It is recommended that Co-ordination Committee should be set up (1) at the level of the State Electricity Boards and (2) at the District level, as suggested in the meeting in Planning Commission in July, 1970.

117. The work of rural electrification though voluminous and involving considerable expenditure, is of repetitive nature. Therefore, there is a very large scope for achieving economy by standardised designs, manufacture and construction practices in the field of rural electrification. The specific suggestions concerning certain major aspects of designs for rural lines and substations which could economise in the rural electrification schemes have been given in the Report of Study Group No. IV. It is recommended that the same may be followed.

118. A special Technical Standards Committee under the aegis of the Rural Electrification Corporation should be formed for simplifying and standardising materials, equipment and construction practices for rural electrification works. This Committee should have a permanent Secretariat and should work in co-ordination with the CW & PC, ISI, REC, manufacturers and Research Organisation.

119. Single phase power distribution is inherently cheaper than 3-phase power distribution and deserves consideration. Indicates the development work already done in India on this. This system is very effective for villages with small loads, especially those with a population of up to 500 (which number about 3.67 lakhs).

120. Break-down in power supply are mostly on account of failures of distribution lines and substations. Standardised plans for operation and maintenance of these should be evolved.

121. Minimum consumption guarantee for agricultural consumers should be reduced to a reasonable figure.

122. There is considerable scope for increasing the load factor in the rural areas.

123. Suitable incentives are required to be provided to encourage the farmers to go in for the use of electric power of the Main Report. In this connection special mention is to be made about the need to set up service stations with mobile squads which should take up work of internal wiring, maintenance, etc. for the rural consumers, on reasonable charges. The State Governments should organise suitable rural technical centres. These could utilise presently unemployed technical personnel. They should be given necessary incentives to offer their services to the farmers. The State Electricity Boards should also set up such centres or assist in their establishment.

124. Rural electrification could be viable and successful if the integrated development of the rural areas done on an intensive basis by Agriculture, Irrigation, Industries Department etc., of the State Government in conjunction with the State Electricity Board.

Expeditious Construction of Power Projects: 125. There are serious shortfalls in achieving the targets for installation of generating capacity and transmission system in the country, year after year, If this trend continues, there are grim prospects of widespread and serious shortages of electric power. Further, on account of inadequacy of advance planning and investigations, there is likelihood of serious power shortage in the 5th and 6th plans also, leading to grave consequences in retardation of industrial and agricultural activity and economic progress. Concerted action on a wide form is essential for correcting this position and making up the lost ground.

Causes of Delay: 126. Causes of delay in the projects taken up for implementation have been identified and are listed in Section 5 of the Report of Study Group No. 5.

Planning: 127. A fairly large programme of construction has to be in hand all the time in order to keep up with the normal load growth. This is in consonance with experience in other countries also.

128. The perspective plan for the next 15 years should be available at any point of time and, every year, such plan should be updated and extended to cover the future 15 years. Advance action in respect of preliminary investigations and designs and estimates should proceed in a continuous manner. The proposals for the next 10 years should indicate details of the specific projects to be undertaken and their time-table of the major stages. The plans for the first 5-7 years should be very definite at any time and should be already under implementation,

129. Planning for electric power should be organised on a nationwide basis. The overall responsibility for planning including investigations are processing of schemes right up to the point of execution should be centralised with the Central Electricity Authority. The existing legislation is adequate for this.

129.1 Each State Electricity Board should have a Planning Cell which will be capable of taking into account the long-range needs for electric energy as well as utilisation of the resources in the best possible manner.

129.2. Similar long-range Planning Cells should also be created in the Regional Electricity Boards, These should be able to coordinate and correlate the plans prepared by the State Cells so as to make the best utilisation of the availability resources in the Region.

129.3 At the Centre, the Planning Commission and the C. W. & P. C. should keep in constant touch with the work and progress of these Planning Cells at the regional and State levels and a long-term power plan should be evolved continuously.

130. There is an urgent need for strengthening the Civil Engineering Organisation in each Electricity Board in order to cope with the large programme of investigations, planning and construction required for hydro projects. An experienced Chief Engineer (Civil) should be appointed for each Board, especially to look after the work of hydro-electric projects. Among other things, he should be in overall charge of a whole time planning and investigation circle.

131. The indigenous manufacturers should plan the manufacture of further large sizes of generation units so that these are available in time when the power system require these, shortly.

Investigations : 132. A massive and continuous programme of field investigations is needed immediately in each region of the country so that the needs of the Fifth and Sixth Plan periods for investigated projects can be fulfilled.

133. The C.W. & P.C. should keep in close touch with these investigations to ensure that these proceed on fruitful lines technically throughout.

134. The finances for project investigations should be provided in the initial stages as "on account grants" in the nature of promotional expenses. These expenses can be reimbursed to the common fund from the project estimate when a project is taken up for execution.

135. Detailed investigations should be entrusted to well-organised Survey and Investigation Units (in each State) equipped for geological as well as other investigations, services of the Research Stations such as C.W.P.R.S., CSMRS, etc. should be utilised for arriving at adequate scientific data, keeping the design engineers associated with the investigation work also proves valuable in ensuring proper orientation of the investigations and avoiding fruitless efforts.

136. Where inter-State development of a resource is indicated, the Regional Electricity Boards should take up the work. Formation of River Valley Authority to take the responsibility for further detailed project investigations and subsequent execution of individual schemes in the certain River Valleys with very large power potentials (according to a time table prescribed by the perspective plan) may also be considered.

137. After the feasibility of a hydro-electric project is established, construction of the minimum access road facilities should be taken up immediately from the 'investigation funds'. This will enable expeditious detailed investigations.

138. When the project is sanctioned, the construction of the access road facilities should be undertaken and completed at the earliest. This will expedite the execution and completion of the project.

Project Preparation: 139. The model proforma circulated by the Planning Commission in consultation with the Ministry of Irrigation and Power, should be followed strictly for the preparation of the project report. This will eliminate protracted correspondence and resultant delays in sanctioning of the projects.

Financing: 140. In order that the Project Authorities can plan and execute the construction programme according to the plan schedule, the finances should be made available as per the phased requirements of the project.

141. Power projects sometimes suffer due to diversion of funds to other purposes by the State Government. This could be discouraged by the Planning Commission by "earmarking" the funds for specific projects at the time of formulation of plan provisions.

142. In the past there has been a great deal of excess expenditure as well as slippages in achievements of targets in the case of both generation and transmis-

sion This is on account of two reasons, viz. :

(i) Underestimation of the cost at the time of preparation and sanction of the project report; and

(ii) Rising costs materials, labour and other services like transport, etc., in the course of project execution.

143. The under-estimation of the cost is mostly due to inadequate investigation and in some cases due to inadequate or incompetent design and engineering. It is, therefore, very essential to have thorough and detailed investigations and sufficient preliminary designs as the basis for the realistic estimates of the time and the cost of project execution.

144. The C.W. & P.C. should be charged with the responsibility for the accuracy of the estimates of time and cost of the project execution. The C.W. & P.C. should organise and equip itself for such work without any delay.

Procurement: 145. Tender specifications should be as detailed as possible and should include listing of all the information such as technical data, requirements of firm deliveries, contractual and financial requirements etc., required of a tender.

146. M/s H.E and M/s B.H.E. should make their quotations thorough and businesslike by furnishing detailed lists of all equipment and accessories they would supply and the supplementary equipment that the project is expected to procure from elsewhere to make the supply complete.

147. A good many items of plant, their anciliaries and other items have been standardised; the purchase specifications should be based on these as far as possible.

148. A model 'general conditions of contract' applicable to public sector and, if possible, to private sector manufacturers; binding on all the parties, would reduce the time between the receipt of the tenders and placing of the orders, and should be prepared and adopted.

149. The manufacturing capability of the two manufacturing units, viz., M/s H.E. and M/s B.H.E. is not sufficient to meet the requirements of the country fully. There is, therefore, no need at present for competitive binding between them.

150. The model technical specifications (prepared by CBI and P Working Group) for each type of hydroelectric turbogenerator set based on each of the technologies adopted by M/s H.E. and M/s B.H.E. should be adopted for ordering of the hydro-electric generating units. Considerable saving of time and effort can thus be effected.

151. It is possible to secure overall economic advantage by grouping the orders placed on the two manufacturing units for different project rationally so as to obtain optimum benefits regarding development and designs. This matter is complex and requires a cautious and informed approach. The planning of the orders may, therefore, be done in consultation with the Ministry of Irrigation and Power and Central Water and Power Commission.

Manufacture of Equipment: 152. The manufacturer should indicate his need of foreign exchange (source as well as the amount) at the time of tender. The concerned Ministries should ensure the release of adequate foreign exchange.

153. The manufacturer should indicate all factors and assumptions on which their promise of delivery period is based. It would be desirable as a contractual obligation for the manufacturers of major items to furnish the project authorities with their PERT network chart for items of their supply including exchange of drawings and data.

154. Manufacturers should attempt to reduce the erection work at site to a minimum by adopting shop assemblies in as large a measure as possible. For this purpose, special wagons/transporters may be devised if necessary for transport to site.

155. The Ministry of Irrigation and Power should be responsible for assigning priorities and programmes for the manufacture of equipment for various projects in consultation with all concerned.

156. There is much scope for standardisation and rationalisation of manufacture of a number of sophisticated items like automatic voltage regulators, excitation equipment, governers for generating sets etc. The manufacturing Units and CW & PC should work jointly to achieve this.

157. In view of the monopoly of M/s. H.E. and M/s B.H.E. in respect of generating plant and equipment, it is imperative to devise a mechanism whereby it can be ensured that the Manufacturing Units will strive towards attaining better efficiencies and producing increasingly superior machines. A Standing Advisory Committee comprised of representatives of the two manufacturers, CWPC, users, consultant and an academician should be set up to decide the targets and coordinate the action in this regard.

Transport Facilities : 158. The Design Organisation of CWPC should survey and catalogue the special transporters available with the various organisations so that the different projects can draw upon these when required.

159. In view of the increasingly large sizes of generating units and other equipment, special transport equipment presently available will not meet all future needs. M/s. BHE and M/s. HE should take up the matter with the Railways for design and construction of special wagons, mobile cranes etc.

Shortages and Breakages in Equipment : 160. Whenever any shortages or breakages are revealed, the project manager should have these inspected on his own and should proceed with ordering of the replacement. The process for making insurance claim and necessary inspection etc., therefore, can proceed separately simultaneously. The procedure of ordering the replacement should be initiated immediately after damage or shortage comes to notice without waiting for acceptance of the claim by the Insurance Company.

Construction Equipment and Plant : 161. The engineer in charge of the project should decide the extent of mechanisation at the design/planning stage after taking the various factors into consideration. The procurement of construction equipment and plant should be initiated well before the start of the execution of the project so that it is available in time.

Construction Contracts : 162. For timely execution of the project it is necessary to draw the overall project schedule as well as the schedules for the construction jobs proposed to be handled on contract before inviting tenders, or in any case, before awarding the contract. Such schedules should define the required data for any significant point of communication of transfer of responsibility between the contractor and other participants on the project.

163. The availability to control a construction project, most elements of which are given on contract, depends largely on the soundness of the contract documents themselves. A loosely defined contract may create considerable dissensions between the contractors and the project management due to individual interpretation of the intent as well as contents of the contract.

164. During the course of execution of the contract, the Project Management should retain full authority under the terms of contract to request any measures that may be necessary for the proper and timely execution of the work. The project personnel should constantly watch the project and evaluate the effect of slippage on the part of any contractor on the rest of the project.

165. Most of the needs of generating plant are going to be met from the indigenous manufacturers M/s. H.E. and M/s. B.H.E. who are not yet sufficiently equipped to undertake erection work of their own equipment. The Electricity Boards should, therefore, build up suitable teams for undertaking the work of installation and commissioning of plant and equipment. Such teams will be of great value to the organisation in arranging overhaul and proper maintenance work also.

166. In the absence of free exchange of ideas between contractors and project officers, there are considerable difficulties regarding measurement or assessment of work done, contractual obligations and responsibility of different parties etc. These difficulties are increasing with the increasing complexity and volume of project construction work. Some organisations like the Institution of Engineers (India) should bring together the contractor firms and project execution people to evolve a common understanding of the problems and to work out possible solutions.

167. The accounting proformae and procedures prescribed for the project works of complexity, particularly the electrical works, do not suit the work involving complex technology. The Ministry of Irrigation and Power should appoint an Expert Committee to go into the methods, detailed rules and proformae and suggest changes for simplifying and rationalising the work in the projects including methods of recording measurements.

168. The consultancy organisations should build up the expertise and capacity for undertaking inspection during manufacture and witnessing of tests on behalf of the projects.

169. The CW & PC should make a comprehensive survey of the facilities available in the country for undertaking quality control "type" and other proving tests and catalogue these for the use of the Project authorities.

Miscellaneous Bottlenecks : 170. The project authorities should be aware of the various possible serious bottlenecks such as land acquisition, rehabilitation, labour strikes, clearances of local/State Authorities etc. and timely action should be taken for tackling these matters at the appropriate level.

Project Organisation and Management : 171. It is essential that every project should be organised from the beginning under a suitable qualified and experienced project manager who is vested with adequate financial and administrative powers including placement of orders.

172. Modern Management methods need to be adopted for efficient and timely execution of the projects. "Systems" approach to the question of project management and control should be adopted. Proper planning of the project work at all stages, marshalling of all the resources (material as well as human) in appropriate combinations at every stage, proper intermeshing of the vast number of different activities by different agencies and monitoring and control of the project by watching the progress of physical achievements as well as spending of funds in a rational manner are the main techniques by which an optimum efficiency and speed can be achieved.

173. PERT/CPM network techniques should be introduced from the earliest possible stages of the project and preferably even to cover the planning stages also. Establishment of PERT cell to cover all projects

of an organisation as well as individual PERT Cells for each project or even its major elements are very desirable.

174. These network techniques have to be integrated in a comprehensive management information and control system. The objectives of this management information system should be primarily achieving on time and on cost completion of each phase of the power project. A model management information system has been given in the Report.

175. Where the project organisation are not adequately equipped, it is advisable to retain the services of an experienced consulting engineer organisation such as the Specialised Engineering Organisation of CW & PC or other Consulting Engineers available in each specialised field.

176. The system of "performance budgeting" should be adopted as an important management tool for monitoring and control of a project.

Marshalling of Resources : 177. Nation-wide survey and planning is necessary to ensure adequate resources for construction projects in respect of construction materials, equipment manufacture, construction machinery and designs and engineering capability.

178. There should be a panel of experts who may be available in the State Electricity Boards, Universities, and other Organisations in the country. Standing arrangements should be made so that the CW & PC or the projects can avail of the expertise of these persons whenever required at short notice.

179. In view of the ever increasing scale of project execution in the field of power, there is an urgent need of expansion of the design units in the Electricity Boards/Undertakings, the Specialised Engineering Organisation of CW & PC and Consulting Engineer Firms.

180. The CW & PC has the dual role of being Consulting Engineers to the power projects and Technical Advisers to the Central Government. There is an urgent necessity to undertake a deliberate programme for building up of the Specialised Engineering Organisation of CW & PC in order to ensure that the design and engineering capability in specific areas of complexity is available.

181. There is an urgent need for developing technical manpower resources to remove scarcity of adequately trained and experienced personnel for manning technical jobs at all levels. This will also help reduce growing unemployment among persons passing through technical institutes.

182. Every effort should be made to accelerate the growth of the capability of M/s HE and M/s BHE and their feeder projects so that the future requirements of plant and equipment for power projects can mostly be met by these.

183. Where M/s HE and M/s BHE cannot cope up with the needs of the power supply industry for enabling it to meet the needs of growth of industry and agriculture, import of plant and equipment to the extent necessary for uninhibited growth of the power sector should be approved.

184. Close collaboration of the Design and Research Organisation in the country should be established for developing designs to get around problems of scarcities of certain materials arising from time to time.

185. Each State Electricity Board should form a pool of construction plant and machinery for all its construction projects. Each project should draw upon this pool in respect of equipment, spares as well as operation and maintenance personnel according to needs. The Regional Electricity Boards should assist by keeping consolidated inventories of the equipment and spares available at different places with different Electricity Boards in the region facilitating better for want of spares. At the national level the CW & PC should take a census of the plant and machinery and its current conditions periodically and make this information available to the Electricity Boards/Construction Projects.

Future Pattern of Project Execution : 186. In view of the ever increasing tempo of project execution in the field of power, the Centre may have to play an increasingly active role. The Centre should take immediate steps to review and strengthen the Central Electricity Authority.

187. For a number of reasons discussed in the report, it would be desirable for the large or inter-State projects to be taken up for execution by the Regional Boards or by the Centre.

188. Presently, the State Electricity Boards are engaged in multifarious activities due to which adequate attention cannot be given to the problems of long-term planning etc. The top management should, therefore, be strengthened and organised by having the State Electricity Boards headed by an experienced Power Engineer as the Chairman and by putting all Members heading two wings of the Board—one being in-charge of planning, construction of power stations and transmission systems of 220 kv and above and other in-charge of construction of transmission and distribution systems upto 132 kv, operation and maintenance and rural electrification etc.

189. A uniform system of accounting needs to be prescribed for use by all Electricity Boards and undertakings so that confusion regarding real figures of cost both financial and economic is avoided.

COMMISSION OF INQUIRY REGARDING THE FACT AND CIRCUMSTANCES RELATING TO THE DEATH OF SHRI DEEN DAYAL UPADHYAYA, 1969—REPORT

New Delhi, Ministry of Home Affairs, 1970. 160p

One Man Commission : Mr. Justice Y. V. Chandrachud.

APPOINTMENT

1. Shri Deen Dayal Upadhyaya, who was elected as the President of the Bharatiya Jan Sangh in December 1967, died during a train journey on the night between the 10th and 11th February 1968.

2. The death occurred in mysterious circumstances and therefore some members of the Parliament asked, during the course of obituary references on the 12th, that the investigation of the matter be entrusted to the Central Bureau of Investigation. The C.B.I. put up two young men—Bharat Lal Dom and Ram Awadh—for trial before the Special Sessions Judge, Varanasi. By his judgment of June 6, 1969, the learned Judge held that Shri Upadhyaya died a homicidal death but he acquitted both the accused of the charge of murder as well as of the charge that they had committed theft after making preparations for causing death. However, he convicted Bharat Lal under Section 379 of the Penal Code for committing theft of Shri Upadhyaya's belonging and sentenced him to a term of four years. Bharat has filed an appeal against his conviction and sentence, which is pending in the High Court of Allahabad.

3. The learned Judge observed in his judgment that the prosecution was unable to prove its case "mainly because of paucity of evidence", that "there have also been deficiencies here and there during the investigation", that as a Criminal Court, his function was merely to decide whether the evidence was sufficient to prove the charges against the accused, that he could not in the very nature of things conduct a probe into the truth of the matter, that the prosecution was unable to offer a satisfactory explanation of some circumstances, that there was no "concrete data" before him to show that the murder was committed for a political motive and that "the offence of murder not having been proved against the accused, the problem of truth about the murder still remains."

4. On June 22, 1969, over seventy member of the Parliament made a written demand that a Judicial Commission be appointed to conduct a further inquiry into the matter so that persons who had committed the murder of Shri Upadhyaya could be brought to book. On August 4, 1969, the Chief Minister of U.P. announced in the State Assembly that the State Government had decided not to file an appeal against the decision of the Special Judge. On August 5, 1969, the Union Home Minister made a statement in the Lok Sabha that the Government had decided to appoint a Commission of Inquiry as desired by some members.

5. Accordingly, the Government of India constituted the Commission of Inquiry vide Ministry of Home Affairs Notification No. 31/13/69—Pol. 1(A) dated October 23, 1969.

TERMS OF REFERENCE

The Commission shall inquire into all the facts and circumstances relating to the death of Shri Deen Dayal Upadhyaya and make its report to the Central Government.

CONTENTS

Part I : Introduction; Scope of the Reference **Part II** : The Fateful Journey; The Strange Story of Mughalsarai; Fateh Bahadur Sing Investigation; Investigation by the C.I.D. and the C.B.I.; Expert Evidence. **Part III** : Sessions Trial; The Shape of the present proceedings. **Part IV** : The Much-maligned Major; When was Shri Upadhyaya last seen alive? Discovery of the body and its possible planting near the pole; Theft of the bedding; Motivation for the murder; Is it political? The Jan Sangh attack on the C.B.I.; Conclusion. **Part V** : Annexures.

CONCLUSION

1. I would like to give here a brief resume of my findings but I must recall that it was not without misgivings that I embarked upon this task. Fortunately my fears proved false. Credit for that must go in a large measure to courtesy and consideration which I received from all quarters. The case was complicated but counsel made it look simple. The care and ability with which Shri C.D. Sheth and Shri Bipin Behari Lall presented their respective cases for the Jan Sangh and Central Bureau of Investigation made my task lighter. But above all, they put their points of view before me

with a certain amount of dispassionateness. They were ably supported by their juniors, Shri Chaudhary, Shri Tiwari, Shri Tripathi and Shri Chaube. I am thankful to them all for their assistance. I must also express my appreciation of the help which I received from Shri B. C. Bhandare, Counsel for the Commission. The shifting of evidence and the spade work which he did aid me greatly.

2. What made the case apparently complicated was a combination of coincidences and a fusion of mysterious circumstances. Every crime presents a problem in some measure but only a few bristle with so many of them that gives to Shri Upadhyaya's murder an eerie complexion.

Look for example at the following facts :

(a) Major Surendra Mohan Sharma's name was taken down by Naik Har Govind Pandey of the R.T.O.'s Office as Major "S.L. Sharma" and his ticket number as 06171 instead of 06172.

(b) Padam Singh, the coach attendant of the Train Service coach took down the name of Major Surendra Mohan Sharma as Major "S.N. Sharma".

(c) Kamal, the Conductor of Sealdah Express, asserted that when he checked up the passengers in the I Class compartment of the F.C.T. bogie at Lucknow, he found a stranger dressed in civilian clothes standing in the unlighted "C" Cabin.

(d) Shri Gauri Shankar Rai, M.L C. who was to travel from Lucknow to Ballia via Varanasi, changed his mind and detrained at Shahganj. He got down from the off-side.

(e) M.P. Singh found at Varanasi that the bathroom near the 'A' Cabin was jammed and could not be opened.

(f) When M.P. Singh got back into the F.C.T. bogie at Mughalsarai after visiting Parcel Office, he saw a stranger standing in the corridor, opposite the "B" Cabin.

(g) That stranger hoodwinked M.P. Singh by feigning to be the son of the passenger who was travelling by the 'B' Cabin (that is, Shri Upadhyaya) and he successfully took away the bedding from the 'B' Cabin.

(h) The thief took away the file also, which was apparently of no value to him. The file was never traced.

(i) The thief did not, however, take away the wrist watch and the sum of Rs. 21, which were on the person of Shri Upadhayaya.

(j) The dead body of Shri Upadhyaya was found lying fully stretched on its back, with left leg over the right and the face fully covered with a shawl.

(k) In the right hand of the dead body was a five rupee note, held in a peculiar way.

(l) The injuries on the person of Shri Upadhyaya presented a unique combination—a head injury over the right ear, imprint abrasions on the shoulder, back and the right buttock, and bilateral fractures of the legs, with the left leg overted and the right leg inverted.

(m) There was no blood in any part of the compartment and none worth the name near the traction pole either. A substance like phenyl was however found near the attendant's seat in the F.C.T. bogie.

(n) The blood-stains on the personal apparel of Shri Upadhyaya had a characteristic pattern. There were blood-stains on the shoulder region only of the two full-sleeved sweaters and the full-sleeved banyan. There were no blood-stains at all on the sleeveless sweater. There were fairly large blood-stains on the shawl.

(o) The members of the shunting team and A.S.M. Prasad made diametrically opposite statements before the C.I.D. and the C.B.I. Their earlier version was that the body was seen at about 2·50 A.M. The version which they gave before the C.B I. was that they saw the body first at about 2.20 A.M.

(p) Even an independent person like Dr. B.R. Chakravarty, Assistant Medical Officer, tampered with the record. A.S.M. Prasad gave him a copy of his memo, asking him to attend the dead body. Dr. Chakravarty, made an endorsement on the original memo stating that he had received the copy at 5·55 A.M., which was correct. He later changed the timing to "3.55 A.M." by altering the figure "5.55" into "3-55".

3. Now, look at the following coincidences :

(1) Originally Shri Upadhyaya was to go to Delhi but in response to the invitation of the Bihar Branch of the Jan Sangh, he decided on the 10th morning to go to Patna. He had a trust with Destiny.

(2) His berth was reserved in the 'A' Cabin of the F.C.T. bogie, where M.P. Singh's berth was also reserved. But he changed from 'A' to 'B' Cabin, by incurring to some extent the displeasure of Shri Gauri Shankar Rai. Shri Rai's luggage was shifted from 'B' to 'C' Cabin without his consent. The result was that Shri Upadhyaya became the sole occupant of the 'B' Cabin.

(3) Shri Rai met Shri Shrivastva at the Lucknow Railway Station. On the latter's advice, Shri Rai got down at Shahganj instead of getting down at Varanasi.

(4) Shri Upadhayaya dashed against a traction pole while falling down from the F.C.T. bogie. There is hardly any other such pole on the particular line, within the vicinity of the particular traction pole.

(5) Major Sharma could have afforded to leave Lucknow on the 11th February as he was required to join his regiment on the 14th but he decided on the 10th that he should leave the same day, and this in spite of his recent marriage which had taken place on

the 17th January.

(6) Though Major Sharma did not travel by the 'C' Cabin where his berth was reserved, another army officer, Subedar Sidh Sing, holding an unreserved ticket, travelled by that cabin.

4. I have dealt with every one of these facts and have endeavoured to offer a rational explanation thereof. I have also discussed the rival theories and have furnished an answer. I hope that I am right in the solution which I have offered to the riddle of Shri Upadhyaya's death.

5. Stated briefly, I have taken the view :

(1) That Shri Upadhyaya was pushed out of the running train when he was standing near the door of the I Class compartment of the F.C.T. bogie.

(2) That he dashed against Traction Pole No. 1276 and died an instantaneous death.

(3) That the injuries found on his person were caused in a single transaction.

(4) That the injuries could not have been caused inside the compartment.

(5) That it cannot be that the murder was committed in the compartment or elsewhere and the dead body laid near the pole in order to stimulate an accident.

(6) That the dead body was discovered at about 2.20 A.M. during the earlier stage of shunting and not at about 2.50 A.M, after the first stage of shunting was over.

(7) That the members of the shunting team made conflicting statements before the C.I.D. and the C.B.I. in order to save themselves and their superior officer B.N. Prasad from a possible charge of negligence.

(8) That B.N. Prasad, the Assistant Station Master, changed his version to accord with truth, his earlier version having been influenced by an anxiety to avoid a charge of remissness in duty.

(9) That the C.B.I. was right in obtaining further statements from these witnesses but the prosecution was not justified in suppressing from the Sessions Court and the Defence, a very material circumstance that the witnesses had made conflicting statements before the C.I.D.

(10) That Dr. B.R. Chakravarty, Assistant Medical Officer, altered the record to show that he had attended to the dead body at 3-55 A.M. though he had not done so till 5-55 A.M., because he wanted to create an impression that he had done his duty promptly.

(11) That the position in which the dead body was lying initially, was definitely disturbed by some one most probably by members of the shunting team.

(12) That this was not done for any ulterior purpose but was done either as a matter of convenience or out of a common human sympathy.

(13) That S.I. Fateh Bahadur Singh further disturbed the position of the body for the purpose of taking a photograph.

(14) That the five rupee note was not planted in the hand of the dead body.

(15) That the body was first identified by Vishwanath Prasad Agarwal at about 10-30 A.M.

(16) That only two and not three photographs of the injuries were taken at the mortuary by K.M. Bhatia of the 'Goras Studio'.

(17) That Shri Upadhyaya was last seen alive at Jaunpur but there is no reliable evidence to show that he was last seen alive at Varanasi.

(18) That no reliance can be placed on the evidence of M.P. Singh or B.D. Kamal for holding that Shri Upadhyaya was or was not alive at Varanasi.

(19) That in the context of the other circumstances, however, it must be held that Shri Upadhyaya was alive at Varanasi.

(20) That Major Surendra Mohan Sharma travelled from Lucknow to Gomoh by the Train Service Coach and not by the F.C.T. bogie of the Sealdah Express.

(21) That in the misdescription of his initials and the ticket number there was nothing more than an error, first on the part of Naik Har Govind Pandey and then on the part of Padam Singh.

(22) That Shri Gauri Shankar Rai got down at Shahganj because it was more convenient to go to Ballia via Shahganj and he got down on the off-side because there was no coolie to carry his luggage.

(23) That apart from M.P. Singh, Shri Upadhyaya, Shri Gauri Shankar Rai and Subedar Sidh Singh, no one else travelled by the I Class compartment between Lucknow and Varanasi.

(24) That the murder of Shri Upadhyaya was accompanied by an immediate theft, which shows that the two are part and parcel of the same transaction.

(25) That the bedding of Shri Upadhyaya was not recovered from a pit.

(26) That there is no reliable evidence to show that the missing file contained any matter of political significance.

(27) That the murder was not committed for political motives.

(28) That neither the left Communists nor Dr. Faridi nor any communalists are connected, directly or indirectly, with the murder, and

(29) That there is no substance in the accusation that the C.B.I. acted mala fide.

6. I have dealt exhaustively with the charge that Shri Upadhyaya's murder was committed for political motives, as that was one of the important points involved in my inquiry. On the 12th February, 1968, some members of the Parliament had expressed a fear on the floor of the House whether in India, politics had

become so unsafe for politicians that one had to pay for one's political beliefs by one's life. I can say with a certain amount of confidence that nothing that has come before me can support the accusation that there was any politics in Shri Upadhyaya's murder.

Undoubtedly, he had political rivals but his death is the rash and extempore handiwork of mere thieves.

7. Before I conclude, a word of praise is due to the staff of the Commission. Shri B.D. Divekar, Shri R.K. Gadagkar, Shri K.M. Kulkarni and Shri G.G. Chavan have put in long hours of work over the past six months. Shri Gadagkar particularly has been of great help, as ever.

8. I must finally record my appreciation of the invaluable assistance which I received from Shri G.S. Nande, Secretary to the Commission. He had to discharge a variety of functions and I am glad to say that he excelled in all that he did. His willing co-operation and resourcefulness made my work so much lighter and enjoyable.

20th October, 1970

(*Sd.*) Y. V. CHANDRACHUD
Commission of Inquiry

EXPERT GROUP ON STATE ENACTMENTS HAVING A BEARING ON COMMERCIAL BANKS LENDING TO AGRICULTURE, 1969—REPORT

Bombay Reserve Bank of India, 1971. 190p.

Chairman : R.K. Talwar.
Members : Shri K. Gopal Rao; Shri K.P.J. Prabhu; Shri H.H. Trivedi; Shri G.V.K. Rao; Shri Ram Sahay; Shri B. Rudramoorthy; Shri P.H. Abhyankar; Dr. C.D. Datey; Shri V.M. Jakhade.
Convenor : Dr. H.B. Shivamaggi.
Joint Convenor : Shri T.V. Ramchandran.

APPOINTMENT

One of the study groups appointed in 1968, by the National Credit Council, to examine the need for adopting area/project approach in implementing schemes for extending commercial bank credit to agriculture including credit for commercially viable projects in the rural electrification and minor irrigation fields, draw attention to legislative and administrative aspects, which had a bearing on the entry of commercial banks, in the field of agricultural credit and felt that some of the provisions in state enactments were somewhat out moded in the light of current requirements of agriculture. It, therefore, recommended that there was need for a study in depth, by an expert Group, of these laws from the point of view of social objectives of such legislation and the need to enlarge the role of commercial banks in meeting the growing credit requirements of agriculture. The need for such a study was also stressed at the seminar on financing of agriculture by commercial banks convened by the Reserve Bank of India in December 1968. In pursuance of these recommendations the Governor of the Reserve Bank of India appointed in September 1969, this expert group.

TERMS OF REFERENCE

(I) To examine the provisions of the State laws relating to abolition of intermediaries, land tenure, and tenancy reforms and similar other enactments which confer different degrees of rights in land on the tenant—cultivators and landholders belonging to backward classes, tribals, etc., with particular reference to right of transferability through sale or mortgage or right to create a charge on land/crops and to suggest modifications, if any, required to facilitate their dealings with the commercial banks.

(II) To examine the state laws relating to agricultural debt relief and regulation of money lending, with particular reference to regulation of interest rates, scaling down of past debts, priority to charges among the different credit agencies, recovery of overdues, etc. and to suggest modifications, if required, in favour of institutional credit agencies;

(III) To examine the provisions of the State legislation imposing ceiling on land holdings, and to suggest modifications, if any, in regard to lands coming into the possession of the institutional credit agencies because of fare closures;

(IV) To examine the provisions of various land reforms legislation relating to the regulations on sale of land applicable to lands coming into the possession of institutional credit agencies during the process of recovery of loans in respect of (a) categories of persons to whom agricultural land could be sold, (b) the price at which land could be sold, (c) leasing out of land temporarily, (d) sale of fragments, (e) right of pre-emption of adjoining landholders, etc, and to suggest amendments or administrative measures for safeguarding the interest of the institutional credit agencies;

(V) To recommend measures for simplification of procedures for registration of documents and of equitable mortgages, recovery or overdues etc., and

(VI) Other related measures (actions which will increase the commercial banks' participation in agricultural development programme;

CONTENTS

Introduction; Background and Formulation of Approach; Land Alienation Rights of Agriculturists; Priority of Charges; Recovery and Other Operational Difficulties of Commercial Banks; Facilities to Agriculturists for Borrowing from Commercial Banks; Summary of Recommendations; Appendices.

RECOMMENDATIONS

It is the context of the massive credit requirements for successful implementation of the new agricultural strategy and the inability of the co-operatives alone to meet the demand, that the multi-agency approach has come to be accepted.

In order that the commercial banks—they have entered this field only recently—are enabled to cater to the credit requirements of as large a number of agriculturists as possible, certain restrictive features of the various State enactments, particularly those relating to right of alienation in land or interest therein, need to be removed.

It is also necessary that certain facilities given to agriculturists borrowing from co-operatives be extended to those who borrow from commercial banks because in our view, these facilities are primarily for the benefit of the individual cultivator-borrower rather than for that of the lending institution. Our recommendations cover all these aspects and we are glad to note that some measures have already been taken by some of the State Governments.

The implementation of our recommendations would involve amendments to a large number of State enactments. In order to expedite action as also to ensure that an unambiguous and clear cut legal framework is provided for the operations of commercial banks in the agricultural sector, a single consolidated piece of legislation would be more advisable. We have therefore, prepared a draft model bill for the purpose, which is given as an Annexure to this report.

A summary of our recommendations is given below.

LEGISLATIVE PROVISIONS

Land Alienation Rights Of Agriculturists

(I) Cultivators who have no rights or have only restricted rights of alienation of their lands or interests therein—such as landholders belonging to scheduled tribes/castes, backward classes/castes, tenant cultivators, fragment holders, allottees of Bhoodan land and of Government Land—should be vested with rights to alienate land/interest in land held by them in favour of banks for the purpose of obtaining loans for agricultural purposes.

(ii) In the case of share-croppers, who form a special category and who do not have any recorded rights in land banks would be able to grant loans only if their status is properly recorded in the record of land rights. Further, they should be enabled to create a charge on the crops raised by them, notwithstanding the fault that they are not the owners of the land over which the crop is raised by them.

Priority of Charges

(iii) The general principle of priority as between institutional credit agencies in regard to loans based on common security, should be as adumbrated in the Transfer of Property Act, 1882. This will ensure that the concept of first charge in favour of co-operatives does not adversely affect commercial banks. However an institutional credit agencies should have priority of charge vis-a-vis private credit agencies.

(iv) The restriction on alienation of land subject to a charge in favour of a co-operative should be relaxed so as to permit subsequent alienation thereof for securing supplementary credit from another institutional credit agency. This would be similar to the provision by which property subject to a charge in favour of a co-operative credit society is allowed to be alienated in favour of a land development bank.

(*v*) On the same basis, where crop loan for current production purposes is granted by one institutional credit agency and term loan for development purposes is granted by another institutional credit agency against common security, priority of security should accrue to the agency providing term loan provided the encumbrance in its favour was made with the knowledge and concurrence of the institution holding the encumbrance for crop loan for current production purposes. The existing priorities under the co-operative legislation as between the Co-operative credit societies and land mortgage banks will remain unaffected.

(vi) As between two institutional credit agencies providing term loans for development purposes against common security, priority of claim should arise according to the point of time of creation of encumbrances.

(vii) On the analogy that the simplified procedure pertaining to the creation of a charge on land/interest in land by declaring in favour of co-operative facilities, expeditious disposal of loan applications, provision should be made to enable agriculturists to create a charge on land/interest therein by declaration in favour of Commercial Banks. Appropriate arrangements should also be made to have such charge noted in the record by rights and in the office of the Sub-Registrar.

(viii) To overcome the prolonged delays involved in securing registration of mortgages created in favour of commercial banks it is necessary to provide that it would be sufficient if a copy of the mortgage deed is sent for registration to the Sub-Registrar. The mortgage so created should also be noted in the record of rights.

Recovery and other operational difficulties.

(ix) Enactments relating to money-lending regulation and debt relief should exclude commercial banks from their purview.

(x) To facilitate prompt recovery by dues of commercial banks without having to resort to protracted and time consuming litigation in civil courts, the State Government should empower an official with authority to issue an order, having the force of a decree of a civil court, for payment of any sum due to a bank by sale of the property charged/mortgaged in favour of the bank.

(xi) As banks may have need to fare-close mortgages of land executed in their favour, bring the property to sale and purchase the property if there are no bidders at auctions conducted for the purpose, they should be permitted to purchase the land and, if necessary, acquire land in excess of the ceiling limit fixed. However, State Governments may fix a time limit within which land acquired by banks is to be sold, ultimate disposal of land by banks will, of course have to be subject to State enactments as regards the persons to whom land can be sold etc.

(xii) In order to facilitate Commercial Banks financing agriculturists through primary agricultural credit societies, the societies should be made eligible to borrow from commercial banks. Further, the commercial banks concerned should be eligible for such facilities as are ordinarily available to a central co-operative bank.

ADMINISTRATIVE MEASURES

(xiii) To enable banks to get adequate and reliable information about the operational holding of an intending borrower and the nature of his interest therein to support his bona fide interest in land and cultivation, the urgency to bring land records up-to-date has been reemphasised.

(xiv) Meanwhile, it is urgently necessary to prepare and maintain interim registers indicating the existence of share-croppers and other informal tenants and the particulars of land cultivated by them; unless this is done, this class of cultivators may not be able to get adequate support from institutional credit agencies.

(xv) As and when land records are brought up-to-date, pass books such as those already in vogue in some States may be issued by State Governments to owners and tenants so that such a pass book can serve as prima facie evidence to the rights in land of an agriculturist and as a starting point to banks to verify such rights and details pertaining to encumbrances thereon.

(xvi) Cultivators borrowing from commercial banks should be exempted from payment of stamp duty, registration fee and charge for issue of non-encumbrance certificate to the extent to which they are eligible for these concessions if they borrow from co-operatives.

(xvii) The number of centres where equitable mortgages can be created in favour of commercial banks for the purpose of agricultural borrowing needs to be increased until such time as the legislative and other measures recommended by the Group are given effect to.

COMMITTEE ON PUBLIC RELATIONS AND PUBLICITY IN PUBLIC UNDERTAKINGS, 1969—REPORT

Delhi, Manager of Publications, 1970. 42p

Chairman : Shri S.K. Ghose

Members : Shri M. L. Bhardwaj; Brig. R. Shreenivasan; Shri Shanker Mitro; Shri B. V. Ranganath (Replaced by Shri S. Almeida); Shri Sanat Lahiri.

Member-Secretary : Dr. Raj K. Nigam.

APPOINTMENT

The Committee on Public Undertakings (1968—69) submitted its 47th Report on Public Relations and Publicity in public undertakings to Parliament in April 1969. The committee recommended, inter alia, that "an expert committee should be appointed to make a detailed study of the organisational structure of the public relations and publicity units in the public undertakings and suggest guidelines for the set-up of such an organisation keeping in view the need to inform the public not only of the products marketed by it but also the functioning of the undertaking".

The committee also suggested that the question of having a joint cadre of public relations officers and publicity officers for public undertakings in the same field or producing similar products or doing the same type of business be examined by the expert committee and that the advice of the expert committee be sought in regard to minimum qualifications and experience required for the posts in the public relations and publicity department of public undertakings. The committee also felt that it might be worthwhile to lay down certain broad guidelines and criteria for determining expenditure on publicity for all public undertakings. Government accepted the committee's recommendations.

In view of the importance attached to public relations and publicity in public undertakings, the Government of India in the Ministry of Finance, Bureau of Public Enterprises, Department of Expenditure appointed a Committee vide their Resolution No. BPE (I&R) 29/69 dated December, 26, 1969.

TERMS OF REFERENCE

(a) To define and formulate clear public relations objectives to public sector undertakings.

(b) To make a detailed study of present organisational structure of the public relations and publicity departments and to suggest guidelines for the setting up of such an organisation;

(c) To examine the question of joint cadre for public relations officers and publicity officers in undertakings in the same field or producing similar products or doing the same type of business ;

(d) To examine the question of minimum qualifications and experience for posts in public relations and publicity departments; and

(e) To evolve guidelines or criteria in regard to expenditure on publicity.

CONTENTS

Introduction; Definitions; Objectives; Organisational Patterns; Joint Cadre of Public Relations Officers; Qualifications; Guidelines; Expenditure; Summary of Conclusions/Recommendations Contained in the Report; Annexures I to V.

RECOMMENDATIONS

Government should lay down management and public relations objectives in clear and specific terms for the public sector as a whole.

Within the parameters of the management and the public relations objectives for the public sector as a whole, each public undertaking should formulate its own management and public relations objectives.

The image of an undertaking in the eyes of its public depends in the ultimate analysis on its performance. Public relations cannot be a substitute for performance.

The chief of the public relations set-up can function effectively only if the reports to the proper decision making level which should be part of top management.

For public relations to be effective the chief of the public relations set-up should be kept fully and constantly informed of all that is happening in his undertaking, its achievements and failures, problems and prospects. He should also take the initiative in the matter of gathering information. The top management of the public undertakings should consider the advisability of setting up public relations committees consisting of the chief executive, Selected heads of departments and the chief public relations executive for properly designing public relations plans.

Each public undertakings must decide for itself the public relations or advertising set-up it needs to implement its public relations and advertising policies. These two units should work in close co-ordination as the public image of a corporate body is also derived from its product advertising,

Government should set up an independent and adequately staffed public relations consultancy organisation to advise public undertakings on public relations strategy and its implementation. This organisation may also be utilised by the Central Government to project the total image of the public sector

A joint cadre for public relations officers in public undertakings is neither necessary nor desirable.

The following minimum qualifications for public relations officers in public undertakings are recommen ded :

(a) a good university degree, preferably in humanities ;

(b) the personality to communicate effectively with a variety of people inside and outside the organisation at various levels ;

(c) capacity for sustained hard work and ability to handle difficult human and organisational problems ;

(d) writing and editing of news items, features and articles; experience of working in an advertising agency, ability to write scripts and commentaries for films and broadcast ; understanding of and ability to utilise various media of mass communication, viz., press, printed material (house magazines, pamphlets leaflets and other company publications), radio, films audio-visual programmes, etc.)

(e) institutional training in public relations would be a very desirable qualification (though persons with such training are not likely to be available in sizeable number for some time yet); and

(f) the persons who had a public relations set-up either in an undertaking or in a plant should have the quality of leadership and the skill to handle creative writers, visualisers and artists to get the best out of them.

The following minimum qualifications for advertising officers in public undertakings are recommended :

(a) a good degree in humanities ;

(b) personality and leadership attributes ;

(c) experience in the advertising agency as in the advertising department of an organisation ;

(d) ability to appreciate the marketing problems of an undertaking and plan an advertising campaign involving various mass media like the press, cinema, commercial radio, printed material ;

(e) skill in liaising and co-ordination advertising work with advertising agencies on the one hand and various departments and sales officers of the organisation on the other ; and

(f) of the head of the advertising set-up should have the managerial ability to head a department, plan and control its work and expenditure.

To meet the demand for trained public relations personnel in the country, the Indian Institute of mass communication or one of the all-India Institutes of management or a university should institute one or more well designed courses in public relations to meet the paucity of competent public relations personnel. The services of the proposed consultancy organisation should be utilised to offer practical training to these trainees.

The Central Information service can continue to be one of the sources for recruitment of public relations officers for the present.

Both in public relations and advertising there should be a periodic evaluation of the results by experts to derive the optimum benefit from the expenditure in terms of human and material resources.

It is not possible to evolve any practical guidelines for expenditure on public relations and advertising. The expen iture should be on the basis of the genuine needs of the undertaking for public relations and advertising.

CHAIRMAN INDEX

INDEX